STUDIES IN CHRISTIAN HISTORY AND THOUGHT

Christ the Mediator of the Law
Calvin's Christological Understanding
of the Law as the Rule of Living
and Life-Giving

STUDIES IN CHRISTIAN HISTORY AND THOUGHT

A complete listing of all titles in this series
will be found at the close of this book

STUDIES IN CHRISTIAN HISTORY AND THOUGHT

Christ the Mediator of the Law
Calvin's Christological Understanding
of the Law as the Rule of Living
and Life-Giving

Byung-Ho Moon

Foreword by David F. Wright

Wipf & Stock
PUBLISHERS
Eugene, Oregon

Wipf and Stock Publishers
199 W 8th Ave, Suite 3
Eugene, OR 97401

Christ the Mediator of the Law
Calvin's Christological Understanding of
the Law as the Rule of Living and Life-Giving
By Moon, Byung-Ho
Copyright©2006 Paternoster
ISBN: 1-59752-782-3
Publication date 6/22/2006
Previously published by Paternoster, 2006

This Edition published by Wipf and Stock Publishers
by arrangement with Paternoster

Paternoster
9 Holdom Avenue
Bletchley
Milton Keyes, MK1 1QR
Great Britain

STUDIES IN CHRISTIAN HISTORY AND THOUGHT

Series Preface

This series complements the specialist series of *Studies in Evangelical History and Thought* and *Studies in Baptist History and Thought* for which Paternoster is becoming increasingly well known by offering works that cover the wider field of Christian history and thought. It encompasses accounts of Christian witness at various periods, studies of individual Christians and movements, and works which concern the relations of church and society through history, and the history of Christian thought.

The series includes monographs, revised dissertations and theses, and collections of papers by individuals and groups. As well as 'free standing' volumes, works on particular running themes are being commissioned; authors will be engaged for these from around the world and from a variety of Christian traditions.

A high academic standard combined with lively writing will commend the volumes in this series both to scholars and to a wider readership.

Series Editors

Alan P.F. Sell, Visiting Professor at Acadia University Divinity College, Nova Scotia, Canada

David Bebbington, Professor of History, University of Stirling, Stirling, Scotland, UK

Clyde Binfield, Professor Associate in History, University of Sheffield, UK

Gerald Bray, Anglican Professor of Divinity, Beeson Divinity School, Samford University, Birmingham, Alabama, USA

Grayson Carter, Associate Professor of Church History, Fuller Theological Seminary SW, Phoenix, Arizona, USA

Contents

	Foreword by David F. Wright	xi
	Preface	xiii
	Acknowledgements	xv
	Abbreviations	xvii

Chapter 1
Introduction: Calvin's Attitude towards the Law — 1
1.1 Exploring Calvin's Christological Understanding of the Law — 1
1.2 Theologizing the Law — 12
1.3 The Thesis and Tasks of Our Study — 18

Chapter 2
The Intellectual Origins of Calvin's Concept of the Law — 23
2.1 The Significance of the Young Calvin's Legal Culture — 23
2.2 *Mos Novus*: A Historical Philological Approach to the Legal Texts — 28
2.3 *Via Moderna* and *Devotio Moderna*: The Merit of Christ and the Role of the Law, and Late-Medieval Spirituality — 38
2.4 Commentary on Seneca's *De Clementia*: A Discovery of the Educational Function of the Law — 47
2.5 Conclusion — 55

Chapter 3
The Formation and Development of Calvin's Christological Understanding of the Law — 60
3.1 The Law in Calvin's Early Writings — 60
3.2 The Development of Calvin's Christological Understanding of the Law in the *Institutes* — 65
3.2.1 Theological Apologia in the First Chapter of the 1536 *Institutes* — 65
3.2.2 Exploring the Soteriological Significance of the Law in the 1539 *Institutes* — 70
3.2.3 *Institutes* 1543-1550 — 74
3.2.4 1559 *Institutes*: Formulating the Whole Process of Salvation in the Light of the Concept of *Christus Mediator Legis* — 77

3.3	Conclusion	82

Chapter 4
Calvin's Concept of *Christus Mediator Legis*: Its Theological Foundation and Scope — 84

4.1	Christ and the Law	84
4.2	*Christus Mediator Legis*	86
4.3	The Necessity of the Mediator of the Law	90
4.3.1	Human Soul Depraved: Knowledge and Conscience	90
4.3.2	Human Soul Depraved: Free Will	92
4.3.3	Free Will to Do Good Works by the Grace of Christ	96
4.4	The Threefold Mediation of the Law	98
4.4.1	Threefold Mediation and Threefold Office	98
4.4.2	*Christus Mediator Reconciliationis*	99
4.4.3	*Christus Mediator Patrocinii*	101
4.4.4	*Christus Mediator Doctrinae*	102
4.5	The Extent of Christ's Mediation of the Law	104
4.5.1	The So-Called *Extra Calvinisticum*	105
4.5.2	"*Deus coram loquutus sit, et tamen per internuncium*": God's Accommodation and Christ's Mediation	111
4.6	Conclusion	119

Chapter 5
Christ's Mediation of the Law in the Old Testament: A Pivotal Approach to Calvin and Judaism — 123

5.1	Introduction	123
5.1.1	Calvin's Criticism of "A New Judaism" of the Papists and the Anti-Judaism of the Anabaptists	123
5.1.2	Calvin and *Veritas Hebraica*	126
5.2	*Calvinus Iudaizans*	130
5.2.1	Not the Presence of the Person but the Personal Presence of Christ: Servetus' Anti-Trinitarian Christology and His Position on the Law	130
5.2.2	Aegidius Hunnius' Critique	139
5.2.3	Calvin's Criticism of Judaism	144
5.3	The Presence and Office of the Mediator in the Old Testament	147
5.3.1	*Praesentia Figurae Personae Mediatoris*	148
5.3.2	The Presence of Christ as the Angel, Jehovah, and Elohim	151
5.3.3	*Christus Caput Angelorum et Ecclesiae*	154
5.4	The Christological Significance of Calvin's Interpretation of the Old Testament Law	157

5.4.1	The Pattern of Interpretation of the First Table Commandments	157
5.4.2	Natural Law and the Second Table Commandments	160
5.5	*Ad Quaestiones et Obiecta Iudaei Cuiusdam Responsio*	163
5.6	Conclusion	170

Chapter 6
Christ the Mediator as the Interpreter and Fulfilment of the Law in Calvin's Exegesis of the Gospels — 173

6.1	Probing Calvin's Christological Understanding of the Law in His Commentary on the Gospels	173
6.2	Christ's Interpretation of the Law	177
6.2.1	"*Ego autem dico vobis*"	177
6.2.2	Calvin's Exegesis in Comparison with Melanchthon's and Bucer's	179
6.2.2.1	You Shall not Kill (Matt. 5:21-26)	181
6.2.2.2	On Adultery and Divorce (Matt. 5:28-32)	184
6.2.2.3	On Oaths (Matt. 5:33-37)	190
6.2.2.4	Love Your Neighbour (Matt. 5:38-48)	191
6.2.2.5	On the Sabbath and Christ's Attitude towards the Tradition of the Elders	194
6.3	"*Non veni ut destruam, sed ut impleam*"	199
6.3.1	Melanchthon's Forensic Understanding	199
6.3.2	Bucer's Spiritual Understanding	201
6.3.3	Calvin's Christological Understanding	204
6.4	The Person and Work of Christ, and the Fulfilment of the Law in Calvin's Exegesis of the Gospels	205
6.4.1	The Manifestation of the Mediator as the Incarnate Word of God	205
6.4.2	The Passion, Resurrection, and Ascension of Christ	208
6.5	Conclusion	210

Chapter 7
***Lex Dei Regula Vivendi et Vivificandi*: Calvin's Dynamic Understanding of the Office and Use of the Law** — 213

7.1	Introduction	213
7.2	*Lex Dei Regula Vivendi*: Calvin's Understanding of the Normative Nature of the Law	214
7.3	The Office and Use of the Law	218
7.3.1	Luther: *Lex Semper Accusat*	218
7.3.2	Melanchthon: From *Lex Accusans* to *Lex Vivendi*	220
7.3.3	Bullinger: From *Lex Vivendi* to *Lex Accusans*	224

7.3.4	Bucer's Holistic Understanding of *Lex Vivendi* and *Lex Accusans*	228
7.3.5	Calvin: From *Lex Vivendi* to *Lex Vivificandi*	231
7.3.5.1	*Duplex Officium Legis*	232
7.3.5.2	*Triplex Usus Legis*	235
7.4	Conclusion	243

Chapter 8
Conclusion: The Coherence between Christology and Soteriology in Calvin's Theology of the Law   246

Bibliography   261
Index of Scripture References   291
General Index   298

FOREWORD

It is well known to all students of the Reformation and the subsequent Reformed tradition of Christian theology that John Calvin distinctively emphasized the role of the law of God for the whole life of Christian people. The 'third' or normative use of the law was in his view its chief use, a position which set Calvin apart from the primary Lutheran stress on the accusatory force of the law for sinful human beings.

The strength of Dr. Byung-Ho Moon's works lies in his demonstration that Calvin grounded this understanding of God's law in Christ's mediation of the law, which made the law not only a rule for living but also something life-giving. One fruit of Dr. Moon's exposition is an enlarged picture of the mediatorial service of Jesus Christ. This is shown to extend in Calvin's writings far beyond his incarnate mediation on behalf of fallen humanity. At the same time in Jesus' Gospels ministry his teaching of and about the law becomes, in Calvin's reading, the revelation of the original import of the law and the righteousness which fulfils it. More surprisingly still, this 'law of living' can even be called 'the law of life-giving (*vivificandi*)', and 'in regenerating us Christ vivifies, gives life to (*vivificat*) the law', as Calvin puts it in his commentary on 2 Corinthians 3:17.

This study exposes, then, unexpected dimensions of Calvin's reflection on the law, and does so by interrogating a very wide sweep of Calvin's writings and by tenaciously sensitive attention to what the Reformer actually says. It is a work of mature Calvinian scholarship, and a testimony to the high quality of serious Calvin studies in Korea.

This book also provides food for thought for Christian circles, not least in Britian but not solely there, which seem intent on reviving a simplistic dichotomy between law and gospel, or even between Old Testament and New – as though the law of God were confined to only the Old Testament. Calvin would prompt those who seek to be Christ's without needing to obey the divine law to reconsider whether they can indeed have Christ without the law, just as even Israel did not have the law without Christ. And Christianity's social witness is certainly on the agenda in this realm of discussion. The grace of law may appear to some an oxymoron, but it is certainly not a contradiction in terms. Living in accordance with God's declared will in his law is not to be sundered, so Calvin counsels, from God's life-giving provision for his children.

David F. Wright
Emeritus Professor of Patristic
and Reformed Christianity,
University of Edinburgh

Preface

This book seeks to give an account of the truth, scope, and validity of Calvin's Christological understanding of the law from the perspective of his concept of *Christus mediator legis*, which is illustrated most lucidly in his commentary and sermon on Galatians 3:19. The book is based on this argument: while Lutherans, sustaining their confessional principle *lex semper accusat*, tend to separate the theological use of the law from its normative use, and while covenant theologians, although paying primary attention to the normative character of the law, regard its peculiar role as merely a preliminary element to establish the mutuality and conditionality of the covenant, Calvin understands the nature of the law as the rule of living (*regula vivendi*) and, from this point of view, deals with the whole office of the law, whether theological or normative, as the rule of life-giving (*regula vivificandi*).

In dealing with the formation and development of Calvin's theology of the law, before turning to specific agendas the book refers initially to the young Calvin's humanistic and legal studies and the influence of the *via moderna* and the *devotio moderna* upon him, and then to his Christological understanding of the law explored in his early catechetical works and the successive editions of the *Institutes*. These studies lay the groundwork for my subsequent inquiry into the theological foundation of the necessity and extent of Christ's mediatorship. It is true that the necessity of the Mediator is primarily discussed negatively in relation to the miserable state of depraved humanity. However, more emphatically, this necessity, for Calvin, is associated with God's grace in accommodating himself to human capacity, even human barbarity in the Old Testament, and the so-called *extra Calvinisticum*, by which he argues for the eternal and continual mediation of Christ according to both his divine and human natures.

From the study of Calvin's position on the law revealed in his controversies with Servetus and his tract *Ad quaestiones et obiecta Iudaei cuiusdam responsio*, the book verifies the wide extent of Christ's mediation, ranging from even before the fall, and the fact that Calvin's literal and historical interpretation of the Old Testament does not witness to any feature of *Calvinus Iudaizans*, but rather to the unique way of his biblical interpretation, which is founded on the concept of Christ's mediation of the law. Then the book examines how Calvin interprets Christ and the law in his exegesis of the Four Gospels in view of the fact that Christ who is the substance of the law becomes its interpreter and fulfilment. Calvin's emphasis here is largely on Christ's appealing to the original nature of the law, which is consistent and eternal throughout history. Finally, before the conclusion that there is a coherence between Christology and soteriology in Calvin's theology of the law is reached, the book examines Calvin's Christological understanding of the law in his exegetical works on Pauline theology, where he distinctively investigates the use and office of the law in the whole process of salvation. It is here sought to verify that as Calvin develops the theological use of the law from its normative use, he claims the continuity between the covenants of works and grace and the unity between *lex vivendi* and *lex vivificandi* in the light of *Christus mediator legis*.

Throughout these studies, the book comes to the conclusion that Calvin's dynamic understanding of the law originates in his dynamic understanding of Christ's mediation of the law as Reconciler, Intercessor, and Teacher; just as from the beginning Christ has been the Mediator of the law, so in its nature, the law is the rule of living and life-giving. This demonstrates why Calvin in his *Institutes* calls the third normative use the principal (*praecipuus*) one and closer to the proper purpose of the law (*in proprium legis finem propius*).

ACKNOWLEDGEMENTS

It is time to express my great gratitude towards many people, without whose help, guidance, and encouragement my book could not have been completed. My sincere appreciation goes to Bundang Church, Doore Scholarship Foundation, Daesung Church, Seongeun Church, and Sion Church. They supported my work both financially and spiritually. My special thanks go out to the Faculty of Divinity of the University of Edinburgh, which paid full tuition for me during my PhD study. I am grateful for financial support and other forms of assistance given to me by Rev. Chiyong Oh in Wangshipri Church, Rev. Joongrim Choi in Dogok Church, KoKos prayer group members, Ross Chapel church members, and my friend Siyeon Park.

I take this opportunity to thank my supervisor, Professor David F. Wright. He read the manuscript with considerable discernment at various stages of its progress, and listened with care and provided careful critique to many of the crucial issues that were eventually incorporated in this book. It was a great pleasure for me to read Latin every week under his wonderful guidance through varying theological documents of the utmost importance. Without his patient academic discipline and insightful suggestions regarding matters of form and content with uniquely warm encouragement the present work would not have been produced to this standard. Dr. Susan Hardman-Moore and Dr. John McDowell at University of Edinburgh have placed me deeply in debt to their discerning reading of this work with keen criticisms and inquiries.

I offer many thanks to those who enlightened and led me to *veritas divina* during my MDiv program in Chongshin Theological Seminary, especially to those who taught me Reformation History and Reformed Theology, Professors Chulwon Suh, Yonggyu Park, Kilsung Kim, and Geontaik Park. Profound thanks go to Professor Richard A. Muller, who taught me the biblical interpretation in the era of the Reformation, Dr. Eugene Osterhaven, with whom I read independently all the chapters of Calvin's *Institutes*, and Dr. I. John Hesselink, who guided my ThM dissertation, "Three Perspectives on Calvin's Concept of Natural Law and Their Relevance for His Commentary on Seneca's *De Clementia*" with tireless thoughtfulness and love. Also, I wish to express my special gratitude for academic dialogues, advice, and warm encouragement I have received from scholars who are sincerely devoted to *Calviniana*, Professor Anthony N. S. Lane, Professor Randall C. Zachman, Professor Herman J. Selderhuis, and Professor Irena Backus with whom I studied the influence of pagan antiquity on sixteenth-century theology in the Institut d'histoire de la Réformation in the University of Geneva.

I am cordially thankful for the constant encouragement and help of my father, Deacon Sangyeon Moon, and my brothers and sisters, Byungchul, Mira, Byungil, Jinja Moon, and for the continuous spiritual and financial support of my parents in law, Rev. Kihaeng Suh and Youngsook Jeong. Finally, to my wife, Sunghee Suh, go the profoundest thanks of all, for supporting and sustaining me for such a long time and in so many places. Also, our children, Wonwook and Maria, receive my thanks and love for their existence, which has been a great joy to me. I also must offer my thanks and love to my mother, Gapsoon Park, who is still waiting for me in glory. This book may be dedicated to the memory of her unfailing love, which always reminds me of the supreme love of God who is working for us through his only Son Christ the Mediator.

ABBREVIATIONS

[ ]: Original Publication
See the Bibliography for Full Citations

ARG	*Archiv für Reformationsgeschichte*
Calvinus Iudaizans	Aegidius Hunnius, *Calvinus Iudaizans*, 1608 [1593]
CC	*Calvin: Commentaries*, ed. and tr. Joseph Haroutunian
CEA	*Calvin's Ecclesiastical Advice*, tr. Mary Beaty and Benjamin W. Farley
Clem.	*Calvin's Commentary on Seneca's De Clementia*, ed. And tr. Ford Lewis Battles and André Malan Hugo
CNTC	*Calvin's New Testament Commentaries*, ed. D. W. Torrance and T. F. Torrance
CO	*Ioannis Calvini opera quae supersunt omnia* (*Corpus Reformatorum*, vols. 29-87)
CR	*Philippi Melanchthonis opera quae supersunt omnia* (*Corpus Reformatorum*, vols. 1-28)
CSA	*Calvin-Studienausgabe*, vols. 1-4, ed. Eberhard Busch, et al.
CTJ	*Calvin Theological Journal*
CTS	*The Commentaries of John Calvin*. Calvin Translation Society Edition.
CTT	*Calvin: Theological Treatises*, ed. J. K. S. Reid
Decades	Heinrich Bullinger, *Sermonum decades quinque, de potissimis Christianae religionis capitibus, in tres tomos digestae*, vol. 2, 1572

DERK	Heinrich Heppe, *Schriften für reformirten Theologie*, vol. 2, *Die Dogmatik der evangelisch-reformirten Kirche*
Dialogorum	Michael Servetus, *Dialogorum de Trinitate*, 1532
Erroribus	Michael Servetus, *De Trinitatis Erroribus libri septem*, 1531
First Catechism	John Calvin, *Catechism or Institution of the Christian Religion* (Latin, 1538), tr. Ford Lewis Battles
HBEM	Heinrich Bullinger, *Sacrosanctum Iesu Christi Domini nostri Evangelium secundum Matthaeum*, 1546 [1542]
HBPE	Heinrich Bullinger, *Commentarii in omnes Pauli Apostoli Epistolas, atque etiam in Epistolam ad Hebraeos*, 1582 [1534]
Inst.	*Institutio christianae religionis* (1559)
1536 *Inst.*	*Institutio christianae religionis* (1536)
1539 *Inst.*	*Institutio christianae religionis* (1539)
1543 *Inst.*	*Institutio christianae religionis* (1543)
1550 *Inst.*	*Institutio christianae religionis* (1550)
LCC	*Library of Christian Classics*
Loci Comm. 1521	Philip Melanchthon, *Loci Communes* 1521
Loci Comm. 1535	Philip Melanchthon, *Loci Communes* 1533
Loci Comm. 1543	Philip Melanchthon, *Loci Communes* 1543
Loci Comm. 1555	Philip Melanchthon, *Loci Communes* 1555
Luther	*Martin Luther's Basic Theological Writings*, ed. Timothy F. Lull
LW	*Luther's Works*, ed. J. Pelikan and H. T. Lehmann
MBEE	Martin Bucer, *In sacra quatuor Euangelia, Enarrationes perpetuae, secundum et postremum recognitae . . .*, 1553 [1536]
MBER	Martin Bucer, *Metaphrasis et enarratio in epist. D. Pauli apostoli ad Romanos . . .*, 1562 [1536]

OS	*Johannis Calvini Opera Selecta*, ed. Peter Barth, et al.
RD	Heinrich Heppe, *Reformed Dogmatics*, ed. Ernst Bizer, tr. G. T. Thomson
Restitutio	Michael Servetus, *Christianismi Restitutio*, 1553
SC	*Supplementa Calviniana*
SCJ	*Sixteenth Century Journal*
TAL	*Treatises against the Anabaptists and against the Libertines*, tr. and ed. Benjamin Wirt Farley
T&T	John Calvin, *Tracts and Treatises*, 3 vols., tr. Henry Beveridge
WA	*D. Martin Luthers Werke, Kritische Gesamtausgabe (Weimarer Ausgabe)*
Wilbur	Michael Servetus, *The Two Treatises of Servetus on the Trinity*, tr. Earl Morse Wilbur
WTJ	*Westminster Theological Journal*

CHAPTER 1

Introduction: Calvin's Attitude towards the Law

1.1 Exploring Calvin's Christological Understanding of the Law

Due to its forensic yet distinctively normative feature, Calvin's concept of the law was regarded by the post-Reformation Reformed theologians as the theological foundation on which they were able to establish their doctrine of the covenant (*foedus, pactum, testamentum*), especially with reference to God's grace and human responsibility.[1] For this reason, in dealing with the

---

[1] There are two striking streams of covenant theology. Reformed Orthodoxy theologians in mainland Europe such as Francis Turretin and Herman Witsius explored covenant theology on the basis of Johannes Cocceius' idea of the covenant of nature and the covenant of grace. Puritan theologians such as William Perkins and John Ball and Scottish covenant theologians represented by Samuel Rutherford were especially keen on the origin and normative validity of the law as they accomplished their own ideal of English Reformation. Heinrich Heppe's monumental work can still be considered the most important textbook for a systematic understanding of covenant theology with the original sources of major Reformed theologians, even though it concentrates on continental theologians. *Reformed Dogmatics: Set Out and Illustrated from the Sources*, ed. Ernst Bizer, tr. G. T. Thomson (London: George Allen & Unwin, 1950, hereafter *RD*). This book originally came out as *Schriften für reformirten Theologie*, vol. 2, *Die Dogmatik der evangelisch-reformirten Kirche* (Elberfeld: Verlag von R. L. Friderichs, 1861, hereafter *DERK*). Heppe's work recalls its English precedents reflecting the tradition of the "marrow" of theology, which reached its most complete form in William Ames, *The Marrow of Theology*, tr. John D. Eusden (Durham, N.C.: Labyrinth Press, 1983). The following collection of major works of J. Wollebius, G. Voetius, and F. Turretin is helpful to understand the doctrine of the law in Reformed Orthodoxy in relation to the formulation of the confessional statements of Dort (1619) and Westminster (1647): John W. Beardslee III, ed. and tr. *Reformed Dogmatics* (New York: Oxford University Press, 1965). For a general overview of the covenant theology of England and Scotland, see R. T. Kendall, *Calvin and English Calvinism to 1649* (New York: HarperSanFrancisco, 1978); Michael McGiffert, "Grace and Works: The Rise and Division of Covenant Divinity in Elizabethan Puritanism," *Harvard Theological Review* 75 (1982), 463-502, and "From Moses to Adam: The Making of the Covenant of Works," *SCJ* 19/2 (1988), 129-155. Concerning the concept of the law among Puritan theologians, see Ernest F. Kevan, *The Grace of Law: A Study in Puritan Theology* (London: Carey Kingsgate Press, 1964). Also, for a comprehensive study of covenant theology, the following works are insightful: David A. Weir, *The Origins of the Federal Theology in Sixteenth-Century Reformation Thought* (Oxford: Clarendon Press, 1990); Richard A.

continuity of theology between Calvin and covenant theologians, scholars have mainly focused on how the covenants (*foedera*) of works and grace were accepted as compatible with the doctrine of the eternal decree of God, how the law preserves its validity in light of Christ's atonement despite the apparent contradiction that was explained, and how the value of the good works of the law (*bona opera legis*) was understood in the whole process of justification and sanctification.[2]

Recent debates on the viability of "two Reformed traditions" in the Reformation, which were evoked by the controversy over the continuity (or discontinuity) between Calvin and Bullinger in their understanding of the covenant, demonstrate that the crucial points of dispute are how the law works continuously with the covenant of grace and how the principle of *sola gratia* invalidates the concept of the covenant of works.[3] Scholars who

---

Muller, "The Covenant of Works and the Stability of Divine Law in Seventeenth-Century Reformed Orthodoxy: A Study in the Theology of Herman Witsius and Wilhelmus à Brakel," *CTJ* 29 (1994): 75-100; Stephen R. Spencer, "Francis Turretin's Concept of the Covenant of Nature," in *Later Calvinism: International Perspectives*, ed. W. Fred Graham (Kirksville, Mo.: Sixteenth Century Essays & Studies, 1994), 71-91.

2 Cf. Peter A. Lillback, *The Binding of God: Calvin's Role in the Development of Covenant Theology* (Grand Rapids: Baker, 2001), 126-141, 194-209, 264-304; James B. Torrance, "The Concept of Federal Theology—Was Calvin a Federal Theologian?" in *Calvinus Sacrae Scripturae Professor: Calvin as Confessor of Holy Scripture*, ed. Wilhelm H. Neuser (Grand Rapids: Eerdmans, 1994), 15-40; Anthony A. Hoekema, "The Covenant of Grace in Calvin's Teaching," *CTJ* 2/2 (1967), 133-161; *RD* 281-300, 371-409. According to Heppe, the Reformed Orthodoxy theologians accept Christ as "the Mediator of the covenant of grace (*mediator foederis gratiae*)" and deal with the *communicatio gratiarum, idiomatum*, and *operationum* in the person and work of Christ in light of the continuity of the covenant of grace (*RD* 410-487, *DERK* 293-351). On the other hand, although Cocceius proclaims both the covenants of works and grace (*foedus operum, foedus gratiae*), he does not seem to maintain the covenant of redemption specifically. He implies the natural origin of the covenant when he says, "Man who comes upon the stage of the world with the image of God, exists under a law and a covenant, and that a covenant of works (*Homo, qui in mundi proscenium prodiit cum imagine Dei, sub lege et foedere et quidem foedere operum exstitit*)" (*RD* 281, *DERK* 207), and "So far as the covenant of works rests upon the law of nature, it may be called the covenant of nature (*Foedus operum, quatenus lege naturae nititur, foedus naturae appellari potest*)" (*RD* 284, *DERK* 208). For the life and theology of Cocceius, Charles S. McCoy and J. Wayne Baker, "The Zenith of Federal Theology: Johannes Cocceius," in *Fountainhead of Federalism: Heinrich Bullinger and the Covenant Tradition with a Translation of De testamento seu foedere Dei unico et aeterno (1534) by Heinrich Bullinger* (Louisville: Westminster/John Knox, 1991), 63-79.

3 The issue of "the two traditions" is suggested by J. Wayne Baker in his book *Heinrich Bullinger and the Covenant: The Other Reformed Tradition* (Athens, Ohio:

oppose the notion of the two traditions are mostly in favour not only of the continuity between Calvin and Bullinger but also of their continuity with later federal theologians. So they point out the unilateral feature of the covenant, which dominates in Calvin, who regards the *foedus legale* in the Old Testament as "a synonym for the old administration of the *foedus gratiae*."[4] On the other hand, scholars who insist on "the other Reformed tradition" of Bullinger emphasize the conditionality of the covenant of works, and differentiate it from the covenant of grace.[5] Meanwhile, a similar issue has been in debate since Paul Helm argued in his book *Calvin and the Calvinists* against R. T. Kendall, who claims that "the central figures of Puritanism such as William Perkins and William Ames derived their theology not from Calvin but from Theodore Beza." Helm criticized Kendall for differentiating Puritan theologians who sustain their view on the ground of "the law before the gospel" from Calvin, who insists on "the gospel before the law."[6]

It is true that covenant theologians made an important contribution to defining and elaborating on such critical issues as the law before the fall, the validity of the law for believers, and the continuity and discontinuity between the Old and New Testaments. One thing to be noted here is that when covenant theologians in Reformed Orthodoxy conceived of placing the gospel prior to the law and sought the origin of this idea in the theology of Calvin, they did not intend to argue for the precedence of the gospel in the process of salvation, as Zwingli did, who spoke of "faith as the foundation on which the law is built,"[7] but rather to point out the principle

---

Ohio University Press, 1980), and "Heinrich Bullinger, the Covenant, and the Reformed Tradition in Retrospect," *SCJ* 29/2 (1998), 359-376. Concerning the position opposed to Baker's, see Lyle D. Bierma, "Federal Theology in the Sixteenth Century: Two Traditions?" *WTJ* 45 (1983), 304-321.

4 Cf. Lyle D. Bierma, *German Calvinism in the Confessional Age: The Covenant Theology of Caspar Olevianus* (Grand Rapids: Baker, 1996), 150-153; Muller, "The Covenant of Works and the Stability of Divine Law in Seventeenth-Century Reformed Orthodoxy," 97.

5 Cf. Baker, *Heinrich Bullinger and the Covenant*, 34-39, 193-215; Robert Letham, "Faith and Assurance in Early Calvinism: A Model of Continuity and Diversity," in *Later Calvinism*, 355-384. Letham says, "A conditional covenant of grace may be the major single factor in precipitating a separation between faith and assurance. A line exists from Bullinger via Musculus and Ursinus to Rollock and Perkins" (383). As Richard A. Muller notes, Baker, treating this agenda, does not take proper consideration of Calvin's exegetical works. *The Unaccommodated Calvin* (Oxford: Oxford University Press, 2000), 155.

6 Paul Helm, *Calvin and the Calvinists* (Edinburgh: Banner of Truth, 1982), 5-6, 9, 61-70, and "Calvin and the Covenant: Unity and Continuity," *Evangelical Quarterly* 55/2 (1983), 65-81.

7 W. P. Stephens, *Zwingli: An Introduction to His Thought* (Oxford: Clarendon Press,

of *sola gratia*, which is engraved in God's decree (*decretum*), by applying it to the covenant of works as well as to the covenant of grace.[8] Therefore, their concern cannot be identified with that revealed through Lutheran controversies over the law and the gospel, i.e., over the role of the law in the process of *poenitentia* (1537-1540), over the realm of the *adiaphora* (1548-1552), and over the normative use of the law called the third use of the law (1556-1557).[9] While for covenant theologians the whole divine *oeconomia* mattered as to the place of the law in its relation to the gospel, Lutheran theologians concentrated on the use of the law in salvation history (*Heilsgeschichte*) and, more specifically, in the process of personal salvation.[10] The revival of the study of Calvin's concept of the law among German scholars which took place in the first half of the twentieth century reflects the influence of the Lutheran controversies over the relationship between the law and the gospel, whereas it does not seem as apparent in the continental covenant theology.[11]

The debates of German scholars for or against Barth's position on natural law and moral law denote the two most distinctive trends in this period. Sharing their legal tradition established on the basis of Luther's two-kingdom theory, they have explored Calvin's understanding of natural law and moral law in the light of their relation to civil (positive) law since the

---

1992), 71. For details, see id., *The Theology of Huldrych Zwingli* (Oxford: Clarendon Press, 1986), 154-69. Concerning the gospel-law order in Zwingli's *De vera et falsa religione commentarius* and its influence on Calvin's theology, Muller, *The Unaccommodated Calvin*, 124-127.

8 By referring to their concept of the absolute and ordained will of God, the late medieval nominalists, who followed the Franciscan theological tradition, tried to explain the compatibility between the covenantal (or conditional) acceptance of God and the principle of *sola gratia*. Cf. Heiko A. Oberman, "Wir Sein Pettler. Hoc Est Verum. Covenant and Grace in the Theology of the Middle Ages and Reformation," in *The Reformation: Roots and Ramifications*, tr. Andrew Colin Gow (Grand Rapids: Eerdmans, 1994), 91-115; Alister E. McGrath, *The Intellectual Origins of the European Reformation* (Grand Rapids: Baker, 1987), 75-85.

9 For the Lutherans' controversies over the law and the formation of their concept of the third use of the law, see Wilfred Joest, *Gesetz und Freiheit: Das Problem des 'tertius usus legis' bei Luther und in der neutestamentlichen Paranese*, fourth ed. (Göttingen: Vandenhoeck & Ruprecht, 1968), 45-55; Gerhard Ebeling, "On the Doctrine of the *Triplex Usus Legis* in the Theology of the Reformation," in *Word and Faith*, tr. James W. Leitch (London: SCM Press, 1963), 62-78; Timothy J. Wengert, *Law and Gospel: Philip Melanchthon's Debate with John Agricola of Eisleben over Poenitentia* (Grand Rapids: Baker, 1997), 177-210.

10 For the formation and influence of Luther's law-gospel doctrine, see Thomas A. McDonough, *The Law and the Gospel in Luther: A Study of Martin Luther's Confessional Writings* (Oxford: Oxford University Press, 1963), 26-38.

11 Cf. I. John Hesselink, *Calvin's Concept of the Law* (Allison Park, Pa.: Pickwick Publications, 1992), 1-6.

publication of the works of Paul Lobstein and Ernst Troeltsch, in which the ethical and social aspects of Calvin's law are identified as *die Lebensregel*.[12] Josef Bohatec pinpointed for the first time the theological foundation of natural law in Calvin. Bohatec examined the influence of natural law upon and its relation to Calvin's concept of the law, in his *Calvin und das Recht*, published in 1934, a year famous for the eruption of the natural law debate between Barth and Brunner.[13]

Brunner established his doctrine of natural law on the ground of the "*analogia entis*" that "God is original, man a derived subject."[14] With this understanding of the *imago Dei*, Brunner argues, "Calvin is not afraid to relate this *lumen naturale* [an immortal soul, a conscience] directly to the Spirit of God."[15] From this perspective Brunner states definitively, "Calvin is concerned to point out that the *lex scripta* has no other function but to make the *lex naturae* effective again. For the *lex naturae* is the will of God."[16] Brunner takes account of the continuity of natural law and the divine law in Calvin by identifying both of them with the will of God.

By citing a famous phrase of Calvin, Barth criticizes Brunner's stance on natural law as it "can only be discussed hypothetically: *si integer stetisset Adam*,"[17] and points out that there is no formal *imago Dei* but "Christ," so we can taste "a *duplex cognitio Domini*, from creation and in Christ."[18] In his article "Nein!" Barth's critique of Brunner's position on natural law (or natural theology in relation to his *analogia entis*) concentrates mostly on Brunner's infidelity to Calvin's *sola scriptura* and *sola gratia*.[19] These

---

12 P. Lobstein, *Die Ethik Calvins in ihren Grundzügen entworfen: Ein Beitrag zur Geschichte der Christlichen Ethik* (Strasbourg: C. F. Schmidt, 1877), esp. 45 ff. Ernst Troeltsch, *The Social Teachings of the Christian Churches*, 2 vols. (London: Allen & Unwin, 1931), 599ff., 866ff. For the implications of Luther's two-kingdom theory for his positions on law, politics, and society, see John Witte, Jr., *Law and Protestantism: The Legal Teachings of the Lutheran Reformation* (Cambridge: Cambridge University Press, 2002) 87-175; Gottfried G. Krodel, "Law, Order, and the Almighty Taler: The Empire in Action at the 1530 Diet of Augsburg," *SCJ* 12/2 (1982), 75-106.
13 *Calvin und das Recht* (Feudigen in Westphalen: H. Boehlaus, 1934), esp. 32-39, 87-93, 97-129. In this book, Bohatec emphasizes the influence of Luther and Christian humanism on Calvin's position on natural law, church and state, etc.
14 Emil Brunner and Karl Barth, *Natural Theology* ("Nature and Grace" by Brunner and the Reply "No" by Barth), tr. P. Fraenkel (London: Geoffrey Bles: The Centenary Press), 23, 55. Brunner distinguishes between the formal and the material *imago Dei*. The quotation refers to the former.
15 Ibid., 42.
16 Ibid., 39.
17 Ibid., 106, cf. 109. Quot. *Inst.* 1.2.1. For Barth's criticism of the formal *imago Dei*, see ibid., 89-90.
18 Ibid., 105, cf. 80-85.
19 Ibid., 79-80, 106-107.

principles were maintained in his ground-breaking article published two years later under the title of "Evangelium und Gesetz." Barth's emphasis was specifically on *sola gratia in Christo*, i.e., on the fact that *Christum in se esse gratiam*, as he says, "The Law is nothing else than the necessary form of the Gospel," and "Jesus Christ, he himself and he alone the grace." Barth's Christological view of the law is basically epistemological. Like Brunner, he admits that "The Law is the manifest will of God." But he lays his emphasis on the question, "Where is the will of God manifest?"[20] While Brunner develops the ontological conception of the law by investigating natural law in the light of *analogia entis* in the *imago Dei*, Barth is initially concerned about the epistemology of the law based on the *analogia fidei* in the person and office of Christ. From this point of view, Barth asserts that Christ himself is the grace of God "in both form and content."[21] The law therefore is not other than the revelation of the event of Christ. "This event is, however, the occurrence of the will of God at Bethlehem, at Capernaum and Tiberias, in Gethsemane, on Golgotha and in the garden of Joseph of Arimathea. Because this occurrence of the will of God, therefore the occurrence of his grace, becomes manifest to us, the Law becomes manifest to us. From what God does for us, we infer what he wants with us and from us."[22] In conclusion, Barth's epistemological understanding of the law is established on the ground that the content of the law is grace, i.e., the incarnate God, Jesus Christ.[23]

Barth's new perspective stimulated many scholars to examine Calvin's law from the perspective of Calvin's Christology and to regard the law as the law of the covenant (*Bundesgesetz*) that is grounded in the incarnation

---

20 Ibid., 77. Cf. Karl Barth, *Church Dogmatics*, vol. 2, *Doctrine of God* 2, tr. G. W. Bromiley, et al. (Edinburgh: T. & T. Clark, 1957), 511-512: "The Gospel itself has the form and fashion of the Law. The one Word of God is both Gospel *and* Law. It is not Law by itself and independent of the Gospel. But it is also not Gospel without Law. It is first Gospel and then Law. It is the Gospel which contains and encloses the Law as the ark of the covenant the tables of Sinai. But it is both Gospel *and* Law. The one Word of God which is the revelation and work of His grace is also Law. That is, it is a prior decision concerning man's self-determination. It is the claiming of his freedom. It regulates and judges the use that is made of this freedom. As the one Word of God, which is the revelation and work of His grace, disposes of man, it is also the impulse directing him to a future that is in keeping with this 'disposing'."
21 Brunner and Barth, *Natural Theology*, 77.
22 Ibid., 77-78.
23 Cf. ibid., 75: "Consequently, God's grace, his grace for our humanity, the goodness, mercy, and condescension in which he is our God and as such accepts us, is Jesus Christ, he himself and he uniquely. Grace, and that means the content of the Gospel, consists therefore simply in the fact that Jesus Christ with his humanity, which he assumed in his birth, preserved as obedience in his death, glorified in his resurrection—he himself and he uniquely intercedes for us with our humanity."

of Jesus Christ.[24] Starting from this perspective, Wilhelm Niesel claims: "Only it ought to have been appreciated that Calvin understands the law from the point of view of its fulfilment in Jesus Christ."[25] In the same vein, H. H. Wolf says that Calvin's special "esteem" of and "emphasis" on the law "was its relation to its *anima* (Christ) and its being included in the covenant of grace."[26]

Meanwhile, Barth's view was criticized by a Lutheran theologian, Werner Elert, who sustained a firm conviction of the "substantive dialectical opposition (*realdialektischer Gegensatz*)" between law and Gospel.[27] Elert's criticism is that, like Barth, Calvin ignored the fact that *lex semper accusat* by defining the law as a "*reigle [règle] de bien vivre et iustement* (a rule of right and just living)"; therefore, according to Calvin even God's judgment becomes God's grace.[28] It seems that Elert follows the misleading understanding of early Lutherans who separated *lex accusans* and *lex vivendi* and would not admit their compatible roles in the whole process of salvation. By revealing the grace-side of the law, Elert, in spite of his critical motivation, consequently played a part in introducing a different image of Calvin to those already accustomed to his dour portrait, which was typically drawn by Reinhold Seeberg who deprecated Calvin's emphasis on the normative use of the law calling it an expression of "fanaticism of submission" saying, "This God of Calvin is the omnipotent

---

24 Wilhelm Niesel, *The Theology of Calvin*, tr. Harold Knight (Philadelphia: Westminster Press, 1956), 92, 95.
25 Ibid., 246. In the new edition of this book Wilhelm Niesel writes: "An ihm hat das Gesetz sein richtendes und strafendes Amt vollendet und, indem das geschah, ist das Gesetz von ihm, dem Einem, erfüllt, der Wille Gottes getan worden." *Die Theologie Calvins* (München: Chr. Kaiser Verlag, 1957), 93. The same view is found in Hugo Röthlisberger, *Kirche am Sinai: Die Zehn Gebote in der christlichen Unterweisung* (Zürich: Zwingli Verlag, 1965), 96-97.
26 *Einheit des Bundes: Das verhältnis von Alten und Neuen Testament bei Calvin* (Neukirchen Kr. Moers: Buchhandlung des Erziehungsvereins, 1958), 50-51, quot. Hesselink, *Calvin's Concept of the Law*, 97.
27 Werner Elert, *Law and Gospel* (Philadelphia: Fortress, 1967), 1, 7-13.
28 Ibid., 47. On the other hand, another Lutheran theologian, Paul Althaus, contrives the concept of "the divine command." He defines it as the original law commanded by God before the publication of the law as he explains the eternity of the will of God. *The Divine Command: A New Perspective on Law and Gospel*, tr. Franklin Sherman (Philadelphia: Fortress, 1966), 6-7, 26-32, 43-47. We should clearly distinguish Calvin's Christological understanding of the law from that of Barth. Barth concentrates on the law in Christ. He fails to explain properly Christ in the law by adhering to the assumption that the law is the form of the gospel. In this respect, Barth's view can be called Christocentric. On the other hand, Calvin pays equal attention to both Christ in the law and the law in Christ. So he deals with the law in its relation to Christ both before and after the incarnation. In this respect, Calvin's view can be considered truly Christological.

Will, ruling throughout the world; the God of Luther is the omnipotent energy of love manifest in Christ."[29]

From the three perspectives founded on the view of natural law we have observed, which are covenant-theological, salvation-historical, and ethical, scholars have dealt with Calvin's concept of the law in certain respects, or sometimes synthetically. However, the first comprehensive examination of the law in Calvin's theology was set forth by I. John Hesselink in his *Calvin's Concept of the Law*.[30] Emil Doumergue's treatment of the law in his epoch-making work is well balanced and paramount in its scope but its focus is centred upon Calvin's *Institutes*.[31] Hesselink derives the dynamic character of Calvin's concept of the law from his definitive statement that "the law is not only an expression of the will of God, it is the will of God."[32] The first part of the definition has been held with reference to the normative nature of the law by Reformers and covenant theologians in the post-Reformation era,[33] but the latter part is so strongly will-oriented that it resounds with God's arbitrariness in *potentia inordinata*, which had been argued by the medieval voluntarists who explored the concept of *voluntas absoluta Dei*.[34] From this perspective, natural law is also defined as "merely one way of expressing God's orderly will for both his creatures and his creation."[35] The influence of the voluntarist tradition (Scotism) on Calvin is highlighted when Hesselink says, "Calvin's concern about the

---

29 Reinhold Seeberg, *Textbook of the History of Doctrines*, vol. 2 (Grand Rapids: Baker, 1952), 416.
30 Cf. Anthony N. S. Lane's review of this book, *Evangelical Quarterly* 70/2 (1998), 165.
31 Emil Doumergue, *Jean Calvin: Les hommes et les choses de son temps*, vol. 6 (Lausanne: G. Bridel, 1926), 181-204.
32 Hesselink, *Calvin's Concept of the Law*, 35. In conclusion of this book, Hesselink claims that the dynamic character of Calvin's concept of the law is derived from his linking of the law to the will of God practically and ethically. Based on this assumption, he describes the dynamic characteristics of Calvin's theology of the law in three ways, i.e., Christ is the example and image of the law, the guidance and leading of the Holy Spirit in understanding and living out the law, and the goal of the law: the restoration of the image of God (278).
33 Cf. Kevan, *The Grace of the Law*, 50-52.
34 For instance, when Zwingli defines the law as "the eternal will of God," more specifically, as "nothing else than teachings as to the will of God, through which we understand what He wills, what He wills not, what He demands, what He forbids," he seeks to identify the law with the expression of *potentia ordinata*. He confirms this by stating immediately thereafter: "But that the will of God is permanent, so that He is never going to change any part of that law which has to do with the inner man, is evident from the words of the Lawgiver Himself." Huldrych Zwingli, *Commentary on True and False Religion*, ed. Samuel Macauley Jackson and Clarence Nevin Heller (Durham, N.C.: Labyrinth Press, 1981), 137-138.
35 Hesselink, *Calvin's Concept of the Law*, 52.

Introduction: Calvin's Attitude towards the Law

unity of law and gospel is thus ultimately a concern about the unity of God's holy will and saving purpose. God is one; therefore his revelation is fundamentally one."[36]

The definition of the law as the expression of God's will helps us to understand in epistemological terms the continuity of God's will, revealed in natural and divine laws, and God's accommodation to human capacity. It also helps to explain the covenant of works from the perspective of *sola gratia*. However, what this definition reveals is more related to the distinctive feature of God's decree that was pinpointed by Reformed theologians in dealing with the sovereign grace of God, than to the law itself and its substantial (*substantialis*) relation to the gospel. When Hesselink designates the law of Moses as the law of the covenant (of grace) and regards the whole law as pointing to Christ on the ground that the law is the will of God,[37] this is not so much a statement on the law itself as on the way in which God's decree is revealed and accomplished in history.[38] It is against this theological background that Hesselink argues for a law-gospel-law paradigm in Calvin's theology.[39] Overall, based on the fact that the law is an expression of the will of God, Hesselink concentrates on the character of Christ as the best interpreter and example of the law as he explains the Christological significance of the law in Calvin's theology.[40]

As in the case of Hesselink, Edward A. Dowey shows his epistemological position on Calvin's law in the light of Calvin's understanding of the knowledge of God the Creator and Redeemer. Dowey affirms that God's law for Calvin is "related closely" to "God's orderly will in creation," but "over against man's freedom God's orderly will is not actualized directly, as in the case of natural events, but through revelation and man's response—that is, God's will has normative value for man."[41] This normative value of God's will revealed in the law, denotes not only the

---

36 Ibid., 160.

37 Ibid., 87-88.

38 For the Christological significance of God's decree, see Richard A. Muller, *Christ and the Decree: Christology and Predestination in Reformed Theology from Calvin to Perkins* (Grand Rapids: Baker, 1988), 35-38.

39 "Law and Gospel or Gospel and Law? Calvin's Understanding of the Relationship," in *Calviniana: Ideas and Influence of Jean Calvin*, ed. Robert V. Schnucker (Kirksville, Mo.: Sixteenth Century Essays & Studies, 1988), 13-32.

40 "Christ, the Law, and the Christian: An Unexplored Aspect of the Third Use of the Law in Calvin's Theology," in *Reformatio Perennis: Essays on Calvin and the Reformation in Honor of Ford Lewis Battles*, ed. B. A. Gerrish (Pittsburgh: Pickwick Press, 1981), 14-20. In dealing with Christ and the law, like Hesselink, Bavinck concentrates on the Christian life following the type of Christ. Cf. John Bolt, "Christ and the Law in the Ethics of Herman Bavinck," *CTJ* 28 (1993), 61-65, 73.

41 The *Knowledge of God in Calvin's Theology*, 3rd ed. (Grand Rapids: Eerdmans, 1994), 222.

precepts but also the promises of the Ten Commandments, however, as Dowey points out, Calvin's high evaluation of the law is directed to "the perfect idea of law which he [Calvin] sees behind them."[42] "The perfect idea of the law," which Calvin designates as "the orderly, harmonious Creator-creature relationship,"[43] is revealed to us sometimes recognizably as the definite rule of life and sometimes unrecognizably as "God's mystery." Therefore, we should turn to God the Redeemer, Christ the Mediator, who is the complete revelation of the law, in order to recognize "the unknowable side of the known God."[44] Dowey's discovery of the normative feature of the law lying between God's revelation and human responsibility stands out, but by treating the relationship between the incarnation of Christ—God's accommodation *par excellence*—and Christ's fulfilment of the law as an epistemologically "dialectic" one,[45] he misses the crucial ontological point of Calvin's Christological understanding of the law, which is based on the fact that Christ is the substance and truth of the law. So, Dowey comes to the same conclusion as Hesselink when he says, "Calvin equates God's orderly will as revealed in creation with the moral law as given to Moses, and the Mosaic moral law with the ethical teachings of Jesus."[46]

While Dowey perceives the law as the expression of the orderly will of God the Creator and from this perspective argues for the substantial unity between the divine moral law and natural law, T. H. L. Parker, in dealing with Calvin's concept of the law, refers mainly to the fact that "the law witnesses to Christ," who is the eternal Word of God (*aeternus Sermo Dei*) hidden *per se* but revealed *in nobis* and *pro nobis*.[47] He does not acknowledge any "mystery" lying between the hidden and revealed will of God, as Dowey does, but maintains the concept of "*Deus absconditus*" considering the fact that "He who is revealed is He who reveals Himself."[48] Thus Parker replaces the epistemological dimension of God's accommodation with the soteriological dimension of God's revelation when he says, "the extra-Biblical revelation is conceived by Calvin purely in reference to salvation in Christ."[49] Parker criticizes Dowey for importing "Brunner's doctrine of responsibility and answerability" thus using Brunner as a basis on which he explains the normative value of the law, i.e., the

---

42 Ibid., 225-226.
43 Ibid., 223.
44 Ibid., 17.
45 Ibid., 14-17, 238-239.
46 Ibid., 230.
47 Calvin's *Doctrine of the Knowledge of God*, rev. ed. (Grand Rapids: Eerdmans, 1960), 36-37, 88-92, 95, 119-120.
48 Ibid., 27-28, 85.
49 Ibid., 55.

necessity of human response.[50] For Parker, there is no room for human reaction through the revelation of the law because there is neither a difference nor a separation between "the revelation of God in Christ" and "the reconciliation of God in Christ."[51] Therefore, the normative characteristic of the law does not originate from the law itself, but from its relation to Christ who is "the eternal Wisdom and Will of God," and "the clear expression of His purpose (*expressa consilii eius effigies*)."[52] Parker attempts to unite God the Creator and God the Redeemer in the light of *Christus pro nobis* and to overcome some epistemological problems in Calvin's theology by concentrating on Christ's mediatorship in the revelation and fulfilment of the law,[53] but his overemphasis on Christ the Redeemer results in the lack of recognition of Christ in the law and the lack of the normative use of the law to reveal God's will not only for believers but also for non-believers. Overall, Parker's view of the law is negative, when he says, "The Commandments witness to Him [Christ] in an indirect manner by convicting of sin."[54]

Calvin gives no full definition of the law, even though he mentions it in two ways, directly yet epistemologically that the law is the expression of God's will, and indirectly yet ontologically that Christ is the truth, substance, soul, and end of the law. These two definitions are not separated because Christ is not only the substance of the law but also the revelation of God's will, i.e., without him there is no true knowledge of God's will.[55] Taking this into account, we can see the existence of "a double aspect of the law," which François Wendel designates as the law which is "peculiar to the people of Israel" and the law which is "oriented towards the Christ."[56] Calvin's Christological understanding of the law is both epistemological and ontological. It, based on the concept of Christ the Mediator of the law, presents both Christ in the law and the law in Christ. This view reflects previous scholars' insights, particularly the major contributions of covenant theologians, but it mostly sheds new light on the study of Calvin's concept

---

50 Ibid., 55-56
51 Ibid., 111.
52 Ibid., 91.
53 Ibid., 99-129. This position of Parker reveals the influence of Barth who writes: "Without the biblical revelation that defines God the Redeemer Calvin sees no real knowledge of God the Creator, and conversely knowledge of God the Redeemer is simply a sharper and clearer seeing of the revelation of God the Creator. Materially the two forms of knowledge are exactly the same. We differentiate them only at once to grasp more truly their essential unity." *The Theology of John Calvin*, tr. Geoffrey W. Bromiley (Grand Rapids: Eerdmans, 1995), 164.
54 Ibid., 95.
55 Cf. Hesselink, *Calvin's Concept of the Law*, 97-101.
56 *Calvin: The Origins and Development of His Religious Thought*, tr. Philip Mairet (London: Collins, 1973), 197.

of the law by considering at the same time the substance and revelation of the law, and the unity and continuity of the law.

1.2 Theologizing the Law

Although a brilliant student of law who was educated by leading scholars of his time, Calvin, unlike Melanchthon, who annotated Cicero's *De officiis* with prolegomena in which he dealt with the nature of the law and presented the exposition of the Decalogue,[57] did not write any specific work on Roman law or common law, except for his *Commentary on Seneca's De clementia*, which contains a noticeable number of legal passages.[58] However, Calvin showed his consistent and deep concern for the law through his doctrinal and exegetical works, and through his tracts and treatises on church polity.[59] Particularly, the registers of the Consistory of Geneva, established by Calvin just after his return to the city in 1541 for "suitable church discipline (*discipline Ecclesiastique convenable*)" according to the legislation of *Les Ordonnances ecclésiastiques*,[60] illustrate how Calvin applied biblical teachings of the law to various civil affairs.[61]

Calvin's Christological view of the law is set out in the academic discourse delivered by Nicolas Cop (1533) and Calvin's preface to Olivétan's French translation of the New Testament (especially the Latin and French preface written in 1534). His special concern for the normative

---

57 *CR* 16.534-679. Melanchthon also deals with the relationship between the Christian doctrine of the law and moral philosophy in his works *Philosophiae moralis epitome*, *Ethicae doctrinae elementa*, and *Enarrationes aliquot librorum ethicorum Aristotelis* (CR 16.1-494).

58 Calvin's *Commentary on Seneca's De Clementia*, tr., intro., and notes by Ford Lewis Battles and André Malan Hugo (Leiden: E. J. Brill, 1969, hereafter *Clem.*), 134*-140*; Ford Lewis Battles, "The Sources of Calvin's Seneca Commentary," in *Interpreting John Calvin*, ed. Robert Benedetto (Grand Rapids: Baker, 1996), 69-72.

59 Cf. Mary Beaty and Benjamin W. Farley, tr., *Calvin's Ecclesiastical Advice* (Louisville: Westminster/John Knox, 1991, hereafter *CEA*). This collection covers a wide range of Calvin's works on church polity from significant theological debates to some then current judicial issues. For the development of church ordinances in Geneva in Calvin's times, see Robert M. Kingdon, "Calvin and Constitutionalism: His Work on the Laws of Geneva," *Pacific Theological Review* 19/1 (1985), 40-53.

60 Quot. Nicolas Colladon, *Vie de Calvin*, CO 21.64.

61 The Consistory took into sincere consideration the regulations of common law, as we can see from the insertion of an article from *Corpus Juris Civilis*, *Codex Iustinianus* under the title *De repudiis* with reference to a case regarding the repudiation of husband or wife to their spouse, saying, "*Consensu licita matrimonia posse contrahi* (Lawful marriage can be contracted by consent)." *Registers of the Consistory of Geneva in the Time of Calvin*, vol. 1. *1542-1544*, ed. Robert M. Kingdon, et al., tr. Wallace McDonald (Grand Rapids: Eerdmans, 2000), 326.

characteristic of the law and its Christological and soteriological relevance is revealed conspicuously in his three catechetical works written around the period of his first stay in Geneva, entitled *Christianae religionis institutio* (1536), *Instruction et confession de foy dont on use en l'Eglise de Genève* (1537), and *Catechismus, sive christianae religionis institutio* (1538). In the first *Institutes* of 1536 he treated the law as a crucial *locus theologicus* whose spirit overarches the whole process of salvation noetically and soteriologically by discussing the two kinds of knowledge and the doctrine of *sola fide* under the title of *"De lege."*[62]

The next stage can be designated as the period in which Calvin's 1539, 1543, and 1550 *Institutes* were written. This decade witnessed Lutheran controversies over antinomianism and the theological realm of *adiaphora*, and the *colloquia* and *disputationes* between Protestants and Catholics.[63] All through these discourses and disputes, both the validity and extent of the law for believers were recognized as enigmas that must be solved in order to establish the true doctrine of salvation. As we can see from the controversy between Calvin and Sadolet, the different understandings of *sola fide* resulted in various opposing views on the office of the law not only in the justification stage but also in the sanctification stage.[64] Calvin

---

62 Scholars, treating the formation of the first chapter of the 1536 *Institutes*, emphasizes the influence of Zwingli's *De vera et falsa religione commentarius* on Calvin's view of the *cognitio Dei ac nostri* and Luther's influence on Calvin's interpretation of the Decalogue. See F. Büsser, "The Zurich Theology in Calvin's *Institutes*," in *John Calvin's Institutes: His Opus Magnum*. Proceedings of the Second South Africa Congress for Calvin Research, 1984 (Potchefstroom: Institute for Reformational Studies, 1986), 135-136; Wilhelm Diehl, "Calvins Auslegung des Decalogs in der ersten Ausgabe seiner *Institutio* und Luthers Catechismen," *Theologische Studien und Kritiken* 70 (1898), 141-162. On the other hand, Wilhelm H. Neuser points out the close connection between *triplex usus legis* and the whole process of salvation, including justification and sanctification, and asserts that in the first chapter of the 1536 *Institutes* "Lutheran sequence of law and Gospel has been destroyed." "The Development of the *Institutes* 1536 to 1559," in *John Calvin's Institutes: His Opus Magnum*, 38.

63 For a survey of colloquies in general, see H. Jedin, *A History of the Council of Trent*, vol. 1 (London: Thomas Nelson, 1957), 372-391; B. Hall, *Humanists and Protestants 1500-1900* (Edinburgh: T & T Clark, 1990), 142-170. With special reference to justification, see Anthony N. S. Lane, *Justification by Faith in Catholic-Protestant Dialogue: An Evangelical Assessment* (Edinburgh: T & T Clark, 2002), 45-85.

64 In his letter to the Genevans written targeting Calvin, Sadolet asserts that there is no faith which is not accompanied by good works because "the true habit of divine righteousness (*verus divinae iustitiae habitus*)" must belong to those justified. Calvin, criticizing this argument, points out the fact that the justified "possesses Christ" and "Christ never is where His Spirit is not (*Christus autem nusquam sine suo spiritu est*)." *A Reformation Debate: John Calvin and Jacopo Sadoleto*, ed. John C. Olin (Grand Rapids: Baker, 1976), 35-36, 68 [altered] (*CO* 5.374, 398).

was involved in these debates mostly by producing letters and theological tracts and treatises, and sometimes by participating in them, and eventually his views were reflected in his later theological works.[65] A most significant example is Calvin's *Acta Synodi Tridentinae cum antidoto*, which was published after the first seven sessions of the Council of Trent in 1547. This work was so brilliant that it established him as the principal advocate of the world of the Reformation.[66]

The three editions of the *Institutes* published during this period illuminate apparently heated issues on the law such as the continuity of the Old and New Testaments, the relation between the law and the gospel, and the validity of the law in relation to double righteousness (*duplex iustitia*) and double imputation (*duplex imputatio*).[67] His commentaries on Romans (1540), I Corinthians (1546), II Corinthians (1547), Galatians to Colossians (1548), and Hebrews (1549) contain his chief arguments about the above subjects. Through these works, Calvin understands the concept of equity from the perspective of God's love revealed in Christ's reconciling work, and deals with *adiaphora* with an emphasis on the interpretation of the law according to its purpose, the only barometer of which is none other than the love of Christ. From this perspective, Calvin strikingly claims the unity of moral law and natural law. Especially, in the *Institutes* of 1543-1550, Calvin devoted many sections to demonstrating how the principles of the divine law should be applied to church polity and discipline and the rule of a magistrate. This reflects Calvin's urgent concern for the ecclesiastical and political consolidation of Geneva.[68]

---

65 As we see later in related sections, the successive editions of Calvin's *Institute* include his several debates with Osiander, Pighius, Stancaro, Biandrata, Servetus, Socinus, etc. For example, like Bucer and Melanchthon, Calvin produced a French edition of Acts of the Regensburg Colloquy, *Actes de Ratisbonne* (*CO* 5.509-684).

66 *CO* 7.365-506. Theodore W. Casteel, "Calvin and Trent: Calvin's Reaction to the Council of Trent in the Context of His Conciliar Thought," *Harvard Theological Review* 63 (1970), 91-117, esp. 100ff.

67 For Calvin, *duplex iustitia* largely denotes *duplex imputatio*, "sola fide non tantum nos sed opera etiam nostra iustificari" (*Inst*. 3.17.10, *CO* 2.598). Therefore, it should be differentiated from the Catholic concept of *duplex iustificatio*, which is based on their synergistic view, and from Osiander's concept of "a twofold righteousness (*duplicis iustitiae*)," which is based on "essential righteousness and essential indwelling of Christ in us (*essentialem iustitiam et essentialem in nobis Christi habitationem*)" (*Inst*. 3.11.10-11, *CO* 2.540-543). Calvin also uses the terms *duplex iustitia* in order to express the twofold (revealed and hidden) justice of God. Cf. Susan E. Schreiner, "Exegesis and Double Justice in Calvin's Sermons on Job," *Church History* 58/3 (1989), 322-338.

68 Calvin wrote *Les Ordonnances ecclésiastiques* (1541) and *Le Catéchisme de l'église de Genève* (1542), and published the Psalter that had been set to verse by Marot (1543) in addition to the publication of the new edition of the *Institutes* (1543) for the

In the following stage of Calvin's life, as we can see for example in his controversy with Osiander over justification, the role of the law in the justification process with reference to Christology was still a vital issue.[69] In his commentaries on the Synoptic Gospels and on the Gospel of John (1553, 1555) and on the Acts of the Apostles (1552, 1554), Calvin argues for the unity of substance (*substantia*) between the law and the gospel by highlighting their Christological relevance and the normative nature of the law as the revelation of the eternal righteousness of God. Calvin's unique understanding of the presence and work of Christ the Mediator is demonstrated prominently in his Old Testament exegeses, especially in his commentaries on Genesis (1554), Isaiah (1551), and in his lectures (*praelectiones*) on the Minor Prophets (1559), Daniel (1561), Jeremiah and Lamentations (1563), and Ezekiel (1564). Some explications present in these works caused Calvin to be accused of being a Judaizer by some of his contemporaries, including Servetus. They centred their criticism mostly on Calvin's historical and literary interpretation stemming from his own Christological perspective. The core of the conflict between Calvin and Servetus is no doubt doctrinal in relation to the Trinity and the person of Christ, but their opposing views originate in their different interpretation of the Old Testament. They accused each other of being a Judaizer, Calvin for his historical approach and Servetus for his literal interpretation that did not take into account Jesus's mediating role in the Old Testament.[70]

---

consolidation of Geneva in the early years after he returned to Geneva. See Bernard Cottret, *Calvin: A Biography*, tr. M. Wallace McDonald (Edinburgh: T & T Clark, 2000), 163-174. William G. Naphy indicates that Calvin's role in this period was "more that of redactor than legislator." *Calvin and the Consolidation of the Genevan Reformation* (Manchester: Manchester University Press, 1994), 85.

69 Andreas Osiander, influenced by the Cabbalistic understanding of the person of Christ, asserts "the connection of Christology with the doctrine of justification by way of Anselm's doctrine of satisfaction." "He equated Christ's human nature with works and his divine nature with faith, and understood the justification of man before God as an inpouring or infusion of Christ's divine nature." See Gottfried Seebaβ, "Osiander, Andreas," in *The Oxford Encyclopedia of the Reformation*, vol. 3. ed. Hans J. Hillerbrand (Oxford: Oxford University Press, 1996), 184a-184b. Osiander kept hold of the Catholic concept of *gratia infusa* in order to explain "the change which Christian faith makes in the life of the believer" as "the indwelling of Christ." His overemphasis on the "perfect" redemption of Christ the Mediator can be understood rightly on this basis. See James Weis, "Calvin Versus Osiander on Justification," *Springfielder* 30/3 (1965), 31-47, esp. 33-35. Cf. Wilhelm Niesel, "Calvin wider Osianders Rechtfertigungslehre," *Zeitschrift für Kirchengeschichte* 46 (1927), 410-430; Trevor Hart, "Humankind in Christ and Christ in Humankind: Salvation as Participation in Our Substitute in the Theology of John Calvin," *Scottish Journal of Theology* 42 (1989), 77-78.

70 Castellio criticizes Calvin as Judaizer mainly as a result of his historical

Calvin's commentaries on the Psalms (1557) and on the last four books of Moses (1563), as well as his sermons on the Psalms and on Deuteronomy dating from 1553 and 1555, demonstrate his positive stance on the normative feature of the law based on the covenant of grace, emphasizing the importance of the law to everyday life. Calvin's mature view of the law is apparent regarding the connection between Christ and the law and the role of the law in the process of justification by faith, outlined in his sermons on Genesis (from 1559), in which he discusses the relation of faith in Christ with the righteousness of the law in the Old Testament. Presumably, for some period before he died, Calvin preached on Christ's teaching of the law in the Sermon on the Mount.[71] In his final commentary on Joshua, published just after he died (1564), once pointing out that God's commandment to establish the cities of refugees clearly showed "how precious human blood is in the sight of God," he observed, "the law was just, equitable, and useful, both in the public and private spheres."[72]

Calvin's increasing concern for the law throughout his life is well demonstrated in his Christological formulation of the law in the successive editions of the *Institutes*. In dealing with Christology in the 1559 *Institutes*, Calvin explains how we can obtain knowledge of Christ our Mediator, revealed and represented by the law (2.7-11), prior to sections on the person and works of Christ (2.12-17). By highlighting the unity and continuity of covenants (*foedera*) and testaments (*testamenta*) in sections where he treats the relation between the law and the gospel (2.9) and between the Old and New Testaments (2.10-11), Calvin testifies to Christ not only being the fulfilment of the law but also the substance and truth of the law. The mentality of this *ordo docendi* of the 1559 *Institutes* appears in the *Harmony of the Books of Moses* as well. In treating the synopsis of the last four books of Moses according to the Decalogue schema, Calvin highlights the precept and promise of the law at the same time, and so demonstrates that the law, which is by nature the rule of living, reveals Christ as its

---

interpretation of the Old Testament law. He argues that Calvin did not know the fact that "The whole law has been transformed by Jesus Christ." See Daniel Augsburger, "Castellio and the Mosaic Law," in *Occasional Papers of the American Society for Reformation Research*, vol. 1 (1977), 169-170.

71 *CO* 46.iii.

72 Comm. Jos. 20:1-6 (240 [altered], *CO* 25.546): "Ita lex tam publice quam privatim iusta et aequa utilisque fuit." All citations of Calvin's commentaries are from the Calvin Translation Society edition for the Old Testament (repr. Grand Rapids: Baker, 1998, vol. 1-15, hereafter *CTS*) and from the Torrance edition for the New Testament (Grand Rapids: Eerdmans, 1960-1972, 12 vols., hereafter *CNTC*). They will be marked as "Comm." with the biblical reference followed by the volume (if distinguished) and page number of the English translation and the Latin citation as found in *Calvin Opera*.

substance, soul, and life. Here Calvin interprets the law as the law of the covenant without losing its historical meaning.[73]

Calvin's Christological stance on the law is revealed prominently once again when he points out the dynamic characteristic of salvation in Book 3 of the 1559 *Institutes*. He deals with regeneration prior to justification claiming that justification and sanctification cannot be separated from each other and, in a strict sense, the most crucial impact of sanctification is our realization of the justified being justified. Initially, he discusses the Holy Spirit (3.1) and faith (3.2), then the regeneration (3.3-5) and the Christian life (3.6-10), and finally the doctrine of justification (3.11-18). These chapters demonstrate that Calvin regards the dynamic relationship between Christ and the law as theologically more crucial to the whole process of justification as he explored it in the first chapter of the 1536 *Institutes* than the view that Christ is the example (*exemplar*) and type (*typus*) set for those trying to live according to God's will revealed in the law by the special illumination of the Holy Spirit. In the same vein, Calvin, calling the doctrine of Christian freedom "*appendix iustificationis*," emphasizes Christian freedom *in* the law rather than Christian freedom *from* the law, and relocates just after justification in the final edition of the 1559 *Institutes* (3.19.1, *CO* 2.613).

Those who regard Calvin's third use of the law as restricted to its purely normative use in the Christian life tend to relate the first theological use to justification and the third normative use to sanctification, the former to Christ's mediation as the Reconciler, the latter to the special work of the Holy Spirit.[74] However, it should be noted that historically the relation

---

[73] T. H. L. Parker argues that Calvin rearranged Moses' four last books into a synopsis called *harmonia* in order "to correct unconvincing relations of time." *Calvin's Old Testament Commentaries* (Louisville: Westminster/John Knox, 1986), 122. This observation is insightful, but not convincing. Presumably, when Calvin commented on the *Harmony* in four categories i.e., preface to the law, the exposition of the law, the supplements, and the end and use of the law, he might have recalled the *Code of Justitinian*, particularly the Justinian *Digest* and *Pandects*, which as the one perfect code included words of cause, regulations and application, and punishments. Professor David F. Wright observes that the value of the *Harmony* lies in his "enlarging of the boundaries of the Decalogue" by "turn[ing] it into a thoroughly Christianized code." "The Ethical Use of the Old Testament in Luther and Calvin: A Comparison," *Scottish Journal of Theology* 36/4 (1983), 475.

[74] Edward A. Dowey, "The Third Use of the Law in Calvin's Theology," *Social Progress* 49/3 (1958), 20-27; Hesselink, *Calvin's Concept of the Law*, 219-221, 251-254; Merwyn S. Johnson, "Calvin's Handling of the Third Use of the Law and Its Problems," in *Calviniana*, 33-50. Johnson relates the first use to "a theological reflection upon humanity," and the third use of the law to "a theological reflection upon God," and argues that the dialectic of the knowledge of God and humanity in Calvin originates from this extrapolation based on the distinction between the law

between law and gospel had been discussed mainly with reference to the role of the law in the whole process of salvation, as we can see most distinctively in the debate between Melanchthon and Agricola over *poenitentia*[75] and in Article 5 of the Regensburg Colloquy, which witnesses that for Calvin's contemporaries the notion of justification (*iustificatio*) was considered closely related to the righteousness of the law (*iustitia legis*) validated in justification and sanctification.[76]

In Calvin's Christological understanding of the law, the character of Jesus Christ as the Mediator who has been working for us is discussed more fundamentally than that as an example or type of the normative application of the law in our life. With the continuous mediation of Christ, God's righteousness revealed in the law is continuously being imputed. Between the unity of God's will and the continuity of God's grace instituted by the divine covenant, there is the continuity of Christ's mediatorship. Therefore, we cannot deal with Calvin's law theologically enough if we do not investigate it from the Christological point of view.

1.3 The Thesis and Tasks of Our Study

As seen above, scholars have tended to explore various views of Calvin's concept of the law from their distinct perspectives. This tendency may be revealed more clearly by those who adhere to Calvin's so-called central

---

and the gospel. In many cases, like here, scholars' misunderstanding of Calvin's *triplex usus legis* comes from their tendency to treat the first and third use as if they represent two different natures of the law.

75 For the historical background and theological reflections, see Wengert, *Law and Gospel*, esp. 25-45, 67-75, 79-102, 156-169.

76 A comparison between Calvin's attitudes towards Article 5 of the Regensburg Colloquy and the Council of Trent (especially its sixth session) is intriguing. Calvin was positive to the concept of *duplex iustitia* in Article 5 even though he was strongly opposed to Catholic understanding of *duplex iustificatio* when he agreed with the phrase "*iustitiam accipit et habet per Christum etiam inhaerentem* (*receoit iustice, et que par Christ il l'ait mesme residente en soy*)" (*CO* 5.526). In the Antidote, however, Calvin criticized the Fathers of Trent because they regarded "the cause of justification (*causa iustificationis*)" as "twofold" "*partim remissione peccatorum, partim spirituali regeneratione*" and explained justification in two ways "*partim imputatione, partim qualitate*" (*CO* 7.448). Calvin's positive attitude towards Article 5 has been asserted by W. H. Neuser, "Calvins Urteil über den Rechtfertigungsartikel des Regensburger Buches," in *Reformation und Humanismus*, ed. M. Greschat and J. F. G Goeters (Witten: Luther-Verlag, 1969), 186-189; Anthony N. S. Lane, "Calvin and Article 5 of the Regensburg Colloquy," unpub., presented International Calvin Congress (Princeton, 2002), forthcoming in *Calvinus Praeceptor Ecclesiae*, ed. Herman Selderhuis (Genève: Droz, 2004), 231-261.

dogma.[77] Those who accept the doctrine of predestination as the central dogma may seek to explain the office and use of the law on the basis of the assurance of faith. Those who think of the union with Christ as central may take issue with the imputation of Christ's righteousness as primary in discussing the role of the law in the context of the whole process of salvation. Meanwhile, those who regard Calvin as the doctor of the Holy Spirit may think of the dynamic characteristic of Calvin's concept of the law as a result of the special illumination of the Holy Spirit and try to associate the normative use of the law with Christian piety.[78]

It does not seem plausible to argue for the centrality of the law in Calvin's theology, even though his dynamic and creative understanding of the relationship between Christ and the law has been considered the very core upon which the whole system of his theology is founded regarding the two kinds of the knowledge of God in the *Institutes*. Calvin's frequent references to the normative nature of the law[79] reflect his firm conviction that Christ is the substance (*substantia*), truth (*veritas*), soul (*spiritus*), and life (*vita*) of the law, as well as its example (*exemplar*) or type (*typus*). In dealing with the Christological meaning of the law, Calvin maintains the concept of Christ the Mediator of the law (*le mediateur de la loy*) by describing it in three ways: Christ as the Mediator of reconciliation (*mediator reconciliationis*), intercession (*patrocinii*), and teaching (*doctrinae*). In so doing, he presents us with an insight through which we can understand why he designates Christ as the substance of the law, on what ground he asserts the normative nature of the law (*lex vivendi*), and from this explores the life-giving office of the law (*lex vivificandi*), and from what perspective he identifies the Holy Spirit that works in and through the law with the Spirit of Christ our Mediator.[80]

---

77 Cf. Charles Partee, "Calvin's Central Dogma Again," in *Calvin Studies III*, ed. John H. Leith (Richmond: Union Theological Seminary, 1986), 39-46.

78 For an example of the perspectival approach to Calvin's concept of the law, see Mary Lane Potter, "The 'Whole Office of the Law' in the Theology of John Calvin," *Journal of Law and Religion* 3/1 (1985), 117-139.

79 E.g., Calvin's definition of the law as "*iuste pieque vivendi norma*" in Comm. Ex. 19:1-2 (1.313, *CO* 24.192), "*pie iusteque vivendi regula*" in Comm. Deut. 6:20-25 (1.363, *CO* 24.225), and "*perfecta vitae regula*" in Comm. Deut. 5:22 (1.333, *CO* 24.205).

80 Calvin, *Sermons on Galatians*, 3:19-20 (453, *CO* 50.543); Comm. Gal. 3:19 (62, *CO* 50.216-217). Concerning the relationship between the law, salvation, and Christ's mediation, see esp. Serm. Acts 7:35-37 (*SC* 8.312-314, 328-330); Gen.15:6 (*SC* 11/2.758-764). All citations of Calvin's sermons are marked as "Serm." with the biblical reference followed by the page number of the English translation (if available) and the volume and page number of the French citation from *Calvini Opera* (*CO*) or *Supplementa Calviniana* (*SC*).

This book plans to examine Calvin's Christological understanding of the law in the light of his concept of *Christus mediator legis*. I will investigate whether there is any unique feature of the law found in the theology of Calvin, mostly by studying his works and sometimes by comparing them with those works of other Reformers' deemed the most influential. My book is based on this argument: while Lutherans regard *lex accusans* as the principal use and separate it from *lex vivendi* in order to keep their principle *lex semper accusat*, and while covenant theologians, although considering much of the normative use of the law, treat the peculiar office and use of the law as merely an important element in explaining the mutuality and conditionality of the covenant, Calvin understands the nature of the law as *regula vivendi* and, from this point of view, deals with the theological use of the law, which had been typically depicted by Lutherans and some Reformed theologians as *officium legis accusantis*, positively as the office of *lex vivificandi*. From this argument, based on the continuity of Christ the Mediator (with reference to the person of Christ) and the continuous mediation of Christ (with reference to the works of Christ), I come to the conclusion that Calvin sustains his dynamic view of the law by claiming the unity of *lex vivendi* and *lex vivificandi*. This study eventually gives an answer to why Calvin calls the third (normative) use of the law the "principal" one (*Inst.* 2.7.12, *CO* 2.261).[81]

Before treating some specific key issues of Calvin's Christological understanding of the law, it would be helpful to study the formation and development of Calvin's theology of the law. This subject can be carried out appropriately through a thorough study of his life and theology. In chapter 2, I will concentrate on the influence of the *via moderna* and the *mos novus* upon the young Calvin's view of the law along with the influence of his legal study. Through the study of the *via moderna*, I examine how late medieval nominalists' Scotism impacted on Calvin, especially with reference to their understandings of God's ordained and absolute will and the merit of Christ. Studying the influence of *mos novus*, the new method of interpreting Roman law established by Calvin's teachers, Pierre de l'Estoile and Andreas Alciati, gives us the clue to solving the origin of Calvin's historical interpretation of the law. The following study of Calvin's *Institutes* in chapter 3 allows us to see the development of his Christological understanding of the law and from this to realize the necessity and validity of our study.

Chapter 4 is devoted to Calvin's concept of *Christus mediator legis*. Firstly, I concentrate on his commentary and sermon on Galatians 3:19.

---

81 All citations of the 1559 *Institutes* are from the Battles translation (Philadelphia: Westminster Press, 1960). The first reference marks the book, chapter, and section number. The second reference is from *Calvini Opera*, which is abbreviated by *CO* followed by the volume and column number.

Then, I treat three types of mediation of Christ, as Reconciler, Intercessor, and Teacher, revealed throughout his works. In particular, with reference to its theological foundation, I ask if the so-called *extra Calvinisticum* is applicable to the realm of the law and if there is any room for *extra legem* in Calvin's theology. These theological agendas lead us to another question, how we should understand Calvin's concept of *Christus mediator legis* in its relation to his favourite theological-rhetorical use of God's accommodation.

The next three chapters are based on Calvin's interpretation of the Old Testament, the Gospels, and Pauline letters, but the subject of each chapter entails particular themes of Calvin's Christological understanding of the law on the basis of his view of *Christus mediator legis*. In chapter 5, I investigate how the law is related to Christ the Mediator in his historical and literal interpretation of the Old Testament. From his controversy with Servetus, I show that although their difference is prominent in the matter of their Christology of the Old Testament, their dispute is basically hermeneutical rather than doctrinal. Besides this, a study of Calvin's treatise *Ad quaestiones et obiecta Iudaei cuiusdam responsio* sheds light on his attitude towards the Jews in the post-biblical era. On the whole, in this chapter, I will verify the extent of Christ's mediation, ranging over the Old Testament, and the fact that Calvin's literal and historical interpretation of the Old Testament in the light of *Christus mediator legis* does not witness to his Judaic tendency, but rather to his unique biblical interpretation.

In chapter 6, I examine Calvin's treatment of Christ's teaching of the law, and the significance of Christ's works for the law and its relevance for his Christological understanding of the law, centred on his commentaries on the Four Gospels. I observe how Calvin identifies God's righteousness revealed in the law with the original meaning of the law in the light of *Christus mediator legis*. Then, by comparing Calvin with Melanchthon and Bucer, who influenced Calvin most prominently by their commentaries on the Gospels, I demonstrate that Calvin's unique understanding of the law is based on his firm conviction of the continuity of the law by linking the law taught by the Mediator with the law fulfilled by the Mediator.

My comparative study of Calvin and other Reformers continues in chapter 7, but here the emphasis is on the use and office of the law for the whole process of salvation. I first deal with the role of the law especially with reference to its role in *poenitentia perpetua* (including repentance in the stage of sanctification). The relationship between the offices of the law, i.e., *lex accusans* and *lex vivendi*, is pinpointed here. Then I deal with Calvin's *triplex usus legis* from the perspective of *Christus mediator legis*. My argument I verify here is that Calvin develops the theological use of the law from its normative use, and furthermore sustains the continuity between *lex vivendi* and *lex vivificandi* by understanding the law in the light of

Christus mediator legis and on this grounds the continuity of the covenants (*foedera*) of works and grace.

In chapter 8, finally, I summarize previous discussions, and give some concluding remarks on the coherence between Christology and soteriology in Calvin's theology of the law, referring especially to his sermons.

CHAPTER 2

The Intellectual Origins of Calvin's Concept of the Law[1]

2.1 The Significance of the Young Calvin's Legal Culture

The influence of Calvin's humanistic and legal studies on his theology has been dealt with by scholars from biographical, rhetorical, and theological aspects. In his interpretation of the law, Calvin was evidently influenced by Christian humanists, Protestant theologians, and by the humanistic jurists who led the *mos novus* (new way) of legal studies. However, it is another task for us to explore how it impacted on his theology. This task is especially difficult, because he did not write any specific work before his conversion dealing with theological position on the law, nor did he write any work after his conversion on his humanistic legal thought and conceptions.[2]

On this account, some scholars have felt a certain hiatus between the periods before and after Calvin's conversion and have had a tendency to overvalue Calvin's sudden conversion (*subita conversio*), which he himself

---

1 The adjective "intellectual" is added in order to differentiate the humanistic background of Calvin's theology of the law from the "spiritual (theological)" foundation of his dynamic understanding of the law, which is sought most significantly in the concept of *Christus mediator legis*.
2 We can hardly find any hermit-character of the late medieval mysticism in Calvin; rather he was quite a social person. He strengthened close personal relationships with his friends, colleagues, teachers, and many acquaintances throughout his life, and devoted his whole life to informing his people of what he was convinced of in the familiar (*familier*), vivid (*vif*), joyful (*joyeux*), elegant (*megnard*), and noble (*noble*) style of writing. Richard Stauffer, *The Humanness of John Calvin*, tr. George H. Shriver (Nashville: Abingdon, 1971), 47-71; Emil Doumergue, *Le caractère de Calvin: l'homme. le systeme. l'église. l'état* (Neuilly: La Cause, 1931), 33-55. Notwithstanding, Calvin did not speak about himself willingly (*De me non libenter loquor*), including his conversion. *Responsio ad Sadoleti Epistolam, CO* 5.389. Calvin's reticence should not be regarded as a revelation of his personal character but understood in the light of his willing devotion to glorify God by denying himself, as we can see from his sermon on Isaiah 53:7-8 (89 [altered], *CO* 35.637), in which he says, once contrasting our sinfulness with God's righteousness, "We glorify God by keeping silent about ourselves (*nous glorifions Dieu en nous taisant*)."

confessed as such in the preface of his commentary on the Psalms, and they have pointed out the discontinuity between his early thought and later theological positions.[3] Meanwhile, other scholars have investigated the influence of Calvin's early studies on his theology, and by this have tried to prove the continuity in his thinking.[4] In doing this, they have depended mostly on Calvin's writings rather than on his life itself. The following observation of Alexandre Ganoczy shows on what ground their assumptions are founded.

> [T]he "I" of Calvin is inseparably tied to his doctrine. This is not the same as with Luther, where the subjective element often "transfigures" the objective element of a statement. Quite the opposite. With Calvin, the objective dominates the subjective. But in dominating the subjective, the objective preserves the reality of the subjective.[5]

Ganoczy perceives Calvin's sudden conversion not as "a sudden or miraculous element in spiritual transformation" but as "a response to a call to reform the Church."[6] A similar approach is also found in the works of

---

3 *CO* 31.21-22. Cf. H. Lecoultre, "La Conversion de Calvin," *Revue de théologie et de philosophie* (1890), 5-30; A. Lang, "Die Bekehrung Johannes Calvins," *Studien zur Geschichte der Theologie und der Kirche* 2 (1897), 1-56; K. Müller, "Calvins Bekehrung," *Nachrichten von der (Königlichen) Gesellschaft der Wissenschaft zu Göttingen* (1905), 188-255; P. Sprenger, *Das Rätsel um die Bekhrung Calvins* (Neukirchen: Neukirchener Verlag, 1960); Wendel, *Calvin*, 38, 44; Danielle Fischer, "Nouvelles réflexions sur la conversion de Calvin," *Etudes théologiques et religieuses* 58 (1983), 203-220. For a survey of scholars' positions on Calvin's conversion, see Williston Walker, *John Calvin: The Organizer of Reformed Protestantism 1509-1564*, 3rd ed. (New York: Schocken Books, 1969), 79-90; Alexandre Ganoczy, *The Young Calvin*, tr. David Foxgrover and Wade Provo (Philadelphia: Westminster Press, 1987), 265; Wilhelm H. Neuser, "Calvin's Conversion to Teachableness," in *Calvin and Christian Ethics*, ed. Peter de Klerk (Grand Rapids: Calvin Studies Society, 1987), 57-77.

4 Cf. Quirinus Breen, *John Calvin: A Study in French Humanism* (Grand Rapids: Eerdmans, 1931), 159-164; Battles, "The Sources of Calvin's Seneca Commentary," 84-85; Basil Hall, "John Calvin, the Jurisconsults and the *Ius Civile*," in *Studies in Church History*, vol. 3, ed. G. J. Cuming (Leiden: E. J. Brill, 1966), 202-216; Charles B. Partee, *Calvin and Classical Philosophy* (Leiden: E. J. Brill, 1977), esp. 13-23; W. Stanford Reid, "John Calvin, Lawyer and Legal Reformer," in *Through Christ's Work: A Festschrift for Dr. Philip E. Hughes*, ed. W. Robert Godfrey and Jesse L. Boyd III (Phillipsburg, N.J.: Presbyterian and Reformed Publishing, 1985), 149-164; Arvin Vos, "Calvin: The Theology of a Christian Humanist," in *Christianity and the Classics: The Acceptance of a Heritage*, ed. E. Helleman (Landham: University Press of America, 1990), 109-118.

5 *The Young Calvin*, 242.

6 Ibid., 251, 266. In the same breath, Ganoczy takes into consideration the influence of

William J. Bouwsma, who explains the continuity in Calvin's life before and after his conversion in the light of his anxiety overarching the whole of his life,[7] in the works of Heiko A. Oberman, who tries to relate the cause of his anxiety to the character of *viator* and link it with the prominent feature of the "refugee Reformation,"[8] in the works of Herman J. Selderhuis, who tries to read Calvin's mind from the notion of asylum (*refugium*), a frequently reoccurring feature in his commentary on the Psalms,[9] and in the works of Olivier Millet, who attempts to portray the "I" of Calvin by referring to the rhetorical meanings of his autobiographical statements and comes to a conclusion similar to that of Oberman and Selderhuis.[10]

Even for scholars who argue for the continuity, it has been regarded as a hard task to prove a specific link between Calvin's early thinking and his later theological views. They are very positive as to the fact that the uniqueness of Calvin's theology should be understood from the background of his early life, but they do not take into serious consideration his theological position before his conversion.[11] This is true of his theology of

---

the *devotio moderna* on Calvin's religious life before his conversion. Ibid., 57-71.

7 *John Calvin: A Sixteenth Century Portrait* (Oxford: Oxford University Press, 1988), 32-48. 230-234. Bouwsma does not consider seriously Calvin's sudden conversion itself; rather, he emphasizes the continuity of Calvin's self. He writes, "Although his [Calvin's] career was filled with accomplishment, his inner life showed few signs of the progress which he associated with godliness; he was still wrestling at the end of his life with the self-doubt, confusions, and contradictory impulses that had been with him from the beginning." Ibid., 9.

8 "*Initia Calvini*: The Matrix of Calvin's Reformation," in *Calvinus Sacrae Scripturae Professor*, 127-154, esp. 129, 154.

9 "Calvin as an Asylum Seeker," in *Calvin's Books: Festschrift for Peter de Klerk*, ed. Wilhelm H. Neuser, et al. (Heerenveen: Groen, 1997), 283-300.

10 *Calvin et la dynamique de la Parole: Etude de rhétorique réformée* (Genève: Editions Slatkine, 1992), 515-554. Seeking the rhetorical meaning of Calvin's sudden conversion in the preface of his commentary on the Psalms by comparing the humanity of Calvin with that of David, Millet observes: "Les motifs de la rhétorique antique, avec son sens de la dignité et de l'efficacité oratoires, rejoignent ceux de la culture chrétienne pour interdire à Calvin toute expression de soi qui ne serait pas soumise aux impératifs de la distinction des genres, à ceux de l'argumentation, ou encore à ceux de l'édification collective des âmes dans de cadre d'une typologie psychologique et spirituelle dont seul le théologien-exégète a les clefs. Sur le plan de l'*ethos* comme sur celui du *pathos*, les traits qui pourraient contribuer à dessiner le portrait de l'auteur ressortissent aux seules règles, formulées par la rhétorique, du discours public" (525).

11 Some scholars have investigated the continuity and discontinuity between the two Calvins by investigating the meaning of his conversion from his own perspective. Most noticeably, Ganoczy examines how Calvin uses the term *metanoia* in his works, and concludes that for him it denotes not "basically detachment (disgust, refusal, break) but attachment (a higher love, acceptance, commitment)," *The Young Calvin*,

the law. They set a high value on his commentary on Seneca's *De clementia* as a humanist's *chef-d'oeuvre*, but they do not pay specific attention to its influence upon his later theological stance on the divine law.[12]

Regardless of biographical arguments on how he started his legal studies and what his attitude towards the law was,[13] Calvin must have been one of the most brilliant law students of his time, who tried to accomplish with amazing ardor and ability his academic goal, i.e., interpreting law in the light of the principle of *ad fontes*. Law was an essential feature in Calvin's life and thought, whether it be God's law or civil law. He attended two colleges of law in Orléans and Bourges, where he studied (Roman) civil law and canon law.[14] Calvin, as a second generation Reformer, realized that law is both indispensable and crucial, like the "sinews" of the body, in the building up of church (cf. *Inst.* 4.10.27-32, esp. 4.10.27) and in organizing the Christian community upon the normative foundation of equity (cf. *Inst.* 4.20.14-21).[15] He definitely regarded the law as the connecting point between epistemology and doctrine, between justification and

---

243. Oberman's conclusion is similar to Ganoczy's in his article, "*Subita Conversio*: The Conversion of John Calvin," in *Reformiertes Erbe: Festschrift für Gottfried W. Locher zu seinem 80. Geburtstag*, vol. 2 (Zürich: Theologischer Verlag, 1993), 279-295. Alister E. McGrath also seems to have an opinion of the twofold meaning of Calvin's conversion, when he explains Calvin's "religious reorientation" as "the transition from a 'consensual' to a 'committed' understanding of religion." *A Life of John Calvin: A Study in the Shaping of Western Culture* (Oxford: Blackwell Publishers, 1990), 75. For the theological meaning of the word "conversion" in Calvin's works, see Walker, *John Calvin*, 71-76; Ford Lewis Battles, "*Calculus Fidei*: Some Ruminations on the Structure of the Theology of John Calvin," in *Interpreting John Calvin*, 141-155; Ganoczy, *The Young Calvin*, 245-252; Oberman, "*Initia Calvini*," 114-115, n. 3.

12 Cf. Louise L. Salley, "A French Humanist's Chef-d'Oeuvre: The Commentaries on Seneca's '*De Clementia*' by John Calvin," *Renaissance Papers* (1968), 41; Ford Lewis Battles, "Against Luxury and License in Geneva," in *Interpreting John Calvin*, 319-328.

13 Cf. Ganoczy, *The Young Calvin*, 64. According to Colladon, Calvin decided "to study law rather than theology, for at that time theology was corrupted in the schools" (*CO* 21. 54).

14 According to Breen, although it is not certain if Calvin took up a study of canon law, taking into account that the College of Orléans offered the course of canon law and the greatest jurists of Calvin's times were usually doctors of both civil and canon law, we are able to confirm the influence of canon law on the young Calvin. *John Calvin*, 137, 139; T. H. L. Parker, *John Calvin: A Biography* (Philadelphia: Westminster Press, 1975), 13; Reid, "John Calvin, Lawyer and Legal Reformer," 152.

15 For the political character of Calvin's Geneva, see John T. McNeill, "The Democratic Elements in Calvin's Thought," *Church History* 18/3 (1949), 153-171.

sanctification, and between the Christian life in the church and in the world.[16]

Not only did Calvin as the Reformer devote his life to establishing ecclesiastical constitutions for the church of Geneva, but he also played a major role in instituting constitutions over the period of the Genevan legal reforms.[17] He was involved as church leader in formulating the articles on moral standards of the 1536 Geneva Constitution and as the author of the 1543 Geneva Constitution, *Ordonnances sur les offices et officiers*.[18] His concern for the application of Geneva laws to their social and religious context was no less significant than his concern for the legislative process itself, as we can see in the registers of the Geneva Consistory.[19] Certainly, he was "a man of law," who discovered that the grace of the law lies in its normative sense.[20] As he says in the *Institutes*, the law "warns, informs, convicts, and lastly condemns," but it also becomes a source of delight because it contains "not only the precepts, but the accompanying promise of grace, which alone sweetens what is bitter" (*Inst.* 2.7.6, 12, *CO* 2.257, 262).

Calvin attended two colleges with the intention of becoming a priest, and two colleges in order to become a lawyer. However, when he published at his own expense his first book on Seneca, he intended to make himself known as a humanist like Budé and Erasmus. These three images—priest, lawyer, and humanist—looked incompatible even to Calvin's contemporaries. Few people lived a life similar to Calvin's. Petrarch,

---

16 Cf. Jean Carbonnier, "Droit et Théologie chez Calvin," in *Johannes Calvin: Akademische Feier der Universität Bern zu seinem 400 Todestag*, ed. Hans Merz, et al. (Bern: Verlag Paul Haupt, 1965), 18-31.

17 For Genevan legal reforms, see E. William Monter, *Calvin's Geneva* (New York: John Wiley & Sons, 1967), 144-155; Josef Bohatec, "Calvin et le code civil à Genève," *Revue historique du droit français et étranger* 4/17 (1938), 229-303; Ernst Pfisterer, *Calvins Wirken in Genf* (Neukirchen: Neukirchener Verlag, 1957), 29-63; Kingdon, "Calvin and Constitutionalism," 40-53. The goal of Calvin's legal Reformation in Geneva is often described as the recovery of King Josiah's theocracy in the Old Testament. Cf. Eugène Choisy, *La Théocratie à Genève au temps de Calvin* (Genève: Ch. Eggimann & Cie, 1897), 23.

18 Robert M. Kingdon, "*Calvinus Legislator*: The 1543 'Constitution' of the City-State of Geneva," in *Calvinus Servus Christi*, ed. Wilhelm H. Neuser (Budapest: Presseabteilung des Ráday-Kollegiums, 1988), 225-227; Reid, "John Calvin, Lawyer and Legal Reformer," 160-162; Monter, *Calvin's Geneva*, 152.

19 For the history and practice of the Geneva Consistory, see Robert M. Kingdon, "Calvin and the Establishment of Consistory Discipline in Geneva: The Institution and the Men Who Directed it," *Nederlands Archief voor Kerkgeschiedenis* 70 (1990), 158-172; Thomas A. Lambert and Isabella M. Watt, "Introduction," in *Registers of the Consistory of Geneva in the Time of Calvin*, vol. 1, *1542-1544*, xvii-xxxv.

20 J. S. Whale, *The Protestant Tradition* (Cambridge: Cambridge University Press, 1955), 164.

Montaigne, and Luther studied law at one time in their lives.[21] However, nobody lived a life so full of religious piety, legal thought, and humanist spirit as Calvin. This uniqueness of Calvin's life gives us a clue to understanding the uniqueness of his theology of the law.

Dealing with the influence of the young Calvin's humanistic and legal studies on the formation and development of his theology of the law, I will concentrate on two subjects with reference to his Christological understanding of the law. First, I will study the humanist jurists of the time. Their influence is crucial in discussing the origin of Calvin's historical-literal interpretation of the law. Secondly, I will examine late medieval views of the righteousness of good works of the law in relation to the idea of the merit of Christ. This study will help us to understand the background of the Christological relevance for the normative use of the law, which is prominent in Calvin's theology of the law. These studies are historically related to the movements of the *mos novus* and the *via moderna*. Especially, with reference to the Christological understanding of the law, the influence of the *devotio moderna*, which pursued Christ-centred spirituality and life, should be considered.

Finally, I will deal with Calvin's commentary on Seneca's *De clementia*, in which the young legal student who tried to make himself known as a Christian humanist like Erasmus deployed his view on one of the crucial issues in his times—the clemency of the magistrate—an idea closely related to the rule of the law, especially to equity and moderation in the legal practice. These elements are of capital importance especially in dealing with Calvin's historical interpretation of the law. Therefore, it is worthwhile to treat them before investigating the Reformer's view of the law as revealed in his early works and in successive editions of his *Institutes*.

2.2 *Mos Novus*: A Historical Philological Approach to the Legal Texts

Scholars have dealt with Calvin's literal interpretation of the Scripture in varying ways, most focusing on his Christocentric biblicism and on his theory of verbal inspiration.[22] In spite of the different approaches, however, they eventually take the same position when they characterize Calvin's biblical interpretation as both historical and Christological. As Richard A. Muller notes, how to find the meaning of "literal" in biblical exegesis must have been a very important agenda for Calvin, as it was for Nicholas of Lyra, who was faithful to the literal meaning of the Scripture by pursuing its

---

21 Cf. Myron P. Gilmore, *Humanists and Jurists: Six Studies in the Renaissance* (Cambridge, Mass.: Harvard University Press, 1963), 67.

22 Cf. Richard A. Muller, *Post-Reformation Reformed Dogmatics*, vol. 2, *Holy Scripture: The Cognitive Foundation of Theology* (Grand Rapids: Baker, 1993), 62-63.

textual and contextual (either historical or Christological) significances based on his theory of a double literal sense (*duplex sensus literalis*), and also for Lefèvre d'Étaples, who believed that there was no specific literal meaning of the Scripture that can be separated from its contextual (spiritual) significance.[23]

On the other hand, another approach to the origin of Calvin's historical and literary interpretation of the Scripture has been suggested by some scholars in the light of the influence of his legal education, which was noticeable in connection to the historical and philological interpretation of the *Corpus* of Roman law.[24] In asserting the similarities between the Mosaic law and the Roman law as to the three kinds of the law—moral, ceremonial, and judicial—the fourfold grouping of the Mosaic codes in his commentary on the four last books of the Pentateuch, the threefold use of the law, and the concept of *iustitia* (in its relation to the concept of *epieikeia*), as Ford Lewis Battles confidently asserts, "what Calvin wrote about the Mosaic law in general, and on justice and equity in particular, was profoundly affected by his early studies in Roman law at the Universities of Orléans and Bourges."[25]

My main concern in this section is not to explore the whole range of the influence of Calvin's legal studies on his theology of the law but to focus on

---

23 Ibid., 44-50, 489-490, and id., "Biblical Interpretation in the Era of the Reformation," in *Biblical Interpretation in the Era of the Reformation: Essays Presented to David Steinmetz in Honor of His Sixtieth Birthday*, ed. Richard A. Muller and John L. Thompson (Grand Rapids: Eerdmans, 1996), 11. Referring to the influence of Lyra and Lefèvre d'Étaples upon Calvin, Muller characterizes the verbal inspiration in the promise-fulfilment hermeneutic of Calvin's Old Testament interpretation as the shift of "paradigm" as "from *littera* to *credenda, agenda*, and *speranda*." "The Hermeneutic of Promise and Fulfillment in Calvin's Exegesis of the Old Testament Prophecies of the Kingdom," in *The Bible in the Sixteenth Century*, ed. David C. Steinmetz (Durham, N.C.: Duke University Press, 1990), 68-82. For the development of the 16th century biblical interpretation from the medieval fourfold exegesis (literal, allegorical, typological, and anagogical), see Philip E. Hughes, "Some Observations on the History of the Interpretation of Holy Scripture," in *Church, Word, and Spirit: Historical and Theological Essays in Honor of Geoffrey W. Bromiley*, ed. James E. Bradley and Richard A. Muller (Grand Rapids: Eerdmans, 1987), 100-106; Parker, *Calvin's Old Testament Commentaries*, 69-82, and *Calvin's New Testament Commentaries*, 2nd ed. (Louisville: Westminster/John Knox, 1993) 93-108; Karlfried Froehlich, "Johannes Trithemius on the Fourfold Sense of Scripture: The *Tractatus de Inuestigatione Sacrae Scripturae* (1486)," in *Biblical Interpretation in the Era of the Reformation*, 23-60, esp. 43.

24 Jack B. Rogers and Donald K. McKim, *The Authority and Interpretation of the Bible* (New York: Harper & Row, 1979), 96-98. Cf. Ford Lewis Battles, "Calvin's Humanistic Education," in *Interpreting John Calvin*, 48-61.

25 Ford Lewis Battles, "Notes on John Calvin, *Justitia*, and the Old Testament Law," in *Interpreting John Calvin*, 307-318, esp. 308.

the new highly context-oriented way of textual interpretation and its influence on Calvin's historical interpretation of the law.[26] This study will enable us to understand the formation of Calvin's Christological understanding of the law as we become aware of some characteristics of his contemporary philological approach to Roman law, according to which the genuine sense of a text was believed to be explored along with its ancient cultural background and the intention of the author of the ancient text.

Roman law had been dealt with as a theme separate from feudal law and canon law since Irnerius opened the era of the so-called glossators by collecting the texts of the *Corpus Juris Civilis* in order to comment on them in the University of Bologna in the twelfth century.[27] The dawn of the revival of Roman law in the sixteenth century began with Lorenzo Valla's (1406-1457) establishment of textual criticism. Renaissance philologists devoted themselves to studying original languages, vocabulary, grammar, and literary structures in order to perfect their historical interpretation of the text.[28] While the glossators meant to comment on Roman law "as if Justinian were still alive and the Roman Empire still a going concern," the Renaissance humanists regarded their task as finding out the original meaning of a text, i.e., that which was most faithful to its own historical and cultural context, by means of textual criticism. Therefore, for the humanists, "the Emperor [Justinian] is no god of law."[29]

---

26 Two works are especially helpful for this study: Michael L. Monheit, "Passion and Order in the Formation of Calvin's Sense of Religious Authority," PhD dissertation, Princeton University, 1988, esp. 242-507; Patrick Le Gal, *Le droit canonique dans la pensée dialectique de Jean Calvin* (Fribourg Suisse: Éditons Universitaires, 1984), esp. 89-161.

27 Quirinus Breen, "The Twelfth-Century Revival of the Roman Law," in *Christianity and Humanism: Studies in the History of Ideas* (Grand Rapids: Eerdmans, 1968), 131-182.

28 Quirinus Breen, "Renaissance Humanism and the Roman Law," in *Christianity and Humanism*, 183-199. The glossators and postglossators had a sense of textual criticism and historical interpretation in pursuing ancient sources (*ad fontes*). They however did not succeed in connecting the literal meaning of a text to its historical context, but only revealed the discrepancy between them, as was found in the case of Bartolus. Monheit, "Passion and Order," 112-124.

29 Breen, "The Twelfth-Century Revival of the Roman Law," 149, and "Renaissance Humanism and the Roman Law," 189. The glossators and postglossators turned to the concept of the "*merum imperium*" as they advocated the authority of the emperor Justinian. Scholars who did not have a legal background such as Valla and Budé opposed this concept as contradictory to their textual criticism. On the other hand, Zasius and l'Estoile, who had a strong jurist background, claimed the continuous validity of this concept with special reference to the judicial power of the emperor of France and the imperial cities of Germany. Alciati also favoured the authority of the emperor even though he did not develop it theoretically. Monheit, "Passion and Order," 106-210, esp., 112-124, 130-147.

Calvin studied Valla's works with the help of his Latin teacher Mathurin Cordier at the Collège de la Marche in Paris.[30] Valla criticized the position of the glossators and postglossators, who believed that a word or expression in a text had a precise and fixed literal meaning, regardless its context, and he applied the knowledge he had on Roman history and Roman rhetorics. Valla showed his special affection for Ciceronianism and his ideal standard of Latin usage was modeled on the best ancient writers.[31] The influence of Valla's humanistic legal interpretation is apparent in Calvin's use of rhetorical skills, his frequent dependence on ancient writers in designating exact meanings of some specific words, and his moral interpretation according to its textual and contextual meaning in his commentary on Seneca's *De clementia*.[32] In particular, Valla's attack on the "Donation of Constantine" in the Decretals of Gratian may have been a definite influence which induced Calvin to realize the fallacy of the papacy as he describes it in the *Institutes* 4.11.23.[33]

It might have been due to the influence of Valla that Calvin moved to Orléans and finally to Bourges from the university of Paris.[34] Both schools were "fountainheads from which the waters of the new spiritual awakening overflowed into every part of the Kingdom of France."[35] However, as far as the Faculty of Law was concerned, the academic character of Orléans, which was headed by Pierre Taisan de l'Estoile (Petrus Stella), and that of Bourges, which was headed by Andrea Alciati (Alciato, Alciat), was quite different.[36]

---

30 Jacques Pannier, *Recherches sur la formation intellectuelle de Calvin* (Paris: Librairie Alcan, 1931), 14-15; *Clem.* 29*; Bouwsma, *John Calvin*, 13.

31 Breen, *John Calvin*, 104-111, and "Renaissance Humanism and the Roman Law," 187-190; Monheit, "Passion and Order," 125-129. Valla does not think that rhetoric and dialectic can be separated from each other. Thomas F. Torrance, *The Hermeneutics of John Calvin* (Edinburgh: Scottish Academic Press, 1988), 112-116.

32 Calvin introduces Valla's annotation of the word "*licentia*" in his commentary on Seneca: "Obseruandum est verbum licentiae hic positum in malam partem, quemadmodum ferè accipitur apud authores: vt Valla annotauit" (*Clem.* 19.24-26). The phrase "*in malam partem*" implies that the word "*licentia*" is regarded as a product of interrogation. This shows the influence of Calvin's law study. Cf. Breen, *John Calvin*, 111-112.

33 Cf. Breen, "Renaissance Humanism and the Roman Law," 188; Monheit, "Passion and Order," 109. Alciati recognized the fraudulency of the Donation of Constantine, but he did not deny the authority of the edict of the emperor. Monheit, ibid., 147. According to Torrance, Calvin's preference for the legal interrogating way rather than Catholic syllogism demonstrates the influence of Valla's humanism. *The Hermeneutics of John Calvin*, 138-139.

34 Le Gal, *Le Droit Canonique*, 61.

35 *Clem.* 21*.

36 Cf. Battles, "Calvin's Humanistic Education," 55-57; Reid, "*John Calvin, Lawyer*

Pierre de l'Estoile (1480-1537), vicar-general (vicaire général) in the diocese of Orléans, exercised a great influence on Calvin not only spiritually as a man of the church but also academically.[37] He did not claim any new way of commenting on the *Corpus Iuris Civilis*. He was inspired by the humanists' great concern for the text itself but was critical of their historical, rhetorical approach to the text and even their own tendency of *ad fontes*. In designating a genuine meaning of a text, he rather shared with the medieval Roman jurists their conviction of the universal applicability of the law and non-contextual literalism based on the assumption of the complex logical construction of the whole text. He was convinced that a word or a passage had its explicit literary meaning and it could be pursued by reading it in the whole text. This is the point that differentiates him from Ulrich Zasius (1461-1535), who, although he criticized Valla's and Budé's humanistic approach, utilized their philological way and allowed for the flexibility of a word by claiming its implicit meaning beyond the text itself.[38]

Stella's way of literary and logical text-reading within the text itself almost certainly influenced Calvin's harmonious interpretation of the Old and New Testaments, and the holistic understanding of the regulations of the law and their historical background in the *Harmony of the Books of Moses*. In particular, Calvin's spiritual (sometimes typological) interpretation of some biblical passages in the Old Testament in the light of the bodily presence of Christ by the work of the Holy Spirit demonstrates the distinctive influence of Stella's logical text reading way of exploring the true meaning of a word or a passage.[39]

The Faculty of Law in Orléans was divided into two sections: civil law employing five professors, and canon law employing three professors. Calvin's study of the *Corpus Iuris Civilis* in Orléans was by way of the glosses of Accursius and Bartholus. Particularly, Bartholus' commentaries on the *Digesta* and *Infortiatum* informed Calvin not only of the *Corpus* itself but also of its practical application to civil law and, furthermore, to

---

and Legal Reformer," 151-152.

37 Doumergue, *Jean Calvin*, 1.130-132; Ganoczy, *The Young Calvin*, 66; Wendel, *Calvin*, 22. Calvin praises de l'Estoile as "quo est praeditus ingenii acumini, qua industria, qua denique juris peritia" in *Praefatio* in *Nic. Chemini Antapologiam* (CO 9.785).

38 Monheit, "Passion and Order," 109-112, 130-200, "Young Calvin, Textual Interpretation and Roman Law," *Bibliothèque d'Humanisme et Renaissance* 59/2 (1997), 268-269, and "Guillaume Budé, Andrea Alciato, Pierre de l'Estoile: Renaissance Interpreters of Roman Law," *Journal of the History of Ideas* 58/1 (1997), 31-34; Reid, "*John Calvin, Lawyer and Legal Reformer*," 151.

39 Cf. Monheit, "Passion and Order," 416-507. The author sets a higher value on Stella's approach than Alciati's, especially with reference to their influence on Calvin's interpretation of the law.

theology.[40] In the following, T. H. L. Parker describes Calvin's study at Orléans, which kept in balance Roman law, civil law, and theology:

> The student would therefore be expected to gain a knowledge of early Church doctrine and in particular of Christology, as well as some acquaintance with the early history of doctrine. It would seem then that Calvin's first theological studies took place not at Paris but at Orléans. But the philosophy of law and the theology occupied in extent only a small part of the *Corpus*. For much of the time he spent in Orléans, Calvin would be concerned with the innumerable material causes of man's dissensions with his neighbours—the disposal of rain-water, rights of way, leases, purchase and possession, marriage and divorce, inheritance—and the decisions which generations of Roman and medieval jurists had given in such disputes.[41]

Calvin's studies with Andrea Alciati (1492-1550) did not last longer than one and a half years,[42] but Alciati's influence on Calvin was still dominant in Calvin's relationships with the jurists who led the principal centre of the *mos gallicus* in the college of Bourges— François le Douaren, François Hotman, and Jacques Cujas.[43] Like Valla and Budé, Alciati introduced the philological way of textual criticism to the legal profession. His contribution, however, is especially prominent in his engrafting this legal

---

40 Parker, *John Calvin*, 13-16. Concerning the mutual influence between Roman law and church law, Guenther H. Haas, *The Concept of Equity in Calvin's Ethics* (Ontario: Wilfrid Laurier University Press, 1997), 22-30, 33-39. Since Rome was re-established as the Christian empire, Roman law had been increasingly revised to conform to Christian principles, as we see clearly in the case of Justinian's *Corpus* (24). In the medieval revival of Roman law Gratian and his successors applied the juristic method of the Roman texts, especially of the *Digest*, to the law of the church (28). This "juristic" method of the glossators and postglossators, which played a key role in the emergence of a system of canon law, was challenged by the philological and historical method (*mos novus*) in the Renaissance era (36-39). So we can presume that in the early sixteenth century the comparative study between Roman law and church law would be regarded as one of the most crucial legal agendas. However, Breen, overvaluing the influence of humanism in Orléans, comments negatively on Calvin's study of canon law. *John Calvin*, 139.

41 Parker, *John Calvin*, 15-16.

42 This was between April of 1529 when Alciati started lecturing and September 1530 when Calvin left the school. Doumergue, *Jean Calvin*, 1.145; Millet, *Calvin et la dynamique de la parole*, 36.

43 Doumergue, *Jean Calvin*, 1.148-149; Donald R. Kelly, *Foundations of Modern Historical Scholarship: Language, Law, and History in the French Renaissance* (New York: Columbia University Press, 1970), 100-115.

humanism onto the study of history.[44] As Emile Doumergue puts it, *"C'était une double nouveauté qui lui permit de 'débarbariser' la jurisprudence et lui mérita le nom glorieux de fondateur de l'école historique."*[45]

Fundamentally, Alciati and Budé took the same position in approving of and applying the historical and philological approach to textual interpretation.[46] However, Budé, the leader of the Gallican way of teaching (*mos docendi gallicus*), was more a Christian humanistic thus biblical in his approach than Alciati who, although he attacked the Italian way of teaching (*mos docendi italicus*), at the same time retained the Italian humanistic freedom.[47] Alciati did not maintain such an uncompromising historicism as Valla did. Just as he believed that the philological approach is not contradictory to the historical background of a text, so he was convinced that the historical meaning of laws does not exclude their spiritual significance, which reveals the intention of their author most prominently.[48] The mediating position of Alciati between the medieval Roman jurists and humanists can be understood from his connection between the "spirit of the laws (*mens legum*)" and the "intention (*voluntas* or *mens*)" of the lawgiver.[49]

We should take care not to overestimate Calvin's negative evaluation of Alciati in his preface to Duchemin's *Antapologia*. Calvin's criticism there was given against Alciati's arrogant attitude towards his former teacher de l'Estoile, but not about his academia itself.[50] We can find the influence of Alciati notable not only in Calvin's commentary on Seneca, in which he interprets some words with historical flexibility rather than focusing on

---

44 Kelly, *Foundations of Modern Historical Scholarship*, 87-100; Breen, *John Calvin*, 140. This approach is prominent in Alciati, *In tres posteriores Codicis Iustiniani libros annotatiunculae* (1513). Clem. 22-24*.

45 Doumergue, *Jean Calvin*, 1.143.

46 Breen, "Renaissance Humanism and the Roman Law," 187.

47 John T. McNeill, *The History and Character of Calvinism* (New York: Oxford University Press, 1954), 18-19; Monheit, "Guillamume Budé, Andrea Alciato, Pierre de l'Estoile," 27-28; Basil Hall, "Calvin and Biblical Humanism," *Huguenot Society Proceedings* 20 (1959-64), 198. According to Hall, Italian humanists owed their concept of freedom to Cicero's *De fato*.

48 Kelly, *Foundations of Modern Historical Scholarship*, 98. In dealing with Budé's and Alciati's interpretation of the *"Ubi decretum"* of the third century Imperial jurist Ulpian, Monheit observes, "Like Budé, . . . for Alciato, too, the recovery of the past could be of immediate, practical exemplary value; but for him this exemplarity lay in the substance of Ulpian's thought. Unlike Budé he closely identified with Ulpian as an ancient *thinker*." "Guillaume Budé, Andrea Alciato, Pierre de l'Estoile," 27.

49 Alciati, *Dispunctiones*, IV, 21 (*Opera*, IV, 208). Quot. Kelly, *Foundations of Modern Historical Scholarship*, 98, n. 29.

50 Ganoczy, *The Young Calvin*, 69. Cf. Breen, *John Calvin*, 52-60.

their linguistic origins, but also on his theological understanding of the law.[51] In the *Institutes*, Calvin claims that the first principle of the law is the spiritual interpretation of the law according to the purpose of the lawgiver and then emphasizes Christ as the interpreter of the law (*Inst.* 2.8.6-7). We should keep in mind that these assertions regarding spiritual interpretation of the law are based on his basic stance on the historical literal interpretation. Under the tutelage of Alciati's *mos novus*, Calvin did not only learn the textual interpretation of the Justinian *Corpus* but also the medieval glossators' practical application of the law article by article to each case;[52] therefore, it must have been a great help in Calvin's legislation of church ordinances and their practical application to each case in the Consistory of Geneva.

In his excellent study on the life and works of Alciati, Paul Émile Viard sees his distinctive achievement in his brilliant usage of the literatures of diverse classical Greek and Latin writers.[53] However, Alciati was not thoroughly learned in the philosophy of language, as was Budé. The influence of *mos Italicus* resulted in Alciati's flexibility, which was revealed sometimes in relation to his view of history, as we see in his acknowledgement of the authority of the emperor in the case of the Donation of Constantine, and sometimes in relation to his acceptance of loose interpretation by the glossators. This mediating position of Alciati caused Calvin and his friends to be disappointed at his first lectures in Bourges.[54]

Guillaume Budé (1468-1540) played a major role in the revival of Roman law in France by annotating some parts of the Justinian *Pandectae* and by writing several important humanistic works. Indisputably, he was a man who enhanced the intellectual level of France in the times of Renaissance. As we see from the debates between his followers and the adherents of Erasmus, which were being held while Calvin was in Orléans and Bourges, he was regarded by some advancing contemporaries as the pride of the Gauls.[55] Calvin and his close friends would have talked about him with some respect and admiration as they were reading his *Annotationes in Pandectas* (1508) and *Annotationes reliquae in Pandectas*

---

51 For the influence of the philological and historical interpretation of Alciati on Calvin, see Monheit, "Young Calvin, Textual Interpretation and Roman Law," 269, 276-282; Le Gal, *Le Droit Canonique*, 64-65.
52 Monheit, "Young Calvin, Textual Interpretation and Roman Law," 266; Parker claims that Alciati "was also a practical lawyer and, like the Bartholists before him, went to the *Corpus* for help in contemporary problems." *John Calvin*, 20.
53 Paul Émile Viard, *André Alciat 1492-1550* (Paris: Société Anonyme du Recueil Sirey, 1926), 229-254.
54 Cf. Parker, *John Calvin*, 20
55 Cf. *Clem.* 27*.

(called by Calvin *Annotationes posteriores*, 1526).[56] Calvin must have remembered these debates when he spoke of Budé "*primum rei literariae decus et columen,*" while he called Erasmus "*literarum alterum decus*" (*Clem.* 42.37-38, ii. 3).

According to Battles, we can find at least ninety-one references to Budé, including seven instances where Calvin names him as reference in Calvin's commentary on Seneca. The references are mostly to his *Annotationes* and *De asse et partibus eius* (1515) concerning legal terms, Roman institutions, political philosophy, and literature. Calvin especially turned to Budé's *Commentarii linguae Graecae* (1530) an erudition on Greek literature and philosophy.[57] Budé raised the issue of equity in the world of jurisprudence from the political-philosophical perspective, based on Aristotle's conception of *epieikeia*.[58] In his commentary on Seneca's *De clementia*, Calvin distinguishes "equity (*epieikeia*)" from "the letter or rigor of the law (*iuri summo seu rigori iuris*)," and insists that there are certain things "not permitted by the common code of living souls (*commune ius animantium*) for man to do to man" (*Clem.* 111.3-9, 112.8-9 [English translation altered]).

This view of the young Calvin reappears in the *Institutes* when he is discussing the principle of synecdoche in the interpretation of the law, saying, "a sober interpretation of the law goes beyond the words (*Ultra verba progredi sobriam legis interpretationem*)" (*Inst.* 2.8.8, CO 2. 272). Budé's historical, philological approach based on his erudition in ancient languages and original sources influenced the young Calvin, who wanted to make his name renowned as a Christian humanist such as Erasmus and Budé himself, but Budé's mystical and allegorical interpretation of major theological issues such as Christology was regarded as unacceptable to Calvin even before his conversion.[59]

Calvin kept a close personal relationship with Budé and his family after his conversion.[60] The influence of Budé's views of Christian philosophy, natural law, and the relationship between the magistrate and his servants still overshadow Calvin's *Institutes*, and, most of all, the influence of his

---

56 Le Gal, *Le Droit Canonique*, 62-63; Breen, *John Calvin*, 139.
57 Battles, "The Sources of Calvin's Seneca Commentary," 69-73, 86.
58 David O. McNeil, *Guillaume Budé and Humanism in the Reign of Francis I* (Genève: Droz, 1975), 23-24; Haas, *The Concept of Equity in Calvin's Ethics*, 36-37.
59 Cf. Battles, "The Sources of Calvin's Seneca Commentary," 73-74; Marie-Madeleine de La Garanderie, "Guillaume Budé, A Philosopher of Culture," *SCJ* 19/3 (1988), 381, 385-386.
60 Cf. Doumergue, *Jean Calvin*, 1.202-203; Jeannine E. Olson, "The Friends of John Calvin: The Budé Family," in *Calvin Studies Society Papers, 1995, 1997: Calvin and Spirituality, Calvin and His Contemporaries*, ed. David Foxgrover (Grand Rapids: CRC Product Services, 1998), 159-168.

philological and historical interpretation dominates in Calvin's wide use of ancient sources. Nevertheless, Calvin probably preferred Alciati, who sought *brevitas* in writing in spite of his erudition and emphasized not only the principles of the philological textual approach but also their practical applications to the various facets of the laws,[61] to Budé, who pursued stylistic grandeur rather than clarity and had a tendency to ignore the practical application of a specific law to a specific case.[62]

Budé believed that there were many contradictions and different realities in the compilation of Roman laws[63] and criticized not only the glosses of the medieval jurists but also the text of Justinian himself as he explored the historical contextual meaning of texts with the spirit of *ad fontes*,[64] whereas Valla claimed the need for the new way of textual criticism by revealing the erroneous approach of the glossators and postglossators and their ignorance of Latin.[65] However, like Valla, Budé was neither a legal practitioner nor a profound philosopher of the law. Calvin was not able to harmonize his literary and historical interpretation of the Scripture with this stance of Budé. Although Budé differentiates Christianity from philosophy, and humanistic interpretation of a text from meditation on the Scripture, his Christian humanism was basically oriented towards a logical contingency rather than the revelation of the text itself. This is why he finally came to the allegorical and mystical interpretation of Scripture in *De studio literarum recte et commode instituendo* (1532), and *De transitu Hellenismi ad Christianismum* (1535). While Erasmus clearly developed Valla's humanistic approach in his annotations on the Gospels, there was no such development by Calvin with regard to Budé.[66]

We can attempt to point out the continuity between Budé and Calvin. Like Quirinus Breen, we can appreciate that Budé revealed "the essential note of the Reformation" when he emphasized that "Christianity is obedience to the commandments of Christ, an imitation of the Master's life upon earth" in *De studio*.[67] Like Josef Bohatec, we can understand this Christ-centred view of Budé from his eschatological view of Christian philosophy and admit its influence on Calvin's theology of the Christian

---

61 Millet, *Calvin et la dynamique de la parole*, 53-55.
62 Le Gal, *Le Droit Canonique*, 62-63; De La Garanderie, "Guillaume Budé, A Philosopher of Culture," 379.
63 McNeill, *Guillaume Budé and Humanism*, 108.
64 Monheit, "Guillaume Budé, Andrea Alciato, Pierre de l'Estoile," 25-26.
65 Monheit deals with the relation between Valla and Budé, only focusing on their similarities, in "Passion and Order," 130-146.
66 Cf. Jerry H. Bentley, "Biblical Philology and Christian Humanism: Lorenzo Valla and Erasmus as Scholars of the Gospels," *SCJ* 8, Supplement (1977), 9-28.
67 Breen, *John Calvin*, 120.

life.[68] We can further argue that Calvin refined Budé's philological approach and applied it to the Scriptures themselves.[69] However, we should keep in mind not to overestimate Budé's theological influence on Calvin. With reference to Calvin's Christ-centred mysticism or spirituality, this was rather more dependent on the theological reformism of Lefèvre d'Étaples.[70] Also, concerning Calvin's biblical interpretation, we should give adequate attention to the influence of Nicholas of Lyra, and with regard to the relation between Word and Spirit, to the influence of late medieval spirituality.

2.3 *Via Moderna* and *Devotio Moderna*: The Merit of Christ and the Role of the Law, and Late-Medieval Spirituality[71]

The significance of the influence of the *via moderna* and the *devotio moderna* upon the young Calvin has been discussed increasingly, because both of these trends have been regarded crucial for the study of the intellectual and spiritual origin of Calvin's theology.

The influence of the voluntarist tradition advocated by the theologians of the *via moderna* in the late medieval era upon Calvin is noticeable in the *Institutes*. Criticizing the Epicurean concept of the idle god, he says, the Epicureans "so apportion things between God and man that God by His power inspires in man a movement by which he can act in accordance with the nature implanted in him, but He regulates His own actions by the plan of His will" (*Inst.* 1.16.4, *CO* 2.147). Also, when criticizing the Stoic concept of fate, he claims that "God's will is the highest and first cause of all things because nothing happens except from his command or permission" (*Inst.* 1.16.8, *CO* 2.152). In his response to Socinus (1555), Calvin takes the voluntarist position, saying, "Apart from God's good pleasure Christ could not merit anything (*nam Christus non nisi ex Dei beneplacito quidquam mereri potuit*)" (*Inst.* 2.17.1, *CO* 2.387).[72] Calvin

---

68 *Budé und Calvin: Studien zur Gedankenwelt des französischen Frühhumanismus* (Graz: H. Böhlaus, 1950), 241, 415-438.
69 Wendel, *Calvin*, 31.
70 Doumergue, *Jean Calvin*, 1.380, 401; Ganoczy, *The Young Calvin*, 74-75.
71 For the concept of "spirituality" in Calvin's times, which usually denoted the Christian life following the type of Christ and worshipping God with the true knowledge of God and man, see Richard C. Gamble, "Calvin and Sixteenth-Century Spirituality: Comparison with the Anabaptists," in *Calvin Studies Society Papers, 1995, 1997*, 32-36.
72 *Responsio ad aliquot Laelii Socini senensis quaestiones*, *CO* 10/1.160. David Willis, "The Influence of Laelius Socinus on Calvin's Doctrines of the Merits of Christ and the Assurance of Faith," in *Italian Reformation Studies in Honor of Laelius Socinus*, ed. John A. Tedeschi (Firenze: F. Le Monnier, 1965), 235; McGrath, *The Intellectual Origins of the European Reformation*, 104-105. In dealing with the office of the law

confirmed this position in a new section added in the 1559 *Institutes* in this way: "In considering Christ's merit, we do not consider the beginning of merit to be in him, but we go back to God's ordinance, the first cause" (*Inst.* 2.17.1, *CO* 2.387).

The influence of the *via moderna* is obvious concerning Calvin's emphasis on the sovereign will and the eternal decree of God, but we should be careful not to overemphasize the influence of the voluntarist tradition upon Calvin's theological position on the relationship between the absolute will of God and the merit of Christ in the process of salvation. As Calvin puts it continuously in response to Socinus:

> [W]henever Christ's grace is joined to God's love. . . . Christ bestows on us something of what he has acquired (*eum de suo quod acquisivit*). For otherwise it would not be fitting for this credit to be given to him as distinct from the Father, namely, that grace is his and proceeds from him (*Inst.* 2.17.2, *CO* 2.387-388).[73]

The theologians of the *via moderna* associated the *ratio meriti Christi* not so much with the truth and extent of Christ's mediation as with the economy of God's omnipotent will.[74] As we see from the works of William Ockham and Gabriel Biel, they concentrated more on Christ as *Legislator* than *Salvator* in dealing with his merit for salvation.[75] This stance reflects the effect of their distinctive understanding of the incarnation of Christ. In dealing with the concept of *Deus manifestatus in carne* in view of the *assumptus*-theory of Peter Lombard, Ockham refers chiefly to the fact that God became man by assuming the "*humanitas*"; but he does not give proper attention to the hypostatic union in the person of Christ as the "*homo*."[76] This Christological lacuna, as Alister E. McGrath calls it, appears in Biel, who grasped the coming of Christ as the *kenosis* of God and claimed that

---

in his book *Beneficio di Christo*, Socinus does not mention its normative use at all. Tedeschi ed., ibid., 49-50.

73 Willis notes that Calvin, by referring to the *acceptatio* of God, points out the sufficiency of the merit of Christ, whereas Scotus leaves more room for another offering. Ibid., 236.

74 Cf. Adolph Harnack, *History of Dogma*, vol. 4 (New York: Dover Publications, 1961), 305-317.

75 McGrath, *The Intellectual Origins of the European Reformation*, 82-83; Heiko A. Oberman, *The Harvest of Medieval Theology: Gabriel Biel and Late Medieval Nominalism* (Durham, N.C.: Labyrinth Press, 1983), 112-119.

76 Alister E. McGrath, "Homo Assumptus? A Study in the Christology of the *Via Moderna*, with Particular Reference to William of Ockham," *Ephemerides Theologicae Lovanienses* 60 (1984), 283-297, esp. 287, 290, 292-297.

the incarnation does not prove the humanity of Christ but his divinity, not the *kenosis* of Christ but the fact that the immutable God became man.[77]

The theologians of the *via moderna* held the Franciscan voluntarist position and highlighted the *ex opere operato* character of the merit of Christ. They were not very concerned about linking the principle of *sola gratia* with the free imputation of the grace of Christ, rather, they sought to take issue with the merit of Christ in the process of applying the axiomatic principle that "*facientibus quod in se est deus non denegat gratiam* (God does not deny grace to those who do what it is in their power to do)" to the whole process of salvation.[78] Inspired by Augustine, who asserted that "*qui creavit te sine te, non justificabit te sine te*,"[79] they referred to the synergistic *facientibus* principle even in the explication of justification "in terms of the concept of the reliability of the *potentia ordinata* with reference to the notion of a 'covenant' or 'contract (*pactum*)' between God and man."[80] It is against this background that they developed their idea of justification in terms of two stages of merit— *meritum de congruo*, which is based on *gratia gratum faciens*, and *meritum de condigno*, which is based on *pura gratia gratis data*.[81]

The congruent merit signifies God's grace infused in every natural man who is able to prepare himself for salvation, voluntarily, by eliminating obstacles and by repentance. It pertains to the first stage of justification, in which the synergism in the *facientibus* principle works totally and individually. At this stage, God binds himself to nothing but to his convenantal promise, not out of his strict justice but out of his liberality (*liberalitas*). In this sense, his will works both absolutely and ordainly.[82]

---

77 In this respect, Oberman says, the feature of the so-called *extra Calvinisticum* for Biel appears as the *kenosis* of God Himself. *The Harvest of Medieval Theology*, 265.
78 Oberman, "Wir Sein Pettler. Hoc Est Verum," 91-115, quot. 104. For the development and application of the axiom "*facientibus quod in se est Deus non denegat gratiam*," see Alister E. McGrath, *Iustitia Dei: A History of the Christian Doctrine of Justification*, 2nd ed. (Cambridge: Cambridge University Press, 1998), 83-91; Heiko A. Oberman, "*Facientibus Quod in se est Deus non Denegat Gratiam*: Robert Holcot O. P. and the Beginnings of Luther's Theology," *Harvard Theological Review* 55 (1962), 317-342.
79 Quot. Oberman, "Wir Sein Pettler. Hoc Est Verum," 106, n. 77.
80 *The Intellectual Origins of the European Reformation*, 81.
81 Heiko A. Oberman, "Duns Scotus, Nominalism, and the Council of Trent," in *The Dawn of the Reformation: Essays in Late Medieval and Early Reformation Thought* (Grand Rapids: Eerdmans, 1992), 211-218.
82 My observation is based on Biel's statement: "Anima obicis remotione ac bono motu in deum ex arbitrii libertate elicito primam gratiam mereri potest de congruo. Probatur quia actum facientis quod in se est deus acceptat ad tribuendum gratiam primam, non ex debito iusticie, sed ex sua liberalitate, sed anima removendo obicem, cessando ab actu et consensu peccati et eliciendo bonum motum in deum tanquam in

The concept of congruent merit helps us to explain the principle of *sola gratia* in the process of justification with respect to the liberality of God and the merit of the believer's conviction of *iustificatio sola fide*, but it does not set forth the objective *opus operatum Christi*—the gratuitous grace of Christ's redemption.[83] Calvin's strict objection to Catholic synergism targets this merely subjective understanding of *sola gratia* in the process of justification (cf. *Inst.* 3.11.13-20, 3.17.1-15).[84]

On the other hand, the condign merit denotes the persistent covenantal grace of God for those already regenerated by congruent merit.[85] The Franciscan theologians of the medieval era who followed the Scotic voluntarist tradition explored this concept in order to explain the perfection of eternal life by referring to the *ordinatio* of God;[86] thus they regarded that as coming out of the strict justice of God, i.e., his equality rather than his liberality and related to his ordained will rather than to his absolute will.[87]

---

suum principium et finem facit quod in se est. Ergo actum remotionis obicis et bonum motum in deum acceptat deus de sua liberalitate ad infundendum gratiam." *Sentences*, II d. 27 q. 1 art. 2 concl. 4k., quot. Oberman, *The Harvest of Medieval Theology*, 172, n. 80.

83 The synergistic position of the *via moderna* was rejected by the theologians of Council of Trent, who argued that "none of the acts which precede justification, whether faith or works, merits the grace of justification." Oberman, "Duns Scotus, Nominalism, and the Council of Trent," 217.

84 Calvin disagrees with the doctrine of the co-operation grace of Lombard and Bernard, and, most greatly, with the nominalists, whom he calls "the more recent Sophists" (*Inst* 2.2.6, *CO* 2.191). For medieval Pelagianism, see Oberman, "'Iustitia Christi' and 'Iustitia Dei': Luther and the Scholastic Doctrines of Justification," in *The Dawn of the Reformation*, 108-114. Oberman presents Luther's criticism of Ockham's Pelagianism and points out that Luther's view of law and gospel starts from his radical re-interpretation of *"facere quod in se est"* (109, 114). For Ockam's attitude towards Pelagianism, see Marilyn McCord Adams, *William Ockham*, 2 vols. (Notre Dame: University of Notre Dame Press, 1987), 1279-1295.

85 Oberman, "Duns Scotus, Nominalism, and the Council of Trent," 214-215.

86 According to Joseph Wawrykow, since the medieval understanding of condign merit, including that of Aquinas, is based not on the foreknowledge of God but on the *ordinatio* of God, Calvin's critique of Aquinas in the *Institutes* 3.22.9 is groundless. "John Calvin and Condign Merit," *ARG* 83 (1992), 80-90. For Aquinas' view of foreknowledge and Scotus' criticism on this, see Jaroslav Pelikan, *The Christian Tradition: A History of the Development of Doctrine*, vol. 4. *Reformation of Church and Dogma (1300-1700)* (Chicago: University of Chicago Press, 1984), 29-30.

87 With regard to the merit for eternal life, "[in congruent merit], there is no equality in value between moral actions and God's payment. Yet God is merciful, and gives more than we deserve"; whereas "in condign merit, there is an equality in value between the morally good act and God's reward. This equality in value is rooted ultimately in God's will." Wawrykow, "John Calvin and Condign Merit," 80-81. According to Oberman, the late medieval nominalists' position on the relationship

Basically, the theologians of the *via moderna* were faithful to this Franciscan tradition.[88] However, with a view to defending their synergistic view of the sacraments, they tended to ascribe the condign merit even to God's *liberalitas*, as they, based on their *pactum*-theory, replaced Aquinas's intellectualistic views on the infused habit of grace and the merit of the sacrament as the secondary cause with the *potentia ordinata Dei*.[89] Although the theologians of the *via moderna* did not deny the existence of created habits itself, they did not accept the Dominican theory of *habitus* as such; their emphasis was shifted from the ontological to the covenantal causality.[90] Their emphasis was not on the qualification of the regenerate but on God's grace upon a *viator*, i.e., God's absolute will (*liberalitas*) in regard to *gratia gratum faciens*.[91]

It might look plausible that Calvin was influenced by the *via moderna* insofar as asserting the dynamic relationship between justification and sanctification and the normative nature and use of the law. However, it should be noted that when Calvin discusses the double grace of God to receive both our persons and our works and emphasizes the third use of the law in the Christian life, he does so on the basis of God's grace to receive our "imperfect" works as righteous, while the theologians of the *via*

---

between *meritum de condigno* and *de congruo* substantially contributed to the final formulation of the decree on justification. "Duns Scotus, Nominalism, and the Council of Trent," 216.

88 Oberman, *The Harvest of Medieval Theology, 173-174*.

89 Cf. Steve Ozment, *The Age of Reform 1250-1550: An Intellectual and Religious History of Late Medieval and Reformation Europe* (New Haven: Yale University Press, 1980), 33-41; Bierma, *German Calvinism in the Confessional Age*, 169. For the dialectic between potentia dei absoluta and potentia dei ordinata in the medieval era and its development in the Reformation, see McGrath, *Iustitia Dei*, 119-128; Francis Oakely, "The Absolute and Ordained Power of God in Sixteenth-and Seventeenth-Century Theology," *Journal of the History of Ideas* 59/3 (1988), 440-457; William J. Courtenay, "The Dialectic of Divine Omnipotence," in *Covenant and Causality in Medieval Thought: Studies in Philosophy, Theology, and Economic Practice* (London: Variorum Reprints, 1984), 1-37; Stephen Strehle, "Calvinism, Augustinianism, and the Will of God," *Theologische Zeitschrift* 48/2 (1992), 221-237.

90 The covenantal causality shows the juridical and volitional facet of the medieval concept of causality. Cf. McGrath, *The Intellectual Origins of the European Reformation*, 82; William J. Courtenay, "Covenant and Causality in Pierre d'Ailly," *Spectrum* 46 (1971), 97-102.

91 McGrath, *The Intellectual Origins of the European Reformation*, 80-81; Oberman, "Wir Sein Pettler. Hoc Est Verum," 105. In dealing with cooperative merit in the Catholic tradition, the prevenience of the actual grace of God (*gratia gratis data*) to congruent merit and the prevenience of the sanctifying grace of God (*gratia gratum faciens*) to condign merit are crucial. But it is not always obvious, as in the case of Biel. Oberman, "Duns Scotus, Nominalism, and the Council of Trent," 204-233.

moderna argue for good works which are merited as "perfect" by the ordained yet absolute will of God. In the following passage, Calvin criticizes them for replacing the merit of Christ with the liberality of God in dealing with the covenant of grace.

> [H]ow deluded the Sophists are, who thought they had neatly got around all these absurdities by saying that works of their own intrinsic goodness are of no avail for meriting salvation but by reason of the covenant (*ex pacti ratione*), because the Lord of his own liberality (*liberalitate*) esteemed them so highly (*Inst.* 3.17.3, *CO* 2.592).[92]

Biel's position on Christ and the law, to provide an example, makes us realize how far it is from Calvin's Christological understanding of the law, even though they look very similar at first. Biel claims that "the Old Law" and "the New Law" are differentiated only by "the difference between *quo* and *qua*"; although the Jews did not know *how* to respond to the Lord, they were fully aware of *what* is the substance and purpose of the law.[93] This recalls the remarkable similarity between Biel and Calvin with reference to their understanding of the substantial unity between the law and the Gospel. Especially when Biel asserts that the sacraments of the New Testament are efficacious not only *ex opere operato* but also *ex opere operantis*, it reminds us of the *ratio* of the continual mediation of Christ in the so-called *extra Calvinisticum*.[94]

However, in spite of these seeming similarities, there is a crucial discrepancy between Biel and Calvin with regard to their understanding of Christ's mediation. As Oberman observes, for Biel, "Indeed, whereas Christ himself is legislator, Moses is only a herald and a promulgator of the law of God. But, again, this is merely a difference of degree, between mediate and immediate, since through Moses God himself gave his law, as clearly appears from the form of the Decalogue."[95] Commenting here on the phrase "*in manu Mediatoris*" in Galatians 3:19, Biel lays more emphasis on the absolute will of God than on the mediatorship of Christ as he points out the fact that both the immediate and the mediate causalities are subject to God's necessity. The same tendency indicates both the intellectualistic and the voluntaristic stream in the medieval era.[96] On the other hand, as far as

---

92 Calvin differentiates "necessity" from "compulsion" (*Inst.* 2.2.5, 2.3.5). For him, there is no room for the concept of *necessitas coactionis*, by which the voluntarists appeal to the self-imposed restriction of God. Cf. McGrath, "Homo Assumptus?" 286, 288.
93 Oberman, *The Harvest of Medieval Theology*, 112.
94 Ibid., 114.
95 Ibid., 115.
96 Ibid., 118. According to Oberman, this position of Biel does not show any difference

Calvin's theology of the law is concerned, the difference between mediate and immediate is not merely quantitative, but lies in the nature, revelation, and fulfilment of the law.[97] In conclusion, the *via moderna* fails to notice the significance of Christ's mediatorship; therefore, its influence on Calvin's Christological understanding of the law is limited.

Regarding the formation of Calvin's theology, the influence of John Major has been discussed significantly by some scholars. Major was known as the person who reconciled the realist and nominalist view of hermeneutics[98] and pursued the unifying of the intellectual and spiritual aspects of Christian philosophy.[99] His influence upon Calvin has been most emphatically presented by T. F. Torrance. According to Torrance, Major's theological and philosophical characteristics are reflected so greatly in Calvin's theological thought that we can hardly deny their close relationship in the Collège de Montaigu.[100] Torrance claims that although there is no general agreement with Reuter's thesis—that Calvin learned a 'new conception of anti-Pelagian and Scotist theology, and a renewed Augustinianism' at Paris under the tutelage of Major—the influence of Major on Calvin was indelible, especially on his study of language.[101] The same position is claimed by Patrick le Gal, who suggests that under the guidance of Major, Calvin was taught the principle of "*fides quaerens*

---

from that of Bonaventura, Aquinas, and Scotus.

97 Heinrich Heppe uses the terms "the *unio immediata*" and "the *unio mediata*" in order to describe the union between the human nature and the person of the Logos and the union with the two natures which is mediated by the Holy Spirit. *RD* 431. If we can apply this distinction to the divine-human relationship, the former represents the mystical relationship between God and man, whereas the latter shows the characteristic feature of Calvin's pietism based on the mediatorship of Christ. On the other hand, Dowey explains "the immediate presence of a mysterious will [of God]" in creation by God's accommodation to human capacity in "God's Creative Word" and to human sinfulness in the office of Christ as the Mediator. *The Knowledge of God in Calvin's Theology*, 7, 10.

98 Torrance, *The Hermeneutics of John Calvin*, 24.

99 Cf. Le Gal, *Le Droit Canonique*, 34-40; Richard, *The Spirituality of John Calvin*, 144-147. Le Gal points up the influence of the *devotio moderna* on Major through Standonck, but Richard does not indicate this point specifically.

100 Torrance, *The Hermeneutics of John Calvin*, 1-57, 80-95.

101 Ibid., 80. Torrance's view is based on Reuter's assumption, explored in *Grundverständnis der Theologie Calvins*, 21, 35-36. Although Reuter continues to argue for the influence of Major upon Calvin in his later work *Vom Scholarem bis zum jungen Reformator*, he gave up his assumption that Calvin attended Major's lectures in the theology faculty. Anthony N. S. Lane, "Calvin's Use of Bernard of Clairvaux," in *John Calvin: Student of the Church Fathers* (Grand Rapids: Baker, 1999), 87-95. Most major biographical works on Calvin basically support Torrance's position. Cf. Ganoczy, *The Young Calvin*, 174; Parker, *Calvin*, 11; McNeill, *The History and Character of Calvinism*, 100; Wendel, *Calvin*, 19.

intellectum," which is essential for establishing the connection between the absolute and ordained powers, the conception of anti-Pelagianism, and the spiritual and constitutional position of the church.[102] McGrath does not agree with Reuter's thesis as such, but takes into consideration his assertion of the influence of the *via moderna* and the *schola Augustiniana moderna* upon Calvin positively, via the works of Gregory of Rimini during his stay at Paris.[103]

As Oberman and Ganoczy point out, there is no historical evidence to clearly verify that Major taught Calvin at Paris and exercised a decisive influence over the formation of his theology.[104] However, it should be noted that Major, influenced by the *schola Augustiniana moderna* as well as by the voluntarist tradition and the late medieval nominalism, seeks to find the *scopus* of the sacred writings not only in Christ's teaching but also in Christ himself, and like Calvin he explores the absolute will of God as one mediated by Christ in its revelation and office.[105] On this Christological basis, the two take a similar position on the unity of the will of God, as seen in Major, who understands *potentia dei absoluta* as a presently active power of God because it is known to us as the divine order by *potentia dei ordinata* as it is revealed in Scripture.[106] Calvin reads the distinction between the *potentia absoluta* and the *potentia ordinata* as a distinction between *potentia ordinata* and *potentia inordinata* and regards all power of God, realized and unrealized, actual and potential, as pertaining to *potentia ordinata*, power ordered by God's justice.[107]

Now it would be helpful to turn to the influence of the *devotio moderna* upon Calvin, which scholars have discussed as another possible element working for the Christological formation of Calvin's theology.[108] In the

---

102 Le Gal, *Le Droit Canonique*, 48-59.
103 McGrath, *The Intellectual Origins of the European Reformation*, 103-106. Concerning the affinity between Augustinianism, Gregori of Rimini, and Calvinism in thought on the will of God, see Strehle, "Calvinism, Augustinianism, and the Will of God," 221-237.
104 Oberman, "*Initia Calvini*," 121-122; Ganoczy, *The Young Calvin*, 174-176.
105 McGrath, *The Intellectual Origins of the European Reformation*, 104-105; Torrance, *The Hermeneutics of John Calvin*, 51.
106 Oakely, "The Absolute and Ordained Power of God in Sixteenth-and Seventeenth-Century Theology," 451.
107 David C. Steinmetz, "Calvin and the Absolute Power of God," in *Calvin in Context* (Oxford: Oxford University, 1995), 49.
108 The characteristics of the *devotio moderna* are: 1) the person of Jesus Christ stands central; 2) the core of the gospel reveals in the life and passion of Christ; 3) the whole approach to the Scripture and Christ should be moralistic and antispeculative; 4) finally, through these efforts, inwardness and interiority should be pursued. John Van Engen, tr., *Devotio Moderna: Basic Writings* (New York: Paulist Press, 1988), "Introduction," 25-27. These elements are also highlighted

Golden Booklet of Christian Life, Calvin highlights that the heart of the Christian life is the following of Christ as the type and example and the meditating on the future life with the firm conviction of eternal union with Christ. This indicates the influence of the modern devotion, especially that of Thomas à Kempis (*Inst.* 3.6-10).[109] We can also find this influence significantly in Calvin's first theological book, *Psychopannychia* (1534).[110]

According to Albert Hyma, Calvin was informed of the new spirituality by those who were influenced by the *devotio moderna*, most significantly Lefèvre d'Étaples and Bucer. It is quite plausible that Calvin's Christological understanding of the law was closely related to d'Étaples' Christ-centred spiritual interpretation of the Bible and Bucer's doctrine of the union with Christ.[111] During his studies at the Collège de la Marche, Calvin esteemed Mathurin Cordier as the model of the ideal master who besides Latin grammar taught his students the pious Christian life in the spirit of the *devotio moderna*.[112] Also, at the Collège de Montaigu, which had taken into itself the soul of mysticism and brethren life since John Standonck, Calvin probably read à Kempis' *De imitatione Christi*, as did Ignatius Loyola.[113] À Kempis contends that knowledge is a source of

---

with reference to the influence of the *devotio moderna* on Calvin through the book of Lucien Joseph Richard, *The Spirituality of John Calvin* (Atlanta: John Knox Press, 1974). The author believes the influence was especially prominent in Calvin's concept of *pietas* and *eruditio* from the 1536 *Institutes* (98).

109 See, esp. *Inst.* 3.6.3, 3.8.5, 3.9.5-6. Most scholars who argue for the influence of the *devotio moderna* through à Kempis' *De imitatione Christi* concentrate on its influence on Calvin's doctrine of the Christian life. Cf. Engen, tr., *Devotio Moderna*, 61.

110 For the influence of *De imitatione Christi* upon Calvin's *Psychopannychia*, see Tavard, *The Starting Point of Calvin's Theology*, 67, 128, 133, 172-173, 172-173. Also, for the eschatological and Christological feature of *Psychopannychia*, see Timothy George, "Calvin's *Psychopannychia*: Another Look," in *In Honor of John Calvin, 1509-64*, ed. E. J. Furcha (Montreal: McGill University Press, 1987), 317-322.

111 *The Christian Renaissance: A History of the "Devotio Moderna,"* 2nd ed. (Hamden, Conn.: Archon Books, 1965), 275-288, 297-299; Alexandre Ganoczy and Stefan Scheld, *Die Hermeneutik Calvins: geistesgeschichtliche Voraussetzungen und Grundzüge* (Wiesbaden: Franz Steiner Verlag, 1983), 35; Philip E. Hughes, "Jacques Lefèvre d'Étaples (c. 1455-1536): Calvin's Forerunner in France," in *Calvinus Reformator* (Potchefstroom: Potchefstroom University for Christian Higher Education, 1982), 107-108. For d'Étaples' attraction to mystical theology, see Philip E. Hughes, *Lefèvre: Pioneer of Ecclesiastical Renewal in France* (Grand Rapids: Eerdmans, 1984), 35-51; Richard, *The Spirituality of John Calvin*, 69-71.

112 Ganoczy, *The Young Calvin*, 57; Cottret, *Calvin: A Biography*, 13-15.

113 Hyma, *The Christian Renaissance*, 236-250; Karl Reuter, *Grundverständnis der Theologie Calvins: Unter Einbeziehung ihrer geschichtlichen Abhängigkeiten* (Neukirchen: Neukirchener Verlag, 1963), 28-37; Le Gal, *Le Droit Canonique*, 31;

human spirit but the *aeterna veritas* lies beyond our reach; therefore, the truth is known to us by the cooperation between God's self-knowledge (*noverim te*) and our self-knowledge (*noverim me*).[114] Upon this knowledge of God and man, à Kempis emphasized the Christian life as one of self-denial, bearing the cross, and following Jesus Christ our master.[115]

2.4 Commentary on Seneca's *De Clementia*: A Discovery of the Educational Function of Law

Calvin wrote his commentary on Seneca's *De clementia* not as a theologian; he did not have any theological purpose. In the words of André Malan Hugo, this commentary is "a perfect specimen of early sixteenth century *classical* scholarship."[116] In spite of the citations of 74 Latin and 22 Greek authors, this commentary contains only seven biblical references.[117] At the same time, by examining the commentary we find evidence of the influence of people and movements described in the previous section.

However, in this work Calvin shows a characteristic feature of *ad fontes* in his times, *Christum praedicare ex fontibus*,[118] by referring to seven church fathers, including Augustine, who is quoted 22 times.[119] So here we encounter with, as Ganoczy notes, "the perspectives of the Christian moralist, a disciple of Paul and Augustine," as well as the rhetorical skills and the historical criticism of a humanist.[120] Calvin must have been

---

Torrance, *The Hermeneutics of John Calvin*, 74. For a study of the devotio moderna in à Kempis' De imitatione Christi, see Pelikan, Reformation of Church and Dogma (1300-1700), 36-38; Hyma, *The Christian Renaissance*, 297-299: Richard, *The Spirituality of John Calvin*, 21-31.

114 Torrance, *The Hermeneutics of John Calvin*, 76; George H. Tavard, *The Starting Point of Calvin's Theology* (Grand Rapids: Eerdmans, 2000), 172-173.

115 Cottret, *Calvin: A Biography*, 31.

116 *Clem.* 19*.

117 Battles, "The Sources of Calvin's Seneca Commentary," 68, 86. However, according to Haas, it cites 56 Latin and 22 Greek writers, and according to Boisset, 55 Latin and 22 Greek writers. Haas, *The Concept of Equity in Calvin's Ethics*, 10; Jean Boisset, *Sagesse et Sainteté dans la pensée de Jean Calvin* (Paris: Presses universitaires de France, 1959), 248. The notable difference of Battles from the others is because he includes all unnamed sources.

118 Cf. David E. Willis, "Rhetoric and Responsibility in Calvin's Theology," in *The Context of Contemporary Theology*, ed. Alexander J. Mckelway and E. David Willis (Atlanta: John Knox Press, 1974), 45.

119 *Clem.* 415 (index). Cf. Doumergue, *Jean Calvin*, 1.222.

120 *The Young Calvin*, 179. Cf. Parker, *John Calvin*, 26-28; William Bouwsma, "The Two Faces of Humanism, Stoicism and Augustinianism in Renaissance Thought," in *Itinerarium Italicum: The Profile of the Italian Renaissance in the Mirror of its European Transformations*, ed. Heiko Oberman and Thomas A. Brady Jr. (Leiden:

familiar with many references of the church fathers through his studies of law.[121]

It is helpful to start our study of Calvin's position on the concept and use of natural law and civil law in the commentary by examining how there he comments on the Stoic concept of God. Stoics identified God with the logos, by which the world was created orderly and has been governed according to the rational laws of nature.[122] Calvin criticizes the Stoics, who saw the necessity of God's providence as subject to fate (*fatum*), and the Epicureans, who maintained the concept of *fortuna* in order to explain the mysterious economy of God and finally engaged in a struggle for the idle God (*Clem.* 5:38 ff).[123] Calvin says that fortune belongs to God but not vice versa because he "takes decisions and lays down the law" (*Clem.* 7.25-28). As he indicates that the word "Fortune" should be replaced by "God" in the axiom "the prince is nothing but the instrument of Fortune" (*Clem.* 7.22-28), Calvin claims that second causality or second causes (intermediate causes) are subject to neither the necessity of fate nor the fortuitous economy of fortune, but to the providence of God.[124] This

---

E. J. Brill, 1975), 9-12; Marcia L. Colish, *The Stoic Tradition from Antiquity to the Early Middle Ages: II. Stoicism in Christian Latin Thought through the Sixth Century* (Leiden: E. J. Brill, 1985), 159-165.

121 Cf. Jean Werckmeister, "The Reception of the Church Fathers in Canon Law," and E. Ann Matter, "The Church Fathers and the Glossa Ordinaris," in *The Reception of the Church Fathers in the West: From the Carolingians to the Maurists*, 2 vols, ed. Irena Backus (Leiden: E. J. Brill, 1997), 51-111.

122 Cf. Marcia L. Colish, *The Stoic Tradition from Antiquity to the Early Middle Ages: I. Stoicism in Classical Latin Literature* (Leiden: E. J. Brill, 1985), 31-34; Partee, *Calvin and Classical Philosophy*, 117: "The Stoics hold that deity expresses itself in the world process which follows a fixed law ($\lambda\acute{o}\gamma o\varsigma$) called fate or necessity ($\epsilon\acute{\iota}\mu\alpha\rho\mu\acute{\epsilon}\nu\eta$) or providence ($\pi\rho\acute{o}\nu o\iota\alpha$, *providentia*)." According to Dietrich Ritschl, "Augustine transformed the Stoic fatum into 'orders of creation' and connected them with his understanding of predestination." "Some Comments on the Background and Influence of Augustine's Lex Aeterna Doctrine," in *Creation Christ and Culture: Studies in Honour of T. F. Torrance*, ed. Richard W. A. McKinney (Edinburgh: T & T Clark, 1976), 73.

123 Cf. Josef Bohatec, "Calvins Vorsehungslehre," in *Calvinstudien: Festschrift zum 400. Geburtstage Johann Calvins*, ed. Reformierten Gemeinde Elberfeld (Leipzig: Verlag von Rudolf Haupt, 1909), 416-427.

124 Cf. Pierre-François Moreau, "Le Stoicisme aux XVII et XVIII siècles: Calvin et le Stoicisme," in *Cahiers de Philosophie Politique et Juridique* (Caen: Publications de l'Université de Caen, 1994), 15-21. Doumergue and Boisset are very critical of the influence of Stoicism on Calvin's view of God's providence. They assert that even in the commentary on Seneca Calvin, as a Christian, criticizes the Stoic view of necessity. Doumergue, *Jean Calvin*, 1.219-222. Boisset, *Sagesse et Sainteté dans la pensée de Jean Calvin*, 248. On the other hand, Wendel acknowledges the Stoic origin of Calvin's view of God's providence, at least "partly." *Calvin*, 29. This view

position of the young Calvin reflects some influence of the conception of covenantal causality and the dialectic between the absolute and ordained will of God in late medieval nominalism.[125]

Natural law had a Greek origin. Its concept had been completed by the Stoics and then passed onto Roman jurists and the Christian church, and became an important principle of the *Corpus Iuris Civilis*, which was actually the church law in Rome (A.D. 534).[126] For Stoics, living according to natural law and the supernatural will of God means to live in accordance with nature.[127] There is no supposed dichotomy between a unitary deity and natural laws (or reason) in their doctrine of the *logoi spermatikoi* (the seminal reasons or seeds of the logos).[128] So when Stoics consider nature or natural law to be "the best guide (*optimam ducem*)" for lawful rule, they relate this not only to legal duty but also to divine piety (*Clem.* 79. 18-22, 115.15).

In the same vein, Cicero says that the notion of equity (*aequitas, epieikeia*) refers to religious piety, spiritual sanctity, and moral justice (*Clem.* 93.19-21). In several places Calvin claims that moral justice is a characteristic feature of equity in relation to judicial proceedings. Citing Quintilian and Cicero, Calvin argues that in the process of interrogation "not the act itself but its quality (*facti qualitas*)" should be considered; and in the process of the application of the law, the law should not be enforced "with the utmost rigor" but "circumstances (*circumstantiis*)" should be taken into consideration if they are subject to equity (*Clem.* 21.28-29, 22.13-14, 17-18). Moreover, in judgment, "equity and right (*aequi bonique*)" should not be subject to "the letter or rigor of the law (*iuri summo seu rigori iuris*)" (*Clem.* 111.5-9). This philological and historical

---

of Wendel is totally supported by P. Marie, "Calvin's God and Humanism," in *Our Reformation Tradition: A Rich Heritage and Lasting Vocation* (Potchefstroom: Potchefstroom University for Christian High Education, 1984): 353-365. Parker, who maintains the early conversion of Calvin, does not think that his humanistic study was so strong as to swerve his faithful attitude towards the teaching of the Scripture "a nail's breath." *Calvin: An Introduction to His Thought* (Louisville: Westminster/John Knox, 1995), 4.

125 Calvin's theological view of God's providence (*Inst.* 1.16-17) is in accordance with his early view in the commentary on Seneca. Concerning second causality, see esp., *Inst.* 1.16.9 and "On How We Ought to Understand the Providence of God by which He Does Everything, and How the Libertines Confound It All When Speaking of It: The First Consequence of the Preceding Article," *TAL* 243-247 (*CO* 7.186-190).

126 Susan E. Schreiner, *The Theater of His Glory: Nature and the Natural Order in the Thought of John Calvin* (Durham, NC: Labyrinth Press, 1991), 73; Breen, *John Calvin*, 67 ff., 134 ff.

127 Haas, *The Concept of Equity in Calvin's Ethics*, 21; Partee, *Calvin and Classical Philosophy*, 67-68; Bouwsma, "The Two Faces of Humanism," 10-12.

128 Colish, *Stoicism in Classical Latin Literature*, 32-34.

interpretation based on *ad fontes* reflects Budé's influence most prominently (cf. *Clem.* 111.3-9).

In the commentary, Calvin shows the influence of jurisconsults, who believed that jurisdiction embraces all sorts of cognizance (*Clem.* 9.11-12). He frequently uses terms related to the court and jurisdiction because he has a firm conviction that proper judicial proceedings are the best way to discover the truth (*Clem.* 21.25 ff; 42.3 ff; 47.2 ff; 87.7 ff; 103.11ff; 111.3 ff; 115. 8 ff; 125.1 ff; 157. 31 ff).[129] This jurisdictional and interrogative interpretation of legal texts was the effect of Calvin's legal studies by which he learned to interpret a text on the ground of its context. Especially, with the knowledge of treating judicial proceedings justly, he must have realized the capital importance of the people in a specific historical context rather than the context itself.

Seneca's view of the nature of humanity is generally pessimistic (cf. *Clem.* 13. 34ff, 46.9-12, 132.15-16). Although human beings have "rational souls" and a "natural disposition from divine spirit" (*Clem.* 32.35; 36.38-39),[130] according to Seneca, "everyone follows the seeds of his own nature" (*Clem.* 33.5). Seneca's negative view of human nature is mostly related to the evil disposition (*affectus*) of humanity rather than its quality (*qualitas*). However, Calvin depicts Seneca as believing in "the rule of reason (*imperio rationis*)" in the human soul, following Plato, and putting a special emphasis on habit (*habitus*), following Aristotle (*Clem.* 17.28-29, 33.2-4, 27.7-39). Aristotle distinguishes *habitus* from *consuetudo*, and says, moral virtues are acquired by *consuetudo*, and *consuetudo* is transformed into the *habitus* of nature (*Clem.* 27.33-34, 38-39).[131] Indisputably, this axiom of Aristotle influenced Aquinas' synergism, which was based on the created habits of the regenerated. Along with *habitus*, in the commentary Calvin shows his view of conscience, by which people examine themselves before God's judgment seat.[132] Metaphors such as a worm and tormentor

---

129 Cf. Willis, "Rhetoric and Responsibility in Calvin's Theology," 48.

130 In the commentary, Calvin refers to Cicero's interpretation of "religion (*religio*)" and differentiate it from superstitions (*Clem.* 150.25-29; cf. *Inst.* 1.12.1). Concerning the influence of Cicero on Calvin's concept of the *cognitio Dei*, see Egil Grislis, "Calvin's Use of Cicero in the *Institutes* 1:1-5—A Case Study in Theological Method," *ARG* 62 (1971), 168-182; Peter J. Leithart, "That Eminent Pagan: Calvin's Use of Cicero in *Institutes* 1.1-5," *WTJ* 52 (1990), 1-12; Serene Jones, *Calvin and the Rhetorical Piety* (Louisville: Westminster John Knox Press), esp. 154 ff.; McGrath, *The Intellectual Origins of the European Reformation*, 36.

131 " . . . moralem virtutem ex consuetudine comparari. . . . consuetudinem in naturae habitum transformari." Both *habitus* and *consuetudo* are translated by Battles and Hugo as "habit" without discrimination, but their meanings in Latin should be differentiated.

132 Cf. David L. Foxgrover, "John Calvin's Understanding of Conscience," PhD dissertation, Claremont Graduate School, 1978, 311-438.

are used here negatively, but the typical metaphor "witness *(testis)*" represents its positive role prominently *(Clem.* 93.30-37, 94.5, Cf. *Inst.* 1.3.3).[133]

Calvin's commentary reveals both the pessimistic and optimistic sides of humanity and especially points out the social character of human beings. This understanding of man reflects the influence of Calvin's legal studies. We cannot find any theological view of total depravity in the commentary, but Calvin shows his basic concern for the common nature of humans by indicating crucial elements of the human soul. His attitude is more Christian than Stoic when he quotes from Augustine in order to attempt to find the cause of the clemency of the prince: "Let us prosecute in them their own wickedness, but let us have pity on the common nature *(misereamur communem naturam)* they share with us" *(Clem.* 11.19-21).[134]

The influence of jurisdiction is revealed noticeably in Calvin's equal emphasis on both the human character as a social man and human responsibility in society. Citing Plato and Aristotle, Calvin points out that mankind has been created as part of society and seeks after a commonality of life as a social animal *(Clem.* 38.34-36, 29.3-5). Calvin also discusses "the common good *(bono gentium),*" and indicates that citing Seneca, "Mankind has been created for mutual assistance *(Homo in adiutorium mutuum generatus est)*" *(Clem.* 29.8-9).[135] The relations between God *(logos),* nature, and humanity are succinctly expressed by Seneca in his *Dialogue*: "The real purpose for which a man exists, the supreme good *(summum bonum),* is to bring himself, as a part of nature, into harmony with the whole, so that he, through virtue, may 'keep company with God'."[136]

---

133 Cf. David Bosco, "Conscience as Court and Worm: Calvin and the Three Elements of Conscience," *Journal of Religious Ethics* 14/2 (1986), 344-345.
134 According to Bouwsma, both Stoicism and Augustinianism have "compatibility" and even "affinity" in that they "were bound up with the ancient rhetorical tradition," and both notions go "back to the yearning of early Christian converts for some bridge between the old world of thought and the new." On the other hand, he points out the clear difference between them in relation to "the biblical understanding of creation" as he says, "the Stoic view of man attributed to him a divine spark or seed, identified with reason, which gave man access to the divine order of the universe, from which the existence, the nature, and the will of God could be known. Stoicism therefore pointed to natural theology." "The Two Faces of Humanism," 5-9.
135 Cf. John H. Leith, *John Calvin's Doctrine of the Christian Life* (Louisville: Westminster/John Knox, 1989), 184-185. According to Leith, Calvin makes very plain that every person has a real responsibility for society, which arises out of the solidarity of humankind and out of the Christian gospel, and when he uses the word "neighbor," it signifies all people including non Christians.
136 Seneca, *Dialogue*, vii.15.5, quot. Hannis Taylor, *Cicero: A Sketch of his Life and*

It is from this understanding of human nature that Calvin explores the relationship between state and law, and the three uses of legal punishment. Calvin looks upon a state as "an assembly or gathering of men associated by law" (*Clem.* 87.8-10). He points this out by citing Cicero, who says, "As our bodies without the mind, so also a state without law, cannot use its parts, which are analogous to sinews and blood and members" (*Clem.* 85.15-16), and by citing Plato, who described "laws as sinews (*nervos*) in man" (*Clem.* 33.1. cf. *Inst.* 4.20.14).

Calvin's interpretation of Seneca's statement on the three uses of punishment[137] refers not only to the use of common law (or civil law) but also to the use of natural law.[138] The first use of punishment is to reform (*emendare*) a man who is convicted. Its need is derived from human nature, which is so corrupt that a man, if his sin is not punished, becomes more vicious and more unbridled (*Clem.* 125.11-12). Proper punishment has an educational function to lead a bad man back onto the right path. Calvin notes that this use corresponds to the Greek words which are translated into "warning," "correction," and "advising," and *monitio* and *animadversio* in Latin (*Clem.* 125.14-16).[139] Cicero considers this admonishing and nourishing function of punishment when he says, "A salutary severity is better than an empty show of clemency" (*Clem.* 23.27-28, Cf. 24.36-37). Concerning the practice of punishment, Calvin notes, for the renewal of sinful men gentleness and clemency are more needed than severe punishment (*Clem.* 126.2-3). The first use of punishment corresponds to the

---

Works, A Commentary on the Roman Constitution and Roman Public Life, Supplemented by the Sayings of Cicero Arranged for the First Time, 2nd ed. (Chicago: A. C. McClurg, 1918), 35.

137 *Clem.* 124.18-21: ". . . alienas iniurias, in quibus vindicandis haec tria lex sequuta est: quae princeps quoque sequi debet, aut ut eum quem punit, emendet: aut ut poena eius caeteros meliores reddat: . . ."

138 Cicero does not differentiate common law from natural law. Cf. Taylor, *Cicero*, 43; Colish, *I. Stoicism in Classical Latin Literature*, 96. For the influence of Cicero's Roman legal thought upon Calvin, see Jean de Savignac, "Une Réédition du '*De Clementia*' de Jean Calvin," *La Revue Réformée* 21/84 (1970), 45; McNeil, *Guillaume Budé and Humanism*, 22-23; Kingdon, "Calvin and Constitutionalism," 41. Calvin's three uses of the law have been compared with the "three uses of church discipline" and the "three uses of punishment" (by Battles) and with "a three-fold shape of natural knowledge" of God (by Grislis). Battles, "Against Luxury and License in Geneva," 325; Grislis, "Calvin Use of Cicero in the *Institutes* 1:1-5," 34.

139 Battles calls the third normative use of the law the pedagogical one and from this point argues that since the first use of punishment is a part of the third use of the law, there is no relation between the first use of the law and the three uses of punishment. Ibid. On the contrary, Hesselink regards the pedagogical office of the law as the core of its first theological use. *Calvin's Concept of the Law*, 231-234.

third use of the law and the third use of church discipline, for the former admonishes believers and urges them on in well-doing and the latter makes men ashamed of their baseness so that they may begin to repent (*Inst.* 2.7.12-13, 4.12.5).[140]

The second use of punishment is to make the rest better by punishing a bad man. According to Plutarch, punishment functions to "deter and restrain some by the chastisement of others." Cicero says, punishment "might for the future establish a warning for all lest anyone be minded to imitate such insanity" (*Clem.* 125.34-35). The essence of this use is well presented by the Greek *paradeigma* and the Latin *exemplum* (*Clem.* 125.26-28). Calvin argues that even for the innocent, clemency is necessary because they come to learn the name of virtue through an equitable punishment (*Clem.* 21.19-24). This use of punishment corresponds to the second use of the law, which deters those not yet regenerate from evil-doing (*Inst.* 2.7.11).[141]

The third use of punishment is to remove bad men in order that the rest may live in greater security (*Clem.* 125.37-126.1). This use was prevalent for ancient people who distinguished between those who are reformable and those who are incorrigible, and thought that, as "the rule of Plato" says, to deprive the incurable of life was to "be doubly beneficial to the rest. For the rest are deterred by their example and also the city is cleansed of wicked men" (*Clem.* 24.2-28).[142] Calvin distinguishes the innocent from the "hopeless" and the "forever lost (*deploratur in perpetuum*)" (*Clem.* 24.15, 21). He says, although a prince should consider his people as his sons and take care of them like a physician, he sometimes kills and cuts "the public ulcer (*ulcus publicum*)" when "public welfare (*publica utilitas*)" demands it and the depravity of men needs to be cured (*Clem.* 96.13-15, 18-20; 109.25-32 [altered]).[143] Accordingly, the third use of punishment corresponds to the first and second uses of church discipline, but it is not related to the use of the law itself (*Inst.* 4.12.5).[144]

---

140 Cf. Battles, ibid.
141 Cf. ibid.
142 Cf. *Clem*, 137*. Plato deals with the second and third uses of the law together, but does not claim the third type of punishment (*Clem.* 24.4-8, 125.38).
143 Cf. *Clem.* 137*-138*. Battles argues that Calvin's remarks about a class of *deplorati* in the commentary have obvious implications for the distinction between the redeemed and the reprobate in his theology. However, the terms used by Calvin, mostly quoted from philosophers, such as "hopeless," "incurable," and "forever lost," designate habitual criminals of the wicked rather than their reprobation. In the commentary Calvin does not pay much attention to the Stoic concept of "wise men," which is based on Stoic fatalism. He rather accepts the Stoic understanding of the human state as more related to Aristotle's concept of *habitus* rather than to human nature (*Clem.* 27.27-39).
144 Battles, "Against Luxury and License in Geneva," 325.

From the previous discussion on the threefold use of punishment, we recognize Calvin's keen awareness of the tension between "personal concern" and "public morality" in Stoic philosophy (*Clem.* 143.20-21). With reference to personal concern, we have found some aspects of the young Calvin's Christian thought, and with reference to public morality, we have seen the great influence of humanist and jurist legal traditions. Calvin demonstrates his stance in considering the interpretation of the law and the application, and the meaning of the law itself and its context at the same time. Therefore, for Calvin, the social character of humans and society itself are equally important. This is why Calvin takes so much interest not only in the literal and historical meaning of a text but also in the character of specific people who live in that context. Calvin's view of the three aims of punishment demonstrates this well.

Calvin finds the key to solving this tension in the clemency of the prince. By emphasizing the divine origin of the power of the prince, Calvin asserts his authority and duty at the same time. In this respect, Calvin calls magistrates God's servants, ministers, and vicars (*Clem.* 1.13, 5.38-6.35, cf. *Inst.* 4.20.4). Therefore, if the prince enters into meditation, he receives the composure of his mind with the conviction that God's providence is the reward of following his conscience (*Clem.* 5.39-6.3). In order to reveal that this idea is not different from "the confession of our religion (*confessio religionis nostrae*)," Calvin adds Romans 13:1, "Power comes from God alone, and those that exist have been ordained by God."[145]

The fact that a prince was endowed with authority from the gods makes him different from other people in his relation to the law. He is in the position not only to distribute God's justice according to the "law of analogy (*ius analogum*)" (*Clem.* 20.11), but also to conduce and contribute to public morality (*Clem.* 143.21). Therefore, the prince is called by Cicero "the living law (*lex animata*)" (*Clem.* 125.4, Cf. *Inst.* 4.20.14). If the law is the sinews of the body called the state, a prince is the mind of the state (*Clem.* 87.15, 26.14-15, 31.25-32).

Calvin uses the rhetoric of accommodation in the commentary in order to explain the interrelationships between the prince and his people, and between the prince and God: "As the people ought to moderate (*attemperare*) themselves to the will of the prince, so should the prince see to it that he keeps Jupiter and the gods propitious. . . . Therefore the prince

---

[145] Concerning Calvin's use of "*nostra religio*" in the commentary, see *Clem.*130*-132*. According to David C. Steinmetz, while Melanchthon insists that there are two grounds for the Christians' obedience to the magistrate: first, reason and natural law; second, God's own ordination of the state and the rule of law. Calvin, focusing on the positive side of political order, argues that there is no other ground but "divine ordination." "Calvin and the Civil Magistrate," in *Calvin in Context*, 202-205.

should consider that he has received his administration of the people from the gods, and is sometime to render an account thereof to them" (*Clem.* 12.22-24, 27-28). Calvin also uses this rhetorical skill when he compares the duty of a prince to the duty of a parent (*Clem.* 97.30ff).

In the following commentary, Calvin clearly expresses the principle of accommodation:

> He [Seneca] reminds the prince of the natural law (*principem legis naturalis*): that he [the prince] treats his subjects as he would have the gods treat himself, for the gods rule him as he himself governs men. But if he lives and breathes by the tenderness of the gods, why shall man not rather be favorable to men and open to their entreaty? (*Clem.* 50.27-31).

Calvin's rhetorical use of accommodation in the commentary is made for a hortatory oration. It is different from the theological rhetorical use of the conception of God's accommodation to human capacity, which was used by Calvin for apologetic, hermeneutical, and pastoral purposes, as well as for rhetorical reasons.[146] However, in the commentary Calvin depicts the prince with metaphors, typically used to describe divine accommodation. The prince is presented as "a shepherd of the people (*pastor populorum*)" (*Clem.* 30.12), "the father of his country (*pater patriae*)" (*Clem.* 97.37, 106.24ff), a "teacher (*praeceptor*)" (*Clem.* 107.36 ff), and a "physician (*medicus*)" (*Clem.* 109.28 ff).[147]

2.5 Conclusion

In his small but very insightful book *Le caractère de Calvin*, Emile Doumergue asserts that the theology of Calvin overcomes *intellectualisme*, whose characteristics are indicated there as extreme literalism and dogmatism, and presents *mysticisme*. With reference to Calvin's *mysticisme*,

---

146 See Ford Lewis Battles, "God Was Accommodating Himself to Human Capacity," *Interpretation* 31/1 (1977), 21; David F. Wright "Accommodation and Barbarity in John Calvin's Old Testament Commentaries," in *Understanding Poets and Prophets: Essays in Honour of George Wishart Anderson*, ed. A. Graeme Auld (Sheffield: Sheffield Academic Series, 1993), 414-415, and "Calvin's Accommodating God," in *Calvinus Sincerioris Religionis Vindex: Calvin as Protector of the Purer Religion*, ed. Wilhelm H. Neuser and Brian G. Armstrong (Kirksville, Mo.: Sixteenth Century Essays & Studies, 1997), 7; Richard C. Gamble, "Calvin as Theologian and Exegete: Is There Anything New?" *CTJ* 23 (1998), 182-183; David L. Puckett, *John Calvin's Exegesis of the Old Testament* (Louisville: Westminster/John Knox, 1995), 112.

147 For Calvin's use of these metaphors in his theological works, see Bouwsma, *John Calvin*, 211-212; Battles, "God Was Accommodating Himself to Human Capacity," 27-31.

Doumergue discusses "the faith of the heart (*la foi du cœur*)" and "the mystical union (*union mystique*).[148] It is surely the case that these two conceptions represent the most significant features of Calvin's pietism, but they cannot be identified with the elements of mysticism. Rather, it should be noted that through his early life Calvin experienced both the intellectualism and the mysticism of his times, and finally reached his own theological pietism.[149] In dealing with the young Calvin's legal and humanistic culture, we should keep in mind that he was a pious Christian who wanted to be a priest even though, as he confessed, his soul was not yet teachable (*ad docilitatem*) to the divine truth.[150]

To a brilliant young student of law, the teaching of the *via moderna*—that it is God's will that those who are justified by the merit of Christ ought to live according to the law so that they finally reach the eternal life—may have looked closely related to the emphasis of the *mos novus* in Roman legal studies which claims that interpretation of the normative imperative of the law should be based on its historical context. The nominalist concept of covenantal causality may have influenced the young Calvin's legal thought. Just as he found out that the nature of the relationship between God and his people is crucial in the covenant, so he found out that designating the meaning of law in relation with the circumstances crucial. Here, we can presume that the nominalist concept of *pactum* helped the young Calvin to take the *via media* between the literal determinism of the glossators and the philological historical approach of the jurisconsults. This is why we should take into special consideration the thought of de l'Estoile, in spite of the definite influence of the *mos novus* on Calvin.

The influence of the young Calvin's synthetic legal position on his theology is considerable in his interpretation of the divine law, which is described characteristically by three principles in the *Institutes*. The first principle, to interpret the law spiritually in accordance with the purpose of the lawgiver, shows the legacy of Alciati's historical interpretation of law (*Inst*. 2.8.6-7). Then, the second principle, that "a sober interpretation of the law goes beyond the words" shows the influence of Budé, as we have seen prominently from his view of equity (*Inst*. 2.8.8-10). Finally, the influence of de l'Estoile is striking in relation to the third principle, when Calvin claims that we should understand the first and second tables of the Decalogue according to their individual purpose but harmoniously because all the commandments are for God's glory—for God's own sake (*Inst*.

---

148 Doumergue, *Le caractère de Calvin*, 64-75.
149 Cf. Boisset, *Sagesse et Sainteté dans la pensée de Jean Calvin*, 327-336.
150 *CO* 31.21. Doumergue gives specific attention to the development of religious piety even before the conversion of Calvin. This position of Doumergue is also demonstrated in his comments on Calvin's commentary on Seneca's *De clementia*. *Jean Calvin*, 1.218-222.

2.8.11-12). Unlike Alciati and Budé, Stella believed that the meaning of a word or a sentence is determined by the text it belongs to, and unlike Zasius, he was convinced that the text itself presents its complete meaning. I do not think that this categorization is always proper, but I believe that it provides sufficient evidence of the intellectual origin of Calvin's dynamic understanding of the law.

Christian humanists in Calvin's times tried to find their way back to the apostolic era. Their slogan *ad fontes* was not just a literary or cultural expression but its aim was to save the church from the papacy and recover the true catholicity of the early church.[151] Although they worshipped God according to the Catholic traditions, they already were imbued with Protestant ideas. They saw scriptural interpretation as the culmination of *ad fontes*. They lived their lives in the era of transition from *ad fontes* to *ad scripturam solam*. So along with the influence of Budé's linguistic and literary interpretation, Alciati's purely philological approach to the text, and de l'Estoile's determinative but practical position on the annotation on the text, we should take into account the religious pietism of the jurists.[152] As we see from the lives of Budé, de l'Estoile, and Major, who was influenced by the *devotio moderna*, the legal and logical mind was not regarded as incompatible with religious spirituality. They did not differentiate legal duty from religious piety and from the covenantal obligation of the chosen people. For the first time, people began to realize that it was more important to elucidate the existence and character of people who are designated by the regulations of the legal texts, rather than the texts themselves. This represents the soul of the Renaissance.

The new understanding of the normative role of the law was influenced by this new perspective on man, "the renaissance man." Calvin probably found the source of the new thought in the ancient philosopher who was known as a Stoic with Christian sympathies, Seneca, who showed throughout his writings "a strong sense of sin, with an accompanying practice of self examination and sensitiveness to conscience."[153]

In the commentary on Seneca's *De clementia*, the prince is depicted not only as the interpreter and executor of the law, but also the law himself. His position is basically understood as the reconciler who resolves the tension between personal virtue and social morality. Also, he is presented as the

---

151 Alister E. McGrath, *Reformation Thought: An Introduction*, 2nd ed. (Grand Rapids: Baker, 1993), 45-46. For the late medieval thought of the unity of the church, see Pelikan, *Reformation of Church and Dogma (1300-1700)*, 69-126.
152 In Calvin's times, the word "jurists" was used to denote not only professional lawyers who studied law but also people who were well read in canon law and civil law as well as Roman law. Michel Reulos, "Les Juristes: En Contact avec Calvin," in *Calvin et ses contemporains*, ed. Olivier Millet (Genève: Droz, 1998), 213.
153 Breen, *John Calvin*, 72.

mediator between God and his people in view of the fact that he does not only rule over his people with an authority which has a divine origin, but has to serve his people because it is a divinely given duty. Meanwhile, man is described as one who longs for the commonality of the society and at the same time should be ruled in order for the public good. People are sinners and are to be reformed by discipline itself.

From this understanding of humanity and society, Calvin deploys his view of law in the commentary. The relationship between law and society is compared to the sinews and soul of the body. The law plays a negative role when it expels people who are incorrigible, but mostly it works for the education and renewal of people. The normative meaning of the law is not always a fixed one but can change according to the historical context. But this does not mean that the norm of a specific law depends on fortuitousness.

In many cases in the commentary, Calvin shows his Christian view *fontibus Christianis*, especially with notable citations from Augustine. Can we, then, find any theological view of the law of the young Calvin in the commentary? From the first *Institutes*, Calvin emphasizes the continuity between natural law and moral law (1536 *Inst.* 1.4, *CO* 1.29).[154] In the 1559 *Institutes*, Calvin discusses the identities of natural law and divine law in their essence not only in the section on the interpretation of the law but also in the section on civil law (*Inst.* 2.8.1, 4.20.16). Thus, Calvin's view of natural law is crucial in understanding his theology of the law. It is worthwhile to investigate the young Calvin's stance on Stoicism, however, the more important task is to prove how it was maintained or abandoned or modified.[155]

Calvin provides many crucial insights we may encounter when we deal with natural law in a theological manner. He reveals the textual and contextual approach to a specific text. He presents various kinds of rhetorical skills which are also found in his later works. He also demonstrates his strong propensity for the normative use of the law. He claims that the reading of texts should strongly take into account the

---

154 All citations of the 1536 *Institutes* are from the Battles translation (rev. ed. Grand Rapids: Eerdmans, 1986). The first reference marks the chapter and section number of the English translation. The second reference is from *Calvini Opera*, which is abbreviated by *CO* followed by the volume and page number.

155 E.g. Alexandre Ganoczy und Stefan Scheld, *Herrschaft – Tugend – Vorsehung: hermeneutische Deutung und Veröffentlichung handschriftlicher Annotationen Calvins zu sieben Senecatragödien und der Pharsalia Lucans* (Wiesbaden: Franz Steiner Verlag, 1982), esp. 30-51; Marianne Carbonnier, "Le droit de punir et le sens de la peine chez Calvin," *Revue d'histoire et de philosophie religieuses* 54/2 (1974), 187-201. In these two articles, the authors argue that Calvin's dynamic understanding of God's providence and law sprang out of his knowledge of Roman law and Stoicism.

specific people in the specific context. These concerns of Calvin are well reflected in his theological works, especially in his commentary on the last four books of the Pentateuch in relation to its structure and its emphasis on God's accommodation to the hardness of heart of the ancient people.[156] With all these concerns, however, we should keep in mind that the Stoic understanding of the law is based on the prominent ethical virtue of moderation rather than on the Christian concept of self-denial, and on the Stoic view of necessity rather than on the Christian doctrine of predestination.[157] Calvin's commentary on *De clementia* does not give us any clue to the origin of his Christological understanding of the law, however, it reveals the young Calvin's resolution to bring together "a fusion of God-given instruction and God-directed history" with the omnipotent providence of God, even though it is not as theological as in his commentary on the Pentateuchal laws.[158]

---

156 Cf. David F. Wright, "Calvin's Pentateuchal Criticism: Equity, Hardness of Heart, and Divine Accommodation in the Mosaic Harmony Commentary," *CTJ* 21/1 (1986), 33-50, and "Accommodation and Barbarity in John Calvin's Old Testament Commentaries," 413-427. For the historical interpretation of Calvin in his commentaries and sermons, see Brian G. Armstrong, "Report on the Seminar: An Investigation of Calvin's Principles of Biblical Interpretation," *Hervormde Theologiese Studies* 54 (1998), 131-142; Danielle Fischer, "L'Élément historique dans la prédication de Calvin: Un aspect original de l'homilétique du Réformateur," *Revue d'histoire et de philosophie religieuses* 64/4 (1984), 365-386.
157 Cf. Moreau, "Le Stoicisme aux XVII et XVIII siècles," 16, 21; Charles B. Partee, "Calvin and Determinism," *Christian Scholar's Review* 5/2 (1975), 127-128; Peter J. Leithart, "Stoic Elements in Calvin's Doctrine of the Christian Life: Part II. Mortification," *WTJ* 55 (1993), 193-200.
158 Quot. Wright, "Calvin's Pentateuchal Criticism," 48.

Chapter 3

The Formation and Development of Calvin's Christological Understanding of the Law

In this chapter we are going to explore the formation and development of Calvin's theology of the law taking into consideration its place and significance in the whole structure of his theology. This is going to be very useful for the overview of Calvin's Christological understanding of the law before we deal it with more specifically in the light of his concept of *Christus mediator legis*.

3.1 The Law in Calvin's Early Writings

The authorship of Nicholas Cop's academic address, delivered on 1 November 1533 (*Concio academica nomine rectoris universitatis Parisiensis, CO* 9.873-876, *CO* 10/2.30-36), has been discussed in relation to whether it was in fact Calvin's first theological work. Some scholars have recognized it as crucial to establishing the time of Calvin's conversion.[1] In this inaugural lecture, the new rector of the University of Paris proclaimed *"philosophia christiana,"* which he designated as *"Christi philosophia"* in view of the fact that our true faith should be established on "Christ, best and greatest, who is the one true intercessor with the Father, to illuminate our minds with his life-giving Spirit."[2] From this perspective,

---

1 Concerning the authorship of this work, scholars have mostly agreed that Calvin at least drafted it or co-operated with Cop upon it since Jean Rott suggested this theory in "Documents strasbourgeois concernant Calvin," *Revue d'histoire et de philosophie religieuses* 44 (1964), 290-305 (text with notes, 305-311). Cf. Joseph N. Tylenda, "Calvin's First Reformed Sermon? Nicholas Cop's Discourse—1 November 1533," *WTJ* 38/3 (1976), 300-310 (translation with notes, 310-318); W. de Greef, *The Writings of John Calvin*, tr. Lyle D. Bierma (Grand Rapids: Baker, 1989), 23, 86-87; Ganoczy, *The Young Calvin*, 80-82; Hans Scholl, "Nicolaus Cop—Pariser Rektoratsrede vom. 1. November 1533," *CSA* 1/1.1-9 (text and translation, 10-25). For scholars such as Parker who uphold Calvin's early conversion, this address is regarded as his first work written as a Protestant, but for scholars such as Bouwsma and Wendel who argue for the continuity of humanistic background and Calvin's late conversion, it is considered to show his "Evangelical humanism position." Parker, *John Calvin*, 30; Bouwsma, *John Calvin*, 15; Wendel, *Calvin*, 40.

2 "The Academic Discourse. Delivered by Nicolas Cop on Assuming the Rectorship of

Cop, sharply critical of *les sophistes de la Sorbonne* who "vilify and contaminate everything, and enclose it within their own sophistical laws,"[3] emphasized the grace of the law as well as the accusing function of the law. He said that "Christ is setting before our eyes his grace and his kindness; and is rightly interpreting Moses' teaching as to how the Law is to be understood,"[4] and that "the Law mentions the mercy of God, but only on a definite condition: provided the Law be fulfilled." Therefore, he claimed, there is no other way but "the promise of Christ " to "live a godly life."[5]

The other example of how Calvin understands the relationship between the law and the gospel in light of the relation of the law to Christ can be found in his French preface to Olivetan's New Testament translation published in 1535 (*A tous amateurs de Iésus Christ, et de son S. Evangile, salut, CO* 9.791-821).[6] In the following lines, he succinctly asserts that Christ is the substance and fulfilment of the law.

> God has confirmed his people in every possible way during their long waiting for the great Messiah, by providing them with his written law, containing numerous ceremonies, purifications, and sacrifices, which were but the figures and shadows (*figures et umbers, figurae et adumbrationes*) of the great blessings to come with Christ, who alone was the embodiment and truth (*le corps et verité, corpus substantia veritas*) of them. For the law was incapable of bringing anyone to perfection; it only presented Christ, and like a teacher spoke of and led to him, who was, as

---

the University of Paris on 1 November 1533," Battles, tr. and ed., 1536 *Inst.*, "Appendix II," 365 (*CO* 10/2.31).

3 Ibid., 364-366 (*CO* 10/2.30-31). Note Calvin's rhetorical expression to accuse the Sorbonne theologians in the following passage including the quotation: "Hoc vitium perditissimi sophistae incurrerunt, qui de lana caprina perpetuo contendunt, rixantur, altercantur, nihil de fide, nihil de amore Dei * * nihil de veris operibus disserunt * *, omnia calumniantur, omnia labefactant, omnia suis legibus, id est, sophisticis coercent" (*CO* 10/2.31). The unknown fragments marked as * * might be suggested as "*nihil de remissione peccatorum, nihil de gratis, nihil de iustificatione,*" and "*Aut si certe disserunt.*" Scholl, tr., "Nicolaus Cop—Pariser Rektoratsrede vom. 1. November 1533," 12.

4 Ibid., 367 (*CO* 10/2.32).

5 Ibid., 369 (*CO* 10/2.34): "Lex misericordiae Dei mentionem facit, sed certa conditione: si impleatur. . . . ex sola Christi promissione, de qua qui dubitat pie vivere non potest et gehennae incendium sibi parat."

6 From 1551 on, the title of the foreword read: *Epistre aux fidèles monstrant comment Christ est la fin de la loy*. The Latin version of this preface was published by Beza in 1576 under the title of *Praefatio in N.T. cuius haec summa est: Christum esse legis finem* (*CO* 9.792-822). De Greef, *The Writings of John Calvin*, 90-92; Ernst Saxer, "Calvins Vorrede zur Olivetanbibel (1535)," *CSA* 1/1.27-32 (text and translation, 34-57).

was said by Saint Paul, the end and fulfillment (*la fin et accomplissement, finis et complementum*) of the law.[7]

Calvin claims emphatically that the law is the rule of living in his early catechetical and confessional works including the 1536 *Institutes* (*Christianae religionis institutio*), the first catechisms in French (*Instruction et confession de Foy dont on use en l'Eglise de Genève* of 1537, *CO* 22.33-74) and in Latin (*Catechismus, sive christianae religionis institutio* of 1538, *CO* 5.317-362),[8] and the *catechismus posterior* in French (*Le Catéchisme de l'église de Genève* of 1542, *CO* 6.9-145) and in Latin (*Catechismus ecclesiae Genevensis* in 1545, *CO* 6.10-146). The normative function of the law was proclaimed in the Genevan confession (*Confession de la foy* of 1536 or 1537, *CO* 22.85-96), which was presented by Farel and Calvin, in Article 3: "[B]ecause his [God's] will is the only principle of all justice, we confess that all our life ought to be ruled in accordance with the commandments of his holy law in which is contained all perfection of justice, and that we ought to have no other rule of good and just living (*reigle de bien vivre et iustement*)."[9]

Calvin called the first catechisms "a brief summary (*summa*) of religion" in the "Letter to the Reader" of the Genevan Catechism in 1545.[10] Although the two catechisms do not contain his characteristic remarks on the threefold use of the law, they touch on very crucial theological issues

---

7 Preface to Olivétan's New Testament, CC 63 (CO 9.801-802). The modern French edition also appears in Jacques Pannier, Épitre a tous amateurs de Jésus-Christ: Préface à la traduction française du Nouveau Testament par Robert Olivetan (1535) . . . avec Introduction sur une édition française de l'Institution dès 1537? (Paris: Fishbacher, 1929), 44. With regard to Calvin's Christological understanding of the law in this preface, Jürgen Quack refers specifically to the influence of Bullinger's covenantal theology in De testamento seu fordere Dei unico et aeterno (1534). "Calvins Bibelvorreden (1535-1546)," in Evangelische Bibelvorreden von der Reformation bis zur Aufklärung (Gütersloh: Gütersloher, 1975), 102-107.
8 Opposing the position of Rilliet and Dufour, who argue that Calvin translated the French *Catechism* into Latin, Rodolphe Peter suggests that the Latin version preceded the French. Olivier Millet, "Le premier 'Catéchisme' de Genève (1537/1538) et sa place dans l'oeuvre de Calvin," in *Catéchismes et Confessions de foi*, ed. Jean Boisset (Montpellier: Université de Montpellier, 1995), 216.
9 The Genevan Confession, *CTT* 26-27 (CO 22.86). For the authorship of this work, see Albert Rilliet, "Notice Historique," in *Le Catéchisme Français de Calvin publié en 1537, réimprimé pour la première fois d'après un exemplaire nouvellement retrouvé, et suivi de la plus ancienne Confession de foi de l'église de Genève, avec deux notices*, ed. Albert Rilliet and Théophile Dufour (Genève, 1878), 52-58; De Greef, *The Writings of John Calvin*, 125.
10 *The Catechism of the Church of Geneva*, *CTT* 90 (*CO* 6.8); Rilliet, "Notice Historique," 22 ff.

regarding the law, which were further developed in his later major writings.[11] As a foreword to his interpretation of the Ten Commandments Calvin points out that the law, which is "the most perfect rule of all righteousness (*perfectissima totius iustitiae regula*)," reveals "the Lord's everlasting will." Then he claims that the sum of the law (*legis summa*) is love. In the following section, entitled "*Quid ex sola lege ad nos redeat*," Calvin defines the nature of the law as "the true pattern of a righteous and holy life and even the most perfect image of righteousness itself (*verum iustae ac sanctae vitae exemplar, adeoque imago iustitiae ipsius absolutissima*)," and says that since the fall this original office of the law never works as desired without "the promise of eternal life." Here Calvin is eager to relate the normative feature of the law to the promise of eternal life contained in our salvation.[12]

Although Calvin does not devote a specific section to the threefold use of the law, he deals with the first and third uses of the law succintly in the sections called "*Legem gradum esse ad Christum*"[13] and "*Per fidem sanctificamur in legis obedientiam*." Especially, the latter shows the Christological origin of the third use of the law very impressively.

> Scripture teaches that for us Christ was made not only righteousness but sanctification as well. . . . The observance of the law does not therefore require our capacity, but rather spiritual power whereby it comes to pass that our hearts are cleansed of their corruption and softened to the obedience of righteousness. Now Christians make a far different use of the law than those without faith can make of it. For where the Lord had engraved on our hearts the love of his righteousness, the outward teaching of law, which previously was accusing us of nothing but weakness and transgression, is now a lantern (*lucerna, une lampe*) for our feet to keep us from wandering away from the straight path. It is our wisdom by which we are formed and instructed to complete uprightness. It is our discipline which does not permit us to abandon ourselves in more wicked license.[14]

It should be noted that Calvin writes this passage in the light of having stated that "Just as Christ by his righteousness intercedes on our behalf with

---

11 *Catechism or Institution of the Christian Religion*, tr. Ford Lewis Battles (from Latin), in I. John Hesselink, *Calvin's First Catechism: A Commentary* (Louisville: Westminster/John Knox, 1997, hereafter *First Catechism*): 7-38. The English translation of the 1537 French *Catechism* to which I refer here is *Instruction in Faith*, tr. and ed. Paul T. Fuhrmann (Philadelphia: Westminster, 1949).
12 *First Catechism* 11-16 (*CO* 5.327-332, *CO* 22.38-46).
13 Ibid., 16 (*CO* 5.332, *CO* 22.45-46). Cf. Hesselink, *Calvin's Concept of the Law*, 13.
14 *First Catechism*, 19-20 (*CO* 5.335-336, *CO* 22.49-50).

the Father, that with him as our sponsor we may be reckoned as righteous, so by the participation in his Spirit he sanctifies to all purity and innocence."[15] Calvin here relates the third use of the law, which is developed along with his doctrine of double grace, to the communication of Christ's righteousness through the working of the Spirit of the Mediator. As we see later, this position of Calvin is prominently shown in his 1539 *Institutes*.[16]

It is obvious from its title that in the Catechism of the Church of Geneva of 1542/45, which is called *Catechismus posterior*, Calvin is more concerned about the practical use of the law in the Christian life than its systematization.[17] This work, termed "*solenne christianae communionis symbolum*," is composed of four parts: faith, law, prayer, and sacrament.[18] The section on the law includes the definitional question and answer—"M: What rule of life (*vivendi regulam*) has he given us? C: His law"—, the interpretation of the Ten Commandments, "a brief compendium of the whole law," and the "*duplex officium legis*."[19] These themes had been introduced in his first Catechism, but here Calvin emphasizes the third use of the law more.[20] It defines the law as "a perfect rule of all righteousness (*perfectam omnis iustitiae regulam*)," ultimately revealing "the form for rightly worshipping God (*formam Dei rite colendi*)."[21]

---

15 Ibid., 19 (*CO* 5.335, *CO* 22.49).
16 Olivier Millet points out that Calvin's first catechisms should be dealt with not so much as the summary of the 1536 *Institutes* as with reference to its relation to both the 1536 and 1539 *Institutes*. His argument is based on the fact that Calvin's ideas in the first catechisms developed partly to the confession of faith in 1536/1537 and partly to the 1536 and 1539 *Institutes*. "Le premier 'Catéchisme' de Genève (1537/1538) et sa place dans l'oeuvre de Calvin," 209-229, esp. 212, 224.
17 The full title of the 1542 French Catechism is *Le Catéchisme de l'église de Genève, c'est a dire le Formulaire d'instruire les enfants en la chrestienté*. Also, its Latin version of 1545 had the same title.
18 *The Catechism of the Church of Geneva*, "Letter to the Reader," 90 (*CO* 6.8), and text, 91-139 (*CO* 6.9-134).
19 *The Catechism of the Church of Geneva*, 107-119 (*CO* 6.51-82), quot. 107, 117-118 (*CO* 6.51-52, 75-76, 79-80).
20 Hesselink, *Calvin's Concept of the Law*, 14. Cf. Nobuo Watanabe, "Calvin's Second Catechism: Its Predecessors and Its Environment," in *Calvinus Sacrae Scripturae Professor*, 230.
21 *The Catechism of the Church of Geneva*, 117-118 (*CO* 6.79-82). Although basically in agreement with the theory of Jacques Courvoisier, who argues for the influence of Bucer's catechisms (1534, 1537) upon Calvin's 1542 *Catechism*, Olivier Millet points out their difference as he comments that while Bucer in his catechisms deals with "*la fois du colloque religieux humaniste et du traité confessionnel*," Calvin there presents "*le résumé vigoureusement économique, parfaitement raisonné et ordonné des chapitres de l'Institution*." "Rendre raison de la foi: Le Catéchisme de Calvin (1542)," in *Aux origins du catéchisme en France*, ed. Pierre Colin (Paris: Desclée,

3.2 The Development of Calvin's Christological Understanding of the Law in the *Institutes*

3.2.1 Theological Apologia in the First Chapter of the 1536 Institutes

According to Jean-Daniel Benoît, the development of Calvin's *Institutes* 1536-1560 was "organic." It was not like adding new blocks upon broken walls but "rather the growth of a living entity, the increase of which is at the same time the concern of all the members of the organism."[22] In dealing with theological *loci* and *disputationes* for the formulation of his Christological understanding of the law, Calvin clearly reveals this tendency.

As has frequently been observed, the first edition of the *Institutes* was written basically to conform to the classical pattern of catechism in the order of *de lege, de fide, de oratione,* and *de sacramentis* under the influence of Luther's *Small and Large Catechisms* of 1529.[23] However, Calvin's concern in this book was not restricted to its catechetical or confessional purpose as had been the case in the schools of the Middle Ages, but he extended the scope to current apologetic agendas such as religious tolerance, false Catholic sacraments, and Christian freedom, including ecclesiastical power and civil government.[24] This is noteworthy, but we should not disregard the fact that in the 1536 *Institutes* Calvin's

---

1989), 194 ff.

22 "The History and Development of the *Institutio*: How Calvin Worked," tr. the editor, in *John Calvin*, ed. G. E. Duffield (Grand Rapids: Eerdmans, 1966), 102.

23 August Lang, "The Sources of Calvin's *Institutes* of 1536," *Evangelical Quarterly* 8 (1936), 134; Benoît, "The History and Development of the *Institutio*," 103; Battles, "Introduction," 1536 *Inst.* xlviii-xlix; Wendel, *Calvin*. 112; Neuser, "The Development of the *Institutes* 1536 to 1559," 36-38; Elsie McKee, "Calvin's 1536 *Institutes*: The Church's Book," in *Calvin Studies III*, 36; McNeill, *The History and Character of Calvinism*, 124-125; Dowey, *The Knowledge of God in Calvin's Theology*, 232. Among these scholars, Wendel, Lang, and Dowey are very positive about the influence of Luther's *Small Catechism* on the order of the 1536 *Institutes*. On the other hand, Neuser, Battles, McNeill, Benoît, and McKee regard it as of great importance that Calvin followed the traditional pattern of Catechism in the late medieval period. From this point of view, Neuser particularly criticizes W. Diehl, who overvalues the influence of Luther's *Large Catechism* on Calvin's 1536 *Institutes*. Cf. Diehl, "Calvins Auslegung des Dekaloges," 141 ff.

24 According to Albert Rilliet, this differentiates Calvin's 1536 *Institutes* and first catechisms from Luther's *Large Catechism* and shows some characteristics of Calvinism in its early stage. Rilliet, "Notice Historique," 42-44. Richard A. Muller notes that the contents of the final chapter of the 1536 *Institutes* are analogous to those of the "table of household duties (*tabula oeconomica*)" which was appended by Luther to the *Small Catechism*. *The Unaccommodated Calvin*, 120.

apologetic was not exclusively concerned with defending of Christian freedom and true ecclesiastical and secular orders but he emphasized the proclamation of "the nature of doctrine (*qualis sit doctrina*)" and "certain rudiments by which those who are touched with any zeal for religion might be shaped to true godliness," as he pointed out in the dedicatory letter to king Francis I of France (1, *CO* 1.9).[25]

Calvin's theological apologia in the 1536 *Institutes* was not so much polemical or formal as doctrinal, and sheds light on the formation and significance of his "Reformed" view of Christian doctrine.[26] This is especially prominent in the first chapter, where Calvin deals with crucial theological doctrines under the title of the law, which, brief as they are, cover the whole schema of salvation, i.e., the knowledge of God the Creator and the Redeemer and the knowledge of man, the righteousness of God revealed in the law, the grace of Christ and the work of the Holy Spirit, justification by faith, and the threefold use of the law. Calvin here relates the two kinds of knowledge to the law, that are the revelation of God's will, and the doctrine of justification to the threefold use of the law.

As regards the formation of Calvin's theology of the law in the 1536 *Institutes*, mentioning of the influence of Luther and Melanchthon has become commonplace in contemporary Calvin studies, regarding the distinction between the two tables of the Decalogue and the relationship between the old law and the new law of Christ.[27] Also, the influence of Bucer and Zwingli on Calvin's normative and spiritual understanding of the law in the 1536 *Institutes* has been persuasively argued for by some scholars, with reference to the former's view of double justification and union with Christ and the latter's moral theology based on the conception of the spiritual duty of the law in his theory of forensic atonement.[28]

---

25 Cf. Benjamin B. Warfield, "On the Literary History of Calvin's Institutes," in John Calvin, *Institutes of the Christian Religion*, tr. John Allen, 7th ed. (Philadelphia: Presbyterian Board of Christian Education, 1936), xv; Harmannus Obendiek, "Die Institutio Calvins als 'Confessio' und 'Apologie'," in *Theologische Aufsätze: Karl Barth zum 50. Geburtstag* (München: Chr. Kaiser Verlag, 1936), 417-431. In dealing with the apologetic character of the 1536 *Institutes*, Obendiek points out Calvin's assertion of the doctrine of Scripture as the doctrine of the living God and Christ (*doctrina Dei viventis ac Christi*) in the light of his biblical interpretation based on the analogy of faith (*fidei analogia*) (418-419).

26 Cf. McKee, "Calvin's 1536 *Institutes*," 35-37.

27 Cf. Ganoczy, *The Young Calvin*, 137, 146-147; Wendel, *Calvin*, 196-204; Paul Wernle, *Der evangelische Glaube nach den Hauptschriften der Reformatoren*, vol. 3, *Calvin* (Tübingen: J. C. B. Mohr, 1919), 8 ff.

28 Cf. McGrath, *Iustitia Dei*, 219-226; Willem van't Spijker, "Calvin's Friendship with Martin Bucer: Did It Make Calvin a Calvinist?" in *Calvin Studies Society Papers, 1995*, 1997, 173-176; Wernle, *Der evangelische Glaube*, 3.22-23, 31-32; G. W. Locher, "Zwingli between Luther and Calvin: Reformation of Faith, Community, and

There are three noteworthy points in the 1536 *Institutes* that seem to reveal Calvin's dynamic position on the understanding of the law. We can say that these points are early indicators of what later matures into Calvin's fixed position on the law.[29] First of all, he concentrates on the instructive role of the law, which is to illuminate our heart so as to make us see the true righteousness of God, and to convict every man of his own unrighteousness. Emphasizing the fact that "the law teaches (*edocet*) God's will," he points out that the instruction of the law is both indicative and imperative. As he puts it, the law "teaches us what perfect righteousness is and how it is to be kept" (1.4, *CO* 1.29).

Calvin's emphasis on the instructive function of the law stems from his conviction that God, who is "himself a just judge," is "merciful and gentle," i.e., a merciful justifier. From this seemingly dialectical attribute of God, Calvin explains the "righteousness" of God, which is ultimately revealed by "the whole righteousness of the law" (1.1, *CO* 1.27). Therefore, the revelation of the law refers not only to the godly life according to the rule of living but also to the renovation of the whole life. As Calvin puts it, "*in lege docetur, vitae perfectionem vere esse iustitiam*" (1.4, *CO* 1.29).

By using the verbs *doceo* and *edoceo* repeatedly here, Calvin shows his dominant interest in the office of the law to reveal and teach how to keep and fulfil (*absolvere*) its rules, rather than in its office to convict (*convincere*) sin. The law reflects our miserable state like "a mirror (*speculum*)," but it also shines with God's grace in imputing his righteousness gratuitously unto us (1.4, *CO* 1.29). Therefore, God reveals by the law both God the Creator and God the Redeemer. As Dr. Hesselink

---

Church," in *Huldrych Zwingli, 1484-1531: A Legacy of Radical Reform*, ed. E. J. Furcha (McGill University, 1985), 28. Many scholars, nevertheless, do not pay special attention to the influence of other theologians such as Bucer and Zwingli on Calvin's theology in the 1536 *Institutes* in their well known biographical and theological works. Cf. Pierre Imbart de la Tour, *Les Origines de la Réforme*, vol. 4, *Calvin et l'Institution Chrétienne* (Paris: Firmin-Didot, 1935), 44-48; Ganoczy, *The Young Calvin*, 151-168, esp., 151-152. Wendel, *Calvin*, 135-136, 137-140, 198; Büsser, "The Zurich Theology in Calvin's *Institutes*," 135-136; Willem van't Spijker, "The Influence of Bucer on Calvin as Becomes Evident from the *Institutes*," in *John Calvin's Institutes: His Opus Magnum*, 109-113. Also, in dealing with Farel's view of the law through his work *Sommaire*, Charles Partee does not mention its influence on Calvin's theology of the law. "Farel's Influence on Calvin: A Prolusion," in *Actes du Colloque Guillaume Farel*, vol. 1, *Communications*, ed. Pierre Barthel, et al. (Genève: Revue de théologie et de philosophie, 1983), 179, 182-185.

29 Francis M. Higman implies the influence of Oliétan's *L'Instruction des enfants* (1533) and Farel's *Pater noster et le Credo* (1524) on Calvin's view of the law in the 1536 *Institutes*. "Farel, Calvin et Olivétan, sources de spiritualité gallicans," in *Actes du Colloque Guillaume Farel*, vol. 1, *Communications*, ed. Pierre Barthel, et al. (Genève: Revue de Théologie et de Philosophie, 1983), 45-61.

observes, in the 1536 *Institutes* "Calvin's concept of the law is viewed by him in direct connection with the revealed will of the Creator-Redeemer God, the God of the gospel."[30]

Secondly, Calvin points out that Jesus Christ came as "the best interpreter (*interpretem*) of the law," not as "the giver (*latorem*)" of another law that might be called "the law of the gospel (*legis evangelicae*)" (1.25, *CO* 1.43). Commenting on the pedagogical function of the fourth commandment, Calvin indicates that "we still retain the truth of the precept which the Lord willed the Jews and us to have forever and in common" (1.13 [altered], *CO* 1.36). In dealing with the continual validity of the law for the Christian life, Calvin emphasizes that with the outward works of the law completed, Christ made our heart affected by the teaching of the law through his Spirit. He calls this persuasion of the heart "a true and living faith (*vera vivaque fides*)" (1.6, *CO* 1.31). Following from his dynamic concept of faith, Calvin points out that the principle of *sola fide* applies to all the benefits of salvation, including "free forgiveness of sins, peace and reconciliation with God, the gifts and the grace of the Holy Spirit" (1.6 [altered], CO. 1.30). In claiming that the right and holy living of the Christian is the special gift of the Holy Spirit, Calvin relates the normative use of the law to the Spirit of Christ on the basis of his doctrine of the union with Christ, the substance and truth of the law (1.6, *CO* 1.31).[31]

Thirdly, Calvin testifies that God justifies us by imputing his righteousness into us so that he may not only liberate us from the bondage of the law to find refuge in Christ, but he also engrave the law on our heart in order for us to live accordingly. As Anthony N. S. Lane observes, "the fact that justification is *by* faith alone does not mean that one can be justified *with* faith alone."[32] Calvin says, "to be Christians under the law of grace does not mean to wander unbridled outside the law, but to be engrafted (*insitos*) in Christ, by whose grace we are free of the curse of the law, and by whose Spirit we have the law engraved upon our hearts [Jer. 31:33]" (1.26, *CO* 1.44). Thus, Calvin's view of the *duplex iustificatio*—justification not only for our soul but also for our good works—means to die to the law and to live again in the law. In the 1536 *Institutes*, Calvin already explores his own understanding of *duplex iustificatio*, which

---

30 Hesselink, *Calvin's Concept of the Law*, 32. Cf. Wernle, *Der evangelische Glaube*, 3.4-23. According to Wernle, with regard to the theological use of the law Calvin discusses the office of the law to reveal, like the mirror (*der Spiegel*), both the knowledge of God the Creator and God the Redeemer; in the same vein, in dealing with the sum of the law—love—in place of the third use of the law, he emphasizes the Christological meaning of the precept and promise (grace) of the law.

31 Therefore, we share "the gifts of Christ" when we are members of his flesh. Cf. Comm. I Cor. 11:1 (246, *CO* 49.487).

32 *Justification by Faith in Catholic-Protestant Dialogue*, 27 (author's italics).

signifies the double imputation of God (1.32, *CO* 1.49). Concerning the value of good works he says, "the works are acceptable to God, and the believers are pleasing to him in these: not that they thus deserve (*merentur*), but because the divine goodness has established this value for them" (1.36 [altered], *CO* 1.53).

In the 1536 *Institutes*, Calvin does not qualify any specific use of the law as proper (*proprius*) or principal (*praecipuus*), but depicts the third use as "no unimportant use (*non mediocrem usum*)" (1.33, *CO* 1.50). However, in his first *Institutes* Calvin already takes special consideration of the third use. He deals with the continual validity of the law for believers before treating the threefold use of the law in an independent section (1.26, 32). Moreover, the following sections, which Battles classifies under the title of justification, are actually related to the third use as a whole (1.34-38). He declares the core of the normative use by indicating that "the law is an exhortation (*exhortatio*) to believers" (1.33, *CO* 1.50).

The law serves to reveal our sin, but it is not only accusing but also instructive, even in the stage of repentance. It is not only legally punitive but also theologically forensic, for "all promises and curses [are] set forth for us in the law itself" (1.6, *CO* 1.31). Calvin follows Bucer and Melanchthon, who separates legal repentance (*poenitentia legalis*) from evangelical repentance (*poenitentia evangelica*) and relate the former to mortification and the latter to vivification (5.12-13, *CO* 1.147-148), but he believes that the only repentance that is true is out of the "true and pure fear of God," which arises from the knowledge of the precepts and promises of the law (5.14-15, *CO* 1.148-150).[33]

In order to bring our attention to the law of grace (*lex gratiae*), Calvin refers to Augustine's famous dictum, which appears in his *Confessions*: "Let him [the Lord] give what he commands, and command what he wills (*Det ille quod iubet, et iubeat quod velit*)" (1.26, *CO* 1.44)."[34] However, it should be noted that unlike Augustine, who emphasizes the work of the Holy Spirit in dealing with God's grace upon the good works of the law, Calvin turns specifically to the forensic righteousness of God fulfilled by the mediation of Christ and Christ's imputation of it (1.38, *CO* 1.54).[35]

---

33 For Calvin's understanding of repentance in the light of union with Christ, see Robert C. Doyle, "The Preaching of Repentance in John Calvin: Repentance and Union with Christ," in *God Who is Rich in Mercy: Essays Presented to Dr. D. B. Knox*, ed. Peter T. O'Brien and David G. Peterson (Sydney: Moore Theological College, 1986), 287-321, esp. 291-298.

34 Johannes van Oort, "John Calvin and Church Fathers," in *The Reception of the Church Fathers in the West*, 666-667.

35 Cf. Jean Cadier, "Calvin et saint Augustin," in *Augustinus Magister*, vol. 2, *Communications* (Paris: Études Augustiniennes, 1954), 1043; Larry D. Sharp, "The Doctrines of Grace in Calvin and Augustine," *Evangelical Quarterly* 52/2 (1980), 86.

Thus, with reference to "satisfaction," Calvin points out that there is no other way but "the prerogative of Christ's blood alone (*solius Christi sanguinis praerogativam*)" (1.37, *CO* 1.53).

3.2.2 Exploring the Soteriological Significance of the Law in the 1539 Institutes

In the 1539 *Institutes*, some parts which belonged to the first chapter of the 1536 *Institutes*, entitled "*De lege*," were developed as independent chapters entitled "*De cognitione Dei*," "*De cognitione hominis et libero arbitrio*," and "*De iustificatione fidei et meritis operum*." The section "*De poenitentia*" was augmented to form a separate new chapter and put before the chapter "*De iustificatione fidei*," thus the repentance-justification framework was formed, which was maintained throughout the later versions. "*De praedestinatione and providentia Dei*" became an independent chapter and was placed after a new chapter "*De similitudine ac differentia veteris ac novi testamenti*." Finally, with a new chapter called "*De vita hominis Christiani*" appearing, all major chapters on the law in the 1559 *Institutes* were already established here.[36]

The *ordo docendi* of the 1539 *Institutes* shows the influence of the commentaries on Romans written by contemporary theologians, especially Melanchthon's published in 1519 and augmented in 1530.[37] The influence of Bucer's Romans commentary (1536) is definitely more recognizable here, with reference to the Christological understanding of the law focused on the union with Christ through the work of the Holy Spirit.[38] Also, the influence of the Zurich theologians is considerable upon Calvin's view of the continuity of the law in the Old and New Testaments, upon the common origin of natural law and the divine law, and upon the doctrine of the civil government in the light of covenantal grace and the duty attached to it.[39] Calvin wrote the new edition of the *Institutes* in order to establish the whole schema of the theological doctrines, so that he "shall have no need to undertake lengthy doctrinal discussions and to digress into *loci communes*"

---

36 Wernle asserts that in the 1536 *Institutes* Calvin treats the whole range of major doctrines in the title of the law and in 1539 these themes are reformulated according to the basic schema of the two kinds of the knowledge of God. *Der Evangelische Glaube* 3.23-24, 166 ff.

37 Ibid., 3.166; Muller, *The Unaccommodated Calvin*, 129-130. Muller notes that the structure of the 1539 *Institutes* "ought to be described not as a movement from catechism to system but as an integration of the catechetical topics and order with the topics and order of Pauline soteriology."

38 Wendel, *Calvin*, 140.

39 Cf. Imbart de la Tour, *Calvin et l'Institution Chrétienne*, 70 ff.; Büsser, "The Zurich Theology in Calvin's *Institutes*," 137-139, 142.

in interpreting the Scriptures. The commentary on Romans was the first "example (*specimen*)" of this intention.[40] Calvin hastened to write a new edition of the *Institutes* from the beginning of 1537 and must have finished writing many parts of it before he visited Strasbourg.[41]

In the 1539 *Institutes*, Calvin gives some very important accounts of the concept and use of the law in the sections on free will (2.76-94, *CO* 1.356-372).[42] Emphasizing that the law has the two sides: "command" and "promise," and works not only as a rule of living but also as a way to grace (2.82, *CO* 1.361), he explains "the three classes (*formis*) of precepts," which basically correspond to the threefold use of the law (2.83, *CO* 1.362). In dealing with the normative use of the law, he highlights the exhortation of the law by adding new passages on it (2.80, *CO* 1.359-360).

Calvin's propensity towards a Christological understanding of the law on the ground of *Christus mediator legis* is clearly noticeable. In treating the connection between Word and Spirit, he declares that the law becomes "the word of life (*verbum vitae*)" when it "shows forth Christ," but it "slays its readers" when it is "apart from Christ (*citra Christum*)" (1.36, *CO* 1.302). In dealing with the divinity of Christ before his incarnation, Calvin points out the work of the Spirit of Christ, who is "Jehovah our Righteousness," in order to explain the revelation of the law in the Old Testament (4.8, 11, *CO* 1.481, 483-484). The 1539 *Institutes* augments Calvin's stance on the soteriologico-historical (*heilsgeschichtlich*) aspect of the law. For example, in the 1536 *Institutes* Calvin, interpreting the word "crucified" in the Apostles' Creed, claims that Christ "had been cursed (*maledicta*) by God's law" (2.14, *CO* 1.69). In the 1539 edition he adds that Christ's crucifixion "was foreshadowed (*adumbratum*) in the law" (4.23, *CO* 1.527).

In the 1539 *Institutes*, some passages on justification which belonged to the first chapter of the 1536 *Institutes* formed a new chapter, "*De iustificatione fidei et meritis operum*," with significant augmentations that

---

40 *OS* 3.6 (*CO* 1.255). Also cited in Parker, *Calvin's New Testament Commentaries*, 10. Concerning the relation between Calvin's Romans commentary and the 1539 *Institutes*, see T. H. L. Parker and D. C. Parker, ed., *John Calvin, Commentarius in Epistolam Pauli ad Romanos* (Genève: Droz, 1999), "Introduction." LIV; Benoît Girardin, *Rhétorique et Théologique: Calvin, Le Commentaire de l'Épître aux Romains* (Paris: Beauchesne, 1979), 241 ff.; Richard Gamble, "Preface," in Richard F. Wevers, *Institutes of the Christian Religion of John Calvin 1539: Text and Concordance*, vol. 1 (Grand Rapids: Meeter Center for Calvin Studies, 1988), vii; Battles, "*Calculus Fidei*," 145.

41 Cf. Wilhelm Niesel, "Descriptio et historia editionum Institutionis latinarum et gallicarum Calvino vivo emissarum," in *OS* 3. XII.

42 All citations of the 1539, 1543, 1550 editions of the *Institutes* are from *Calvini Opera*, which is abbreviated by *CO* preceded by the chapter and section number and followed by the volume and page number.

help us understand Calvin's concept of the law regarding its soteriological significance.

First, he augments some passages on the perfection of righteousness, specifically on God's grace that allows our good works to be seen righteous. "The complete observance of the law is perfect righteousness before God," but "the teaching of the law is far above human capacity" (3.91, *CO* 1.426-427); therefore, "not rejecting our imperfect obedience, but rather supplying what is lacking to complete it, he causes us to receive the benefit of the promises of the law (*legalium promissionum*) as if we had fulfilled their condition" (3.92, *CO* 1.427).

Secondly, Calvin argues that although those whose sins are forgiven thus regarded as righteous in front of God are liberated from the bondage of the law, they are still to live according to the teaching of the law (3.104, *CO* 1.435). He criticizes Bucer and Melanchthon who interpret the phrase "*deleto quod contra nos erat, chirographo in decretis*" in Colossians 2:14, focusing on its literal meaning, by asserting that although their interpretations are rightly based on the distinction between the moral and ceremonial laws and between the accusatory and instructive functions of the law, they do not pay proper attention to the fact that in this verse Paul argues for the merit of Christ's blood-sacrifice in which the continual validity of the law is sustained rather than annulled (3.105, *CO* 1.435-438).

Thirdly, Calvin underscores the third use of the law by emphasizing that obedience to the law is the gift of grace. He argues that humans are incapable of living according to the law, which is "the rule of perfect righteousness (*perfectae iustitiae regula*)." Our obedience is like "the payment of a debt"; however, God promises a "reward" of "eternal life" for it; "He therefore yields his own right when he offers a reward for our obedience." From this point of view, "the perfect teaching of righteousness that the Lord claims for the law has a perpetual validity" (3.2-3.6, *CO* 1.371-375). In the 1539 edition, Calvin emphasized the third use and the validity of the first two uses concerning believers and nonbelievers. For the first time he regards the third use of the law the "principal" use, which "pertains more closely to the proper purpose of the law" (3.101, *CO* 1.433).[43]

Calvin introduces a new metaphor: "the scales of the law (*legis trutinam*)" in addition to the law being "a mirror (*speculi*)" used in the 1536 edition to explain the punitive function of the law which is to inform us of our miserable state and convict the "presumption of fictitious righteousness" (3.94, *CO* 1.429). He adds new arguments about our incapacity to meet the perfection of God's righteousness and the truth of justification in Christ. He says, "in the precepts of the law, God is but the rewarder of perfect righteousness, which all of us lack, and conversely, the

---

43 "Tertius usus, qui et praecipuus est et in proprium legis finem propius spectat, . . ."

severe judge of evil deeds. But in Christ his face shines, full of grace and gentleness, even upon us poor and unworthy sinners" (3.94-3.98, *CO* 1.428-431, quot. 3.97). In spite of his elaborate explanation of the righteousness of the law in the process of justification, Calvin indicates that this kind of teaching should be "far from abusing the law (*legi contumeliosa*)" and says, "the grace of God, which nourishes us without the support of the law, becomes sweeter, and his mercy, which bestows this grace upon us, becomes more lovely" (3.96, *CO* 1.430). Calvin closes this section by indicating that the first use refers even "to the reprobate" (3.98, *CO* 1.431).

As to the second use of the law, there was no specific augmentation except to point out that the law works as "tutelage (*paedagogia*)" and "a halter (*retinaculum*)" "even for the children of God" (3.100, *CO* 1.432-433). It seems that this reflects the influence of Lutheran antinomian controversies. Afterwards no other augmentation for the first two uses was made except for an addition of one section in relation to the second use in the 1543 *Institutes*.

With regard to the third use of the law, Calvin says that owing to the function of "teaching (*doctrina*)" and "exhortation (*exhortatione*)" of the law, believers are "to learn more thoroughly each day the nature of the Lord's will" and are "to conform and accommodate (*componat et accommodet*)" themselves to "their master's ways (*mores domini*)." In order to express this use of the law more figuratively, Calvin uses a new metaphor of "a constant sting (*assiduus aculeus*)," and implies that what David sings of the nature of the law in Psalm 119 and what Paul teaches in Romans are "what it [the law] can of itself confer upon (*conferre*) man" rather than "what use the law serves (*praestet*) for the regenerate" (3.101, *CO* 1.433). Calvin connects the knowledge of God to living according to the law more specifically than in the 1536 *Institutes* when he deals with human free will. He says that *spiritualis perspicientia* consists in "knowing God, His will towards us, and the way of framing our life according to it" (2.37, *CO* 1.327).[44] Also, in the 1539 *Institutes* he argues that by the precepts of the law, which is a rule of life (*vitae regula*), we are "converted to God," "bidden to honor God," and finally we "remain under God's grace" (2.82-83, *CO* 1.361-362). He devoted a new section to criticizing the Libertine sect and John Agricola, who maintained the annulment of the old law and denied the function of the law in the process of salvation (3.102, *CO* 1.433-434).

In the 1539 *Institutes*, Calvin reinforced the critique of 1536 against the view that "Christ was another Moses, the giver of the law of the gospel" by

---

44 "Deum nosse, eius erga nos voluntatem, et formandae secundum illam vitae rationem." This sentence is augmented in 1559 in this way: "Deum nosse, paternum erga nos eius favorem, in quo salus nostra consistit, et formandae secundum legis regulam vitae rationem" (*Inst.* 2.2.18, *CO* 2.200).

dealing with the continuity of the law in the light of the purpose of the lawgiver. He criticizes some contemporaries for having thought "that Christ added (*adiicere*) to the law when he only restored (*restituit*) it to its integrity" and of "the perfection of the law of the gospel, that it far surpasses the old law—in many respects a most pernicious opinion!" (3.9, *CO* 1.376).[45] Furthermore his interpretation of Colossians 2:13-14 argues that the substance of old ceremonies has not been destroyed by the blood offering of Christ although their practices were annulled (3.105, *CO* 1.435-438). Calvin's argument for the agreement between the Old and New Testaments was deployed against Servetus and the Anabaptists who tried to eliminate any Christological significance from the Old Testament law.[46]

It should be noted that although Calvin sustained his view of law and gospel, and the role of the law in the whole process of salvation, which was asserted in the 1536 *Institutes*, he here elaborated on more precisely the "promises and threats" of the law. He stressed how far humans are from "the sufficiency of the law" and accordingly how great the grace of God is (3.3-6, *CO* 1.372-375). He then explained three principles of spiritual interpretation of the law (3.7-14, *CO* 1.375-380) and Jesus Christ's teaching of the law (3.80-88, *CO* 1.421-425). Finally, he concludes that the commandments of the law regulate "all the duties of piety and love (*omnia pietatis et dilectionis officia*)" (3.81, *CO* 1.421).[47]

3.2.3 Institutes 1543-1550

In the 1543 *Institutes* Calvin dealt with religious vows and monasticism in a separate chapter called "*De votis*" and with the doctrine of faith in a new chapter called "*De fide*." In the new versions, the 1543 and 1550 *Institutes*, Calvin added current debates on the doctrine of the church and civil government extensively.[48] The newly written sections on the doctrine of angels (3.24-43, *CO* 1.497-503) and on images, where Calvin distinguished *latria* and *dulia* in order to testify the true worship of God (3.24-43, *CO* 1.384-397), revealed his special concern for major issues concerning the

---

45 Cf. McNeill points to Melanchthon and Aquinas as these theologians in footnote 12 at *Inst.* 2.8.7.

46 Cf. Willem Balke, *Calvin and the Anabaptist Radicals*, tr. William Heynen (Grand Rapids: Eerdmans, 1981), 97-122; Doumergue, *Jean Calvin*, 4.4; Battles, "*Calculus Fidei*," 159; Karl H. Wyneken, "Calvin and Anabaptism," *Concordia Theological Monthly* 36/1 (1965): 18-29.

47 The title of the first French version of the *Institutes*, published in 1541, which is the translation of the 1539 *Institutes*, shows the book is "*une somme de piété*" and "*de salut.*" Cf. Doumergue, *Jean Calvin*, 4.3.

48 Cf. Benoît, "The History and Development of the *Institutio*," 107-108; Neuser, "The Development of the *Institutes* 1536 to 1559," 45-46.

church.[49] With a large number of passages cited from the early church fathers, especially from Augustine, this edition of the *Institutes* can be rightly called the "most patristic."[50]

There is no specific augmentation regarding the third use of the law in the 1543 *Institutes*, but in dealing with the perfection of Christian life Calvin points out the complex working of the law for believers by indicating that man is *simul iustus et peccator* (2.63-66, *CO* 1.348-350). In the same vein, in the chapter on repentance, he emphasizes "the duties of piety toward God, of charity toward men in the whole of life, holiness and purity" (9.10 [altered], *CO* 1.692).

In 1543 Calvin added a new section on the second use of the law, paying special attention to Galatians 3:24, "the law was for the Jews a tutor (*paedagogum*) unto Christ" (3.100, *CO* 1.432-433). In his commentary on this verse, published later in 1548, Calvin focused on the first use of the law by using two metaphors, i.e., "a mirror (*speculo*)" with a view to pointing out the use of the law to reveal our unrighteousness and "the grammarian of pupils (*grammaticus puerorum*)" in order to explain the function of the law to enlighten our heart by "the theology of faith."[51] In the 1543 *Institutes*, however, Calvin relates this verse not only to the first use of the law but also to the second use. He says that even for some of the elect who have not yet been regenerated by the "chaste and pure fear (*timore casto et puro*)" of God, the law serves to keep them from committing sins by threatening them with punishment "in such a way that the bridle of the law restrained them [God's sons] in some fear and reverence toward God until, regenerated by the Spirit, they began wholeheartedly to love him" (3.100, *CO* 1.432-433).

The fact that Calvin clearly acknowledges the expansion of the second use to the elect yet to be regenerated is not irrelevant to his understanding of the church. In the 1543 *Institutes*, Calvin distinguished the invisible church which is composed of the "children of God" from the visible church which is composed of "the whole multitude of men spread over the earth who profess to worship one God and Christ," and says that in the visible church "are mingled many hypocrites who have nothing of Christ but the

---

49 Calvin also refers to the Second Council of Nicea (787) in order to criticize Catholic idol worship (1543 *Inst.* 3.37, *CO* 1.393). The 1543 *Institutes* clearly shows the influence of the theological discussions in Worms and Regensburg, especially the influence of the agreement of the colloquy of Regensburg (1541). Cf. P. Fraenkel, "Trois passages de l'*Institution* et 1543 de leurs rapports avec les colloques interconfessionnels de 1540-41," in *Calvinus Ecclesiae Genevensis Custos*, ed. Wilhelm H. Neuser (Frankfurt a. M.: Peter Lang, 1984), 149-157; Neuser, "The Development of the *Institutes* 1536 to 1559," 46; Jean Cadier, "Calvin and the Union of the Churches," tr. P. Rix, in Duffield, ed., *John Calvin*, 121-122.

50 Van Oort, "John Calvin and Church Fathers," 675-676. Cf. Neuser, "The Development of the *Institutes* 1536 to 1559," 47.

51 Comm. Gal. 3:24 (66-67, *CO* 50.220).

name and outward appearance. There are many ambitious, greedy, envious persons, evil speakers, and some of quite unclean life. Such are tolerated for a time either because they cannot be convicted by a competent tribunal or because a vigorous discipline does not always flourish as it ought to" (8.8, *CO* 1.542).[52] Thus we become aware that Calvin's convincing statement supporting the application of the second use of the law not only to the reprobate but also to the elect corresponds to his consistent emphasis on the visible church since the 1539 *Institutes*.[53]

In the same vein, Calvin, deploying the two-kingdom theory in the 1543 *Institutes*, points out that since human laws are "consonant with God's word," even people who are regenerated spiritually should obey them faithfully (12.16, *CO* 1.840). In treating the power of lawmaking in the chapter of *De traditionibus humanis*, Calvin asserts that "in his law the Lord has included everything applicable to the perfect rule of the good life, so that nothing is left to men to add to that summary" (13.7, *CO* 1.843).[54] Calvin refers to the close relationship between the law of God in the visible church and civil law, when he justifies the right of the government to wage war; not only do "both natural equity and the nature of the office dictate" this but also "the Holy Spirit declares such wars to be lawful by many testimonies of Scripture" (20.10. *CO* 1.1109).

We find a striking number of passages on church law added in the 1550 *Institutes*. Calvin there explains the origin and content of conscience in more detail in connection with the power of legislation and Christian freedom. He argues that law is "the outward forum (*externum forum*)" working through "the forum of conscience (*forum conscientiae*)" in which we are led to "an awareness of divine judgment (*sensum divini iudicii*)." With the adoption of this principle in the realm of Christian freedom and civil law, Calvin confirms that the second use of the law refers not only to non-believers but also to believers who are not yet regenerated. Also, in dealing with this so-called political use of the law, he points out that this tutelage (*paedagogia*) of the law to control outward activity (*opus exterius*) by the fear of punishment makes people recover their reverence towards God (*Inst.* 2.7.10-11, *CO* 2.260-261). Calvin's positive attitude towards the political use of the law originates in his dynamic view of conscience, which

---

52 For Calvin's understanding of the church as *corpus mixtum*, see Herman J. Selderhuis, "Church on Stage: Calvin's Dynamic Ecclesiology," in *Calvin and the Church*, ed. David Foxgrover (Grand Rapids: CRC Production Services, 2002), 51-54.

53 This position of Calvin sheds light on why he emphasizes so sharply human responsibility in dealing with predestination. Cf. Doumergue, *Le Caractère de Calvin*, 108-124.

54 "Quod ad perfectam bene vivendi regulam pertinebat, id totum sic complexus est Dominus lege sua, ut nihil hominibus reliquerit, quod ad summam illam adderent."

works as "a certain mean (*medium*) between God and man."[55] The function of human conscience is to lead us to fear punishment, to learn the will of God in our lives by making us realize the rule of right and godly living. In this regard, the difference between the first and second uses of the law lies not so much in their theological foundation as in their effect on humans.

In the 1543 and 1550 *Institutes* Calvin elaborates a practice of the law, which he defines in the 1536 *Institutes* as "a silent magistrate (*mutum magistratum*)" (1536 *Inst*. 6.47, *CO* 1.237), not only for the government of society but also for the ministry of the church. He pays special attention to the inner state of man as well as to the outward observance of the law in dealing with the use of the law by emphasizing human conscience. Even in his doctrine of predestination, Calvin does not emphasize the invisible church more than the reality of the visible church. This high view must have been of much value for the rule of God's law in Geneva.

3.2.4 1559 Institutes: Formulating the Whole Process of Salvation in the Light of the Concept of Christus Mediator Legis

In the 1559 *Institutes*, Calvin restructured his whole doctrinal system according to the quadripartite division of the Apostles' Creed,[56] which had been treated along with the doctrine of faith in the same chapter since 1536 and had been divided into three chapters since 1543.[57] The new edition, which he believed was founded on a "suitable order and method (*ad aptissimam methodum, en ordre et méthode bien propr*),"[58] has innumerable transpositions but does not show any essential diversion from the previous views on major doctrines.[59] The chapters of the new edition are arranged in this order: the revelation of God's righteousness or the knowledge of God the Creator (1), the misery of fallen man (2.1-5), fallen man ought to seek redemption in Christ (the necessity of a Mediator) (2.6), the law (2.7-11), and justification (3.2). Except for the fact that in the new edition Christology (2.12-18) and the doctrine of the Holy Spirit (3.1),

---

55 Cf. Wendel, *Calvin*, 117.
56 Benoît, "The History and Development of the *Institutio*," 109; Wendel, *Calvin*, 121-122. According to Muller, in the 1559 *Institutes* Calvin successfully integrated the credal model, already present within the *Institutes*, with the catechetical model and, above all, with the basic outline of Pauline *loci*, with all its organizational patterns drawn from the Apostles' Creed. *The Unaccommodated Calvin*, 137-138.
57 Since the 1543 *Institutes*, Calvin had divided the chapter on the Apostles' Creed into three parts yielding a chapter on faith, God, creation; another chapter on Christ and the Holy Spirit; and a final chapter on the church, forgiveness of sins, and the resurrection.
58 Muller, *The Unaccommodated Calvin*, 132-133, 245 (n. 87).
59 Doumergue, *Jean Calvin*, 4.9-10; Neuser, "The Development of the *Institutes* 1536 to 1559," 51-52.

which had been dealt with as parts of the Creed, were placed between the doctrine of the law and justification, the new order remarkably corresponds to the arrangement of the themes deployed in the first chapter of the 1536 *Institutes* entitled "*De lege.*"

Theologians have debated if there is any uniqueness in Calvin's view of *ordo salutis*, considering the sequence of faith (3.2)-repentance (3.3-5)-Christian life (3.6-10)-justification by faith (3.11-18) in book 3 of the 1559 *Institutes*. These chapters demonstrate Calvin's dynamic understanding of salvation as a whole, but when it comes to the doctrinal significance of the order of salvation, Calvin's remarks are concentrated in the last part, which deals with the principle of *sola fide*. On the other hand, chapters on the first three themes are mostly devoted to their biblical references and their significance in the Christian life. The earlier versions also show the same tendency. Through the successive editions of the *Institutes*, Calvin deals with the whole range of the doctrine of salvation in the name of the doctrine of justification by faith. In this respect he calls the chapter on Christian freedom (3.19), which follows chapters on justification by faith, "*appendix iustificationis*" in 1559.

Calvin understands the concept of justification dynamically, as related to the whole process of salvation. From this perspective, he understands the continual imputation of the grace of Christ not only for our justification but also for our sanctification. When Calvin applies the Chalcedonian formula—distinguished but not separated—to the relation between justification and sanctification, this is also relevant to the theological and normative use of the law. Therefore, in spite of Calvin's successful integration of the credal model in 1559, replacing the remaining elements of the catechetical model since 1536 in *ordo docendi*,[60] with regard to *ordo doctrinae salvificae* he was persistent in the sequence "law-justification by faith" in his holistic view of justification. In this respect, Calvin does not have the concept of the order of salvation found in Reformed Orthodoxy. He applies the law-faith order not only to justification but also to sanctification. This shows the dynamic feature of his doctrine of salvation most clearly.[61]

Whereas in the 1539 *Institutes* Calvin pays primary attention to the continuity of the Old and New Testaments in dealing with the soteriological significance of the law, in the final edition he focuses on the relationship between Christ and the law in the light of the concept of Christ's mediation of the law. He devotes a new chapter to treating the necessity of Christ the Mediator, entitled "*Homini perdito quaerendam in Christo redemptionem*

---

60 Cf. Muller, *The Unaccommodated Calvin*, 135; Wendel, *Calvin*, 120-121.
61 Cf. Cornelis Graafland, "Hat Calvin einen Ordo salutis gelehrt?" in *Calvinus Ecclesiae Genevensis Custos*, 221-244, esp. 240-242; Michael Beintker, "Calvins Denken in Relationen," *Zeitschrift für Theologie und Kirche* 99 (2002), 122-127.

esse" (*Inst.* 2.6).[62] Also, he augments sections to point out the mediation of Christ in dealing with the law as the law of the covenant (*Inst.* 2.7-8). Particularly, he refers to Christ's mediatorship in claiming the continuity of the law and the gospel in the new chapter called "*Christum, quamvis sub lege Iudaeis cognitus fuerit, tamen in evangelio demum exhibitum fuisse*" (*Inst.* 2.9).

In the following passage, enlarged in 1559, Calvin shows the foundation of his view of *Christus mediator legis*.

> Indeed, because Christ had not yet been manifested, it is necessary to understand the Word (*sermonem*) as begotten of the Father before time [cf. Ecclus. 24:14, Vg.]. But if that Spirit, whose organs were the prophets, was the Spirit of the Word (*sermonis spiritus*), we infer without any doubt that he was truly God. And Moses clearly teaches this in the creation of the universe, setting forth this Word as intermediary (*intermedium*). . . . For here we see the Word understood as the order or mandate of the Son (*pro nutu vel mandato filii*), who is himself the eternal and essential Word of the Father (*Inst.* 1.13.7, *CO* 2.95).

He emphasizes the continuity and the dynamic characteristic of the law from the Christological perspective. As he puts it, "since God cannot without the Mediator be propitious toward the human race, under the law Christ was always (*semper*) set before the holy fathers as the end to which they should direct their faith" and "the kingdom finally established within the family of David is a part of the law" (*Inst.* 2.6.2, 2.7.2, *CO* 2.250, 254). The law reveals "the form of religion (*formam religionis*) handed down by God through Moses" and "if the figures of the law (*legales figurae*) are separated from its end (*finem*), one must condemn it as vanity" (*Inst.* 2.7.1 [altered], *CO* 2.252-253). Calvin here uses terms such as "*umbra*," "*figura*," and "*typus*" in order to express the Christological significance of the law in the Old Testament (*Inst.* 2.7.1. *CO* 2.252-254).[63] Particularly in dealing with the historical significance of the law in the light of the mediation of Christ (the Word), Calvin frequently refers to the concept of God's accommodation to human capacity and barbarity.[64]

---

62 Thus, in the 1559 *Institutes*, "Calvin moves from his discussion of the nature of the image of God in humanity directly to the renewal of the image of God in Christ." Jane Dempsey Douglass, "The Image of God in Humanity: A Comparison of Calvin's Teaching in 1536 and 1559," in *In Honor of John Calvin*, 191.

63 Calvin uses the word *typus* in place of the *figura* which is used in the Vulgate and Erasmus' translation of verses 6 and 11 of I Corinthians 10 (*CO* 49.456, 460).

64 The following references in the 1559 *Institutes* reveal that God's accommodation refers not only to the use of the law but also to the creation and fulfilment of the law. *Inst.* 1.13.1 (1539), 1.14.3 (1543/1559), 1.14.11 (1543), 1.17.13 (1539), 2.6.4 (1559),

Calvin did not significantly augment or revise the existing contents on Christian life and Christian freedom in 1559, but he explicitly focused on their relevance for the doctrine of salvation, especially in relation to the role of the law for the whole process of salvation. He begins the doctrine of the Christian life by indicating that "the object of regeneration" is "a harmony and agreement between God's righteousness and their obedience," and "the law of God contains in itself that newness by which his image can be restored in us" (*Inst.* 3.6.1, *CO* 2.501).[65] Through the two passages, augmented anew for the doctrine of Christian freedom, Calvin emphasized the believer's willing obedience to the law which is due to the living grace of Christ the Mediator (*Inst.* 3.19.1, 13, *CO* 2.613, 622).[66]

In order for us to gain a better understanding of Calvin's view of the continual validity of the law for the regenerate, it is worth examining his position on the role of the law in the process of repentance. In the 1536 *Institutes*, Calvin asserted that true repentance arises from the true fear of God through faith, mainly in the course of criticizing false Catholic sacraments, but extended his scope of criticism to Lutheran theologians (Melanchthon and Bucer) (5.12-13, *CO* 1.147-148). In the edition of 1539, Calvin focused on the theological meaning of repentance working in the process of salvation, reflecting his criticism of the Anabaptists who believed themselves spiritual (5.1, *CO* 1.685-687).[67] Calvin in 1543 augmented remarks on "the duties of piety" in the life of a Christian in dealing with continual repentance (2.63-66, *CO* 1.348-350 and 9.10, *CO* 1.692). Finally, in the 1559 edition of the *Institutes*, Calvin augments some passages on the normative use of the law. As he puts it, "briefly, the more earnestly any man measures his life by the standard of God's law, the surer are the signs of repentance that he shows" (*Inst.* 3.3.16, *CO* 2.446).[68] Stating this, Calvin points to "the Jesuits," who followed Ignatius Loyola's

---

2.10.6 (1539), 2.11.13 (1543), 2.16.2 (1539), 4.1.5 (1559), 4.1.8 (1539), 4.14.3 (1536), 4.17.1 (1543), 4.17.6 (1539).

65 "Scopum regenerationis esse diximus, ut in vita fidelium appareat inter Dei iustitiam et eorum obsequium symmetria et consensus, atque ita adoptionem confirment qua recepti sunt in filios. Etsi autem novitatem illam qua imago Dei in nobis instauratur, lex ipsius in se continet, ..."

66 In the first passage augmented, Calvin criticizes people who ignore the true doctrine of Christian freedom as fellows of "Lucianic men (*Lucianici homines*)" (*Inst.* 3.19.1, *CO* 2.613). In the second passage augmented, Calvin's tone becomes more radical and apologetic (*Inst.* 3.19.13, *CO* 2.622).

67 The Anabaptists' view of man is helpful to understanding their position on the validity of the law. Cf. 1539 *Inst.* 2.67, *CO* 1. 350-351.

68 "Denique quo maiore quisque studio vitam suam exigit ad normam legis Dei, eo certiora poenitentiae suae signa edit."

position on exterior and interior penance, as the "companions" of the Anabaptists (*Inst* 3.3.2, *CO* 2.436).[69]

We have seen that Calvin's view of repentance should be differentiated from the Catholic sacramental understanding, which was eventually promulgated by the Council of Trent, and from the views of the Anabaptists and the Jesuits, as well as from Lutherans, who would be properly placed in the middle between the Catholics and the Anabaptists. Through the successive editions of the *Institutes*, Calvin consistently sustained his own view of repentance. In its relation to the use of the law, the doctrine of repentance has been regarded as a crucial issue for the designation of the right relationship of law and gospel and for the categorization of three kinds of divine covenant. Calvin did not follow Zwingli's gospel-law framework, but upheld the precedence of the law in the order of salvation in spite of his conviction of the same substance between law and gospel—Christ.[70] The twofold office of the law, which can be depicted typically as *lex accusans* and *lex vivendi*, is crucial in the early stage of salvation with special reference to repentance because from this concept we can approach the nature of the law more closely in light of the fact that Christ is the substance and truth of the law.

In the 1559 *Institutes*, with the insertion of the words "*extra controversiam esse debet*" Calvin confirmed his on-going assertion since 1539 that "repentance not only immediately follows faith, but is also born of faith (*Poenitentiam vero non modo fidem continuo subsequi, sed ex ea nasci*)" (*Inst*. 3.3.1 [altered], *CO* 2.434).[71] Calvin relates the gospel to the whole process of salvation in view of the fact that Christ is the fulfillment of the law, and understands the threefold use of the law from this perspective. For Calvin, with regard to the use of the law, whether it is punitive or normative, only the sequence "faith-repentance" is applicable (*Inst*. 3.3.2, *CO* 2.435-436). He believes the law and the gospel always work together, although the grace of God working without the support of the law becomes "sweeter (*suavior*)" and "more lovely (*amabilior*)" (*Inst*. 2.7.7, *CO* 2.258-259).

In conclusion, in the 1559 *Institutes*, the dialectic between the fact that Christ is "the truth (*veritas*)" of the law (*Inst*. 2.7.1, *CO* 2.253) and the fact that Christ is "the fulfilment or end of the law (*complementum legis, vel*

---

69 Cf. McNeill's footnote 8 at the same section.

70 Neuser affirms "the sequence of Christology (Gospel) first and then the law" in the 1559 *Institutes* by adhering to the order of chapters in the second and third book on Christ and the law, and justification and sanctification. "The Development of the *Institutes* 1536 to 1559," 50.

71 Calvin in this section reiterates the statement "the sum of the gospel is held to consist in repentance and forgiveness of sins," which existed from 1536 (1536 *Inst*. 5.15, *CO* 1.149, cf. *Inst* 3.3.19, *CO* 2.449-450).

finem)" (Inst. 2.7.2, *CO* 2.254), demonstrates that the dynamic feature of Calvin's understanding of the law is based on his unique thought of *Christus mediator legis*. This dialectic leads us to the proper understanding of Calvin's equally unique position on the relation of *lex vivendi* and *lex vivificandi*.

3.3 Conclusion

Calvin's position on Christ and the law, presented consistently in his early writings and the successive editions of the *Institutes*, may well be regarded as his distinctive answer to the critical question of the late medieval era about the merit of Christ and good works. As opposed to the radical perspective of Luther, who clearly separated law and gospel, Calvin tried to explain the dialectic between law and gospel by pointing out the normative nature of the law itself, which is not different from the gospel *circa essentiam*.[72] As a Christian who experienced a sudden conversion by which his heart was made teachable to the truth of God, Calvin realized that what has been changed since the fall is not the truth or teaching of the law itself but the status and quality of humanity. So, the reason the gospel was given was not for any change or destruction of the law, but for the salvation of fallen humanity, which does not bring the denial of the law but the total overcoming of human depravity.

Therefore, with Christ's coming as the Mediator, the revelation of the law has become perfect as a rule of living (*regula vivendi*), and moreover as a rule of life-giving (*regula vivificandi*). Calvin clearly asserts that Christ, as the substance of the law, fulfilled the law. He believed that there is no other proper way to learn the normative meaning of the law but through the mediation of Christ. Christ, who fulfilled the demands of the law, leads us to the perfection of our life that we may live according to the law, but through this grace. This is the very point by which Calvin has solved the riddle of *meritum de condigno* and *meritum de congruo*.

Calvin holds to his position steadfastly, to distinguish the unchangeable nature of the law, which is the rule of right and godly living, from its variable significance to man before and after the fall. He regards the third normative use of the law as the principal one, from this stance, understands the "accidental" use of the law, which is called the theological use. Calvin's adherence to the unchangeable nature of the law is derived from his conviction of the unity and continuity between natural law and the moral law of God. Aquinas suggested a hierarchy of law in oder to describe the relationship between natural and divine law,[73] whereas Gratian maintained

---

72 Cf. Imbart de la Tour, *Calvin et l'Institution Chrétienne*, 86-87.
73 For the hierarchy of the law, see Thomas Gilby, tr., *Saint Thomas Aquinas: Philosophical Texts* (Oxford: Oxford University Press, 1967), 357, n. 1; Oberman,

their unity for the legitimate claims of customary practices of the positive law, which he believed to be the expression of natural equity.[74] However, these approaches were focused mostly on the similarity of natural law and the divine command before the fall. Calvin extends this horizontal stance on the nature of the law by adding the concept of continuity to the unity of the law before and after the fall, with no reliance on any optimistic philosophical view of man, which had been suggested since Aristotle and adopted by the Stoics and the medieval Scholastics. Calvin's understanding of the unity of the law is based on the fact that Christ is the substance of the law. The continuous validity of the law is argued by Calvin not on the ground of the ability of human reason, but based on his view of the total depravity of man and *sola gratia* of Christ our Mediator. Calvin's understanding of the whole structure of the law does not rely on any legal hierarchy, which is actually based on the hierarchy of divine and human reason, but on the dialectic between Christ as the substance and truth of the law and Christ as the fulfilment of the law. Calvin's early works and his successive editions of the *Institutes* demonstrate impressively how he sought to explore the hermeneutic and theology of the law by the concept of *Christus mediator legis*.

The Harvest of Medieval Theology, 90-91: "In view of the 'intellectualism' of Thomas Aquinas, it is not surprising that for him God's will is only a partner in the operation of the intellect in establishing the hierarchy of eternal law, natural law, and positive law. . . . Duns Scotus stresses the direct dependence of all law on God's will without, however, endangering the hierarchy of eternal, natural, and positive law."

74 Cf. James A. Brundage, *Medieval Canon Law* (London: Longman, 1995), 154-155. The author asserts that "the Canonist, unlike Roman lawyers, also taught that laws ceased to have effective force when the reason that had prompted them ceased to exist" (173).

CHAPTER 4

Calvin's Concept of *Christus Mediator Legis*: Its Theological Foundation and Scope[1]

4.1 Christ and the Law

The relation between Christ and the law has been regarded as a crucial issue in demonstrating the substantial unity of law and gospel (cf. *Inst*. 2.9), and as the hermeneutical centre by which the continuity and discontinuity between the Old and New Testaments can be explained (cf. *Inst*. 2.10-11).[2] In regard to its ethical significance, this subject has been discussed in relation to Calvin's doctrine of the Christian life, in which he emphasizes living according to the example and pattern of Christ (cf. *Inst*. 3.6-10).[3] Scholars who share these positions mostly link Christ's mediation to the law only in view of the fact that Christ fulfilled the law, on the basis of their conviction that for Calvin the law is the law of the covenant.[4]

On the other hand, scholars who are concerned about Calvin's doctrine of atonement and the so-called *extra Calvinisticum* consider the incarnation

---

1 The title *"Christus mediator legis"* is the Latin translation of the phrase *"le Mediateur de la Loy"* which appears in Calvin's *Sermons on Galatians* 3:19-20 (453, CO 50.543).
2 Cf. Hesselink, *Calvin's Concept of the Law*, 155-215, 222-230, 251-253; Johnson, "Calvin's Handling of the Third Use of the Law and Its Problems," 42-45; Andrew J. Bandstra, "Law and Gospel in Calvin and in Paul," in *Exploring the Heritage of John Calvin*, ed. David E. Holwerda (Grand Rapids: Baker, 1976), 11-39; John H. Leith, "Creation and Redemption: Law and Gospel in the Theology of John Calvin," in *Marburg Revisited: A Re-examination of Lutheran and Reformed Traditions*, ed. Paul C. Empie and James I. McCord (Minneapolis: Augsburg Publication, 1966), 141-152; Edmond Grin, "L'unité des deux Testaments selon Calvin," *Theologische Zeitschrift* 17 (1961), 175-186.
3 Cf. *Inst*. 3.6.3 (*CO* 2.503): "Christ, through whom we return into favor with God, has been set before us as an example (*exemplar*), whose pattern (*formam*) we ought to express in our life. What more effective thing can you require than this one thing?" For the use of the law in the Christian life, see Hesselink, *Calvin's Concept of the Law*, 278-286; Ronald S. Wallace, *Calvin's Doctrine of the Christian Life* (Edinburgh: Oliver and Boyd, 1959), 112-122; Leith, *John Calvin's Doctrine of the Christian Life*, 45-60.
4 Cf. Niesel, *The Theology of Calvin*, 92-94; Hesselink, *Calvin's Concept of the Law*, 97-101, 161-165.

of Christ to be the prerequisite for their theories. Accordingly, although they are keen to acknowledge Christ's mediation before the incarnation, they do not show a positive view of Christ's mediation of the law in the Old Testament. Some base their theory of atonement on the conception that Christ is our legal substitute through his redemptive death, so they view Christ's mediation resticted to fulfilling the law.[5] Others explain the wide extent of Christ's mediation with regard to both the divine and human natures even beyond his ascension in terms of the so-called *extra Calvinisticum*. Their view is restricted to the historical presence and action of Christ as the Mediator, not to mention its sacramental significance.[6]

In the *Institutes*, Calvin deals with the unity of the person of Christ on the basis of *communicatio idiomatum*, focusing on how the divine and human natures of the Mediator co-operate rather than on how the two sets of properties communicate, that is, on *communio naturarum* itself (*Inst.* 2.14.1-3).[7] Even in interpreting the deity of the second person of the Trinity, Calvin points to the *hypostasis* of the "intermediary (*intermedium*)" rather than the divine essence itself (*Inst.* 1.13.7, *CO* 2.95).[8] Also, Calvin,

---

5   Cf. Paul van Buren, *Christ in Our Place: The Subsitutionary Character of Calvin's Doctrine of Reconciliation* (Edinburgh: Oliver and Boyd, 1957), 3-11; J. F. Jansen, *Calvin's Doctrine of the Work of Christ* (London: James Clarke, 1956), 70: Robert A. Peterson, *Calvin's Doctrine of the Atonement* (Phillipsburg, N.J.: Presbyterian and Reformed Publishing, 1983), 21-26.

6   Cf. David. E. Willis, *Calvin's Catholic Christology: The Function of the So-Called Extra Calvinisticum in Calvin's Theology* (Leiden: E. J. Brill, 1966), 67-73, 124-125, 140-141; Stefan Scheld, *Media Salutis: Zur Heilsvermittlung bei Calvin* (Stuttgart: Franz Steiner Verlag, 1989), 28-41; Peterson, *Calvin's Doctrine of the Atonement*, 11-17. For the formation and development of the so-called *extra Calvinisticum*, see Jan Rohls, *Reformed Confessions: Theology from Zurich to Barmen*, tr. John Hoffmeyer (Louisville: Westminster/John Knox, 2000), 102-117.

7   Cf. Doumergue, *Jean Calvin*, 4.214-223; Joseph N. Tylenda, "Calvin's Understanding of the Communication of Properties," *WTJ* 38/1 (1975), 54-65. Concerning the difference between the Lutheran and the Calvinist view of *communicatio idiomatum*, Willis, *Calvin's Catholic Christology*, 8-25. Gottfried W. Locher claims that both Zwingli and Calvin base their position on the *communicatio idiomatum* on the so-called *extra Cavinisticum*. "The Shape of Zwingli's Theology: A Comparison with Luther and Calvin," *Pittsburgh Perspective* 8 (1967), 17-19, 25-26.

8   Cf. *Confessio de Trinitate propter calumnias P. Caroli*, *CO* 9.706-707: "Quod ad Christum peculiariter attinet, duabus ipsum naturis constare affirmamus. Nam antequam carnem indueret, verbum illud aeternum fuit ex patre ante saecula genitum, verus Deus unius cum patre essentiae, potentiae, maiestatis, adeoque Iehova, qui a se ipso semper habuit, ut esset, et aliis subsistendi virtutem inspiravit. . . . Itaque scripturae, tametsi proprietates illas distincte nobis considerandas proponunt, dum Christo interdum quod solius est Dei, interdum quod hominis est tribuunt, earum tamen coniunctionem quae in Christo subest tanta religione exprimunt, ut eas quandoque inter se communicent: ut quum sanguine Dei acquisitam ecclesiam (Act.

commenting on the word "*Logos*," concentrates on its "twofold relation to God and men." From this perspective, he translates it not into *verbum* but into *sermo*.[9]

As was noted, the emphasis of the theory of atonement is put on *Christus ad nos*, whereas that of the so-called *extra Calvinisticum* on the presence of *Christus in se*.[10] How then should we harmonize these two positions on the ground of *Deus manifestatus in carne* and then apply them to the mediation of Christ in the Old Testament? Tracing the issues raised by this question it should be most crucial to examine Calvin's Christological understanding of the law. He suggests no direct answer to this question yet illustrates it most comprehensively in his concept of *Christus mediator legis*.

4.2 *Christus Mediator Legis*

Calvin uses the concept of "mediator" widely throughout his *Institutes*, exegetical works and apologetic treatises.[11] It appears mostly as "the Mediator" or "mediator" to denote Christ's sole mediatorship, except for some cases, where it points to the office of a priest, Moses, Aaron, David, Abraham, Nazarites, etc. On the other hand, the plural form of the word,

---

20, 28) et filium hominis in coelo fuisse dicunt (Ioann. 3, 13), quo tempore adhuc in terris agebat (qui tropus veteribus ἰδιωμάτων κοινωία dicus est) verum omnium clarissime veram Christi substantiam enarrant illi loci, qui simul utramque naturam complectuntur, quales in evangelio Ioannis exstant quamplurimi. Christum ergo verum Deum et verum hominem Dei filium esse asserimus, etiam secundum humanitatem, etsi non ratione humanitatis."

9 Comm. Jn. 1:1 (1.7-9, *CO* 47.1-4). Cf. Comm. Jn. 14:10 (2.78, *CO* 47.326): "[Q]uia non simpliciter disputat Christus, quia sit in se, sed qualis debeat agnosci a nobis, virtutis potius quam essentiae elogium est."

10 The relation between *Christus in se* and *Christus ad nos* has been dealt with as a crucial theme for the arguing of the immanent presence of the Logos in the creation and, more specifically, in the order of nature, since Origen, who explored the Logos Christology. Cf. Willis, *Calvin's Catholic Christology*, 49-60. In dealing with the person of Christ, Calvin seeks to link the economy of the Trinity with the divine-human relationship. Cf. Philip Walker Butin, *Revelation, Redemption, and Response: Calvin's Trinitarian Understanding of the Divine-Human Relationship* (Oxford: Oxford University Press, 1995), 74-75; David J. Engelsma, "Calvin's Doctrine of the Trinity," *Protestant Reformed Theological Journal* 23 (1989), 34-37.

11 In the 1559 *Institutes*, Calvin uses the term mediator at least 96 times (*mediator* 21, *mediatoris* 39, *mediatorem* 19, *mediatore* 12, *mediatori* 4, *mediatores* 1) and other related terms such as *medius, medium, intercedente*, etc. In the 1539 *Institutes*, Calvin uses the word mediator 19 times in its various forms. Wevers, *Institutes of the Christian Religion of John Calvin 1539*, 20.m-21.m. Calvin uses the word *mediator* in at least 129 passages in the commentaries and lectures on the Old Testament and 14 times in prayers, which appear in his lectures on the Minor Prophets, and in at least 132 passages in the commentaries on the New Testament.

"mediators," is seen mostly in its apologetics, in order to reveal the fallacy of the Judaic and Catholic concepts of the intercession of priests and saints,[12] which Calvin believes follow the Platonic concept of angel.[13] Sometimes the mediation of men and angels is mentioned, almost unexceptionally, with the note that Christ is the chief Mediator who rules over them.[14] Characteristically, Calvin claims the mediation of specifically denoted Old Testament figures to clarify its significance in presenting the true Mediator, and the mediation of the Angel with reference to the presence of the Mediator.[15]

Calvin turns to the relationship between the deity (*deitas*) of the Son of God and the divinity (*divinitas*) of Christ the Mediator in order to demonstrate the uniqueness of Christ's mediatorship. He explains the deity of Christ as the Son of God from the economic-Trinitarian viewpoint in the chapter on the Trinity by referring significantly to the existence and work of the divinity of Christ in his intercession not only for the whole process of salvation but also for the creation of the universe as its author (*autor*) (*Inst.* 1.7-13).

Also, in his controversies with the Polish ministers Francesco Stancaro and Giorgio Biandrata, who asserted that "Christ is not a Mediator, except according to the flesh," Calvin insists that Christ's mediatorship according to both natures refers not only to *Deus manifestatus in carne*, but also to the Word of God before the incarnation (cf. *Inst.* 2.14.3).[16] Criticizing Biandrata's anti-Trinitarian position, Calvin says, "the Mediator, God-man, is truly the Son of God according to both natures by reason of their union; but properly in respect of the divinity, because the Word is of the Father before all ages."[17] Calvin especially points to "*modus communicationis*"

---

12 Cf. Comm. Gen. 8:20 (1.281, *CO* 23.138); Ex. 3:2 (1.61, *CO* 24.35-36); Jos. 5:13-14 (87-88, *CO* 25.463-464); Dan. 7:27 (2.77, *CO* 41.85); Zech. 12:8 (358, *CO* 44.332); Col. 2:18 (338-340, *CO* 52.111-112); *Articles Agreed upon by the Faculty of Sacred Theology of Paris, with the Antidote*, *T&T* 1.94 ("*de orandis sanctis*," *CO* 7.23), 1.96 (on the intercession of the saints, *CO* 7.25-26); *The Necessity of the Reforming the Church*, *T&T* 1.130, 154-159, 191-192, 195 (*CO* 6.462, 480-483, 504-505, 507).

13 Cf. Comm. Jer. 11:13 (2.93-95, *CO* 38.112-113); Dan. 2:11 (1.133, *CO* 40.569).

14 Cf. Comm. Gen. 18:2 (1.470, *CO* 23.251); Gen. 20:7 (1.526, *CO* 23.290); Gen. 28:12 (2.113, *CO* 23.391); Ex. 23:20 (1.403, *CO* 24.251); Jos. 5:13, 14 (87-88, *CO* 25.463-464).

15 Cf. Comm. Gen.12:3 (1.349, *CO* 23.117-118); Gen. 16:10 (1.433, *CO* 23.228); Gen. 18:2 (1.470, *CO* 23.251); Gen. 22:2 (1.563-565, *CO* 23.313-314); Ex. 30:23 (2.224, *CO* 24.446); Lev. 16:3 (2.315, *CO* 24.501-502); I Cor. 10:9 (209, *CO* 45.459); Heb. 1:5 (11, *CO* 55.15). Serm. Deut. 9:25-29 (417b-420b, *CO* 26.724-730).

16 Beza, *Life of John Calvin*, *T&T* 1.116-117.

17 Joseph N. Tylenda, "The Warning that Went Unheeded: John Calvin on Giorgio Biandrata," in "John Calvin's Response to the Questions of Giorgio Biandrata," *CTJ* 12 (1977), 62 [altered] (CO. 9.332): "Mediator Deus et homo, vere est filius Dei

between God and humanity regarding the unity and continuity of the deity and divinity of Christ in order to defend the deity of the Mediator against Stancaro, who distorted the condescension of God with his own tendency to Arianism and insisted on Christ's mediation not only between God and us but also between God the Father and God the Son.[18]

Calvin believes that the names Adonai, Elohim, and Jehovah refer to Christ's mediatorship. Adonai expresses the messenger nature of Christ's mediatorship.[19] Elohim refers to the person of the Mediator (*persona mediatoris*) who has divine power and glory,[20] and the name Jehovah (Jahweh) reveals Christ as Saviour and Leader.[21]

Calvin maintains the versatility and continuity of Christ's mediatorship that started before the time of the Old Testament and has been in operation ever since. He declares that Christ was revealed not only as the substance, soul, light, and truth of the law, but he is also the end of the law, even for the people of the Old Testament.[22] With regard to Christ's mediation of the law before the incarnation, he argues that the law served not only to represent Christ but also to reveal the presence of Christ as the Mediator in the Old Testament. For instance, in dealing with the ancient Jewish priesthood, he points out that if there were no mediation of Christ, the blood offering of priests would be futile, and mentions that Jesus Christ is the eternal High Priest.[23] Calvin demonstrates in many instances that Christ's presence as the Mediator is not restricted to some narratives related to the appearance of the Lord as angel or in visions of the Prophets, rather,

---

secundum utramque naturam ratione unionis, proprie tamen divinitatis respectu, quia sermo est ante saecula ex patre."

18 Joseph N. Tylenda, "Christ the Mediator: Calvin versus Stancaro," *CTJ* 8/2 (1973), 5. This article includes the translation, "How Christ is the Mediator: A Response to the Polish Brethren to Refute Stancaro's Error," 11-16 (*CO* 9.337-42); id., "The Controversy on Christ the Mediator: A Response to the Polish Nobles and to Francesco Stancaro of Mantua," in "The Controversy on Christ the Mediator: Calvin's Second Reply to Stancaro," *CTJ* 8/1 (1973), 146-157 (*CO* 9.349-58, quot. *CO* 9.350). These two articles including translations are hereafter cited as "First Response to Stancaro" and "Second Response to Stancaro" respectively.

19 Comm. Mal. 3:1 (568-569, *CO* 44.461-462); Dan. 9:18 (2.181, *CO* 41.157).
20 Comm. Ps. 45:6-7 (2.178-183, *CO* 31.451-454).
21 Comm. Ex. 14:19 (1.248-249, *CO* 24.153); Zech. 3:3-4 (87, *CO* 44.171).
22 Cf. Comm. Ex. 28:42 (2.205-206, *CO* 24.435-436); Isa. 29:11-12 (2.322, *CO* 36.492); Eze. 16:61 (2.176-178, *CO* 40.395-396).
23 Comm. Gen. 4:5 (1.196, *CO* 23.86); Ex. 29:38-46 (2.295, *CO* 24.490); Lev. 17:1 (2.260, *CO* 24.468-469); Ps. 119:108 (4.482, *CO* 32.261); Hab. 2:5 (84, *CO* 43.535-536); Serm. Deut. 33:9-11 (1202a-1209b, *CO* 29.142-155); Isa. 53:12 (140-152, *CO* 35.679-688).

he applies Christ's headship of the church to the people of the Israelites, which is called the ancient church.[24]

In his sermon on Galatians 3:19-20, indicating "that Our Lord Jesus Christ was the mediator of the Law (*que nostre Seigneur Iesus Christ a esté le Mediateur de la Loy*)," Calvin argues that "the continual (*tousiours*) Mediator" has reference there not only to the Jews but also to the Gentiles, and not only to the theological use of the law for justification but also to the normative use of the law for sanctification.[25] From this dynamic understanding of Christ's mediation of the law, Calvin understands the continuity of Christ's mediatorship in the Old and New Testaments. As he puts it:

> [I]f we consider how our Lord Jesus Christ was the mediator in the publishing of the law (*Mediateur pour publier la Loy*): it showeth unto us, that if he be our advocate (*advocat*) at this day, it will be a good and sufficient discharge for us: insomuch that although God have pronounced his sentence of cursing against us, yet we must not be dismayed at it, nor so overpassed with heart grief and anguish of mind, as though the mischief were incurable: but assure ourselves that our Lord Jesus Christ will very well agree to both twain, that is to wit, both make us ashamed that we may learn humility, and therewithal also make us sure of our salvation. And therefore let us learn, that whensoever we be beaten down, there is none other means to raise us up again, but to know that the selfsame person which was ordained to be the mediator for the publishing of the law, is now manifested unto us at this day with the same commission, and will make us to perceive it by experience.[26]

In the following, I will study first how Calvin deals with the necessity of Christ the Mediator in relation to the nature of the law and the human capacity to live according to the law. Then, I will examine the extent of Christ's mediation of the law by concentrating on the extent of Christ's mediatorship. To this end, I will deal first with how Calvin understands Christ's mediation in terms of both divine and human natures in the Old Testament as well as in the New Testament, the relationship between God's accommodation and Christ's mediatorship, and the scope of the so-called *extra Calvinisticum*.

---

24 Gen. 17:13 (1.456, *CO* 23.243); Ex. 23:20 (1.403, *CO* 24.251); Jos. 5:13-14 (87, *CO* 25.463-464); Matt. 11:2 (2.2, *CO* 45.299); I Cor. 10:9 (209, *CO* 49.459); Serm. Gal. 1:6-8 (52, *CO* 50.302-303).
25 Serm. Gal. 3:19-20 (452-453, *CO* 50.541). Cf. Serm. Gal. 3:19-20 (456, *CO* 50.544): "Il nous a donné sa Loy, il nous a donné son Evangile ne pensons pas qu'en cela il y ait nulle repugnance, mais le tout s'accorde bien."
26 Serm. Gal. 3:19-20 (454-5, *CO* 50.543).

4.3 The Necessity of the Mediator of the Law[27]

4.3.1 Human Soul Depraved: Knowledge and Conscience

Unlike Osiander, who infers with the firm conviction of the existence of substantial righteousness (*substantialis iustitia*) that even if the fall had not taken place, Christ would still have become man, Calvin sees the need for a Mediator in filling the huge gap between the imperative of the law and our state of total[28] individual[29] depravity[30] (*Inst.* 2.12.6, *CO* 2.345; 3.11.5, 10. *CO* 2.536-537, 540-541). He refers particularly to the soteriological meaning of the faculty of human soul, comprising the intellect and the will, rather than to its philosophical or metaphysical significance.[31]

Calvin distinguishes "spiritual insight" in three ways: the knowledge of God, the knowledge of his favor towards his people, and the knowledge of how to frame our life according to the rule of law (*Inst.* 2.2.18, *CO* 2.200).[32] The first two types of knowledges are related to such lofty wisdom about the existence and mercy of God that even the greatest geniuses are blinder than "moles" to be able to recognize them (*Inst.* 2.2.18-21, quot. 2.2.18, *CO* 2.200). On the other hand, with reference to the third one, Calvin acknowledges the noetic function of natural law, restricting it to the role of conscience (*Inst.* 2.2.22-24).

In the *Institutes*, Calvin explores the office of conscience in relation to the knowledge of the Second Table commandments (*Inst.* 2.2.24, *CO* 2.205). He turns to the forensic term "witness (*testis*)" in order to describe the normative aspect of the noetic funtion of conscience, which makes us

---

27 Calvin's frequent references to the necessity of the Mediator are related mostly to Christ's incarnation. Cf. Comm. Ex. 3:2 (1.61, *CO* 24. 35-36); Num. 17:8 (4.127, *CO* 25.231); Isa. 63:17 (4.359, *CO* 37.405); II Tim. 1:5 (292, *CO* 52.348); Serm. Deut. 32:11-15 (1122a-1127b, *CO* 28.696-708).

28 *Inst.* 2.1.9, *CO* 2.184: ". . . totum hominem quasi diluvio a capite ad pedes sic fuisse obrutum, ut nulla pars a peccato sit immunis; ac proinde quidquid ab eo procedit in peccatum imputari."

29 *Inst.* 2.2.1, *CO* 2.185: ". . . peccati dominatum, ex quo primum hominem sibi obligatum tenuit, non solum in toto genere grassari, sed in solidum etiam occupare singulas animas, . . ."

30 As regards human depravity, Calvin obviously rejects traducianism, which was supported by Servetus who, according to Calvin, tried to introduce the Manichaean error of the soul's emanation (*Inst.* 1.15.5, 2.14.8, *CO* 2.139-140, *CO* 2.360-361). Cf. *Inst.* 2.1.7, McNeill's footnote 10; *Inst.* 1.15.5, McNeill's footnote 15.

31 Cf. Richard A. Muller, "Fides and Cognitio in Relation to the Problem of Intellect and Will in the Theology of John Calvin," *CTJ* 25/2 (1990), 215-216.

32 ". . . spiritualem illam perspicientiam, quae tribus potissimum rebus constat, Deum nosse, paternum erga nos eius favorem, in quo salus nostra consistit, et formandae secundum legis regulam vitae rationem."

aware of our duty before God to live according to his will revealed in the law.[33] The following definition of conscience demonstrates its relation to the theological use of *adiaphora*, the third type of Christian freedom, which strikingly reveals the dynamic character of the normative use of the law.

> For just as when through the mind and understanding men grasp a knowledge (*notitiam*) of things, and from this are said "to know (*scire*)," this is the source of the word "knowledge (*scientiae*)," so also when they [believers] have a sense of divine judgment (*sensum divini iudicii*), as a witness (*testem*) before the Judge's tribunal, this sense is called "conscience (*conscientia*)." For it is a certain mean (*medium*) between God and man, because it does not allow man to suppress within himself what he knows, but pursues him to the point of convicting him . . . . Therefore, this awareness which hales man before God's judgment is a sort of guardian appointed for man to note and spy out all his secrets that nothing may remain buried in darkness. Whence that ancient proverb: "Conscience is a thousand witnesses" (1550 *Inst.* 13.3, *CO* 1.841, *Inst.* 3.19.15, *CO* 2.623-624).[34]

Calvin here verifies that the term *conscientia* originates from *scientia* (or *notitia*) and denotes *sensus divini iudicii*.[35] He distinguishes this sense of divine judgment from *sensus divinitatis*—the knowledge of "*Deum et quod Dei est*" (*Inst.* 2.2.19, *CO* 2.201). The former denominates *semen iustitiae*,[36] while the latter signifies *semen religionis*.[37] In this way, Calvin keenly designates the role of conscience within the realm of the intellect, although it is very closely associated to the function of the will to decide right from wrong.[38]

---

33 1536 *Inst.* 1.4, *CO* 1.29: "[C]onscientia, quae nobis intus testis sit eorum quae Deo debemus, nobisque quid bonum sit, quid malum proponat, atque ita nos accuset reosque teneat, dum nobis ipsi conscii sumus, non esse, ut decuit, officio nostro defunctos." For the noetic function of natural law in conscience, see Dowey, *The Knowledge of God in Calvin's Theology*, 65; William Klempa, "Calvin and Natural Law," in *Calvin Studies IV*, ed. John H. Leith and W. Stacey Johnson (Davidson, N.C.: Davidson College Presbyterian Church, 1988), 10-13; Pelkonen, J. Peter. "The Teaching of John Calvin on the Nature and Function of the Conscience," *Lutheran Quarterly* 21/1 (1969): 74-88.
34 The same definition of conscience appears in 1550 *Inst.* 13.3 (*CO* 1.841) and *Inst.* 4.10.3 (*CO* 2.868-869).
35 Cf. *Inst.* 1.15.2 (*CO* 2.135): "Certe conscientia, quae inter bonum et malum discernens, Dei iudicio respondet, indubium est immortalis spiritus signum."
36 Comm. Rom. 2:15 (48, *CO* 49.38).
37 Comm. Jn. 1:5 (1.12, *CO* 47.6).
38 Cf. Randall C. Zachman, *The Assurance of Faith: Conscience in the Theology of Martin Luther and John Calvin* (Minneapolis: Fortress, 1993), 102: "Calvin

Conscience enables us to conceive "the natural light of righteousness" as "a law," but it does not implant into our heart "a full knowledge (*cognitionem*) of the law."[39] In spite of the noetic function of conscience, if we are not "convinced (*persuasi*) of Christ's grace" by the special illumination of the Holy Spirit, we are not at all able to recognize the promises of the law (*Inst.* 3.19.15, *CO* 2.264).[40] Therefore, conscience itself cannot lead us to the full knowledge of the instruction and exhortation of the law, and it merely makes us *inexcusabilis* because of our ignorance (*Inst.* 2.2.22, *CO* 2.204).[41] Although by conscience we are able to perceive the will of God for us, neither can we have any good will to live according to it without the help of the Holy Spirit (*Inst.* 2.2.25-27), nor are we led to the knowledge of our salvation, which is composed of a sense of individual wretchedness (*propriae miserae sensus*), the knowledge (*agnitio*) of Christ, and the knowledge of the grace of Christ with solid confidence.[42]

4.3.2 Human Soul Depraved: Free Will

In dealing with the soteriological significance of the faculty of the human soul, Calvin clearly distinguishes the function of the intellect from that of the will.[43] He is not so positive about the volitional function of natural law

---

associates conscience (*conscientia*) with consciousness (*conscius*) or awareness (*sensus*), whereas Luther associates conscience with the syllogism of practical reason, possibly indicating the Platonic versus Aristotelian influences in their anthropologies."

39 Comm. Rom. 2:14-15 (47-49, *CO* 49.37-39). For scholars' various positions on natural law, see Hesselink, *Calvin's Concept of the Law*, 56-60.

40 By using the word *persuasio*, Calvin generally points to the special illumination of the Holy Spirit, especially that of the Spirit of Christ the Mediator: "Et sane certo sciunt; sed divinae veritatis persuasione confirmati magis, quam rationali demonstratione edocti" (*Inst.* 3.2.14, *CO* 2.410); "In summa, vere fidelis non est, nisi qui solida persuasione Deum sibi propitium benevolumque patrem esse persuasus, de eius benignitate omnia sibi pollicetur; nisi qui divinae erga se benevolentiae promissionibus fretus, indubitatam salutis exspectationem praesumit" (*Inst.* 3.2.16, *CO* 2. 411). David E. Willis deals with the concept of *persuasio* as closely related to the office of conscience to make people wary of the judgment of God and lead to good behaviour. "Persuasion in Calvin's Theology: Implications for his Ethics," in *Calvin and Christian Ethics*, 83-94.

41 Cf. Comm. Rom. 1:20 (31, *CO* 49.23-24).

42 *The Necessity of Reforming the Church*, *T&T* 1.133-134 (CO 6.464-465).

43 Dowey asserts that both "*sensus divinitatis*" and "*conscientia*" belong to the intellect, which is clearly differentiated from the will. *The Knowledge of God in Calvin's Theology*, 32, 72. On the other hand, Dennis E. Tamburello argues that for Calvin, the word "will" in a large sense includes "knowledge" and "understanding" and "will" is different from "intellect" inasmuch as the latter is "a desire to know God in *essentia*." From this perspective, Tamburelo understands the believer's union with Christ in

as about its noetic function. He does not think that "Themistius' rule," that man does not sin if he knows the truth, can be always applied to human behaviour, because people tend to commit sins out of evil desires despite their consciousness of their sinfulness (*Inst.* 2.2.23, *CO* 2.204). While the intellect refers to the revelation of God's will, the will refers to God's will itself. Accordingly, Calvin, treating free will, gives his primary attention to the relationship between [human] *voluntas* and [divine] *necessitas*.[44]

Man, who fell into the state of *non posse non peccare* after the fall, lost both freedom "from sin" and freedom "from misery." However, he still has freedom "from necessity" (*Inst* 2.2.5, *CO* 2.190) in the light of the fact that "he sins of necessity, yet sins no less voluntarily (*dum necessario peccat, nihilo tamen minus voluntarie peccare*)" (*Inst.* 2.4.1, *CO* 2.224, cf. 2.5.1, *CO* 2.230).[45] Calvin makes clear this position by citing Bernard, who writes: "Hence, neither does necessity, although it is of the will, avail to excuse the will, nor does the will, although it is led astray, avail to exclude necessity. For this necessity is as it were voluntary" (*Inst.* 2.3.5, *CO* 2.214).[46]

Calvin's theology as the "union of wills." *Union with Christ: John Calvin and the Mysticism of St. Bernard* (Louisville: Westminster/John Knox, 1994), 35-40, 105. Muller also notes the close relation between the will and the understanding as he points out their soteriological significance in Calvin's theology. He says that the will is placed "between the intellect and the senses." "Fides and Cognitio," 216.

44 Lane translates *voluntas* as "will" and *arbitrium* as "choice." "Introduction," in *The Bondage and Liberation of the Will: A Defence of the Orthodox Doctrine of Human Choice against Pighius*, ed. Anthony N. S. Lane, tr. G. I. Davies (Grand Rapids: Baker, 1996), xxxii.

45 Cf. *The Bondage and Liberation of the Will*, 69-70; *Calvin's Calvinism: Treatises on the Eternal Predestination of God and the Secret Providence of God*, tr. Henry Cole, repr. (Grand Rapids: Eerdmans, 1950), 332-335 (CO 9.311-312).

46 ". . . nec necessitas (quum voluntaria sit) excusare valeat voluntatem, nec voluntas (quum sit illecta) excludere necessitatem. Est enim necessitas haec quodammodo voluntaria." Calvin's understanding of the relation between *voluntas* and *necessitas* becomes the centre of Brümmer and Helm's debate over the influence of Bernard on Calvin's view of free will. Vincent Brümmer, "Calvin, Bernard and the Freedom of the Will," *Religious Studies* 30 (1994), 437-455; Paul Helm, "Calvin and Bernard on Freedom and Necessity: A Reply to Brümmer," *Religious Studies* 30 (1994), 457-465. According to Brümmer, Bernard clearly distinguishes necessity from compulsion and claims the existence of a "kind of necessity from which the will remains free in spite of sin" (446). He thinks that Bernard's "freedom from necessity" is not different from what Calvin refers to as "freedom from compulsion" (447). Against this view, Helm argues that "to be free from compulsion is, for Calvin, not to be indeterministically free, but to be psychologically free, to be acting in accordance with one's preferences. Such psychological freedom may be consistent with either metaphysical necessity or contingency, and Calvin opts for the former" (461). Anthony N. S. Lane concludes after detailed reserarch that Calvin's distinction between necessity and

Calvin thinks that God's will, whether absolute or ordained, is subject to no necessity, other than the necessity of his own plan, so he does not accept the distinction between *potentia absoluta* and *potentia ordinata* (*Inst.* 1.16.9, *CO* 2.153).[47] With regard to the reason why God gave an imperfect will to the first humans, he states in the same vein, "no necessity was imposed upon God of giving man other than a mediocre and even transitory will, that from man's fall he might gather occasion for his own glory" (*Inst.* 1.15.8, *CO* 2.143).[48] There are "the wisdom that resides with God and the portion of wisdom God has prescribed for men" (*Inst.* 1.17.2, *CO* 2.155).[49] The necessity is hidden in "the best reason (*optima ratio*)" of God. Therefore, it is not perceived as such by the measure of human understanding (*Inst.* 1.17.1, *CO* 2.154, cf. 2.2.12).

Calvin denotes freedom from necessity as the state in which man acts voluntarily upon the wisdom which is prescribed for him and revealed to him. Man is subject to the necessity of God but free from it when he lives according to the revealed will of God.[50] This position of Calvin is derived from his firm conviction that God's will revealed in the law is not contradictory to his will which is hidden from us.[51] Calvin writes:

> Therefore, since God assumes to himself the law (*ius*) of ruling the universe, which is unknown to us, let our law (*lex*) of soberness and moderation be to assent to his supreme authority, that his will may be for us the sole rule of righteousness, and the truly just cause of all things. Not, indeed, that absolute will of which the Sophists babble, by an impious and profane distinction separating his justice from his power— but providence, that determinative principle of all things, from which

---

coercion was not drawn from Bernard. *Calvin and Bernard of Clairvaux*, Studies in Reformed Theology and History New Series, no. 1 (Princeton: Princeton Theological Seminary, 1996), 100.

47 In his sermon on Job 23:1-7, Calvin accuses the Sorbonne doctors' assertion that God has an absolute or lawless power as a diabolical blasphemy invented in hell (415a, *CO* 34. 399-340). For Calvin's rejection of the distinction between the absolute and the ordained power of God, see Steinmetz, "Calvin and the Absolute Power of God," 45-50.

48 Cf. Anthony N. S. Lane, "Did Calvin Believe in Free Will?" *Vox Evangelica* 12 (1981), 72-75.

49 Cf. Richard Stauffer, "Quelques aspects insolites de la théologie du premier article dans la prédication de Calvin," in *Calvinus Ecclesiae Doctor*, ed. Wilhelm H. Neuser (Kampen: Kok, 1978), 50; Schreiner, "Exegesis and Double Justice in Calvin's Sermons on Job," 322-338.

50 Mary Potter Engel explains this in two ways, from the perspective of God and from the perspective of man. *John Calvin's Perspectival Anthropology* (Atlanta: Scholars Press, 1988), 140-144.

51 Cf. *Calvin's Calvinism*, 306-316 (*CO* 9.302-306).

flows nothing but right although the reasons have been hidden from us (*Inst.* 1.17.2 [altered], *CO* 2.156).

For Calvin, what freedom from necessity signifies is nothing different from freedom "in" necessity.[52] It is none other than for us to adjust our law of moral living to the divine rule of righteousness and by this to inquire into the hidden will of God. Calvin's view of the relationship between *voluntas* and *necessitas* gives us a crucial clue to understand the origin of his equal emphasis upon both God's grace and human will, and both God's sovereignty and human freedom. Calvin's emphasis here is on God's glory rather than on God's sovereignty (cf. *Inst.* 1.15.8). On this ground, we can understand the basic principle of Christian ethics for which Calvin argues as follows, against his opponents who misunderstood the true relationship between God's grace and human free will (cf. *Inst.* 2.5.1-19): "nothing good can arise out of our will until it has been formed again (*reformata*); and after it is formed again (*reformationem*), in so far as it is good, it is so from God, not from ourselves" (*Inst.* 2.3.8 [altered], *CO* 2.218). Calvin's view of free will and freedom from necessity eventually make us realize how we, as fallen man, preserve confidence in living according to the will of God, and in what way Christ still mediates for our normative life. Here are Calvin's words:

> I say that the will is effaced; not in so far as it is will, for in man's conversion what belongs to his primal nature remains entire. I also say that it is created anew; not meaning that the will now begins to exist, but that it is changed from an evil to a good will (*Inst.* 2.3.6, *CO* 2.215).[53]

---

52 This position of Calvin was charged with fatalism by his contemporary opponents (Pighius, Hesshusius, Castellio, and Bolsec) and even by his friends, most notably by Melanchthon. Cf. Egil Grislis, "Seneca and Cicero as Possible Sources of John Calvin's View of Double Predestination: An Inquiry in the History of Ideas," in *In Honor of John Calvin*, 29.

53 "Voluntatem dico aboleri, non quatenus est voluntas; quia in hominis conversione integrum manet quod primae est naturae. Creari etiam novam dico, non ut voluntas esse incipiat, sed ut vertatur ex mala in bonam." There have been some debates related to this passage, whether the reformation of the will pertains only to its form or extends to its matter. Muller and Lane approach this issue on the assumption that Calvin here shows the influence of Aristotle. They claim the former view. Richard A. Muller, "Scholasticism, Reformation, Orthodoxy, and the Persistence of Christian Aristotelianism," *Trinity Journal* (1998), 92-93; Lane, "Introduction," in *The Bondage and Liberation of the Will*, xxiv-xxvi. On the other hand, Ronald N. Frost, a Lutheran theologian, traces it with an emphasis on the influence of Luther upon Calvin, and denies any kind of formal reformation of human will by regeneration. "'Scholasticism, Reformation, Orthodoxy, and the Persistence of Christian Aristotelianism': A Brief Rejoinder," *Trinity Journal* 19 (1998), 99-101, and

4.3.3 Free Will to Do Good Works by the Grace of Christ

In dealing with free will with special reference to human ability to live according to rule of the law (*Inst.* 2.5.4-11),[54] Calvin strictly opposes Ockham's view of a co-operating grace that "grace is denied to no one who does what is in him (*eam [gratiam] nemini denegari facienti quod in se est*)," and follows Augustine's formula, "the grace of God is efficacious of itself" (*Inst.* 2.3.10, *CO* 2.220). In doing so, Calvin takes into consideration the new state of the regenerate, *non posse peccare*, which is superior to the state of original human beings, *posse non peccare* (*Inst.* 2.3.13, *CO* 1.222-223).[55]

Calvin's negative view of "*quod in se*" is due to his recognition of the dilemma that humans face between the divinely ordered duty and their lack of ability to carry it out. This miserable state is pinpointed by the fact that God orders not what we can do but what we ought to (*non quid possint homines sed quid debeant*). Notwithstanding, Calvin refers in detatil to the *gratia tota* not only for our salvation but also for good works. For this purpose, he quotes Augustine: "God does not measure the precepts of his law according to human powers, but where he has commanded what is right, he freely gives to his elect the capacity to fulfill it" (*Inst.* 2.5.4, *CO* 2.232, cf. 2.5.7, 9).[56]

The law was given as the rule of living. However, no one reaches the perfection of God's righteousness by keeping the law perfectly because God does not measure the precepts of the law according to our ability. Therefore, it is God's grace that he wants us to live according to the rule of life prescribed in the law and "requires only what is within our power." God accommodates himself not to our natural capacity but to our capacity renewed by his grace, so he makes us free from necessity even though we

---

"Aristotle's Ethics: The Real Reason for Luther's Reformation?" *Trinity Journal* 18 (1997), 223-241.

54 Cf. *The Bondage and Liberation of the Will*, 40-42 (*CO* 6.259-260), 116-119 (*CO* 6.312-313), 141-142 (*CO* 6.329-330), 165-170 (*CO* 6.346-350), 206-207 (*CO* 6.376-377), *et passim*.

55 On this ground, Augustine asserts, "Faith achieves what the law commands (*fides impetrat quod lex imperat*)" (*Inst.* 2.5.7, *CO* 2.235). For the influence of Augustine upon Calvin concerning the superiority of the *novissima libertas* in the state of *non posse peccare* to Adam's original freedom in the state of *posse non peccare*, especially with reference to its significance after the resurrection of godly people, see David F. Wright, "*Non posse peccare* in this life? St. Augustine, *De correptione et gratia* 12:33," in *St Augustine and his Opponents, Other Latin Writers*, Studia Patristica, vol. 38 (Leuven: Peeters, 2001), 348-353.

56 "[U]bi Deum legis suae praecepta non humanis viribus metiri docet, verum ubi iussit quod rectum est, gratis dare implendi facultatem suis electis." This argument between Augustine and the Pelagians is presented by Calvin precisely in *The Bondage and Liberation of the Will*, 141-142 (*CO* 6.329-330), 166 (*CO* 6.347).

are always subject to his necessity, which is hidden for us (*Inst.* 2.5.6-7, *CO* 2.234-235). Therefore, the reconciling grace of Christ is taken into consideration with reference to the exhortative office of the law (*Inst.* 2.5.5, *CO* 2.233-234).

By the bare precepts (*nuda praecepta*) of the law, we are taught merely our spiritual death, but with the grace poured upon us, the law itself reveals the promises of the free imputation of the righteousness of Christ the Mediator. Through the promises of the law not only are we converted to God but we are also persuaded to love the precepts (*Inst.* 2.5.10).[57] When Calvin talks about the grace (or promise) of the law, he is concerned not only with God's grace to reveal the precepts and promises of the law, but also with God's grace to enable us to live according to the rule of the law.[58] Calvin's view of good works can be understood on the ground of his dynamic understanding of the relation between the precepts and promises of the law. Good works are not our works but God's because they come "from the pure prompting of the Spirit (*ex mero spiritus instinctu*)" (*Inst.* 2.5.15, *CO* 2.243). They are commanded to believers out of necessity because they cannot sin (*non posse peccare*) anymore. This does not mean that the regenerate have the free will to do good works by themselves; it rather means freedom from necessity, i.e., freedom to do good works voluntarily without coercion.[59] This kind of necessity is made known only to the people who are guided and directed by the Spirit of Christ the Mediator, who is the fulfilment of the law (*Inst.* 2.5.15-19).

Calvin's treatment of free will regarding Christ's mediation of the law makes us anticipate his later emphasis on the normative use of the law as the principal one, his own view of double justification, and his view of the

---

57 For the precept and promise of the law, cf. *Inst.* 2.5.10, 2.7.12, 2.9.3, 3.17.1-15; Comm. Ex. 19:1-2 (1.313-316, *CO* 24.192-194), Lev. 18:5 (3.201-289, *CO* 25.1-58).

58 Calvin distinguishes between *lex nuda* and *lex tota* according to whether the law is clothed with the grace of Christ the Mediator or not. Cf. *Inst.* 2.7.2, *CO* 2.255; Comm. Deut 29:29 (1.412, *CO* 24.256). He argues that "where the whole law is concerned (*de tota lege*), the gospel differs from it only in clarity of manifestation" (*Inst.* 2.9.4, *CO* 2.312). As we see in the following commentary on Psalm 19:8 (1.322, *CO* 31.201), the bare law signifies the letter of the law itself which does not contain the promise of God's grace in it: "Without Christ (*extra Christum*) there is in the law nothing but inexorable rigour, which adjudges all mankind to the wrath and curse of God . . . without the promise of grace, it strictly and rigorously exacts from us the duty which we owe to God; but David, in praising it as he here does, speaks of the whole doctrine of the law, which includes also the gospel, and, therefore, under the law he comprehends Christ." For the use of these two terms, see Hesselink, *Calvin's Concept of the Law*, 158, 170-172.

59 This position is described by Dewey J. Hoitenga, Jr. as "Calvin's soteriological voluntarism." *John Calvin and the Will: A Critique and Corrective* (Grand Rapids: Baker, 1997), 51-52.

relationship between *regula vivendi* and *regula vivificandi*. Calvin has a firm conviction of Christ's saying, "Without me you can do nothing" (John 15:5) (*Inst.* 2.5.4, CO. 2.232). Upon this foundation, he delves into the reality of human free will after the fall and the positive function of the law for the people who are regenerated by the grace of Christ the Mediator.

4.4 The Threefold Mediation of the Law

4.4.1 Threefold Mediation and Threefold Office

In the following commentary on Galatians 3:19, Calvin classifies the mediatorial office of Christ into *mediator reconciliationis, mediator patrocinii,* and *mediator doctrinae*:

> As He is the Mediator of reconciliation, by whom we are accepted of God, and the Mediator of intercession, through whom the way is opened for us to call upon the Father, so He has always been the Mediator of all teaching, because by Him God always revealed Himself to men.[60]

Calvin deals with the first two kinds of mediation as the office of a priest and the third as the office of a prophet in the Catechism of the Church of Geneva (1542).[61] He had expressed his view of the threefold office of Christ (*Christi munus triplex*) since the 1539 *Institutes* (4.2, CO 1.513-514), but most parts of the office of Christ were augmented in the 1559 *Institutes*.[62]

In 1559, Calvin relates the prophetic office of Christ to the mediation of teaching in view of the fact that "the prophetic dignity in Christ leads us to know that in the sum of doctrine (*summa doctrinae*) as he has given it to us all parts of perfect wisdom are contained" (*Inst.* 2.15.2, CO 2.363). He describes the priestly office as representing the reconciliation and intercession of Christ. In asserting this view, he returns to the insight that in Christ both priest and sacrifice belong to the same person (*Inst.* 2.15.6, CO 2.366-377). In dealing with the kingly office of Christ, Calvin emphasizes

---

60 Comm. Gal.3:19 (62, *CO* 50.216-217): "Sicuti ergo mediator est reconciliationis, per quem accepti sumus Deo, mediator patrocinii, per quem accessus nobis patet ad patrem invocandum: ita mediator semper fuit omnis doctrinae: quia per ipsum semper Deus se hominibus patefecit."

61 *CTT* 96 (*CO* 6.21-22). Calvin expresses a two-office view of Christ (king and priest) in the 1536 *Institutes* (2.14, *CO* 1.69) and in the 1537/8 catechism (*First Catechism* 22, *CO* 5.338).

62 For the development of Calvin's concept of the threefold office of the Mediator, see Klauspeter Blaser, *Calvins Lehre von den drei Ämtern Christi, Theologische Studien* 105 (Zürich: EVZ Verlag, 1970), 7-23.

Christ's rule over both the whole body of the church and each individual member, also pointing out "the perpetuity of the church" and the "blessed immortality" of believers (*Inst.* 2.15.3, *CO* 2.363-364). With reference to this office, Calvin pays much attention to Christ's continual mediation for the godly and right living of the Christian (*Inst.* 2.5.14, *CO* 2.364-365). Christ's kingly office is especially denoted when he is described as the chief of the angels, who rules angels and menservants.[63] This office does not seem to belong to any specific type of mediation, but to the whole process of mediation.[64] In his commentary and sermon on Galatians 3:19-20, Calvin argues that Christ's mediation ranges through the whole process of the law, i.e., its creation, publication, interpretation, and use. Moreover, he asserts Christ's mediation to be pertinent to the whole process of salvation.[65] In this respect, the threefold office of Christ refers completely to Christ's threefold mediation of the law.[66]

4.4.2 Christus Mediator Reconciliationis

When Calvin deals with the reconciling work of Christ as part of the priestly office, he focuses chiefly on the merit of Christ's redemptive death. However, for Calvin, the concept of Christ's mediation of reconciliation

---

63 Calvin points out the office of Christ as the head of the angels in order to explain Christ's mediation before the fall. Cf. "First Response to Stancaro," 13 (*CO* 9.338); "Second Response to Stancaro," 147 (*CO* 9.350).

64 The third type of mediation is relevant to Willis' "*mediation as sustenance*" in that "the performance of sustaining mediation means that the Eternal Son's full equality of nature with the Father was not diminished just because the Father ordered the universe through him." *Calvin's Catholic Christology*, 70.

65 In the sermon on Gal. 3:19-20 (448-455, *CO* 50.539-544), these points are strongly proclaimed with reference to Christ's mediation of the law: that "a Mediator" in the passage should be interpreted as denoting Christ rather than Moses, that in Old Testament times Christ appeared as the Mediator in the form of "the Angel," that Christ's mediation refers not only to his reconciling work but also to his office to enable us to live according to the law voluntarily, that Christ as "the continual Mediator" has been working not only for the Jews but also for the Gentiles today, and that the extent of Christ's mediation of the law is manifested throughout its publication, teaching, and fulfilment.

66 According to Blaser, in the context of Calvin's *Institutes* the threefold office of Christ is expressed in three ways: *das Freiheitsamt*, which signifies Christ the eternal Word (*Wort*) who makes us free by his truth, *das Gehorsamsamt*, which signifies the person of Christ (*Wesen*) who intercedes between God and us as he humbles himself and becomes obedient to death, and *das Lebensamt*, which signifies the work (*Werk*) of Christ who accepts us as righteous and leads us to eternal life by imputing his righteousness to us. *Calvins Lehre von den drei Ämtern Christi*, 24-44. These three aspects of the office of Christ correspond respectively to each of the characteristic features of the threefold mediation of Christ.

refers to the Old Testament as well. The ancient people also felt the necessity of a Mediator, because they were aware that without propitiation, the law did not bring them near God. God's mercy-seat was commanded to be built in order to reveal the grace of the Mediator. "For as long as the law stands forth before God's face it subjects us to His wrath and curse; and hence it is necessary that the blotting out of our guilt should be interposed, so that God may be reconciled with us."[67] Calvin comments that if all the sacrifices of the fathers were not "directed to the Mediator" and did not look to "the medium of a reconciliation," they "differ in no respect from mere profane butchery."[68]

Calvin argues that we cannot discern any merit of Abel which differentiates him from his brother Cain but his firm conviction of the grace of Christ. As he puts it, "the chief point of well-doing, for a pious person, is relying on Christ the Mediator, and on the gratuitous reconciliation procured by him."[69] There is no true piety without the perception of the grace of the Mediator, for we cannot contemplate God himself and his providence without the knowledge of his will, that he gives mercy to his people through the hand of his Son. By giving the name *Immanuel* to Christ, God the Father shows his everlasting will towards his people, to give eternal life to them. Therefore, Christ is properly called *Immanuel* because of his mediatorship.[70]

Calvin repeatedly refers to the nature of the lawgiver (*natura legis latoris*) for the purpose of illustrating the nature and purpose of the law. Mostly, in these cases, he points to God's mercy as revealed in Christ's reconciliation.[71] Thus, when the law reveals God's will, it also reveals its accomplishment by the mediation of his Son. "God interposed His Son to reconcile Himself to us because He loved us."[72]

---

67 Comm. Ex. 25:17 (2.156, *CO* 24.406).
68 Comm. Ex. 29:38-41 (2.293-295, *CO* 24.489-491). For the sacrifices pointing to the propitiatory sacrifice of Christ, cf. Comm. Lev. 1:1-17 (2.323-326, *CO* 24.506-508); Lev. 17:1 (2.260, *CO* 24.468); Gen. 8:20 (1.281, *CO* 23.138); Ps. 119:108 (4.482, *CO* 32.261): "It was the design of God, by that ceremony, to testify to the fathers that no prayers were acceptable to him, but those which were joined with sacrifice, that they might always turn their minds to the Mediator."
69 Comm. Gen. 4:7 (1.201, *CO* 23.89).
70 Comm. Isa. 8:10 (1.274. *CO* 36.173); Matt. 1:23 (1.68-69, *CO* 45.68-69).
71 Cf. *Inst.* 2.8.51, 59; Comm. Deut. 26:17-19 (1.361, *CO* 24.224); Deut. 13:5 (2.75, *CO* 24.356); Ex. 20:4-6 (2.107, *CO* 24.376); Ex. 34:17, et al. (2.117, *CO* 24.283); Deut. 4:12-18 (2.120, *CO* 24.384-386); Ex. 25:8-15 (2.150-155, *CO* 24.403-405); Ex. 25:31-39 (2.163-165, *CO* 24.409-411); Ex. 26:31-37 (2.175, *CO* 24.417); Ex. 20:13, et al. (3.21, *CO* 24.612-613); Deut. 24:16 (3.50-51, *CO* 24.631); Deut. 24:14-15 (3.114, *CO* 24.671); Deut. 10:17-19 (3.118, *CO* 24.674); Ex. 20:17, et al. (3.187, *CO* 24.718); Deut. 29:22-28 (3.280, *CO* 25.51).
72 Comm. I Jn. 4:10 (292, *CO* 55.354): "[F]ilium suum interposuit Deus, ad se nobis

4.4.3 Christus Mediator Patrocinii

Christ's office as the Mediator of intercession between God and man is relevant to all the laws that foreshadow Christ, who is the reality and substance of them.[73] For if a ceremony were held with no expectation of Christ, it bears only a "bare sign (*nudo symbolo*)" because nothing can make it worthy except Christ's intercession.[74] As Calvin puts it:

> But as we have elsewhere seen in what manner blood atones for souls, i.e., in a sacramental manner, upon which it must be observed that what properly belongs to Christ is thus transferred by *metonomy* to figures and symbols, yet in such a way that the similitude should neither be empty nor inefficacious; for in so far as the fathers apprehended Christ in the external sacrifices, atonement was truly exhibited in them (*quatenus in externis sacrificiis Christum apprehenderunt patres, illic vere exhibita fuit expiatio*).[75]

Christ's mediation of intercession is well expressed in Calvin's use of the sacramental terms "lift one's heart higher (*sursum corda*)" in relation to the function of the sacrifices in the Old Testament (*Inst.* 4.17.36 [altered], *CO* 2.1039, cf. 4.17.18, *CO* 2.1016-1017).[76] This concept is prominent in the

---

reconciliandum, quia nos amabat."
73 For the *umbra-veritas* (*substantia*) analogy in the Pentateuch, cf. Ex.12: 46 (1.467, *CO* 24.292, on the Passover); Ex. 27:20-21, et al. (2.167, *CO* 24. 411-412, on the lamps upon the candlestick); Ex. 26: 1-37 (2.171-176, *CO* 24.414-417, on the tabernacle); Ex. 27:1-8 (2.177-178, *CO* 24.418-419, on the burnt offerings); Ex. 28:42-43 (2.205-206, *CO* 24.435-436, on the Levitical priesthood); Ex. 30:25-33 (2.224, *CO* 24.446-447, on an oil of holy anointment); Lev. 21:1-12 (2.227-230, *CO* 24.448-450, on the purity of priests); Ex. 29.38-41 (2.296-297, *CO* 24.490-491, on burnt offerings); Lev. 16: 7-11 (2.316-317, *CO* 24.502-503, on two goats offered in sacrifice); Lev. 16:16 (2.318-319, *CO* 24.503-504, on an atonement for the holy place); Lev. 1:1-17 (2.323-326, *CO* 24. 506-508, on sacrifices); Lev. 2:1-10 (2.328-329, *CO* 24.509-510, on a grain offering and meat-offering); Lev. 6:1-7 (2.356-362, *CO* 24.525-529, on reconciliation of sin); Lev. 22:17-21 (2.378-381, *CO* 24.540-541, on the offering for a vow and a free will offering); Ex. 20:8 (2.435, *CO* 24.577, on Christ and the Sabbath); Ex. 31:13-17 (2.442-444, *CO* 24.583-584, on the Sabbath and circumcision); Lev. 23:10-23, 34-35 (2.456-458, 462-463, *CO* 24.591-592, 594-595, on the year of Jubilee). For the *umbra-veritas* (*substantia*) analogy in the New Testament, cf. *Inst.* 2.7.16 (*CO* 2.264); Comm. Col. 2:17 (337-338, *CO* 52.110-111); Matt. 5:17 (1.180, *CO* 45.171); Heb. 9:6-12 (117-120, *CO* 55.107-110).
74 Comm. Ex. 30:1-9 (2.182, *CO* 24.421).
75 Comm. Lev. 17:10-14 (3.31, *CO* 24.619-620).
76 Cf. *Inst.* 2.7.1, *CO* 2.253: "Yet that very type shows that God did not command sacrifices in order to busy his worshipers with earthly exercises. Rather, he did so that he might lift their minds higher (*altius erigeret eorum mentes*)"; Comm. Ex.

mediation of prayer.[77] Calvin calls prayer "an intimate conversation of the pious with God" and says, "we should lift up our minds (*tollendas esse sursum mentes*) to a pure and chaste veneration of Him" (*Inst.* 3.20.16, *CO* 2.642). Further, he points out that due to the merit of Christ the Mediator God regards our prayer as worth listening to and offers all good things.[78]

Christ's mediation as "the eternal intercessor (*deprecatorem*)" is represented notably by the priestly office, to purify and nourish people into the perfection of life as well. It is on this ground that Calvin regards the grace of Christ as the foundation of the eternal beatitude (*Inst.* 2.15.6, *CO* 2.367),[79] and takes into consideration the priestly office of the Mediator and God's accommodation in Christ's kingly office at the same time as he deals with the *sursum corda* of believers (cf. *Inst.* 2.15.5).

4.4.4 Christus Mediator Doctrinae

This type of mediation, which is closely related to Christ's office as Prophet, is based on the fact that we have no knowledge of God *extra Christum*.[80] We can find this kind of mediation most distinctively in Calvin's commentary on Genesis 28:12, where he comments that the chief

---

12:21-22 (1.221, *CO* 24.221): "We elsewhere see that the Paschal lamb was a type of Christ, who by His death propitiated His Father, . . . And there is no doubt that by this visible symbol He raised up their minds to that true and heavenly Exemplar (*extulerit ad verum et coeleste exemplar*), whom it would be absurd and profane to separate from the ceremonies of the law."

77 "John Calvin's Response to the Questions of Giorgio Biandrata," 59-60, 62 (*CO* 9.329-330). Cf. Comm. Ps. 50:14-15 (2.269-274, *CO* 31.500-503); Dan. 9:23 (2.194, *CO* 41.166); Matt. 6:9 (206, *CO* 45.196); Serm. Isa. 53:12 (140-152, *CO* 35.679-687); Deut. 11:26-32 (482a-488b, *CO* 27.135-149); *Forms of Prayer for the Church*, *T&T* 2.101 (*CO* 6.175); *Catechism of the Church of Geneva*, *T&T* 2.73 (*CO* 6.89-90).

78 Cf. *Inst.* 3.20.1 (*CO* 2.625); *First Catechism* 27 (*CO* 5.343).

79 Cf. Comm. Ex. 28:1-43 (2.191-193, *CO* 24.426-427); Ex. 30:23-24 (2.222-224, *CO* 24.445-446); Lev. 21:17-21 (2.239-240, *CO* 24.456); Lev. 16:3-6 (2.315-316, *CO* 24.501-502); Hos. 8:4 (283, *CO* 42.364).

80 Cf. Comm. Jn. 5:27 (1.132, *CO* 46.118); Jn. 6:45 (1.165, *CO* 46.150); Jn. 10:7 (1.260, *CO* 46.238); Jn. 10:15 (1.266, *CO* 46.243); Jn. 17:3 (2.136-137, *CO* 46.376-377); Jn. 17:8 (2.139-140, *CO* 46.379-380). Willis reminds us of the *totus-totum* in the so-called *extra Calvinisticum* when he comments that "Calvin does not say we have no knowledge of God *extra hanc carnem*; he says we have no knowledge of God *extra Christum*." From this point of view, he argues that the characteristic feature of Calvin's doctrine of the knowledge of God is "beyond the humanity, to the divinity." *Calvin's Catholic Christology*, 109, 114. Augustine also takes the position that we have no other way to the true knowledge of God but Christ the Mediator. Cf. Robert E. Cushman, "Faith and Reason," in *A Companion to the Study of St. Augustine*, ed. Roy W. Battenhouse (New York: Oxford University Press, 1956), 304-310.

angel of God who appeared on Jacob's ladder revealed the sign (*signum*) of Christ the incarnate. He fleshes out the presence of the Mediator *etiam extra carnem* as he points out "the fact that the body of Christ is finite in no way prevents his filling the heavens, since his grace and power spread over all." By understanding the connection between the mediation of Christ before and after the incarnation from this shadow-reality framework, Calvin maintains that we can understand that in Christ the eternal image (*aeterna imago*) of the Father was revealed even to the ancient people.[81]

Commenting on II Corinthians 4:4, Calvin writes: "When Christ is called the image of the invisible God the reference is not merely to His essence (*essentia*), because He is, as they say, co-essential with the Father, but rather to His relationship to us because He represents the Father to us."[82] Calvin here refers to the *persona* of the Mediator rather than to the immanent-Trinitarian view of the *co-essentia* of the Trinity. Therefore, Calvin claims that man is not created according to the image of Christ but through the mediation of Christ, as he debated with Osiander who, refusing to accept the distinction between the divine essence and the divinity (*divinitas*) of the *hypostasis* of the Son, insisted that the incarnation was the infusion of the divine essence to humanity (*Inst.* 2.12.6-7, *CO* 2.344-347).[83]

---

81 Comm. Gen. 28:12 (2.112, *CO* 23.391). Cf. Comm. Col. 1:15 (308-309, *CO* 46.84-85); Jn. 1:18 (1.25, *CO* 46.19); Jn. 14:10 (2.78, *CO* 46.326); Heb. 1:5 (10-12, *CO* 55.14); Isa. 6:1 (1.201, *CO* 36.126). For Calvin's Christological understanding of the image of God, see Hans Helmut Esser, "Zur Anthtopologie Calvins Menschenwürde—Imago dei Zwischen Humanistischem und Theologischem Ansatz," *Hervormde Theologiese Studies* 35/1-2 (1979), 33-34, 38-39; J. Faber, "Imago Dei in Calvin: Calvin's Doctrine of Man as the Image of God in Connection with Sin and Restoration," tr. J. D. Wielenga, in *Essays in Reformed Doctrine* (Alberta, Canada: Inheritance Publications, 1990), 264-267; Randall C. Zachman, "Jesus Christ as the Image of God in Calvin's Theology," *CTJ* 15/1 (1990), 45-62.

82 Comm. II Cor. 4:4 (55-56, *CO* 50.51). Cf. Serm. Deut. 5:17 (165, *CO* 26.333). Calvin writes that not only must we acknowledge that we "are formed in the image of God," but we must also remember that we "are members of our Lord Jesus Christ and that there exists [now] a more strict and sacred bond than the bond of nature which is common in all human beings."

83 Osiander's position on the person of Christ is based on the assumption that the divine essence cannot take on humanity. He understands the eternal existence of the Son of God as featured by the eternal presence of the divine essence invariably throughout, before, and after incarnation. Therefore, he argues, although man is not depraved, Christ would become flesh. As a result, Osiander denies the necessity of the coming of Christ as the Mediator, because he believes that man, being created by the image of Christ, bears the original righteousness infused through his divine essence. Osiander's contention is not based on the free imputation of the righteousness of Christ but on the fact that "we are righteous together with God (*nos una cum Deo iustos esse*)" (*Inst.* 3.11.5-12, quot. 3.11.11, *CO* 2.541). For the debate between Calvin and Osiander over the image of God, see J. Faber, "Imago Dei in Calvin:

Christ's mediation of teaching is well presented in the character of priest, whom Calvin describes not only as a messenger but also as an interpreter of the doctrine of the law.[84] In the following, Calvin demonstrates how the Levitical priest mediates for his people as a type of the true Mediator.

> What the Scripture sometimes relates, as to the inquiries made by Urim and Thummin, it was a concession made by God to the rudeness of His ancient people. The true Priest had not yet appeared, the Angel of His Almighty counsel, by whose Spirit all the Prophets spoke, who, finally, is the fountain of all revelations, and the express image of the Father; in order then that the typical priest (*umbratilis sacerdos*) might be the messenger (*internuncius*) from God to man, it behoved him to be invested with the ornaments of Christ. Thus even then believers were taught in a figure, that Christ is the way by which we come to the Father, and that He also brings from the secret bosom of His Father whatever it is profitable for us to know unto salvation.[85]

4.5 The Extent of Christ's Mediation of the Law

Calvin claims that the eternal presence of Christ as the Mediator ranges from before the fall: "Certainly, the eternal λόγος was already mediator from the beginning, before Adam's fall and the alienation and separation of the human race from God."[86] He states: "Even if man had remained free from all stain, his condition would have been too lowly for him to reach God without a Mediator" (*Inst.* 2.12.1, *CO* 2.340).[87] It is surely the case that Calvin contends that Christ's mediation ranges over the whole of history after the fall throughout his theological and exegetical works.[88] He

---

Calvin's Doctrine of Man as the Image of God by Virtue of Creation," in *Essays in Reformed Doctrine*, 234-239; Peter Wyatt, *Jesus Christ and Creation in the Theology of John Calvin* (Allison Park, Pa.: Pickwick Publications, 1996), 39.

84 Comm. Deut. 17:8-11 (2.262-265, *CO* 24.470-471, quot. 262, *CO* 24.470). That Christ is the interpreter of the law (*interpres legis*) demonstrates the character of Christ the Mediator of all teaching most significantly. Cf. Lev. 10:9-11 (2.235, *CO* 24.453); Num. 35:1-3 (2.249, *CO* 24.462); Jn. 3:13 (1.71-72, *CO* 47.62).

85 Comm. Ex. 28:4-8 (2.198, *CO* 24.430-431).

86 "Second Reply to Stancaro," 147 (*CO* 9.350): "[Nam] certe λόγος aeternus iam ab initio ante lapsum Adae, et alienationem ac dissidium humani generis a Deo, fuit mediator."

87 "Quamvis ab omni labe integer stetisset homo, humilior tamen erat eius conditio quam ut sine mediatore ad Deum penetraret." Cf. Tylenda, "First Response to Sancaro," 12 (*CO* 9.350): "[N]ot only after Adam's fall did he begin to exercise his office of mediator, but since he is the eternal Word of God, both angels as well as men were united to God by his grace so that they would remain uncorrupted."

88 Cf. Comm. Gen. 18:13 (1.475, *CO* 23.254); Ex. 3:2 (1.61, *CO* 24.35-36); Isa. 19:20

claims that "since God cannot without the Mediator be propitious toward the human race, under the law Christ was always set before the holy fathers as the point (*obiectum*) to which they should direct their faith" (*Inst*. 2.6.2 [altered], *CO* 2.250). Moreover, Christ's mediation refers to the office and use of the law in the whole process of personal salvation. In the following commentary on Acts 17:18, Calvin points this out in opposition to the false concept of mediators argued by the Gentiles. He says,

> Christ as the Mediator . . . teaches that salvation must be sought from Him alone; that it [our faith] bids us seek the expiation, by which we may be reconciled to God, in His death; that it teaches that men, who had previously been unclean and in the grip of sin, are restored and renewed by His Spirit, to begin to live righteous and holy lives; lastly, that, from such beginnings, which make it clear that the Kingdom of God is spiritual, it finally lifts our minds to the hope of the future resurrection.[89]

In the following section, I will deal with the function of the so-called *extra Calvinisticum* in Calvin's theology with respect to Christ's mediation according to both the divine and human natures before the incarnation and after the ascension, and God's accommodation through the mediation of Christ with respect to the issue of the *extra-legem* related to Calvin's understanding of the absolute will and the ordained will of God.

4.5.1 The So-Called Extra Calvinisticum

The so-called *extra Calvinisticum* has been developed through the controversies of the Reformed and Lutherans, who criticized Calvin's understanding of the bodily presence of the bread as opposed to their view of *communicatio idiomatum* and scorned it as "*extra Calvinisticum*."[90] The notion has been supported in the light of the fact that Calvin makes use of *etiam extra carnem* to take account not only of the doctrine of the Holy Supper but also of his Christology leading to Christ's mediation with regard to both his natures even after his ascension.

In his fundamental study on this subject, David Willis seeks the doctrinal origin of the so-called *extra Calvinisticum* based on the distinction between *Christus totus* and *Christus totum* from the early church fathers and

---

(2.75, *CO* 36.344); Isa. 63:17 (4.359, *CO* 37.405); Matt. 1:23 (1.69, *CO* 45.69); Jn. 5:46 (1.143, *CO* 47.129); Jn. 16:23-24 (2.125-128, *CO* 47.367-369); Jn. 16:26 (2.129-130, *CO* 47,371); Heb. 8:5 (107, *CO* 55.99); Serm. Matt. 26:36-39 (65, *CO* 46.846); Matt. 26:67-27:10 (114, *CO* 46.886); Gal. 3:13-14 (407-408, 412, *CO* 50.515, 518); Gal. 3:15-18 (423-437, *CO* 525-534).

89 Comm. Acts 17:18 (2.108, *CO* 48.406).

90 Willis, *Calvin's Catholic Christology*, 1-25.

ecumenical councils and, of most importance, from Augustine and Lombard, and evinces its great significance for Calvin's dynamic understanding of Christ's mediatorship.[91] Oberman's view of the extra dimension of Calvin's theology is more comprehensive than that of Willis, ranging over *extra ecclesiam, extra coenam, extra carnem, extra legem,* and *extra praedicationem*.[92] He also explores the influence of Calvin's view of *etiam extra carnem* on his position on the continual mediation of Christ. As he puts it:

> The *extra calvinisticum* serves to relate the eternal Son to the historical Jesus, the Mediator at the right hand to the sacramental Christ, in such a way that the 'flesh of our flesh' is safeguarded. Rather than hiding secret divine resources, which mark a divide between the incarnate Christ and fallen man, the *extra calvinisticum* is meant to express both the reality of the *kenosis* and the reality of the Ascension. The theological motive is the *caro vera*, the religious motive is the *spes resurrectionis*.[93]

Following the *consensus Tigurinus* of 1549, Calvin defends against both the Catholic view of transubstantiation and the Lutheran concept of *ubiquitas*, the believer's partaking of the body and blood of the Lord, which is "spiritual" but "real."[94] He pays specific attention to the continual mediation of Christ with regard to both natures[95] and turns to the principle of *"totus ubique, sed non totum"* in order to explain it.[96] He manifests this principle in the 1559 *Institutes*: "since the whole Christ is everywhere, our Mediator is ever present with his own people, and in the Supper reveals himself in a special way, yet in such a way that the whole Christ is present, but not wholly" (*Inst* 4.17.30 [altered], *CO* 2.1032).[97]

While Lutheran theologians such as Joachim Westphal and Tileman Heshusius employed the concept of *ubiquitas* in order to explain the local presence (*localis praesentia*) of Christ's body, Calvin called on the principle of the *totus non totum* presence of Christ's body to elicit the

---

91 Ibid., 26-60, 67-78.
92 Oberman, "The 'Extra' Dimension in the Theology of Calvin," 239-258.
93 Ibid., 249. From this perspective, Oberman explains "Calvin's shift of accent from a natures-Christology to an offices-Christology, converging towards a Mediator-theology" (253).
94 *Exposition of the Heads of Agreement, T&T* 2.239-240 (CO 9.32).
95 Ibid., 240-244 (*CO* 9.33-36).
96 The influence of Augustine and Lombard on Calvin's distinction between *Christus totus* and *Christus totum* is clearly shown in *Inst* 4.17.30 (*CO* 2.1031-1032) and *Last Admonition to Joachim Westphal,* and *The True Partaking of the Flesh and Blood of Christ*. Cf. Willis, *Calvin's Catholic Christology*, 29-33, 44-49.
97 "Mediator [ergo] noster quum totus ubique sit, suis semper adest; et in coena speciali modo praesentem se exhibet, sic tamen ut totus adsit, non totum."

omnipresence of the human nature of Christ after his ascension in relation to his continual mediation. Following Augustine, Calvin argues that "the flesh of Christ is to be worshipped in the person of the Mediator."[98] That is, regarding the sole mediatorship of Christ, he pointed to the fact that in Christ *sacrificium* becomes *sacerdos*. Although his debate with Lutheran theologians was concentrated on the meaning of the Lord's Supper, Calvin extends the *totus-totum* distinction to the mediation of Christ. He says, "the Mediator, God and man, is whole everywhere, but not wholly (*totus ubique, sed non totum*), because in respect of his flesh he continued some time on earth and now dwells in heaven," and "because his empire and the secret power of his grace are not confined within any limits."[99]

Also, while Lutherans developed their theory of *communicatio idiomatum* for the reason of the transformation of properties, whose insight originated from Luther's view of *ubiquitas*, Calvin deals with it in the light of the *totus-totum* distinction (*Inst*. 1.14.1-3, cf, 4.17.29-30).[100] Calvin distinguishes the unity of the *hypostasis* of Christ from the union of properties. He relates unity (*unitas*) to *totus*, and union (*unio*) to *totum*, as he argues, "although the two natures form the one person of the Mediator, the properties (*proprietates*) of each remain distinct, since union is a different thing from unity."[101] From this point of view, Calvin asserts, "Christ our Mediator is everywhere entire, but not as to His flesh, which is confined within its own limits, while His power is infinite, and its operation felt on earth as well as in heaven."[102] According to Calvin, not only the *unitas* but also the *unio* is always and everywhere present. So he sometimes

---

98 *Last Admonition to Joachim Westphal*, *T&T* 2.468 (*CO* 9.231).
99 Ibid., *T&T* 2. 418, 457 (*CO* 9.195, 223). Cf. *Last Admonition to Joachim Westphal*, *T&T* 2.452, 465, 488-489, 465 (*CO* 9.223, 229, 246-247); *The True Partaking of the Flesh and Blood of Christ*, *T&T* 2.515 (*CO* 9.476).
100 Cf. Willis, *Calvin's Catholic Christology*, 8-25.
101 *The Best Method of Obtaining Concord*, *T&T* 2.576 (*CO* 9.520). As Willis demonstrates with reference to the thinking of Lombard, the distinction between *totus-totum* is "between Christ as the second *hypostasis* of the Trinity, the Eternal Son of God, and Christ the second *hypostasis* with what he united to himself in the Incarnation." *Calvin's Catholic Christology*, 35.
102 Comm. Jer. "To the Illustrious Prince" (1.xx, *CO* 19.75): "Christum mediatorem esse ubique integrum , sed non carnis respectu quae finibus suis continetur, quum infinita sit eius potentia et operatio in terra non minus quam in coelo sentiatur." Cf. *Inst*. 2.13.4 (*CO* 2.352): "For even if the Word in his immeasurable essence (*essentia*) united with the nature (*natura*) of man into one person (*personam*), we do not image that he was confined therein. Here is something marvelous: the Son of God descended from heaven in such a way that, without leaving heaven, he willed (*voluit*) to be born in the virgin's womb, to go about the earth, and to hang upon the cross; yet he continuously filled the world even as he had done from the beginning (*ut semper mundum impleret, sicut ab initio*)!"

uses expressions such as "the deity keeps silent" or "at rest" with reference to the biblical passages which seem to refer only to the human nature of Christ.[103]

We should remember that when Calvin discusses *etiam extra carnem*, he does so both from the connection of *unitas-unio* with reference to the second person of the Trinity and from the connection of *totus-totum* with reference to the eternal presence of the Son of God with regard to his two natures. Calvin's understanding of the continuity of the person of Christ in *etiam intra carnem* and in *etiam extra carnem* stems from his conviction that the Son of God was begotten as the Mediator from the beginning and will continue to mediate for us until our glorification by his second coming. As we see from Calvin's commentary on the Tabernacle in the Old Testament, two meanings of the body are always significantly noted. First, the body of Christ itself is the way to heaven: "He is said to have made through His body a way (*iter*) to ascend into heaven because He consecrated Himself to God in that body: in it He was sanctified to be true righteousness and in it He prepared Himself to make His sacrifice." Second, he still mediates for us in the body: "He intercedes (*intercedit*) for us in heaven because He has put on our flesh and consecrated it as a temple to God the Father and has sanctified Himself in it to make atonement for our sins and gain for us eternal righteousness."[104]

Calvin illustrates Christ's mediation *etiam extra carnem* by referring to the continual distribution of the body and blood of the risen Christ by the special work of the Holy Spirit, designated as the Spirit proceeding from Christ, that is, as the Spirit of Christ.[105] The eucharistic concept of *sursum corda* is declared for the purpose of taking account of the continual mediation of Christ for the sanctification and, ultimately, glorification of the saints.[106] Here are Calvin's words, preached on Christ's headship of the church:

---

103 Cf. Comm. Matt. 14:23 (2.151, *CO* 45.440-441); Lk. 19:41 (2.295, *CO* 45.576); Matt. 24:36 (3.99, *CO* 45.672).
104 Comm. Heb. 9:11 (120, *CO* 55.110).
105 Cf. Acts 2:33 (24, *CO* 48.47): "Utrumque enim recte dicitur, quod a se ipso miserit Christus spiritum, et a patre. A se ipso misit: quia aeternus est Deus. A patre: quia quatenus homo est, a patre accipit quod in nos transfundat. . . . quod Christus quasi inter Deum et nos medius, accepta ex patris manu dona manu sua nobis tradat." For Calvin's view of the Spirit of Christ, cf. *Inst.* 1.13.7, 2.7.2, 2.8.57, 3.1.2 (*CO* 2.94-95, 254, 307, 394-395); Comm. Jn. 14:16 (2.82, *CO* 47.329); Rom.1:4 (16-17, *CO* 49.10-11); II Cor. 3:6 (41-43, *CO* 50.39-41).
106 Jn. 17:12 (2.142, *CO* 47.382): "While He dwelt on earth He had no need to borrow power from elsewhere to keep His disciples; but all this relates to the person of the Mediator, who appeared for a time under the form of a Servant. But now He tells the disciples to raise their minds direct to heaven (*recta in coelum sensus suos attollere*) as soon as they begin to be deprived of the outward help. From this we

It is not enough then for us to come to seek in him [Christ] the supply of the good things that we lack that he may impart them to us, but in the first place, he presents himself, and says, "Here is my body which is delivered up for you, here is my blood which will be shed for the remission of your sins." And this is done in order that we should know that he dwells in us by the power of the Holy Spirit; that we live by his own substance; that it is not said here without cause that the union of the body proceeds from him (*la liaison du corps procede de luy*) and that he is its provision; and that when we lack the graces and gifts that belong to our spiritual life, we must draw them out of that fountain. And when we resort to him with perseverance in the faith of the gospel, we shall feel ourselves more and more strengthened and confirmed in all these graces, even until he has rid us of all our imperfections and infirmities so that we may enjoy his heavenly glory with him.[107]

So far, we have discussed the so-called *extra Calvinisticum*, focusing on the relevance of the principle of *totus ubique sed non totum* for Christ's mediation after the ascension in relation to the bodily presence of Christ in the Lord's Supper. Can we apply this eucharistic idea to Christ's mediation before the incarnation in Calvin's theology? A study of Christ's mediation of the law in the Old Testament in the light of the so-called *extra Calvinisticum* presents us with an insight to grasp the doctrinal foundation upon which Calvin's historical and literary interpretation of the law is based. The presence of Christ the Mediator before the incarnation is suggested most persuasively by the conception of the eternal nativity (*nativitas*) of the Son, based on the inner begetting in the Trinity.[108] From this perspective, Calvin argues for Christ's mediation according to both the divine and human natures (*Inst.* 2.14.3, *CO* 2.354-355)[109] and the

---

conclude that Christ keeps believers today no less than before, but in a different way, because divine majesty is displayed openly in Him." Cf. *Last Admonition to Joachim Westphal*, *T&T* 2.390 [altered] (*CO* 9.174): "Hence, too, we infer that whenever he says he will be present, it is by a proper attribute of Godhead. For although he adheres to his body as Mediator, yet the Spirit is the bond of sacred union, who, raising our souls upwards by faith (*sursum fide attolens*), inspires life into us from the heavenly head."

107 Serm. Eph. 4:15-16 (404, *CO* 51.592).
108 Cf. *Second Defense of the Faith Concerning the Sacraments in Answer to Joachim Westphal*, *T&T* 2.301 (*CO* 9.87-88).
109 In his book *Calvin's Catholic Christology*, Willis claims that "the primary sense of Mediator for Calvin is *Deus manifestatus in carne*. When he speaks of the Mediator, without any explicit or contextual qualifications, Calvin means the One Person formed by the *assumptio carnis*. Even in restricting 'Mediator' to this, however, Calvin is especially cautious to see that the divinity's part in the mediation

believer's union with God through his or her union with Christ. As Calvin puts it:

> Thus perfect unity (*perfecta unitas*) was taught by the Mediator: while, we remaining in him, he remained in the Father, and remaining in the Father, remained in us—thus, advancing us to unity with the Father, since while he is naturally in the Father in respect of nativity, we are naturally in him, and he remains naturally in us. That there is this natural unity (*naturalis unitas*) in us, he himself thus declared, Whoso eateth my flesh and drinketh my blood, abideth in me, and I in him (John vi. 56.)[110]

As seen here, Calvin identifies the spiritual unity with the natural unity from the standpoint of the so-called *extra Calvinisticum*.[111] It reflects his eucharistic theology as well as his stance on the presence and work of Christ as Mediator before his incarnation. From this perspective, Calvin, identifying the angel who appeared to Jacob in his dream as Christ, says that "the fact that the body of Christ is finite, does not prevent him from filling heaven and earth, because his grace and power are everywhere diffused."[112] Also, in the same vein, he asserts that "when Christ anciently appeared in human form (*forma hominis*), it was a prelude to the mystery (*praeludium mysterii*) which was afterwards exhibited when God was manifested in the flesh."[113] Although Christ was not yet the Mediator in the flesh (*carne*), "whenever he manifested himself to the fathers, Christ was the Mediator between God and them,"[114] and he revealed "a pattern (*specimen*) of his future mission."[115] There seems to be every reason to

---

is not denied" (68). In this respect, Willis continues to say, Calvin argues for Christ the Mediator "before the Incarnation even prior to and apart from the Fall" (69).
110 *The True Partaking of the Flesh and Blood of Christ*, T&T 2.540 (*CO* 9.494).
111 Cf. *Inst*. 1.13.24, *CO* 2.111: "For from the time that Christ was manifested in the flesh, he has been called the Son of God, not only in that he was the eternal Word begotten before all ages from the Father, but because he took upon himself the person and office of the Mediator, that he might join us to God."
112 Comm. Gen. 28:12 (2.113, *CO* 23.391).
113 Comm. Jos. 5: 14 (87-88, *CO* 45.464). In his book *Calvin's Catholic Christology*, Willis demonstrates his positive position on the mediation of Christ before the incarnation (68-71. 124-125). However, he does not claim the revelation—presence and representation—of the humanity of the Mediator in the Old Testament. He says, "Before the movement of the Eternal Word towards us, there was no human side of Jesus to which the Word could be added to make One Person; the human nature of Jesus had no separate existence apart from or prior to the *assumptio carnis*" (72).
114 Comm. Gen. 18:13 (1.475, *CO* 23.13).
115 Comm. Ex. 23:20 (1.404, *CO* 24.252). Cf. Comm. Ex. 3:2 (1.61, *CO* 24.35-36); Ps 132:10 (5.153, *CO* 32.347); Isa. 19:20 (2.75, *CO* 36.344); Dan. 7:13 (2.40-44, *CO* 41.59-62); Dan. 8:15 (2.111-112, *CO* 41.109-110); Matt. 28:18 (3.250, *CO* 45.821);

assume that this special emphasis on the presence of Christ the Mediator before the incarnation originates in his conviction of the spiritual but real (bodily) omnipresence of Christ throughout history.

4.5.2 "*Deus coram loquutus sit, et tamen per internuncium*"[116]: God's Accommodation and Christ's Mediation

"The teaching of the law is far above human capacity" (*Inst* 2.7.3). Human beings tend to measure their capacity by the precepts of God's law, and as a result to accommodate them to the capacity of their own will.[117] This fallacy is founded on their arrogant conviction that God *must* accommodate what belongs to him to human capacity because he is love. However, God's accommodation, as understood by Calvin, refers not so much to the precepts of the law as to God himself.[118] The precepts of some case laws in the Old Testament, which we call the tribal law of the Israelites, were given according to the capacity of the ancient people, to their barbarity, so that they did not fall into eternal death by abandoning all attempt at morality. On the other hand, the precepts of moral laws, whose nature is eternal and unchangeable, were given not according to human capacity but according to the necessity of God. In the former case, the character of God is represented by God who compromises, whereas in the latter case, God who condescends.[119]

In Ford Lewis Battles' well-known article "God Was Accommodating Himself to Human Capacity," the late church history professor and translator of the *Institutes* describes God's self-portraits as three, Father, Teacher, and Physician, for the purpose of taking account of Calvin's rhetorical use of the divine accommodation. With reference to "Physician," Battles turns to God's accommodation in Christ as he argues, "the cross of Christ is God's medicine for us."[120] Battles deals with the incarnation of Christ particularly in the last section of the article independently, calling it

---

II Tim. 1:5 (292, *CO* 52.348); Heb. 8:5 (107, *CO* 55.99); Heb. 8:6 (108, *CO* 55.99-100).

116 Comm. Deut. 5:4 (1.341, *CO* 24.211).

117 Comm. Rom. 8:3 (158, *CO* 49.138): "It is, therefore, absurd to measure human strength by the precepts of the law, as if God, in demanding what is just, had regarded the character and extent of our powers."

118 For example, God reveals "himself" as expressed as father, teacher, physician, and even God the drunkard, etc. Battles, "God Was Accommodating Himself to Human Capacity," 27-31; Wright, "Calvin's Accommodating God," 3-10.

119 Cf. Jon Balserak, "'The Accommodating Act Par Excellence?': An Inquiry into the Incarnation and Calvin's Understanding of Accommodation," *Scottish Theological Journal* 55/4 (2002), 417-421.

120 Battles, "God Was Accommodating Himself to Human Capacity," 31.

"the accommodating act par excellence."[121] There he emphasizes the accommodatory act of Christ's intermediation.[122]

Expounding I Peter 1:20 on the manifestation of the blood of Christ which was foreknown before the foundation of the world, Calvin demonstrates the character of Christ as the Mediator along with the divine accommodation.

> Since God is incomprehensible, faith can never reach to Him, unless it had immediate regard to Christ. There are two reasons why faith cannot be in God, unless Christ intervenes as a Mediator (*medius*). First the greatness of the divine glory must be taken into account, and at the same time the littleness of our capacity. Our acuteness is very far from being capable of ascending so high as to comprehend God. Hence all thinking about God without Christ is a vast abyss which immediately swallows up all our thoughts.... The second reason is that, as faith ought to unite us to God, we shun and dread every access to Him, unless a Mediator (*mediator*) comes who can deliver us from fear, for sin, which reigns in us, renders us hateful to God and Him in turn to us.... It is evident from this that we cannot believe in God except through Christ, in whom God in a manner makes Himself little (*quodammodo parvum facit*), in order to accommodate Himself to our comprehension (*ut se ad captum nostrum submittat*), and it is Christ alone who can make our conscience at peace, so that we may dare to come in confidence to God.[123]

God's accommodation is revealed by Christ's mediation by which we are taught the knowledge of God and have access to God's majesty. Further, Calvin asserts the accommodation of Christ himself for us, as he comments on Christ coming as the witness of his Father. "By distinguishing Himself from the Father He accommodates Himself to the capacity of His hearers (*se auditorum captui accommodat*). He does this for the sake of His office; for at that time He was the Father's minister, and so He asserts that the Father is the Author of all His doctrine."[124]

Calvin gives more detailed explanation on God's accommodation in Christ's mediation as he deals with his kingly office, which he believes is spiritual in nature and pertains to the perpetuity of the whole body of the church and to the immortality of each individual member (*Inst.* 2.15.3, *CO* 2.363). God's accommodating act in the mediation of Christ is seen by

---

121 Ibid., 36.
122 Ibid., 38. Peter Opitz regards Christ's mediation according to both the divine and human natures as the accommodation of the Word of God. *Calvins Theologische Hermeneutik* (Neukirchen: Neukirchener Verlag, 1994), 132-134.
123 Comm. I Pet. 1:20 (250, *CO* 55.226-227).
124 Comm. Jn. 8:17 (1.212-213, *CO* 47.194).

Calvin as relating not only to God's condescension in Christ but also to our enhancement through his [Christ's] grace. It is noted both that God "wills to rule and protect the church in Christ's person" (*Inst.* 2.15.5, *CO* 2.365) and that Christ "shares with us all that he has received from the Father. Now he arms and equips us with his power, adorns us with his beauty and magnificence, enriches us with his wealth" (*Inst.* 2.15.4, *CO* 2.364). As Calvin comments,

> Why did he take the person of the Mediator? He descended from the bosom of the Father and from incomprehensible glory that he might draw near to us. All the more reason, then, is there that we should one and all resolve to obey, and to direct our obedience with the greatest eagerness to the divine will (*nutum*)! (*Inst.* 2.15.5, *CO* 2.366).

In addition, God's accommodation means his receiving our imperfect obedience, compensating for the lack with his own merit. As Calvin states, "not rejecting our imperfect (*semiplenam*) obedience, but rather supplying what is lacking to complete it, He causes us to receive the benefit of the promises of the law as if we had fulfilled their condition" (*Inst* 2.7.4, *CO* 2.255-256).

Calvin sees the characteristic feature of Christ's mediation of the law as embodied in the law itself, whose significance as a rule of life is found not only in its precept but also in its promise. Once the promise of the law is revealed, one recognizes that it needs to be fully observed, despite the fact that it is beyond his or her ability. With this intention, Calvin cites Augustine, who says, "the usefulness of the precepts is great if free will is so esteemed that God's grace may be the more honored" (*Inst.* 2.5.7, *CO* 2.235). With regard to God's accommodation through the mediation of Christ the Mediator, it is not our capacity as such but rather our capacity to which we are converted by the proper grace of God.

The relation between Christ's mediation and God's accommodation is stated even more expressively in Calvin's commentary on Deuteronomy (29:29; 30:11-14). Expounding 29:29, "The secret things belong unto the Lord our God; but those things which are revealed belong unto us and to our children for ever, that we may do well the words of this law," Calvin comments that the reason why God set forth the doctrine openly in the law but allowed his counsel (*consilium*) to be hidden and incomprehensible (*occultum et incomprehensibilem*) was that God reveals things which are profitable to us and retains to himself secret things which neither a concern nor a profit for us. Calvin argues that the doctrine of the law itself, the rule of just and pious living (*pie iusteque vivendi regula*), is perpetual, but God sometimes makes it obscure in order to grade himself "down to the measure of our understanding (*ad modulum ingenii nostri demisit*)." In the doctrine of the law, God declares his will, which is the will accommodated to human capacity.[125]

In the commentary on Deuteronomy 30:14, "But the word is very nigh unto thee, in thy mouth, and in thy heart, that thou mayest do it," Calvin demonstrates that the divine will, accommodated to human limited capacity, is the free imputation of God's righteousness by the grace of Christ our Mediator, which is the catalyst of the gospel. This gratuitous grace is due to God's fatherly indulgence (*paterna indulgentia*) to receive our imperfect obedience pleasantly and to relax the rigorous requirement of the law.[126] Therefore, the true will of God who accommodates himself to human capacity cannot be revealed unless we are aware of Christ's mediation of the law. That is, only from the perspective of *Christus mediator legis* can we grasp God's accommodation to human capacity, sinfulness, and barbarity.[127] In the following sermon, Calvin preaches how God accommodated himself to the limited human capacity and sinfulness as the living God, whose definite revelation is described as the presence of the eternal Son of God as the Mediator.

> Because we are not yet participants in the glory of God, thus we cannot approach him; rather, it is necessary for him to reveal himself to us according to our rudeness and infirmity (*rudesse et infirmite*). The fact remains that since the beginning of the world when God appeared to

---

[125] Comm. Deut. 29:29 (1.410-412, *CO* 24.255-257). Cf. Wright, "Calvin's Accommodating God," 19: "The revealed God is always still for Calvin the partly hidden God, for all knowledge of God is accommodated knowledge—which means knowledge tailored to our measure and hence knowledge curtailed. We must make do with the prattling of God until hereafter he speaks to us face to face."

[126] Comm. Deut. 30:11-14 (1.412-414, *CO* 24.257-258). Cf. Serm. Deut. 5:28-33 (284-285, *CO* 26.417): "Now therein we are readily informed that God wills to draw us to himself, but we must not infer that men can merit anything by serving God. For the papists, when they hear passages like these, stress their merits and suppose that God is obligated to them in the same proportion. On the contrary, God clearly wishes to show us that he is ready to accommodate himself to us along human lines, that he only wants to induce us to obey him."

[127] For variable accommodation of God, see Battles, "God Was Accommodating Himself to Human Capacity," 19-38; Wright, "Calvin's Pentateuchal Criticism," 33-50, "Accommodation and Barbarity in John Calvin's Old Testament Commentaries," 412-426, "Calvin's 'Accommodation' Revisited," in *Calvin as Exegete*, ed. Peter De Klerk (Grand Rapids: Calvin Studies Society, 1995), 171-182, and "Calvin's Accommodating God," 3-19. Calvin's rhetorical use of the divine accommodation with reference to the divine discourse to the rude and ignorant people (*rudes et ignorants*) appears prominently in his sermons on Job. Cf. Millet, *Calvin et la dynamique de la parole*, 97; Balserak, "'The Accommodating Act Par Excellence'?" 415.

mortal men, it was not in order to reveal himself as he was, but according to men's ability to receive him. We must always keep in mind that God was not known by the Fathers. And today he does not appear to us in his essence (*en son essence*). Rather he accommodates himself (*s'accommode*) to us. That being the case, it is necessary for him to descend according to our capacity in order to make us sense his presence with us. . . . For if God does not reveal himself to us in as lofty a manner as our ambition requires, remember that it is for our profit and salvation that he does so.[128]

In dealing with the accommodated will of God, it should be noted that the single will of God, which is hidden and incomprehensible, is sustained in spite of its varying revelations.[129] God's accommodation to the ancient

---

128 Serm. Deut. 5:4-7 (53 [altered], *CO* 26.248). God's accommodating act is depicted more vividly and decisively in Calvin's sermons on the Ten Commandments than in his commentaries. Cf. Serm. Deut. 5:4-7 (56, *CO* 26.251, God's accommodation to our weakness); Deut. 5:8-10 (69, *CO* 26.261, God's accommodation to our "ignorance," "anger," "wrath," and "indignation"); Deut. 5:8-10 (77, *CO* 26. 267, God's accommodation to our nature, by hiding "his naked essence"); Deut. 5:11 (83, *CO* 26.271, God's accommodation in our using his name); Deut. 5:16 (135, *CO* 26.310, God's accommodation to our ignorance: He "spoke in the rough language"); Deut. 5:17 (153, *CO* 26.323: "God spoke in a gross and uncultured manner in order to accommodate himself to the great and the small and the less intelligent"); Deut. 5:17 (155 [altered], *CO* 26.324: "And seeing that he had descended so low (*est descendu si bas*), there is no one so ignorant who cannot understand what the law contains"); Deut. 5:22 (241-242, *CO* 26.387: "God has so truly accommodated (*conformé*) himself and stooped (*abbaissé*) to our smallness . . . Therefore, let us keep in mind that our Lord has not spoken according to his nature"); Deut. 5:23-27 (257, *CO* 26.397: "God accommodates himself to our lowliness and weakness (*s'accommode à nostre petitesse et infirmité*). For when it pleases him to send us his Word which must be preached to us and when we have men like ourselves who are his messengers, he therein expresses his concern for what is fitting and useful to us"); Deut. 5:28-33 (285, *CO* 26.417: "God clearly wishes to show us that he is ready to accommodate himself to us along human lines, that he only wants to induce us to obey him").
129 Concerning "the single will of God," see Wright, "Calvin's Accommodating God," 13-15, 18-19: "Condescension is the hallmark of all the dealings that God the transcendent has had with humanity. That is why the motif, or cluster of motifs, of divine accommodation takes us to the heart of Calvin's theology. . . . Yet God remains in control throughout, but at the cost of self-limitation, sometimes to such an extent that the true knowledge of God and his will is largely veiled. That is why there is uncanny similarity at times, as I said earlier, between allegory and accommodation. . . . The real truth was as much masked as exposed by the text" (18-19). Cf. Comm. Deut. 25:5-10 (3.178, *CO* 24.172): "Since we now understand the intention (*finem*) of the law, we must also observe that the word brethren does

people is the expression of God's grace given in accordance with the requirements of the age, which correspond to "the childhood of the Church (*pueritia ecclesiae*)."[130] It is for the hardness of heart of the rude and uncivilized people.[131] In particular, through the limited application of the

---

> not mean actual brothers, but cousins, and other kinsmen, whose marriage with the widows of their relative would not have been incestuous; otherwise God would contradict Himself."

130 Cf. Comm. Ex. 25:8-15 (2.154-155, *CO* 24.404-405).

131 For God's accommodation to the barbarity of the ancient people, cf. Comm. Lev. 11:2 (2.61, *CO* 24.347, on the clean animals): "Afterwards, when God imposed the yoke of the Law to repress the licentiousness of the people, He somewhat curtailed this general permission, not because He repented of His liberality; but because it was useful to compel in this way to obedience these almost rude and uncivilized people (*rudes fere et indomitos*)"; Lev. 17: 10-14 (3.31, *CO* 24.619-620, on eating blood): Calvin here points to God's accommodation to barbarity for the purpose of keeping the ancient people from falling into more aggravated barbarism, commenting that "this mode of instruction was necessary for a rude people, lest they should speedily lapse into barbarism"; Ex. 21:18-19 (3.40, *CO* 24.624, on smiting together): "Whenever . . . God seems to pardon too easily, and with too much clemency, let us recollect that He designedly deviated from the more perfect rule (*ab optima regula*), because He had to do with an intractable people (*indomabili*)"; Deut. 20:12-14 (3.53, *CO* 24.632, on making war): "It has already been stated, that more was conceded to the Jews on account of their hardness of heart (*pro cordis duritie*), than was justly lawful for them"; Num. 35:19-27 (3.65, *CO* 24.639, on "the revenger of blood himself"): "[S]ince this indulgence [of punishments by private will] was conceded on account of the people's hardness of heart (*duritiem*), God here reminds them how needful it was to provide an asylum for the innocent, because all murderers would else have been indiscriminately attacked"; Lev. 18:26-30 (3.74, *CO* 24.646, on keeping the whole statutes and judgments of God): "The exhibition of His severity, which He had referred to, might indeed have sufficed for the instruction (*erudiendos*) of His people; but in order to influence them more strongly He at the same time adduced the way pointed out to them in the law, which would not suffer them to go astray, if only they refused not to follow God"; Deut. 22: 23-27 (3.79, *CO* 24.649, on the adultery of a virgin pledged to be married): "Although . . . the terms are accommodated to the comprehension of a rude people (*ad captum rudis populi accommodatur sermo*), it was the intention of God to distinguish force from consent"; Ex. 21:7-11 (3.81, *CO* 24.650, on the fact that "the sanctity of the marriage vow" is greater than the slave covenant): "[A]lthough God is gracious in remitting the punishment, still He shows that chastity is pleasing to Him, as far as the people's hardness of heart (*durities*) permitted." Calvin here also alludes that it is God's accommodation to the barbarity of the ancient people to allow them to sell their children for the relief of their poverty (3.80, *CO* 24.650); Deut. 24:1-4 (3.93, *CO* 24.657-658, on divorcement): God did not punish divorce because the perverseness of their heart was so great that it "could not be restrained from dissolving a most sacred and inviolable tie [the bond of union between husband and wife]"; Ex. 22:1-4 (3.140, *CO* 24.687-688, on

theory of *adiaphora* to the ancient people, Calvin distinctively shows God's accommodation to the barbarity of the ancient people.

Calvin distinguishes clearly Christian freedom and its use, as he deals with the realm of *adiaphora* (*Inst.* 3.19.7-13). The core of this theory is represented by the distinctive teleological and deontological attitudes towards the use of what is allowed, i.e., the distinction between "an offense given (*scandalum datum*)" and "one received (*acceptum*)" (*Inst.* 3.19.11. *CO* 2.619).[132] It is known that Calvin's application of *adiaphora* to the use of images in the church, which is related to the second commandment, is very limited in comparison to that of Luther and Melanchthon[133] as we can see it in his commentary on the last four books of the Pentateuch, in which he claims that God accommodated to the barbarity of ancient people because of their hardness of heart and of the incompleteness of the revelation in the Old Testament era.

Regarding Leviticus 18:18, "Neither shalt thou take a wife to her sister . . . ," Calvin mentions the principle of *adiaphora* negatively with reference to its use for the ancient people. As he puts it:

> Since from long custom it is established that cousins-german (*consobrinus*) should not marry, we must beware of giving scandal lest

---

the law of restitution): "Now follow the civil laws, the principle of which is not so exact and perfect; since in their enactment God has relaxed His just severity in consideration of the people's hardness (*duritiem*) of heart"; Ex. 21:1, et al (3.160, *CO* 24.701, on the freedom of slaves in the seventh year): "[But] the tie of slavery could not only be loosed by divorce, that is to say, by this impious violation of marriage. There was then gross barbarity (*barbaries*) in this severance, whereby a man was disunited from half of himself and his own bowels. . . . The sanctity of marriage therefore gave way in this case to private right; and this defect is to be reckoned amongst the others which God tolerated on account of the people's hardness (*duritiem*) of heart."

132 Cf. Zachman, *The Assurance of Faith*, 229-243. For Calvin's Understanding of the *adiaphora*, see Edward A. Meylan, "The Stoic Doctrine of Indifferent Things and the Conception of Christian Liberty in Calvin's *Institutio Religionis Christianae*," *Romanic Review* 28 (1937), 135-145; Thomas W. Street, "John Calvin on Adiaphora: an Exposition and Appraisal of his Theory and Practice," PhD dissertation, Union Theological Seminary, 1955.

133 Calvin declares the principle of *adiaphora* with reference to the second commandment in Comm. Ex. 23:24 (2.387, *CO* 24.546): "I admit indeed that whatever tends to foster superstition should be removed, provided we are not too rigorously superstitious in insisting peremptorily on what is in itself indifferent (*medium*)." For Calvin's position on the second commandment, see James R. Payton Jr., "Calvin and the Legitimation of Icons: His Treatment of the Seventh Ecumenical Council," *ARG* 84 (1993), 222-241; Carlos M. N. Eire, *War Against the Idols: The Reformation of Worship from Erasmus to Calvin* (Cambridge: Cambridge University Press, 1986), 195-233; Zachman, *The Assurance of Faith*, 238-243.

too unbridled a liberty should expose the Gospel to much reproach; and we must bear in mind Paul's admonition, to abstain even from things lawful when they are not expedient (I Cor. 10: 23).[134]

Also, as to "objects of vow," Calvin points out that the principle of *adiaphora* is only applicable when it is legal. He says,

> [I]nasmuch as there is an intermediate degree (*medius gradus*) between that which God has expressly prescribed and forbidden, it might be objected that it was allowable to make a vow in respect to things which are called indifferent (*indifferentes*). My reply to this is, that since the principle ought always to be maintained by the godly, that nothing is to be done without faith (Rom. 14:23), it must ever be considered whether a thing is agreeable to God's word, otherwise our zeal is preposterous.[135]

Calvin uses the *adiaphora* in a strictly limited way in the interpretation of the Old Testament law, for he believes that to practise it is not yet suitable for the ancient people who are in the childlike and barbarous state. Calvin's comment on the prohibition of shaving the way the uncircumcised did, reflects how Calvin limits the use of *adiaphora* even in the realm of the indifferent, because he maintains that the ancient people were in a childlike and barbarous state; therefore the use of *adiaphora* was not suitable for them.

> The same thing was also commonly practised by others; inasmuch as the world is easily deceived by the exposure of parades. But though this were a thing in itself indifferent (*medium*), yet God would not allow His people to be at liberty to practise it, that, like children, they might learn from these slight rudiments, that they would not be acceptable to God, unless they were altogether different from uncircumcised foreigners, and removed themselves as far as possible from following their examples; and especially that they should avoid all ceremonies (*ritus*) whereby their [the uncircumcised's] religion was testified to. For experience teaches how greatly the true worship of God is obscured by anything adscititious, and how easily foul superstitions creep in, when the contrivances (*commenta*) of men are tacked on to the word of God.[136]

---

134 Comm. Lev. 18:18 (3.105, *CO* 24.665).
135 Comm. Deut. 23:21-23 (2. 414, *CO* 24.564).
136 Comm. Lev. 19:27-28 (2.51-52 [altered], *CO* 24.341). I translates the words *pomparum objectu* literally into "by the exposure of parades" in order to distinguish its meaning from that of *ritus*. Also we need to take care that the word *commenta* should be translated as "contrivances," "inventions," and "devices," etc. It should not be translated as "comments."

4.6 Conclusion

As a rule of just and godly living, the law makes us aware of our limited capacity and causes us to realize the necessity of the Mediator. Further, the law reveals the promise of the coming of Christ as the Mediator. As well as that, Christ mediates the law as the Reconciler to satisfy its demand, as the Intercessor to recover the communion between God and us by eliminating its curse, and as the Teacher to reveal its true nature.

God accommodates himself not to the natural state of people, which is totally depraved because of the fall, but to the state of people renewed by the mediation of Christ. Therefore, with respect to the law, God's accommodation to human capacity, sinfulness, and barbarity should be taken into account on the basis of the fact that Christ is the Mediator of the law.

God is subject to no necessity but that of his own plan. He is the law to himself. Therefore, he is not subject to the law either. God's will remains beyond the regulation of the law, but is not contradictory to his wisdom. In commenting on a case law on the guilt-by-association system, Calvin says,

> [S]urely our natural common sense (*communis sensus naturae*) dictates that it is an act of barbarous madness to put children to death because they hate their father. If any should object to what we have already seen, that God avenges "unto the third and fourth generation," the reply is easy, that He is a law unto Himself (*eum sibi esse legem*), and that He does not rush by a blind impulse to exercise vengeance, so as to confound the innocent with the reprobate, but that He so visits the iniquity of the fathers upon their children, as to temper extreme severity with the greatest equity (*aequitate*). Moreover, He has not so bound Himself by an inflexible rule as not to be free, if it so pleases Him, to depart from the Law; as for example, He commanded the whole race of Canaan to be rooted out, because the land would not be purged except by the extermination of their defilements; and, since they were all reprobate, the children, no less than their fathers, were doomed to just destruction. Nay, we read that, after Saul's death, his guilt was expiated by the death of his children (II Sam. 21:2), still, by this special exception, the Supreme lawgiver did not abrogate what He had commanded; but would have His own admirable wisdom (*consilio*) acquiesced in, which is the fountain from whence all laws proceed.[137]

Calvin here asserts that although some regulations of judicial case laws are not in accordance with those of natural law and moral laws, the consistency of God's will towards his people should not be denied. Even

---

137 Comm. Deut. 24:16 (3.50-51 [altered], *CO* 24.631).

the act of God, which cannot be justified by any regulation of the whole law, should be regarded as done according to God's wisdom and the great divine equity. Speaking of death in dealing with another case law, "He that smiteth a man, so that he die," Calvin comments that there is no concept of Stoic fatalism allowed, but nothing is done without God's secret counsel (*arcano Dei consilio*). God takes away life even from an innocent man according to his will without any reason comprehensible to us. God's providence, therefore, should not be philosophized (*philosophari*) according to our measure.[138] The secret counsels of God found in some cases of judicial laws and historical events are beyond our measure, but show God's will to deliver his people from eternal death and to nurture them. No other reason is suggested by Calvin, but God's accommodation to the barbarity of his people because of the hardness of their heart.[139]

Therefore, the reality and significance of God's accommodation cannot be recognized fully and definitely unless it is by the mediation of Christ. With reference to the law, God's accommodation signifies none other than Christ's mediation of the law not only for its revelation but also for its fulfilment. For Calvin, the Word denotes not only the deity of the second person of the Trinity and the divinity of the incarnate Son, but also the *hypostasis* of the Son as the Mediator, the peculiar properties (*proprietates*) of "wisdom (*sapientia*), counsel (*consilium*), and the ordered disposition (*dispensatio*) of all things" (*Inst.* 1.13.18, *CO* 2.105). The Word denotes both the essence of God and the property of the Son of God at the same time, because it is "understood as the order or mandate of the Son (*pro nutu vel mandato*), who is himself the eternal and essential Word of the Father" (*Inst.* 1.13.7, *CO* 2.95). Therefore, no secret counsel of God has been revealed in any other place but in the Word since the "hidden and inward (*arcana et interior*)" begetting of the Son before time.[140]

Christ is the substance of the law, the expression of the will of God. Also, as the Mediator, Christ reveals and accomplishes the precepts of the law. Therefore, for Calvin the *etiam extra legem* is related not so much to God's absolute will itself as to his accommodation revealed by it. Just as the revelation of God had been present by the inward begetting of the Son of God during the time before the incarnation, so Christ had been working as the Mediator even before he was manifested as the Mediator. This being so, not only God's will in the law but also God's will *etiam extra legem*—even *extra legem*—is revealed solely by the mediation of Christ the Son of God. In this respect, Calvin differentiates himself from late medieval nominalists,

---

138 Comm. Ex. 21: 12 (3.36-38, *CO* 24.622-623).
139 Comm. Ex. 21: 18 (3.39-40, *CO* 24.623-624).
140 Cf. Comm. Heb. 1:5 (11, *CO* 55.15).

who equated God's rule *extra legem* with the rule of the absolute or ordained will of God.[141]

For Calvin, Christ's mediation of the law is understood as the typical expression of God's accommodation to his people by the imputation of the grace of his Son. The nature or soul of the law is unchangeable because it reveals the eternal righteousness of God. No one can satisfy its demand, but with the grace of the Mediator, God deems our status and our works as worthwhile to receive. God lowers himself and stoops to the imperfect obedience of his people by enhancing them through the grace of his Son. Calvin explains Christ's mediation according to two natures, not by the *communicatio idiomatum*, which is based on the absoluteness of God's will, but by the principle of *totus ubique, sed non totum*.[142] From this perspective, he maintains Christ's mediation before the incarnation, even before the fall. Polish theologians such as Stancaro and Biandrata did not rightly understand the unity and continuity between the deity of the eternal Son of God and the divinity of Christ the Mediator because of their anti-Trinitarian tendency, so they could not accept Christ's mediation according to the divine and human nature.

Christ reveals the law, and the law reveals Christ. Although the emphasis of the Old Testament is more on Christ in the law and is more on the law in Christ in the New Testament, Calvin grasps these two at the same time in dealing with the relation between Christ and the law. When Christ in the law and the law in the Christ are revealed at the same time by the mediation of Christ, we can overcome the voluntarist view of *extra legem* and truly understand God's accommodation par excellence.

Although many critical theological issues on Christ's mediation of the law concentrate on the person of the Mediator in the Old Testament, Calvin's chief concern, which was shown in his debates with Stancaro and Biandrata, is rather related to its significance for the glorification of the chosen people. Calvin's concept of *Christus mediator legis* reveals the characteristic feature of the Reformation of refugees.[143] The zenith of God's accommodation is found in the fact that God sent his only Son into

---

141 For the similarity between Calvin and the late medieval theologians in their view of *extra legem* and their resort to the ordained will of God, see Oberman, "The 'Extra' Dimension in the Theology of Calvin," 256-257.

142 The principle of the bodily presence of *Christus totus-non totum* had been developed and supported by Augustine, Lombard, and Aquinas, for the purpose of eliciting the continual mediation of Christ according to two natures. However, this tendency was changed by the theologians of the medieval voluntarist circle from Duns Scotus to Gabriel Biel, who emphasized the *communicatio idiomatum* based on the absoluteness of God's will. Willis, *Calvin's Catholic Christology*, 40-43.

143 Cf. Heiko A. Oberman, "One Epoch-Three Reformations," in *The Reformation: Roots and Ramifications*, 217-220.

the world as a *viator*, like us. Christ will not reveal his glory fully until the end of his journey. Therefore, we should be careful not to fall into false humility and try to separate the divinity from Christ the incarnate. Here are the words of Calvin:

> As long as Christ sustains the role of mediator, he does not hesitate to submit himself to the Father. He does this not because his divinity had lost its rank when he was clothed in the flesh but because he could not in any other way interpose himself as intermediary between us and the Father without the Father's glory, in the present dispensation, becoming clearly visible in the person of the mediator. Nor should Christ's saying that he is less than the Father (John 14:28), a statement concerning his humanity, be referred to the whole person; neither does he unite his humanity with the Father's divinity, but links the present state with the future, in which the glory of his divinity will be perfectly revealed. Now, the entire divinity is denoted under the name of the Father, whose plenitude is in Christ (Col. 1:19; 2:9), and that not only is the distinction between the persons of the Father and the Son to be maintained, but also that admirable counsel of God by which it came about that God's only begotten Son should descend to us.[144]

---

[144] "First Response to Stancaro," 15 (*CO* 9.340-341): "quia non dubitat Christus ipse quoties mediatoris personam sustinet, patri se subiicere: non quod divinitas eius gradum suum amiserit, dum carne fuit vestita: sed quia se aliter medium inter nos et patrem interponere non potuit, quin dispensationis ordine supra ipsam mediatoris personam emineret patris gloria. Nec vero quod pronunciat Christus se patre minorem esse (Ioann, 14, 28), sic de humanitate intelligitur, quin ad totam personam spectet. Neque enim suam humanitatem cum patris divinitate confert: sed statum praesentem cum futuro, in quo manifestanda perfecte erat divinitatis suae gloria. Nam sub patris nomine hic notatur tota divinitas, cuius plenitude in Christo habitat (Col. 1, 19 et 2, 9): ut non tantum tenenda sit distinction inter patris et filii personas, sed admirabile illud Dei consilium, quo factum est ut filius Dei unigenitus as nos descenderet." Cf. Comm. I Cor. 15:27 (325-327, *CO* 548-549); *Inst.* 2.14.3 (*CO* 2.354-355); "Seconde Response to Stancaro," 152 (*CO* 9.354).

CHAPTER 5

Christ's Mediation of the Law in the Old Testament: A Pivotal Approach to Calvin and Judaism

5.1 Introduction

In this chapter, we are going to explore Calvin's Christological understanding of the law focusing on the person and work of Christ the Mediator in the Old Testament. Despite his critical position on Judaic monotheism and Jewish literal interpretation, Calvin was accused of a Judaizer by some theologians, most significantly by Servetus and Hunnius, because of his historical interpretation of the Old Testament. The following study will be devoted to verifying how Calvin interprets the Mosaic law historically yet spiritually maintaining firmly his economic-Trinitarian position in the light of the concept of *Christus mediator legis*.

5.1.1 Calvin's Criticism of "A New Judaism" of the Papists and the Anti-Judaism of the Anabaptists

Calvin's criticism of the Catholic view of the church in the *Institutes* centres specifically on its distorted formalism. He accuses the Romanists of displaying certain outward appearances (*larvae*), in a similar fashion to the Jews who boasted of temples, ceremonies, and priesthood (*Inst.* 4.2.3, *CO* 2.769). He claims that the Roman Church constitutions distort and deny the truth of the law and enslave believers by bringing Jewish vexations upon the conscience (*Inst.* 4.10.1-32, esp. 4.10.10, 30).

Calvin, passing judgement on the Catholic tonsure as an imitation of the purification of the Nazarites, rebukes the Papists as those who are raising up "another Judaism" and keep practising "the old Judaism," which the Jews were allowed temporarily by God, who "accommodated (*accommodaret*)" himself to their limited human capacity and barbarity (*Inst.* 4.19.26, *CO* 2.1085). He expresses his view of "a new Judaism" definitely in the following, as he criticizes the papal doctrine of worship, which is based on their improper discrimination between *dulia* and *latria*.

> A new Judaism (*novus iudaismus*), as a substitute for that which God had distinctly abrogated, has again been reared up by means of numerous

puerile extravagancies, collected from different quarters; and with these have been mixed up certain impious rites, partly borrowed from the heathen, and more adapted to some theatrical show than to the dignity of our religion. The first evil here is, that an immense number of ceremonies, which God had by his authority abrogated, once for all, have been again revived. The next evil is, that while ceremonies ought to be living exercises of piety (*viva pietatis exercitia*), men are vainly occupied with a number of them that are both frivolous and useless. But by far the most deadly evil of all is, that after men have thus mocked God with ceremonies of one kind or other, they think they have fulfilled their duty as admirably as if these ceremonies included the whole essence of piety and divine worship (*tota vis pietatis et cultus Dei*).[1]

Calvin further refers to the Christological significance of the sacraments by adducing the false doctrine of Catholic ceremonies, which he believes work in order to hide Christ rather than to set him forth as the substance of the sacraments (*Inst.* 4.10.14). It is the focal point of his argument that the Catholic false sacraments do not bear the promise of Christ declared by the Word of God, which is the crucial element not only regarding the sacraments set by Christ in the New Testament but also the ancient Jewish sacraments (*Inst.* 4.14.20-26). In commenting on the coat of Aaron, Calvin expresses his view against the Catholic formalism once again. He asserts that "this is the true perpetuity of the ceremonies, that they should rest in Christ, who is their full truth and substance (*veritas et substantia*)." He goes on to criticize the Papists because

> they have dared to obscure the brightness of the gospel with a new Judaism (*novo Judaismo*). They were altogether without the means of proving their priesthood, and so their easiest plan was to envelop their vanity in an immense mass of ceremonies, and, as it were, to shut out the light by clouds. So much the more diligently, then, must believers beware of departing from the pure institution of Christ, if they desire to have Him for their one and eternal Mediator.[2]

---

1 *The Necessity of Reforming the Church*, T&T 1.131-132 [altered] (*CO* 6.463). Cf. *Inst.* 2.8.33 (on the observing days of the Jews), 4.5.5 (on Jewish ceremonies and Catholic ordination), 4.10.11, 13, 14 (on Judaism and Roman constitutions on ceremonies), 4.19.26 (on the purifications of the Nazarites), and 4.19.31 (on Catholic ceremony of anointing and Jewish ceremonies).
2 Comm. Ex. 28:42 (2.205-206, *CO* 24.436).

This stance of Calvin recalls, as he puts it in the 1536 *Institutes*, that the true worship of God in divine sacraments is "to hunger for, seek, look to, learn, and study Christ alone"(4.52, *CO* 1.139; *Inst.* 4.18.20, *CO* 2.1065).[3]

On the other hand, Calvin's criticism of the Anabaptists (Catabaptists) centres chiefly on their attitude towards the validity of the Old Testament law as far as their relationship with Judaism is concerned. He regards them as the new followers of Marcion who definitely separated the law from the Gospel.[4] Calvin calls these people who insist on "soul sleep" and "celestial flesh" but deny infant baptism "certain madmen of the Anabaptist sect" in the 1539 *Institutes* (7.1, *CO* 1.802),[5] and later categorizes Servetus as a follower of this sect in the 1559 *Institutes* (2.1.10, *CO* 2.313).

In a chapter added anew in the 1539 *Institutes* called "*De similitudine veteris et novi testamenti*," Calvin declares his position on the continuity of the law succinctly but implicatively: "The covenant made with all the patriarchs is so much like ours in substance and reality that the two are actually one and the same. Yet they differ in the mode of dispensation (7.2, *CO* 1.802; *Inst.* 2.10.2, *CO* 2.313)."[6] Then he goes on to explain the three chief points of the similarity between the Old and New Testaments:

> [First] they [the Israelites] were adopted into the hope of immortality; and assurance of this adoption was certified to them by oracles, by the law, and by the prophets. Secondly, the covenant by which they were bound to the Lord was supported, not by their own merits, but solely by the mercy of the God who called them. Thirdly, they had and knew Christ as Mediator, through whom they were joined to God and were to share in his promises (1539 *Inst.* 7.2, *CO* 1.803; *Inst.* 2.10.2, *CO* 2.314).

Calvin here pointedly emphasizes the historical presence of Christ as the Mediator alive throughout the whole of salvation history. It is on this basis that he develops the dynamic relationship between the universal church, individual churches, and individuals as well as the continuity of the church and the sacramental significance of various symbols of the ancient church (4.50, *CO* 1.543; *Inst.* 4.1.2, 9, *CO* 2.747, 754). He distinctively expresses his position again in a newly added sentence in 1559 at the outset of this chapter: "the patriarchs participated in the same inheritance and hoped for a

---

3 "Unum duntaxat Christum esurire, quaerere, spectare, discere, ediscere nos oportet."
4 Cf. Tertullian, *Adversus Marcionem*, I.19, quot. W. H. C. Frend, *The Rise of Christianity* (Philadelphia: Fortress Press, 1984), 214.
5 Cf. Benjamin W. Farley, *TAL*, "Introduction," 13-35.
6 "Patrum omnium foedus adeo substantia et re ipsa nihil a nostro differt, ut unum prorsus atque idem sit; administratio tamen variat."

common salvation with us by the grace of the same mediator" (*Inst.* 2.10.1, *CO* 2.313).[7]

As we have seen, the main focus of Calvin's criticism of the Romanists is their lack of knowledge of the law in Christ, whereas, in the case of the Anabaptists is their failure to see Christ in the law. Calvin's recognition of both Christ in the law and the law in him sheds light on his stance on Jewish monotheism and Jewish literal interpretation of the law. How then does one grasp the ad-hoc significance and validity of the law from the Trinitarian point of view in Old Testament interpretation? This might have been the question that made Calvin turn to the historical presence and works of Christ as Mediator in the Old Testament and explore the concept of Christ's mediation of the law throughout the whole of salvation history *extra etiam carnem*.

5.1.2 Calvin and Veritas Hebraica

No clear evidence supports that Calvin personally met any Jewish person throughout his life.[8] The Jewish issue was not prevalent in his time, at least politically. The turmoil of Christian anti-Semitism had already settled when Calvin visited Strasbourg, the city of Bucer and Capito. In Geneva, the mass expulsion of the Jews was completed by the end of the fifteenth century.[9]

Calvin widely read Jewish literature and was very well learned in Jewish thought,[10] as demonstrated by his frequent quotations from Hebrew

---

7 ". . . patres eiusdem nobiscum haereditatis fuerint consortes, et eiusdem mediatoris gratia communem salutem speraverint, . . ."
8 Salo W. Baron assumes that Calvin may have encountered Josel of Rosheim during his visit to Frankfurt in 1539 and this chief defender of German Jewry may have been Calvin's counterpart in *Ad quaestiones et obiecta Iudaei cuiusdam responsio*. "John Calvin and the Jews," in *Ancient and Medieval Jewish History: Essays by Salo W. Baron* (New Brunswick: Rutgers University Press, 1972), 347. Gottfried W. Locher does not agree with Baron's view. "Calvin Spricht zu den Juden," *Theologische Zeitschrift* 23 (1967), 186, n. 7. On the other hand, there is an opinion that when Calvin visited Ferrara in 1535 or 1536 he might have had some contact with Jewish scholar Abraham Farissol. Phillip Sigal, *The Emergence of Contemporary Judaism*, vol. 3 (Allison Park, Pa.: Pickwick Publications, 1986), 61.
9 Cf. Robert Bonfil, "Aliens Within: The Jews and Antijudaism," in *Handbook of European History, 1400-1600*, vol. 1, *Late Middle Ages, Renaissance, and Reformation*, ed. Thomas A. Brady Jr., et al. (Grand Rapids: Eerdmans, 1994), 263-302.
10 Cf. Comm. Dan. 2:44-45 (1.185, *CO* 40.605): "I have had much conversation with many Jews: I have never seen either a drop of piety or a grain of truth or ingenuousness—nay, I have never found common sense in any Jew. But this fellow, who seems so sharp and ingenious, displays his own impudence to his great

scholars such as Ibn Ezra (1092-1167), David Kimchi (1160-1232), Rashi (1040-1105), etc., and by his erudition about the etymology of the Hebrew language.[11] In many cases, Calvin, expounding the Old Testament, refers to both Jewish and Christian sources at the same time when exploring the original meaning of a biblical term. In so doing, he prefers the Hebrew text to the Septuagint.[12]

Although not so *peritus* as Reuchlin, Calvin was quite learned in Hebrew as well as in Greek and classical Latin.[13] Simon Grynaeus and Wolfgang Capito helped him along Hebrew studies during his stay at Basel and Strasbourg.[14] Calvin was not immersed in the mystery of the Hebrew language itself, as Reuchlin had been in his work *The Miracle-Working Word*,[15] rather, he was mainly concerned with how to read the Bible in the original language with etymological, grammatical, and contextual preciseness.[16]

Calvin did not share the political concern of earlier Reformers in relation to the mass conversion and mass expulsion of the Jews.[17] The anti-Judaism

---

disgrace." Calvin here talks about Isaac Abravanel (1437-1508) whom he calls "a certain Rabbi Barbinel" (1.183).

11 E.g. Comm. Ex. 1:1-7 (1.19-24, *CO* 24.9-12). For Calvin's citation of the Rabbinical sources, see Hans-Joachim Kraus, "Israel in the Theology of Calvin—Towards a New Approach to the Old Testament and Judaism," *Christian Jewish Relations* 22 (1989), 75; Darryl Phillips, "An Inquiry into the Extent of the Abilities of John Calvin as a Hebraist," D. Phil. dissertation, Oxford University, 1998, 361-366.

12 Cf. Puckett, *John Calvin's Exegesis of the Old Testament*, 56-64.

13 Cf. Max Engammare, "*Joannes Calvinus Trium Linguarum Peritus*? La Question de l'Hébreu," *Bibliothèque d'Humanisme et Renaissance* 58/1 (1996), 35-42; Wilhelm Vischer, "Calvin, exegete de l'Ancien Testament," *Revue Réformée* 18/69 (1967), 8-11. Heiko A. Oberman appreciates Reuchlin as "the only truly *trilinguis*" among his contemporaries. *The Roots of Anti-Semitism: In the Age of Renaissance and Reformation*, tr. James I. Porter (Philadelphia: Fortress, 1984), 20.

14 For Calvin's study of Hebrew, see J. Baumgartner, *Calvin Hébraïsant et Interprète de l'Ancien Testament* (Paris: Librairie Fischbacher, 1889), 5-26; Phillips, "An Inquiry into the Extent of the Abilities of John Calvin as a Hebraist," 14-17.

15 Heiko A. Oberman, "Reuchlin and the Jews: Obstacles on the Path to Emancipation," in *The Impact of the Reformation*, 147-150. According to R. Gerald Hobbs, "Hebrew was held in high esteem throughout the Christian Middle Ages" since Augustine had claimed "the historic primacy of Hebrew, 'the primitive language of the human race'." "*Hebraica Veritas and Traditio Apostolica*: Saint Paul and the Interpretation of the Psalms in the Sixteenth Century," in *The Bible in the Sixteenth Century*, 85.

16 Engammare, "Joannes Calvinus Trium Linguarum Peritus?" 47-60. The author properly distinguishes between Calvin's ability in l'hébreu rabbinique and in l'hébreu biblique and says, "Quant à l'hébreu biblique, il est indéniable que Calvin le connaissait relativement bien" (58).

17 As Oberman observes, "the dangerous fanaticism of Christian anti-Judaism is rooted in the inability to decide between these [the] two aims of mass conversion and mass

debates in the early sixteenth century reflect the "new socio-cultural and religious entity" which had been formed since the Middle Ages.[18] The controversies between the Jewish convert Pfefferkorn and the Christian Hebraist Reuchlin and between Luther and Josel of Rosheim in the Diet of Augsburg of 1530 raised politically significant theological agendas.[19] Early writings of Luther and Sebastian Münster showed their special concern for the mass conversion of the Jews by proclaiming the truth of the Bible.[20] However, as we see from Luther's later works and Bucer's *Judenratschlag* (the Cassel Advice), as time went by the Jewish issue among Reformers became more radically political which they believed to be related to the interpretation of civil law.[21] However, on the whole, the Reformers were keen to distinguish between the political significance of anti-Semitism and

---

expulsion." "Three Sixteenth-Century Attitudes toward Judaism: Reuchlin, Erasmus, and Luther," in *The Impact of the Reformation*, 87. For the expulsion and conversion of the Jews in the Renaissance and Reformation era, John Edwards, *The Jews in Christian Europe 1400-1700* (London: Routledge, 1988), 11-65.

18 Bonfil, "Aliens Within," 276.

19 Cf. Oberman, "Reuchlin and the Jews," 141-170; Jerome Friedman, *The Most Ancient Testimony: Sixteenth-Century Christian-Hebraica in the Age of Renaissance Nostalgia* (Athens, Ohio: Ohio University Press, 1983), 69-98; Salo W. Baron, *A Social and Religious History of the Jews: Late Middle Ages and Era of European Expansion*, vol. 13, *Inquisition, Renaissance, and Reformation* (New York and London: Columbia University Press, 1969), 223-225.

20 Martin Luther, *Daß Jesus Christus ein geborner Jude sei* (WA 11.307 ff, 309 f, 314 f., 1523); Sebastian Münster, *Christiani hominis cum Judeo pertinaciter prodigiosis suis opinionibus et Scripturae violantibus interpretationibus addicto colloquium* (Basilae, 1929). Cf. Jerome Friedman, "Sebastian Münster, the Jewish Mission, and Protestant Antisemitism," *ARG* 70 (1979), 242-246; Hans J. Hillerbrand, "Martin Luther and the Jews," in *Jews and Christians: Exploring the Past, Present, and Future*, ed. James H. Charlesworth (New York: Crossroad, 1990), 129-130.

21 Martin Luther, *Wider die Sabbather an einen guten Freund* (WA 50.312-37, 1538), *Von den Juden und ihren Lügen* (WA 53.417-552, 1543), *Vom Schem Hamphoras und vom Geschlecht Christi* (WA 53.579-648, 1543), *Von den letzten Worten Davids* (WA 54.28-100, 1543); Martin Bucer, *Ob Christlicher Oberkeit gepuren muge, das die Judden under den Christen geduldet, und wo sie zůdulden, welcher gestalt und mais en Martin Bucers Deutsche Schriften*, vol. 7. ed. Rob. Stupperich (Gütersloh/Paris, 1964), 343-361. Cf. Hillerbrand, "Martin Luther and the Jews," 130-132; Baron, *Inquisition, Renaissance, and Reformation*, 225-229; Jerome Friedman, "Protestants, Jews, and Jewish Sources," in *Piety, Politics, and Ethics: Reformation Studies in Honor of George Wolfgang Forell*, ed. Carter Lindberg (Kirksville, Mo.: Sixteenth Century Journal Publishers, 1984), 140-142, and "Sebastian Münster, the Jewish Mission, and Protestant Antisemitism," 250; W. Nijenhuis, "Bucer and Jews," in *Ecclesia Reformata: Studies on the Reformation* (Leiden, E. J. Brill: 1972), 42-49. For Bucer's position on Canon Law, civil law, and their relationship with the law of God, see Christoph Strohm, ed. *Martin Bucer und das Recht* (Genève: Droz, 2002).

the significance of the Jews in salvation history.[22] For Bucer, this tendency is especially apparent. In his commentary on the Psalms, he shows favour for the Jews referring to Jewish sources from the historical and philological point of view. He also asserts, in his commentary on Romans, that there is a permanent place for Israel with respect to God's plan of salvation. Calvin was influenced significantly by Bucer's concept of "*corpus christianum*" founded on his understanding of the believer's mystical union with Christ in *De regno Christi*, rather than by his legal position on the Jews proclaimed in *Judenratschlag*.[23]

As has been noted, Calvin frequently makes Judaism a subject of discussion in dealing with Catholic formalism and the Anabaptists' Marcionite view of the Bible. He reveals his position on Judaism, though neither explicitly nor directly, as he contradicts some theologians who have denied the deity or divinity of Christ such as Caroli, Biandrata, Stancaro, and Servetus, etc.[24] More than anything else, his work *Ad quaestiones et obiecta Iudaei cuiusdam responsio* demonstrates his stance on the Jews and Judaism with lucid brevity. Throughout these cases, Calvin differentiates his position on biblical interpretation from Jewish literal interpretation, and argues how far his doctrine of the Trinity originates in Judaic monotheism. Why then was Calvin accused of being a Judaizer by Servetus in his day and by Hunnius later?

---

22 Cf. Nijenhuis, "Bucer and Jews," 49-65; Gerald Hobbs, "Martin Bucer on Psalm 22: A Study in the Application of Rabbinic Exegesis by a Christian Hebraist," in *Histoire de l'exégèse au XVIe siècle: Textes du Colloque International Tenu à Genève en 1976*, ed. Olivier Fatio and Pierre Fraenkel (Genève: Droz, 1978), 144-163.

23 Baron, *Inquisition, Renaissance, and Reformation*, 280-281; Willem van't Spijker, "Bucer's influence on Calvin: church and community," in *Martin Bucer: Reforming church and community*, ed. David F. Wright (Cambridge: Cambridge University Press, 1994), 42-43, and "The Influence of Bucer on Calvin as Becomes Evident from the *Institutes*," 106-132, esp. 129-132.

24 The radical Reformers' Jewish monotheistic tendencies motivated their critical debates with Reformers, the subjects of which ranged from the proper usage of the Hebrew alphabet to the doctrines of the Holy Supper, infant baptism, Christology, and the Trinity. Cf. George Huntston Williams, *The Radical Reformation*, 3rd ed. (Ann Arbor, Mic.: Edwards Brothers, 1992), 897-942.

5.2 Calvinus Iudaizans[25]

5.2.1 Not the Presence of the Person but the Personal Presence of Christ: Servetus' Anti-Trinitarian Christology and His Position on the Law

After he was tried by the fourteen ministers of the Genevan council in the middle of September of 1553, Servetus wrote a brief paragraph with his signature[26] and a letter to Calvin[27] in which he expressed his defiance towards the charges made against him. Servetus inserted them as a conclusion to his marginal comments on the prosecution document, a list of thirty-eight *Sententiae vel propositiones* excerpted from his writings by Calvin.[28] In this brief paragraph, Servetus reaffirmed his anti-Trinitarian position on the *hypostasis* of Christ, by indicating that no solid passage of the Scripture teaches either the invisible Son or the distinction between Father and Son.[29]

Servetus revealed this same position in the first part of the letter, but on this occasion touching the origin of his dogmatic much more fundamentally. Servetus demurred towards the Genevan Reformer:

> The main principle of which you are ignorant is that every action comes about through contact. Neither Christ, nor God Himself, acts on anything which He does not touch. Indeed, He would not be God if there were anything that escaped His contact. You dream up imaginary qualities, like the servitudes of lands. Neither the power of God, nor the grace of God, nor any such thing is in God which is not God Himself; nor does God send a quality into any part in which He Himself is not present. God, therefore, is truly in everything. He acts in everything, and He touches

---

25 The term "Judaizing" has often been used with regard to Jews who have become Christians (*conversos*) but in many cases it has represented a sarcastic and pejorative attitude of an accuser towards his or her opponent in intra-Christian polemics. Cf. Louis Israel Newman, *Jewish Influence on Christian Reform Movements* (New York: Columbia University Press, 1925), 1-4; Baron, "John Calvin and the Jews," 340-341.
26 *CO* 8.553, footnote b.
27 *CO* 8.799-800.
28 *Sententiae vel propositiones excerptae ex libris Michaelis Serveti, quas ministri ecclesiae Genevensis . . .*, *CO* 8.501-508. The refutation of Geneva ministers on these 38 charges and Servetus' responses to them together with his comments on specific parts underlined by him appear in *Brevis cavillatonum refutatio, quibus Servetus errores sibi a nobis obiectos diluere tentavit*, *CO* 8.535-554. Also, the introductory observation of the ministers appears in *Brevis refutatio errorum et impietatum Michaelis Serveti a ministris ecclesiae Genevensis magnifico senatui sicuti iussi fuerant oblata*, *CO* 8.519-522.
29 *CO* 8.553, footnote b.

everything. Everything is from Him, through Him, and in Him. When, therefore, the Holy Spirit acts in us, His deity is in us and He touches us.[30]

This passage helps us to unveil Servetan modalism and leads us to discover the radical theological divergence between Servetus and Calvin. It demonstrates that Servetus regards the presence of the unique property of each person of the Trinity as the personal appearance of the same essence (*essentia*) of God. The incarnation of Christ denotes the transformation of the human matter into God in the process of the intermingling of the deity of God with human flesh, and thus the hypostatic union (*unio*) in the person of Christ denotes the substantial unity (*substantialis unitas*) of divinity and humanity. In the same vein, the believer's union with Christ is understood as the indwelling of the deity of God in Christ by the work of the Holy Spirit.

In the latter part of the letter, following this discussion on the Trinity, Servetus pointed out another significant error of Calvin regarding the continuous validity of the law. Servetus claimed the abrogation of the law in the new era of grace when he accuses Calvin of being a Judaizer by using unleavened bread for Holy Supper.[31] The Genevan ministers strongly opposed Servetus' position on the law in the final statement of the thirty-eight charges,[32] which must have made Calvin to accuse him of being a follower of the Anabaptist sect in the 1559 *Institutes* (2.1.10, *CO* 2.313). Servetus did not accept this charge. Moreover, he criticized Calvin's position on the law claiming that it sounds like that of "some Mohammedan or pseudo-Jew."[33] It is ironical that Servetus, who was charged chiefly

---

30 Philip E. Hughes, ed. and tr., *The Register of the Company of Pastors of Geneva in the Time of Calvin* (Grand Rapids: Eerdmans, 1966), 284-285 (*CO* 8.799-800): "Hoc est principium maximum, quod tu ignoras, Omnis actio fit per contactum. Nec Christus, nec Deus ipse agit in rem aliquam quam non attingit. Imo iam nos esset ipse deus, si esset res aliqua fugiens contactum eius. Qualitates imaginarias tu somnias, quasi servitutes agrorum. Nec virtus dei, nec gratia dei, nec quicquam eiusmodi est in deo, quod non sit ipsemet deus: nec mittit deus qualitatem in partem aliquam, in qua non sit ipsemet. Est igitur vere deus in omnibus, agit in omnibus, et attingit omnia. Omnia ex ipso, per ipsum, et in ipso. Cum igitur spiritus sanctus in nobis agit, deitas ipsius in nobis est et nos tangit."

31 *CO* 8.800: "Quare vos hodie in azimis iudaizatis?"

32 *CO* 8.552: "Legem Dei sic abolet, ut cuique suus afflatus sit vivendi regula." For a detailed description of the proceedings, see R. Willis, *Servetus and Calvin: A Study of an Important Epoch in the Early History of the Reformation* (London: Henry S. King, 1877), 314-445; Richard Wright, *An Apology for Dr. Michael Servetus: Including an Account of His Life, Persecution, Writings and Opinions* (Wisbech: Printed by F. B. Wright, 1806), 126-260; Doumergue, *Jean Calvin* 6.337-345.

33 *CO* 8.694-695: "Mosaicam legem in eadem nobis qua et Iudaeis fore observatione contendis, iniuriam ei et contumeliam fieri dicens, si de eius regula sit quidquam

because of his affinity to Judaic and even Muslim monotheism, reproached Calvin for his positive interpretation of the law as Judaic.[34] In the following, I will examine whether there is any relation between Servetus' view of the continuous validity of the law and the office of Christ, the character of which is designated by him crucially with reference to his unique understanding of the person of Christ and the believer's union with Christ.[35]

The influence of contemporary Judaism and his "marrano" background upon Servetus[36] was set forth most prominently in his edition of the *Santis Pagnini Polyglot Bible* (1542), where he interpreted some of the most typical messianic passages in the Old Testament in the historical and literal sense and argued that "the literal prophetic sense refers to Christ."[37] This attitude of Servetus towards biblical interpretation was most significantly embodied in his *magnum opus*, *Christianismi Restitutio* (1553). As Jerome Friedman observes, "The rabbinic literature found in all his writings took on new meaning in the *Restitution*. Where in the past Jewish thought was used to snipe at Christian thought, Servetus was now able to incorporate this literature into his new Christian system."[38]

As noted by Doumergue, it is extremely hard to understand Servetus' position on the Trinity,[39] but it is much harder to define clearly its relation to Judaism. Although Servetus sustained his radical monotheistic view on the Trinity throughout his works, he persistently differentiated it from Judaic monotheism. In the beginning part of *De Trinitatis Erroribus* (1531), he expressed his opposition to the Jews who acknowledged Jesus but denied that he was Christ. Also, he devoted the initial part of *Dialogorum*

---

immutatum. Videor hic mihi Mahometum audire, aut pseudoiudaeum aliquem."
34 For example, Calvin criticized Servetus for his interpreting Isaiah 53 as referring to Cyrus instead of Jesus. *CO* 8.497: "Quia singulis excutiendis tempus non dabatur: in primis obiectum est caput Iesaiae LIII cuius perspicuitas quum Iudaeis quamlibet impudentibus ansam calumniandi praeciderit, his falsarius ausus est ad Cyrum torquere." For the Jewish background of Servetus' doctrine of God, see Newman, *Jewish Influence on Christian Reform Movements*, 572-588.
35 The several epistles of Servetus "elaborate this anti-Mosaic tendency on the part of the anti-Trinitarian." Newman, *Jewish Influence on Christian Reform Movements*, 592.
36 Jerome Friedman, *Michael Servetus: A Case Study in Total Heresy* (Genève: Droz, 1978), "Glossary," 144. For Jewish elements in Servetus' early career, see Newman, *Jewish Influence on Christian Reform Movements*, 511-519.
37 "Michael Villanovatus to the Reader," in Wright, *An Apology for Dr. Michael Servetus*, 310-312 (quot. 303).
38 Friedman, *Michael Servetus: A Case Study in Total Heresy*, 12-13, esp. 13.
39 Doumergue, *Jean Calvin*, 6.224.

de Trinitate (1532) to the argument that the Logos and Elohim and Christ were one and the same.[40]

With reference to the person of Christ, Servetus clearly opposed Judaic monotheism in his comments on some parts of the selected passages and groups of passages from Tertullian, Irenaeus, and the supposed *Epistula Petri* prefaced to the Pseudo-Clementine *Homilies*.[41] Referring to Tertullian's *Against the Jews* and Irenaeus's *Concerning the Human Person of the Word*, Servetus argued that he who spoke to Abraham, Aaron, and Moses in the shape of man was the Son of God (*filium dei*), the Word of God (*verbum dei*), Jesus himself (*Iesus Ipse*), the man Jesus Christ (*homo Iesus Christus*) who was visible (*visibilis*).[42] Servetus claimed again, commenting on the apostle Peter, that the true prophet Jesus who appeared to Moses and struck the Egyptians was the Word of God, the personal Son (*personalis filius*), the man Jesus Christ (*homo Iesus Christus*).[43]

In dealing with the presence of the Son of God, especially in the Old Testament, throughout the passages from the early fathers, Servetus was concerned mainly about the meaning of the term *persona*, which he believed to denote *personalis repraesentatio*[44] or *Christi facies iam hypostatice relucens*.[45] He interpreted John 1:1, "In the beginning was the Word," as "there was a proclamation in the deity representing (*repraesentans*) Jesus Christ."[46] The true form of the man Jesus Christ (*forma vera hominis Iesu Christi*),[47] the visible person (*persona visiblis*) of the Son in the Word, which is his true hypostasis (*subsistentia vera*), is permanent and unchangeable.[48] Servetus was accused by the Genevan ministers of claiming that Christ, the Son of God, was eternal in the very

---

40 *Erroribus* 2a ff. *Dialogorum* A2a ff. Michael Servetus, *The Two Treatises of Servetus on the Trinity*, tr. Earl Morse Wilbur (Cambridge, Mass.: Harvard University Press, 1932, hereafter Wilbur), 6 ff., 189 ff.

41 "Ex Tertulliano," "Loci ex Irenaeo, de humana Verbi persona," and "Loci ex Petro apostolo et Clemente discipulo," *CO* 8.507-515. The refutation of Genevan ministers on these passages, *CO* 8.522-535. For Servetus' use of Irenaeus in his doctrine of Tertullian, compared with that of Tertullian, see David F. Wright, "Calvin and Servetus in Dispute over Irenaeus," 1-21, forthcoming from the Center for Reformation Studies, Emanuel University of Romania.

42 *CO* 8.508, 512. In translating the documents of the proceedings (*CO* 8.501-553), I consulted Hughes' translation (*The Register*, 233-285), along with the translation of the 38 final articles and Servetus' replies presented by Willis (*Servetus and Calvin*, 406-417) and Wright (*An Apology*, 181-201).

43 *CO* 8.514.
44 *CO* 8.507.
45 *CO* 8.509.
46 *CO* 8.512.
47 *CO* 8.510.
48 *CO* 8.511, 513-514.

flesh which was visible and resplendent.⁴⁹ Therefore, the incarnation of Christ signifies "the same face of Christ through which God was seen is now seen."⁵⁰

This view was different not only from Judaic monotheism because of acknowledging the presence of the Son of God, but also from the traditional doctrine of the Trinity because he identified the personal (*personalis*) presence of Christ with the presence of the person (*persona*) of Christ. His own Trinitarian view was manifest most predominantly in his response to the first charge of the *Sententiae vel Propositiones*: "In the essence and unity of God there is no real distinction of three invisible entities. But there is a personal distinction between the invisible Father and the visible Son."⁵¹ Servetus persistently sustained his conviction of the *non realis sed personalis* distinction in the Trinity throughout the process of the trial and in his last words,⁵² and when he was finally burnt on the fire, his prayer, in spite of Farel's exhortation for his conversion, reflected his conviction. "Jesu, Thou *Son of the eternal God*, have compassion upon me!" He would never confess Jesus Christ as *the eternal Son of God*.⁵³

Servetus disapproved of the doctrine of the eternal deity of Christ. "From the beginning Jesus Christ was man with God in his own person and substance."⁵⁴ Servetus explaining the incarnation points out that "the one and same deity of the Father was communicated to the Son Jesus Christ immediately and corporeally."⁵⁵ He also asserted that the body of Christ is different from ours because he received into his body the body of God, the

---

49 *CO* 8.532: ". . . Christi caro aeterna fuerit in idea relucente."

50 *CO* 8.512: ". . . eandem faciem Christi per quam Deus visus est, et nunc videtur"; *CO* 8.522: "Nam si visus est semper filius, necesse est semper fuisse filium."

51 *CO* 8.515: ". . . in ipsa Dei essentia et unitate non esse realem trium invisibilium rerum distinctionem. Sed personalem esse invisibilis patris et visibilis filii distinctionem." Servetus continues to express his conviction that in this way the Trinity is most piously (*sanctissime*) believed. Based on this confession of Servetus, Castellio upbraided Calvin for his religious intolerance. "Contra libellum Calvini in quo ostendere conatur haereticos iure gladii coercendos esse," in Roland H. Bainton, *Concerning Heretics . . . An anonymous work attributed to Sebastian Castellio* (New York: Morning Side Heights, 1935), 286.

52 Cf. "Michael Servetus' Speech before he was burnt at Geneva, concerning the true knowledge of God and his Son," in Wright, *An Apology for Dr. Michael Servetus*, 244-255.

53 Willis, *Servetus and Calvin*, 484, 487; Roland H. Bainton, *Hunted Heretic: The Life and Death of Michael Servetus 1511-1553* (Boston: Beacon Press, 1953), 214.

54 *CO* 8.502: "Iesum Christum hominem ab initio apud Deum fuisse in propria persona et substantia."

55 *CO* 8.504: "Unam et eandem deitatem quae est in Patre communicatam fuisse filio Iesu Christo immediate et corporaliter."

element uncreated (*elementum increatum*).[56] On this ground, since Servetus believed that the presence of the deity of God in the Son denotes the existence of the substantial and personal Son, which he identifies with the person of Christ, he claimed that "from eternity God produced this Son from His own substance."[57]

Just as in the case of the use of the term *persona*, Servetus understood the *hypostasis* of the Son of God as denoting a visible appearance (*visibile spectrum*) of that which hypostatically subsists in God (*id quod in Deo hypostatice subsistit*), which he regarded as the true substance (*vera substantia*) of God.[58] Therefore, for Servetus, each person of the Trinity is differentiated from the others not by its peculiar *hypostasis*, the unity (*unitas*) of person, but by the hypostatical union (*unio*). Servetus regards the conception of the unity of person separated from the personal union as imaginary and merely speculative. In response to the Genevan ministers who differentiated union from substantial unity, Servetus claimed:

> Wherever there is substantial union there is unity. Just as the rational soul and the flesh is one man, so God and man is one Christ.[59]

Accordingly, the incarnation is nothing else than the transformation (*transformatio*) of the human matter into God and the intermingling (*immiscere*) of the created human element and the uncreated divine element, which I previously mentioned.[60]

In dealing with the person of the Holy Spirit, Servetus maintains that the union between the divine and human breath of the soul (*halitus animae*) of Christ is the unity of the Holy Spirit.[61] He denies the existence of the hypostasis of the Holy Spirit before the advent of Jesus Christ. Just as he understands the person of Christ as *hypostasis visibilis*, so he understands

---

56 *CO* 8.504: ". . . in Christo esse [elementa] creata et increata, et substantiam Spiritus Dei, ipsi carni substantialiter communicatam."

57 *CO* 8.516: "Deum de sua substantia ab aeterno protulisse filium hunc."

58 *CO* 8.517, 546. Cf. *CO* 8.505 (XXV).

59 *CO* 8.545: "Ubicunque est substantialis unio, ibi est unitas: sicut anima rationalis et caro unus est homo, ita Deus et homo unus est Christus." Cf. Servetus, *Restitutio* 16: "Christus vero est naturali nativitate Deus, naturaliter genitus de substantia Dei. Tota patris deitas, adoratio Dei, et visio Dei, est in Christo vero Deo"; ibid., 702: "Nam incorporea et invisibilis illa res, quae vobis est filius, non est vere mortua: id vero corpus, quod re ipsa mortuum est, vobis non est filius."

60 *CO* 8.504: "Rorem illum coelestem virgini obumbrantem, et semini eius et sanguini sese immiscentem transformasse in Deum humanam materiam." In responding to this, Servetus argues that "Transformatio est ibi glorificatio et illustratio" (CO 8.517). Cf. *Dialogorum* B6a (Wilbur 209): "Quid aliud est incarnationis mysterium quam hominem Deo miscere?"

61 *CO* 8.503. Cf. *CO* 8.504 (XXI).

the person of the Holy Spirit as *hypostasis perceptibilis*.[62] Servetus distinguishes the Holy Spirit of Christ from the spirit of deity (*spiritus deitatis*) which was implanted in all things from the beginning.[63]

As was seen in the first part of the letter which Servetus inserted at the end of the document of the proceedings, he was convinced of the indwelling of the deity of God in all creatures. Based on this seemingly neo-Platonic and even pantheistic view, Servetus argues for the existence of the substantial deity (*deitas substantialis*) in angels and in the elect from the beginning.[64] He asserts that in the law, just as the Word represented the visible Son in deity, so the angels, which are resplendent, foreshadowed Christ.[65] Servetus turns to the hypostatic union between the soul and the body in order to explain the believer's union with Christ. In the passage cited earlier from the apostle Peter, Servetus maintains that when God made man, he implanted his divinity in us.[66] In the following opinion of the Genevan ministers this position of Servetus is expressed more definitely: "both our soul and the Holy Spirit of Christ have an elementary substance essentially joined to themselves, just as the Word has flesh joined to himself."[67]

In conclusion we can say that it is not from the hypostatic union (*unio*) between the divine and human nature of the person (*persona*) of Christ but from the substantial unity (*unitas substantialis*) of the deity (*deitas*) of Christ[68] that Servetus argues for the continuity between the Word and *Deus manifestatus in carne* claiming that there is no unique property (*proprietas*) of Christ which designates the second person of the Trinity but the peculiar appearance of "the Son of the eternal God."[69] This position was

---

62 *CO* 8.505, 517.
63 *CO* 8.506: "Omnibus insitum esse ab initio spiritum deitatis ex Dei halitu." Cf. *CO* 8.516: "Christus in se una persona est, sed in eo est vere spiritus sanctus, qui etiam persona est."
64 *CO* 8.506 (XXXIII, XXXIV). Ernst Wolf calls this position of Servetus "spiritualistisch-pantheistische Verbum-Spiritus-Christologie." "Deus Omniformis: Bemerkungen zur Christologie des Michael Servet," in *Theologische Aufsätze: Karl Barth zum 50. Geburstag* (München: Chr. Kaiser Verlag, 1936), 464.
65 *CO* 8.506: ". . . nunquam fuisse in lege Deum vere adoratum, sed angelos adumbrantes Christum adoratos fuisse." For the origin of the office of angels, cf. *Dialogorum* A5c-d (Wilbur 195-196).
66 *CO* 8.514: "Deus quum fecisset hominem ad imaginem et similitudinem suam, . . . esse nobis insitam divinitatem, . . ."
67 *CO* 8.506: ". . . et animam nostram, et ipsum Christi Spiritum sanctum sibi essentialiter iunctam habere eiusmodi elementarem substantiam, sicut Verbum sibi iunctam habet carnem."
68 Cf. *Dialogorum* A2b (Wilbur 190): ". . . eandem esse hodie in carne Verbi substantiam"; Wolf, "Deus Omniformis," 457.
69 *Dialogorum* A3a (Wilbur 190): "Ut probarem quod Verbum illud sit ipse Christus,

predominant from his early works on the errors of the Trinity. Servetus says,

> the Word was in the law as a prefiguring of Christ; the Word was the shadow, and Christ is the truth. John, both in his Gospel and in his Epistle, says of the Word, was; but now, after its being manifested, there is no such Word but the very being itself of which the Word was a type. For we never read of the Word, is, but, was. But now there is the Son, Jesus Christ, because what was in the Word exists as flesh, and the Word became flesh; that is, the Person became a being (*persona facta est res*), the shadow became light, as Paul says, Our glorifying became truth; that is, just as we gloried in the Word, so it was in fact. The Word, which was in the law as a shadow, was given through Moses; truth came through Christ. There was then a Word concerning the being which now is; that is, the being itself did not exist, but there was a Word concerning it, like a conversation about an absent being, which was then being represented by the Word.[70]

We cannot find here any room for the mediatorship of Christ in the Old Testament because Servetus does not approve of the presence of Christ who is true God and man, even though he admits that the substantial deity already existed not only in the soul but also in the body of Christ.[71] He did not accept that the law itself had already revealed the presence of Jesus Christ as the Mediator in addition to its representing his future coming.[72]

---

dicebam Logon et Elohim idem fuisse." Cf. *Dialogorum* B4a (Wilbur 206): "Christ came forth into the world not after the manner of creatures, but being conceived by the Holy Spirit, being brought forth not out of nothing, but out of the very *hypostasis* of God, and being born of God's Substance through the Substance of the Word incarnate and made flesh (*ex ipsa Dei hypostasi eductus, et ex Dei substanatia genitus, per incarnatam et carnem factam Verbi substantiam*)."

70 *Erroribus*, 93a (Wilbur 143-144): ". . . quod Verbum illud erat in Lege, Christi praefiguratio, Verbum illud erat umbra, et Christus est veritas. Ioannes tam in Evengelio quam in epistola de Verbo dicit, erat, nunc autem post manifestationem, non est tale Verbum, sed res ipsa, cuius illud Verbum erat typus, nunquam enim de Verbo illo legimus, est, sed erat, nunc autem est filius Iesus Christus, quia id quod erat in Verbo, caro extitit, et Verbum caro factum est, id est, persona facta est res, umbra facta est lux, sicut dicit Paulus, gloriatio nostra, veritas facta est, id est, ita fuit in re, sicut fuimus Verbo gloriat. Verbum quod in lege erat, umbra factum est veritas. Sicut subdit, Lex, id est, umbra per Moysen, veritas per Christum, de re quae nunc est, tunc erat Verbum, id est, non erat res ipsa, sed de ipsa Verbum, tanquam de re absente sermo, quae eo Verbo tunc praesentabatur, . . ."

71 *CO* 8.502: "Non solum in anima, sed et in carne Christi est substantialis deitas."

72 Cf. *Dialogorum* A3a (Wilbur 190): ". . . quicquid in lege visum est, umbram vocare, ut corpus, id est, veritas ipsa sit Christi."

For Servetus, the word *persona* does not signify an entity as *hypostasis* but rather reveals the form or disposition of a personal entity. Accordingly, the person of Christ is understood only as its visible revelations, which advanced in history. As he puts it, "The different mysteries of Christ are threefold; before the incarnation in a shadow, in the incarnation in infirm body, after the resurrection in glory and power."[73] Just as the Word that was (*erat*) in the law (*in lege*) disappeared with the advent of Christ, so the law of Moses was abolished by its fulfilment in Christ.

Servetus outlined his quite negative and dispensational view of the law in a series of letters he wrote to Calvin in 1546-1547. He regarded the Mosaic Law as given to serve its temporal office to meet the needs of the ancient barbarity[74] and was annulled when it was fulfilled by Christ just as the ancient covenant came to its end by the proclamation of the new covenant in Jeremiah 31.[75] The whole law of Moses, including the Decalogue, was abolished with the coming of the new era in which the work of the Spirit of Christ prevails.[76] Even people who are justified by the living faith are led to Christ without any knowledge of the law, and now natural law compensates for the role of the law to reveal sin.[77] In treating the

---

73 *Restitutio* 457, tranlation from Friedman, *Michael Servetus: A Case Study in Total Heresy*, 65: "Triplex est differentia mysteriorum Christi, ante incarnationem in umbra, per incarnationem in corporis infirmitate, post resurrectionem in gloria et potentia."

74 *Epistola* 25, *CO* 8.702: "Mosaica lex, ut tu censes, erat lex inertibus saxis data, lex irrationalis, lex impossibilis, tyrannica. Ita miseros et rudes populos, te iudice, in equuleo exercebat tunc Deus, sicut tyrannus Diomedes in lecto ferreo, ut equis essent in pabulum."

75 *Epistola* 23, *CO* 8.699: ". . . Nihil ergo nunc damnationis est nobis insitis Christo Iesu, vero libertatis assertori, qui a lege decalogi, quae erat lex peccati et mortis, nos liberos reddidit. Etenim quod lex illa praestare non poterat, ipse praestitit, legem ipsam nos destruentem tollens. Adde adhuc locum unum, ut omnino cognoscas, decalogi legem nunc esse sublatam. Foedus initum cum patribus, quando egrediebantur de Aegypto, sublatum docet Ieremias cap. 31. Hoc autem fuit foedus decalogi."

76 *Epistola* 23, *CO* 8.697: "Absque lege illa decalogi, per quam erat cognitio peccati, ut ibi ait, chirographum nobis contrarium per decreta Christus delevit (Coloss. 2). Chirographus mandatorum dicitur decalogus digito Dei scriptus. Chirographus est, quo scripto obligamur ad aliquid faciendum, et contrarius est nobis, quando transgredimur. Tota ergo lex scripta Iudaeis erat chirographus nunc sublatus."

77 *Epistola* 23, *CO* 8.698: ". . . quamdiu viva fide ei credimus. Ex hac sola fide poterat quis iustificari, etiam ignorans legem Mosis. Sunt qui decalogi vim sustinent, moralia dicentes esse leges naturae perpetuas. Quibus illud obiicimus: Quod ex natura perpetuum est, non est ex Mose, quum fuerit ante Mosen. Si haec naturae dictamina dicas, non dabis eis vim legis maledicentis, quum nesciretur maledictio talis, nisi per legem, nec ira talis, nisi per legem. Sublata ergo est lex, et nos non sumus sub lege, nec sub eius ira."

annulment of the law, Servetus especially emphasizes the universal work of the Spirit of Christ, and on this basis he asserts that the spiritual norm of Christ supersedes the teaching of the law of Moses.[78] Servetus differentiates the doctrine of the Spirit, which he calls *lex Christi*, *lex spiritus*, and *lex fidei*, from the doctrine of the law.[79] In explaining the unique feature of the new law of Christ, he turns to his own understanding of the union with Christ, which, as we have seen, is founded on his view of the hypostatic union that signifies the substantial unity between the humanity of the believer with the deity of Christ.[80]

5.2.2. Aegidius Hunnius' Critique

As we have seen, Servetus' criticism of Calvin's Judaic interpretation of the law was founded on his peculiar understanding of the progress of revelation, which was derived from his dispensational Christology based on the concept that *"persona facta est res."* On the whole, however, with reference to the Trinity and the person of Christ, Servetus accused Calvin of denying the deity of the soul implanted in all creatures along with Simon Magus[81] and following the merely speculative papist Trinity.[82]

On the other hand, the Lutheran theologian, Aegidius Hunnius (1550-1603), criticized Calvin's position on Christ in the Old Testament claiming that it was Judaic.[83] His criticism of Calvin's exegesis reached its climax in

---

78 *Epistola* 23, *CO* 8.699: "Imo scopus eius est, sublatam esse legem, ut initio capitis praemittit, legem decalogi semper intelligens, et de ea exemplum dans. Ex lege illa, sicut ex caeremoniis, nobis nunc superest spiritualis ratiocinatio. Superest cognitio impleti mysterii, et cognitio peccati: quam etiam cognitionem uberiorem in nobis facit nunc spiritus sanctus universaliter docens, omnia opera carnis esse peccata. Non solum legis illius scriptae vim et iugum sustulit Christus: sed et contra legem hanc peccati, quae est membris nostris innata, validum dedit mortificationis spiritus auxilium."

79 *Epistola* 24, *CO* 8.701.

80 *Epistola* 24, *CO* 8.702: "Ut autem melius intelligas, in hac spirituali Christi doctrina non esse illud vinculum, nec servitutis praeceptum, sed liberaliter oblatam gratiam, et coeleste donum: perpende totum adventus Christi evangelicum gaudium et laetitiae nuncium a lege procul distinctum. . . . Docentur regenerari ex aqua et spiritu sancto: alioqui extra regnum manere. Docentur carnem et spiritum mortificare. Docentur diligere, et in coena Christi communicare, ut cibo coelesti servent vitam coelestem."

81 *CO* 8.514, 515, 518 (XXX, XXXV), et passim.

82 *CO* 8.507. Cf. *Restitutio* 670: "Whoever truly believes that the pope is Antichrist, will also truly believe that the papist Trinity, paedobaptism and other sacraments of the papacy are the doctrines of demons." I owe the citation to Wright, "Calvin and Servetus in Dispute over Irenaeus," 8.

83 Calvin in his letter to Farel in April 1539 claimed that the Lutheran attitude towards ceremonies "was not far from Judaism (*non procul esse a iudaismo*)." *CO* 10/2.340.

his tract, *Calvinus Iudaizans* (1593),[84] which was written in response to the Reformed theologian David Pareus (1548-1622).[85] Here the Wittenberg theologian revealed the errors of Calvin's anti-Christological interpretation of some of the verses which contain Messianic prophecies claiming that they reveal the influence of Judaism upon him.[86]

Hunnius' criticism starts with Calvin's interpretation of the word Elohim in Genesis 1:1. He claims that Calvin understands the plural form of the word not as describing the three persons (*personas*) in God, but as signifying "those powers (*virtutes*) which God put forth (*exseruit*) in creating the world."[87] Calvin believes that since Genesis 1:2 clearly refers

---

84 Aegidius Hunnius, *Calvinus Iudaizans, Hoc est: Iudaicae Glossae et Corruptelae, quibus Iohannes Calvinus illustrissima Scripturae sacrae loca et Testimonia, de gloriosa Trinitate, Deitate Christi, et Spiritus sancti, cum primis autem vaticinia Prophetarum de Adventu Messiae, nativitate eius, passione, resurrectione, ascensione in caelos, et sessione ad dextram Dei, detestandum in modum corrumpere non exhorruit. Addita est corruptelarum confutatio* (Wittenberg: Vidua Mattaei Welaci, 1593). The text I use here is Aegidius Hunnius, *Calvinus Judaizans, Opera Latina*, vol. 2 (Frankfurt a. M.: Impensis Iohan. Iacobi Porsij Bibliopolae, 1608), cols. 635-690. *Calvinus Iudaizans* comprises two parts. In the first part the author is concerned mainly with Calvin's anti-Trinitarian view revealed in his exposition of the word Elohim in the Old Testament. The second part is devoted chiefly to proving the errors of Calvin's Judaic literal interpretation of Old Testament prophecies concerning "vaticinia de Nativitate et adventu Messiae" (654.b-), "vaticinia de passione et morte Christi" (664.c-), and "vaticinia Prophetarum de gloriosa resurrectione Christi ex mortuis" (677.d-690.c).

85 Aegidius Hunnius, *Articulus de Trinitate, per quaestiones et responsiones pertractatus solide, et indubitatis testimoniis sacrarum literarum contra quamvis haereticorum veterum et recentium blasphemas strophas et corruptelas firmissime communitus* (Frankfurt a. M.: Johannes Spies, 1589); David Pareus, *In Quartam Explicationum Catecheticarum Partem, De Gratitudine, Praefatio, in Miscellanea Catechetica* (Johannes Tornaesius, 1622), 177-193. Pareus' response to Hunnius' *Calvinus Judaizans* is found in *Libri Duo: I. Calvinus Orthodoxus de Sacrosancta Trinitate: et de aeterna Christi Divinitate. II. Solida Expositio XXXIIX. Difficillimorum Scripturae Locorum et Oraculorum: et de recta ratione applicandi Oracula Prophetica ad Christum. Oppositi Pseudocalvino Iudaizanti nuper a quodam emisso* (Neustadt: Matthaeus Harnisch, 1595). For other works related to Hunnius-Pareus debates, see David C. Steinmetz, "The Judaizing Calvin," in *Die Patristik in der Bibelexegese des 16. Jahrhunderts*, ed. The author (Wiesbaden: Harrassowitz, 1999), 135 (n. 2), 136 (n. 6); Ken Schurb, "Sixteenth-Century Lutheran–Calvinist Conflict on the Protevangelium," *Concordia Theological Quarterly* 54/1 (1990), 44-45, n. 15.

86 Cf. Baumgartner, *J. Calvin Hébraïsant et Interprète de l'Ancien Testament*, 37-39; Puckett, *John Calvin's Exegesis of the Old Testament*, 4-7; Steinmetz, "The Judaizing Calvin," 138-139; Schurb, "Sixteenth-Century Lutheran-Calvinist Conflict on the Protevangelium," 33 ff.

87 In *CTS*, the word "*exseruit*" is translated as "exercised." The translator may have

to the third person of the Trinity (the Spirit of the Elohim), if we suppose three persons to be here denoted, we will involve ourselves in the error of Sabellius, for "it will follow, both that the Son is begotten by himself, and that the Spirit is not of the Father, but of himself." Thus Calvin asserts that the plural form of Elohim in the first verse denotes not so much the three persons of God as the working of God's power "included in his eternal essence (*essentia*)."[88]

Criticizing Calvin's view, Hunnius says, "Indeed the fact that that name Elohim is sometimes given to each person individually is sought only from a sort of *rei ratio* which is no other than from the mystery of the beatific Trinity." He demonstrates here emphatically his immanent Trinitarian position.[89]

Also, as regards the repetitive use of the word "the Lord" ("*Jehova . . . a Jehova*") in Genesis 19:24, Calvin comments that the repetition is "emphatic (*emphatica*)" and in both cases the word *Jehova* denotes "the Deity of Christ," which is different from the interpretation of the Jews. Here Calvin is concerned with God who acts by the hand of his Son and with the significance of the Scripture in the historical context. He says that "the design of Moses" to repeat the same word "was to raise the minds of the readers to a more lively contemplation of the hand of God."[90] As expected, Hunnius accuses Calvin of ignoring that this repetition indicates "the argument of proving the Trinity, that there are plural persons within God."[91]

Hunnius again criticizes the way Calvin interprets "Elohim" in his commentary on Genesis 35:7. Calvin claims that his interpretation is consistent with "a higher doctrine (*superior doctrina*)" manifest in Genesis 28:12, in which he comments on the ladder as "the symbol (*symbolum*) of

---

confused it with *exercuit*. Hunnius' criticism reminds us of Calvin's criticism of Judaism: "the Jews [who] turned their backs and made the name Elohim fit also the angels and the powers (*potestates*)" (*Inst.* 1.13.9, *CO* 2.96).

88 Quotations from Comm. Gen. 1:1 (1.71-72, *CO* 23.15). Cf. Richard Stauffer, *Interprètes de la Bible: Études sur les Réformateurs du XVIe* (Paris: Éditions Beauchesne: 1980), 76-77. The Old Testament scholar Hengstenberg basically follows Calvin's interpretation of the word Elohim. Comm. Gen. 1:1 (1.72, n. 1).

89 The text, including the passage I quote, is: "Quod vero nomen illud Elohim, interdum uni singulatim personae tribuitur, petitur huiusce quoque rei ratio non aliunde, quam ex illo beatae Trinitatis arcano. Pater Elohim dicitur, quia non solitarie Deus est sine Filio, Spirituque Sancto, sed una cum his, adeoque in Trinitate Deus est: ita ut vox Elohim in hoc quoque personali significatu respectum mutuum illum pluralitatemque divinarum hypostasewn involuat. Unde fit, ut πρώτως personis simul iunctis, secundario autem personis singulis exposito tam sensu atque modo attribuatur." Hunnius, *Calvinus Iudaizans*, col. 638b-c.

90 The quotations above are from Comm. Gen. 19:24 (1.512-513, *CO* 23.277-278).

91 Hunnius, *Calvinus Iudaizans*, col. 639d: ". . . argumentum probandae Trinitatis, quod nimirum in Deo plures sint personae, . . . "

Christ," who is "the only Mediator."[92] This is Hunnius' comment: "It is clearly obvious that Calvin unjustly by his gloss robs this testimony of its proof of the Holy Trinity against the Jewish people."[93]

In the following we are going to look at why Hunnius called Calvin a Judaizer. In his commentary on Genesis 3:15, Calvin interprets the word "וזרעה (her seed, *semen mulieris*)" not as a singular noun referring to Christ, but as a collective noun (*nomen collectivum*) referring to the people of God.[94] Calvin does not deny that ultimately the phrase denotes the coming of Christ as Saviour and as head of the church, but he tries to point out the fact that the promise has been handed down through the ages.[95] He believed that the woman's seed could be interpreted according to three stages of history as: all men (against snakes), all men (against the devil), and Christ as the victor of all men (i.e., the head of the church).[96] Calvin emphasizes "our" victory through the victory of Christ on the ground of the continuity of the church in the Old and New Testaments. In contrast with Calvin, Hunnius asserts that the promise refers to only one seed, who is Christ, as was promised to Abraham later on.[97]

Referring to Micah 5:2, "But thou, Beth-lehem Ephratah, though thou be little among the thousands of Judah, yet out of thee shall he come forth unto me that is to be ruler in Israel; whose goings forth have been from of old, from everlasting," Hunnius declares the eternal generation and essence of Christ, and the two natures in the person of Christ.[98] And he cites and rejects Calvin's commentary on this verse:

> Some, I know, pertinaciously maintain, that the Prophet speaks here of the eternal essence (*essentia*) of Christ; and as for myself, I willingly own that the divinity (*divinitatem*) of Christ is here proved to us; but as this will never be extorted from the Jews, I prefer taking the words simply as they are—that Christ will not come forth unexpectedly (*repente*) from Bethlehem, as though God had previously determined nothing respecting him. But others bring a new refinement,—that the Prophet uses the plural

---

92 Comm. Gen. 35:7 (2.237-239, CO23.468-469); Gen. 28:12 (2.112-114, *CO* 23.390-392).

93 Hunnius, *Calvinus Iudaizans*, col. 640d: ". . . luculenter apparet, immerito Calvinum hoc testimonium, probandae contra Iudaeos sacrosanctae Trinitatis, glossa futili sua enervare."

94 For the debate between Hunnius and Pareus over Genesis 3:15, see Schurb, "Sixteenth-Century Lutheran –Calvinist Conflict on the Protevangelium," 31-40.

95 *CO* 23.71: ". . . ita per continuam aetatum seriem promittitur victoria soboli humanae. Generaliter ergo semen interpretor de posteris."

96 Schurb, "Sixteenth-Century Lutheran–Calvinist Conflict on the Protevangelium," 30.

97 Quotations above from Hunnius, *Calvinus Iudaizans*, cols. 655c-656d, and Calvin, Comm. Gen. 3:15 (1.169-171, *CO* 23.70-71).

98 Hunnius, *Calvinus Iudaizans*, col. 646c.

number, his goings forth (*egressus*), to designate the twofold nature of Christ (*duplicem Christi naturam*): but there is in this an absurdity; for the Prophet could not properly nor wisely mention the human nature of Christ with the divine, with reference to eternity.

Unlike earlier church interpreters, Calvin here does not put emphasis on the eternal divinity of Christ but rather pays primary attention to a present "*consolatio*" which God gave to his people.[99] He points out the fact that Christ will not "suddenly (*repente*)" come to this world in order that the Jews could understand and receive him as the Messiah. Moreover, while Hunnius points up the plurality of the word "*egressus*" in order to explain the two natures of Christ, Calvin turns to the interpretation of the Hebrews themselves. He says that it "is a common thing in Hebrew to use the plural form for a singular number."

Calvin, in expounding Micah 5:2, avoids both the extremes of Christian spiritual interpretation and Jewish literal interpretation. He takes proper consideration of the Jews—both the biblical and contemporary—, but he stubbornly rejects certain Rabbis' assertion that "the Messiah was created before (*primogenitus*) the creation of the world" as "insipid fables." The following shows the *via Calvini* which is most Christian and faithful to the context:

The prophet shows simply, that even before the world was made Christ was chief, as he is also called the First-born of every creature, for by him all things were created, (Col. i. 15) and the same Word of God, by whom the world was created, is to be the Head of the Church (*caput ecclesiae*), and by him what had been lost is to be recovered. We now then comprehend what the Prophet meant by saying, the goings forth of Christ are from eternity (*egressus Christi esse aeternos*). But I would not concede to the Jews, that only by the perpetual appointment of God the going forth of Christ has been from the beginning, or from all ages: but two things must be noticed by us,—that Christ, who was manifested in the flesh that he might redeem the Church of God, was the eternal Word, by whom the world was created,—and then, that he was destined by the eternal counsel of God to be the first-born of every creature, and especially to be the Head of the Church, that he might restore a fallen world by his grace and power.[100]

---

99 Quotations from the lecture on the first part, Comm. Mic. 5:2 (294-298 [altered], *CO* 43.365-367).

100 Quotations from the lecture on the second part, Comm. Mic. 5:2 (298-301, *CO* 43. 367-369).

In the passage cited Calvin directs our focus on Christ's presence and work in the Old Testament. Calvin was motivated by the salvation of the church (*salus ecclesiae*) that we may see Christ as Mediator and the relation between Christ and the law. Calvin's Christological interpretation of the Old Testament reaches its summit in his commentary on "the majesty of the name of Jehovah" in Micah 5:4, in which he emphasizes the two natures of Christ and his coming as the Messiah, along with his headship of the church: "Though Christ is God manifested in the flesh, he is yet made subject to God the Father, as our Mediator and the Head of the Church in human nature: he is indeed the Mediator between God and us."[101]

5.2.3 Calvin's Criticism of Judaism

In spite of his radical criticism, Hunnius did not intend to call Calvin Arian.[102] In fact, the dispute between Hunnius and Pareus mainly focused on Calvin's historical interpretation, which was faithful to the literal and literary meaning of the Scripture. Calvin himself had the same problem as Hunnius regarding Servetus: distinguishing the biblical exegesis from the dogma.

The influence of the Jewish literal interpretation on Servetus' biblical interpretation is extensive,[103] but the impact of Judaic monotheism on his anti-Trinitarian position is much more overwhelming. Calvin defines the word *persona* as "a subsistence in God's essence, which, while related to the others, is distinguished by an incommunicable quality" (*Inst.* 1.13.6, *CO* 2.94).[104] He frequently uses the word in order to express not only the entity of person but also its office, and sometimes in order to define the whole person in the Trinity.[105] On this account, he has often been accused of "Judaizing," as we have seen in the case of Hunnius. However, in whatever

---

101 Comm. Mic. 5:4 (305 [altered], *CO* 43. 371): "Et Christus quamvis sit Deus manifestatus in carne, tamen dum nobis mediator describitur et ecclesiae caput in natura humana, subiicitur Deo patri. Est enim medius inter Deum et nos."

102 Hunnius, *Calvinus Iudaizans*, col. 636a: "Non accuso Calvinum Arianismi, sicut Grabius impudenti ore me immerentem teterrimae huius haereseos accusavit."

103 Cf. Jerome Friedman, "Servetus and the Psalms: The Exegesis of Heresy," in *Historie de l'exégèse au XVIe siècle*, 175-178; Newman, *Jewish Influence on Christian Reform Movements*, 536-559.

104 "Persona igitur voco subsistentiam in Dei essentia, quae ad alios relata, proprietate incommunicabili distinguitur." For Calvin's theological use of the terms *substantia, hypostasis, persona,* see Irena Backus, "'Aristotelianism' in Some of Calvin's and Beza's Expository and Exegetical Writings on the Doctrine of the Trinity, with Particular Reference to the Terms οὐσια and ὑποστασις," in *Historie de l'exégèse au XVIe siècle*, 351-360.

105 J. Raitt, "Calvin's Use of *Persona*," in *Calvinus Ecclesiae Genevensis Custos*, 280-286.

way the word is used by Calvin, it conveys "the personal dynamic behind the office."[106]

On the other hand, Servetus, who understands the three persons of the Trinity as the three peculiar personal appearances and the peculiar property (or quality) of each person as the peculiar form in which the deity intermingles with the flesh and soul of Christ, turns to Jewish concepts of *middoth* and *schechina* in order to explain his own view of the Trinity. Servetus believes that the Jews use *persona* and *facies* interchangeably.[107] The meaning of *middoth* should be differentiated from that of *proprietas* in Christian theology. For *middoth* signifies something which is in God as produced by God.[108] It corresponds to the *elementum creatum* in Servetus.[109] In addition, in order to express the peculiar personal presence of each person of the Trinity, Servetus refers to the Jewish *schechina*, which signifies indwelling or inhabitation.[110] Based on this understanding of the person, Servetus argues that the Jews also had the "Christian" concept of the Messiah.[111]

---

106 Ibid., 282. David E. Willis finds this dynamic from the eucharistic relationship between the terms *persona* and *substantia*. "Calvin's Use of *Substantia*," in *Calvinus Ecclesiae Genevensis Custos*, 289-301.

107 *Restitutio* 108: "This is a clear issue for the Hebrews; what we call person (*persona*), they call image (*facies*)." Translation from Friedman, *Michael Servetus: A Case Study in Total Heresy*, 123.

108 *Restitutio* 700: ". . . three middoth, three properties (*proprietates*) are said by the Hebrews to be in God; produced from God, not separating things." Translation from Friedman, *Michael Servetus: A Case Study in Total Heresy*, 122. For Calvin's criticism of Servetus, Biandrata, and Stancaro over their understanding of the person of the Mediator, see Jill Raitt, "The Person of the Mediator: Calvin's Christology and Beza's Fidelity," *Occasional Papers of the Society for Reformation Research*, vol. 1 (1977), 55-58.

109 Cf. n. 62 (*CO* 8.504) of this chapter.

110 *Dialogorum* A7a-b (Wilbur 197); *Restitutio* 74: "The rabbis called divinity *schechina* from the verb *schachan* which signifies inhabitation (*inhabitare*). Therefore the divinity of Christ is an inhabitation of God (*inhabitatio Dei*)." Translation from Friedman, *Michael Servetus: A Case Study in Total Heresy*, 124. In fact, the word *middoth*, for the Jews, is related to the qualities of God rather than to the person, and the word *schechina* does not mean "the indwelling of Christ in God" but "the nature of God's presence in the Tabernacle, the Temple, and even within each person." Cf. Jerome Friedman, "Michael Servetus: The Case for a Jewish Christianity," *SCJ* 4/1 (1973), 103.

111 *Restitutio* 134. ". . . the Hebrews said in this sense, the messiah is from the beginning, not because of some sophistical Trinity, but because his person and visible form subsisted in God." Translation from Friedman, "Michael Servetus: The Case for a Jewish Christianity," 94-95. In this article, Friedman, after investigating some passages of Servetus' *Biblia Sacra ex Santis Pagnini Tralatione*, concludes that "Throughout his theological writings, both the Targums of Onkelos and of

It is helpful to sample some cases of Calvin's criticism of Servetus' interpretation of the presence of Christ in the Old Testament in order to further confirm their difference. Calvin, expounding "the appearance (*aspectus*) of a man" in Ezekiel 1:26, argues that Servetus misinterprets this as signifying "the appearance of the figurative Son (*figurativus filius*)," that is, "a man figured in divine essence (*homo figuratus in essentia divina*)."[112] In the same vein, Calvin, commenting on "the Angel" in Hosea 12:4, criticizes Servetus "who imagined that Christ was from the beginning an angel, as if he was a phantom of man (*phantasma hominis*), and as if he was another exterior person, having the essence divided from the Father separately."[113]

On the other hand, in his commentary on Ezekiel 1:26, Calvin emphasizes that not the form of Christ, but Christ "himself" appeared in the form of man, though not yet made man.[114] Also he interprets "the Angel" in Hosea as the presence of Christ the Mediator. "Christ, though he was God, was also a Mediator; and as a Mediator, he is rightly and fitly called the angel or the messenger (*nuntius*) of God, for he has on his own accord placed himself between the Father and men."[115] From these two commentaries, we recognize that for Calvin the entity of the Son of God in the Old Testament not only represents the coming Mediator but also signifies the presence of the Mediator as God in the form (*forma*) of God and man.

Servetus understands that the Greek title *Christos* signifies a mediator between God and men, the man Christ Jesus.[116] Also, as seen previously, he recognizes that Christ's appearance as a man in the Old Testament represents the presence of a mediator as the figuration of man, the state similar to that of an angel. He understands the person of Christ from the vantage point of the progress of revelation influenced by neo-Platonic thought and thus maintains that God cannot mediate between God and man. Therefore, he regards the presence of the Son in the Old Testament as

---

Jonathan are often cited, and it is through the use of these works that Servetus' interest in Judaica is most apparent. More than any other type of literature, this source is consistently used to support the Spaniard's notion of Christ as an emanation or aspect of the Father rather than as a sepate entity" (99). Concerning the influence of Jewish mysticism Cabbalah on Servetus, however, the author is not so positive (99-110).

112 Comm. Eze. 1:25-26 (1.97, *CO* 40.54).
113 Comm. Hos. 12:3-5 (421, *CO* 42.455). Cf. Servetus, *Restitutio* 108: "Angelus in persona Dei tota lege loquitur."
114 Comm. Eze. 1:25-26 (1.99, *CO* 40.55): ". . . tunc Christum in forma hominis, quamvis nondum esset homo."
115 Comm. Hos. 12:3-5 (421 [altered], *CO* 42.455).
116 *Erroribus* 4a (Wilbur 9): "Mediator Dei et hominum homo Christus Iesus."

merely a figure or a form of Jesus Christ.[117] On the contrary, Calvin, who believes in the historical presence of Christ as the eternal Son of God and God who acts in history by the hand of the Mediator, asserts that only God can mediate between God and man. This is what most strikingly differentiates Calvin from Servetus and Judaism. According to Calvin's commentary on the chief angel who appeared to Abraham: "[W]henever he manifested himself to the fathers, Christ was as the Mediator between God and them; who not only bears the person of God in respect to the Word, but is also truly and essentially God."[118]

5.3 The Presence and Office of the Mediator in the Old Testament

Calvin's *via media* in Old Testament interpretation has been suggested from the perspective of its relation to Judaism since J. Baumgartner published *Calvin Hébraïsant et Interprète de l'Ancien Testament*. The author there asserts that Calvin successfully overcame the weaknesses and errors of both Christian and Jewish interpreters and was keen to keep himself away from contemporary Christian Judaism as well as from Roman Catholicism.[119] Also it is argued that in his Old Testament exegesis Calvin takes into consideration the specific historical context of the text prior to quest for its Messianic and eschatological meaning.[120] The same view, although in a

---

117 Cf. *Restitutio* 109: "Persona Christi ibi ostenditur, dicens se esse ab aeterno formatam. Figuratio erat Christi, relucentia, expressio quaedam. Generatio erat in Deo ipsa cogitatio et exhibitio, ad generationem Christi tendens. Loquitur ibi sapientia in parabola, et figurate loquutione, cum sapientiam gereret persona Christi, qui est in Deo ab aeterno formatus, expressione quadam genitus, et creatus. Sed creatus dicitur, quia particeps creaturae. Genitus personaliter, personalis filius: atque ita personaliter formatus."

118 Comm. Gen. 18:13 (1.475 [altered], *CO* 23.254): "[Q]uoties se patribus manifestavit, Christum fuisse quasi intermedium, qui non tantum verbi respectu sustinet Dei personam, sed vere et essentialiter Deus est."

119 Baumgartner, *Calvin Hébraïsant et Interprète de l'Ancien Testament*, 35-36: "[Calvin] montrera en peu de mots l'erreur des interprètes chrétiens et, par la même occasion, la faiblesse des interprétations juives, et il le fera de la manière la plus équitable et la plus impartiale. Il faut se rappeler qu'à son époque les rabbins dominent l'exégèse de l'Ancien Testament, que les principaux hébraïsants du seizième siècle ont été formés à leur école ou à celle de juifs convertis; le premier venu n'était pas capable de battre en brèche leurs idées en matière d'explication des Écritures. Nous n'avons qu'à rappeler le nom du grand Reuchlin et ses travaux sur la Kabbale pour montrer quelle importance on attachait alors aux interpretations et aux systèmes de rabbins. Calvin, avec son rare bon sens, avec cette sagacité critique qui savait se déblayer la route au travers de toutes les broussailles de la tradition tant juive que romaine, Calvin n'y va pas de main morte."

120 Ibid., 39-40: ". . . la préoccupation constante de bien placer les textes dans leur milieu historique avant de chercher en eux une portée plus éloignée, messianique ou

different way, is expressed by T. H. L. Parker when he observes: "[P]age after page he can look like *Calvinus Judaeus* and then suddenly show that, in his voluntary exile among the men of the Old Covenant, living with them in shades and shadows, he has not forgotten the Sun of righteousness who, as he himself already knows, will in their future rise with healing in his wings."[121] More recently, in his book *John Calvin's Exegesis of the Old Testament*, David L. Puckett describes Calvin's *via media* more characteristically, placed "somewhere on the continuum that stretches from Hunnius to Servetus."[122]

In fact, through the studies undertaken in the previous sections of this chapter, this middle position of Calvin has been examined and illuminated especially with reference to his Christological stance. In the following sections I will deal with several characteristic features of the person and work of Christ as the Mediator on the Old Testament and their reflection in Calvin's interpretation of the law.

5.3.1 Praesentia Figurae Personae Mediatoris

As has been noted, Calvin refers mainly to the presence and work of Christ as the Mediator in order to verify his eternal sonship. In dealing with the significance of the incarnation in his commentary on Matthew 1:23, he points out that Christ has performed "*officium mediatoris*" from the beginning, before he put on the title *Immanuel* in his new person.[123] Also in his commentary on Isaiah Calvin emphasizes the perpetual presence of Christ as the Mediator in order to identify the one who was prophesied to be Saviour.[124]

As regards the person of Christ before the incarnation, especially in association with his mediatorship, Calvin first designates the fullness of the deity dwelling in him and then turns to his spiritual but real bodily presence. This line of thought is demonstrated in his commentary on Genesis 28:12 in which he makes use of the so-called *extra Calvinisticum* for the purpose of taking into account the "*Deus*" *in carne manifestatus*. As

---

eschatologique."
121 Parker, *Calvin's Old Testament Commentaries*, 7.
122 Puckett, *John Calvin's Exegesis of the Old Testament*, 7. Also the following book is useful for the comprehensive understanding of Calvin's middle position. Jack Hughes Robinson, *John Calvin and the Jews* (New York: Peter Lang, 1992).
123 Comm. Matt. 1:23 (1.69, *CO* 45.69).
124 Comm. Isa. 19:20 (2.75, *CO* 36.344): "He has always been the Mediator (*perpetuus mediator*), by whose intercession all blessings were obtained from God the Father; and now that he has been revealed, let us learn that nothing can be obtained from God but through him." Comm. Isa. 63:17 (4.359, *CO* 37.405): "To the ancient fathers also he was indeed the Mediator, but we have everything clearer and plainer; because they were still kept amidst the darker shadows."

he puts it, "The fact that the body of Christ is finite, does not prevent him from filling heaven and earth, because his grace and power are everywhere diffused."[125] Further, it deserves taking into consideration that it is on this doctrinal foundation that Calvin understands the believer's union with Christ (*unio cum Christo*) in the Old Testament. He argues that Moses wishes to state both the fact that "the fullness of the deity dwelt in the person of the Mediator (*plenam deitatem residere in mediatoris persona*)" and that "Christ not only approached unto us, but clothed himself in our nature (*induit naturam nostram*), that he might make us one with himself."[126]

This position of Calvin is clearly different from that of Servetus who, being pantheistic, denies the person (or *hypostasis*) of Christ as the Mediator and regards the union with Christ as the infusion of the universal deity into the believer. While Servetus interprets the visible presence (*ocularis praesentia*) of Christ as the appearance of the figurative Son (*Filius figurativus*), Calvin, on the contrary, maintains that it denotes the prefiguration (*praefiguratio*) of the person of Christ the Mediator and highlights its sacramental significance.[127] Particularly, Calvin shows a strong tendency to apply the so-called *extra Calvinisticum* to the personal presence of Christ in dealing with the sacramental significance of the Old Testament ceremonies.

In the following commentary on the burnt offering given as a sin-offering in Leviticus 4:22-24, Calvin tells us what he means by "the sacramental mode of speaking"[128] by claiming that this ceremony signifies not only the presence of Christ but rather also his mediatorial office.

> [A]s now in baptism sins are sacramentally (*sacramentaliter*) washed away, so under the Law also the sacrifices were means of expiation, though in a different way; since baptism sets Christ before us as if He were present (*praesentem*), whilst under the Law He was only obscurely foreshadowed (*obscure adumbratus*). Improperly indeed what applies to Christ only is transferred to the signs, for in Him alone was manifested to us the fulfillment of all spiritual blessings, and He at length blotted out sins by His one and perpetual sacrifice.[129]

---

125 Comm. Gen. 28:12 (2.113, *CO* 23. 391): "Nec obstat quod Christi corpus finitum est, ut coelum et terram minime impleat: quia ubique diffusa est eius gratia et virtus."
126 Comm. Gen. 28:12 (2.113, *CO* 23. 391).
127 Cf. Comm. Ex. 13:21-22 (1.236, *CO* 24.145).
128 Comm. Ex. 13:21-22 (1.236, *CO* 24.145).
129 Comm. Lev. 4:22-24 (2.345 [altered], *CO* 24.519). Cf. Lev. 1:1-4 (2.324, *CO* 24.507).

In dealing with the Old Testament sacraments as the prototypes of the sacraments in the *Institutes* (4.14.20-26, 4.15.9), Calvin argues that those sacraments established by the law of Moses bore Christ in them as their material (*materia*) or substance (*substantia*) (4.14.16, *CO* 2.952-953).[130] He admits that the presence of Christ in Jewish ceremonies was shadowy, but definitely denies that they had no reality (*solidum*), for he is convinced of the presence of the power of Christ working inwardly in believers in the ancient times (*Inst.* 4.14.25, *CO* 2.960).[131]

The holy fathers believed in Christ as the head and foundation of the covenant (*caput et fundamentum foederis*) and tried to direct their lives towards the Mediator.[132] They believed that as God promised to Abraham, Christ was ordained to be their Mediator.[133] Thus, they lived and died in their faith in the Mediator, although he was not yet manifested.[134] With the perception of the sacramental presence of Christ in the ceremonies, they not only held themselves to faith in the Mediator[135] but also experienced "a taste (*gustum aliquem*)" of his grace.[136] Therefore the faith of the fathers is different from the faith of the faithful who belong to a better covenant (*potior foedus*), but only with respect to its form (*formam*), and not to its substance (*substantiam*).[137]

---

130 "Christum sacramentorum omnium materiam, vel, si mavis, substantiam esse dico: quando in ipso totam habent suam soliditatem, nec quidquam extra ipsum promittunt."

131 "Paulum non ideo umbratiles facere caeremonias quod nihil haberent solidi; sed quia eorum complementum, usque ad Christi exhibitionem, quodammodo suspensum erat. Deinde non de efficacia, sed potius de modo significandi hoc intelligendum esse dico. Donec enim manifestatus est in carne Christus, omnia signa velut absentem eum adumbrabant, utcunque virtutis suae suique adeo ipsius praesentiam fidelibus intus exsereret."

132 Comm. Jn. 5:46 (1.143, *CO* 47.129).

133 Serm. Gal. 3:13-14 (407-408, *CO* 50.515): "Vray est que nostre Seigneur Iesus Christ n'estoit point encores apparu au monde, quand la promesse gratuite a esté donnee à nostre Pere Abraham: mais c'est assez que desia il avoit esté constitué nostre mediateur, à fin que par son moyen les hommes fussent reconciliez à Dieu"; Serm. Gal. 3:13-14 (412, *CO* 50.518): "D'autant donc que desia du temps d'Abraham nostre Seigneur Iesus Christ a esté ordonné mediateur, à fin que Dieu fust appaisé envers nous parson moyen, et quand nous venons en son nom requerir grace qu'elle nous soit apprestee, et que nous ne soyons point frustrez de nostre attente: . . . "

134 Comm. II Tim. 1:5 (292, *CO* 52.348).

135 Comm. Heb. 8:5 (107, *CO* 55.99): "There was a real spiritual meaning in everything, in that Moses was commanded to do every thing according to the original pattern which was heavenly. . . . these practices [Old Testament ceremonies] were to hold the people to faith in the Mediator."

136 Comm. Dan. 8:15 (2.112, *CO* 41.110).

137 Comm. Heb. 8:6 (108, *CO* 55.99-100).

For Calvin, concerning the temporal use of the ceremonial law, no Platonic concept of the progress of revelation is considered applicable except for God's accommodation to his people according to their capacity, need, and barbarity. Most significantly, the ancient ceremonies, practices, and God's various types of revelation teach us of God who acts in his own Son, the Mediator—God's accommodation par excellence.[138] The only difference between the old and new covenants is that for ancient fathers Christ was revealed not as the very one (*pro ipso*), but in the form (*in forma*) of the coming Mediator.

5.3.2 The Presence of Christ as the Angel, Jehovah, and Elohim

In order to explain both the work of Christ and his presence as the Mediator in the Old Testament, Calvin particularly points to his appearance as the Angel before the fathers and prophets, which he believes to be closely related to the hypostasis of the Son of God denoted by the names Jehovah and Elohim.[139] Note his commentary on "the Angel of the Lord" who appeared before Moses in a flame of fire in Exodus 3:2.

> [T]he ancient teachers of the Church have rightly understood that the Eternal Son of God is so called in respect to his person as Mediator, whose figure he bore from the beginning, although he really took it upon him only at his Incarnation. And Paul sufficiently expounds this mystery to us, when he plainly asserts that Christ was the leader of his people in the Desert (1 Cor. x. 4.). Therefore, although at that time, properly speaking, he was not yet the messenger of his Father, still his predestinated appointment to the office even then had this effect, that he manifested himself to the patriarchs, and was known in this character. Nor, indeed, had the saints ever any communication with God except through the promised Mediator. It is not then to be wondered at, if the

---

138 Cf. Stephen D. Benin, *The Footprints of God: Divine Accommodation in Jewish and Christian Thought* (Albany: State University of New York Press, 1993), 187-197, 210-211. This significant work of the Jewish theologian on God's accommodation and Judaism contains a chapter devoted to Calvin's understanding of the divine accommodation. Although insightful, the author's view is not in line with the real Calvin's at least on the following two points. First, the author overemphasizes that the characteristic of Calvin's concept of the divine accommodation denotes a revival of Chrysostom's *oikonomia*. As a result, he is misled to argue that Calvin tends to lose the sense of *raison d'être* which is prominent in Jewish thought. Secondly, the author, concentrating on the special work of the Holy Spirit, does not pay proper attention to God's accommodation in Christ in both the Old and New Testaments.

139 Cf. *Confessio de Trinitate propter calumnias P. Caroli, CO* 9.708-710 ("De Christo Iehova").

Eternal Word of God, of one Godhead and essence with the Father, assumed the name of "the Angel" on the ground of his future mission.[140]

A syllogism is suggested here: Christ bore the figure of the person of the Mediator (*figura personae mediatoris*) from the beginning. Christ fulfilled the role effectively (*vigebat*) even before the incarnation. Therefore, Christ was called the eternal Son of God regarding the person of the Mediator (*respectu personae mediatoris*). Calvin calls this a mystery (*mysterium*), characterizing the presence and ministry of the Angel as those of Christ the Mediator.[141]

Calvin links the character of the Angel to Jehovah and Elohim. The Hebrew Jehovah represents the whole essence (*essentia*) of all the three persons of God. At the same time, it indicates the character of Christ as the Mediator.[142] The name stands for the redemptive work of "the Angel" in the Old Testament, who led the people in the desert.[143] On Hosea 12:3-5, Calvin comments:

> Christ, the eternal Wisdom of God, did put on the character of a Mediator, before he put on our flesh. He was therefore then a Mediator, and in that capacity he was also an angel. He was at the same time Jehovah, who is now God manifested in the flesh.[144]

---

140 Comm. Ex. 3:2 (1.61-62 [altered], *CO* 24.35-36): ". . . recte senserunt veteres ecclesiae doctores, aeternum Dei filium ita vocari, respectu personae mediatoris, quam licet vere demum una cum carne susceperit, figuram tamen gestavit ab initio. Et Paulus huius mysterii nobis idoneus est interpres, qui palam asserit (1. Cor. 10, 4) Christum fuisse ducem populi in deserto. Quanquam ergo tunc, proprie loquendo, nondum nuncius patris erat, praedestinatio tamen ad officium iam tunc ita vigebat, ut patribus sub hoc habitu cognoscendum se exhibuerit. Nec sane alia unquam sanctis fuit communicatio cum Deo quam per mediatorem promissum. Itaque nihil mirum si aeternus Dei sermo, unius cum patre deitatis et essentiae, nomen angeli mutuatus sit futurae legationis respectu."

141 Cf. Alexandre Ganoczy. *Ecclesia Ministrans: dienende Kirche und kirchlicher Dienst bei Calvin* (Freiburg: Herder, 1968), 108-113. In dealing with Calvin's interpretation of the presence of the Angel in the Old Testament, Ganoczy does not consider seriously its Christological significance, which is based on the unity and continuity of Christ's mediatorship, but merely points up its significance as the theophany of God.

142 Cf. Comm. Eze. 1:25, 26 (1.99, *CO* 40.55); Jos. 5:13-14 (87-88, *CO* 25.463-464): "In the books of Moses the name of Jehovah is often attributed to the presiding Angel, who was undoubtedly the only-begotten Son of God. He is indeed very God, and yet in the person of Mediator by dispensation, he is inferior to God."

143 Comm. Ex. 14:19-20 (1.248-249, *CO* 24.153).

144 Comm. Hos. 12:3-5 (421, *CO* 42.455): "Christus enim aeterna Dei sapientia induit personam mediatoris, antequam induceret carnem nostram. Fuit ergo nunc mediator, et eo respectu fuit etiam angelus. Interea fuit etiam Iehova qui nunc est

Similarily, the meaning of the Hebrew Elohim represents angels and gods as a collective noun, it denotes the economy of the Trinity rather than the fact that they are in the same essence. At the same time, it defines a peculiar property of Christ; it reveals not only his divine majesty, but also his character as the Mediator. In the same vein, Calvin comments that when the Psalmist seeks the mercy of God (Elohim), he looks upon him as "the only true God" and "the servant of God and our brother (*servus Dei et frater noster*)." He also regards him not only as the almighty God but also as "God manifested in the flesh"—"the head of the Church, the author and protector of our welfare (*salutis nostrae custos et praeses*)."[145] In this case, the name "Elohim" reveals the character of Christ as our Lord, i.e., Jehovah, who "is shown to us not as he is in himself, but as he is toward us (*non quis sit apud se, sed qualis erga nos*)" (*Inst.* 1.10.2, *CO* 2.73).

Calvin often interprets the word Elohim as denoting the whole essence of God or the mutual relations between the persons, but mostly he focuses on the office of a specific person in the economy of the Trinity. In commenting on Genesis 1:26, "Let us make (*faciamus*) man," Calvin first indicates what this phrase says about the office of "counsellor (*consultor*)," and then argues that the reason why the author used the plural form was to emphasize, in opposition to Jewish thinking, that God does not look for his counsellors outside, e.g., on the earth or among the angels: "since the Lord needs no other counsellor, there can be no doubt that he consulted himself (*secum ipse deliberet*)." More emphatically this is described as follows:

> [T]here exists a plurality of Persons in the Godhead. God summons no foreign counsellor; hence we infer that he finds something distinct within himself; as, in truth, his eternal wisdom and power reside within him.

"Something distinct within himself (*intus eum aliquid distinctum*)"; this expression signifies the peculiar property (*proprietas, proprium, qualitas*) of each *hypostasis* or *persona*. Office (*officium*) cannot be separated from person because a particular office designates a particular property. Therefore, the Son of God is properly called "eternal wisdom and power (*aeterna sapientia et virtus*)."[146]

Even before the person of the Mediator was manifested, his property had already been revealed clearly through his presence and works in the Old Testament. Characteristically, Calvin describes this state as the presence of the figure of the person of the Mediator.[147] In the figure of Christ, the

---

Deus manifestatus in carne." Cf. Comm. Zech. 3:3-4 (87, *CO* 44.171).
145 Comm. Ps. 45:6-7 (2.178-183, *CO* 31.451-454).
146 Comm. Gen. 1:26 (1.91-93 [altered], *CO* 23.25).
147 Cf. Comm. Ps. 132:10 (5.153, *CO* 32.347). The Psalmist here depicts the character

humanity of the Mediator was already revealed as the property of the Son of God.[148] Therefore no other gods or angels could become human legitimately except for the eternal Son of God.[149] For Calvin, there is no room either for the concept of the personal presence of the figurative Christ or for the transformation of the substantial deity in the flesh, both of which were claimed persistently by Servetus.[150]

5.3.3 Christus Caput Angelorum et Ecclesiae

Several scholars have dealt with Calvin's doctrine of the unity of the church mainly in its relation to the unity of God's people and the divine covenant, which is prominently explored in his commentary on Romans 9-11 and *Institutes* 2:10-11.[151] They pay special attention to the continuity of the true or spiritual Israel (the *ecclesiola* in *ecclesia*), which is grounded in the pre-existent Christ.[152] We have demonstrated that Calvin verifies the eternal sonship of Christ by referring to his mediatorship whose characteristic is most strikingly revealed in the fact that he is the Angel, Jehovah, and Elohim. Based on this economic-Trinitarian understanding of the pre-existent Christ, Calvin defines him as the leader of God's people and the head of the church, that is the Mediator of the church. The following

---

of Christ as "*umbratilis mediator, qui exorandi fiduciam populo daret.*"

148 Comm. Eze. 1:25-26 (1.99-100, *CO* 40.55): "The whole deity, then, appeared to his Prophet, and that too in the form of a man, but yet neither the Father nor the Holy Spirit appeared, because the persons begin to be considered when the peculiar property of Christ is shown forth (*quia in rationem venire incipiunt personae, ubi ostenditur quid peculiare sit vel proprium Christo*)."

149 Comm. Gen. 48:16 (2.429, *CO* 23. 585): "We must remember what the Apostle says to the Hebrews, (ii. 16,) that 'he took not on him the nature of angels,' so as to become one of them, in the manner in which he truly became man; for even when angels put on (*induerunt*) human bodies, they did not, on that account, become (*facti sunt*) men."

150 Cf. Comm. Eze. 1:25-26 (1.97-100, *CO* 40.53-57). Here Calvin also criticizes the heresy of George Blandrata; Ps. 45:6-7 (2.183, *CO* 31.453-454); Hos. 12:3-5 (421, *CO* 42.455).

151 Cf. I. John Hesselink, "Calvin's Understanding of the Relation of the Church and Israel Based Largely on His Interpretation of Romans 9-11," *Ex Auditu* 4 (1988), 59-69; J. Marius J. Lange van Ravenswaay, Calvin und die Juden—eine offene Frage?" in *Reformiertes Erbe: Festschrift für Gottfried W. Locher zu seinem 80. Geburtstag*, vol. 2, 183-194; L. Schümmer, "Le Mystère d'Israël et de l'Église, postérité d'Abraham," *Irénikon* 1988/2, 207-242; Wolf, *Die Einheit des Bundes*; Mary Potter Engel, "Calvin and the Jews: A Textual Puzzle," *Princeton Seminary Bulletin*, Supplementary Issue no. 1 (1990), 106-123.

152 Hesselink, "Calvin's Understanding of the Relation of the Church and Israel," 66; Engel, "Calvin and the Jews," 114. Schümmer, "Le Mystère d'Israël et de l'Église," 240.

commentary on an angel coming up before Zechariah allows us to understand Calvin's dynamic position on the church.

> [T]his chief angel was the Mediator and the Head of the Church; and the same is Jehovah, for Christ, as we know, is God manifested in the flesh. There is then no wonder that the Prophet should indiscriminately call him angel and Jehovah, he being the Mediator of the Church, and also God. He is God, being of the same essence with the Father; and Mediator, having already undertaken his Mediatorial office, though not then clothed in our flesh, so as to become our brother; for the Church could not exist, nor be united to her God without a head. We hence see that Christ, as to his eternal essence (*respectu aeternae suae essentiae*), is said to be God, and that he is called an angel on account of his office (*respectu officii*), that is, a Mediator.[153]

Calvin emphasizes the headship of Christ over the church by referring to the fact that he is the head and chief of angels.[154] It is true that angels are appointed to do a particular work of God and have a divine majesty, but only on condition that they serve Christ as their master.[155] No mediatorial office can be undertaken by angels independently if they are not led by Christ the sole Mediator. Calvin finds the Platonic philosophy unacceptable which admits many mediators between gods and men. As he puts it, "it is brought about only through Christ's intercession that the angels' ministrations come to us" (1543 *Inst.* 5.38, *CO* 1.503; 1559 *Inst.* 1.14.12 [altered], *CO* 2.126).[156]

---

153 Comm. Zech. 1:18-21 (57, *CO* 44.152). The last part of the passage quoted, "*respectu autem officii vocetur angelus, quatenus scilicet est mediator, sed diverso respectu*," can be rendered more literally in this way: "however, for the sake of his office he is called angel, so far as he is deservedly a Mediator, but in different regard."
154 Cf. Comm. Gen. 18:2 (1.479, *CO* 23. 251); Gen. 19:1 (1.495, *CO* 23. 267); Gen. 28:12 (2. 113, *CO* 23. 391); Zech. 12:8 (358, *CO* 44.332).
155 Comm. Gen. 16:10 (1.432-433 [altered], *CO* 23.228): "That the angel here promises to do what is peculiar to God alone, involving no absurdity, for it is sufficiently usual of God to lead his ministers whom he sends in his own person, that the authority of their word may appear the greater. I do not, however, disapprove of the opinion of most of the ancients; that Christ the Mediator has always been present in all the oracles, and that this is the cause why the majesty of God is ascribed to angels."
156 Cf. Comm. Jer. 11:13 (2.93-95, *CO* 38.112-113); Dan. 2:11 (1.133, *CO* 40.569). Concerning Augustine's criticism of the Platonic concept of mediator, see St. Augustine's *City of God*, book 8, in *A Select Library of the Nicene and Post-Nicene Fathers of the Christian Church*, ed. Philip Schaff, vol. 2, repr. (Grand Rapids: Eerdmans, 1993), 144-165.

Calvin claims that the main office of angels is their intercession between God and his people, and their leader is Christ (the Angel). In so doing he asserts that Christ is the head of the church.[157] Calvin, looking upon the church as a family or a household (*domesticus*), insists that as soon as we are grafted (*inserimur*) into the body of Christ we become members of it and constitute the *familia Dei*.[158] The truth of the symbol of circumcision is regarded as an initiation into the family.[159] Therefore, he argues against the Rabbis, "separating the Church from the Mediator is like leaving dead a mutilated body apart from its disjoined head."[160]

Calvin bases the continuity and unity of the church on the eternal mediatorship of Christ,[161] and in order to explain it, he frequently refers to the fact that Christ is the head of the church.[162] He sees the historical and eschatological significance of the church in the light of the historical presence and eternal glorification of our Lord who describes himself as "one with his Father in his person as mediator inasmuch as he is our head."[163]

---

157 Cf. Comm. Ex. 14:19 (1.248-249, *CO* 24.153); Ex. 23:20 (1.403, *CO* 24.251); Jos. 5:13 (87, *CO* 25.463).

158 Comm. Ps. 89:30 (3.439, *CO* 31.822).

159 Comm. Gen. 17:13 (1.456, *CO* 23.243).

160 Comm. Dan. 7:27 (2.77 [altered], *CO* 41.85): "Ergo quum separant ecclesiam a mediatore, perinde est ac si truncato capite relinquerent corpus mutilum, et mortuum."

161 Comm. Gal. 4:1-2 (71, *CO* 50.224). Calvin argues for the continuity of the church of God taking into account the fact that the Jews "held the same doctrine as ourselves, were joined with us in the true unity of faith, placed reliance with us on the one Mediator (*unius etiam mediatoris fiducia nobiscum fretos*), called on God their Father, and were governed by the same Spirit." For Calvin's Christological understanding of the unity and continuity of the church, see W. McKane, "Calvin as an Old Testament commentator," *Nederduitse Gereformeerde Theologiese Tydskrif* (1984), 254-256; Danielle Fischer, "Ministères et instruments d'unité de l'Eglise dans la pensée de Luther et de Calvin," *Istina* 30 (1985), 14-17.

162 Comm. Gen. 20: 7 (1.526, *CO* 23. 290); Ex. 3:15 (1.75, *CO* 24.45): "[S]ince, in the coming of Christ, the truth of the covenant made with Abraham was shown forth, and was thus demonstrated to be firm and infallible, its memory was rather renewed than destroyed; and that thus it still survives and flourishes in the Gospel, since Abraham even now ceases not to be the father of the faithful, under the one head (*sub uno capite*)."

163 Comm. Jn. 17:21 (2.148, *CO* 47.387). Cf. S. H. Russell, "Calvin and the Messianic Interpretation of the Psalms," *Scottish Journal of Theology* 21 (1968), 37-47. Regarding "the threefold reference" of the Psalmist among David, Christ, and his church, the author asserts, "the master-key of Calvin's exegesis of the messianic elements in the Psalms is the solidarity of Christ and His members both before and after the incarnation" (41-42). He also points out that the Davidic kingdom is not only "a mere *representation* of that of Christ" but it also shows that "the substance

It hardly is plausible that we should find the origin of Calvin's doctrine of the unity and continuity of the church in any influence of a Judaistic Messianistic concept of the church and the Platonic analogy of shadow (*skia, umbra*) and substance (*substantia*) prior to his firm conviction of the continuity of Christ's mediatorship throughout history.[164] As David Steinmetz puts it in one of his "Ten Theses" of Reformation-era biblical interpretation, although the meaning of a text is not confined within its *ad hoc* significance and in this respect the pre-critical exegesis has its own limitation, "the importance of the Old Testament for the church is predicted upon the continuity of the people of God in history, a continuity which persists in spite of discontinuity between Israel and the church."[165] Calvin sometimes seems to adhere very strictly to a peculiar office of the Triune God to pinpoint Christ as the Mediator of the church, but he is always keen enough not to confuse the entity of the person (*persona*) of Christ with his personal (*personalis*) presence in history. In this respect, we may say that Calvin's *via media* is placed somewhere between Servetus and Hunnius.

5.4 The Christological Significance of Calvin's Interpretation of the Old Testament Law

5.4.1 The Pattern of Interpretation of the First Table Commandments

We have examined the great significance of Calvin's concept of *Christus mediator legis* for his Old Testament theology studying how the law reveals the presence of Christ as the Mediator and represents his future coming at the same time. How then was the position of Calvin reflected in his interpretation of the law in the Old Testament? Calvin's exposition of the law was given mainly in three genres, i.e., sermons, lectures, and commentaries. His approach varies in accordance with each genre.[166] However, his interpretation of the Ten Commandments that belong to the First Table presents a remarkably consistent pattern.

We can start exploring the pattern by examining his commentary on the second commandment concerning the burnt-offering in Leviticus 1:1-4,

---

of His kingdom must be in some way regarded as *present*" (42, italics mine).

164 Cf. Hans-Joachim Kraus, "Calvin's Exegetical Principles," *Interpretation* 31/1 (1977), 17, and "Israel in the Theology of Calvin," 80-82. In dealing with the unity of the church in the scope of *familia Dei, ecclesia aeterna*, and *eadem ecclesia*, Kraus refers largely to the influence of Calvin's humanist studies.

165 David C. Steinmetz, "The Superiority of Pre-Critical Exegesis," *Theology Today* 37 (1980-1981), 27-38, and "Theology and Exegesis: Ten Theses," in *Histoire de l'exégèse au XVIe siècle*, 382.

166 Cf. Parker, *Calvin's Old Testament Commentaries*, 9-41.

which shows a typical example.[167] First, Calvin seeks for the simplicity (*simplicitas*) of a text according to its context (*ex contextu*).[168] He avoids using allegories (*allegoriis ludere*); rather investigates the social and religious context of the Jewish concept of the burnt offering. He comments: "This, then, was the first rule of obedience, that men should not offer indiscriminately this or that sacrifice, but bulls or bull-calves of their herds, and male lambs or kids of their flocks." Overall, in the first stage, as Puckett observes, Calvin tries to understand the context in which the document was originally produced, giving primary attention to "the original writer's contemporaries."[169]

His special concern for historical biblical context carries on in the next stage, but from the spiritual perspective in which Calvin pursues a spiritual meaning of the law viewed by the lens of the original addressees. It is pointed out that even the ancient people believed that "unless they directed their faith to Christ, whatsoever came from them would be rejected." Thus, the spiritual meaning of the burnt offering is described in this way: "since the sacrifices were figures (*figurae*) of Christ, it behooved that in all of them should be represented (*repraesentari*) that complete perfection of His whereby His heavenly Father was to be propitiated."[170] Both the fact that Christ himself is revealed in the law and that in Christ the truth of the law—the will of God—is revealed are equally considered at this stage.[171] Calvin highlights the fact that God's face (*facies*), which indicates Christ as the living and express image of God, shone forth in the law.[172] At this point Calvin claims that Christ not only designates the norm of each law as "the sole standard (*unica regula*)," but also reveals himself as the substance of the law.[173]

---

167 Comm. Lev. 1:1-4 (2.323-325 [altered], *CO* 24.506-507).
168 Comm. Lev. 3:16-17 (2.335, *CO* 24.514).
169 Puckett, *John Calvin's Exegesis of the Old Testament*, 67-68. According to Puckett, for the "simple lexicological observation" in this stage, Calvin considers these four criteria: the opinion of Jewish commentators, etymology, biblical usage, and context (64-72).
170 Cf. Ibid., 84: "Calvin's belief that all of scripture is a witness to Christ as the mediator between God and man is nowhere more evident than in his condemnation of Jewish exegesis."
171 Cf. Comm. Ex. 13:1-2, et al. (1.477-481, *CO* 24.298-301); Ex. 30:11-16 (1.481-484, *CO* 24.301-302); Deut. 26:1-11, et al. (1.492-497, *CO* 24.307-311).
172 Comm. Ex. 20:3, et al. (1.419, *CO* 24.262): ". . . true and pure religion was so revealed in the Law, that God's face (*Dei facies*) in a manner shone forth (*tradita*) therein."
173 Quot. *Inst*. 1.1.1-2 (*CO* 2.31-32). Cf. Comm. Ex. 12:1-2 (1. 458, *CO* 24.286); Ex. 12:5-11 (1.462, *CO* 24.289): ". . . duplicem huius sacramenti fuisse usum: quia in recordatione praeteriti beneficii populum exercuerit, et spem aluerit redemptionis futurae."

While in the first two stages Calvin deals with the law before the coming of Jesus Christ and how the predestined promise of Jesus Christ worked for the Old Testament people, in the third stage he comments on the fulfilment of the law in Christ who is its reality, truth, and substance.[174] As Calvin puts it in the commentary, "there was a price of satisfaction in the ancient sacrifices which should release them from guilt and blame in the judgment of God; yet still not as though these brute animals availed in themselves unto expiation, except in so far as they were testimonies of the grace to be manifested by Christ." In this stage, both the *umbra-substantia* analogy and God's accommodation to human capacity (especially to the barbarity of the ancient people) are to be taken into consideration in order to explain both the temporal validity and the continual significance of the ceremonial law.

Then in the final stage of the interpretation, Calvin claims the continuity between law and Gospel with his argument for the continuity and unity of the church. He frequently refers to the wide extent and continual validity of Christ's mediatorship in their relation to the unity of the covenant in the Old and New Testaments.[175] With reference to burnt offering, the continuity is revealed in the following: "Thus the ancients were reconciled to God in a sacramental manner by the sacrifices, just as we are now cleansed through baptism." Before closing each individual commentary, Calvin generally demonstrates its pedagogical significance. In so doing, Calvin maintains, as Parker notes, that "the context of any single book is the rest of the Holy Scripture. No book can be interpreted as if it stood outside the Bible."[176]

Calvin's commentary on the blood of burnt offerings gives us another good example of the pattern of his interpretation of the First Table commandments.[177] First, he writes about the significance of blood for the ancient people, as the "medium whereby the covenant was established and confirmed." Secondly, he reveals the spiritual meaning by indicating the fact that the covenant "was sealed with the blood of Christ in type and shadow (*umbra et typo*)." Thirdly, he says that "the true and genuine nature of the Sacraments" was made complete in Christ; therefore, Catholic sacraments which are devoid of the substance of Christ are "dumb sacraments (*muta sacramenta*)." Finally, Calvin concludes that the principle of "gratuitous reconciliation" is prevalent throughout the whole Scripture.

This pattern is also prominently shown in Calvin's commentary on the tithes, which we briefly presents: the tithes were given to priests as representatives (*vicarios*), an office of representative is allocated to Christ, Christ fulfils the office (*munus*) and now possesses the dignity (*dignitas*) alone, finally, the meaning of the tithes is that the tithes belonged to God

---

174 Cf. Comm. Zech. 1:18-21 (57, *CO* 44.152).
175 Cf. Comm. Ex. 29:38-41 (2. 293-297, *CO* 24.489-491).
176 Parker, *Calvin's Old Testament Commentaries*, 81.
177 Comm. Ex. 24:5-8 (3.319-321 [altered], *CO* 25.74-76).

originally but he gave them to the priests as his representatives in Old Testament times and to Christ the Mediator in the new covenant.[178]

We do not need to enumerate all the relevant commentaries here,[179] but his commentary on the keeping of the Sabbath deserves presenting before we move on to the next section because it is of great help in understanding his commentary on Jesus's teaching on the Sabbath in the Gospels, which I deal with in the next chapter. Calvin first investigates the literary and historical meaning of the fourth commandment. Even for the ancient Jews, he comments, the true meaning of the Sabbath was conceived as "the sum of sanctification, viz., the death of the flesh, when men deny themselves and renounce their earthly nature, so that they may be ruled and guided by the Spirit of God." Then, he says that the fathers directed themselves to Christ who is the "body" and "substance" of the Sabbath. Then Calvin mentions that the Sabbath is fulfilled by Christ as he quotes a verse from Romans 6:4: "Our old man is crucified with Christ." Finally, he refers to the continual significance of the law as he argues that "we have an equal necessity (or need, *necessitas*) for the Sabbath with the ancient people, so that on one day we may be free, and thus the better prepared to learn and to testify our faith."[180]

5.4.2 Natural Law and the Second Table Commandments

Since the commandments of the Second Table are related mostly to the regulations of the moral law whose validity is continuous, Calvin's commentaries and sermons on them are more concentrated on their nature and extent than their relation to Christ the Mediator. His focus shifted from the representation of Christ the Mediator in the law and Christ's fulfilment of the law to what "*Christus certissimus interpres*" says in the Gospels[181] and what he "shows (*ostendit*)"[182] and "teaches (*docet*)."[183] Therefore, it does not seem that the pattern of the interpretation of the First Table applies to the Second Table.[184] What Calvin pursues here is the examination of the

---

178 Comm. Num. 18:20-24 (2.277-281, *CO* 24. 479-481).
179 This typical pattern is dominant in these commentaries of Calvin: Lev. 20:25-26, et al. (2. 58-68, *CO* 24.345-351, on the clean and unclean beasts); Ex. 25:8-15 (2.150-155, *CO* 24.403-405, on the sanctuary); Ex. 28:4-8 (2.195-197, *CO* 24.429-430, on sacerdotal garments); Lev. 26:3-8 (3.214-219, *CO* 25.12-15, on the blessings of the law).
180 Comm. Ex. 20:8 (2.434-437 [altered], *CO* 24.576-579).
181 Comm. Ex. 22:28 (3.18, *CO* 24.610).
182 Comm. Lev. 19:33 (3.118, *CO* 24.674).
183 Comm. Deut. 10:17-19 (3.119, *CO* 24.674).
184 In commenting on "the eating of blood" in relation to the sixth commandment, Calvin takes a similar position as he does in interpreting the First Table, but his commentary here is not on the precept of the commandment but rather on the

true meaning of the law derived "from the judgment of Christ (*ex Christi sententia*)"[185]

In the commentaries on the Second Table Calvin frequently makes use of the three principles of the interpretation of the law which are founded on the spiritual interpretation of Christ (*Inst.* 2.8.7, *CO* 2.271).[186] The introduction of the sixth commandment demonstrates that Calvin turns to such principles as "synecdoche" and "the opposite affirmation (*contrariam affirmationem*)" in order to read the will of God, who is the spiritual lawgiver, in the law.[187] In particular, in arguing the original nature of each commandment, Calvin makes use of varying notions which stemmed from the order of nature or natural law,[188] such as "*conscientia*,"[189]

---

signification of the blood itself. Comm. Lev. 17:10-14 (3.31-32, *CO* 24.619-620).

185 Comm. Ex. 22:25 (3.129 [altered], *CO* 24.681).

186 The three principles of the interpretation of the moral law was established in the 1539 *Institutes* and remained without augmentation. See 1539 *Inst.* 3.7-14 (*CO* 1.375-380); *Inst.* 2.8.6-12 (*CO* 2.270-275).

187 Comm. Ex. 20:13, et al. (3.20-22, *CO* 24.612-613). Cf. Comm. Ex. 20:15, et al. (3.111, *CO* 24.669).

188 Scholars who clearly distinguish between natural law and the order of nature and refer human depravity after the fall only to the former tend to see the office of natural law negatively. Cf. August Lang, "The Reformation and Natural law," in *Calvin and the Reformation*, ed. William P. Armstrong, repr. (Grand Rapids: Baker, 1980), 68-72; Niesel, *The Theology of Calvin*, 42-43, 102-103; T. F. Torrance, *Calvin's Doctrine of Man* (London: Lutterworth Press, 1952), 164; Arthur C. Cochrane, "Natural Law in Calvin," in *Church-State Relations in Ecumenical Perspective*, ed. Elwyn A. Smith (Louvain: Duquesne University Press, 1966), 184, 187. On the other hand, scholars, who emphasize the noetic function of natural law to reveal God's will in the creation and providence and regard the law as an authoritative witness of natural law, tend to deal with it comprehensively ranging over the order of nature and natural equity. They usually understand the office of natural law positively as they link it with the noetic function of conscience. Cf. Bohatec, *Calvin und das Recht*, 2-3; Günter Gloede, *Theologia Naturalis bei Calvin* (Stuttgart: Verlag von W. Kohlhammer, 1935), 178-203; Dowey, *The Knowledge of God in Calvin's Theology*, 65-70; David Little, "Calvin and Prospects for a Christian Theory of Natural Law," in *Norm and Context in Christian Ethics*, ed. Gene H. Outka and Paul Ramsey (New York: Charles Scribner's Sons, 1968), 196, id., "Natural Law Revisited: James Luther Adams and Beyond," *Union Seminary Quarterly Review* 37/3 (1982), 218-219; Klempa, "Calvin and Natural Law," 7; John T. McNeill, "Natural Law in the Teaching of the Reformers," *Journal of Religion* 26 (1946), 181-182; Susan Schreiner, "Calvin Use of Natural Law," in *A Preserving Grace: Protestants, Catholics, and Natural Law*, ed. Michael Cormartie (Grand Rapids: Eerdmans, 1997), 73, and *The Theater of His Glory*, 17-18, 30-32; Paul Helm, "Calvin and Natural Law," *Scottish Bulletin of Evangelical Theology* 2 (1984), 9-11.

189 Comm. Deut. 24:14-15 (3.114, *CO* 24.671).

"*humanitas*," [190] "*aequitas*," [191] and "*caritatis regula* (or *normam caritatis*)."[192]

In the commentary on the Second Table in the *Harmony of the Books of Moses*, we can find a significant number of statements related to natural law[193] and those that illuminate the influence of his study of law.[194] This is true of his sermons on the Second Table of the Ten Commandments.[195] According to Calvin, the law is nothing else than "a testimony of natural law"[196] and its regulation is in accordance with the Roman laws.[197] Calvin

---

190 Comm. Deut. 24:14-15 (3.114, *CO* 24.671); Ex. 22:25 (3.126-127, *CO* 24.679-680).
191 Comm. Deut. 24:6 (3.122, *CO* 24.677).
192 Comm. Ex. 20:15, et al. (3.110 [altered], *CO* 24.669); Ex. 22:25 (3.132 [altered], *CO* 24.682).
193 Cf. Comm. Ex. 20:12 (3.6-12, *CO* 24.602-606); Ex. 21:15-17 (3.14, *CO* 24.607); Lev. 19:32 (3.18-19, *CO* 24.610); Ex. 20:13 (3.20-21, *CO* 24.611-613); Lev. 19:14 (3.24, *CO* 24.614); Deut. 24:16 (3.50, *CO* 24.631); Ex. 20:14 (3.68-69, *CO* 24.641); Ex. 22:19, et al. (3.73-74, *CO* 24.645-646); Deut. 24:1-4 (3.93, *CO* 24.657-658); Lev. 20:18 (3.95, *CO* 24.659); Lev. 18:1-18, et al. (3.97-103, *CO* 24.660-663); Lev. 20:11-12 (3.107, *CO* 24.666); Ex. 22:25, et al. (3.126-133, *CO* 24.679-683); Deut. 23:24-25 (3.150, *CO* 24.695); Deut. 15:1-2 (3.154, *CO* 24.697).
194 For Calvin's knowledge of Roman law and common law in *Harmony of the Four Last Books of Moses*, cf. Comm. Deut. 21:18-20 (3.15-16, *CO* 24.607-608, on the power of life and death over his children and on the process of a trial); Lev. 14:17-21 (3.35-36, *CO* 24.621-622, on the law of retaliation); Ex. 21:14 (3.38-39, *CO* 24.623, on the wide difference between slaying a man presumptuously and with guile and the regulation of Roman law on the punishment enacted for wounds and blows); Deut. 25:1-3 (3.48-50, *CO* 24.630, on the punishment); Num. 35:16-18 (3.63, *CO* 24.638, on the regulation of the *Lex Cornelia* on the voluntary and involuntary murder); Deut. 22:22 (3.78, *CO* 24.648-649, on adultery); Lev. 18: 6-17 (3.99, *CO* 24.661, on incest); Lev. 19:35-36, et al. (3.120, *CO* 24.675, on measures); Deut.19:14 (3.121, *CO* 24.676, on the land-mark); Ex. 22:1-4 (3.140-142, *CO* 24.687-689, on punishment regulated in Twelve Tables); Ex. 22:7-8 (3.146, *CO* 24.692, on a deposit). Even though Haas devotes one chapter to "Equity in the Commandments of the Second Table" in his book *The Concept of Equity in Calvin's Ethics*, he does not deal with those of the First Table separately because he considers the equity to be related mainly to the Golden Rule of Matt. 7:12, 93-106.
195 Calvin frequently refers to nature or natural law in his sermons on the Second Table: Deut. 5:16 (136, 137, 139, 141, 142, 145, 148-150, *CO* 26.309 ff.); Deut. 5:17 (153, 154, 155, 156, 157, 162, 164, 165, *CO* 26.321ff.); Deut. 5:18 (169, 181, *CO* 26.334 ff.); Deut. 5:19 (189, 191, 192, 197, *CO* 26.346 ff.).
196 *Inst*. 4.20.16 (*CO* 2.1106): "Iam quum Dei legem, quam moralem vocamus, constet non aliud esse quam naturalis legis testimonium, et eius conscientiae quae hominum animis a Deo insculpta est, tota huius, de qua nunc loquimur, aequitatis ratio in ipsa praescripta est."
197 Comm. Lev. 18:6 (3.99, *CO* 24.661): "The Roman laws accord with the rule prescribed by God, as if their authors had learnt from Moses what was decorous and agreeable to nature."

frequently uses the concept of natural law in his commentary on the Sermon on the Mount in order to point out that Christ's teaching of the law ultimately reveals the original nature (or righteousness) of the law which is not different from the teaching of natural law.[198] A typical pattern of Calvin's interpretation of the Second Table strikingly reflects that of the new teaching of Jesus in the Sermon on the Mount. First, Calvin deals with the original nature of each commandment. In so doing, he is much concerned with the will of God towards his people, which he often calls the original righteousness. Then, he mentions natural laws related to each commandment, most significantly equity, moderation (*moderatio*), and the rule of love. Finally, he refers to what Christ says of the unity of the original nature of the law and natural law.

Calvin keenly applies this pattern of interpretation to his historical and literary exegesis of the moral law. With an emphasis on the continuity of the original nature of moral law, he refers to the mediatorship of Christ particularly as *mediator omnis doctrinae*. Although Christ was not manifested yet as the Mediator, he had already undertaken his mediatorial office effectively to reveal and instruct the truth of the law as its interpreter and to make his people turn their heart towards God as the Intercessor.[199] Although Christ was present as *figura mediatoris*, the ancient people believed him as the eternal Son of God by his peculiar mediatorial office not only to lead his people but also to teach them a rule of living in accordance with the specific historical environment in which they were living.

5.5 *Ad Quaestiones et Obiecta Iudaei Cuiusdam Responsio*

We are going to treat this tract because it has been regarded as the other document of Calvin which contains direct addresses to the Jews, along with the one known as the fourth preface to Olivétan's French translation of the Bible.[200] The authorship of this preface which begins with the clause

---

198 Cf. Comm. Matt. 5:25 (1.186-187, *CO* 45.177, "*moderationem et aequitatem*"); Matt. 5:43 (1.197-198, *CO* 45.187, "the course which nature herself dictates," "the common tie of nature," "the natural order," "a general rule of the Law," "the teaching of common sense"); Matt. 5:44 (198, *CO* 45.188, "*lex caritatis*"); Matt. 5:46 (1.200, *CO* 45.190, "humanity"); Matt 5:48 (1.200, *CO* 45.190, "the sense of equality (*aequalitatem*)"); Matt. 7:1 (225, *CO* 45.214, "*caritatis regulam*").

199 Cf. *Inst*. 2.8.1 (*CO* 2.206): "the Jews not only learned from the law what the true character of godliness (*vera pietatis ratio*) was; but also that, since they saw themselves incapable (*impares*) of observing the law, they were in dread of judgment drawn inevitably though unwillingly to the Mediator."

200 Locher, "Calvin Spricht zu den Juden." 180-193; Mary Sweetland Laver, "Calvin, Jews, and Intra-Christian Polemics," PhD dissertation, Temple University, 1988, Appendix I, "'Calvin Speaks to the Jews': Two Controversial Documents," 220-

"V.F.C. à nostre allié et confédéré le peuple de l'alliance de Sinai, Salut" is still uncertain.[201] In spite of some persuasive references, I cannot find there any evident characteristic feature that enables us to ascribe its authorship definitely to Calvin in considering its style or its theological tone.[202] Therefore, in the following I will only treat *Ad quaestiones*.

It is worthwhile to identify the Jewish interlocutor for the right understanding of the historical and theological background of the tract.

---

228. This dissertation contains the English translation of *Ad quaestiones* (229-261) and of the preface (262-281). The German translation of *Ad quaestiones* with its text appears in "Zu den Fragen und Einwürfen irgendeines Juden," tr. Achim Detmers, *CSA* 4.366-405.

201 Scholars' various views on the authorship have been suggested on the basis of their unique interpretation of the initials V.F.C., e.g., as *Votre Frère Calvin* (Droz), as *V*iret, *F*arel, *and C*alvin (Reuss, Locher), and as *V*(W)olfgang *F*abricius *C*apito (Roussel, White). Cf. De Greef, *The Writings of John Calvin*, 92; E. Reuss, "Fragments littéraires relatifs à l'histoire de la Bible française," *Revue de théologie* 3 (1865), 217-252, and 4 (1866), 1-48, 281-322; Eugénie Droz, *Chemins de l'hérésie: Textes et documents*, vol. 1 (Genève: Slatkine, 1970), 108-115 (with a facsimile from the Neuchâtel Bible); Locher, "Calvin Spricht ju den Juden," 187-188. Locher claims that Olivétan himself wrote the preface, but as a composite work with the three men; Bernard Roussel, "Francois Lambert, Pierre Caroli, Guillaume Farel ... Et Jean Calvin (1530-1536)," in *Calvinus Servus Christi*, 40-41: "On y relève de multiples auto-citations de ses oeuvres par Capiton, et l'écho de débats strasbourgeois des années 1528-1534. De plus le style de ce texte mis en français à partir d'un original latin (lui-même traduit de l'allemand?) est incompatible avec ce qu'on peut lire dans le même volume et qui est indubitablement de Calvin"; Robert White, "An Early Reformed Document on the Mission to the Jews," *WTJ* 53 (1991), 93-108. esp. 102-104. White maintains the authorship of Capito by identifying his theological position on such doctrines as Christ's mediatorship, the covenant of grace, and the similarity between the Old and New Testaments.

202 Some points are to be presented in order to explain why I take the negative position on Calvin's authorship of this preface. Most significantly, its theological positon is quite different from that revealed in Calvin's earlier prefaces to the Olivétan Bible. For example, its author refers to Seneca's view of man addressed to the Jewish audience rather than to the Christian concept of total depravity in order to explain the still-remaining ability of man to do good works according to his will in the grace of God (Laver, 262-268). The author claims that the promise of the law is related to the "charges of sin," and thus as denoting the promise of the merit of good works (Laver, 275). On this ground, in dealing with the "letter" and "spirit" of the law, the author only takes into account the work of the Holy Spirit through the law. No statement on Christ's fulfilment of the law based on the shadow-substance framework is presented (Laver, 280). Cf. "John Calvin's Latin Preface to Olivétan's French Bible (1535)," tr. Ford Lewis Battles from Latin (*CO* 9.787-790), 1536 *Inst.* 373-377; "Preface to Olivétan's New Testament: Epistle to the Faithful Showing that Christ Is the End of the Law," *CC* 58-73.

Rabbi Josel of Rosheim has been suggested as the person. This assumption is supported by Calvin's participation in the debate on the Torah in Frankfurt in 1539. However, we can hardly presume that there was such a critical theological debate between one of the most renowned Jewish scholars and a relatively young Christian pastor from Strasbourg who attacked him with a "violent, angry and menacing" harangue.[203] Another view has suggested that Calvin's *Ad quaestiones* was influenced by Sebastian Münster's Hebrew-Latin diglot of the Gospel of Matthew, which contains the annotations of *Sefer Nizzahon*, and considers "a certain Jew" to be the unknown author of *Sefer Nizzahon*.[204] The feasibility of view depends on the fact that the structure of the tract almost concurs with that of Calvin's commentary on Matthew, the structure of which in turn is remarkably similar to Münster's Matthew diglot. It does not, however, refer seriously to Calvin's use of theological terms and his theological characteristics, nor does it take much consideration of the influence of contemporaries on Calvin's commentary on the *Harmony of the Gospels*, especially of the influence of Bucer, the affinity of whose biblical interpretation to Christian Judaism is significant.[205]

Therefore, most scholars who characterize this work as the one by which Calvin expresses his position on some crucial theological themes related to the biblical Jews rather than a wayward polemic against contemporary Jews have argued that the Jewish interlocutor was created by the imagination of Calvin.[206] Those questions raised by the interlocutor are mostly with the intention of criticizing the lack of continuity in Christian theology with the Old Testament. They range over the person and work of Christ, the relation of law and gospel, and the state of the Jews in the New Testament. In response to these questions, Calvin refers consistently to Old Testament passages in order to verify the continuity of Christian theology. Therefore, when we read this tract, we should pay special attention to "its academic character."[207] If we regard this work as a letter, as Beza did, the recipients would be Christians themselves rather than certain Jews.[208]

Ad quaestiones may well be divided into three parts. Some of the first articles deal with the meaning of the coming of Christ. At the outset, the Jewish interlocutor asks about the paradox that Christ who came "to cleanse

---

203 Baron, "John Calvin and the Jews," 346-349, 352. Quot. Josel's *Diary*.
204 S. G. Burnett, "Calvin's Jewish Interlocutor: Christian Hebraism and Anti-Jewish Polemics during the Reformation," *Bibliothèque d'Humanisme et Renaissance* 55/1 (1993), 117-118, esp. 118.
205 Ibid., 120.
206 Locher, "Calvin Spricht zu den Juden," 180-186, esp. 186, n. 7.
207 Jacques Courvoisier, "Calvin et les Juifs," *Judaica* 2 (1946), 204.
208 Ibid.

men from sins" "increased the sin of the Jews."[209] Calvin's response is that Christ as the Son of God already came as "the light of life" not only to the Jews but also to the Gentiles, but they "turned the light into shadows by their own wickedness."[210] Therefore, Calvin argues, the wrath of God was not natural but provoked by the Jews, who made "a death-bringing poison out of medicine."[211] In the same vein, Calvin's answer to the question about the abrogation of the law raised in Qs. 2 and 4 is as follows: "Certainly a clear change of external worship is shown under the reign of the Messiah; however, the law is not destroyed in this way, nor is a point of it diminished. Rather, indeed this is the true ordinance (*sanctio*) of the law: not an empty spectacle exposed to the eyes in the old forms but a spectacle of things which signified the substance shown forth in Christ."[212] In defense of the continuity of the law, Calvin rests on the *umbra-substantia* analogy as he uses such words related to the sacraments as *umbra, figura, substantia, symbolum* and the verb *significare*.[213]

The second part consists of questions related to Jewish literal interpretation, including Qs. 5, 8, 10, 12, and 13. Calvin here affirms his spiritual, but not allegorical, interpretation of the Bible. For instance, in answering the question about the length of Jesus's lying dead on earth, Calvin, reminding us of his favorite rhetorical "synecdoche," asserts that "in examples, full conformity is not essential, nor are they absurd if something dissimilar is noted."[214] In responding to the question why people did not have the power to move a mountain when they prayed in spite of the promise of Christ, Calvin says, criticizing the Jewish literal interpretation, that "if there were to be any grain of wit and sane intelligence in those

---

209 *CO* 9.657: ". . . ut mundaret homines a peccatis, . . . auxerit peccatum Iudaeorum, . . ." I refer to the English translation of *Ad quaestiones* by Rabbi Susan Frank, which appears as an appendix in Laver's dissertation, but all quotations in this book are basically my translation. "Calvin, Jews, and Intra-Christian Polemics," 229-261.
210 *CO* 9.657: ". . . sua malitia lucem vertisse in tenebras."
211 *CO* 9.658.
212 *CO* 9.659: "Certe clara externi cultus mutatio sub regno Messiae ostenditur: neque tamen hoc modo dissolvitur lex, vel apex unus ex eo minuitur: quin potius haec vera est legis sanctio, non fuisse in veteribus figuris obiectum oculis inane spectaculum, sed eorum quae significabant exhibitam in Christo substantiam." Frank translates "*sanctio*" as "holiness" (Laver, 233). The word "*sanctio*," which means "sanction," "decree," or "ordiance," should be differentiated from "*sanctimonia*."
213 *CO* 9.958, 961. Cf. Calvin Augustine Pater, "Calvin, the Jews and the Judaic Legacy," in *In Honor of John Calvin,* 266-286.
214 *CO* 9.665: ". . . in exemplis plenam conformitatem exacte non requiri, nec absurdum esse, si quid dissimile notetur."

beasts, they could learn without controversy that the word of Christ, in which they hunt after absurdity, is the most truthful."²¹⁵

The third part, including all of the remaining questions, converges on the person and office of Christ as the Mediator. Calvin, accusing the Jews of thinking of the incarnation as the transformation of God into human flesh, claims that "we believe that he was manifested in the flesh but is still like himself."²¹⁶ Then, in order to explain harmoniously the eternal deity of the Son of God and his incarnation he refers to his own concept of *communicatio idiomatum*, which is based on the so-called *extra Calvinisticum* (Cf. *Inst*. 2.14.1-2). He says that "inasmuch as Christ is God, he transfers the vivifying power of his Spirit to human nature."²¹⁷

First, the Jewish interlocutor raises questions about the presence of Christ as the Son of God in the Old Testament by asking about the difference or superiority of the Son of God over angels (Qs. 6, 7). In responding to them, Calvin argues that Christ is differentiated from other angels, who are called the sons and ministers of God, considering the fact that he is "the Son" of God and "the Angel"—the chief of angels. Citing David's and Solomon's words, Calvin points out that the superiority of Christ is witnessed by them, that only the Son of God is prophesied legitimately as the future Son of man.²¹⁸ Also, as the Angel, Christ is called "the leader and guardian of people (*ducem populi et custodem*)."²¹⁹

Secondly, in responding to Qs. 11, 16 about the visibility of the deity of Christ after the incarnation, Calvin claims that God's "divine essence" is visible only to the spiritual eyes "in the person of Christ."²²⁰ This answer recalls the *totus Christus, non totum* in Calvin's theology of the Lord's Supper. We participate in the whole person of Christ spiritually, not in a carnal sense because he is not ubiquitous but now dwells in heaven. In giving an answer to the question about how Christ felt hunger and had his own will (human will) if he was the same as God, Calvin refers again to his unique concept of *communicatio idiomatum*. He says that "because it was somewhat useful for him to be recognized by us as a brother, to whom the condition of human life was common, he immediately returned to what is proper to humans. Not because the infirmities of the human nature were

---

215 *CO* 9.666: "Si granum salis vel sanae intelligentiae in istis pecudibus esset, sine controversia verissimum esse cognoscerent Christi dictum, in quo absurditatem venantur."
216 *CO* 9.660: "Neque enim, ut somniant Iudaei, credimus Deum esse mutatum, sed in carne manifestatum, et interea sui similem."
217 *CO* 9.660: ". . . quatenus Deus est, in humanam naturam vivificam spiritus sui potentiam transfundit."
218 *CO* 9.662.
219 *CO* 9.662.
220 *CO* 9.665-666, 669-670.

overcome except to that extent that by his own pure will he lowered himself to be like us."[221]

Thirdly, another question is raised about the relation between Christ and the paschal lamb in Q. 15. In response to this question, Calvin claims that Christ was foreshadowed by "the figure (*figura*)" not only of the paschal lamb and of all sacrifices but also of all priests and of the kingship in the Davidic family. He asserts that "God foreshadowed something far superior in the whole legal worship" even to the ancient people and made them look for the Mediator Christ. Then, he accuses the Jews of having the false conviction that in order to communicate with God "more Christs should be found by us."[222]

Although Calvin's responses to the third sets of questions contain significant remarks on the person and work of Christ as the Mediator, he does not use the word mediator at all before Q. 19, "If Christ was God, why, while he prayed, did he say to his Father that he would perform his will?"[223] This question is a crucial one for the Jews because it touches on their doctrine of the mediation of priests and angels in prayer and sacrifices founded on the Torah, and even on their view of the coming Messiah. In the response to this question, Calvin demonstrates his unique understanding of *communicatio idiomatum* based on the so-called *extra Calvinisticum*:

> They indeed do not here accuse us at all of what an Apostle declares with fear, that Christ died of the weakness of the flesh but rose again in the power of the Spirit (I Peter 3:18). In Christ the office of the Mediator which could not be performed without his obedience should always be observed by us in this way that he could not fulfill the obedience unless he had humiliated himself. Christ, therefore, not only accepted being weak according to the human nature, but he assuming the form of a slave made himself empty not because anything at all was lost from his eternal power or became less but because his divinity kept itself silent until he showed the full obedience to his Father in the person of man. In this way, these two sentences concur: "I lay down life away from Myself, that I

---

221 *CO* 9.668: "[Sed] quia non minus utile erat, fratrem a nobis agnosci, cui nobiscum humanae vitae conditio esset communis, ad ea quae propria sunt hominis, statim reversus est. Non quod in eo dominatae sint humanae infirmitates, nisi quatenus mero suo arbitrio se submisit, ut nobis esset similis."

222 *CO* 9.669: "[Ergo] in toto legali cultu aliquid praestantius adumbravit Deus. . . . plures nobis reperiendos Christos."

223 *CO* 9.671: "Si ille fuit Deus, quare dum oraret dixit patri suo, ut faceret voluntatem suam?" This question is based on the Prayer of Jesus at Gethsemane in Matthew 26:36-42. Cf. Burnett, "Calvin's Jewish Interlocutor," 123, "Appendix: Index of Quotations in Calvin's Response."

may take it up again" and "Father, glorify Your Son" (John 10:17 and John 17:1).[224]

Then, in responding to Q. 20, "'Total dominion of heaven and earth were given to me.' Who then gave it to him?,"[225] Calvin asserts, referring to Psalm 45:8, that from the beginning Christ the Son of God performed the office of the Mediator (*munus mediatoris*) of intercession between God and man both as the king and as Elohim in both his humanity and divinity.[226] He insists: "To be sure, if Christ had not assumed in his human himself our poverty and nakedness, that sort of giving would have been superfluous."[227] In Q. 21, the interlocutor asks how the divine nature of Christ is sustained if he takes true humanity. Calvin finds the answer in the word *persona*, which

---

224 *CO* 9.671: "Hic vero nihil nobis obiectant quod non intrepide apostolus praedicet, Christum ex infirmitate carnis mortuum esse, qui resurrexit in virtute spiritus (1. Pet. 3, 18). In Christo semper nobis observandum est mediatoris munus, quod praestare non potuit sine obsequio, sicuti nec obsequio potuit defungi, quin se humiliaret. Christus ergo secundum hominem non modo infirmus esse sustinuit, sed assumpta servi forma exinanivit se ipsum, non quod ex aeterna eius virtute quidquam decesserit, vel fuerit imminutum, sed quia quietam se continuit eius divinitas, donec in hominis persona plenam obedientiam patri suo praestaret. Hoc modo conveniunt duae istae sententiae: Ego a me ipso animam meam pono et iterum sumam eam, item: pater glorifica filium tuum (Ioann. 10, 17; Ioann. 17, 1)." Calvin translates the latter part of I Peter 3:18 as "*mortificatus quidem carne, vivificatus autem Spiritu.*" Passive participles *mortificatus* and *vivificatus* denote the economy of the Trinity in the death and resurrection of Christ. The passage quoted in *Ad quaestiones* is from his commentary on the verse: ". . . *etsi passus est propter infirmitatem carnis, resurrexit in virtute spiritus*" (*CO* 55.264). The word "*resurrexit*" itself should not be translated as passive, although it includes the meaning of "*vivificatus*" theologically. The same fault is found in the translation presented in Laver, "Calvin, Jews, and Intra-Christian Polemics," 256. Calvin's understanding of *communicatio idiomatum* of the two natures of Christ in his mediation is well expressed in the phrase "*quietam se continuit eius divinitas.*" Cf. Comm. Lk. 19:41 (2.295, *CO* 45.576): "His Deity rested (*quievit*) and in a sense hid (*abscondit*) Itself, lest It should hinder Him as Mediator" (2.295, *CO* 45.576); Matthew 24:36 (3.99, *CO* 45.672): "the two natures in Christ were so conformed in one Person that each retained what was proper (*proprietas*) to it: in particular the Divinity was silent (*quievit Divinitas*) and made no assertion of itself whenever it was the business of the human nature to act alone in its own terms in fulfilment of the office of Mediator."
225 *CO* 9.672: ". . . datum est mihi omne dominium coeli et terrae? Quis enim dedit ei?"
226 Cf. Comm. Ps. 45:8-11 (2.184-190, *CO* 31.454-457). Calvin here comments that the kingdom of Solomon stands for the kingdom of God, which is the Church of Christ.
227 *CO* 9.672: "Certe nisi Christus cum hominis persona inopiam nostram vel nuditatem in se sumpsisset, supervacua esset ista donatio."

represents the unity (*unitas*) of the two natures in the *hypostasis* of Christ rather than in their physical union (*unio*).[228] The unity of the person of Christ, this is the core of Calvin's argument.

The last two questions are concerned with the contradiction between Christ's condemnation of Judas Iscariot and his promise of salvation. The Jewish interlocutor asks about the probability of the salvation of the Jews. Calvin's response emphasizes that God accomplishes his providence with the intermediation of even a mere vicious man, but this is not incompatible with the fact that Christ submits himself to his Father's will voluntarily. There is no conflict between God's providence and Christ's voluntary accomplishment of his will on the cross: "The sacrifice [therefore] had to be a voluntary one. But it was brought about by the secret and wonderful plan of God that the very one who met his death voluntarily should be dragged by sinners to the cross."[229] Recalling the final words of Christ on the cross which are about asking for forgiveness for the Jewish people, the Jewish interlocutor asks if this sin of theirs can be forgiven in the final question, with a word of petition: "However, if the Father and the Son are the same and have the same will, certainly this sin would be forgiven since Christ himself forgave it."[230] Calvin has already presented theological answers to this question in his responses to Qs. 19 and 22. So here he just touches on God's rule on reward and punishment. He indeed confirms that God's plan, God's rule, and Christ's mediation cannot be in discord with each other at all.

5.6 Conclusion

As we have seen, several crucial themes we examined regarding Christ and the law in Calvin's Old Testament interpretation are discussed in *Ad quaestiones*. Overall in this significant work, Calvin concentrates on the continuity of Christ's mediatorship concerning creation and redemption in order to explain *Deus manifestatus in carne*. On this basis, he argues that Christ's fulfilment of the law does not mean either annulment or abrogation of the law, instead, it signifies the manifestation of the substance of the true

---

228 *CO* 9:673: "Dicimus, sicuti anima et corpus hominem unum efficiunt, ita Christum ex duabus naturis constare: non quod similitudo omni ex parte conveniat, sed quia apta et concinna est ad exprimendam personae unitatem."

229 *CO* 9.674: "Sacrificium igitur voluntarium esse oportuit: arcano autem et admirabili Dei consilio factum est, ut idem qui sponte mortem obibat, ab impiis traheretur ad crucem." Note Calvin's own title of *Inst.* 1.18 (CO 2.167): "Deum ita impiorum opera uti, et animos flectere ad exsequenda sua iudicia, ut purus ipse ab omni labe maneat."

230 *CO* 9.674: "Si autem pater et filius idem sunt, et est illis eadem voluntas, esset certe condonata haec iniquitas, quum ille ipsemet condonaret."

ordinance of the law. He explains the union (*unio*) of the two natures of Christ in terms of the unity (*unitas*) of his person which is revealed most prominently in his own concept of *communicatio idiomatum*. Calvin understands *communicatio idiomatum* the way in which the two natures of Christ work as the Mediator. In this respect, the extent of the so-called *extra Calvinisticum* reaches to the person of Christ the Mediator even before his incarnation.

The tract has no date, preface or conclusion, but is very well organized. It is also theological and academic as well as biblical. It is like a dialogue between the Old Testament and the New. Mainly concerned about the Old Testament, Calvin does not quote from Romans 9-11. However, he affirms that the grace of our Lord is not only for the Gentiles but also for the Jews indiscriminately. He is concerned much about the salvation-historical significance of the betrayal of Judas and the great sin of the Jewish people, but he does not point out the superiority of the sinfulness of the Jews. Rather, he indicates the fact that not only the Jews but also the Gentiles rejected the Son of God who came as the light from the beginning. His tone is far from "violent, angry and menacing."[231]

If we take the position that this tract was written by Calvin in his later years, as the editors of *Corpus Reformatorum* believed, we may well presume that it was written in response to Servetus' criticism of the Judaizing Calvin. Unquestionably, both Calvin and Servetus were influenced by Jewish literal interpretations of the Old Testament. Calvin was keen enough to match the historical and literary interpretation with his Christology in the Old Testament by referring to the concept of *Christus mediator legis* on the basis of the understanding of the so-called *extra Calvinisticum*. Convinced that Christ performed his mediatorship effectively even before his incarnation, Calvin was able to develop his positive and dynamic stance on the law without losing the continuity of the law.

On the other hand, Servetus, who was significantly influenced by the Jewish Cabbalistic understanding of the person of Christ, was so accustomed to the dispensational conception of revelation that he could not match Christ in the law in the Old Testament with the law in Christ in the New Testament. Thus, for him, the barbarity of the ancient Jewish people

---

231 Baron, "John Calvin and the Jews," 347. Baron's criticism is derived mostly from his prejudice against Calvin's temperament. He says that this "violent, angry and menacing" man described in Jesel's *Diary* "would quite fit" the temperament of Calvin, who attended the debate as Bucer's "faction." The following expressions reveal Baron's stance more vividly: "Calvin was temperamentally far from inclined to give any opponent an equal chance . . ."; "It would quite fit Calvin's temperament to have made a menacing speech against . . ."; ". . . his customary rancor."

defines the character of the law as such. No divine accommodation is suggested except for their immaturity. He could not admit to the concept of the grace of the law before the law of Christ was proclaimed by his coming. Basically, Servetus' negative view of the law is founded on his anti-Trinitarianism. In this respect, his doctrine of the law cannot be called biblically-Jewish. Rather, it can be properly called philosophically-Judaic. He must have believed that his pantheistic understanding of the person of Christ, which he equates with his personal presence, corresponds to the neo-Platonic concept of the progress of revelation. He endeavored to apply this *ratio* to the *veritas* of the Bible in the course of expounding it as literally as possible. His anti-Trinitarianism was the fruit of this task. In fact, when he accused Calvin of Judaizing, it was more related to the *ratio* of the law than to its *veritas*.

Hunnius' criticism in his *Calvinus Iudaizans* was associated with the *ratio*, in this case, that of the Trinity and Christology in the Old Testament. He did not criticize Calvin's Arianism, but his historical interpretation focused on the original addressees. The Wittenberg theologian, who was influenced by his predecessor Luther's Christo-typological interpretation of Messianic narratives and prophecies in the Old Testament, took issue with Calvin's practice in Old Testament exegesis: to read a text according to its context and then to link its contextual meaning with a theological dogma, which is a typical pattern in Calvin's commentary on Genesis 3:15. Hunnius was not keen to understand the fact that when Calvin talks about the economy of God, he actually denotes the mediation of Christ the Son of God in the Old Testament. In short, while Hunnius takes into consideration the existence of the Trinity in terms of its *ratio*, Calvin is concerned about its significance in terms of its economy and *veritas* (truth or reality).

Calvin's tract *Ad quaestiones* demonstrates outstandingly Calvin's midway position between Servetus and Hunnius. With reference to Christology in the Old Testament, Calvin emphasizes the office of Christ as the Mediator, but, unlike Servetus, he does not equate the personal presence of Christ with his person. Even though he definitely acknowledges the existence of the three persons of God in the Old Testament, unlike Hunnius, he understands it through their specific office and economy. With reference to the law, although Calvin emphasizes Christ's fulfilment of the law, unlike Servetus, he believes that the law played a positive role in the life of the ancient Jewish people. Calvin does emphasize the spiritual meaning of the law in the Old Testament, but unlike Hunnius he makes more use of the law in the historical context through the mediation of Christ than of just its typological and sometimes allegorical use. Against this theological background, we can rightly understand Calvin's criticism both of the "new Judaism" of Catholicism and of the anti-Judaism of the Anabaptists. In fact, strictly speaking, there is no *via media*; there is only *medius noster*, Christ our Lord.

CHAPTER 6

Christ the Mediator as the Interpreter and Fulfilment of the Law in Calvin's Exegesis of the Gospels

A study of the work and teaching of Christ the Mediator in the Four Gospels is crucial for exploring Calvin's Christological understanding of the law from both the perspectives of the *umbra-substantia* and the promise-fulfilment analogies because it touches specifically on how Christ as the substance of the law interprets the original nature of the law, which Calvin defines the eternal righteousness of God revealed in the law, and how Christ as the fulfilment of the law accomplishes the demand of the law. This chapter will be devoted to this study, especially focusing on the relationship between Christ's mediation of teaching and reconciliation.

6.1 Probing Calvin's Christological Understanding of the Law in His Commentary on the Gospels

Calvin's commentary on the Synoptic Gospels was his first major work to be published after the dramatic downfall of the former first syndic Ami Perrin and his party.[1] Calvin dedicated it to the presidents and the Council of Frankfurt, to whom also his opponent Joachim Westphal had recently dedicated his book on the Lord's Supper.[2] Unlike his contemporaries such as Bucer, Bullinger, and Melanchthon, Calvin began his commenting with the Epistles and, in turning to the Gospels, wrote on John before the Synoptics.[3] Though Calvin's motivation for choosing this route through the

---

1 For the expulsion of Perrin and his partisans from Geneva, see Cottret, *Calvin: A Biography*, 198-199; McNeill, *The History and Character of Calvinism*, 177.
2 "Dedicatory Epistle," *CNTC* 1.vii-ix (*CO* 15.710-712). Westphal published *Collectanea sententiarum D. Aurelii Augustini de coena Domini* in Frankfurt and dedicated it to its city council. In opposition to this work, Calvin published *Defensio sanae et orthodoxae doctrinae de sacramentis* (*CO* 9.5-36) in January 1555. The publication of this treatise was delayed because of the censorship of the Council of Geneva. This caused him to postpone writing the commentary on the Synoptic Gospels. Cf. De Greef, *The Writings of John Calvin*, 100-101, 191-192; Jean-François Gilmont and Rodolphe Peter, *Bibliotheca Calviniana: Les œuvres de Jean Calvin publiées au XVIe siècle*, vol. 2 (Gèneve: Droz, 1994), 55/9 (588).
3 Parker, *Calvin's New Testament Commentaries*, 31, 60-84. Cf. Gilmont and Peter,

New Testament remains unclear, Parker observes that Calvin might have intended to see the life and work of Christ in the light of the teaching of the Epistles and the Fourth Gospel.[4] Calvin designates the first three Gospels as the "body (*corpus*)," which contain "all the duties (*partes*) of the Mediator," and the Gospel of John as its "soul (*animam*)" and "a key (*clavem*) to open to the understanding of others."[5]

With reference to Christ's mediation of the law, the peculiarity of the Gospels demonstrates not only the fact that the Son of God is manifested as the Mediator in the person of *Deus manifestatus in carne* but also the fact that he, who is the substance of the law, reveals and fulfils the eternal righteousness of the law. When Christ teaches the original meaning of the law in the Sermon on the Mount and several narratives related to its authority and validity, he actually reveals himself, that is, his person and office as the Mediator. So, whenever Christ is manifested as the interpreter of the law in the Gospels, he is manifested as the fulfilment of the law at the same time. How then should we deal with the *ad hoc* significance of Christ's teaching of the law before its fulfilment?

Dieter Schellong keenly approaches this question with the assumption that Calvin's exegetical stance was taken "between the biblical text and the concrete position of the evangelical church in the era of the counter-Reformation" in his book *Das evangelische Gesetz in der Auslegung Calvins*,[6] which was published as a part of his main work, *Calvin's Auslegung der synoptischen Evangelien*. He emphasizes in the former work that Christ was not merely "the proclaimer of the new law (*ein Verkünder neuer Gesetz*)," but rather gave the new teaching of the law "to accommodate himself to human beings (*den Menschen zu akkommodieren*)," specifically, *den Menschen "der Gemeinde*."[7]

Schellong holds, in reference to the ethical significance of the law for *der Mensch der Gemeinde*, that Calvin does not discriminate between a godly person and a worldly person as Luther does, but rather refers to the dual nature of man, which is finally overcome by the grace of Christ the Mediator.[8] Influenced by Bohatec, Schellong farther asserts that Calvin

---

Bibliotheca Calviniana, 2.53/5 (483): "Il est donc vraisemblable que Calvin a présenté au Conseil de Genève son commentaire de Jean et la 'glose ordinaire' de Robert Estienne." See also David F. Wright, "Robert Estienne's *Nova Glossa Ordinaria*: A Protestant Quest for a Standard Bible Commentary," in *Calvin: Erbe und Auftrag. Festschrift für Wilhelm H. Neuser zum 65. Geburtstag*, ed. Willem van't Spijker (Kampen: Kok, 1991), 41-43.

4 Parker, *Calvin's New Testament Commentaries*, 35.
5 "The Theme of the Gospel of John," *CNTC* 4.6 (*CO* 47.VII).
6 (München: Chr. Kaiser Verlag, 1968), "Einleitung," 9.
7 Ibid.
8 Ibid., 10-11: "Calvin konnte den Weg der Zweiteilung der Person nicht mitgehen."

bases the continuity of the law on the common ground of natural law, and explores it in view of the affinity between the precepts (*praecepta*) of the law and the divine counsels (*consilia*), as well as between the law (*Gebot*) and the divine instruction (*Ratschlag*).[9]

Schellong makes two points concerning Calvin's historical interpretation of Christ's teaching of the law in the Gospels: "first, Calvin emphasizes the law of Jesus in the time of his public mission before the fulfilment of his mediatorial office; second, Calvin regards the demand of the law as pertaining to a specific person in a specific situation, so that we must detach it therefrom [i.e., from its historical particularity] and identify from it its general useful essence."[10] On this basis, Schellong argues, in his book *Calvins Auslegung der synoptischen Evangelien*, that Christ's "radicalization (*Radikalisierung*)," which is examined by Calvin in his commentary on the Gospels, overall features none other than a transformation of man through "the inner teaching of Christ."[11]

Calvin's historical and literal interpretation of the Gospels occasionally causes some Christological problems. In dealing with Calvin's Christology in his commentary on the Synoptic Gospels, Johannes L. Witte claims that although Calvin maintains the oneness of the two natures of Christ and the person of the divine Word, he has a kindred spirit with Nestorius in that he considers the human nature not as coming "from the person of the Word who became man (*auf die Person des menschgewordenen Wortes*)" but as "an independent whole (*ein autonomes Ganzes*)."[12] According to Witte, Calvin, influenced by the school of Antioch, refuses to accept the deification of the humanity of Christ, but instead refers to the work of the Holy Spirit in order to explain Christ's mediation according to both the divine and human natures. The unity between the divine and human nature in Christ is so loosened that the humanity of Christ does not play an essential role in the process of sanctification; so Christ unites God's people to himself and to his Father through the pouring out of his power, which is the power of the Holy Spirit, "always and exclusively (*immer und ausschließlich*)."[13] In this respect, Witte claims, Calvin rejects the

---

9 Ibid., 16-17, 18. In this respect, Schellong insists, Calvin's ethical understanding differs from Luther's political understanding of the law founded on his two-kingdom theory.

10 Ibid., 20-21.

11 (Müchen: Chr. Kaiser Verlag, 1968), 254-255, 271-273. Cf. Hiltrud Stadtland-Neumann, *Evangelische Radikalismen in der Sicht Calvins: Sein Verständnis der Bergpredigt und der Aussendungsrede* (Matth.10) (Neukirchen: Neukirchener Verlag, 1966), 11, 14. The author argues for Christ's radicalization on the basis that he is both the judge and the Reconciler at the same time.

12 "Die Christologie Calvins," in *Das Konzil von Chalkedon: Geschichte und Gegenwart*, ed. Alois Grillmeier (Würzburg: Echter-Verlag, 1954), 510-511. 515-516.

13 Ibid., 515-516, 529.

mediation between Christ in heaven and the faithful on earth taking place without the "personification (*Verdinglichung*)" of the power of the Holy Spirit through the Word of God and sacraments.[14]

Witte's view is completely different from that of David E. Willis, who maintains that "*Deus manifestatus in carne* . . . does indeed function to protect the fact that Jesus was Mediator as God manifested in the flesh, and that in the flesh he was never less God than he was before this fleshly manifestation. *Deus manifestatus in carne* serves also, however, to indicate the reality of both natures, their distinction, and their unity in the person of the Mediator Jesus Christ."[15] As studied before in chapter 4, Calvin understands the *communicatio idiomatum* as the way in which the two natures of Christ work in the whole process of his mediation in the light of the so-called *extra Calvinisticum*. Therefore, when Christ undertakes his mediatorial office, the power of the Spirit which proceeds from his divinity works together with the Holy Spirit who acts as the bond of the two natures.[16]

Accordingly, Willis insists that Calvin's Christology is "'Spirit-Christology' in the sense that it is so much a *Filioque-Christology*" and "Christ's existence and ordering reality beyond the flesh are in large measure to be accounted for Pneumatologically."[17] Christ's mediation in both his natures supports his voluntary subjection to the Father, the silence of the divine nature in the works which belong to the humanity of Christ, the existence of the Spirit working within the divine nature of Christ, which is often called by Calvin the Spirit of Christ, and finally the divine-human relationship moderated by the Mediator.[18]

Each of these three scholars' views gives us an insight for our inquiry into Calvin's understanding of the person and work of Christ in the Gospels. Schellong teaches the continuity between the Word of God and the word of the incarnate Christ, and the ethical, evangelical, and contextual significance of his teaching and application of the law. Witte refers to the special work of the Holy Spirit in order to explain the union of the two natures of Christ especially with reference to his mediation as *Deus manifestatus in carne*. In so doing, both scholars are keen to distinguish the

---

14 Ibid., 528.

15 *Calvin's Catholic Christology*, 63.

16 Ibid., 84. Willis is not convinced that Calvin differentiates the Spirit of Christ from the Spirit of God. According to Krusche, although Calvin acknowledges the peculiarity of the Spirit of the Eternal *Sermo* as the Spirit of the Mediator, he claims no differentiation between the Spirit of God and the Spirit of Christ. *Das Wirken des Heiligen Geistes nach Calvin*, 128-129.

17 Ibid., 82-83.

18 For Christ's mediation, the divine-human relationship, and the work of the Holy Spirit, see Butin, *Revelation, Redemption, and Response*, 62-75.

Spirit of Christ and the Spirit of God, but they are not concerned about linking their thought with Calvin's peculiar understanding of *communicatio idiomatum*, which is based on the so-called *extra Calvinisticum*. Willis picks up this point and from it seeks to explain the continual mediation of Christ, which sheds light on our study of the relationship between Christ the interpreter and the fulfilment of the law.[19]

In the following, reflecting on these theological observations, I will first examine Calvin's interpretation of Christ's teaching of the law with great emphasis on the influence and role of Christ the Mediator. At this stage I am mainly concerned with the continuity of the law and the *ad hoc* significance of Christ's interpretation of the law. In the following section I will investigate the meaning of Christ's fulfilment of the law presented in Calvin's interpretation of Matthew 5:17-18. With reference to the fulfilment of the law, the fact that Christ is the substance and truth of the law will be especially taken into consideration. Then, finally, I will deal with the life and work of Christ, centred on its significance for the continual mediation of the law.

Throughout this chapter, I will concentrate primarily on Calvin's exegesis of the Gospels, but in the first two sections I will compare Calvin's position with those of Melanchthon and Bucer to show its characteristics more clearly.

6.2 Christ's Interpretation of the Law

6.2.1 "Ego autem dico vobis"

Through his teaching of the law in Matthew 5:17-48 Christ reveals not only the true meaning of the law but also his authority as the Son of God, which is authenticated by the typical expression in six antitheses, "*Audistis quoniam dictum est antiquis, . . . Ego autem dico vobis, . . .*" It is worthwhile starting with Matthew 5:20 before we treat each individual teaching, because although Calvin, like Bucer, deals with this verse along with the following teaching of the sixth commandment, he regards it as a common introduction to the other five teachings.

In commenting on verse 20 along with the following verses, Calvin accuses the Pharisees and Scribes of "perverse teaching" by which they

---

19 Cf. Ganoczy, *Ecclesia Ministrans*, 45-61. Like Willis, Ganoczy refers to the so-called *extra Calvinisticum* in order to explain Calvin's dialectical position on the person of Christ after the incarnation in accordance with the Chalcedonian formula. In doing so, however, Ganoczy turns to the dialogue between *Gottes Göttlichkeit* and *Gottes Menschlichkeit* (*Deus manifestatus in carne*) rather than the hypostatic union between *Gottnatur Christi* and *Menschennatur Christi*.

bound the divine law only to "the outward duties."[20] More specifically, he identifies the Scribes who "struggled to besmear the teaching of the Gospel as playing havoc with the Law" and the Pharisees who "were not satisfied with the plain text (*simplici litera*), but claimed to have a key to elicit hidden senses."[21] Whereas the Pharisees fabricate the righteousness of the law and make it their own by distorting its precepts, Calvin comments, Christ never wished to "change," "innovate," or "correct" them.[22] As he puts it,

> Christ is not to be made into a new Law-giver, adding anything to the everlasting righteousness of His Father, but is to be given the attention of a faithful Interpreter, teaching us the nature of the Law, its object, and its scope.[23]

Regarding the continuity of the law, some key features should be noted. First, Calvin emphasizes the eternal normativeness of the law. The law reveals and works as "the precepts of holy and godly living (*pie sancteque vivendi praecepta*)."[24] Secondly, the righteousness of the law is different from that of the temporary political and civil one, which is bound only to outward offices, because it is spiritually engraved within our heart.[25] Thirdly, the spiritual nature of the law denotes the eternal righteousness of God, which is revealed ultimately and fulfilled by Christ the Mediator. Therefore, the law contains both the precepts and promises. In this respect Calvin argues: "The beginning of righteousness was once handed down in the Law, but its perfection was taught in the Gospel."[26] Thus, commenting on the phrase "*Ego autem dico vobis*," Calvin claims that "He [Christ] does not set His answer against the precept of Moses, but against the popular fiction of the scribes."[27]

---

20 Comm. Matt. 5:20 (1.182 [altered], *CO* 45.173-174).
21 Comm. Matt. 5:20 (1.182-183, *CO* 45.173-174).
22 Comm. Matt. 5:21 (1.183, *CO* 45.174): ". . . atqui nihil minus propositum Christus habuit quam aliquid *mutare* vel *novare* in legis praeceptis. . . . Quod autem nihil in eius praeceptis *corrigere* voluerit Christus, . . ." (italics mine).
23 Comm. Matt. 5:21 (1.184, *CO* 45.175): ". . . neque enim fingendus est Christus novus legislator, qui ad aeternam patris sui iustitiam aliquid addat, sed tanquam fidus interpres audiendus est, ut sciamus qualis sit lex, quorsum tendat, et quousque pateat."
24 Comm. Matt. 5:21 (1.183 [altered], *CO* 45.174).
25 Comm. Matt. 5:21 (1.184 [altered], *CO* 45.175).
26 Comm. Matt. 5:21 (1.183. *CO* 45.174): ". . . Iustitiae initium traditum olim fuisse in lege, perfectionem vero in evangelio doceri: . . ."
27 Comm. Matt. 5:22 (1.184 [altered], *CO* 45.175).

6.2.2 Calvin's Exegesis in Comparison with Melanchthon's and Bucer's

Calvin's commentary on the Sermon on the Mount shows his lucid brevity of style and his zeal for the edification of church.[28] In dealing with the so-called Synoptic problems, Calvin prefers Augustine's position to Osiander's, when he says that the Sermon on the Mount and the Sermon on the Plain in Luke 6 have the same origin.[29] Here I study Bucer's and Melanchthon's commentaries on Matthew 5:17-48 and on some related verses in the Gospels, not only because these books have been believed to be a significant influence on Calvin's commentaries on the Gospels,[30] but also because, as Parker observes, "they also represented a distinctive literary tradition and had imposed this tradition on the commentary form."[31] I will accordingly refer to Luther's commentary on the Sermon on the Mount, especially in discussing the origin of these Reformers' works.[32]

In the note of dedication of his commentary on Romans to Simon Grynaeus of Basel, Calvin appreciates three Reformers "among so many scholars of pre-eminent learning"[33]: Melanchthon illustrated major points with excellent knowledge and skill; Bullinger expounded doctrine with an ease of expression; and, Bucer, to whom Calvin paid most homage, was superseded by no one in his precise and diligent interpretation of the

---

28 Z. N. Holler, "Calvin's Exegesis of the Sermon on the Mount," in *Calvin Studies III*, 5. Calvin cites from Augustine on three occasions, from Chrysostom twice, and Erasmus once. He regularly refutes the Papists but not so severely as he does in his *Institutes* 1559.

29 Comm. Matt. 5:1 (1.168, *CO* 45.160): "Both Evangelists had the intention of gathering into one single passage the chief headings of Christ's teaching, that had regard to the rule of godly and holy living." Cf. Schellong, *Calvins Auslegung der synoptischen Evangelien*, 43-67; Henk Jan de Jonge, "Sixteenth-century Gospel Harmonies: Chemnitz and Mercator," in *Théorie et pratique de l'exégèse*, ed. Irena Backus et Francis Higman (Genève: Droz, 1990), 156. In his commentary on the harmony of the Synoptic Gospels (1537), Andreas Osiander claims that "each evangelist had preserved the correct chronological order." He is opposed to Augustine who argues that "none of the evangelists could be deemed to have preserved the true, historically correct order of the events narrated."

30 Cf. Parker, *Calvin's New Testament Commentaries*, 60-84; Schellong, *Calvins Auslegung der synoptischen Evangelien*, 9-42.

31 Parker, *Calvin's New Testament Commentaries*, 61.

32 *Wochenpredigten über Matth. 5-7* (1530/2). *Das fünffte, Sechste und Siebend Capitel S. Matthei gepredigt und ausgelegt* (1532), *WA* 32.299-544. Luther's concept of the law is precisely described in *Von den guten Werken* (1520), *WA* 6.196-276.

33 The scholars mentioned here might be Valla, Ficino, Colet, Lefévre d'Etaples, Erasmus, Luther, Zwingli, and Oecolampadius, etc. Cf. Fritz Büsser, "Bullinger as Calvin's Model in Biblical Exposition," in *In Honor of John Calvin*, 68. For the survey of the three Reformers' exegetical methods in their New Testament commentaries, see Parker, *Calvin's New Testament Commentaries*, 73-77.

Scripture.³⁴ Calvin then critically evaluates Melanchthon and Bucer, for the former neglected many points and the latter was too verbose,³⁵ and says that as a compensation for these weaknesses he "decided to treat every point with such brevity."³⁶

Melanchthon lectured on the Gospel of Matthew in 1519-1520 and eventually published a collection in 1523 as *Breves Commentarii in Matthaeum*. It followed the traditional method of catechism: composed of *quaestio et enarratio, obiectio,* and *responsio*.³⁷ As he is in his commentary on Romans and *Loci Communes* which were lectured and written in the same period, in his commentary on Matthew Melanchthon "is deliberately applying to the understanding of the Bible a method the details of which he had originally evolved for the treatment of any document in general."³⁸

Bucer, like Calvin, comments on the Gospel of Matthew verse by verse, but in a noticeably subject-oriented manner.³⁹ His commentary is full of brilliant insights, which are quite logical, precise, and ranging over the whole of the Bible. He does not seem to simplify his view into conformity with any specific theological stream. Sometimes his ardent desire to allow both antithetical themes together makes him verbose and even complicated. Even so, he does not lose his own logical consistency. Calvin's assessment of Bucer's commentary on Romans is quite applicable here: "Bucer is too verbose (*prolixior*) to be read quickly by those who have other matters to deal with, and too profound (*sublimior*) to be easily understood by less intelligent and attentive readers."⁴⁰ In his case, the problem is related not so much to *brevitas* as to *facilitas*. Calvin, in the argument for his

---

34 "John Calvin to Simon Grynaeus," *CNTC* 8.2 (*CO* 10/2.403-404).
35 *CNTC* 8.3 (*CO* 10/2.404).
36 *CNTC* 8.3 (*CO* 10/2.405): "Praesertim quum ita omnia succincte perstringere iustituerem, ut non magnam temporis iacturam facturi essent lectores apud me legendo quae in aliis habentur."
37 Philip Melanchthon, *Annotationes in Evangelium Matthaei*, in *CR*, vol. 14.
38 Parker, *Calvin's New Testament Commentaries*, 62-64 (quot. 64).
39 Martin Bucer, *In sacra quatuor Evangelia, Enarrationes perpetuae, secundum et postremum recognitae. Quibus inspersi sunt syncerioris Theologiae Loci communes, ad Scripturarum fidem simpliciter et nullius cum insectatione tractati: adiectis etiam aliquot locorum tractationibus, et copiosissimo* (Oliva Roberti Stephani, 1553, hereafter MBEE). This book is the Geneva reprinting of the third edition (Basel 1536). Bucer's original commentary on Matthew, Mark, and Luke was published in Strasbourg in 1527, and was revised together with the edition of John in 1530. For the general introduction of this work, see Jacques Courvoisier, *Une traduction francaise du commentaire de Bucer sur l'évangile selon Saint Matthieu* (Paris: Librairie Félix Alcan, 1933).
40 "John Calvin to Simon Grynaeus," *CNTC* 8.3 (*CO* 10/2.404).

commentary on the *Harmony of the Gospels*, says that although he at times "dissents" from Bucer, he "imitates (*sum imitatus*)" Bucer.⁴¹

Bucer's influence on Calvin is worth taking into special consideration in dealing with Calvin's commentary on the Synoptic Gospels. Since Wilhelm Pauck designated Bucer as "the father of Calvinism," scholars have been concerned with the relation between Bucer and Calvin with special respect to their ecclesiology including church offices, church discipline, and sacraments, and sometimes in regard to their attitude towards union with Christ, Christ the Mediator, and the Holy Spirit.⁴² Even August Lang's earlier work on Bucer's commentary on the Gospels reflects this tendency.⁴³ It may not be absurd to ascribe the reason for this phenomenon to over-emphasis on *De regno Christi*.⁴⁴ Bucer did not write any book alike Calvin's *Institutes* and Melanchthon's *Loci Communes*, but his theological views are inexhaustibly presented throughout his massive exegetical works. As far as I know, there has been no single work which deals with the relation between Bucer and Calvin solely with respect to their theology of the law, in spite of the presence of available sources.⁴⁵

6.2.2.1 YOU SHALL NOT KILL (MATT. 5:21-26)

Now let us move on to Calvin's commentary on Christ's teaching of the commandments of the Second Table and compare it with those of

---

41 "The Theme of the Gospel of Jesus Christ," *CNTC* 1.xiv (*CO* 45.4). For the influence of Bucer's commentary on the Gospels upon Calvin's 1536 *Institutes*, see van't Spijker, "The Influence of Bucer on Calvin as Becomes Evident from the *Institutes*," 109.

42 Wilhelm Pauck, "Calvin and Butzer," *Journal of Religion* 9/2 (1929), 237-256, esp. 256; David F. Wright, ed., *Martin Bucer: Reforming church and community* (Cambridge: Cambridge University Press, 1994); Willem van't Spijker, *The Ecclesiastical Offices in the Thought of Martin Bucer*, tr. John Vriend and Lyle D. Bierma (Leiden: E.J.Brill, 1996); Amy Nelson Burnett, "Church Discipline and Moral Reformation in the Thought of Martin Bucer," *SCJ* (1991), 439-456; W. P. Stephens, *The Holy Spirit in the Theology of the Martin Bucer* (Cambridge: Cambridge University Press, 1970).

43 A. Lang, *Der Evangelienkommentar Martin Butzers und die Grundzüge seiner Theologie* (Leipzig, 1900); repr. Aalen: Scientia, 1972.

44 Cf. Wilhelm Pauck, "Editor's Introduction," in *Martin Bucer, De regno Christi*, LCC 19.155-173; Willem van't Spijker, "The Kingdom of Christ According to Bucer and Calvin," in *Calvin and the State*, ed. Peter de Klerk (Grand Rapids: Calvin Studies Society, 1993), 109-132, and Victor A. Shepherd, "Reponse," ibid., 133-137.

45 Cf. Hermann Schlingenseipen, *Die Auslegung der Bergpredigt bei Calvin* (Berlin: Emil Ebering, 1928), 3, 18-19. The author deals with Calvin's doctrine of the Christian life and the unity between the natural order of love and the law of Christ (*Gebote Christi*) in comparison with Erasmus, Stapulensis (Lefévre d'Etaples), Francis Lambert, Zwingli, Bucer, Luther, and Melanchthon.

Melanchton and Bucer. According to Calvin, Christ's teaching of the sixth commandment in this passage reveals "love (*caritas*)" as its own righteousness,[46] and in the same vein, "*fraterna concordia*"[47] and "*moderatio et aequitas.*"[48] He claims that if kept perfectly, the law is not merely "a preliminary to true righteousness,"[49] but "completes (*absolvat*) a righteous life."[50] Calvin interprets this passage in a more simple sense and criticizes the Papists, who established the purgatory by allegorizing Christ's teaching.

He first emphasizes Christ as the faithful interpreter of the law who reveals the eternal righteousness of God. Then, he refers to the authority of Christ to fulfil the law.[51] Finally, he points out the *ad hoc* significance of Christ's teaching, as he puts it, "Christ cites the words of the law, but He accommodates (*accommodat*) Himself to the common capacity of people."[52] Calvin regards Christ's using synecdoche in vv. 23 and 24 as serving the same end with his accommodation.[53]

On the other hand, Melanchthon, expounding this passage, is concerned chiefly with the difference (*discrimen*) between the gospel and the law, whereas Calvin concentrates on the eternal righteousness of God as the true and perfect meaning of the law.[54] Melanchthon's criticism of the Pharisees' and the Scribes' formalism does not aim so much at their attitude towards the law as at their attitude towards the gospel.[55] He tends to equate the internal (spiritual) meaning of the law with the gospel.

Melanchthon enumerates *poenitentia, fides, invocatio*, and *consolatio* in order to show the superiority of the gospel and to point out the difference between the teaching of hypocrites and of Christians.[56] Following Luther's

---

46 Comm. Matt. 5:21 (1.184 [altered], *CO* 45.175).
47 Comm. Matt. 5:23-24 (1.186, *CO* 45.177).
48 Comm. Matt 5:25 (1.186, *CO* 45.177).
49 Comm. Matt. 5:21 (1.183, *CO* 45.174).
50 Comm. Matt. 5:21 (1.183 [altered], *CO* 45.174).
51 Comm. Matt. 5:22 (1.184 [altered], *CO* 45.175): "Christus ad suam autoritatem, cui merito cedere debet omnis vetustas, populum revocat: . . ."
52 Comm. Matt. 5:21 (1.184 [altered], *CO* 45.174).
53 Comm. Matt. 5:23-24 (1.186, *CO* 45.177).
54 *CR* 14.586.
55 *CR* 14.587: "[Et] nihil dicebant de vera poenitentia, de vera humilitate, de Christo, de iusticia fidei, et de gratia, vel de illis veris consolationibus, de quibus concionantur Prophetae in promissionibus."
56 *CR* 14.589. In his interpretation of the first commandment Calvin mentions four specific elements of the true worship of God, "adoration, trust, invocation, and thanksgiving" (*Inst.* 2.8.16, *CO* 2.277-278). Calvin criticizes those who interpret the teachings of Christ and the apostles which are clearly related to the Second Table in the light of the *ratio* of the First Table (*Inst.* 2.8.52, *CO* 2.304). According to McNeill (*Inst.* 2.8.52. footnote 57), this comment refers especially to Melanchthon's view in

negative position on the law, Melanchthon here adheres only to the accusing function of the law.[57] Unlike Calvin, who emphasizes the normative use of the law for godly life, Melanchthon stresses "that we are justified by the Son of God, not by our fulfilment of the law."[58]

Melanchthon treats the kerygma of vv. 23-24 regarding the "*tota religio*," which comprises "promise," "precepts of moral works," and "ceremonies."[59] With reference to the practice of the law, he says, these three correspond to "faith," "good conscience in moral works," and "ceremonies with proper knowledge."[60] Melanchthon's attitude here becomes very polemical. He even cites Plato and Cato to defend his assertion against the false teaching of the Pope and monks.[61] He earnestly endeavors to verify the significance of the doctrine of the church for the Christian life. However, he does not take into proper consideration the law as the rule of right and godly living.[62]

Bucer, commenting on v. 20, accuses the Pharisees, Sadducees, and Essenes of alienating themselves from the kingdom of God by replacing the law with the shadow of the law,[63] and argues that the original righteousness of the sixth commandment denotes the single law—love (*dilectio*).[64] Bucer points out the distinction between the precept of the law and its practice, and deploys the concept of *pietas* based on their dynamic relation. He defines Christian piety as throwing away all kinds of carnal desire and living according to the guidance of the Spirit of Christ in pursuit of eternal spiritual felicity rather than the present external prosperity.[65]

Unlike Melanchthon, who understands the righteousness of the law as either preliminary or assimilated to the gospel, Bucer concentrates on the

---

his *Annotationes in Evangelium Mattaei* (1523), 46a.

57 CR 14.589: "Taxavit et recens [Dominus Doctor Martinus], quia Deus vult agnosci peccatum, quod intus in corde haeret, et vult expavescere, vult nos agnoscere gratuitam remissionem peccatorum, et iusticiam propter Filium."

58 CR 14.591: ". . . quod simus iusti propter Filium Dei, non propter nostram impletionem legis."

59 *CR* 14.592.

60 *CR* 14.595.

61 CR 14.592.

62 Melanchthon has the similar positive position on the interpretation of this fifth commandment as Calvin. *Loci Communes* 1555, 110-112 (*CR* 22.234-236).

63 *MBEE* 48b: "Abstulerant clavem scientiae, ut alibi illis Dominus opprobrat, sibi vendicata docendi interpretandique Legem facultate, et suffundentes sibiipsis et aliis in Lege per se lucida tenebras, tam seipsos, quam alios a regno Dei alienabant."

64 *MBEE* 48b: "Quemadmodum finis et consummatio Legis, adeoque et germanae iustitiae, dilectio est, ita hanc Christus ubique unice urget, quam denique vel solam suis cum ubique, tum iamiam migraturus ex hac vita, per novum suum et unicum praeceptum, commendat."

65 *MBEE* 49b.

eternal righteousness of the law working through the Spirit of Christ. Placing great emphasis on the Spirit of Christ, Bucer points out that Christ's office precedes the work of the Holy Spirit *in ordine*, but *in re* Christ himself is still working as the Mediator through his Spirit.[66] Bucer equally emphasizes God's grace and love, in contrast with Melanchthon, who focuses on specifically God's grace. According to Bucer, the teaching of Christ is that the sixth commandment works not only to make people aware of their miserable state and to make them seek the grace of Christ, but also to make believers live according to the rule of love following Christ. Thus, through our union with Christ, God wants us to be united equally both with the grace of Christ and his love.[67]

6.2.2.2 ON ADULTERY AND DIVORCE (MATT. 5:28-32)

Calvin's view of marriage and divorce has attracted scholars' academic interest, at first historically but recently more theologically. That interest has increased markedly since the first volumes of the Registers of the Consistory of Geneva were published in plain French and then translated into English.[68] Disputed promises to marry, married life, adultery, divorce, and remarriage had been the most frequent cases facing the Consistory since the 1541 Marriage Ordinance left the government of marriage and family life to the Consistory and to the Small Council.[69]

Adultery and divorce are dealt with differently, because whereas the former concerns both physical and spiritual chastity, the latter is mostly associated with the civil institution, even though marriage has been regarded as a religious issue with reference to its character as *sacramentum* since Augustine.[70] In dealing with divorce in Matthew 19, Calvin claims that the core of Christ's teaching in this narrative is expressed strikingly by the marriage commandment in Genesis 2:24. He regards this "perpetual

---

66 *MBEE* 49a.
67 *MBEE* 50a: "Adeo vult Deus in summa gratia et charitate esse coniunctos."
68 Cf. Robert M. Kingdon, *Adultery and Divorce in Calvin's Geneva* (London: Harvard University Press, 1995); John Witte Jr., "Between Sacrament and Contract: Marriage as Covenant in John Calvin's Geneva," *CTJ* 33 (1998), 9-75.
69 Cf. Lambert and Watt, *Registers of the Consistory of Geneva in the Time of Calvin*, vol. 1. *1542-1544*, "Introduction," xxi; Witte, "Between Sacrament and Contract," 20. For the development and practice of ecclesiastical and civil ordinances in Geneva, see Witte, ibid., 19-33.
70 Cf. Joel F. Harrington, *Reordering Marriage and Society in Reformation Germany* (Cambridge: Cambridge University Press, 1995), 50. Augustine designates a "triple good (*triplex bonum*)" resulting from the conjugal bond as procreation, fidelity, and sacrament, when he says, "*Haec omnia bona sunt propter quae nuptiae bonae sunt, proles, fides, sacramentum*" (*Corpus scriptorum ecclesiasticorum latinorum* [*CSEL*] 41:27). For the relation of marriage and the church up to the Reformation era, see ibid., 48-100.

law" as different from the Law of Moses regulating the permissiveness of divorce with a certificate in Deuteronomy 24:1-4 because the former regulates "the order of creation (*ordo creationis*)" and denotes "the inward law of God," i.e., "the rule of love (*caritatis regula*)," but the latter was given as "the polity and external order" to meet the temporal need to rule the hardness of heart of the Hebrews.[71]

Calvin's view of marriage is very positive yet strict.[72] He reckons the marriage commandment of Genesis 2:24 as "a sure law on the sacred and dissoluble bond of marriage."[73] It was not given as a compensation for human desire but as "the order of nature" before the fall to establish "the indivisible society." Therefore, the natural bond (*nexus*) of marriage is not less dissoluble than the bond of family; the former even precedes the latter.

No exception is allowed from the rule that "if a man divorces his wife the divine bond is broken."[74] Calvin does not regard the only type of divorce allowed by the Lord in v. 9 as its exception because he believes that a rotten body contaminated by adultery cannot be called a part of the body and so it should be cut off.[75] This rule applies to both parties because no party is the lord of the body (*dominus corporis*). The faith of the wife[76] or anything disagreeable such as serious diseases and leprosy cannot be a proper cause of divorce because "God instituted marriage for the common welfare of the human race."[77]

Calvin sees the role of marriage very positively: "when our nature had become corrupt, marriage began to be a medicine (*medicina*), and it is not surprising if there is some bitter taste mixed with sweetness."[78] Throughout the successive editions of the *Institutes*, he emphasizes the feature of marriage as "a remedy (*remedium*)."[79] He claims that remarriage should be

---

71 Comm. Matt. 19:3, 4, 7-8 (2.243, 244, 246, *CO* 45.528, 530).
72 For Calvin's view on practical matters in marriage, see *Projet d'Ordonnance sur les Mariages* (CO 10/1.33-44); *Quaestiones matrimoniales* (*CO* 10/1.231-244, *CEA* 121-136).
73 Comm. Matt. 19:3 (2.243, *CO* 45.527).
74 Comm. Matt. 19:4 (2.243-244, *CO* 45.528): ". . . divinum vinculum abrumpi, si vir ab uxore divortium faciat."
75 Cf. Jeffrey R. Watt, "The Control of Marriage in Reformed Switzerland, 1550-1800," in *Later Calvinism*, 35.
76 Comm. Matt. 19:9 (2.246-247, *CO* 45.531).
77 Comm. Matt. 19:10-11 (2.248, *CO* 45.532): "Atqui si coniugium instituit Deus in communem humani generis salutem, licet quaedam minus grata secum trahat, non ideo protinus spernendum est."
78 Comm. Matt. 19:10-11 (2.249, *CO* 45.531).
79 1536 *Inst.* 1.19 (*CO* 1.39). From 1539, Calvin pointed out the necessity (or need) of marriage more strongly: ". . . illam ipsam coniugalem in necessitates remedium esse ordinatum, ne in effraenem libidinem proruamus" (1539 *Inst.* 3.63, *CO* 1.410, *Inst.* 2.8.41, *CO* 2.296). Cf. Harrington, *Reordering Marriage and Society in Reformation*

allowed to widows and widowers,[80] and to divorced men and women if they are not bound either to "unlawful and frivolous divorces" or to "voluntary divorce (*voluntaria divortia*)."[81]

Therefore, no civil authority has priority to dissolve this sacred knot: "the magistrate who gives a man permission to divorce his wife is abusing his power."[82] Upbraiding the Pharisees who "were wrong in taking a rule for godly and holy life from the civil code," Calvin claims:

> The laws of the state are deflected from time to time by human morality, but when God presents a spiritual law, He does not consider what men can do, but what they ought to do (quid possint homines, sed quid debeant). So perfect and complete righteousness is contained therein, although we may lack the means to live up to it.[83]

Calvin's position on the civil law is consistent. He admits its reality but he believes that it should be guided and corrected by the spiritual law of God.[84]

Bucer's position on marriage and divorce is very similar to Calvin's regarding his emphasis on the eternal law of love, the need for severe punishment against marital crimes, and the positive attitude towards remarriage.[85] Calvin avoids Bucer's verbosity and "curious modernity"[86] on divorce and remarriage but shows an affinity to the principle of marriage

---

Germany, 53-54. Since the argument of Gratian in the *Decretum* and Peter Lombard in the *Sentences*, the *sacramentum* and the *remedium* had been the problematic dual ideals of marriage in the western church. Both the canonists had extended Augustine's triplex bonum politically with respect to the *remedium* and religiously with respect to the *sacramentum*.

80 Comm. Matt. 19:4 (2.244, *CO* 45.528).
81 Comm. Matt. 19:9 (2.247-248, *CO* 45.531, 532).
82 Comm. Matt. 19:6 (2.244, *CO* 45.529).
83 Comm. Matt. 5:31 (1.190, *CO* 45.180).
84 From some critical biblical texts, Calvin recognizes the legitimacy of divorce in order to avoid greater sins, such as incest and polygamy, e.g., Gen. 29:29, Mal. 2:14, and Deut. 24:1-4. Witte, "Between Sacrament and Contract," 45, n. 143. For the influence of his legal study and contemporary Reformers such as Bucer, Melanchthon, and Farel upon Calvin's concept of marriage, see Bohatec, *Budé, und Calvin*, 127-148; Breen, *John Calvin*, 40-66, 86-99.
85 Bucer's position on the principle and practice of marriage and divorce appears precisely in *De Regno Christi* 2.16-47 (Wendel edition, 153-236, *LCC* translation, which does not include ch. 22-46, 317-333).
86 David F. Wright, tr. and ed., *Common Places of Martin Bucer* (Appleford: Sutton Courtenay Press, 1972), 12. Concerning his liberal sanctioning of divorce and remarriage, see esp. *MBEE* 148b ff.

which is "mutual love and fidelity."[87] In spite of their similarity, however, their difference is also notable, especially in relation to Bucer's distinction between the kingdom of Christ (*regnum Christi*) and the kingdom of the world (*regnum mundi*).[88]

In commenting on Christ's teaching of the meaning of adultery, Bucer relates the seventh commandment to the tenth. Just as Calvin catches a delicate "distinction between intended will (*consilium*) and concupiscence (*concupiscentiam*),"[89] Bucer argues that a man who has perverse cupidity in the heart already commits adultery and has a propensity to violate a female neighbour against the commandment of the love of neighbour.[90] Like Calvin, Bucer realizes that the inward law does not speak of what we can do but of what we ought to do. Christ's teaching on adultery is far beyond human ability, which is totally debilitated by the fall. Whence he recommends us "to hasten to run to our restorer Christ."[91]

Based on the following features, Bucer emphasizes the grace of Christ in dealing with marriage and divorce. The first thing we should note is that Bucer does not differentiate the law taught by Christ from the law fulfilled by Christ. In commenting on Matthew 5:31-32, he says, "Since Christ expounded the precept against all perverse desires and impurities, he without doubt carried out most faithfully all things by which he restored the true knowledge of the precept and fulfilled this part of the law profoundly."[92]

The second point is that Bucer applies Christ's teaching only to the elect who belong to the kingdom of Christ. He insists in his commentary on Matthew 19 that sometimes marriage and divorce should be dealt with by secular authority rather than by church ordinances because although the regulations of civil law are not different from ecclesiastical orders where their principle is concerned, some variations should be considered with

---

87 H. Selderhuis, *Marriage and Divorce in the Thought of Martin Bucer*, tr. John Vriend and Lyle D. Bierma (Kirksville, Mo.: Thomas Jefferson University Press, 1999), 368.
88 Witte claims that Calvin's early view takes after Luther's two-kingdom theory whereas his later view reflects Bullinger's covenantal doctrine of marriage, but he does not mention Bucer's influence specifically: "Between Sacrament and Contract," 36-59.
89 *Inst.* 2.8.49 [altered] (*CO* 2.302).
90 *MBEE* 50a: "Unde videtur illud Ad concupiscendum, sic intellexisse, Qui ex prava concupiscentia mulierem modo fuerit intuitus ut damnasse intelligas quemlibet aspectum natum ex concupiscentia, non solum eum qui ad concupiscendum et quaerendum illicitam voluptatem instituitur."
91 *MBEE* 50b: ". . . ad Christum nostri innovatorem accurramus avidius."
92 *MBEE* 51a: "[Itaque] quum tractaret praeceptum contra stuprum et omnem impudicitiam, exequutus est procul dubio quam diligentissime omnia, quibus germanum praecepti intellectum restitueret, er hanc partem Legis penitus impleret."

reference to their application.[93] Commenting on Christ's words, "*Regnum meum non est de hoc mundo*," Bucer claims that Christ's teaching on divorce only refers to the elect (*electis*), not to the common people who are bound to civil orders because various things can happen in secular society that necessarily (*necessario*) require divorce. He also argues that no progress in the republic can be achieved if there is no severe punishment for adultery such as death sentence, public disgrace, and physical torment.[94]

Another characteristic of Bucer is found in the fact that he understands an eschatological dimension of the law Christologically. Commenting on celibacy in Matthew 19:10-12, he uses the words "*regnum caelorum*" as many as 14 times in two pages. He says that Christ's teaching of celibacy shows "a certain form (*specimen*) of the future life in heaven."[95] He describes the kingdom of heaven as none other than "the place where Christ governs more expansively and communicates with more people."[96] Bucer here shows a strong tendency to regard Christ's teaching as the present revelation of a future thing, whereas Calvin puts more emphasis on its significance for the original addressees.

Apparently, Calvin believes that the true meaning of the law which Christ taught in the Gospels is from the beginning and will last till the end without change, but he is very aware of the delicate distinction in dispensation between the law taught by Christ in the Sermon on the Mount and the law finally fulfilled by him on the cross. Calvin's historical interpretation of the law is consonant with his theological position on the law. On the other hand, for Bucer, "the analogy of faith (*fidei analogia*)" is considered first, then "the office of Christ," and finally "what Christ wanted to respond to and teach appropriately in each place," which was given "for the progress of piety most profitably and most persuasively."[97] This position is reflected apparently in his definite stance on divorce: "Unless there is no highest necessity by which we are compelled, we should not permit divorce."[98]

---

93 *MBEE* 147b ff.
94 *MBEE* 148b-149a: "Postremo quia omnino quaedam in vita humana saepe incidunt, quae necessario divortium requirunt, et de his vel novae leges condendae, vel veteres revocandae erant."
95 *MBEE* 150b-151a.
96 *MBEE* 150b: ". . . regnum caelorum, hoc est ut Christus latius regnet, et pluribus communicetur, . . ."
97 *MBEE* 150a: "Spectanda igitur fidei analogia est, spectandum quid officium Christi, spectandum denique quid proprie in unoquoque loco respondere et docere voluerit: et quod nusquam respondere et docere alia potuerit quam quibus in omnibus pietas quam commodissime et suavissime promoveatur."
98 *MBEE* 150a: "Discamus ergo hinc primum ut a divortio abhorreamus quam maxime, neque unquam id nobis nisi summa necessitate compulsi permittamus."

In spite of their differences, both Bucer and Calvin are convinced that the eternal righteousness of the law is revealed by Christ through his teaching on marriage and divorce. However, this is not true of Melanchthon, who relates the new teaching of Christ mainly to the revelation of the gospel rather than to the original righteousness of the law. He says that Christ's teaching on adultery in Matthew 5:27-30 is given in relation to "the doctrine of sin, grace, and new obedience."[99] Chastity (*castitas*) is identified with living in "pure (*castus*) Spirit" as "a member of Christ"[100] and marriage is regarded as making "a sweet society," i.e., "the church."[101] He argues that divorce results from original and other sins which have brought about domestic calamities.[102] Therefore, he argues, "the soul of the Gospel (*mentem Evangelii*)" is "to return marriage to the original institution: two will be into one body."[103]

Melanchthon is more generous than Calvin in the permission of divorce. He deals with men and women who abandon their spouses for a long time without a valid reason as no better than adulterers and adulteresses.[104] He approves a divorce from a spouse who is naturally unable to get married because such marriage is not marriage.[105] However, his attitude towards divorce is strict. No disease, even leprosy, can be a proper reason for divorce. For, just as parents should not abandon sons and daughters because of their diseases, so men and women should not abandon their spouses because of weaknesses.[106] Overall, Melanchthon focuses on the grace of God in the gospel. He deals with chastity as a natural virtue of marriage and asserts that it is given only by God as "a gift (donum)."[107] In this sense, he says, the real consolation is to ask for God's mercy in living according to his will in marital life.[108]

---

99 *CR* 14.596. Melanchthon's position on practical matters in marriage and divorce appears precisely in a section which has been regarded as an appendix to the third edition of *Loci Communes* (1543), *LCC* 19.247-259.
100 *CR* 14.599, 600.
101 *CR* 14.602.
102 *CR* 14.602.
103 *CR* 14.603.
104 *CR* 14.604.
105 *CR* 14.605: ". . . quando aliqua persona natura non est idonea ad coniugium, . . . talis coniunctio non est coniugium."
106   *CR* 14.605.
107   *CR* 14.597.
108 *CR* 14.605-606: "Tales impatientes sciant voluntatem Dei esse, quod debeant petere consolationem a Deo, et Deo obedire in tali afflictione, et debeant manere apud aegrotantes, et nequaquam ab eis discedere." Cf. *Loci Communes* 1555, 112 (*CR* 22.237).

6.2.2.3 ON OATHS (MATT. 5:33-37)

In his *Institutes*, Calvin relates oaths to God and to a neighbour to the fourth and the ninth commandment. There, he investigates the theological meaning of swearing focused on its relation to true worship and love of neighbour (*Inst.* 2.8.23-27, 48, *CO* 2.283-287, 301). In his commentary on Matthew 5:33-37, Calvin offers no further theological observation, with reference to his Christological understanding of the law, however, he demonstrates his typical pattern of exegesis. In v. 33, he insists that this law, according to "its original (*germana*) interpretation," should regulate not only religious vows but also personal contracts and promises, and not only perjury but also trivial oaths by the name of God.[109] When Christ says in v. 34, "Swear not at all," he "does not refer to the substance (*substantiam*) at all but to the form (*formam*),"[110] and in opposition to the Anabaptists' literal interpretation, he claims, "So we must abstain from all unnecessary liberty in swearing, for when is is compelled by a right reason, the Law not only allows the oath but explicitly enjoins it."[111]

Calvin maintains this view in spite of Christ's teaching in v. 37, which seems to prohibit taking oaths. He comments that Christ teaches "the simplicity which nature dictates," but he overcomes the merely literal meaning of the text.[112] He refers to the concept of *adiaphora*, when he says that "it does not follow that we may not legitimately take an oath as often as necessity demands it, for the use of many things is innocent, though their source be vitiated."[113]

Bucer emphasizes that those who have received the Spirit of Christ excel in making oaths. He indicates that ancient people were allowed and even encouraged by the law to swear to God and to neighbours, as we can see from many faithful oaths of the disciples of the Lord.[114] He severely criticizes the obstinacy of certain Anabaptists who were against any kind of oath whether religious or political.[115] Here Bucer again emphasizes the

---

109 Comm. 5:33 (1.190-191, *CO* 45.181).
110 Comm. 5:34 (1.191 [altered], *CO* 45.182).
111 Comm. 5:34 (1.191 [altered], *CO* 45.182). Calvin criticism's on the Anabaptists' literal interpretation is briefly shown: ". . . vocem unam morose urgendo totum sermonis tenorem clausis oculis praetereunt." Calvin's criticism of the Anabaptists' view of the oath is precisely presented in *TAL* 92-105 (*CO* 7.92-102).
112 Comm. 5:37 (1.193, *CO* 45.183).
113 Comm. 5:37 (1.193, *CO* 45.183): "Neque tamen sequitur, quin licitum sit iurare quoties id *necessitas* postulat, quia purus est multarum rerum *usus*, quarum vitiosa est *origo*" (italics mine).
114 *MBEE* 51b-52a: "A veteribus discipuli acceperant, satis ex fide cum proximo actum, si quod quis iurasset per Dominum, etiam praestitisset: Christus autem voluit docere id satis non haberi, sed oportere Christianos ea inter se fide et dilectione esse, ut nihil omnino iuramento apud eos locus relinqueretur, quippe unoquoque de alio etiam iniurato, optime sentiente et sperante."
115 *MBEE* 51b.

continual work of the Spirit of Christ. As he puts it, "Christ did not come to prescribe a new reason of living by his words, but rather to give explanation of the thing itself which was prescribed in the law and by the Prophets, by bestowing his Spirit which he earned for us by his death."[116]

Melanchthon's commentary is doctrinal and polemical. He defines, "To swear is to keep something said in the invocation of God."[117] A valid oath comprises *"veritas," "invocatio Dei," "confessio,"* and *"promissio."*[118] The Papists' oath to the saints and the Pope is invalid "because the saints are not to be invoked."[119] He accuses the Pope of "taking for himself the authority to forgive so that people cannot make promises by swearing legitimately."[120] Melanchthon's polemic against the Anabaptists is based on his strict discrimination between the law and the gospel. He argues that Christ forbids us to take an oath that is related to the gospel, e.g., the remission of sin, the purity of the heart, etc. On the other hand, he is quite positive on the political oath. He says that "legitimate oath is the bond of civil obedience and judgments."[121] To be short, oaths regarding our salvation are worthless. They are not oaths at all.[122] Other religious oaths can be valid according to the law, but political oaths are subject to political orders.

6.2.2.4 LOVE YOUR NEIGHBOUR (MATT. 5:38-48)

The last two antitheses contain Christ's teaching of the Mosaic Law on the law of talio (*lex Talionis*) and the love of neighbour. The law of talio had been regarded as the basic principle for punishment in civil law. Christ's response to this forensic principle is so revolutionary that Julian and others alike, as Calvin says, slandered him for making "a complete reversal of law and order."[123] Whereas other Reformers deal with this passage with respect

---

116 *MBEE* 52a: ". . . Christumque non venisse ut novam vivendi rationem praescriberet verbis, sed daret re ipsa potius exprimere, quam abunde in Lege et Prophetis praescripsit, donato in hoc suo Spiritu, quem nobis morte sua meruit: . . ."
117 *CR* 14.607: "Iuramentum est asseveratio alicuius dicti cum invocatione Dei."
118 *CR* 14.607-608.
119 *CR* 14.609: ". . . quod Sancti non sint invocandi."
120 *CR* 14.611: ". . . quod Papa sibi sumsit autoritatem absolvendi homines, ne faciant promissa legitimo iuramento."
121 *CR* 14.613: ". . . legitimum iusiurandum, quod est vinculum civilis obedientiae et iudiciorum."
122 *CR* 14.612: "Et quae iuramenta sint irrita, nec revera sint iuramenta." When Melanchthon claims a principle, *"Iuramentum non sit vinculum iniquitatis,"* he means by the false oath not only an oath committing sin but also an impossible oath. *Loci Communes* 1555, 92 (*CR* 22.212-213).
123 Comm. Matt. 5:39 (1.194, *CO* 45.184): ". . . leges et iudicia funditus everteret."

to practical issues such as "recourse to law" and "usury," etc., Calvin concentrates on the more essential and theological aspects of it.[124]

Accusing the Scribes of restricting the word neighbour (*proximus*) to one's friends, Calvin argues that it corresponds to the order of nature to love people as friends without discrimination.[125] He comments that Christ restores "the true and original meaning of the law"—"love (*caritas*)." The order of nature which commands mutual communication among us is still valid in spite of our total depravity because "the common nature unites (*conciliat*)" all men in general. Thus, the law of love is called "a general rule of the Law (*generale praeceptum legis*)."[126]

We cannot satisfy the demand of the law of charity and be perfect by our own ability. The necessity of obedience is not enjoined by perfection where human capacity is concerned. The Papists distorted this truth for the defense of their doctrine of perfection by devising the concept of "counsels (*consilia*)," which are construed as the law whose precepts are transformed by human reason to adjust it to human capacity.[127]

Not only should the perfection of the law not be measured by human criterion but also it should not be restricted by human capacity. As Calvin puts it, "Perfection [is used] here, not in the sense of equality (*aequalitatem*), but in relation to its likeness (*similitudinem*). However far we are from God regarding our capacity, yet we are said to be perfect as He is, as long as we aim for the same goal, that He presents us with in Himself."[128] Christ shows us the reality and the extent of perfection. He reveals in advance by what criteria we shall be judged in the last judgment. They are not something to be agreed upon by us but something suggested to us by God. Therefore, "Christ wishes us to be imitators of His fatherly goodness and kindness."[129]

Although the necessity of perfection is imposed on us and made to be our goal, we are not qualified to meet it. However, "the free gifts of God are presented as a reward by way of encouraging us to do what is right."[130]

---

124 In dealing with Luke 6:35 as a parallel verse, Calvin notes that to attach usury excessively to this sentence is absurd. Comm. Luke 6:35 (1.196, *CO* 45.186). However, Calvin, treating usury, appeals mainly to the epistles of Seneca rather than biblical passages. "On Usury," *CEA* 83-87 (*CO* 10/1. 245-249).

125 Cf. *Inst.* 2.8.55 [altered] (*CO* 2.306): "[W]e ought to embrace the whole human race without exception in a single feeling of love; here there is no distinction between barbarian and Greek, worthy and unworthy, friend and enemy, since all should be considered in God, not in themselves."

126 Comm. Matt. 5:43 (1.197-198 [altered], *CO* 45.187-188).

127 Comm. Matt. 5:44 (1.198-199 [altered], *CO* 45.188-189). Cf. *Inst.* 2.8.56 (*CO* 2.306).

128 Comm. Matt. 5:48 (1.200, *CO* 45.190).

129 Comm. Matt. 5:45 (1.199, *CO* 45.189).

130 Comm. Matt. 5:45 (1.200 [altered], *CO* 45.189).

Calvin claiming this points out the fact that by the work of "the same Spirit" we are made sons of God.[131] Criticizing the Catholic concept of counsels regarding the commandment to love our enemy in the *Institutes*, Calvin indicates that the distinction between "the law of the Spirit of life (*lex Spiritus vitae*)" and "the law of sin and death (*lex peccati et mortis*)" does not lie in the difference of the precept of the law but in the dispensation of Christ's redemptive work. He finds the answer for the dilemma between *quid possint homines* and *quid debeant* in the mediation of Christ. He states:

> To be Christians under the law of grace does not mean to wander unbridled outside the law, but to be engrafted in Christ, by whose grace we are free of the curse of the law, and by whose Spirit we have the law engraved upon our hearts [Jer. 31:33]. This grace Paul called "law," not in the strict sense but alluding to the law of God, with which he was contrasting it [Rom. 8:2] (1536 *Inst.* 1.26, *CO* 1.44, *Inst.* 2.8.57, *CO* 2.307).

Melanchthon defeats the Catholic concept of counsels by examining Christ's teaching of tolerance in Matthew 5:38-41.[132] He says the people not allowed to punish who are not regenerated through penitence because it stems from their heart's vengeance and hatred. Therefore, Christ's teaching is "*praeceptum, et non tantum consilium.*"[133] He basically does not allow usury, but a proper setting of interest rate can be legally acceptable if it does not originate from greed (*rapacitas*). Then, it is a donation (*donatio*) and not a loan (*mutatio*).[134]

In dealing with this passage, Bucer mainly focuses on how Christ's teaching, the kernel of which he believes to be "the tolerance of soul," is applied to church discipline and civil order "inwardly (*penitus*)."[135] He argues that the tolerance of the government should correspond "to the

---

131 Comm. Matt. 5:45 (1.200, *CO* 45.189). Cf. Comm. Matt. 19:9 (2.247, *CO* 45.531).

132 In his sermon on Matt. 5:21, Luther expresses his view against the Catholic concept of counsels. He says that the perfect forgiveness, presented in the crucifixion, is not "recommended" but "commanded" (*LW* 21.75). In the 1521 edition of *Loci Communes* Melanchthon criticizes the Catholic Schoolsmen's view of counsels by referring to their interpretation of Matt. 5:44 (59, *CR* 21.126). In the 1535 and 1543 editions, he does not mention at all who he argued with. However, in the 1555 edition, he points to the Anabaptists as those who take the position that "A counsel is a doctrine, not a commandment; it does not demand a work, even though it praises the work as blameless and useful" (*Loci Communes* 1555, 130, *CR* 22.283-284).

133 *CR* 14.616-417.

134 *CR* 14.622-629.

135 *MBEE* 53a.

tolerance of Christ on the cross." If not for the guidance of "the Spirit of Christ," no magistrate would be able to properly understand "the will of God." Therefore, true piety begins with the knowledge of "the intention (*sententia*) of Christ."[136] Bucer accepts usury on the condition that it is not contrary to Christian piety.[137] Overall, in commenting on Christ's saying, "Love your enemies," Bucer concentrates on to what extent "the doctrine of pure love (*dilectionis*)" is applied to "the religion of Christ."[138]

6.2.2.5 ON THE SABBATH AND CHRIST'S ATTITUDE TOWARDS THE TRADITION OF THE ELDERS

Christ's controversies on the Sabbath with the Pharisees and the Scribes illuminate his position on their tradition most strikingly. The contrast between a few Gentiles who were converted to Christian faith and the Jews who stuck to their traditions is already notable in the Gospels. According to Calvin, this contrast is prominent with reference to their attitude towards God's Word. A centurion who confessed Christ as the true and only God believed that the heavenly authority of Jesus Christ came from "the actual Word." He did not attach it to "His bodily presence," but rather to "the authority of the Word."[139] On the other hand, the Pharisees and the Scribes infringed "the simple and pure Word of God" by their leaven.[140] They are described as abandoning the "perfect holiness" of the law and binding themselves to "empty traditions." The elders misused the freedom to obey the law and replaced it with "a license to give commands."[141] Thus, Calvin calls the traditions of the elders "secondary laws invented by scrupulous men."[142] In dealing with the debate on the custom of washing before a meal, he asserts that Christ allows ceremonies to be used "in moderation (*mediocritate*)" according to their true purpose, not as "bare signs (*nudis signis*)." "A figure (*figura*)" itself becomes "scandal (*offendiculo*)" when it is substituted with God.[143] Calvin here shows an aspect of the theological use of *adiaphora*.

---

136 *MBEE* 54b.
137 *MBEE* 56a-56b.
138 *MBEE* 57a-57b. For the Reformers' views of usury, see Eric Kerridge, *Usury, Interest and the Reformation* (Aldershot: Ashgate, 2002), 23-52.
139 Comm. Matt. 8:8-10 (1.249-250, *CO* 45.236-237).
140 Comm. Matt 16:12 (2.181, *CO* 45.469).
141 Comm. Matt. 15:1 (2.156, *CO* 45.446).
142 Comm. Matt. 15:2 (2.158, *CO* 45.448).
143 Comm. Luke. 11:37-41 (2.100-101, *CO* 45.392-393). Calvin uses indiscriminately the words "*offendiculum*" and "*scandalum*" in his commentary on Luke 14:3-4 (2.102, *CO* 45.394). For the definition of scandal, cf. Calvin, *Concerning Scandals*, 7-12 (*CO* 8.9-14).

According to the Gospels, Christ was faithful to keeping the law. He kept the Jewish festivals and the Sabbath.[144] Christ's teaching was not contradictory to the law but rather based on it as illustrated by the two witnesses required in the Law of Moses recurring in John 8:17-18.[145] The kernel of Christ's teaching on the Sabbath is represented in the following two sayings: "The Son of man is Lord of the Sabbath" in Matthew 12:8, Mark 2:28, and Luke 6:5, and "My Father works even until now, and I work" in John 5:17. The former controversial statement mainly refers to the necessity of the observance of the Sabbath, which is described most impressively in Christ's saying, "The Sabbath was made for man, not man for the Sabbath" in Mark 2:27. On the other hand, the latter concerns the substance of the Sabbath which will be fulfilled in the future.

In treating the meaning of Christ's teaching of the Sabbath, Calvin suggests five arguments by which he verifies the difference between Christ's interpretation, which is faithful to "the mind of the Legislator" and the Pharisees' "malicious and implacable superstition."[146] Calvin comments:

---

144 Jesus' positive attitude towards the law is presented characteristically in the following narratives of the Synoptic Gospels: the story of the leper healed by Jesus (Matt. 8:1-4; Lk. 5:12-14), violation of the laws of defilement (Lk 7:14, 8:54, 10:28-37), Jesus' desire to observe the Passover feast in Jerusalem (Mk 14:12-16), and the strict observance of the Sabbath during flight from Jerusalem in the last days (Matt. 24:20). For reference, see Robert Banks, *Jesus and the Law in the Synoptic Tradition* (Cambridge: Cambridge University Press, 1975). Calvin frequently points out the soteriological significance of Christ's obedience to the law. Cf. Comm. Jn. 5:1 (1.116 [altered], *CO* 47.104): "He [Christ] must be subject to the Law in order to redeem us all from its bondage."

145 Christ frequently appeals to the authority of the law in the Gospel of John, particularly in defense of his Sabbath work (7:21-24), in defense of his claim to be the Son of God (10:34-36), and in defense of the authority of his teaching (5:31-47, 6:45, 8:12-20). For Christ and the law in the Gospel of John, see Severino Pancaro, *The Law in the Fourth Gospel: The Torah and the Gospel, Moses and Jesus, Judaism and Christianity according to John* (Leiden: E. J. Brill, 1975).

146 Richard B. Gaffin, dealing with the fourth commandment in his ThM thesis "Calvin and the Sabbath" (Westminster Seminary, 1962), concentrates on its origin in natural law with reference to its extent and its spiritual meaning regarding its practical uses. He points to the compliance between the teaching of the *Institutes* and his commentary on Gen. 2:2. His focus, however, is on "the exposition itself" rather than on Calvin's theological understanding of the Sabbath (29). On the other hand, in the following two articles the authors emphasize Calvin's spiritual interpretation of the fourth commandment in comparison with the Puritan understanding of the Sabbath, which is in some respect traced back to Jewish formalism. Richard Müller, *Adventisten-Sabbat-Reformation: Geht das Ruhetagsverständnis der Adventisten bis auf die Zeit der Reformation Zurück? Eine Theologiegeschichtliche Untersuchung* (Malmö, Sweden: GWK, 1979), 62-91;

The only purpose of the Sabbath was that the people might sanctify themselves to God and practice a true, spiritual worship, and that they might be released from all earthly business and join together in holy assemblies.[147]

The first argument originates in the principle that "the ceremonies do not violate the law as long as godliness (*pietas*) is unharmed." Ceremonies were given to satisfy the necessity of a true and spiritual worship, not vice versa. So, "what was forbidden for a certain purpose necessity (*necessitas*) made lawful (*licitum*)." In the case of David and his followers who ate the sacred bread, the necessity was associated with the saving of their lives by which God would be worshipped.[148]

The second argument originates in the principle that "the duties of godliness (*pietatis officia*) are not in conflict with one another." Calvin widely interprets by synecdoche the holy duties such as offerings, circumcision, and the worship of God. He argues that "when the Law commands men to abstain from their work it does not forbid holy work."[149] The third argument is that although the ceremonies of the law serve the true worship of God in the first place, their purpose and intent are not discordant with the righteousness of the commandments of the Second Table. Calvin explains this by noting the precedence of the love of God to the love of neighbour yet the concurrence in their dispensation.[150]

The fourth argument demonstrates the characteristic of the mediation of Christ as the interpreter of the law. His teaching does not yet point to his fulfilment of the law, but signifies that the Spirit of Christ is already working among his people. Although he is still subject to the law, he himself has the power to designate its true and spiritual meaning. Christ says that "For the Son of man is Lord of the Sabbath." Calvin explains this passage as follows:

John H. Primus, "Sunday: The Lord's Day as a Sabbath—Protestant Perspectives on the Sabbath," in *The Sabbath in Jewish and Christian Traditions*, ed. Tamara C. Eskenazi (New York: Crossroad, 1991), 98-121. For Calvin and contemporaries' views of the Sabbath, see Daniel Augsburger, "Calvin and the Mosaic Law," PhD dissertation, Strasbourg University, 1976, 248-284.

147 Comm. Mk. 2:24 (2.28, *CO* 45.324): "Atqui haec tantum fuit sabbati ratio, ut populus se Deo sanctificans ad verum et spiritualem cultum se exerceret: deinde ut solutus ab omnibus terrenis negotiis sacros conventus liberius ageret."
148 Comm. Matt. 12:3-4 (2.29, *CO* 45.324).
149 Comm. Matt. 12:5-6 (2.29 [altered], *CO* 45.324-325).
150 Comm. Matt. 12:7 (2.29-30, *CO* 45.325).

Here He [Christ] says that power is given to Him to free His people from the necessity of keeping the Sabbath. 'The Son of man,' He says, 'because He is Lord, has the power to regulate the Sabbath and other legal ceremonies.' And indeed, outside Christ the Law is wretched slavery (*servitus*) from which He alone releases those to whom He freely grants the Spirit of adoption (*adoptionis spiritus*).[151]

The fifth argument is based on Christ's words, "The Sabbath was made for man, not man for the Sabbath." Calvin believes that by this teaching Christ does not mean to speak about the abrogation of the law but rather about its "proper use (*rectus usus*)."[152] Especially, Calvin points out that here Christ accommodates himself to the original addressees.[153] He indicates again that although Christ claimed his authority as the Lord of the Sabbath, "the full time of its abrogation was not yet come, for the veil of the Temple had not yet been rent."[154]

Based on these arguments, Calvin argues for the righteousness of the healing of Christ on the Sabbath by pointing out that it was "a divine work (*divinum opus*)." Calvin frequently refers to this concept in his commentaries.[155] It may be defined as "the work of God in accordance with the law."[156] First, it is God's "work." Calvin appreciates Christ's healing as the "substantial perfection" of the Sabbath. Secondly, it is "God's" work, because the healing power proceeds from his divinity. Thirdly, it is the work of God "in accordance with the law." It is the work of God who subjects himself to the bondage of the law. The authority of Christ to heal the sick is that of the servant rather than that of the victor. Christ reveals himself as "the author of salvation (*salutis autorem*)," but not yet the fulfilment of salvation.[157]

Calvin finds the true meaning of the Sabbath for the people of God, not in the fact that they should do what is right for themselves but in the fact

---

151 Comm. Matt. 12:8 (2.30 [altered], *CO* 45.325-326).
152 Comm. Mk. 2:27 (2.30, *CO* 45.326). Cf. Léopold Schümmer, "Le Sabbat, le Dimanche: Un jour pour Dieu, un jour pour l'homme," *Revue Réformée* 45/181 (1994): 39-51.
153 Comm. Matt. 12:5-6 (2.29, *CO* 45.325): "Christ adapting (*accommodat*) Himself to His hearers. . . ."; 12:7 (2.29, *CO* 45.325): "Christ accommodates (*accommodat*) this verse to His own time . . ."
154 Comm. Mk. 2:27 (2.30, *CO* 45.326). In the French version, the last part of the citation—"*quia velum templi nondum scissum erat*"—does not appear. *CTS* 16/2.51, n. 3.
155 Comm. Matt. 12:9 (2.31, *CO* 45.327), Lk. 14:1-6 (2.102, *CO* 45.394), Jn. 5:17 (1.123, *CO* 47.110), 5:19 (1.125, *CO* 47.112).
156 Comm. Jn. 5:17 (1.123, *CO* 47.110-111): "In hoc capite insistit Christus, non turbari divinis operibus sanctam quietem quae lege Mosis mandata est."
157 Comm. Jn. 5:17 (1.123-124, *CO* 47.110-111).

that they should make themselves ready by taking spiritual rest (*quies spiritualis*) so that the Lord may work in them through his Spirit (*Inst.* 2.8.34, *CO* 2.291-292).[158] He argues that by his teaching, Christ demonstrates the "substance" of the fourth commandment to the Pharisees who "chase a shadowy righteousness" and "stick to the form (*forma*)."[159] Commenting on Jesus's teaching of the Sabbath, Calvin also points out Christ the Mediator who works for his people in order to fulfil the righteousness of the law. The necessity of the divine work on the Sabbath is enjoined to the people of God, but only on the condition that Christ as the Lord of the Sabbath mediates for them. In this respect, Christ is called "the end (*finem*) and soul (*animam*) of the law."[160]

Melanchthon's assertion of the four aspects of the Sabbath in his commentary on John 7:21-24 is quite different from Calvin's five arguments: first, the observance of the Sabbath should be spiritual, not literal; secondly, in order to celebrate the Sabbath we should mortify the flesh and spiritually become a new being; thirdly, because the Sabbath came from the spiritual law, no literal observance can satisfy its demand; fourthly, therefore, no one is justified by the righteousness of the law before God, but the law is fulfilled by faith.[161] He interprets the narrative on the Sabbath in the light of the gospel with which he replaces the inward, spiritual righteousness of the law. Although he mentions the revelation of eternal righteousness by the coming of the Messiah, he glimpses at its significance for the Jews of his time.[162] In dealing with the healing of Jesus on the Sabbath, Melanchthon refers to "the principle of Christian liberty" rather than to the positive meaning of its commandment.[163] Thus, his point is related mostly to the validity of the ceremonies of the Sabbath.[164]

Bucer emphasizes that the true righteousness of the Sabbath is "solid love (*dilectio*)," which is founded on "the perfect and solid knowledge of Christ who is the eternal life."[165] Like Calvin, he asserts that "when necessity requires, nothing is impious (*quum necessitas cogeret, nihil erat impii*)."[166] However, he fails to see the relation between the spiritual rest of

---

158 This teaching reflects on the three meanings of the spiritual observance of the Sabbath in the *Institutes* 2.8.28, 34.
159 Comm. Matt. 12:9 (2.31, *CO* 45.327).
160 Comm. Jn. 5:46 (1.143, *CO* 47.129).
161 *CR* 14.1111.
162 *CR* 14.851.
163 *CR* 14.1093, 1098.
164 *CR* 14.851. Melanchthon relates this commandment mainly to "*ministerium docendi et administrandi ceremonias divinitus institutas*" (*Loci Communes* 1535, *CR* 21.394; *Loci Communes* 1543, 64, *CR* 21.700; *Loci Communes* 1555, 96, *CR* 22.216).
165 *MBEE* 110b.
166 *MBEE* 110b.

the Sabbath and Christ's mediatorial work for his people. Thus, he distinguishes between the Sabbath as rest and the Sabbath as salvation, and believes that the proclamation of Christ's lordship of the Sabbath concerns only the latter.[167] Like Melanchthon, he mentions "the freedom of the Gospel (*libertas Evangelii*)" instead of the positive rule of the law in dealing with the true significance of the Sabbath commandment for the people of God.[168]

6.3 "*Non veni ut destruam, sed ut impleam*"

6.3.1 Melanchthon's Forensic Understanding

According to Luther, Christ's proclamation of the fulfilment of the law in Matthew 5:17-19 is not about the substantial fulfilment of the righteousness of the law, but about its perfect revelation. It is "not about life, but about doctrine." It denotes not the perfection of the Christian life, but the perfect righteousness of the law.[169] It is but the full revelation of a way of life according to which we ought to live in the gospel in the new era. In this respect, it is related to the specific use of the law rather than the eternal substance of the law.[170]

Melanchthon, following Luther's thinking, leaves no room for the fulfilment of the moral law in addition to the concept of the gospel, and claims that Christ's fulfilment of the law denotes on the whole the *umbra-substantia* analogy in the fulfilment of the ceremonial law. He argues that the promise of God's grace is "signified (*obsignata*)" by the law, but fulfilled by the gospel. It should be noted that he does not say that the law reveals or includes the promise in it, just signifies it. The voice of the law (*vox legis*) merely imposes our weakness, whereas the promise of the gospel heals us, working as "the medicine (*medicina*)."[171] Therefore, for Melanchthon, Christ's fulfilment of the law denotes the fact that the gospel fulfils the promise signified by the law. In this respect, he calls Christ's words, "*non veni ut destruam, sed ut impleam*," "the most solemn statement

---

167 *MBEE* 110b.
168 *MBEE* 112a-113b. Bucer's concept of the Sabbath is also found in his commentary on John 5:1-18, 7:19-24. *Enarratio in Evangelion Iohannis (1528, 1530, 1536)*, *Martini Buceri Opera Latina*, vol. 2, ed. Irena Backus (Leiden: E. J. Brill, 1988), esp. 213-214, 295-297; *De regno Christi* ("The Sanctification of Holy Days"), *LCC* 280-282. For Bucer's spiritual interpretation of the Sabbath, see Marijn de Kroon, "Freedom and Bondage," in *Calvin's Books*, 271-282.
169 *LW* 21.67, 72.
170 *LW* 21.69-70.
171 *CR* 14.581-582.

concerning the law (*de lege*)."[172]

Using this argument, Melanchthon explains Christ's fulfilment of the law in four ways: first, by completing the demand of the law through obedience; secondly, by bearing the punishment through which we become righteous before God; thirdly, by restoring us so that we can live according to the law; finally, by teaching the necessity of observation and by rooting out Pharisaic errors.[173] Referring to the second way as "most admirable," Melanchthon points out that Christ fulfilled the "types and symbols (*typi et signa*)" foreshadowed by ceremonial laws by accomplishing God's wonderful decree and imputed his righteousness into us.[174] Melanchthon refers specifically to "the intervening compensation (*compensatione interveniente*)" of Christ.[175] Here he does not distinguish between moral and ceremonial laws but explains the Decalogue, in terms of the *umbra-substantia* analogy. The only difference he implies is that with reference to the fulfilment of the moral law, the first way is more relevant than the second way.[176]

With reference to the third way of the fulfilment of the law, Melanchthon turns to the special work of the Holy Spirit in order to explain the spiritual function of the law. The Holy Spirit illuminates our hearts so that we may receive the law into our hearts and live according to the wisdom and will of God. Melanchthon frequently refers to the special work of the Holy Spirit in dealing with the penitent use of the law ranging over justification and sanctification.[177] Typically, in the first edition of *Loci Communes* he contrasts the law—the will of God—with the Holy Spirit—the living will of God.

> The law is the will of God; the Holy Spirit is nothing else than the living will of God and its being in action (*agitatio*). Therefore, once we have been regenerated by the Spirit of God, who is the living will of God, we will spontaneously that very thing which the law used to demand.[178]

---

172 *CR* 14. 582, 584 (italics mine).
173 *CR* 14.583: "Primum, suae propriae obedientiae perfectione, quia solus Christus perfecte facit legem. Secundo, solvendo poenas pro nobis. Tertio, efficiendo legem in nobis, dans Spiritum sanctum, et regenerans nos, et restituens nobis vitam aeternam, ut ita fiat lex in nobis, quia oportet nostras voluntates congruere cum sapientia et voluntate Dei. Quarto, quia ipse eam etiam docet et illustrat, et testatur obedientiam esse necessariam."
174 *CR* 14.585.
175 *CR* 14.584.
176 *CR* 14.584-585.
177 Cf. *Loci Communes* 1555, 123-128 (*CR* 22.250-256).
178 *Loci Communes* 1521, 123 [altered] (*CR* 21.195). Melanchthon defines the law as "the will of God (*sententia Dei*)" and the Decalogue as "the eternal will of God (*aeterna sententia Dei*)" (*CR* 14.581, 582).

In fact, when he defines the law as the will of God, he means the precept of the law, and more specifically, its accusing function. Thus, what is engraved into our hearts by the special illumination of the Holy Spirit is none other than the precept of the law which reveals our sin and accuses us. Even when he says, in the fourth way, "Christ fulfils the law by teaching," Melanchthon still sticks to the use of the law to lead us "to repentance by disclosing our sin.[179]

6.3.2 Bucer's Spiritual Understanding

Bucer's commentary on Matthew 5:17-19 is quite wordy yet precise, and its scope is quite wide yet logically arranged. First he deals with three reasons why Christ gave this instruction to his disciples. He touches mainly on the significance of the fulfilment of the law and the continuity and discontinuity between the Law of Moses and the teaching of Christ. Then, he discusses Christian freedom as the fruit of the fulfilment of the law with emphasis on Christian piety. Finally, he deals with the two uses of the law which are equivalent to the first and third uses of the law in Calvin. Treating each of these themes, Bucer concentrates on how the righteousness of the law, which is fulfilled by Christ, operates in the Christian life through the Spirit of Christ.

In dealing with the three reasons, Bucer first indicates that all of the perfection of the law was accomplished by Christ, the Mediator of the new covenant. Christ restored the solid and internal righteousness of the law by his Spirit.[180] Since the law was fulfilled by Christ through the work of his Spirit, it bears "the righteousness of the Spirit (*iustitiam Spiritus*)," and believers ought to live in "*pietas solida et spiritualis*."[181] So the following is suggested as the message of Christ: "In fact, for the purpose of completing everything through the Spirit I [Christ] will give my power in abundance, delivering it from the Father, to those deserving my death."[182]

Regarding the second reason, Bucer emphasizes that Christ's fulfilment of the law is "actually for the sake of our office (*nostri profecto officii*)." Christ encourages us towards "the desire of a more sanctified life." He gives us an example to which we should respond by living a godly life.[183]

---

179 *CR* 14.586.
180 *MBEE* 44a: ". . . ab admiratione externarum rerum, ad cultum solidae atque internae iustitiae suos revocare."
181 *MBEE* 44a.
182 *MBEE* 44b: ". . . tum virtutem meis per Spiritum omnia perficiendi, quem mea ipsis morte merebor, et a Patre mittam, suppeditabo."
183 *MBEE* 44b.

Bucer affirms again that Christian piety is living "relying on the Spirit of Christ."[184]

Bucer, treating the third reason based on v. 19, concentrates on God's will towards his people who belong to "the kingdom of heaven," which he calls "the Republic of the faithful which is governed by Christ the Lord with his Spirit."[185] Bucer identifies people who belong to the kingdom of heaven as "the Church of God (*Ecclesia Dei*)" and claims that they must "desire to live according to God's will alone."[186]

In contrast with Melanchthon, Bucer, referring to the continuity of the law, concentrates on the character of the moral law, which he describes as "*doctrina et vitae institutio.*"[187] He says that the new law of Christ in Galatians 3:19 is "the precept of the Decalogue and a series of primary orders concerning the love of neighbour."[188] In the same vein the judicial and ceremonial laws are regarded fulfilled by Christ as "*doctrina pietatis et iustitiae Dei.*"[189] In his polemic against Calvin over the use of ceremonies, Bucer claims that a ceremony itself is pious if it is used humbly and those who are persuaded by the Holy Spirit that they belong to the kingdom of Christ can make use of the ceremonies in a true way.[190] He claims that the ancient people with whom the Spirit of Christ communicated also knew the internal meaning of the ceremonial law.[191] Therefore, there is no distinction between the Old and New Testaments as far as the substance (*substantia*) of the law is concerned. The difference is rather in the fact that the ancient

---

184 *MBEE* 44b. According to Marijn de Kroon, for Bucer, the word *pietas* is the key that "proves to give access to the complex building of his theology, which impresses the reader with the abundance and richness of its thought but frequently also perplexes the interested visitor." *Bucer en Calvijn* (Zoetemeer: Meinema, 1991), 93-94, quot. Selderhuis, *Marriage and Divorce*, 360.

185 *MBEE* 44b: ". . . regnum caelorum . . . sanctorum Rempublicam, quam Christus Dominus suo Spiritu moderatur."

186 *MBEE* 44b: "Magnum ergo et hoc stimulum habet ad impellendos nostros animos, quo ad Dei voluntatem vivere unice studeamus."

187 *MBEE* 45a.

188 *MBEE* 45a: "Adhaec minima mandata intelligit, ut satis patet, quae in Mosche continentur: quae enim hic subiecit, non nova praecepta sunt, sed praeceptorum Decalogi explicationes, et primarii mandati de diligendo proximo, series."

189 *MBEE* 45b.

190 Cf. *Consilium Theologicum Privatim Conscriptum, Martini Buceri Opera Latina*, vol. 4, ed. Pierre Fraenkel (Leiden: E. J. Brill, 1988), 143-147: "Caeremonia ritus est religiosus—tum per se pius, quando divinitus ad pietatis usum institutus est: per se impius, si a Sathana institutus sit ad impietatis usum" (143).

191 According to van't Spijker, for Bucer, "the entire Old Testament points to Christ in a typology that is not primarily noetic but ontic." *The Ecclesiastical Offices in the Thought of Martin Bucer*, 40-41.

people lived according to the law "with the immature Spirit given (*donato Spiritu puerili*)."[192]

Bucer features the Spirit of Christ in its two specific aspects—Spirit of freedom and its office. The Spirit of Christ makes people free from the outward observance of the law to follow "the order (*iussum*) of Christ" "willingly (*libere*) from the Spirit of Christ."[193] Bucer points out the theological meaning of the life of Christ the Mediator in explaining the presence of the living Spirit of Christ in the following passage with a strong rhetorical reiteration.

> Christ alone fulfilled the law, and accomplishes and completes it every day among his people. He fulfilled it when he rescued the law from the haze of the Pharisees' interpretation by giving an explanation of the law, and restored it to its fine and genuine splendour. He fulfilled it when he alone expressed the law fully in his life, being made the unique perfect example of that which we all seek to emulate. He fulfilled it finally and fulfils it every day, when he gives his Spirit to us even now, which he earned by his death; by this Spirit it is pleasing and possible to live according to the law.[194]

In dealing with the work of the Spirit of Christ, Bucer emphasizes its character as "the Spirit of sons (*Spiritus filiorum*)." He particularly defines the living Spirit of Christ (*Spiritus vivificans*) working for the sanctification of believers as "the loving spirit of the law (*legis amantem spiritum*)."[195] By the Spirit of Christ we discern what is lawful (*fas*) and what is unlawful (*nefas*) in a spiritual sense.[196] Thus, as he puts it, "The whole law should be completed and fulfilled in us by this very Spirit of Christ."[197]

Bucer deals with how the whole law aims at true piety through its spiritual use. As a result, his focus is more on the continuity of the law and its use than on Christ's fulfilment of the law as the Mediator. Bucer, regarding Christian piety, consistently refers to the work of the Spirit of

---

192 *MBEE* 45b.

193 *MBEE* 46a.

194 *MBEE* 46b: "Hanc solus implevit, et quotidie in suis implet atque consummat. Implevit, quum per subiectam Legum explanationem, fumo Pharisaicarum interpretationum illam exemit, et suo vero et germano splendori restituit. Implevit quum unus illam vita sua plene expressit, factus unicum eius, quod aemulemur universi, absolutum exemplum. Implevit denique et implet eam quotidie, quum suis Spiritum, quem morte sua meruit, etiam donat: quo et ipsis secundum eam vivere et libeat et liceat."

195 *MBEE* 47.

196 *MBEE* 47b.

197 *MBEE* 48a: ". . . totam [quoque] Legem in nobis hoc ipso Spiritu Christi perficiendam implendamque."

Christ, but he does not give much consideration to the continuity of Christ's mediatorship. When he says that "the reality of the internal law is the Spirit of Christ," he is concerned with the inner dispensation of the law rather than the fact that Christ is its substance and truth.[198] We may call this extensive spiritual use of the kerygma of Christ's fulfilment of the law, going back to the time before the incarnation, an extra dimension of Bucer's theology of the law.[199]

6.3.3 Calvin's Christological Understanding

Calvin's commentary on Matthew 5:17-19 characteristically features his pursuit of brevity and facility in writing. It is not polemical. He mentions the Jews but not the Papists or the Anabaptists.[200] He does not try to formulate the doctrine of the law, but simply pursues the intention of the author. He does not quote at all from the Letters of Paul. Only one verse is cited with theological intention, Jeremiah 31:33, which is noted for its revelation of a new covenant.

Overall, like Luther, Calvin takes the position that these words of Christ concern not the perfection of life but the perfection of teaching; thus, they are related to *quid debeant homines* rather than to *quid possint.*[201] However, it should be noted that, in so doing, while Luther emphasizes the priority of the gospel to the law, Calvin points out the perfect revelation of the eternal truth of the law and its continual validity.[202] He regards Christ's fulfilment of the law as the recovery of "the whole system of religion (*totum religionis statum*)."[203]

In dealing with the fulfilment of the law, Calvin separates the doctrine of the law from its ceremonies. The doctrine of the law is eternal and unchangeable because it reveals "*iustitia Dei*" as "*pie sancteque vivendi regula.*" The "practice (*usus*)" of ceremonies was abrogated although their

---

198 *MBEE* 45b: ". . . res internae Legis, hoc est spiritus Christi."
199 For Bucer's spiritual interpretation of the Bible, see Van't Spiker, *The Ecclesiastical Offices in the Thought of Martin Bucer*, 48-49, 57-58; Ganoczy and Scheld, *Die Hermeneutik Calvins*, 76-87.
200 Only once does Calvin polemicize against the Papists, but without noting their identity. Comm. Matt. 5: 19 (1.181-182, *CO* 45.173): "When Christ keeps out of His Kingdom such men as accustom others to condemn the Law, then it is a fantastic folly for them not to be ashamed of remitting, by blasphemous indulgence, the absolute demands of God, and calling them venial sins, in order to do away with the justice of the Law."
201 Comm. Matt. 5:17 (1.178, *CO* 45.170).
202 Comm. Matt. 5:18 (1.181, *CO* 45.172): ". . . the word accomplished is not related to men's life, but to the solid truth of doctrine (*solidam doctrinae veritatem*), . . ."
203 Comm. Matt. 5:17 (1.179, *CO* 45.170).

"significance (*significatio*) was given further confirmation";[204] their form is lost like a "shadow," although their "effect (*effectum*)" is sustained.[205] When Calvin argues for the substantial unity of the law with the gospel, he refers to this eternal doctrine of the law, which reveals "*legislatoris consilium et finem.*"[206]

Calvin, claiming the substantial (*substantialis*) unity and continuity between the law and the gospel with regard to the fulfilment of the law, seeks their link in Christ's continual mediation of the law. He accepts the *hypostasis* of the Word of God as signifying Christ's eternal sonship as the Mediator.[207] Therefore, the differentiation between the doctrine of the law and the gospel is derived from the varying economies of Christ the Mediator in accordance with different dispensations in history. As we have seen in his interpretation of the true meaning of the Sabbath, when Calvin explores the spiritual meaning of the law he takes into account that Christ still mediates for us. In conclusion, for Calvin, Christ's fulfilment of the law denotes the full revelation of the Christological meaning of the law. As he puts it:

> Truly He fulfilled the deadness of the letter by reviving it with His Spirit, and eventually displaying in actual fact (*re ipsa*), what had till then been indicated figuratively (*sub figuris*).[208]

6.4 The Person and Work of Christ, and the Fulfilment of the Law in Calvin's Exegesis of the Gospels

6.4.1 The Manifestation of the Mediator as the Incarnate Word of God

Calvin believes that the incarnation is of great significance because through it the clear knowledge of the Son of God as the Mediator was revealed.[209] He claims that "Jesus" signifies the revelation of the substance of the law which had been foreshadowed figuratively.[210] The incarnation is regarded as the coming of the time for the full manifestation of the Mediator who had

---

204 Comm. Matt. 5: 17 (1.180, *CO* 45.171).
205 Comm. Matt. 5: 19 (1.181 [altered], *CO* 45.173).
206 Comm. Matt. 5: 17, 19 (1.180-181, *CO* 45.172-173).
207 Comm. Matt. 5: 17 (1.179, *CO* 45.171-172).
208 Comm. Matt. 5: 17 (1.180, *CO* 45.171).
209 Comm. Lk. 1:32 (1.24-25, *CO* 45.27-28).
210 Comm. Lk. 1:31 (1.24, *CO* 45.27). In dealing with Christ's mediatorship, Calvin criticizes those who follow Arius and the cabbalists because they deny the lordship of Christ as Jehovah and looks upon him as an angel. Cf. Matt. 1:21 (1.64, *CO* 45.64-65); Jn. 1:1 (1.8-9, *CO* 47.2-3).

been promised to the ancient fathers.[211] The other significance of the incarnation is that the church in the person (*persona*) of Christ is renewed (*instauratur*) through it.[212]

Calvin's understanding of the Word (*sermo*) sheds light on our study of his position on the continual mediation of Christ. The Word is of the same essence with the God, but as "the eternal wisdom (*sapientia*) and will (*voluntas*) of God" has a *hypostasis* distinct from the Father.[213] So, as proclaimed in a sermon, in the Word, "God's plan is God."[214] The *hypostasis* of the Word denotes Christ's mediatorship as the Son of God. Thus, its office was revealed most significantly as "the life-giving light."[215] To the Word belongs "life united with the light of understanding (*luce intelligentiae*)."[216] Therefore, by the eternal Word of God the knowledge of salvation was taught even to the ancient people; and "the force and effect of this redemption, which was once displayed in Christ, were in fact shared by all generations."[217]

The peculiar property of the Word also signifies the substance and truth of the law. In the following commentary on John 1:17, "For the law was given through Moses; grace and truth came through Jesus Christ," Calvin argues that the law is the shadow of the body, but contains the truth of the body.

> The Evangelist certainly means that the Law contained a mere shadowed (*adumbratam*) image of spiritual blessings, but in Christ they show their wholeness (*solide*). Whence it follows that if you separate the Law from Christ nothing remains in it save empty figures (*inanes figuras*). This is why Paul says in Col. 2.17 that the shadow (*umbras*) is in the Law, but the body (*corpus*) is in Christ. But it must not be supposed that anything false was shown in the Law; for Christ is the soul (*anima*) which quickens (*vivificat*) what would otherwise have been dead in the Law.[218]

In dealing with the life of Christ, Calvin frequently refers to Christ's mediatorship in order to explain his divine sonship. In commenting on the

---

211 Comm. Lk. 1:26 (1.21, *CO* 45.24).
212 Comm. Lk. 1:32-33 (1.25-26, *CO* 45.28-29). Cf. Comm. Lk. 1:35 (1.29, *CO* 45.31).
213 Comm. Jn. 1:1 (1.7-9, *CO* 47.1, 3).
214 Serm. Jn. 1:1-5 (20, *CO* 47.470-471): ". . . le conseil qui est en Dieu, il est vrayement Dieu."
215 Comm. Lk. 1:78 (1.50, *CO* 45.52): ". . . nihil esse vivificae lucis in mundo extra Christum."
216 Comm. Jn. 1:4 (1.11 [altered], *CO* 47.5).
217 Comm. Lk. 1:68 (1.45, *CO* 45.46): "[Respondeo], vim et effectum huius redemptionis, quae semel in Christo fuit exhibita, saeculis omnibus fuisse communem."
218 Comm. Jn. 1:17 (1.24-25 [altered], *CO* 47.18).

name "Immanuel," he claims that Christ performed the office of the Mediator so that the ancient people could be united with God.[219] In commenting on the transfiguration of Christ, Calvin describes him as "the only teacher (*doctorem*) of the church" and "Reconciler."[220] In the following commentary on Christ's baptism, Calvin points out his willing obedience for the sake of accomplishing his office as the Mediator. He says, "the reason for Christ's undergoing baptism was to offer His Father full obedience, while the particular reason, was to consecrate baptism in His own body, that it might be common between Him and us."[221] In the same vein, Calvin comments on Christ's circumcision,[222] temptation in the wilderness,[223] and many verses related to Christ's obedience to the law.[224] In commenting on the Beatitudes and the Lord's Prayer, Calvin emphasizes spiritual obedience to the law through the mediation of Christ.[225] This also refers to most narratives of Christ's controversies relating to Jewish tradition, as I have already noted in the section that deals with Christ's teaching on the Sabbath.

---

219 Comm. Matt. 1:23 (1.69, *CO* 45.69).
220 Comm. Matt. 17:5 (2.201, *CO* 45.488). Cf. Comm. Lk. 2:46 (1.108, *CO* 45.105).
221 Comm. Matt. 3:13 (1.130, *CO* 45.125): ". . . baptismi ratio fuit Christo, ut plenam obedientiam praestaret patri: specialis autem, ut baptismum consecraret in suo ipsius corpore, ut nobis communis cum eo esset."
222 Comm. Lk. 2:21 (1.81, *CO* 45.80). Calvin points out the twofold meaning of Christ's circumcision, which is related to Christ's obedience to the law—"God wished His Son to be circumcised that He might come under the Law, for circumcision was a solemn symbol by which Jews were initiated into the observance of the Law"—and Christ's abrogation or fulfilment of the law—"Though its [the law's] abrogation depends on the death and resurrection of Christ, this was something of a preliminary, that God's Son underwent circumcision."
223 Comm. Matt. 4:1-2 (1.133-136, *CO* 45.128-131). Calvin, commenting on the temptation, emphasizes Christ's intervention for us: "Christ was tempted as the Representative (*persona*) of all the faithful" (135, *CO* 45.130).
224 Cf. Comm. Lk. 2:22-24 (1.89-90, *CO* 45.87-89); Lk. 2:49 (1.109, *CO* 45.106-107); Lk. 4:16-22 (1.146-147, *CO* 45.140-143); Matt. 8:1-4 (1.242-246, *CO* 45.230-233). For Christ's observance of the law, see Max Dominicé, *L'humanité de Jésus d'après Calvin* (Paris: Éditions "Je Sers," 1933), 159-174.
225 Comm. Matt. 5:1-12 (1.168-174, *CO* 45.159-166). In commenting on the Beatitude, Calvin writes that "the philosophy of Christ's disciples," which he calls "Christ's paradox," is totally different from "Stoic paradoxical understanding of happiness" because the former is based on the mediation of Christ, which is taught "in the school of the cross" (169-170, 173, *CO* 45.161, 165). For Christ's intercession in the Lord's Prayer, cf. Comm. Matt. 6:9, 12 (1.206, 211, *CO* 45.196, 200-201).

6.4.2 The Passion, Resurrection, and Ascension of Christ

As well as his commentaries, a series of Calvin's sermons on the passion (including the resurrection) and ascension of Jesus Christ constitute good sources to gain an understanding of his position on Christ's fulfilment of the law.[226] Calvin sees the death of Christ as the fulfilment of his mediatorial work. In his sermon on Christ's pronouncement in John 19:30, "It is done, all is fulfilled," Calvin points out the fact that "He had acquitted Himself of His whole duty as Mediator."[227] Calvin differentiates the sacrifice of Christ on the cross as "the body (*corpus*)" from old sacrifices which were "shadows (*umbras*)."[228] He also describes Christ the Mediator as "the Sun of righteousness (*le soleil de iustice*), because He acquired life for us by His death."[229]

In his sermons on the passion of Christ, Calvin puts great emphasis on the continuous mediation of Christ.[230] He does not see it merely as "an example and a mirror (*exemple et miroir*)" but concentrates on its impact upon his people "by the power of His Holy Spirit."[231] In order to explain this, he refers to the eucharistic theology on the bodily presence of Christ in the Lord's Supper.[232] In the same vein, commenting on Matthew 27:51, "the veil of the temple was rent in twain," he asserts that "as the substance of the shadows and the reality was fulfilled, all legal figures were transformed into spirit."[233] Also, the living sacrifice of Christ was given as a "visible (*visibile*)" one, but "spiritually (*spiritualiter*)";[234] that through the practice of the Lord's Supper "the Holy Spirit brings us back to what is

---

226 "It is quite probable that Calvin preached the entire text of the Synoptic Gospels in the series of sermons" (*CO* 46, "Notice Preliminaire," iii). However, only 45 sermons on the first part of the Gospels (up to Matt. 5:11, 12; Lk. 6:22-26) have remained. Notwithstanding, fortunately invaluable sermons have been preserved on the nativity, passion, and ascension of Jesus Christ our Lord along with *Congrégation sur la Divinité de Iésus-Christ* (*CO* 47.465-484), *Sermons sur la Passion de Nostre Seigneur Iésus-Christ* (*CO* 46.833-954), *Sermons de l'Ascension de Nostre Seigneur Iésus-Christ* (*CO* 48.585-622).

227 Serm. Matt. 27:45-54 (161, *CO* 46.924): ". . .qu'il s'estoit acquitté de tout devoir de Mediateur, . . ."

228 Comm. Jn. 19: 30 (2.183-184, *CO* 47.419). Cf. Serm. Matt. 27:45-54 (162-163, *CO* 46.924-925).

229 Serm. Matt. 27:45-54 (154 [altered], *CO* 46.918). Cf. Comm. Matt. 27:45 (3.206, *CO* 45.778).

230 Serm. Matt. 26:36-39 (65, *CO* 46.846); Matt. 26:40-50 (80-81, *CO* 46.858-860); Matt. 25:51-66 (97, *CO* 46.872); Matt. 26:67-27:10 (114-116, *CO* 46.886-888).

231 Serm. Matt. 26:36-39 (63 [altered], *CO* 46.843-844).

232 Serm. Matt. 26:36-39 (64-65, *CO* 46.845); Matt. 27:45-54 (156-157, *CO* 46.920); Matt. 27:55-60 (175, *CO* 46.935).

233 Comm. Matt. 27:51 (3.211, *CO* 45.782): ". . . quia iam umbrarum substantia et veritas completa erat, figuras legales in spiritum conversas esse."

234 Comm. Matt 27:51 (3.211, *CO* 45.782).

visible in the death of Christ."²³⁵ Through the action of his Spirit, the Mediator Christ becomes not only the end of the law but also the reality of its promises.²³⁶

Calvin refers to the special work of the Holy Spirit in order to explain the continual presence and work of Christ as the Mediator through his resurrection and ascension. In these cases, the Holy Spirit is designated as the Spirit of Christ. The benefit of the resurrection is that the believers can share in the body and blood of Christ through the Lord's Supper.²³⁷ The benefit of his ascension is that the believers can be in communion with the Intercessor Christ.²³⁸ He writes:

> Just as God is through all and in all things invisibly, Jesus Christ communicates Himself to us. And when we are united to Him, our souls are nourished by the substance of His body (although He is up there in heaven), but this is done by the power of faith and by the Holy Spirit. For Jesus Christ does not descend corporally.²³⁹

Further, Calvin deals with the coming of the Holy Spirit on the day of Pentecost in the light of the believer's union with Christ, and explains it with the eucharistic theology of the bodily presence of Christ in the bread,²⁴⁰ the declaration that now we have Christ as "the Mediator in person (*en personne*)" by his Spirit, whereas the ancient fathers had him in various "types and shadows (*figures et ombres*)."²⁴¹ By identifying the Spirit poured out on the disciples on the day of Pentecost with the Spirit by which Christ had baptized his disciples, Calvin suggests that the Spirit of Christ is the Spirit working through his mediatorial works.²⁴² In commenting on the last teaching of Christ on the coming of the Holy Spirit, Calvin says that as "our Mediator and Intercessor" Christ "obtains from the Father the grace of the Spirit; but inasmuch as He is God, He bestows that grace from Himself (*a se ipso*)." He continues to say that the Spirit of Christ, Comforter (*Paracletus*), makes us believe in him as our eternal

---

235 Serm. Matt. 27:45-54 (156, *CO* 46.920).
236 Comm. Lk. 24:47 (3.235-236, *CO* 45.818).
237 Serm. Matt. 28:1-10 (194-96, *CO* 46.952-954).
238 Serm. Acts 1:9-11 (236-240, *CO* 48.617-621). The *exaltatio* of Christ refers to both the divine and human nature. Comm. Phil. 2:10 (251-252, *CO* 52.29-30).
239 Serm. Acts 1:9-11 (240, *CO* 48.620): "Et quand nous sommes unis à luy, nos ames sont nourries de la substance de son corps (combien qu'il soit là haut au ciel), mais cela se fait par la vertu de la foy et par le S. Esprit. Car Iesus Christ ne descend point corporellement." Cf. Comm. Acts 1:11 (1.34-36, *CO* 48.12-14).
240 Serm. Acts 2:1-4 (250-257, *CO* 48.629-636).
241 Serm. Acts 2:13-17 (265, *CO* 48.642). Comm. Acts 2:17-21 (1.56-62, *CO* 48.31-37).
242 Comm. Acts 1:5 (1.27, *CO* 48.6-7). Cf. Comm. Jn. 14:20 (2.84, *CO* 47.331).

"Patron (*patronus*)."²⁴³ Then follows the commentary on Christ's words, "Abide ye in my love":

> Some quite foolishly infer from these words that there is no efficacy in the grace of God unless it is supported by our steadfastness. I do not allow that the Spirit demands from us only what we are capable of (*quae facultatis nostrae sunt*). Rather, He shows us what we ought to do (*quid fieri oporteat*), so that if we have no strength we may seek it elsewhere. Likewise, when Christ here exhorts us to perseverance, we must not rely on our own efforts and industry (*marte et industria*), but pray to Him who commands us, to confirm us in His love.²⁴⁴

6.5 Conclusion

As a result of our examination, we have learned about each of the three Reformers' unique positions on Christ's fulfilment of the law, which are sometimes distinguished not so much by their theological stance as by the extent of their emphasis. Melanchthon persists in his gospel-centred position. Like Luther, he does not deal positively with the normative use of the law. He is concerned about the accusatory (*accusans*) office of the law even when he talks about the use of the law for believers. Thus, Christ's fulfilment of the law is characterized as the fulfilment of the demand of the law itself, and Christ's continual mediation of the law is regarded as groundless because the law is already fulfilled enough for its peculiar function to urge us to repent. In this respect, he refers to the *umbra-substantia* analogy of the ceremonial law even in explaining the fulfilment of the moral law.

On the other hand, Bucer deals with Christ's fulfilment of the law, concentrating on the moral law. For him, the fulfilment of the law is none other than its spiritualization by the work of the Spirit of Christ.²⁴⁵ It signifies the inner function of the law in Christian piety. Referring to the union with Christ, Bucer emphasizes not only the communication of his grace but also the communication of his love. In this regard, Bucer's understanding of the law is basically normative and dynamic. However, Bucer does not refer to the continual mediation of Christ in order to explain the continual validity of the law, but is concerned with the varying

---

243 Comm. Jn. 14:16 (2.82, *CO* 47.329).
244 Comm. Jn. 15:9 (2.97 [altered], *CO* 47.342).
245 Cf. van't Spijker, *The Ecclesiastical Offices in the Thought of Martin Bucer*, 48-49: "Bucer's doctrine of the Holy Spirit gets its prior signification from his Christology. The Holy Spirit is the Spirit of Christ and Christ alone disposes over Him. . . . Christ himself speaks, and works all things in the elect, just as he, after all, lives in them by his Spirit."

dispensation of the Holy Spirit.[246] With reference to the fulfilment of the law, on the whole Bucer takes into consideration the spiritual use of the law for the people who belong to the new covenant rather than the spiritual significance of the substantial fulfilment of the law.[247]

Unlike Melanchthon and Bucer, Calvin understands Christ's fulfilment of the law both as the clear revelation of the substance of the law and the fulfilment of its righteousness on the cross, and explains it as the manifestation of the Mediator and the fulfilment of his mediatorial office. He deals with the meaning of the life and work of Christ in the Gospels in the light of his continual mediatorship. Calvin understands the gospel not only as "the solemn proclamation of the presence of the Son of God revealed in the flesh to renew a fallen world, to restore men from death into life" but also as the good news about "Christ's working (*defunctum*) out of the office of Mediator."[248] He argues that the perfect righteousness of the law is taught in the gospel because it reveals Christ as the substance of the law.[249] The substance of the law does not only denote its fulfilment on the cross. As Calvin puts it, "the birth, death and resurrection of Christ contain in themselves the whole sum of our salvation, indeed are so much its substance (*materia*)."[250] Based on this dynamic understanding of Christ's fulfilment of the law, Calvin understands the agreement of the law and the gospel and the character of the law as the whole system of religion.

Calvin asserts the continuity between the Word of God and the word of Christ, not merely on an ethical basis, as Schellong observes, but substantially (*substantialiter*), on the basis of the continuity of the person and work of Christ the Mediator. It is true that Calvin emphasizes the

---

246 In linking the working of the Holy Spirit with Christ's mediatorship, Bucer's focus is "more on the work than on the person of Christ." Ibid., 39.

247 Cf. Cornelis Graafland, "Alter und neuer Bund: Calvins Auslegung von Jeremia 31, 31-34 und Hebräer 8, 8-13," in *Reformiertes Erbe: Festschrift für Gottfried W. Locher zu seinem 80. Geburtstag*, vol. 2 (Zürich: Theologischer Verlag, 1993), 135-145. According to the author, in dealing with the old and new covenants, Calvin emphasizes the unity between the substance of the law with that of the gospel by relating it to the unity between the Old and New Testaments, whereas Melanchthon points out the abrogation of the law as he explains the revelation of the gospel, Bullinger underscores the difference between the old and new covenants by referring especially to the temporality of the Old Testament law although he maintains their continuity, and Bucer focuses on the universal aspect of the law as he explores its spiritual meaning.

248 "The Theme of the Gospel of Jesus Christ," *CNTC* 1.xi-xii (*CO* 45.2). Cf. Comm. Acts 1:1 (1.21, *CO* 48.1-2); Serm. Acts 1:1-4 (198, *CO* 48.586): ". . . le sommaire de l'Evangile est comprins en ces deux mots, c'est ascavoir que Iesus Christ a enseigné et qu'il a fait: . . ."

249 Comm. Matt. 5:21 (1, 83, *CO* 45.174).

250 "The Theme of the Gospel of Jesus Christ," *CNTC* 1.xii (*CO* 45.2).

historical presence of Christ, and sometimes the independence of his humanity, but this cannot be ascribed totally to the influence of the school of Antioch as Witte maintains. Calvin understands the unity of the person of Christ in the light of his own concept of the *communicatio idiomatum*, by which he explains the co-operation of the two natures on the basis of the so-called *extra Calvinisticum*.

In exploring the *hypostasis* of Christ from the perspective of the dynamic of his mediatorial office, Calvin refers to the properties of the Word of God, which he presents both as the counsel of God and as the life-giving light. These two demonstrate the property of *Deus manifestatus in carne* both as interpreter and as fulfilment of the law. For Calvin, the fact that Christ is the substance of the law is always taken into consideration together with the fact that the law is the expression of the will of God. As the Mediator of the law, Christ not only reveals, teaches, and fulfils the will of God, but he also reveals himself and fulfils his own office as the second person of the Trinity.

CHAPTER 7

Lex Dei Regula Vivendi et Vivificandi: Calvin's Dynamic Understanding of the Office and Use of the Law

7.1 Introduction

In the previous chapters, we examined the relationship between Christ and the law in Calvin's theology in the light of the fact that Christ is the Mediator of the law. Our main focus was the revelation of the presence of Christ in the law and its representation of him in the Old Testament and Christ's interpretation and fulfilment of the law in the Four Gospels. These themes reflect Calvin's Christological understanding of the law most distinctively, characterized as both Christ in the law and the law in Christ.

Now I will examine the soteriological significance of the law in Calvin's theology, that is, Christ's mediation of the law for justification and sanctification, described by Calvin as the communication of the righteousness of Christ, who is the head of the church. In treating this subject, I will concentrate on the office and use of the law with reference to Calvin's own understanding of the double grace of God to accept both our persons and our imperfect works as righteous by imputing Christ's righteousness to us.

As we see from the debate between Melanchthon and Agricola over *poenitentia*, the sixteenth century Lutheran controversies over the law featured the necessity of the law for *vera poenitentia* and the compatibility between the principle of *justificatio sola fide* and the enduring validity of the law for the Christian life. In spite of their different positions, they finally came to the agreement that the law still works for the regenerate, yet, without discarding their assumption that *lex semper accusat*. They consequently acknowledged the normative use of the law for the faithful in a negative sense of continual repentance.

On the other hand, Calvin deals with the office and use of the law in the light of the continual mediation of Christ for justification and sanctification. He distinguishes the nature (*natura*) of the law clearly from the natural (*naturalis*) use of the law. Since the fall, the law plays its natural role to accuse and convict sinners in order to restrain them. However, the law, as the law of the covenant, plays its theological role to teach people the righteousness of God so that they may long for Christ as Saviour and be led to eternal life. Calvin explains the double grace of God with an emphasis on the normative nature of the law and Christ's mediation in the whole process of salvation.

When we pay very close attention to Calvin's consistent reference to the normative nature of the law for the explanation of the theological background of the threefold use of the law, we can reach the true understanding of his view of the office and use of the law and evade the false argument of Lutheran theologian such as Elert, who claimed that Calvin is ignorant of the theological use of the law—*lex accusans*—and concentrates only on the moral aspect of the law, the law as the rule of a right and godly living.[1]

In the following, I will first deal with Calvin's normative understanding of the nature of the law as *lex vivendi*. Then, I will deal with how the law, *lex vivendi*, works as *lex accusans* and *lex vivificandi* in the whole process of salvation, giving primary attention to the relation between Calvin's dynamic understanding of the law based on Christ's mediation and his dynamic understanding of salvation based on his doctrine of union with Christ. In treating this subject, I will compare his position with those of his contemporary Reformers whose great influence upon him he mentions in the preface of his commentary on Romans—Melanchthon, Bullinger, and Bucer. Also, I will refer to Luther's view of the office and use of the law in order to pursue the theological foundations of these Reformers. Finally, I will interpret the threefold use of the law in Calvin's *Institutes* 2.7.6-13 from his unique perspective on the twofold office of the law examined in the previous sections.

7.2 *Lex Dei Regula Vivendi*: Calvin's Understanding of the Normative Nature of the Law

According to Calvin the law consists of the Ten Commandments, which is the rule of godly and righteous living, and of a form of religion on which the Mosaic Law was founded, that is the covenant of grace made with the seeds of Abraham (*Inst* 2.7.1, *CO* 2.252).[2] As the promulgation of the rule of a just and pious life, which was initially delivered to Adam and Eve in the Garden of Eden,[3] the Ten Commandments enforce "the perfect doctrine

---

1 Elert, *Law and Gospel*, 7, 11.
2 For Calvin's definition of the law as the rule of pious and right living (*regula vivendi pie et recte*), cf. *Confession of Faith* (1536), 26-27 (*CO* 9.694, 22.86); *The Catechism of the Church of Geneva*, 107 (*CO* 6.51-52); "The Preface," *CTS* 2/1.xvi, xvii (*CO* 24.5-6); Comm. Ex. 19:1-2 (1.313, *CO* 24.192); Matt. 5:19 (1.181, *CO* 45.172-173); Rom. 7:11 (145, *CO* 49.126).
3 Comm. Gen. 2:16 (125, *CO* 23.44): ". . . the only rule of living well and rationally (*unica bene et cum ratione vivendi regula*), that men should exercise themselves in

of piety and righteousness," which signifies the moral law as a whole.[4] Calvin distinguishes the moral law from the ceremonial and political law, but he maintains that the ceremonies supplement the rule of pious life, which is characterized by "the spiritual worship" in the First Table, and the political laws related to the Second Table help us with living according to "the rule of a good and upright life."[5]

As the rule of life, the truth of the law is eternal, but since the fall people have lost their ability to live according to it. Originally the law was good and perfect, but it "accidentally (*accidentale*) became the minister of death."[6] With the coming of sin into the world, the office of the law, without diminishing its nature as *lex vivendi*, was transformed to play a theological role for the salvation of God's people. As Calvin puts it in his sermon on Ephesians, after stating that the Decalogue is the summary and perfection of the Christian life, which is persuaded by faith (related to the instruction of the First Table) and illuminated by love (related to the instruction of the Second Table), the life submitted to the instruction of the moral law is to look towards Christ the Mediator who is the express image of God.[7] In the same vein, in his sermon on the Synoptic Gospels, Calvin argues that the Decalogue regulates the rule of worshipping God and loving neighbours in the firm conviction of the reconciling grace of Christ, and that the truth and substance of the law are embodied in the mediatorial office of Christ.[8]

Throughout his works, Calvin puts a balanced emphasis upon the normative and theological office and use of the law. He accuses people who advocate free will, asserting that the law (or the whole Bible) is nothing other than "a rule of living" (*Inst* 2.5.7, *CO* 2.235). They are criticized for adhering to "the natural use of the law (*l'usage naturel*)" working merely as a bridle to hold back our wicked desires and lusts.[9] The use of the law which is taken into theological consideration may not correspond to the natural use of the law in punishment, which Calvin deals with in his commentary on *De clementia*.[10]

According to Calvin, the theological use of the law for the conversion and continual nurturing of the human soul is related to the restoration of the image of God (*Inst.* 1.15.1-8, *CO* 2.134-143). Although the conditionality

---

obeying God."
4 Comm. Ex. 19:1-2 (1.313, *CO* 24.192).
5 "The Preface," *CTS* 2/1.xvi-xvii. Calvin tends to equate the law of God with the moral law, e.g., *Inst*. 4.20.16 (CO2.1106).
6 Comm. Gen. 2:16 (126, *CO* 23.45); Gen. 3:8 (161, *CO* 23.65).
7 Serm. Eph. 1:15 (84-87, *CO* 51.312-315).
8 Serm. Lk. 1:75 (*CO* 46.189-190). Cf. Serm. Isa. 32:6 (*SC* 3.120-122).
9 Serm. I Tim. 1:7 (44b-45a, *CO* 53.47-48).
10 *Clem.* 143.20-21.

of the law was overcome by the death of Christ, its peculiar normative feature as *lex vivendi* continues to work as the criterion by which we should judge good from evil. He writes:

> Although the Law is a testimony of God's gratuitous adoption, and teaches that salvation is based upon His mercy, and invites men to call upon God with assured faith, yet it has this peculiar property, that it covenants conditionally (*sub conditione paciscitur*).[11]

In this passage Calvin does not relate the word "*conditio*" to the merit of our good works, but underscores the validity of the righteousness of the law still working in spite of the promise of the gratuitous grace of Christ in the divine covenant. In fact, the conditionality of the covenant rests on the mutuality between the precept and promise of the law. Therefore, "*conditio*" means the way in which the law, as *lex vivendi*, works for the salvation of people as *lex accusans* by making them look for the grace of Christ in "reverence and fear (*reverentia et timor*)."[12]

The law regulates *quid debeant homines*, but not *quid possint*.[13] As Calvin puts it in the 1536 *Institutes*, "in God's law we must have regard not for the work but for the commandment" (1.28, *CO* 1.46).[14] The law regulates not "our might, power, or ability, but our duties." Notwithstanding, what the law requires of us is the righteousness accommodated to angels and to his people.[15] The law reveals not only God's will towards his people, that they ought to live a right and holy life according to the instruction of the law, but also the "eternity, power, wisdom, goodness, truth, righteousness, and mercy" of the lawgiver (1536 *Inst*. 1.1, *CO* 1.27).

From the proper understanding of the relationship between these two aspects of the law, each of which represents the precept and promise of the law individually, we can realize that Calvin points out the fact that the righteousness of the law reveals the eternal will of God towards our salvation when he proclaims in his first catechism, "In God's law is given the most perfect rule of all righteousness, which is for the best of reasons to be called the Lord's everlasting will."[16] Thus, the law is not "a preliminary

---

11 Comm. Ex. 19:1-2 (1.313 [altered], *CO* 24.192-193).
12 Comm. Ex. 19:1-2 (1.313-315, *CO* 24.192-194). For the sanctions and promises of the law, cf. Comm. Rom. 3:22 (73, *CO* 49.60); *Inst*. 2.5.10 (*CO* 2.237-238), 3.17.6 (*CO* 2.594-595).
13 Cf. Comm. Matt. 5:31 (1.190, *CO* 45.180).
14 "... in lege Dei non opus respiciendum, sed mandatum."
15 Cf. Serm. Deut. 28:1 (88-89, *CO* 28.353); Job 10:16-17 (186a-187, *CO* 33.496-499); Job 23:1-7 (412a-416b, *CO* 34.331-344).
16 *First Catechism* 11 (*CO* 5.327).

(*tirocinium*) to true righteousness" but "the beginning (*initium*) of righteousness."[17] It is surely the case that the righteousness of the law, in Calvin's judgment, should be differentiated from the higher righteousness (*iustice plus haute*) of God. The law itself does not reveal the secret providence of God, but points to the double grace of God for justification and sanctification.[18] With reference to justification, the righteousness of the law instructs people on the principle of the righteousness of faith by revealing the eternal righteousness of God accomplished by his Son Christ the Mediator.[19] Likewise, with reference to sanctification, the righteousness of the law denotes that one who is in union with Christ ought to live according to the instruction of the law through the continual communication of his righteousness.[20]

In dealing with "the grace of the law" in his sermon on Deuteronomy, Calvin explains the significance of the righteousness of the law for the whole process of salvation in three ways. First, he is concerned with the normative aspect of the law: Men should keep the whole corpus of the law; Since men cannot meet the perfect righteousness of the law because of their sinfulness, God gave his Son whom he had decreed as a remedy before the publication of the law; In the grace of Christ God receives their life and their imperfect works as righteous.[21] Then, he takes into consideration the righteousness of the law in view of the promise of the law: The law regulates not what men can do, but what they ought to do; The law, however, teaches that the promise of the law refers to the continual mediation of Christ both for justification and for sanctification; Therefore, men who are in union with Christ by the communication of the Spirit of Christ can live according to the law and this leads to eternal life.[22] The first two aspects of the righteousness of the law are based on the fact that the law is the law of the covenant: The righteousness of the law is subject to the unconditional mercy of God in the covenant of grace; Even the promise which is conditional rests on the fatherly love of God; Therefore, the reward of good works is due to the grace of God who receives our imperfect works as righteous.[23]

As observed, Calvin deals with the nature of the law very positively as the rule of life. With regard to the knowledge of the law, he emphasizes God's accommodating grace to reveal his own righteousness through the

---

17 Comm. Matt. 5:20 (1.183, *CO* 45.174).
18 Serm. Job 10:16-17 (186a-187, *CO* 33.496-499).
19 Comm. Rom. 10:4-5 (222-224, *CO* 49.196-198).
20 Serm. Deut. 26:25 (300b-302b, *CO* 26.491-495).
21 Serm. Deut. 27:24-26 (63-76, *CO* 28.335-345).
22 Serm. Deut. 28:1-2 (78, *CO* 28.345-357).
23 Serm. Deut. 27:11-15 (21-29, *CO* 28.306-312).

law, instead of inducing fear of his punishment.[24] As the rule of a pious and upright life, the law plays its theological role in the whole process of salvation. Thus, according to Calvin, the perception of the normative nature of the law should be placed prior to the knowledge of its theological use for justification as *lex accusans* and for sanctification as *lex vivificandi*, by which he understands the use of the law for the believer's perfection in eternal life.

7.3 The Office and Use of the Law

7.3.1 Luther: Lex Semper Accusat

In his treatise, *The Freedom of a Christian*, Luther strictly distinguishes between "commandments and promises," and argues like Calvin that the commandments show not what we can do but what we ought to do.[25] He does not admit that the promise of the law works in the process of salvation,[26] and writes: "Repentance proceeds from the law of God, but faith or grace from the promise of God. . . . Accordingly man is consoled and exalted by faith in the divine promise after he has been humbled and led to a knowledge of himself by the threats and the fear of the divine law."[27] Since Luther does not acknowledge the promise of the law, he equates the righteousness of the law working in the process of justification with the merit of the works of the law, and differentiates it from "Christ's righteousness," which he calls "alien righteousness," i.e., "the righteousness of another, instilled from without" in a sermon of Palm Sunday (1519) entitled *Two kinds of Righteousness*.[28] The reason why Luther was so critical of the positive use of the law in his early works was that he based his argument on the clear distinction between Christ's righteousness and the righteousness of the law.[29] Luther declares in his *Heidelberg Disputation* article 1, "The law of God, the most salutary doctrine of life, cannot advance man on his way to righteousness, but rather hinders him"[30]

---

24 Cf. Benoît Girardin, *Rhétorique et Théologique: Calvin le Commentaire de l'Épître aux Romains* (Paris: Éditions Beauchesne, 1979), 342, 350, 354.

25 *Martin Luther's Basic Theological Writings*, ed. Timothy F. Lull (Minneapolis: Fortress Press, 1989. hereafter *Luther*), 600: ". . . the commandments show us what we ought to do but do not give us the power to do it."

26 *Luther*, 601: ". . . the promises of God belong to the New Testament. Indeed, they are the New Testament."

27 *Luther*, 616.

28 *Luther*, 155. 157.

29 *Luther*, *Disputation against Scholastic Theology*, esp. 18-19 (articles 70-89), and *Heidelberg Disputation*, esp. 30-49 (theological theses 1-28).

30 *Luther*, 33-34.

Lex Dei Regula Vivendi et Vivificandi 219

Luther sustained his view of the twofold use of the law throughout his life although in a few places he mentions the use of the law in the life of a Christian.[31] As Ebeling observes, for Luther "the absolute center of gravity is located in the *usus theologicus*, which really alone deserves to be called *usus legis*," and "the distinction of law and Gospel encroaches on the doctrine of the *usus legis*."[32] In his 1519 and 1535 Galatians commentaries, Luther consistently points out the negative office of the law that it gives rise to the fear of punishment in order to explain the two uses of the law. In his commentary on Galatians 4:3, he writes:

> . . . the Law is a custodian, because, since the letter of the Law compels the unwilling to do its works for fear of punishment, it compels them at the same time to acknowledge this reluctance and to run to Christ, who gives the spirit of freedom.[33]

Like Calvin, Luther interprets "an intermediary" in Galatians 3:19 as Christ, but he does not mention Christ's mediation of the law, but indicates that he is "the Mediator of a better covenant."[34] He concludes that this verse says that we are led to Christ the Mediator by our consciousness of the fact that there is nothing more "hateful," "odious," and "intolerable" than the law.[35]

In his commentary on Galatians 3:20, Luther merely emphasizes Christ's abolition of the wrath of the law. He writes:

> That Mediator is Jesus Christ. He does not change the sound of the Law, as Moses did; nor does He cover it with a veil or lead me away from a view of the Law. But He sets Himself against the wrath of the Law and abolishes it; in His own body and by Himself He satisfies the Law.[36]

Then, he concludes:

---

31 In Ebeling, "On the Doctrine of the *Triplex Usus Legis*," 62-65, Luther is said to have clearly taught the *usus triplex legis* at the conclusion of his *Second Disputation against the Antinomians* (1538): "Why should the law be taught? The law is to be taught for the sake of discipline . . . that by this pedagogy men might come to Christ. . . . Secondly, the law is to be taught in order to expose sin. . . . Thirdly, the law is to be retained so that the saints may know which works God requires" (*WA* 391, 485). However, according to Elert, these sentences represent a forgery from Melanchthon's 1535 *Loci Communes*. *Law and Gospel*, 38-39.
32 Ebeling, "On the Doctrine of the *Triplex Usus Legis*," 71, 78.
33 *LW* 27.286.
34 *LW* 27.271-272, 319.
35 *LW* 27.320.
36 *LW* 27.325.

Therefore the Law cannot do anything except that with its light it illuminates the conscience for sin, death, judgment, and the hate and wrath of God . . . Therefore the principal purpose of the Law in theology is to make men not better but worse; that is, it shows them their sin, so that by the recognition of sin they may be humbled, frightened, and worn down, and so may long for grace and for the Blessed Offspring.[37]

Like Calvin, Luther has the conception that apart from the matter of justification, the law is "holy, righteous, good, spiritual, divine, etc."[38] However, he does not admit the grace of the law in its normative use for the Christian life because he believes that those who are regenerated by the Holy Spirit may live with the living faith (*fides viva*), not having to rest on the instruction of the law.[39] Luther finds no room for the positive aspect of Christ's mediation of the law, but only his annulment of its slavery. Accordingly, he can find no use for the continual validity of the law in the Christian life, particularly with reference to its theological use. Luther's basic assumption is applicable to the whole process of salvation, that "the Law and Christ are mutually contradictory and altogether incompatible."[40]

7.3.2 Melanchthon: From Lex Accusans to Lex Vivendi

Melanchthon's debate with Agricola over *poenitentia* was evoked by the first statement of Luther's *Ninety-Five Theses* (1517): "the entire life of believers to be one of repentance (*poenitentia*)."[41] Along with the motto established in the *Apology to the Augsburg Confession*, "*lex semper accusat*,"[42] this very comprehensive statement prompted the early Lutheran theologians to raise questions about the theological use of the law concerning continual repentance in the whole process of salvation.

Melanchthon was faithful to the sequence of *lex-poenitentia-fides*.[43] He argued that the knowledge of the law is necessary for repentance, without

---

37 *LW* 27.327.
38 *LW* 27.365 (Galatians 4:3).
39 Doumergue, *Jean Calvin*, 4.195-196; Karl-Heinz zur Mühlen, "Law," in *The Oxford Encyclopedia of the Reformation*, 2.405a. By the concept of *fides viva* Luther seeks to overcome Catholic doctrine of *habitus*. Cf. B. A. Gerrish, *Grace and Reason: A Study in the Theology of Luther* (Oxford: Clarendon Press, 1962), 92-99.
40 *LW* 27.366.
41 *Luther*, 21. In the same vein, in his work *Discussion of Poenitentia* (1518) Luther proclaims that "the best *poenitentia* is the new life." Quot. Wengert, *Law and Gospel*, 16.
42 4.285, in *The Book of Concord*, trans. and ed. Theodore G. Tappert (Philadelphia: Fortress, 1959), 50. Cf. Elert, *Law and Gospel*, 7, 11.
43 Cf. *Loci Communes 1521*, *CR* 21.153-154: "Hic satis sit monuisse hoc opus legis initium esse poenitentiae, quo spiritus dei terrere ac confundere conscientias solet. . .

which faith is nothing but a foolish dream.[44] Agricola adhered to the sequence of *fides-poenitentia*. He allowed no room for the concept of legal repentance because he believed that faith should precede repentance and thus no theological use of the law should be proposed in evangelical repentance.[45]

Agricola asserts that what makes people repent (*poenitentiam agere*) is not the office of the law, but the faith of people who are in fear ("*fides minarum*"). God's people love his righteousness and live according to his will because they are illuminated by "the spontaneous Spirit of Christ." Therefore, the regenerate should not turn to the instruction of the law when seeking the accomplishment of their righteousness any more.[46] This position is very similarly to Luther's early polemical position on the law.

On the other hand, Melanchthon derives legal repentance from the concept of the righteousness of the law, and distinguishes it from evangelical repentance.[47] Three facts are considered with reference to the righteousness of the law: We are justified by perfect obedience to the law; No one can satisfy the demand of the law; Therefore, the law should be fulfilled by someone else instead of us. With the perception of the righteousness of the law, according to Melanchthon, we are led to legal repentance, and then with the true and living faith we are led to evangelical repentance.[48] As Melanchthon puts it, in his *scholia* to Exodus 20 (1525), "The knowledge of the law is absolutely necessary because we cannot discover nor experience the gospel in our hearts without it!"[49]

Melanchthon acknowledges the wide use of the law in the process of salvation, but as he maintains the use of the law for continual repentance in the Christian life, which acts independently from the working of the gospel, he sustains his negative view of the nature of the law as *lex semper accusans*. He understands the first two uses of the law as being "to coerce the flesh and to terrify the conscience (*coercere carnem et terrere conscientiam*),"[50] and the third use of the law as the application of the first two uses of the law to the Christian life, that is, the legal instructions for

---

Et sicut hinc nempe a peccati cognitione vita Christiana auspicanda est, ita a legis officio Christiana doctrina auspicanda est."
44 Wengert, *Law and Gospel*, 23, 79. This view is presented precisely in Melanchthon's Latin version of the *Visitation Articles* of 1527, his catechism called *Etliche Sprüche*, and *Scholia in Epistolam Pauli ad Colossenses*, published in 1527, 1528, and 1534.
45 Ibid., 18-22. This view is well presented in Agricola's catechisms called *Elementa pietatis congesta: Christliche Kinderzucht and Hendertdreißig gemeine Fragestücke, and Die Epistel an die Colosser S. Pauls* published in 1527.
46 Ibid., 90-93, 126-138.
47 Girardin, *Rhétorique et Théologique*, 339.
48 Wengert, *Law and Gospel*, 71, 101-102.
49 Ibid., 71.
50 Ibid., 91-93, 101.

good works and its impact upon daily penance rather than to the teaching and exhortation of the law in seeking a godly life.

Melanchthon discusses the threefold use of the law for the first time in his 1534 *Scholia* on Colossians.[51] He writes: "God gave the law for these three reasons: to coerce the flesh and to terrify or humble. The third reason pertains to the righteous, that they may practice obedience (*ad cohercendam carnem, et ad terrendum seu humiliandum. Tertia ad iustos pertinet, ut exerceant obedientiam*)."[52] He develops the normative use of the law for the believer on the basis of the double grace of God to justify both our person and our imperfect obedience.[53] He is keen to link the third use to the Christian freedom to willingly obey God's will.[54] However, he fails to understand the third use of the law in terms of its dynamic relation to the continual mediation of Christ. He is more concerned about the function of conscience than the believer's communication with the grace of Christ when he deals with the office of the law.

Although there is no specific place which directly refers to the threefold use of the law, Melanchthon's commentary on Romans (1532) presents us with its theological foundation very systematically. Melanchthon concentrates on the law's role in repentance, which he defines as to realize God's wrath and punishment, through this to come to the state of true confession and contrition, and to give up our merit and the righteousness of good works.[55] For the sake of repentance, according to him, the law serves merely as a voice accusing us of our sins ("*vox legis accusantis nos*") and reveals no promise.[56]

In dealing with the use of the law in the process of repentance, Melanchthon often refers to the inner judgment of conscience that works prior to faith[57] and expresses his negative view of the law by adhering to

---

51 In his second lecture on Paul's letter to the Colossians 2:17 (1527), Melanchthon explicitly declares his view of the twofold use of the law—"to keep the fleshly man under control" and "to inspire fear, to condemn us and to humble us." Melanchthon, *Paul's Letter to the Colossians*, tr. D. C. Parker (Sheffield: The Almond Press, 1989), 65-66. The same view also appears in his commentary on Colossians 2:20, ibid., 68-69.

52 Wengert, *Law and Gospel*, 195-196. The phrase "*exercere obedientiam*" is also found in *Loci Communes* 1535 (*CR* 21.406), 1543 (*CR* 21.719), and 1555 (*CR* 22.255).

53 Ibid., 179-191, quot. 182.

54 Ibid., 198.

55 *CR* 15.581: "Hic ergo cum fatetur Propheta se esse peccatorem, et addit exclusivam, tantum, abiicit dignitatem propriam, agnoscit se habere immunditiem pugnantem cum lege Dei, ac se reum esse ac meritum iram Dei et poenas. Haec confessio quid sit, in vera contritione pii experiuntur. In his pavoribus excutitur arrogantia et fiducia propriae dignitatis, seu iusticiae legis."

56 *CR* 15.582.

57 Melanchthon regards the conscience as the place in which we realize God's

the dictum, which is derived from a principle of common law, that "the law reveals, but does not remove sin (*Lege tantum ostendi peccatum, non tolli*)." He thinks that the "*duplex usus*" is common to the whole law including the Mosaic law but natural law, which he defines as follows: "the first is political, to coerce carnal men outwardly, and the second pertains to the judgment of God and to conscience, that is to accuse and frighten conscience."[58] In the same vein, in dealing with the second use of the law (the theological use) throughout the editions of his *Loci Communes*, Melanchthon devotes most passages to the exposition of the inner judgment of the law focused on the fear and terror of the conscience, but gives no direct statement on the office of the law to make people to look for Christ as their Mediator. Likewise, he claims that Galatians 3:24 points to the first use of the law and pays more attention to the word "schoolmaster" than to the words "unto Christ."[59]

Just as Melanchthon refers to the fear of judgment arising in the conscience in order to explain the second use of the law, so he does likewise in order to explain the third use of the law for the continual repentance of the believer. Commenting on sanctification in Romans 6, he argues that mortification without faith is terror, but the terror of God's children, which is accompanied by faith and the knowledge of Christ, will make them worship God and do good works.[60] When Melanchthon says, "Truly the beginning of the new and eternal life is new and spiritual obedience," he is concerned mainly with the power of the gospel rather than with the normative use of the law.[61]

As noted in his commentary on the phrase, "*lex efficit iram*," in Romans 4:15, Melanchthon differentiates "*promissio legis*" from "*promissio gratiae*," and thinks that the former only signifies God's reward for good works, whereas the latter contains the core of the gospel. So he argues that the promise of the law works solely to lead us to repentance.[62] He believes

---

redemptive and reconciling grace (*CR* 15.587). He argues that "conscience is erected by faith when in faith it recognizes the mercy of God (*conscientia fide erecta, cum agnovit misericordiam fide propositam*)," (*CR* 15.593)."

58 *CR* 15.585: "... alter est politicus, scilicet foris coercere homines carnales.... Alter usus non est politicus, sed pertinet ad iudicium Dei et ad conscientiam, scilicet accusare et perterrefacere conscientiam."

59 *Loci Communes* 1521, *CR* 21.149-153; *Loci Communes* 1535, *CR* 21.405: "Secundum officium ac proprium legis divinae et praecipuum est, ostendere peccata, accusare, perterrefacere et damnare conscientias"; *Loci Communes* 1543, *CR* 717-719; *Loci Communes* 1555, *CR* 22.250-255. Melanchthon here describes the second use of the law as "*Zornpredigt* (preaching the wrath of God)" (250).

60 *CR* 15.636: "... mortificatio sine fide est terror ... terrores cum fide et notitia Christi, sunt timor filialis seu vera contritio, et fiunt cultus Dei et bonum opus: ..."

61 *CR* 15.635: "Incoatio vere novae et aeternae vitae est nova et spiritualis obedientia."

62 *CR* 15.603-604.

that the promise of the law is related to the righteousness of the law, and the promise of grace to Christ the Mediator. He points out freedom from the bondage of the law and voluntary obedience to the law in relation to the normative use of the law, but for him the law still serves to evoke not the grace of God but the fear of God (*timor dei*). In conclusion, for Melanchthon, like the first two uses of the law, the third use also indicates an aspect of *lex accusans*. The vital difference to remember is that the first two uses of the law signify God's works through the power of the law, but the third use signifies our works through the norm of the law.[63] This feature shows the shift of Melanchthon's emphasis, from *lex accusans* to *lex vivendi*.

7.3.3 Bullinger: From Lex Vivendi to Lex Accusans

Because Bullinger explores the nature of the law in terms of its relation to the office and use of the law from the standpoint of his covenantal theological understanding, I will here deal with his commentary on the Sermon on the Mount[64] where he mainly refers to the original meaning of the law and its continuity between the Old and New Testaments, along with his commentary on the Epistle to the Romans[65] and with his great sermons called *Decades*.[66]

Concerning the nature of the law in his commentary on Matthew, Bullinger points out the perpetual validity of the precepts of the law for all the people in the old and new covenants.[67] As he puts it,

---

63 Cf. Wengert, *Law and Gospel*, 195-196.
64 Bullinger, *In Sacrosanctum Iesu Christi Domini nostri Evangelium secundum Matthaeum* (1546, Zürich, hereafter *HBEM*). Cf. Parker, *Calvin's New Testament Commentaries*, 71-72, 226. Bullinger confessed in his *Diarium* that he had been nourished by Chrysostom's Homilies on Matthew and what Jerome wrote on Matthew, the writings of Ambrose, Origen, and Augustine, along with Luther's major theological tracts and especially Philip Melanchthon's first edition of his *Loci Communes*.
65 Bullinger gave lectures on the Epistle to the Romans twice, in Kappel (1526) and in Zürich (1533). Here I use his second lecture *Commentarii in omnes Pauli Apostoli Epistolas, atque etiam in Epistolam ad Hebraeos* (Zürich, 1582, hereafter *HBPE*), which was originally published in 1534. This publication was followed by that of his book *De testamento seu foedere Dei unico et aeterno* which was published in the same year (1534). Cf. Büsser, "Bullinger as Calvin's Model in Biblical Exposition," 70-71.
66 For Bullinger's covenantal understanding of the continuity of salvation history, see David C. Steinmetz, *Reformers in the Wings: From Geiler von Kaysersberg to Theodore Beza*, 2nd ed. (Oxford: Oxford University Press, 2001), 93-99.
67 *HBEM* 8.178b: "Lex vero perpetua est, omni tempore valens, et omnibus hominibus praecepta vitae praescribens."

The law of God is the perpetual and best will of God, written by this finger of God and explained and published to the people through Moses, by which all human beings would know the will of God (what they should do in their whole life and what they should leave out) and do what they have come to know, that is, wholly depending on His will to live according to what God has prescribed.[68]

Bullinger calls the eternal will of God revealed in the law the righteousness of the law, which prescribes not only the eternal decree of God's salvation but also the divine norm of life.[69] He states:

The law was first enacted by the Lord in order that it may set before our eyes sin and the kind of people we are by nature, lead us to Christ through this way as a teacher, and order the duties of life. Therefore, those who learn by the law that they are sinners and unjust people, and have no trust in their own strength catch the true and genuine sense of the law and are converted to Christ whom the law promised.[70]

Bullinger believes that the "marrow (*medullam*)," "end (*finem*)," and "spirit (*spiritum*)" of the law were already revealed to the ancient fathers in the era of the Old Testament, even though they were not communicated with "the liberal and spontaneous Spirit of Christ."[71] He especially emphasizes the work of the Spirit of Christ in order to explain the fulfilment of the righteousness of the law for the whole process of salvation. He comments:

[However] the Spirit of Christ, who is conferred on believers through their faith, does not release a person from the law but subjects him to it:

---

68 *HBEM* 3.54b: "Lex enim dei est perpetua et optima dei voluntas, in hoc digito dei exarata et exposita per Mosen vulgataque, quo omnes homines dei voluntatem (quid in omni vita sua faciant, et quid omittant) cognoscant, et cognitam faciant, id est, toti ab ea pendentes ita ut deus praescripsit vivant." A similar definition of the law is found in Heinrich Bullinger, *Sermonum decades quinque, de potissimis Christianae religionis capitibus, in tres tomos digestae*, vol. 2 (Zürich, 1572, hereafter *Decades*), 2.1.36a: "Lex aliud non est quam declaratio divinae voluntatis, praescribens quid facias aut quid omittas."

69 *HBEM* 3.54b: " . . . totius vitae regula et faciendorum omittendorumque formula."

70 *HBEM* 3.56a: "Est autem lex lata a domino, primum quidem ut peccatum et quales natura simus ob oculos statuat, et per hunc modum ceu paedagogus ad Christum deducat: deinde ut officia vitae praescribat. Verum ergo et genuinum legis sensum capiunt, qui ex lege peccatores et iniustos sese esse cognoscunt, ac ideo de suis diffisi viribus, ad eum convertuntur quem lex promisit Christum."

71 *HBEM* 3.55a-55b.

so that he should furnish obedience to God not as compelled (that people under the law are used to be) but as spontaneous and free. Thus, a Christian fulfills the law, but through Christ and in the Spirit of Christ.[72]

Therefore, in those who have not the Spirit of Christ and walk according to flesh, in them not even justification of the law is fulfilled.[73]

Consequently, the Christian's fulfilment of the righteousness of the law is the embodiment of the righteousness of Christ which works through the work of his Spirit.[74]

The impact of this understanding of the nature of the law based on the promise in the covenant of grace is well demonstrated in Bullinger's understanding of the threefold use of the law which is explored in the eighth sermon of the third decade of sermons (1550). What he calls "*praecipuum et proprium legis officium*" is similar to the second use of the law in Luther and Melanchthon, but more positive and comprehensive. He argues that apart from convicting us of our sins, the law describes the true and absolute righteousness of God in the doctrine of justification. In this sense, he says, it takes up the office of the gospel. Referring to Galatians 3:24, "the law was our schoolmaster," he affirms that the law leads us to Christ the Saviour and declares "Christ and life in Christ (*Christum et in ipso vitam*)." The law teaches the holy will of God as a whole, i.e., "not only the basic principles of righteousness but also the very true and absolute righteousness (*non tyrocinia tantum iustitiae, sed ipsam veram et absolutam iustitiam*)." Further, he mentions the pedagogical function of the ceremonies of the law to reveal Christ and his mysteries as a guide and schoolmaster (*ductio et paedagogia*).[75]

Bullinger's second use of the law is similar to Calvin's third use. Like Calvin, he points out the use of the law as the rule of a godly and upright life. The law teaches "*quid sequantur vel quid fugiant iustificati in fide per Christum, et quomodo pii rite colant deum.*" Citing many passages from Psalms, Bullinger stresses that the precepts of the law are also applied "for the exhortation and consolation (*exhortationem et consolationem*)" of the

---

72 *HBEM* 3.54b: "[Sed] et spiritus Christi, qui confertur per fidem credentibus, legi dei non eximit hominem, sed subdit: non ut coacta (quod solent qui sub lege sunt) sed spontanea et libera deo obsequia praestet. Complet itaque legem homo Christianus, sed per Christum et in spiritu Christi."

73 *HBEM* 3.54b-55a: ". . . ergo in quibus nullus Christi spiritus est, et qui secundum carnem ambulant, in iis nulla etiam legis iustificatio impletur."

74 *HBEM* 3.56a: "Christus ergo est iustitia Christianorum, et communicat hic nobiscum iustitiam suam per fidem: unde apostoli appellarunt etiam fidem iustitiam Christianorum. Simul autem per fidem datur nobis spiritus Christi quo regeneramur."

75 *Decades* 3.8.136a-137b.

regenerate. Thus, this normative office of the law encompasses "*doctrinam perfectissimam et fidei in Deum et omnium bonorum operum.*"[76] Then, what Bullinger calls the third use of the law, which is "*coercere petulantes,*" is similar to the first use of the law in Luther. However, unlike Luther and Melanchthon, the negative office of the law to give rise to the fear of punishment is related only to its political use. He quotes I Timothy 1:8, "the law is good if one uses it properly," as the most relevant verse, like Luther, Melanchthon, and Calvin.[77]

Bullinger's interpretation of the role of *paedagogus* in Galatians 3:24 demonstrates his understanding of the office and use of the law based on the continual grace of the divine covenant. The law teaches not only the gratuitous grace of Christ for our justification but also the godly life according to the inspiration of the "liberating and spontaneous Spirit of Christ," which he equates to "the spirit of the law (*spiritus legis*)."[78] In his Romans commentary, he describes the righteousness of the law as "the mind of the law (*mens legis*)," by which the law teaches and inspires "*pietatem, fidem, innocentiam et charitatem.*"[79] He particularly shows his strict antipathy to the merit of the works of the law for justification,[80] but he does not deny the fact that the office of the law to reveal the rule of life precedes the accusing role of the law in the process of justification. Bullinger refers to the fact that the law is the expression of God's will towards his people, which is represented by the restoration of the image of God in relation to the third use of the law in Calvin, for explaining the first use of the law. Bullinger's covenantal understanding of the law is clearly shown when he asserts that although as the declaration of God's will the law was revealed to the ancient fathers, if there is no death of Christ, there is no revelation of God's will.[81]

---

76 *Decades* 3.8.137b-138a.

77 *Decades* 3.8.138a.

78 *HBPE* 287-288. Bullinger took the same position in his first lecture on Romans. Cf. Susi Hausammann, *Römerbriefauslegung zwischen Humanismus und Reformation: Eine Studie zu Heinrich Bullingers Römerbriefauslegung von 1525* (Zürich: Zwingli Verlag, 1970), 256-258.

79 *HBPE* 23, 46.

80 *HBPE* 26-27: ". . . the whole righteousness and works of ours are like the rag of a menstruous woman (*omnes iustitiae vel opera nostra sicut pannus mulieris menstruatae*)." This expression is inspired by the phrase in Latin Vulgate Isaiah 64:6, "filthy rags (NIV, *vestimentum inquinatum*, Calvin)." In the *Institutes*, Calvin quotes this Vulgate translation from Bernard of Clairvaux (3.2.25).

81 *HBPE* 45: "Per legem autem nolim intelligas voluntatem Dei, sed id quod legis indicio agnoscitur, peccatum. Hoc enim beneficio mortis Christi extinctum iacet."

7.3.4 Bucer's Holistic Understanding of Lex Vivendi and Lex Accusans

Bucer's commentary on Romans (1536) along with his commentary on the Synoptic Gospels (1527, 1530, 1536) is of capital importance in revealing his theology of the law.[82] Bucer's position on the law in these two commentaries is consistent although the latter concentrates more on the original meaning of the law and the continuity of the substance of the law in the Old and New Testaments than the former where he stresses the relationship between the law and the Gospel, and on the continual validity of the law in justification and sanctification. Although Bucer's commentary is holistic and sometimes "too verbose to be read quickly," basically he is faithful to the text and gives very precise and refined presentations on *loci theologici maiores*.[83] Just as we can call Calvin's *Institutes* "an extended commentary on Romans,"[84] we may consider Bucer's commentary on Romans to be a small *Institutes* of the Christian religion, even though it is relatively weak in its doctrine of the church and civil government.

In his commentary on Romans, Bucer explains his dynamic view of the office and use of the law from the concept of the righteousness of God (*iustitia dei*). Expounding Romans 1:17, he underscores that Christ does not only give us new life, but pours his Spirit into our heart to live according to the teaching of the law with the eager desire for true and solid righteousness. The righteousness of God, therefore, embraces the concept of "the just and justifying God (*deus et iustus et iustificans*)."[85] Citing Augustine's words, "*Bona opera sequi iustificatum, non praecedere iustificandum*," Bucer gives an account of the *triplex iustitia* inspired by "the three kinds of eternal life."[86] The first righteousness is to receive eternal life by the merit of Christ, the second is to receive the Spirit of sonship that makes us cry out "Abba, Father," the third signifies that the

---

82 We cannot discover in Bucer any comprehensive treatment of the law either in *De regno Christi* or in "A brief summary of Christian doctrine." The order of articles related to the doctrine of the law in "A brief summary of Christian doctrine" is very similar that of Calvin's 1536 *Institutes*, that is., article 2. Knowledge of God and of Christ, Article 3. Knowledge of Man, Article 4. True Repentance, Article 5. Redemption and Justification. Wright, *Common Places of Martin Bucer*, 78-79.
83 "John Calvin to Simon Grynaeus," *CNTC* 8.3 (*CO* 10/2.404).
84 Battles, *Calculus Fidei*, 145.
85 Metaphrasis et enarratio in epist. D. Pauli apostoli ad Romanos . . . (Basileae, 1562, hereafter MBER), 50-51. This book was originally published as a part of Metaphrases et enarrationes perpetuae epistolarum D. Pauli Apostoli . . . (Strasbourg, 1536).
86 "*Bona opera sequi iustificatum*" was a very controversial issue among Lutherans in the middle of the sixteenth century as to its relevance for Augustine's thought that "We are reputed righteous on account of the fulfillment of the law affected in us by the Holy Spirit." Melanchthon was once accused by his colleagues of supporting it. Wengert, *Law and Gospel*, 180.

people who are blessed with "good things (*bona*)" are to reveal God's righteousness by their "deeds (*facta*)."[87]

As Professor Wright points out, Bucer demonstrates his "distinctive approach to the doctrine of justification, viz., his refusal to separate the imputing from the imparting of righteousness, that is, the gift of pardon and reconciliation from the production of the godly life in us through the Holy Spirit."[88] In dealing with the principle of *iustificatio sola fide* in his commentary on the phrase, "*per legem enim cognitio peccati*," in Romans 3:20, Bucer shows his strict position on "*non iustificari ex operibus legis, sed ex fide Iesu Christi.*"[89] However, even in this case, he refers to the normative use of the law which is most strikingly depicted in Psalms 19 and 119. When he argues that the whole law makes known "the free giver (*largitorem*) of eternal life" and instructs people in the truth that "anyone who believes will have eternal life," by eternal life Bucer means the perfection of the whole process of salvation.[90] Therefore, the office of the law presented here features both *lex accusans* and *lex vivendi*.

The same position of Bucer is found in his commentary on the phrase "*sine lege iustitia dei manifestata est*" in Romans 3:21. With the intention to highlight the total grace of God in our salvation, he first pays attention to the fact that "*lex accusat et condemnat [peccatum]*." However, he is keen not to discard the normative significance of the law in repentance. As he puts it, "*sine lege*" means "*pro, non ex observatione legis.*"[91] He confirms his position by citing Augustine, who writes, "The righteousness of God which is given without the law, is not manifested without the law.[92]

Admittedly, "The law teaches righteousness; faith which persuades us into true righteousness, therefore, makes the law firm."[93] When the law leads the elect to true repentance, it reveals not only "the knowledge of sin (*cognitio peccati*)" but also "the doctrine of upright life (*doctrinam vitae rectae*)."[94] Based on this dynamic view of the relationship between faith and the office of the law, Bucer reaffirms that justification is the partaking of the righteousness of God (*communio iustitiae*).[95]

---

87 *MBER* 119.
88 Wright, *Common Places of Martin Bucer*, 159.
89 *MBER* 183-184.
90 *MBER* 190.
91 *MBER* 185.
92 *MBER* 186: "Iustitia [ergo] Dei sine lege, non sine lege manifestata est." Bucer here refers to Melanchthon's concept of double righteousness in order to corroborate his position on the normative use of the law.
93 *MBER* 212: "Lex sane iustitiam docet; Fides igitur cum iustitiam veram adducit, legem stabilit."
94 *MBER* 210.
95 *MBER* 191: ". . . in voce iustificationis, ut superius diximus, eius quoque doni significatio, quo nobis iustitia communicatur, praecipuum licet sit, quod ea vox

God's righteousness, which is imputed by the grace of Christ, is imparted by the power of the Spirit of Christ not only to us but also to the godly people in the Old Testament. Both the incarnation and death of Christ and the whole office of the Mediator were foreshadowed and prefigured in the law by the work of the Spirit of Christ. Bucer calls this *"mysteria Christi."*[96] In the Old Testament, the mystery of Christ was revealed as a type, but in the new covenant its substance was revealed in the body of Christ. Bucer designates the Holy Spirit as the Spirit of Christ in order to point out that the spiritual order of Christ is not under the law but under the grace of Christ the Mediator. Therefore, we are now justified "by faith in the Mediator *(fide mediatoris)*," and God's righteousness is communicated to us "by the Spirit of faith *(spiritu fidei).*"[97] So, those to whom God's righteousness is imparted take part in the divinity of Christ.[98]

The law reveals the divine will of God, which is to teach us the truth of salvation and Christian piety.[99] True piety means to "die to the law and be united to Christ *(nos legi mori, et iungi Christo)*." When people are united with Christ, the Spirit of Christ "makes the law our husband, in other words, a teacher so that the law, which is the interpreter of the divine will, may deservedly lead and moderate our entire life."[100] This very positive view of Bucer on the continual validity of the law for the regenerate is derived from his firm conviction of God's grace which justifies and accepts the believer's imperfect works as perfect.

Like Melanchthon, Bucer acknowledges the independent office of the law of legal repentance. He says that the law itself reveals our sins so that we flee to the grace of God even without the inspiration of the Spirit of Christ.[101] However, no one who is not persuaded by the Spirit of Christ can be led to the true salvation and righteousness because the Spirit of Christ is

---

exprimit, nostri absolutio in iudicio dei, peccatorum condonatio, vitaeque aeternae gratuita adiudicatio."

96 *MBER* 204-209.

97 *MBER* 198-200.

98 *MBER* 211: ". . . quod talibus divinitatis suae donat esse participes, hoc est, solidae iustitiae: qui et hac de causa vasa misericordiae dicuntur, parata ad gloriam."

99 *MBER* 348: ". . legem, cum sancta, iusta, et bona sit, ut quae voluntatis divinae de nobis, sanctae, iustae et bonae expressio sit, sanctis omnibus quandiu hic vivunt salutarem esse, meditarique in ea, ad instaurationem pietatis valere plurimum. Erudit ad salutem, et quavis sui parte: studereque ei, absoluit hominem Dei, ut instructus sit ad omne opus bonum."

100 *MBER* 345: ". . . spiritu Christi. . . . Hic facit legem maritum nostrum, alibi paedagogum. Nam lex quae est interpres bonae voluntatis Dei, merito omnem vitam nostrum regere et moderari debet: . . ."

101 *MBER* 350: "Sic lex sola, Christo non adflante suum spiritum, qui peccatum in nobis opporimat, et ad iustitiam impellat, in primis vero ad fiduciam in bonitatem Dei per Christum erigat, nihil quam augere peccatum, et nos occidere poterit."

"*spiritus adoptionis.*" Also, without the Spirit of Christ there is no "justification of the law (*iustificatio legis*)" because the Spirit of Christ is "*spiritus verae iustitiae.*"[102] Only by the Spirit of Christ can believers be emancipated from the law because it is "*spiritus libertatis.*"[103] Bucer acknowledges that the law itself (*lex per se*) serves to make people realize that they ought to *agere poenitentiam*; however if there is no special illumination of the Spirit of Christ it is merely an "occasion (*occasio*)" that has no fruit.[104]

Bucer calls the law "the doctrine of piety and righteousness (*doctrina pietatis atque iustitiae*),"[105] and the Decalogue "the perfect doctrine of piety (*doctrinam pietatis perfectam*)."[106] The most striking feature of Bucer's understanding of the normative use of the law is that he applies the concept of the communication of the righteousness of God, which he developed in the course of expounding justification by faith.[107] Bucer does not give any specific attention either to *lex accusans* or to *lex vivendi*, but believes that both are working together inspired by the Spirit of Christ "to increase, destroy, and condemn sin (*peccatum augere, occidere, condemnare*)" and "to vivify, manifest wisdom, restore, and illuminate (*vivificare, praestare sapientiam, restituere, illuminare*)" the perfection of the righteousness of God, that is, the eternal heavenly life.[108]

7.3.5 Calvin: From Lex Vivendi to Lex Vivificandi

As Calvin mentions in his note of dedication, if we understand the Epistle to the Romans, "we have a passage opened to us to the understanding of the whole scripture."[109] In no other work does he express his view of the office and use of the law in relation to its significance for the whole process of salvation more systematically, and with such brevity, than in his commentary on Romans. Calvin made great efforts to augment and refine this first biblical commentary throughout his life for "the common good of the Church" (1540, 1551, 1556).[110] The vital importance of this

---

102 *MBER* 374.
103 *MBER* 383. Cf. *MBER* 384: ". . . nulla earum legum satis, nisi quae fide certa ut lex Dei excipitur."
104 *MBER* 215.
105 *MBER* 216.
106 *MBER* 358-360.
107 *MBER* 481. Cf. Melanchthon, CR 15.688.
108 *MBER* 363.
109 "John Calvin to Simon Grynaeus," *CNTC* 8.2 (*CO* 10/2.403); T. H. L. Parker, *Commentaries on Romans 1532-1542* (Edinburgh: T & T Clark, 1986), 1-83; Akira Demura, "Two Commentaries on the Epistle to the Romans: Calvin and Oecolampadius," in *Calvinus Sincerioris Religionis Vindex*, 165-166.
110 "John Calvin to Simon Grynaeus," *CNTC* 8.3 (*CO* 10/2.404). For the development

commentary has been recognized by scholars who have noted its influence upon the 1539 *Institutes*, especially with reference to its *ordo docendi* which also reflects the impact of Melanchthon's Romans commentary.[111] In the following, I will examine Calvin's understanding of the office of the law concentrating on Christ's mediation of the law for the whole *ordo salutis*, the idea which is mainly inspired by his dynamic concept of salvation expressed in his commentary on Romans.

7.3.5.1 DUPLEX OFFICIUM LEGIS

In his works Calvin often refers to the twofold office of the law which comprises *lex accusans* and *lex vivendi*.[112] In his treatise against the libertines, Calvin argues for the perpetual validity of the law by indicating its office to arouse the fear of God's judgment and to teach the rule of life.[113] In the 1539 *Institutes*, he discusses the office of the law under the title of "the three classes of precepts (*tribus praeceptorum formis*)," commanding us to be converted to God, to live according to the law, and to remain under God's grace. He claims that not only does the law serve to accuse our sin so that we may look for the grace of the Mediator, but it also works for our daily sanctification and perfection in the end, the state of which he favours depicting as the eternal heavenly life (1539 *Inst.* 2.83, *CO* 1.362, *Inst.* 2.5.8, *CO* 2.235-236). He repeats the definition of *duplex legis officium* in his Catechism of the Church of Geneva (1545)[114] and in sermons on I Timothy.[115]

In spite of his manifestation of the twofold office of the law, Calvin regards *lex accusans* as the subsequent result of *lex vivendi*. As noted typically in the 1559 *Institutes*, "[T]he Jews not only learned from the law

---

of the successive editions of Calvin's Romans commentary, see T. H. L. Parker, *Commentarius in Epistolam Pauli ad Romanos*, "Introduction," XI-XVII.

111 Ibid., LIV; Muller, *The Unaccommodated Calvin*, 118-139.

112 Calvin does not always seem to use the words "*officium*" and "*usus*" discriminately. He uses these two words at the same time in order to express the threefold use of the law in *Inst.* 2.7.6. However, the former is more related to the nature of the law and the latter to its effect and efficacy.

113 *TAL* 271-272 (*CO* 7.206-207): "There are two things to consider in the law. That is to say, the teaching, which is the rule for right living. . . . The second point is its rigor, since it declares to us that whoever fails in a single point will be cursed, and it promises salvation only to those who perfectly observe its commandments . . . ."

114 *CTT* 118 (*CO* 6.79-82). Here Calvin clearly proclaims "the double office of the law (*duplex legis officium*)," which serves both to accuse people of their sins so that they may long for salvation in the Lord and to teach "a perfect rule of righteousness (*une reigle parfaicte de tout bien, perfectam iustitiae regulam*)."

115 Serm. I Tim. 1:5 (44a, *CO* 53.47); I Tim. 1:8 (51a, *CO* 53.53-54). Here Calvin describes the twofold office of the law as teaching "the doctrine of salvation" and "a rule to live well and holily."

what the true character of godliness (*vera pietatis ratio*) was; but also that, since they saw themselves incapable of observing the law, they were in dread of judgment drawn inevitably though unwillingly to the Mediator" (*Inst.* 2:8:1, *CO* 2.266). In his sermon on Genesis called *Sermon de la justification*, Calvin points out the positive aspect of the punitive function of the law: to make known the righteousness of God by instructing his people in the rule of right living.[116]

The law, whether it works as *lex vivendi* or *lex accusans*, plays its pedagogical role. The law teaches "the way of reconciliation between God and men" (*Inst.* 1.6.2, *CO* 2.54). Through the law we seek Christ's grace (*Inst.* 1.9.3, *CO* 2.71), and try to imitate "Christ's image" (*Inst.* 2.12.4, *CO* 2.342). Thus, the law of the Lord is "the very school (*scholam*) of God's children" (*Inst.* 1.6.4, *CO* 2.55), and "Christ is the inner school master (*interior magister*)" (*Inst.* 3.1.4, *CO* 2.397).[117] The whole divine law reveals the promise of God. Therefore, as Calvin puts it in his commentary on Deuteronomy 5:2, the teaching (*paedagogia*) of law "must be accounted a peculiar blessing, and a very high honour to be taken into the covenant by God."[118]

On the other hand, Luther's interpretation of the same verse is quite different from Calvin's. He regards the covenant in Horeb as the covenant of the law, and asserts that "the New [the covenant of grace] is founded wholly on the promise of the merciful and faithful God, without our works; but the Old is founded also on our works. Therefore Moses does not promise beyond the extent to which they keep the statutes and judgments."[119] According to a Lutheran theologian, Walter R. Bouman, Luther understands the Decalogue in a narrow sense as "a folk law" called "*Sachsenspiegel* of the Jews," which, as the formal revelation of "universal natural law," has no covenantal promise in it; thus, the promise of the law refers only to the "Torah," which he designates as the gospel revealed in the law.[120] While Calvin tries to look for the grace of the law from its normative nature on the basis of the covenant of grace, Luther keeps the righteousness of the law within the righteousness of good works and

---

116 Serm Gen. 15:6 (*SC* 11/2.756-758): "Vray est que la Loy nous monstre bien que c'est de justement vivre, et d'acquerir justice si nous en estions capables, comme nous traitterons plus au long ici apres" (757).

117 With regard to Calvin's first use of the law, Potter emphasizes its character as the "tutor of righteousness," "The 'Whole Office of the Law' in the Theology of John Calvin," 118-123.

118 Comm. Deut. 5:1-3 (1.340-341, *CO* 24.210).

119 *LW* 9.63.

120 In this respect, only the "Torah" works as a "guide" in the Old Testament and as an "exhortation (*paraenesis*)" in the New Testament. "The Concept of the 'Law' in the Lutheran Tradition," *Word & World* 3/4 (1983), 416-417, 420-422.

equates the nature of the law with that of natural law which works primarily for the condemnation of sin and accusation. Therefore, although both Reformers are faithful to Pauline theology, the difference between their views of the law is "denotive" rather than "connotative" and "theological" rather than "semantic."[121]

For Calvin, the righteousness of the law does not refer merely to the reward and punishment received according to the merit of good works. It has its negative side: it reveals human sinfulness and wickedness. However, mostly it is used positively, in relation to the restoration of the original nature of the law. It is argued that just as the Gospel becomes accidentally (*per accidens*) the occasion (*occasio*) of death but is not the cause (*causa*) or material (*materia*) of death, so does the law.[122] He denies that the law is "the material cause of death (*mortis materiam*)" although he acknowledges that the death "is brought upon us by sin through the occasion (*occasione*) of the law."[123] *Lex accusans* is regarded as accidental and occasional because as "*via recte vivendi*" the original nature of the law is holy, good, and just.[124]

Accordingly, the occasional use of the law is derived from its proper use to instruct people in the rule of life and finally bring them to the eternal heavenly life. Calvin comments on "*mortui estis Legi*" in Romans 7:4 as to take off the curse and bondage of the law to be clothed with "the newness of life" and "holiness and righteousness," which is but restoration of the original meaning of the law. Therefore, people who unite themselves with Christ by a sacred bond are willingly subject to his law because the law of Christ corresponds perfectly to the nature of the law.[125] Likewise, Calvin claims the everlasting validity of the law with regard to the normative nature of the law, which he defines as the eternal righteousness of God revealed in the law.[126]

In his commentary on "the new commandment" and "the old commandment" in I John 1:7-8, Calvin asserts that the eternal will of God had been revealed before the coming of Christ into the world. He writes:

---

121 My view here is opposite to that of Dowey and Hesselink. Dowey, "Law in Luther and Calvin," 148, 153; Hesselink, *Calvin's Concept of the Law*, 218, and "Luther and Calvin on Law and Gospel in Their Galatians Commentaries," *Reformed Review* 37(1984), 69-82.
122 Comm. II Cor. 3:6 (42, *CO* 50.40); II Cor. 3:7 (44, *CO* 50.41).
123 Comm. Rom. 7:13 (146, *CO* 49.127). Cf. Comm. II Cor. 3:7 ff. (43-45, *CO* 50.41-43).
124 Comm. Rom. 7:9-12, (143-145, *CO* 49.125-127).
125 Comm. Rom. 7:4 (139-140, *CO* 49.121).
126 Comm. Rom. 7:2-3 (139-140, *CO* 49.120-121).

[T]he Gospel should not be received as a recently born teaching, but as what has proceeded from God and as His eternal truth. It is as if he said, You must not measure the antiquity of the Gospel by the date at which it is brought to you. For in it is revealed to you the eternal will of God. Therefore, not only did God give you this rule of a holy life (*pie vivendi regulam*) when first you were called to the faith of Christ, but the same has always been determined and prescribed by Him.[127]

7.3.5.2 TRIPLEX USUS LEGIS

7.3.5.2.1 The First Use of the Law

We should bear in mind that when Calvin deals with the threefold use of the law, he refers to the whole law (*lex tota*) which is spiritual and clothed with the grace of God by Christ's mediation of the law.[128] It has been accepted as something of a commonplace in contemporary Calvin studies that the first use of the law is theological in the sense that it leads people to Christ (justification) and the third use is normative because it is related to progress in the daily Christian life (sanctification). Also, it is generally accepted that the second use of the law is political and thus related to outward activity.[129]

In categorizing these three uses, scholars are mostly interested in varying *effects* of the three uses of the law themselves, but inadequately consider their relation to Christ the Mediator, which Calvin developed most significantly in several sections (2.6.1-2.7.5) just before the *triplex usus legis* is handled in the *Institutes* (2.7.6-13).

In the *Institutes*, the first use of the law is described in this way: "while it shows God's righteousness, that is, the righteousness alone acceptable to God, it warns, informs, convicts, and lastly condemns, every man of his own unrighteousness" (2.7.6).[130] Similarly, in his sermon on Genesis 15:6, Calvin points out that the law makes us examine our life, throws us into despair of ourselves, and eventually makes us seek salvation in Christ.[131]

---

127 Comm. I Jn. 1:7 (248, *CO* 55.313).
128 There is no room for *lex nuda* in Calvin's threefold use of the law (*Inst.* 2.7.2, *CO* 2.254).
129 Cf. Doumergue, *Jean Calvin*, 4.191-193; Hesselink, *Calvin's Concept of the Law*, 217-257; Dowey, "The Third Use of the Law in Calvin's Theology," 20-27; Johnson, "Calvin's Handling of the Third Use of the Law and Its Problems," 33-50; Victor A. Shepherd, *The Nature and Function of Faith in the Theology of John Calvin* (Macon, Ga.: Mercer University Press, 1983), 137-156.
130 ". . . dum iustitiam Dei ostendit, id est, quae sola Deo accepta est, suae unumquemque iniustitiae admoneat, certiorem faciat, convincat denique ac condemnet."
131 Serm. Gen. 15:6 (*SC* 11/2.758): "Ainsi donc voilà comme la Loy nous doit faire entrer en l'examen de toute nostre vie, que nous n'ayons que desespoir en nous, et que par ce moyen nous soyons solicitez de cercher nostre Seigneur Jesus Christ

Unquestionably, by the first use of the law Calvin means that the office of the law is to make people realize their weakness and impurity and flee to Christ the Mediator. It corresponds to Luther's and Melanchthon's second use of the law, which they call *usus theologicus*.[132]

However, in contrast with these two theologians who are mainly concerned about the punitive function of the law, with reference to the theological use of the law Calvin emphasizes the revelation of the law itself rather than its subsequent effect.[133] The punitive function of the law is not merely instrumental, but rather existential.[134] He uses two metaphors: "scale (*trutina*)" and "mirror (*speculum*)" (*Inst.* 2.7.6, 7, *CO* 2.257-258). They are not adopted in order to express the fear and wrath of God, but to shed light on the original office of the law to reveal the rule of right and godly living. What Calvin means by the first use of the law is not different from the expression of the general rule by which the law works: the nature of the law is "holy," "just," and "good," but because of the fall it becomes a curse to the human race as its precepts are beyond human capacity. However, the condemnation of the law is neither substantial nor ultimate because as the precepts of law initially make people disheartened, simultaneously the promises of the law comfort them when they call on Christ the Mediator in order to be saved (*Inst.* 2.5.4-11, 2.7.1-5).[135]

The first use of the law therefore is to make people realize who they are and convert themselves from their righteousness of good works to the righteousness imputed by the grace of Christ the Mediator. It refers to "*adventitia qualitas*" of humanity (cf. *Inst.* 2.1.11, *CO* 2.184), but it is based on the original nature of the law, which signifies the rule of a godly and upright life. The characteristic feature of the theological or punitive use of the law is consequently described as follows:

> In the precepts of the law, God is but the rewarder of perfect righteousness, which all of us lack, and conversely, the severe judge of evil deeds. But in Christ his face shines, full of grace and gentleness, even upon us poor and unworthy sinners (*Inst.* 2.7.8, *CO* 2.259).

---

pour le commencement de nostre justice."
132 Cf. Ebeling, "On the Doctrine of the *Triplex Usus Legis*," 62-78, esp. 75-78.
133 Luther describes it as the nature of this punitive use "to denounce and to increase sin, but for the purpose of righteousness; and to kill, but for the purpose of life." *LW* 27.361 (Commentary on Galatians 1535, 4:3). In his 1521 *Loci Communes* (*CR* 21.152), Melanchthon declares that "*proprium legis opus est peccati revelatio, aut ut clarius dicam peccati conscientia.*"
134 Cf. Robert A. Gessert, "The Integrity of Faith: An Inquiry into the Meaning of the Law in the Thought of John Calvin," *Scottish Theological Journal* 13/3 (1960): 258-260.
135 Quot. Comm. Rom. 7:12 (145 *CO* 49.127).

In conclusion, for Calvin, the first use of the law denotes not only the office of the law to lead people to Christ, but also the revelation of the substance of the law by Christ's mediation. It denotes the use of the law to convince us that "the righteousness of Christ is efficacious to justify us (*Christi iustitiam esse efficacem ad nos iustificandos*)."[136]

7.3.5.2.2 The Second Use of the Law

The second use of the law refers to "outward activity (*exteriori opere*)," not as to its cause, but as to its effect (*Inst*. 2.7.10).[137] With reference to the way in which the law works, the second use is not different from the first use because it also serves to reveal and instruct the truth of the law as "a tutor (*paedagogus*)."[138] Therefore, the political use of the divine law should be differentiated from the tutelage (*paedagogia*) of common law which can work towards no theological conversion (*Inst* 2.7.11).[139]

7.3.5.2.3 The Third Use of the Law

The law still works "among believers in whose hearts the Spirit of God already lives and reigns." Calvin explains the third use of the law (*usus in renatis*) in two ways: the office of teaching (*doctrina*) and exhortation (*exhortatio*). In the first case, the law continually plays a role to inform the regenerate of its precepts so that they may "make fresh progress toward a purer knowledge of the divine will (*Domini voluntas*)." Likewise, the law continually fulfils a pedagogical function for believers.[140] This is the process in which God's people are aware of his will and "conform and accommodate (*componat et accommodet*)" to it. The will of God corresponds to what Calvin defines as "the law of God" and "the law of the mind" in his commentary on Romans 7:21-23. He says, "the law of God" is "the rule of righteousness by which our life is rightly formed," and "the law

---

136 Comm. Rom. 5:18 (117, *CO* 49.101).
137 Cf. Hesselink, *Calvin's Concept of the Law*, 245-251; Denis Müller, *Puissance de la Loi et limite du Pouvoir* (Paris: Éditions Michalon, 2001), 20-27.
138 In this sense, Donald MacLeod depicts the first two uses of the law commonly as "a constant penitent." "Living the Christian Life—1. Luther and Calvin on the Place of the Law," in *Living the Christian Life*. Papers read at Westminster Conference (Huntingdon, 1974), 9.
139 Calvin acknowledges the same nature of the divine law and natural law (cf. *Inst*. 2.8.1, 4.20.16, *CO* 2.267, 1106). However, exploring the two-kingdom theory, he admonishes people not to mix up "the political order" with "the gospel teaching on spiritual freedom." See 1543 *Inst*. 12.15 (*CO* 1.839), 20.2 (*CO* 1.1101-1102).
140 In this respect, Battles calls Calvin's third use of the law "the pedagogical" one. "Against Luxury and License in Geneva," 325.

of the mind" is "the readiness of the faithful mind to obey the divine law," which is "our conformity to the law of God."[141]

Regarding exhortation, the law works for believers more positively: "by frequent meditation upon it to be aroused (*excitetur*) to obedience, be strengthened (*roboretur*) in it, and be drawn back (*retrahatur*) from the slippery path of transgression." The office of exhortation is beyond the noetic instruction of the law; its efficacy is rather volitional. Believers who are taught the precepts of the law are persuaded by the Holy Spirit of the accompanying promises of grace and as a result they make themselves ready to live according to God's will. In this case the law reveals the promise that Christ as the Mediator is still working for the believer's holy and just living. Calvin uses such metaphors as "a whip (*flagrum*)" and "a constant sting (*assiduus aculeus*)" positively in order to illustrate this quickening use of the law (*Inst.* 2.7.12, *CO* 2.261-262).[142]

We can hardly find any definite difference between Bucer and Calvin with reference to the effect of the normative use of the law itself until we come to investigate its doctrinal significance for justification and sanctification. Calvin defines justification as acceptance by God through "the imputation of Christ's righteousness (*imputatio iustitiae Christi*)" (*Inst.* 3.11.2, *CO* 2.534). It denotes the state of man who is "received into communion with Christ" and "clothed (*vestitus*) with Christ's righteousness" (*Inst.* 3.17.8, *CO* 2.596). Calvin understands on this basis the double grace of God by which he receives our person and our works, which is declared in his first catechism (1537, 1538)[143] and developed in his 1543 *Institutes*, where he says, "*sola fide non tantum nos, sed opera etiam nostra iustificari*" (1543 *Inst.* 10.70, *CO* 1.787, *Inst* 3.17.10, *CO* 2.598).

Calvin's commentary on Romans exhibits his doctrine of justification in more detail. The definition of justification is more specific: "communion in the death of Christ (*communionis cum morte Christi*)," which extends from the beginning of regeneration to participation in the eternal life.[144] He also describes it as the process of "establishing a common likeness (*mutua*

---

141 Comm. Rom. 7:21 (152, *CO* 49. 133): "Legem Dei, quae sola proprie sic nuncupatur, quia est iustitiae regula, qua vita nostra recte formatur. Huic coniungit legem mentis, sic appellans propensionem fidelis animae ad obedientiam divinae legis: quia est quaedam nostri cum lege Dei conformatio."

142 From the 1536 Institutes, Calvin suggests the continual office of the law for the believers as "eos officii sui admonendo ad sanctitatis et innocentiae studium excitet . . . docere et exhortari et stimulare ad bonum" (1536 *Inst.* 6.2, *CO* 1.196, *Inst*. 3.19.2, *CO* 2.614).

143 *First Catechism* 21 (*CO* 5.336-337).

144 Comm. Rom. 6:7 (126, *CO* 49.108). Cf. Comm Rom. 6:3 (122, *CO* 49.105).

similitudo) between ourselves and the Redeemer."[145] Calvin points out that the gift of justification is not "a quality (*qualitatem*) with which God endows us," but "the free imputation of righteousness."[146]

God's grace of free imputation reveals the continual imparting of newness of life, which is most strikingly represented in the concept of the communication of the righteousness of God.[147] The gospel provides the firm conviction of the fact that the righteousness of God is communicated (*communicatur*) to us in Christ.[148] By "in Christ" Calvin highlights not only the fact that Christ intercedes between God and his people by his Spirit, but particularly the fact that the righteousness becomes "a quality (*qualitatem*)" of Christ, so it belongs "properly (*proprium*)" to Christ.[149] Therefore, there is no other way for us to own the fruits of righteousness—sanctification and eternal life—apart from being engrafted into Christ.[150]

In his commentary on Romans, Calvin does not present the clear distinction between the righteousness of God and the righteousness of Christ, but with reference to the latter he emphasizes the merit of the blood of Christ, by which we are cleansed from sin, sanctified, and ultimately led to eternal life. In particular, Calvin, describing the Spirit of Christ as "life-giving (*vivificam*)," takes into account the whole of life including rebirth, regeneration, and eternal life.[151] Calvin confirms this as he comments that "the life-giving power exists in the Spirit of Christ, which is able to

---

145 Comm. Rom. 6:10 (127, *CO* 49.109).
146 Comm. Rom. 5:17 (117, *CO* 49.100). God's righteousness is neither infused (*infusa*) nor transfused (*transfusa*), but imputed grace (*gratia imputata*). This is the point by which Calvin attacked Osiander who argued for "essential righteousness (*essentialis iustitia*)." Cf. *Inst.* 3.11.5, 10 (*CO* 2.536-537, 540-541); *Contra Osiandrum* (*CO* 10/1.166): "Essentialem iustitiam sibi nulla ratione imaginatus est. Nam etsi eo trahit scripturae testimonia, quae Deum in nobis habitare asserunt, et nos unum cum ipso fieri: nihil tamen inde probatur, quam arcana spiritus virtute, dum coalescimus in Christi corpus, uniri simuo Deo. Adde, quod essentialis illa communicatio ex Manichaeorum deliriis sumpta est. Nec video quomodo excusari possit hoc absurdum, essentialem Dei iustitiam esse accidens, quod adesse nunc homini possit, nunc abesse."
147 Cf. Comm. Rom. 6:1 (121, *CO* 49.103): "[T]hose who imagine that Christ bestows free justification upon us without imparting newness of life shamefully rend Christ asunder."
148 Comm. Rom. 1:17 (28, *CO* 49.20); Rom. 3:21 (70, *CO* 49.57); Rom. 3:22 (73, *CO* 49.60).
149 Comm. Rom. 5:19 (118 [altered], *CO* 49.101).
150 Comm. Rom. 6:22-23 (136, *CO* 49.118). This thinking is already evident in his response to Sadolet, where Calvin emphasizes the imputation of the righteousness of Christ and the special working of the Spirit of Christ in the practice of love (*caritas*) in faith. Cf. Helmut Feld, "Um die reinere Lehre des Evangeliums: Calvins Kontroverse mit Sadoleto 1539," *Catholica* 36 (1982), 168-180.
151 Comm. Rom. 8:2 (157, *CO* 49.137).

overwhelm our mortality."[152] The living and life-giving (*viva et vivifica*) Spirit of God points to the Spirit of the Mediator that frees us from the bondage of the law and makes us to decide to live according to the law.[153] Thus the exhortation of the law is put out of us by the continual mediation of Christ, as put forward in the following:

> The interpreters who understand that those who have been renewed by the Spirit of Christ fulfil the law, introduce a misrepresentation which is completely foreign to Paul's meaning. As long as believers sojourn in the world, they do not make such progress that the righteousness of the law (*iustificatio legis*) is full or complete in them. We must, therefore, apply this phrase to forgiveness, for while the obedience of Christ is imparted to us, the law is satisfied, so that we are accounted just. The perfection which the law demands was exhibited in the flesh for this reason, that its rigorous demand should no longer have the power to condemn us. But because Christ communicates His righteousness (*iustitiam*) only to those whom He joins to Himself by the bond of His Spirit (*spiritus sui vinculo*), Paul mentions regeneration again, lest Christ should be thought to be the minister of sin.[154]

It is unlikely that in the cited passage Calvin means to categorize Bucer as one of "the interpreters" whom he must have defined as antinomians. Nevertheless, it should be noted that Bucer like the antinomians has a tendency to overestimate the enduring work of the Holy Spirit. We might presume that this is because of his conviction, as Alister E. McGrath notes, that "the man who is justified by faith will necessarily be justified by works."[155] Calvin shares this conviction with Bucer,[156] too, yet based on the believer's union with Christ: "Christ justifies no one whom he does not at the same time sanctify. These benefits are joined together by an everlasting and indissoluble bond (*perpetuo et individuo nexu*), so that those whom he illumines by his wisdom, he redeems; those whom he

---

152 Comm. Rom. 8:10 (165 [altered], *CO* 49.145): ". . . vim vivificandi in spiritu Christi inesse, quae ad mortalitatem nostram absorbendam valeat."
153 Cf. Comm Jn. 1:17 (1.25, *CO* 47.18): "Christus enim anima est quae vivificat quod alioqui esset in lege mortuum"; II Cor. 3:7 (45, *CO* 50.43).
154 Comm. Rom. 8:4 (160, *CO* 49.140). Calvin here uses the words *iustitia* and *iustificatio* interchangebly. Cf. Parker, *Commentaries on Romans 1532-1542*, 196.
155 "Humanist Elements in the Early Reformed Doctrine of Justification," *ARG* 73 (1982), 12.
156 Cf. Lane, "Calvin and Article 5 of the Regensburg Colloquy," 19-27 (pages shown in the paper presented in Calvin Congress).

redeems, he justifies; those whom he justifies, he sanctifies" (*Inst.* 3.16.1, *CO* 2.586).[157]

Both Calvin and Bucer underline the continual work of the Spirit of Christ, but for Calvin, Christ's continual mediation for believers is at work throughout the whole process of salvation. Like Bucer, who argues "*pro, non ex observatione legis*," Calvin regards good works as of capital importance in the life of a Christian as he states: "we are justified not without works yet not through works (*non sine operibus, neque tamen per opera*), since in our sharing in Christ, which justifies us, sanctification is just as much included as righteousness" (*Inst.* 3.16.1, *CO* 2.586). However, Bucer, although points out the blessing of God as the free giver of eternal life (*largitor vitae aeternae*) in dealing with the righteousness of good works, concentrates on the work of the Holy Spirit, once given by God, rather than on the believer's continual communion with the righteousness of Christ by the work of his Spirit.

On the phrase "the law is spiritual" in Romans 7, Bucer comments that the law was originally given as "the law of life (*legem vitae*)," but after the fall it becomes "life-giving (*vivificam*)" when it is governed by the Spirit of Christ who is the life-giver (*vivificator*).[158] He here highlights the power of the Holy Spirit to renew everything and to recover eternal life, but he does not mention Christ's mediation of the law regarding the way in which the law plays a life-giving role for Christians. We can find a similar statement of Calvin to Bucer's in his commentary on II Corinthians 3: that the law "will come alive and be life-giving (*vivam and vivificam*) only if it is inspired by Christ." Calvin calls Christ "the spirit of the law (*spiritum eius* [*legis*])" and "the life of the law (*legis vita*)." Then he says,

> Christ in regenerating us gives life to the Law and shows Himself to be the source of life, just as the soul is the source from which all man's vital

---

157 McGrath highlights the difference between Bucer and Calvin regarding the *ordo salutis* claiming that "where Bucer links the first and second justifications [the *iustitia impii* and the *iustitia pii*] on the basis of the regenerating activity of the Holy Spirit, Calvin relates them on the basis of the beliver's *insitio in Christum*." *Iustitia Dei*, 224. For the comparison between the *ordo salutis* in Bucer: *electio-iustificatio impii-iustificatio pii-glorificatio* and in Calvin: *electio-unio mystica* (*iustificatio, sanctificatio*)-*glorificatio*, see McGrath, *Iustitia Dei*, 221-226, and "Humanist Elements in the Early Reformed Doctrine of Justification," 10-17. As McGrath points out, regarding the *ordo salutis*, it must be noted that Calvin explains the doctrine of predestination and its impact on the Christian life in view of the believer's personal union with Christ. Cf. *Calvin's Calvinism*, 134-140 (*CO* 8.319-323); François Wendel, "Justification and Predestination in Calvin," in *Readings in Calvin's Theology*, ed. Donald K. McKim (Grand Rapids: Baker, 1984), 169-178.

158 *MBER* 363.

functions spring. Christ is therefore, so to speak, the universal soul of all men not as regards His essence, but as regards His grace. Or, to put it another way, Christ is the Spirit because he animates us with the life-giving power of His Spirit (*vivifica spiritus sui virtute*).[159]

By designating Christ as the life and spirit of the law, Calvin supremely witnesses the working of the law as the rule of life and life-giving through the inspiration of the Spirit of Christ the Mediator. Also, by attesting that Christ is "the end (*finem*)" and "the only aim (*scopum*)" of the law, Calvin sets the foundation of the liberation from the bondage of the law seen in the previous verse.[160] In conclusion, the law, which is a rule of living (*regula vivendi*), works as a life-giving rule (*regula vivificandi*) for believers by the Spirit of Christ the Mediator. This is what Calvin means by the exhortatory use of the law, which demonstrates the essence of Calvin's third use of the law.

For Calvin, the Spirit of Christ works for the whole process of salvation as the Spirit of the Mediator. Therefore, the special work of the Holy Spirit should not be thought of as merely related to the third use of the law, just as the merit of Christ should not be associated merely with the first use.[161] It is absurd to see the third use of the law as the "pastoral application" of the first two uses, and try to apply it to both believers and non-believers.[162] It is even more absurd to affirm the "transformation" of the law in Christ in order to explain the theological foundation of the normative use of the law from the Christological point of view.[163]

In dealing with the third use of the law, Hesselink is keen to derive the theological foundation of the normative use of the law from the fact that Christ is the soul, life, and fulfilment of the law. Hesselink here finds the answer to the question why in dealing with the Christian life Calvin prefers using the word "Christ" rather than the word "the law" in order to point up

---

159 Comm. II Cor. 3:17 (48-49, *CO* 50.45-46).
160 Comm. II Cor. 3:16 (48, *CO* 50.45).
161 Hesselink, *Calvin's Concept of the Law*, 251; Ralph R. Sundquist, Jr., "The Third Use of the Law in the Thought of John Calvin," PhD dissertation, Columbia University, 1970; Augsburger, "Calvin and the Mosaic Law," 96-100.
162 Cf. William H. Lazareth, "Love and Law in Christian Life," in *Piety, Politics, and Ethics*, 116. The author evaluates the third use of the law in the *Fomula of Concord* (VI).
163 Johnson, "Calvin's Handling of the Third Use of the Law and Its Problems," 42. He develops this idea in his article read in Calvin Studies Society. There he affirms that "for Calvin the law itself is transformed by Christ, . . . *Christ removes from the law its demand character* (the author's italics)." "Calvin's Ethical Legacy," in *The Legacy of John Calvin: Papers Presented at the 12th Colloquium of the Calvin Studies Society, 1999*, Ed. David Foxgrover (Grand Rapids: CRC Product Services, 2002), 68-69.

the character of the law as the norm or rule of godly living.[164] From this perspective, Hesselink criticizes Hugo Röthlisberger, who regards the law and Christ as two different norms in Christian life, and Wernle, who accuses Calvin of Christianization of the law by concentrating only on its normative aspect.[165] Hesselink emphasizes the special illumination of the Holy Spirit in order to explain the normative use of the law, but he does not pay specific attention to the fact that Calvin defines the Holy Spirit working for the normative use of the law as the Spirit of Christ who is still mediating for his members as the head. Overall, Hesselink, dealing with the relationship between Christ and the law, is more concerned about *Christus exemplar legis* than *Christus Mediator legis*. So he fails to distinguish the exhortation of the law from the instruction of the law.[166]

7.4 Conclusion

As seen above, by presenting the continual validity of the law in the light of the concept of *Christus mediator legis* Calvin deals with the whole office and use of the law without losing the significance of the original nature of the law, which is righteous (before the fall) and life-giving (after the fall). In developing the concept of *lex vivificandi* in the light of the Spirit of Christ the Mediator, who is still working according to both his natures in the bodily presence *totus-non totum*, Calvin sets the theological foundation for Christ's mediation of the law even before his incarnation in the Old Testament. The vivifying nature of the law sheds light on why Calvin calls the third use of the law the "principal (*praecipuus*)" one and "more closely related to the proper purpose of the law (*proprium legis finem*)" (*Inst.* 2.7.12, *CO* 2.261).

The law not only instructs the godly people with a rule of living, but it exhorts them to live according to it.[167] Therefore, the offices of the law are both pedagogical and normative. The revelation of the law is sometimes frightening and sometimes encouraging, but the nature of the law is holy, good, and righteous. The first two uses denote the fundamental use of the

---

164 "Christ, the Law, and the Christian," 18.
165 Ibid., 15-16.
166 *Calvin's Concept the law*, 278-281, and "Christ, the Law, and the Christian," 13-14. The same position on Calvin's third use of the law is found in Shepherd, who concentrates on Christ as the image of God *par excellence* in dealing with the relation between faith and the law. *The Nature and Function of Faith in the Theology of John Calvin*, 152-171.
167 Hesselink takes the position that only the third use of the law for Calvin refers to the normative use of the law (*lex vivendi*). He basically follows Emil Doumergue's view that as regards the first two uses of the law Calvin and Luther are in complete accordance with each other. Hesselink, *Calvin's Concept of the Law*, 255; Doumergue, *Jean Calvin*, 4.192.

law for believers and non-believers. There is a difference between their effects, but the way in which the law works is completely the same. On the other hand, the third use of the law refers to the continual validity of the law for believers. It basically signifies the pedagogical use, but its characteristic feature is shown in the office of *lex vivificandi*.

If we can admit any intrinsic and transformative tendency in Calvin's theology of justification, it is derived from the dynamic of Christ's mediation. Calvin defines faith as "the instrument by which we receive Christ, in whom righteousness is communicated to us," and comments that if we do not embrace God's grace not only for justification but also for sanctification, we have only "a mutilated faith (*mutila fide*)."[168] He does not believe that justification and sanctification are separated although they are distinguished. Nor does he acknowledge the concept of legal repentance itself because he does not believe in the existence of mortification which is not followed by vivification.[169] When Calvin defines justification as the communication of the righteousness of God in Christ, he presupposes the precedence of union with Christ who brings about justification and sanctification in the *ordo salutis*.

While in his commentary on Romans Calvin demonstrates mainly the theological foundation upon which the concept and use of the law is based, in his commentary on Psalms he elucidates remarkably the blessings of the law. Expounding the inner instruction of the law, he especially emphasizes that it is the Spirit of the Mediator who persuades the soul of the Psalmist so that he may open his eyes not only to the precepts of the law but also to its promises. Likewise he believes that the Psalmist delights in the law with a conviction that in Christ *lex vivendi* becomes *lex vivificandi*.[170] Before

---

168 Comm. Rom. 3:22 (73, *CO* 49.60); Rom. 8:13 (167, *CO* 49.147). Calvin asserts that faith justifies "because it leads us into fellowship with the righteousness of Christ (*quia in communicationem iustitiae Christi nos inducit*)" (*Inst*. 3.11.20, *CO* 20.550).

169 Calvin epitomizes his argument by stating that "man dies to himself that they may begin to live to God (*hominem sibi mori ut Deo vivere incipiat*)" (*Inst*. 3.3.3, *CO* 2.436).

170 Commenting on the phrase "the marvellous things of thy law" in Ps. 119:18, Calvin writes that "not only the ten commandments are included in the term law, but also the covenant of eternal salvation, with all its provisions, which God has made. And knowing, as we do, that Christ, 'in whom are hid all the treasures of knowledge and wisdom,' 'is the end of the law,' we need not be surprised at the prophet commending it, in consequence of the sublime mysteries which it contains, Col. ii.3; Rom. x. 4" (4.413-414, *CO* 32.222). Calvin, expounding Psalm 119, repeatedly refers to the internal illumination of the Holy Spirit in order to explain the internal instruction of the law. Cf. Comm. Ps. 119:12 (4.410, *CO* 32.219, "*spiritu iudicii*"); 119:18 (412, *CO* 32.221, "*singulari spiritus gratia*"); 119:26 (420, *CO* 32.226, "*interior magister Dei spiritus*"); 119:27, 33 (420, 424, *CO* 32.226, 228, "*intelligentiae spiritu*"); 119:34 (425, *CO* 32.229, "*coelestis spiritus luce*"); 119:64

closing the section on the doctrinal significance of the third use of the law, he confirms this: "[In the Psalms] David especially shows that in the law he apprehended the Mediator, without whom there is no delight or sweetness (*oblectatio vel suavitas*)" (*Inst.* 2.7.12, *CO* 2.262).[171]

(449, *CO* 32.242, "*arcana mentis illustratione spiritus*"); 119:125 (5.5, *CO* 32.270, "*arcano spiritus instinctu*").

171 For the sweetness (*dulcedo, suavitas*) of the law, see I. John Hesselink, "Calvin, Theologian of Sweetness," *CTJ* 37 (2002), 325-327.

CHAPTER 8

Conclusion: The Coherence between Christology and Soteriology in Calvin's Theology of the Law

Calvin resorts to the special illumination of the Spirit of Christ the Mediator for the explanation of the spiritual blessings of the law, described most impressively in his commentary on the Psalms, which he calls "the anatomy of all parts of the soul."[1] He takes the position that the soul is the immortal and incorporeal substance (*substantia immortalis et incorporea*) in which the seed of religion (*religionis semen*) dwells, and, from this point, argues that just as Christ sustained the *hypostasis* of God and man after his ascension, so the human soul is eternal after death and keeps shining forth the image of God (*Inst* 1.15.6, *CO* 2.182-183).[2] In identifying the spiritual character, and correspondingly the spiritual interpretation of the law, Calvin takes into consideration the *substantia* of man itself as well as the working of human *ratio* consisting of understanding and will. Specifically, as far as the office and use of the law is concerned, he gives primary attention to the regeneration and eternity of the soul rather than to its varying faculties.[3]

Calvin seeks to substantiate the spiritual character of the law by exploring the concept of *Christus mediator legis* on the basis of the

---

1 "The Author's Preface," *CTS* 4/1.xxxvii (*CO* 31.15). For the spiritual interpretation of the law in Calvin's commentary on the Psalms, see book 7.4.
2 Cf. Comm. I Cor. 15:12-13 (318, *CO* 49.542): ". . . Christus non sibi mortuus est, neque resurrexit, sed nobis: ergo ipsius resurrectio hypostasis nostrae est: et quod in eo factum est, oportet in nobis quoque impleri." Calvin sees the soul not merely as the *qualitas*, but rather as the *substantia* of man. Cf. Comm. I Cor. 15:39 (336, *CO* 49.556), 15:44 (337-338, *CO* 49.557-558); *Psychopannychia, CO* 5.177-178, 203. Calvin's idea of the eternal substance of the soul demonstrates the influence of Plato. However, Calvin, unlike Augustine who followed Plato's position, does not think that the soul is always subject to the body, even though he is totally in agreement with Augustine as to the total depravity of human soul after the fall (*Inst* 1.15.8, *CO* 2.186-187). It is on this basis that Calvin develops his doctrine of the immortality of the soul after life. Heinrich Quistorp, *Calvin's Doctrine of the Last Things*, tr. Harold Knight (Richmond: John Knox Press, 1955), 55-107. For the epistemological, ethical, and eschatological influence of the Platonic body-soul dualism on Calvin's theology, see Wilhelm Schwendemann, *Leib und Seele bei Calvin: Die erkenntnistheoretische und anthropologische Funktion des platonischen Leib-Seele-Dualismus in Calvins Theologie* (Stuttgart: Calwer Verlag, 1996), esp. 201-210.
3 For the faculty of human soul (understanding and will), see book 4.3.

normative nature of the law and its characteristic shape as the law of the covenant.[4] He proposes the concept of moral law (*lex moralis*) as ranging over the whole law including both *cultus* in the First Table and *caritas* in the Second, and examines the covenantal significance of the law in the course of answering the question of how the law, the nature of which is characterized as *regula vivendi*, works as *regula vivificandi*.[5] Thus, the spiritual office of the law refers not only to the spiritual regeneration of each individual person but also to the fulfilment of the kingdom of God by Christ's mediation of the law as Teacher, Priest, and King.[6]

Although we do not actually have any works of Calvin written before his conversion that might tell us directly what he thought of the divine law, there seems to be every reason to assume that his special emphasis on the inner working of the law originates from his early legal studies, by which he gained the erudition of ancient literature and philosophies as well as the knowledge of Roman law. Calvin's literal yet spiritual interpretation of the law, which emphasizes its *ad hoc* significance, reflects the influence of the historical and philological interpretation of the jurists of the *mos novus*, represented by Aciati and Budé and the influence of de l'Estoile's literary and logical text-reading method.[7] As seen in his commentary on Seneca's *De clementia*, the young Calvin was already keen to distinguish equity from the letter of the law and to link natural law with the divine law in terms of the concept of conscience.[8] In addition, it may be quite plausible for us to suggest the influence of the *via moderna* and the *devotio moderna* upon Calvin's Christological understanding of the law with reference to the covenantal understanding of *meritum Christi* and the *unio mystica cum Christo*.[9] Especially, with reference to the influence of the *via moderna*, we must keep in mind the fact that Calvin, by referring to the dynamic feature of Christ's mediation, overcame the late medieval theologians' view of covenantal causality, which they had developed in dealing synergistically with the relationship between *patum* and *meritum* on the basis of their unique interpretation of the axiom *facientibus quod in se est deus non denegat gratiam*.[10]

---

4 For the Christological interpretation of the normative nature of the law, see book 4.1-2, 7.2.
5 For the relationship between *lex vivendi* and *lex vivificandi*, see book 7.3.5.
6 For the threefold office of the Mediator and the threefold mediation, see book 4.4.1.
7 For Calvin's legal studies, see book 2.1.
8 Olivier Millet, "Le thème de la conscience libre chez Calvin," in *La liberté de conscience (XVIe - XVIIe siècles)*, ed. Hans R. Guggisberg, et al. (Genève: Droz, 1991), 21-37, esp. 22-29; Irena Backus, "Calvin's Concept of Natural and Roman Law," *CTJ* 38 (2003), 7-26, esp. 12-19, 25-26. For Calvin's concept of natural law in his commentary on Seneca, see book 2.4.
9 For the influence of the *devotio moderna* and the *via moderna*, see book 2.3.
10 According to Alister E. McGrath, Luther overcame this attitude of the theologians of

When Calvin argues for the spirituality of the law by referring to its original normative nature, he turns to the fact that Christ is the substance and soul of the law.[11] He believes that the divine law works as such when it is mediated by Christ and consequently clothed with his grace. The grace of the law is not so much related to its individual effect upon justification and sanctification but associated with its essential relevance for the union with Christ which precedes both of them.[12] Therefore, there is no room for the concept of legal repentance that is independent of faith, as the one which is merely preliminary to evangelical repentance.[13] The following commentary expounds this far-reaching grace of the law mediated by Christ.

> I therefore take this defence [*iustificatio sola fide*] of Paul to refer not only to ceremonies, not only to what are called moral precepts, but to the whole law in general. The moral law is truly confirmed and established through faith in Christ, since it was given to teach man of his iniquity, and to lead him to Christ, without whom the law is not fulfilled. The law proclaims what is right in vain, yet it accomplishes nothing but the increase of inordinate desires, in order to finally bring greater condemnation upon man. When, however, we come to Christ, we first find the exact righteousness of the law (*legis iustitia*) in Him, and this also becomes ours by imputation (*per imputationem*). In the second place we find sanctification in Him, by which our hearts are shaped to keep the law. True, we keep it imperfectly, yet at least we are aiming at keeping it. The argument is the same in the case of ceremonies. These cease and vanish away when Christ comes, but they are truly confirmed by Him. In themselves they are empty and shadowy images, and will be found to possess reality (*solidi aliquid*) only in reference to a better end (*meliorem finem*). Their highest confirmation, therefore, lies in the fact that they have attained their truth (*veritatem*) in Christ. Let us, therefore, also remember to preach the Gospel in such a way that we establish the law by our manner of teaching, but let the only support of our preaching be that of our faith in Christ.[14]

---

the *via moderna* by his theology of the cross. *Luther's Theology of the Cross: Martin Luther's Theological Breakthrough* (Oxford: Basil Blackwell, 1985), esp. 86-92, 104-119, 126-128, 148-175.

11 Cf. Comm. Jn. 1:17 (1.25, *CO* 47.18).

12 In this respect, Calvin equates repentance with regeneration. Cf. *Inst* 1539, 5.8 (*CO* 1.690), *Inst* 3.3.9 (*CO* 2.8): "Uno ergo verbo poenitentiam interpretor, regenerationem, cuius non alius est scopus, nisi ut imago Dei, quae per Adae transgressionem foedata, et tantum non obliterata fuerat, in nobis reformetur." For *ordo salutis* in Calvin's theology, see book 7.3.5.

13 For Calvin's view of legal and evangelical repentance, see book 3.2.

14 Comm. Rom. 3:31 (81 [altered], *CO* 49.67-68).

For Calvin, Christ's mediation ranges throughout the whole of history. "Right from the beginning God made no communication with men except by Christ. For there is no relationship between God and us unless the Mediator is present to procure His favour for us."[15] From the beginning, Christ has had the power of the lawgiver and worked as the Mediator of intercession and teaching.[16] In view of Christ's eternal mediatorship, Calvin claims that *si integer stetisset Adam*, Christ would not have become man in flesh.[17] Originally, the role of the law was to reveal God's will as the rule of right living. After the coming of sin into the world, however, it began to perform its theological office as *lex accusans*.

For depraved humanity, what the true and inward law regulates is not so much *quid homines possint* as *quid debeant*. Notwithstanding, the law requires the righteousness accommodated to the state of the regenerate.[18] The law initially reveals God who is judge, then subsequently God who is father. This is true of both the Old and New Testaments. When the law was published, Christ had already been ordained to be killed on the cross by the eternal decree of God. Therefore, the whole promise of the law is founded on the grace of Christ. There is no conditionality in the covenant of God, whether it is the covenant of grace or the covenant of works, although the regulation of the law is sometimes conditional.[19] The imputation of the righteousness of God pertains to the justification of our imperfect works as well as to the justification of our persons. Sometimes the promise of the law is prescribed conditionally, but even on these occasions God's reward is due to the grace of Christ communicated to godly people. As Calvin puts it:

> When we are made partakers (*participes*) of Christ, we are not only ourselves righteous, but our works also are counted righteous in the sight of God (*non ipsi solum iusti sumus, sed opera iusta reputantur coram Deo*), because any imperfections in them are obliterated by the blood of Christ. The promises, which were conditional (*conditionales*), are fulfilled

---

15 Comm. Acts 7:30 (190 [altered], *CO* 48.144). For Christ's mediation before the fall, see book 4.2, 4.5.1.
16 Cf. Comm. Heb. 7:12 (96, *CO* 55.89): "Et Christus dum instituitur sacerdos, legislatoris etiam potestate instruitur, ut novi testamenti minister sit ac interpres."
17 For Calvin's critique of Osiander who maintains that Christ was ordained to come to the world regardless of human depravity, see book 4.3.1.
18 For God's accommodation and the mediation of Christ, see book 4.5.2.
19 Cf. Comm. Ex. 19:1-2 (1.313, *CO* 24.192-193): ". . . quamvis lex testimonium sit gratuitae adoptionis, et salutem fundatam esse doceat in Dei misericordia, hominesque invitet ad Deum certa fide invocandum, hoc tamen habere proprium et peculiare quod sub conditione paciscitur."

to us also by the same grace, since God rewards our works as perfect, inasmuch as their defects are covered by free pardon.[20]

Calvin criticizes Schoolmen belonging to the so-called *via moderna* as "some modern theorists," for they, like Augustine, regarded these two propositions as standing separately, that "man is justified by faith through the grace of Christ" and that "he is justified by the works which proceed from spiritual regeneration."[21] It is true that Calvin takes the strictly negative position on the merit of good works regarding justification,[22] but he does not sustain *nuda fides*. Rather, he maintains the concept of living faith (*fides viva*) by which godly people reach the eternal heavenly life as they live according to the instruction of the law through the grace of Christ the Mediator.[23] The works "of the law" have promise in them, and "the reward for works depends on the free promise of the law."[24] With regard to what brings about justification there is a distinct contradiction between the law and the gospel, and between faith and good works, but "there is no good works without faith."[25]

Calvin's Christological understanding of the law features both Christ in the law and the law in Christ. The law represents Christ as its truth and substance and reveals his eternal presence as the Mediator at the same time. The former aspect is distinctively signified by the *umbra-substantia* analogy,[26] and the latter by the promise-fulfilment framework.[27] They are

---

20 Comm. Rom. 3:22 (73, *CO* 49.60).
21 Comm. Rom. 3:21 (71-72, *CO* 49.218). Cf. Demura, "Two Commentaries on the Epistle to the Romans: Calvin and Oecolampadius," 172-173.
22 Cf. Comm. Rom. 2:13 (47, *CO* 49.37); Rom. 3:20 (69-70, *CO* 49. 56-57); Rom 3:27-28 (78-79, 49.64-66); Comm. Gal. 3:10-14 (52-56, *CO* 50.207-210).
23 Lane, *Justification by Faith*, 26-39. Cf. *Inst.* 3.15.3-4, 3.17.3-10 (on the validity of good works) and *Inst.* 3.18.5 (on the reward for good works).
24 Comm. Rom. 3:20 (69-70, *CO* 49.56-57).
25 Serm. Gen. 15:6 (*SC* 11/2.758-759): "Et pourquoy donc est-ce que sainct Paul trouve une telle contrarieté entre la Loy et l'Evangile? C'est au regard de nous justifier. Autant en est-il entre la foy et lex oeuvres. Il y a contrarieté entant que les oeuvres sont merites. Et qui plus est, nous ne pouvons faire *nulle bonne oeuvre sinon par foy*, comme nous l'avons desja touché, et sera encores deduit plus au long. Car la cause et l'effet ne sont pas contraires, mais quand nous voulons establir quelque merite en nos oeuvres, c'est à dire que nous voulons qu'elles doivent valoir pour nous aquerir grace devant Dieu, et que soyent une satisfaction pour nos pechez, brief, qu'elles nous servent à salut, c'est pour ruiner du tout la foy, et par ce moyen-là elle est aneantie." Calvin refers especially to James in order to explain this position. Serm. Gen. 15:6 (*SC* 11/2.780-785). Cf. Ganoczy and Scheld, *Die Hermeneutik Calvins*, 194-201. The authors argue that Calvin's frequent reference to James reflects the influence of Stoicism on him.
26 For the *umbra-substantia* analogy, see book 5.3-4.

distinguishable, but they are co-operative. On the basis of this dynamic understanding of the relationship between Christ and the law, Calvin develops his dynamic position on the office and use of the law in the process of salvation.[28]

Calvin understands justification (*iustificatio*) in relation to the righteousness of God (*iustitia Dei*). He defines justification as to be reckoned (*censetur*) righteous by the communication of the righteousness of God.[29] The righteousness of God refers not only to the will of God for an orderly life for his people, but also to the full recovery of the image of God.[30] It is called the righteousness of Christ (*Christi iustitia*) because it is fulfilled by Christ and imputed to us as gift (*gratuita iustitiae imputatio*) by his grace.[31]

Justification thus denotes communion (*communio*) with Christ who imparts his life to his members if they hold true and genuine communication (*communicatio*) with him. In this respect, justification signifies not only the free imputation of the righteousness of Christ but also the continual governing of his Spirit.[32] Calvin seeks the righteousness of the law (*iustitia legis*) in the fact that "Christ communicates His righteousness only to those whom He unites with Himself by the bond of His Spirit."[33] As Calvin repeatedly claims in his sermons on Job, the righteousness of the law, which is accommodated to our capacity, should be differentiated from the higher righteousness (*iustice plus haute*) of God. The law itself does not reveal the secret providence of God, but points to the double grace of God for justification and sanctification.[34] Therefore, only when we are clothed (*vestiemur*) with the righteousness of Christ does the law reveal the way of right living by which we are led to the perfection of eternal life.[35] Accordingly, for Calvin, the righteousness of the law is equated with the righteousness of Christ imputed by his continual mediation

---

27 For the continual mediation of Christ in salvation history, see book 6.3-4.
28 For the dynamic understanding of the office and use of the law, see book 7.3.5.
29 Comm. Rom. 1:17 (28, *CO* 49.20); Rom. 3:22 (73, *CO* 49.60). Cf. H. Paul Santmire, "Justification in Calvin's 1540 Romans Commentary," *Church History* 33 (1964), 298-303; Lane, *Justification by Faith*, 21-26.
30 Cf. Santmire, "Justification in Calvin's 1540 Romans Commentary," 295-297.
31 Comm. Rom. 5:17 (117, *CO* 49.100).
32 Comm. Gal. 2:19 (42-43, *CO* 50.199).
33 Comm. Rom. 8:4 (160, *CO* 49.140): ". . . suam iustitiam nullis communicat Christus, nisi quos spiritus sui vinculo sibi coniungit, . . ." Cf. Girardin, "Rhétorique et Théologique," 345.
34 Cf. Serm. Job 10:16-17 (186a-187, *CO* 33.496-499), 11:1-6 (195b ff., *CO* 33.521 ff), 13:16-22 (238a-b, *CO* 33.633-634), 15:11-16 (273a-b, *CO* 33.726-727), 23:1-7 (412a-416b, *CO* 34.331-344), 27:1-4 (455b, *CO* 34.447-448).
35 Comm. Rom. 7:9-11 (144-145, *CO* 49.125-127); Rom. 8:3 (160-161, *CO* 49. 138-139).

of the law according to both the divine and human natures, the theological foundation based on the so-called *extra Calvinisticum*.[36]

Calvin sought harmony between the Christological and soteriological understandings of the law throughout his successive editions of the *Institutes*. In the first revision of 1539, he re-arranged what he dealt with in the first chapter of the 1536 *Institutes* in terms of the credal order according to the salvation-historical order, i.e., the two kinds of knowledge of God, the principle of justification by faith, and the concept and use of the law. Then, through the considerable addition and augmentation in the editions of 1543 and 1550, he pursued the origin of the power of church law and the role of civil law by invoking the unity and continuity between the divine law and natural law. Finally, in the *ordo docendi* of the 1559 edition, he set out the Christological and soteriological formation of the law by linking Christ's fulfilment of the law with the continual validity of the law for believers by the concept of Christ's mediation of the law.[37]

Several sermons of Calvin demonstrate the coherence between Christology and soteriology in his theology of the law impressively.[38] Referring to David as the figure of Christ and expounding his meditation on the law as glorifying the redemptive work of the Lord, Calvin in his sermon on Psalm 89 pays specific attention to the great and perfect instruction of the law as the way (*chemin*) to eternal life through the grace of Christ. In the first part, he initially mentions the twofold office of the law to reveal our sins and to teach us how to apply ourselves to the service of God. In so doing, he rests on the merit of Christ who fulfilled the law. Following this Christological observation, he indicates the soteriological significance of the law by linking the righteousness of the law with the righteousness of Christ who is the head of the church.[39] The same position is sustained in the second part, but more focused on the Christian life. Calvin touches on the natural office of the law as revealing God's punishment, but immediately proceeds to note the profit and instruction of the law springing from the grace of Christ. Then he again resorts to the believer's union with Christ for the explanation of the continual validity of the law for the godly

---

36 For Christ's mediation of the law and the the so-called *extra Calvinisticum*, see book 4.5.1.

37 For the development of Calvin's Christological understanding of the law, see book 3.2.

38 We find an insight into the coherence between Christology and soteriology in Calvin's theology, argued most notably concerning the relationship between book 2 and book 3 of the *Institutes*, in the recent work of Dawn DeVries, where the author explores this agenda in view of the relationship between *Christus praesens extra nos* and *in nobis. Jesus Christ in the Preaching of Calvin and Schleiermacher* (Louisville: Westminster/John Knox, 1996), 96.

39 Serm. Ps. 89:31-39 (*SC* 7.65-67).

life.⁴⁰ Finally, he finishes the sermon by pointing up the grace of the law originating from Christ's freely imputed grace.⁴¹

Calvin's sermon on the name "Jesus" in the Synoptic Gospels provides another example. With reference to the *meritum Christi*, he argues that as its substance and truth Christ fulfilled and vivified the law through his Spirit.⁴² Then, following this Christological observation, he takes account of the office and use of the law in the process of salvation by underscoring the continuity of the mediation of the eternal Son of God and the continual work of his Spirit.⁴³

It is time to turn to four distinctive characteristics demonstrated in some passages of Calvin's sermons setting forth his well-balanced Christological and soteriological understanding of the law in order to verify Calvin's emphasis on the fact that the Christ who fulfilled the law is still working for us as the Mediator. The first characteristic by which we may discover his dynamic understanding of the relationship between Christ and the law is his view of the unity and continuity of the church.⁴⁴ Calvin identifies the church as the seed of Abraham belonging to Christ their head.⁴⁵ From this point, he explains the communion of the saints and Christ's mediation according to both his natures.⁴⁶ By referring to Christ's headship of the church, Calvin especially points out that the ancient fathers were aware of Christ as the substance of the law and moreover they were partakers of his righteousness through the special illumination of the Holy Spirit.⁴⁷ He attributes the headship of the church to Christ because he both governs and mediates for his members. In doing this, he bases Christ's government on his mediating grace.⁴⁸

---

40 Serm. Ps. 89:31-39 (*SC* 7.67-70).
41 Serm. Ps. 89:31-39 (*SC* 7.70-72).
42 Serm. Lk. 1:33 (*CO* 46.80-81): "Car Iesus Christ en [de la loy] est la fin, comme il le dit en l'autre passage. Et puis encores en l'autre passage, C'est luy qui en est l'ame et l'esprit. Car c'est une chose morte que la Loy, et mesmes tous les Prophetes, sinon que tout soit vivifié par nostre Seigneur Iesus Christ, et que nous cognoissions que c'est en luy que tout gist et consiste, et qu'il est la vertu et substance de toutes les figures et ombrages qui ont este anciennement."
43 Serm. Lk. 1:31-35 (*CO* 46.73-86). Calvin here accuses Servetus of denying the existence of the eternal Son of God and his presence as the Mediator (*CO* 46.79-80).
44 For the unity and continuity of the church as the body of Christ, see book 5.3.3.
45 Serm. Gen. 15:4-5 (89-93, *SC* 11/2.741-743); Ps. 147:18-20 (*SC* 7.11-15); Gal. 3:18 (430-437, *CO* 50.529-534).
46 Serm. Acts 7:36 (*SC* 8.312-313); Eph. 1:21 (112-114, *CO* 51.336-338); Eph. 3:16 (282-283, *CO* 51.485-486).
47 Serm. Eph. 1:17-18 (107-110, *CO* 333-336); Eph. 4:16 (402-404, *CO* 51.591-592); Eph. 5:30 (600-604, *CO* 51.767-772).
48 Serm. Eph. 1:21-23 (114-126, *CO* 51.333-350, esp. 118-119, *CO* 51.343-344). Cf. Selderhuis, "Church on Stage: Calvin's Dynamic Ecclesiology," 54-59.

Just as Calvin explains the unity of the church by the headship of Christ, so he explains its continuity by the continual mediation of Christ.[49] Calvin demonstrates this stance most clearly in dealing with the meaning of ceremonies. The ceremonies were established by temporary ordinances, but their substance is eternal and unchangeable.[50] Without the life-giving grace and mercy of Christ the Mediator, the temple and the tabernacle would be meaningless.[51] On this occasion, Christ is not only the substance but also the perfection of ceremonial laws,[52] and as long as we are in communion with Christ, we shall be instructed by the same truth of the ceremonies of the law.[53] Also, the continual validity of the moral law is depicted in the light of the continuity of the church because it plays its original role only for those who have the righteousness of Christ.[54]

Now, we can appropriately take into consideration the continuity of Christ's mediation of the law as another significant characteristic.[55] Calvin believes that although the law is distinguished from the gospel with respect to its economy, their substance is one and the same. Especially, in order to explain the soteriology of the Old Testament, Calvin resorts to the ad-hoc significance of Christ's mediation on the basis of the so-called *extra Calvinisticum*. Calvin takes the position that even before the fall Christ worked as the Mediator to reconcile men to God and to join them to the angels of heaven.[56] In his sermons on Melchizedek, Calvin explains the continuity of Christ's mediation by comparing it with the office of Melchizedek. Melchizedek represents Christ as the Son of God who performed his mediatorial office as Priest and King from the pre-Mosaic period.[57] It is argued that the knowledge of salvation was given before the publication of the law, and the Mediator Christ already worked for the believers.[58] Also, referring to the eternal priesthood of Melchizedek,

---

49 Serm. Mic. 3:11-4:9 (*SC* 5.104-137).
50 Serm. Deut. 27:2-6 (9-13, *CO* 28.298-301).
51 Serm. Ps. 48:9-15 (*SC* 7.58-59, 62-63); Acts 7:42-44 (*SC* 8.355-363); Acts 7:53 (*SC* 8.383); Gal. 4:9-10 (552-559, *CO* 50.603-607).
52 Serm. Mic. 4:9 (*SC* 5.134-136).
53 Serm. Gal. 1:22 (140-141, *CO* 50.354); Gal. 2:4 (158-162, *CO* 50.365-367).
54 Serm. Eph. 5:8-9 (512-513, *CO* 51.687-689).
55 For the continuity of Christ's mediation in salvation history, see book 5.3.3.
56 Serm. Eph. 3:9 (261-262, *CO* 51.466): "Notons bien donc que tout a esté creé en Iesus Christ, quand il a esté ordonné chef des Anges et des hommes: voire encores que nous n'eussions point eu besoin de Redempteur, si est-ce que desia nostre Seigneur Iesus Christ avoit esté establi pour nostre chef. Il n'avoit que faire de vestir nostre nature, ni de s'offrir en sacrifice pour la redemption des pecheurs: mais quoy qu'il en soit, si ne laissoit-il point d'avoir desia cest office de reconcilier Dieu avec les hommes et les conioindre avec les Anges du ciel."
57 Serm. Gen. 14:18 (*SC* 11/2.703-707).
58 Serm. Gen. 14:18 (*SC* 11/2.705-706, 709-714).

Calvin explains Christ's mediation after his ascension "in the person of the Mediator (*en la personne du mediateur*)."[59]

Calvin does not associate Christ's mediation merely with the effect of his office, but presents it as the believer's participation in his substance by the power of his Spirit.[60] He explains the omnipresence of Christ the Mediator with emphasis on our participation in his body and soul, which are distinguishable but not separated because they are made of the same substance. He acknowedges no transfiguration taking place in the personal presence of the Mediator after his ascension according to both the divine and human natures, but argues for his spiritual yet real presence by referring to the so-called *extra Calvinisticum*. Thus, Calvin explains the continuity of the church by the eternal headship of Christ throughout the old and new covenants.[61]

Another characteristic feature by which Calvin explores the soteriological significance of Christ's mediation of the law in his sermons is that he frequently refers to the special illumination of the Spirit of Christ in order to explain the law. He depicts the Spirit of Christ as the spirit of perfection, the spirit of the fear of God, the spirit of purity, the spirit of all righteousness, and the spirit of truth.[62] Moreover, due to the spiritual government of Christ over our hearts through his Spirit, the realm of Christ's kingship and priesthood is regarded as extending to the spiritual kingdom of God.[63] The peculiar feature of the Spirit of Christ is presented prominently in relation to its operation to make godly people partakers of his righteousness, to lift up their heart so that they stand before the Father with confidence, and ultimately, to lead them to the perfection of eternal life.[64]

It is surely the case that Christ is, in Calvin's judgment, the life (*vie*) and soul (*ame*) of the law. This claim is based on the fact that by the special illumination of the Spirit of Christ, the law, which is "the word of life (*parolle de vie*)" and "the living word (*parolle vivante*)," performs its orginal office as *regula vivendi* and its theological office as *regula vivificandi*.[65] Two further points should be noted here. First, the life-giving office of the law is suggested on the basis of the free imputation of the righteousness of Christ the mediator through the special illumination of his

---

59 Serm. Gen. 14:19 (*SC* 11/2.715-716). Cf. Comm. Heb. 5:6 (62-63, *CO* 55.60-61).
60 Serm. Eph. 4:10 (360, *CO* 51.552): ". . . non pas que nous soyons creez de sa substance, mais que par la vertu de son sainct Esprit il fait decouler en nous la substance de son corps et de son sang, dont nous sommes rassasiez: . . ."
61 Serm. Eph. 4:10 (353-360, *CO* 51.546-554).
62 Serm. Deut. 9:17 (404b-405b, *CO* 26.697-701); Eph. 1:1 (14, *CO* 51.251).
63 Serm. II Sam. 8:15 (418-426, SC 1.244-249).
64 Serm. Eph. 3:14-19 (285-302, *CO* 51.485-502).
65 Serm. Acts 7:38 (*SC* 8.328); Matt. 1:22 (*CO* 46.259).

Spirit.⁶⁶ Secondly, and more specifically, in this respect, a true submission to God's will revealed in the law, denotes that the believer lives according to the type of Christ inspired by his Spirit.⁶⁷ Calvin reflects these two points when he explains the end of the law in these three ways in his sermon on I Timothy: the law teaches the rule of living rightly; the law reveals the promise of God to the godly people who belong to the seeds of Abraham; the law makes the elect assured of their salvation.⁶⁸

The final characteristic which is to be explored as the application of the three features I have raised, shows the significance of Christ's mediation of the law in the double imputation of God in order to accept both our persons and our imperfect works as righteous. Calvin does not regard the first and third uses of the law clearly separated because he thinks that both are derived from the theological and normative office of the law. He relates the doctrine of salvation mainly to the first use and the regulation of the law to live well and in a holy way to the third use, but he is firmly assured that unlike the second use of the law, both are founded on the believer's union with Christ and on the continual imputation of his righteousness, which is invoked by the spiritual operation of the law.⁶⁹

The original purpose of the law is pedagogical. The whole law, including ceremonial laws, was given for edification or instruction in order to restore and make the image of God within us perfect.⁷⁰ The original nature of the law is normative, yet life-giving.⁷¹ The righteousness of the law should be distinguished from the higher righteousness of God. The grace of salvation was revealed on Mount Sion, and the law came from the gospel of Christ which had been present before the publication of the law.⁷² The name "Immanuel" suggests to Calvin that the continual presence and communication of Christ adheres to the role of Mediator.⁷³ The substance which the law reveals is primarily "*nostre medecin spirituel*" which heals us by communicating Christ's righteousness to us.⁷⁴ The grace of Christ as a remedy (*remede*) refers to the whole process of salvation. The positive aspect of Christian freedom is founded on the fact that to die to the law in Christ is to die in the gospel, that is, when clothed by the grace of the Mediator, "a deadly death (*mort mortelle*)" becomes "a quickening death

---

66 Serm. Acts 7:38 (*SC* 8.329-330).
67 Serm. Eph. 4:24 (437-441, *CO* 51.621-625).
68 Serm. I Tim. 1:5 (26b-37b, *CO* 53.29-40, esp. 28a-28b, *CO* 53.31-32).
69 Serm. Eph. 2:10 (165-169, *CO* 51.383-386).
70 Serm. Acts 7:44 (*SC* 8.359-363); Eph. 2:14-15 (191-197, *CO* 51.405-412).
71 Serm. Acts 5:20 (*SC* 8.154-156).
72 Serm. Ps 48:2 (*SC* 7.51); Mic. 4:2 (*SC* 5.107, 114-120).
73 Serm. Matt. 1:23 (*CO* 46.266-269); Deut. 7:21 (336a-337a, *CO* 26.563-565).
74 Serm. Gen. 15:6 (*SC* 11/2.747-750); Acts 5:13-16 (*SC* 8.140-147).

(*mort vivifiante*)."⁷⁵ Accordingly, Christian freedom is nothing else than to believe in Christ's mediation during the whole process of salvation.⁷⁶

These four characteristics feature the varying aspects of Christ's mediation of the law. As the Mediator of reconciliation, Christ accepts both our persons and our imperfect works by imputing his righteousness to us. In so doing, Christ reveals himself as the fulfilment of the law. As the Mediator of all teaching, Christ interprets and reveals the original meaning of the law so that we may ultimately be aware of its substance and truth. As the Mediator of intercession, finally, Christ prays for us and makes us lift up our hearts to God. Through the continual intercession of Christ, who is the head, the regenerate are instructed and exhorted to live according to the law.⁷⁷

As Ronald S. Wallace indicates, for Calvin, preaching is "a means whereby Christ establishes His rule in the hearts of His people."⁷⁸ As a result of the observations above, we recognize that Calvin's concept of *Christus mediator legis* bears both Christological and soteriological significance and ranges over not only the realm of salvation history but also the whole process of personal salvation. Thus Calvin's concept of *lex vivificandi* is due to his linking the normative nature of the law and Christ's mediation of the law, which in turn demonstrates the theological foundation of Calvin's dynamic understanding of the law.

Like Calvin, both Melanchthon and Bucer have a dynamic view of salvation based on the double imputation of Christ. However, Melanchthon fails to grasp the internal relationship between the righteousness of Christ and the righteousness of the law because he believes that the law always works primarily as *lex accusans* prior to faith.⁷⁹ Bucer's Christological understanding of the law is similar to that of Calvin, since both teach the embodiment of the grace of Christ in the law by the work of the Spirit of Christ. They both argue that the normative character of the law is not abandoned even when it performs its punitive office. However, with regard to the continual mediation of Christ in the course of the soteriological application of the grace of Christ to the office and use of the law, the difference between them is rather prominent. While Calvin points out the coherence between Christology and soteriology concerning the office and use of the law by the concept of Christ's mediation, Bucer only refers to the continuing efficacy of the law which is sustained and revealed by the gospel

---

75 Serm. Gal. 2:17-18 (271-280, *CO* 50.433-439, quot. 270-280, *CO* 50.438-439).
76 Serm. Gal. 5:1-3 (642-662, *CO* 50.655-670, esp. 644-646, *CO* 657-659).
77 For the threefold mediation of the law, see book 4.4.2-4.
78 Ronald S. Wallace, *Calvin's Doctrine of the Word and Sacrament* (Edinburgh: Oliver and Boyd, 1953), 85.
79 For Melanchthon's view of the law, see book 6.3.1, 7.3.2.

for the sake of explaining the normative use of the law for the regenerate.[80] This characteristic feature of Bucer has fundamental affinity to Bullinger's covenantal understanding of the law. We should keep in mind that for Bullinger it is the frame of the promise and fulfilment of the law in salvation history that is primarily considered as opposed to its Christological origin, i.e., the substance of the law.[81]

It can be properly argued that Calvin's literary and historical interpretation of the law was influenced by his Christological understanding of the law based on Christ's mediation of the law and on its soteriological application. Calvin differentiates his biblical interpretation from Jewish literal interpretation.[82] For him, the historicity of the law reflects the historical presence and office of the Mediator and his historical biblicism is supported by the dynamic nature of Christ's mediation. Accordingly, the true meaning of each individual law should be pursued in view of its Christological relevance.[83]

Calvin's peculiar position on the law originates from his view of its nature and substance rather than from his attitude towards the office and use of the law. His stance on the theological use of *adiaphora*, to take but one example, clearly bears witness to this point.[84] Luther's and Melanchthon's assertion of the wide extent of *adiaphora* is due to their negative view of the law as *lex accusans*. Because the regenerate have living faith (*fides viva*) to submit themselves to the rule of the law voluntarily, both Reformers argue, they are not obliged to its bondage any longer.[85] This assertion is based on their conviction that external, indifferent things can be sufficiently ruled by natural law and civil law.[86] Calvin also accepts the

---

80 For Bucer's view of the law, see book 6.3.2, 7.3.4.
81 For Bullinger's view of the law, see book 7.3.3.
82 For the historical interpretation of the law in the Old Testament, see book 5.4.
83 For the Christological understanding of the law in the Old Testament, see book 5.2-3, 6.
84 For the theological use of the principle of *adiaphora* in relation to God's accommodation, see book 4.5.2.
85 With regard to the validity of the law, Benjamin B. Warfield sees the difference between Luther and Calvin in the fact that while Calvin emphasizes the inner testimony of the Holy Spirit in dealing with the Christian life, Luther concentrates more on the liberty of the Christian man. *Calvin and Augustine* (Philadelphia: Presbyterian and Reformed Publishing, 1956), 105-106.
86 Steinmetz explains why Luther was generous about the extensive use of images in the church in this way: "Natural law requires that God alone be honored and worshiped. The prohibition of images, on the other hand, is a time-bound application of this principle to the situation to the Jews." "The Reformation and the Ten Commandments," *Interpretation* 43/3 (1989), 261. Similarly to Luther, Melanchthon admits the wide realm of *adiaphora* as to the validity of civil law in his commentary on Colossians 2:20. He writes: "Indeed, such traditions as specified fastings,

concept of living faith, but on the basis of Christ's continual mediation for believers.

Calvin's view of living faith is different from those of Luther and Catholic theologians. Luther believes that there is no specific regulation of the law that is needed for the Christian life because "a living faith 'spontaneously' fulfils the demands of divine law."[87] On the other hand, Catholic theologians view a living faith as based on *iustitia inhaerens*, which parallels the *fides efficax caritate* that is testified in Galatians 5:6. For them, *fides viva et efficax* signifies the qualification or status of a believer rather than a persuasion of heart by imputed grace.[88] Adhering to the normative nature of the law, Calvin insists that Christian freedom from the bondage of the law refers only to its occasional or accidental office. Therefore, in regard to the original nature of the law, Christian freedom signifies freedom in the law rather than freedom from the law. From this

---

festivals, forms of dress, have this one end function. It is to control and govern unrighteousness or inexperienced people, such as children and the common people." *Paul's Letter to the Colossians*, tr. D. C. Parker, 68.

87 Luther distinguishes "a living faith" from "a justifying faith." While the former is related to "the doing of good works," which he calls the third element of the Christian life, the latter is related to "repentance or contrition and grief, and faith," which he calls the first two elements. *Instructions for the Visitors of Parish Pastors in Electoral Saxony, LW* 40.275, 277.

88 In his letter to the Genevans, Sadolet points out living faith as the faith accompanying hope and love: "Est enim amplum et plenum vocabulum Fides, nec solum in se credulitatem et fiduciam continet, sed spem etiam et studium obediendi Deo, et illam, quae in Christo maxime perspicua nobis facta est, principem et dominam christianarum omnium virtutum caritatem: qua in caritate proprie et peculiariter spiritus sanctus inest, vel potius ipse est caritas" (*CO* 5.374-375). For Sadolet's argument for the supremacy of *caritas* in obtaining eternal life, see V. E. d'Assonville, "Observations on Calvin's Responsio to Cardinal Sadoletus's Letter to the Genevans," in *Calvinus Servus Christi*, 156-157. Calvin also does not maintain bare faith secluded from love and takes a similar position as Sadolet in *Inst.* 3.2.41-43 (*CO* 2.431-434). However, in explaining the living faith, Calvin appeals specifically to the special work of the Spirit of Christ and the believer's union with Christ rather than the inner working of faith itself. In his reply to Sadolet, Calvin especially emphasizes this point: "Nam si Christum possidet qui iustitiam est adeptus, Christus autem nusquam sine suo spiritus est, inde constat, gratuitam iustitiam cum regeneratione necessario esse coniunctam. Proinde si rite intelligere libet, quam sint res individuae, fides et opera, in Christum intuere: qui, ut docet apostolus, in iustitiam et sanctificationem datus nobis est (I Cor. 1, 30). Ubi ergo cunque ista quam gratuitam praedicamus fidei iustitia est, illic est Christus. Ubi Christus, illic spiritus sanctificationis: qui animam in vitae novitatem regeneret" (*CO* 5.398). Concerning the concept of *fides viva et efficax* (*la foy vive et efficace*) in Article 5 of the Regensburg Colloquy (*CO* 5.525), Lane, "Calvin and Article 5 of the Regensburg Colloquy," 13-16.

perspective, he admits the wide extent of the use of the law for the Christian life, but strictly restrains the realm of *adiaphora*.[89] This stance of Calvin is evoked by his conviction of Christ's continual mediation of the interpretation, work, and exhortation of the law.

Some reflections on Calvin's sermons on Christ and the law lead us to the conclusion that his concept of *Christus mediator legis*, based on his normative understanding of the nature of the law, refers not only to the person of Christ the Mediator, who is represented and finally revealed as the substance and truth of the law, and his fulfilment of the law, but also to the office and use of the law for the whole process of salvation and its practices in the Christian life, distinctively with reference to the theological use of *adiaphora*. Due to Christ's mediation for the instructive and pedagogical office of the law (Christ's mediation as Teacher), Calvin's epistemology, explored by the framework of the knowledge of God and men, reveals its uniquely dynamic feature with reference to the teaching (*doctrina*) of God's accommodation to human capacity. Due to Christ's mediation in the theological use of the law (Christ's mediation as Reconciler), the law, which has a normative nature as *lex vivendi*, works as *lex accusans* and *lex vivificandi* at the same time for the total restoration of the image of God among the regenerate. Thus, we can recognize that the conditionality of the covenant cannot be divorced from its mutuality, which rests totally on the principle of *sola fide* and *sola gratia*. Finally, due to Christ's mediation for the perfection of eternal life in the Christian life (Christ's mediation as Intercessor), the believer's communion with the body of Christ and continual communication with his righteousness is set forth and vouchsafed. Therefore, Christian freedom signifies the believer's fulfilment of the law of Christ by bearing his yoke (Matt. 11:28) with firm conviction of his continual mediation.[90] This is the core and culmination of Calvin's Christological understanding of the law in terms of his concept of *Christus mediator legis*.   *Soli Deo Gloria in Aeternum*!

---

89 Zachman explains the difference between Luther's and Calvin's view of *adiaphora* by his reference to their peculiar stance on conscience. *The Assurance of Faith*, 229-243, esp. 242-243. For the different view of *adiaphora* between Calvin and Melanchthon in their letters, see Timothy Wengert, "'We Will Feast Together in Heaven Forever': The Epistolary Friendship of John Calvin and Philip Melanchthon," in *Melanchthon in Europe*, ed. Karin Maag (Grand Rapids: Baker, 1999), 33-36. Also, for Melanchthon's view of *adiaphora*, see Clyde L. Manschreck, "The Role of Melanchthon in the Adiaphora Controversy," *Archiv für Reformationsgeschichte* 48/1 (1957): 165-182.

90 Serm. Gal. 6:2 (811-816, *CO* 51.68-72).

BIBLIOGRAPHY

I. WORKS BY CALVIN
A. Primary Sources

Ioannis Calvini opera quae supersunt omnia.* Ed. Guilielmus Baum, Eduardus Cunitz, and Eduardus Reuss. 59 vols. *Corpus Reformatorum*, vols. 29-87. Brunswick: C.A. Schwetschke, 1863-1900.

Ioannis Calvini Opera Selecta. Ed. P. Barth and W. Niesel. 5 vols. München: Kaiser, 1926-1936.

L. Annei Senecae . . . libri duo de clementia . . . commentariis illustrati. In Calvin's Commentary on Seneca's De Clementia. Trans., intro., and notes by Ford Lewis Battles and André Malan Hugo. *Renaissance Text Series*, vol. 3. Leiden: E. J. Brill, 1969.

Supplementa Calviniana. Sermons inédits. Ed. Erwin Mühlhaupt et al. Neukirchen: Neukirchener Verlag, 1936-. Texts used in the book are vol. 1, *Predigten über das 2. Buch Samuelis*; vol. 3, *Sermons sur le Livre d'Isaïe chapitres 30-41*; vol. 5, *Sermons sur le Livre de Michée*; vol. 7, *Psalmenpredigten, Passions-, Oster-, und Pfingstpredigten*; vol. 8, *Sermons on the Acts of the Apostles Chapters 1-7*; vol. 11/1, *Sermons sur la Genèse chapitres 1,1-11,4*; vol. 11/2, *Sermons sur la Genèse chapitres 11,5-20,7*.

*TEXTS FROM CALVINI OPERA

Institutes

Christianae religionis institutio, totam fere pietatis summam, et quidquid est in doctrina salutis cognitu necessarium, complectens; omnibus pietatis studiosis lectu dignissimum opus, ac recens editum, 1536.	1.1-252
Institutio christianae religionis nunc vero demum suo titulo respondens, 1539.	
Institutio christianae religionis nunc vero demum suo titulo respondens, 1543.	1.253-1152
Institutio totius christianae religionis, 1550.	
Institutio christianae religionis, in libros quatuor nunc primum digesta, certisque distincta capitibus, ad aptissimam methodum: aucta etiam tam magna accessione ut propemodum opus novum haberi possit, 1559.	2

Commentaries

Commentarii in Epistolam Pauli ad Romanos, 1540/1551/1556.	49.1-292
Iohannis Calvini Commentarii in priorem Epistolam Pauli ad Corinthios, 1546.	49.293-574
Ioannis Calvini Commentarii in secundam Pauli Epistolam ad Corinthios, 1548.	50.1-156
Ioannis Calvini Commentarii in quatuor Pauli Epistolas: Ad Galatas, ad Ephesios, ad Philippenses, ad Colossenses, 1548.	50.157-268; 51.137-240; 52.1-132.
Ioannis Calvini Commentarii in utramque Pauli Epistolam ad Timotheum, 1548	52.241-396
Ioannis Calvini Commentarii in Epistolam ad Hebraeos, 1549.	55.1-198
Ioannis Calvini Commentarii in Epistolas Canonicas, unam Petri, unam Ioannis, unam Iacobi, Petri alteram, Iudae unam, 1551.	55.201-500
Commentariorum Ioannis Calvini in Acta Apostolorum, liber I, 1552.	48.1-317
In Evangelium secundum Iohannem, Commentarius Iohannis Calvini, 1553.	47.1-458
In primum Mosis librum, qui Genesis vulgo dicitur, Commentarius Iohannis Calvini, 1554.	23.1-622
Commentarius Ioannis Calvini in Acta Apostolorum, liber posterior, 1554.	48.317-574
Harmonia ex tribus Evangelistis composita, Matthaeo, Marco et Luca; adiuncto seorsum Iohanne, quod pauca cum aliis communa habeat. Cum Calvini Commentariis, 1555.	45
In librum Psalmorum, Iohannis Calvini Commentarius, 1557.	31, 32
Ioannis Calvini Commentarii in Isaiam prophetam. Nunc demum ab ipso authore rocogniti, locupletati, magnoque labore et cura expoliti. Additi sunt duo indices: prior rerum et sententiarum, posterior vero locorum utriusque Testamenti, quos in his commentariis ipse author interpretatur, aut opposite ad sensum suum accommodat, 1559.	36.19-37.454
Mosis libri V. cum Ioannis Calvini Commentariis: Genesis seorsum; reliqui quatuor in formam harmoniae digesti, 1563.	24.1-25.416
Ioannis Calvini in librum Iosue brevis commentarius, quem paulo ante mortem absolvit. Addita sunt quaedam de eius morbo et obitu . . ., 1564.	25.417-570

Lectures (*Praelectiones*)

In Hoseam prophetam, Io. Calvini Praelectiones a Ioanne Budaeo et sociis auditoribus assiduis bona fide exceptae, 1557.	42.182-514
Ioannis Calvini Praelectiones in duodecim prophetas (quos vocant) minores . . ., 1559	42.176-44.498
Ioannis Calvini Praelectiones in librum prophetiarum Danielis, Ioannis Budaei et Caroli Ionuillaei labore et industria. Additus est e	40.529-41.304

regione versionis Latinae Hebraicus et Chaldaicus textus, 1561.
Ioannis Calvini Praelectiones in librum prophetiarum Ieremiae et   37.469-39.646
Lamentationes, Ioannis Budaei et Caroli Ionuillaei labore et industria exceptae, 1563.
Ioannis Calvini in viginti prima Ezechielis prophetae capita Praelectiones, Ioannis Budaei et Caroli Ionuillaei labore et industria   40.21-516
exceptae, 1565.

Sermons

Plusieurs sermons touchant la divinité, humanité, et nativité de nostre Seigneur Iésus Christ. . . ., 1558.	35.595-688; 46.829-968; 47.459-484; 48.585-664
Sermons sur les deux Epistres S. Paul à Timothée, et sur l'Epistre à Tite, 1561.	53, 54
Sermons sur le V. livre de Moyse, nommé Deutéronome, 1562.	25.573-29.232
Treze sermons traitans de l'élection gratuite de Dieu en Iacob, et de la réiection en Esau. . . ., 1562.	58.1-206
Soixantecinq sermons sur l'harmonie ou concordance des trois Evangelistes. . . ., 1562.	46.1-826
Sermons sur l'Epistre S. Paul apostre aux Ephésiens, 1562.	51.241-862
Sermons sur le Livre de Iob. . . ., 1563.	33.1-35.514
Sermons sur l'Epistre S. Paul apostre aux Galatiens, 1563.	50.269-51.136

Other Theological Writings

Concio academica nomine rectoris universitatis Parisiensis scripta, 1533.	9.873-876
A tous amateurs de Iésus Christ, et de son S. Evangile, salut, 1535.	9.791-822
Confessio de Trinitate propter calumnias P. Caroli, 1537.	9.703-710
Confession de la foy laquelle tous bourgeois et habitans de Geneve et subiects du pays . . . , [1536 or 1537].	22.77-96
Instruction et confession de foy don't on use en l'église de Genève, 1537.	22.25-74
Catechismus, sive christianae religionis institutio, 1538.	5.313-362
Jacobi Sadoleti Romani Cardinalis Epistola ad senatum populumque Genevensem, qua in obedientiam Romani pontificis eos reducere conatur. Ioannis Calvini Responsio, 1539.	5.363-416
Les Actes de la iournée imperiale, tenue en la cité de Regespourg, aultrement dicte Ratispone . . . sur les différens qui sont auiourdhuy en la religion, 1541.	5.509-684
Vivere apud Christum non dormire animis sanctos, qui in fide Christi decedunt (Psychopannychia), 1542.	5.165-232
Le Catéchisme de l'église de Genève, 1542. .	6.1-145
Defensio sanae et orthodoxae doctrinae de servitute et liberatione	

humani arbitrii adversus calumnias Alberti Pighii Campensis, 1543.	6.225-404.
Supplex exhortatio ad invictissimum Caesarem Carolum quintum et illustrissimos principes, aliosque ordines, Spirae nunc imperii conventum agentes. Ut restituendae ecclesiae curam serio velint suscipere. Eorum omnium nomine edita qui Christum regnare cupiunt, 1543.	6.453-534
Articuli a facultate sacrae theologiae Parisiensi determinati super materiis fidei nostrae hodie controversis. Cum antidoto, 1544.	7.1-44
Brièvè instruction pour armer tous bons fidèles contre les erreurs de la secte commune des anabaptistes, 1544.	7.45-142
Catechismus ecclesiae Genevensis, hoc est, formula erudiendi pueros in doctrina Christi, 1545.	6.1-146
Contre la secte phantastique et furieuse des libertins, qui se nommnent spirituelz, 1545.	7.145-248
Projet d'ordonnance sur les mariages, 1545.	10/1.33-44
De scandalis quibus hodie plerique absterrentur, nonnulli etiam alienantur a pura evangelii doctrina, 1550.	8.1-84
Contra Osiandrum, 1551.	10/1.165-167
De aeterna Dei praedestinatione, qua in salutem alios ex hominibus elegit, alios suo exitio reliquit; item de providentia qua res humanas gubernat, Consensus pastorum Genevensis ecclesiae, a Io. Calvino expositus, 1552.	8.249-366
Sententiae vel propositiones excerptae ex libris Michaelis Serveti, quas ministri ecclesiae Genevensis partim impias ac in Deum blasphemas, partim profanis erroribus et deliriis refertas esse asserunt: omnes vero a verbo Dei, et orthodoxae ecclesiae consensu prorsus alienas, 1554.	8.501-508
Michaelis Serveti responsio ad articulos Ioannis Calvini, 1554.	8.507-518
Michaelis Serveti epistolae triginta ad Ioannem Calvinum gebennensium concionatorem, 1554.	8.645-714
Brevis refutatio errorum et impietatum Michaelis Serveti a ministris ecclesiae Genevensis magnifico senatui sicuti iussi fuerant oblata, 1554.	8.519-554
Defensio sanae et orthodoxae doctrinae de sacramentis eorumque natura vi fine usu et fructu, quam pastores et ministri Tigurinae ecclesiae et Genevensis. . . ., 1555.	9.5-36
Responsio ad aliquot Laelii Socini senensis quaestiones, 1555.	10/1.160-165
Secunda defensio piae et orthodoxae de sacramentis fidei contra Ioachimi Westphali calumnias, 1556.	9.41-120
Quaestiones matrimoniales, 1557.	10/1.229-244
Ultima admonitio Ioannis Calvini ad Ioachimum Westphalum, 1557.	9.137-252
Calumniae nebulonis cuiusdam, quibus odio et invidia gravare conatus est doctrinam Ioh. Calvini de occulta Dei providentia. Ioannis Calvini ad easdem responsio, 1558.	9.269-318

Ad quaestiones Georgii Blandratae responsum Ioannis Calvini, 1558.	9.321-332
Responsum ad fratres Polonos, quomodo mediator sit Christus, ad refutandum Stancaro errorem, 1560.	9.333-342
Ministrorum ecclesiae Genevensis responsio ad nobiles Polonos et Franciscum Stancarum Mantuanum de controversia mediatoris, 1561.	9.345-58
Dilucida explicatio sanae doctrinae de vera participatione carnis et sanguinis Christi in sacra coena ad discutiendas Heshusii nebulas, 1561.	9.457-518
Optima ineundae concordiae ratio, si extra contentionem quaeratur veritas, 1561.	9.518-524
Ad quaestiones et obiecta Iudaei cuiusdam responsio Ioannis Calvini, [undated].	9.653-674

B. Modern Editions and Translations

The Academic Discourse. Delivered by Nicolas Cop on Assuming the Rectorship of the University of Paris on 1 November 1533. In *John Calvin: Institutes of the Christian Religion (1536)*. Appendix 3. Trans. and annot. Ford Lewis Battles. Rev. ed. Grand Rapids: Eerdmans, 1986: 363-372.

Against the Fantastic and Furious Sect of the Libertines Who Are Called "Spirituals." In *John Calvin: Treatises against the Anabaptists and against the Libertines*. Trans. and ed. Benjamin W. Farley. Grand Rapids: Baker, 1982: 187-326.

The Bondage and Liberation of the Will: A Defence of the Orthodox Doctrine of Human Choice against Pighius. Ed. Anthony N. S. Lane. Trans. G. I. Davies. Grand Rapids: Baker, 1996.

Brief Instruction for Arming All the Good Faithful against the Errors of the Common Sect of the Anabaptists. In *John Calvin: Treatises against the Anabaptists and against the Libertines*. Trans. and ed. Benjamin W. Farley. Grand Rapids: Baker, 1982: 36-158.

Calvin: Commentaries. Trans. and ed. Joseph Haroutunian. *Library of Christian Classics*, vol. 23. Philadelphia: Westminster, 1958.

Calvin: Institutes of the Christian Religion. Ed. John T. McNeill. Trans. Ford Lewis Battles. *Library of Christian Classics*, vols. 20-21. Philadelphia: Westminster, 1960.

Calvin's Calvinism: Treatises on the Eternal Predestination of God and the Secret Providence of God. 2 vols. in 1. Trans. Henry Cole. London: Wertheim and Mackintosh, 1856-1857; repr. Grand Rapids: Eerdmans, 1950.

Calvin's Ecclesiastical Advice. Trans. Mary Beaty and Benjamin W. Farley. Louisville: Westminster/John Knox, 1991.

Calvin's New Testament Commentaries. Ed. David W. Torrance and Thomas F. Torrance. 12 vols. Grand Rapids: Eerdmans, 1959-1972.

Calvin-Studienausgabe. Ed. Eberhard Busch et al. Neukirchen: Neukirchener Verlag, 1994-2002. Vol. 1/1, 2, *Reformatorische Anfänge (1533-1541)*; vol. 2, *Gestalt und Ordung der Kirche*; vol. 3, *Reformatorische Kontroversen*; vol. 4, *Reformatorische Klärungen*.

Calvin: Theological Treatises. Trans., intro., and notes by J. K. S. Reid. *Library of*

Christian Classics, vol. 22. Philadelphia: Westminster, 1954.
Catéchisme de Calvin (1537) and *Confession de foi de l'Eglise de Genève* (1537). In *Le Catéchisme français de Calvin, publiée en 1537, reimprimé pour la première fois, avec deux notices par Albert Rillet and Théophile Dufour*. Geneva: H. Georg, 1878: 1-122.
Catechism or Institution of the Christian Religion. Trans. and intro. Ford Lewis Battles. Pittsburgh: Pittsburgh Theological Seminary, 1972; rev. ed. 1976; reissued I. John Hesselink, *Calvin's First Catechism, A Commentary: Featuring Ford Lewis Battles' translation of the 1538 Catechism*. Louisville: Westminster/John Knox, 1997: 1-38.
The Commentaries of John Calvin. 46 vols. Edinburgh: Calvin Translation Society, 1843-1855; repr. 22 vols. Grand Rapids: Baker, 1979.
Commentarius in Epistolam Pauli ad Romanos. Ioannis Calvini Opera Exegetica, vol. 1. Ed. T. H. L. Parker and D. C. Parker. Genève: Droz, 1999.
Concerning Scandals. Trans. John W. Fraser. Grand Rapids: Eerdmans, 1978.
The Controversy on Christ the Mediator: A Response to the Polish Nobles and to Francesco Stancaro of Mantua by the Ministers of the Church of Geneva. Trans. Joseph Tylenda. *Calvin Theological Journal* 8/2 (1973): 146-157.
The Covenant Enforced. Sermons on Deuteronomy 27 and 28. Trans. Arthur Golding. (1583). London: Henry Middleton, 1583; rev. ed. James B. Jordan. Tyler, Tex.: Institute for Christian Economics, 1990.
Épitre a tous amateurs de Jésus-Christ: Préface à la traduction française du Nouveau Testament par Robert Olivetan (1535) . . . avec Introduction sur une édition française de l'Institution dès 1537? Ed. Jacques Pannier. Paris: Fishbacher, 1929.
How Christ is the Mediator: A Response to the Polish Brethren to Refute Stancaro's Error. Trans. Joseph Tylenda. *Calvin Theological Journal* 8/1 (1973): 11-16.
Institutes of the Christian Religion of John Calvin: 1539, Text and Concordance. 4 vols. Ed. Richard F. Wevers. Grand Rapids: Meeter Center for Calvin Studies, 1988.
Institutes of the Christian Religion (1536). Trans. and Annot. Ford Lewis Battles. Rev. ed. Grand Rapids: Eerdmans, 1986.
Institution de la religion chrétienne [1560]. Ed., intro., and notes by Jean-Daniel Benoit. 5 vols. Paris: J. Vrin, 1957-1963.
Instruction et confession de foy don't on use en l'eglise de Geneve, Catechismus seu Christianae religionis Institutio ecclesiae Genevensis. Ioannis Calvini Scripta Ecclesiastica, vol. 2. Ed. Anette Zillenbiller and Marc Vial. Genève: Droz, 2002.
Instruction in Faith (1537 Catechism). Trans. and notes by Paul T. Fuhrmann. Philadelphia: Westminster, 1949.
John Calvin's Response to the Questions of Giorgio Biandrata. Trans. Joseph Tylenda. *Calvin Theological Journal* 12/1 (1977): 54-62.
John Calvin's Sermons on Isaiah's Prophecy of the Death and Passion of Jesus Christ. Trans. T. H. L. Parker. London: James Clake, 1956.
John Calvin's Sermons on Melchizedek and Abraham. Trans. Thomas Stocker. London, 1592; reissued. Audubon, N. J.: Old Paths Publications, 2000.
John Calvin's Sermons on 2 Samuel Chapters 1-13. Trans. Douglas Kelly. Edinburgh: Banner of Truth, 1992.

John Calvin's Sermons on the Deity of Christ. Trans. Leroy Nixon. Grand Rapids: Eerdmans, 1950; 2nd ed. Audubon, N. J.: Old Paths Publications, 1997.

John Calvin's Sermons on the Ten Commandments. Ed. and trans. Benjamin W. Farley. Grand Rapids: Baker, 1980.

John Calvin's Tracts and Treatises. 3 vols. Trans. Henry Beveridge. Edinburgh: Calvin Translation Society, 1844-1851; repr. Grand Rapids: Eerdmans, 1958.

The Mystery of Godliness and Other Select Sermons. New York: S. & D. A. Forbes, 1830; reissued, Grand Rapids: Eerdmans, 1950; repr. Morgan, Pa.: Soli Deo Gloria Publications, 1999.

A Reformation Debate: John Calvin and Jacopo Sadoleto. Trans. Henry Beveridge. In *John Calvin's Tracts and Treatises*, vol. 1. Edinburgh: Calvin Translation Society, 1844-1851: 3-68; new ed. John C. Olin. Grand Rapids: Baker, 1976.

Sermons of Maister Iohn Calvin upon the Booke of Job. Trans. Arthur Golding: London: George Bishop, 1574; facsimile repr. Edinburgh: Banner of Truth, 1993.

Sermons of M. Iohn Calvin upon the Fifth Booke of Moses called Deuteronomeie. Trans. Arthur Golding. London: Henry Middleton, 1583; facsimile repr. Edinburgh: Banner of Truth, 1993.

Sermons of M. John Calvin on the Epistles of S. Paule to Timothie and Titus. Trans. L(aurence). T(omson). London: George Bishop, 1579; facsimile repr. Edinburgh: Banner of Truth, 1983.

Sermons on the Epistle to the Ephesians. Trans. Arthur Golding, London, 1577; rev. trans. Leslie Rawlinson and S. M. Houghton. Edinburgh: Banner of Truth, 1973.

Sermons upon the Epistle of Saint Paul to the Galatians. Trans. Arthur Golding. London, 1574; reissued, Audubon, N. J.: Old Paths Publications, 1995.

Thirteen Sermons of Maister Iohn Calvin, Entreating of the Free Election of God in Iacob, and of Reprobation in Esau. A treatise wherein every Christian may see the excellent benefits of God towards his Children, and his marvellous iudgements towards the reprobate. Trans. Iohn Fielde. London, 1579; reissued, Audubon, N. J.: Old Paths Publications, 1996.

Two and Twentie Sermons of Maister Iohn Calvin, in which Sermons is most religiously handled, the hundredth and nineteenth Psalme of David, by eight verses aparte, according to the Hebrewe Alphabet. Trans. Thomas Stoker. London, 1580; reissued, Audubon, N. J.: Old Paths Publications, 1996.

II. OTHER PRIMARY SOURCES

Bucer, Martin. *Common Places of Martin Bucer*. Trans. and ed. David F. Wright. *The Courtenay Library of Reformation Classics*, vol. 4. Appleford: Sutton Courtenay Press, 1972.

Consilium Theologicum Privatim Conscriptum. Martini Buceri Opera Latina, vol. 4. Ed. Pierre Fraenkel. Leiden: E. J. Brill, 1988.

Enarratio in Evangelion Iohannis (1528, 1530, 1536). Martini Buceri Opera Latina, vol. 2. Ed. Irena Backus. Leiden: E. J. Brill, 1988.

— *In sacra quatuor Euangelia, Enarrationes perpetuae, secundum et postremum recognitae . . .*, [Geneva] 1553.

— *Metaphrasis et enarratio in epist. D. Pauli apostoli ad Romanos* . . ., Basel, 1562.
Bullinger, Heinrich. *Commentarii in omnes Pauli Apostoli Epistolas, atque etiam in Epistolam ad Hebraeos.* Zürich, 1582.
— *Sacrosanctum Iesu Christi Domini nostri Evangelium secundum Matthaeum.* Zürich, 1546.
— *Sermonum decades quinque, de potissimis Christianae religionis capitibus, in tres tomos digestae,* vol. 2. Zürich, 1572.
Hunnius, Aegidius. *Calvinus Iudaizans, Hoc est: Iudaicae Glossae et Corruptelae, Quibus Iohannes Calvinus illustrissima Scripturae sacrae loca et Testimonia,* . . . (Wittenberg, 1595). In *Opera Latina*, vol. 2. Frankfurt a. M.: Impensis Iohan. Iacobi Porsij Bibliopolae, 1608.
Luther, Martin. *D. Martin Luthers Werke. Kritische Gesamtausgabe.* 66 vols. Weimar: Hermann Böhlaus Nachfolger, 1883-1987.
— *Luther's Works.* 56 vols. Ed. Jaroslav Pelikan and Helmut Lehmann. St. Louis: Concordia/ Philadelphia: Fortress Press, 1955-1986.
— *Martin Luther's Basic Theological Writings.* Ed. Timothy F. Lull. Minneapolis: Fortress Press, 1989.
Melanchthon, Philip. *Loci communes theologici* (1521). Trans. Lowell Satre. In *Melanchthon and Bucer.* Ed. Wilhelm Pauck. *Library of Christian Classics*, vol. 19. Philadelphia: Westminster, 1969.
— *Loci Communes 1543.* Trans. J. A. O. Preus. St. Louis: Concordia, 1992.
— *Melanchthon on Christian Doctrine: Loci Communes 1555.* Trans. and ed. Clyde L. Manschreck. New York: Oxford University Press, 1965.
— *Paul's Letter to the Colossians.* Trans. D. C. Parker. Sheffield: The Almond Press, 1989.
— *Philippi Melanchthonis opera quae supersunt omnia.* 28 vols. Ed. C. G. Bretschneider and H. E. Bindseil. Halle/ Braunschweig: C. A. Schwetschke, 1834-1860.
Servetus, Michael. *Christianismi Restitutio.* Vienne, 1553.
— *De Trinitatis Erroribus libri septem.* Hagenau, 1531; facsimile repr. Frankfurt a. M.: Minerva G.M.B.H., 1965.
— *Dialogorum de Trinitate.* Hagenau, 1532; facsimile repr. Frankfurt a. M.: Minerva G.M.B.H., 1965.
— *The Two Treatises of Servetus on the Trinity.* Trans. Earl Morse Wilbur. Cambridge. Mass.: Harvard University Press, 1932.

III. SECONDARY LITERATURE

Adams, Marilyn McCord. *William Ockham.* 2 vols. Notre Dame: University of Notre Dame Press, 1987.
Althaus, Paul. *The Divine Command: A New Perspective on Law and Gospel.* Trans. Franklin Sherman. Philadelphia: Fortress, 1966.
Augsburger, Daniel. "Calvin and the Mosaic Law." PhD dissertation. Strasbourg University, 1976.
— "Castellio and the Mosaic Law." In *Occasional Papers of the American Society for*

Reformation Research, vol. 1 (1977): 167-173.

Ames, William. *The Marrow of Theology*. Trans. John D. Eusden. Durham, N.C.: Labyrinth Press, 1983.

Armstrong, Brian G. "Report on the Seminar: An Investigation of Calvin's Principles of Biblical Interpretation." *Hervormde Theologiese Studies* 54 (1998): 131-142.

Backus, Irena. "'Aristotelianism' in Some of Calvin's and Beza's Expository and Exegetical Writings on the Doctrine of the Trinity, with Particular Reference to the Terms οὐσια and ὑπόστασις." In *Histoire de l'exégèse au XVIe siècle: Textes du Colloque International Tenu à Genève en 1976*. Ed. Olivier Fatio and Pierre Fraenkel. Genève: Droz, 1978: 351-360.

— "Calvin's Concept of Natural and Roman Law." *Calvin Theological Journal* 38 (2003): 7-26.

Bainton, Roland H. *Concerning Heretics . . . An anonymous work attributed to Sebastian Castellio*. New York: Morning Side Heights, 1935.

— *Hunted Heretic: The Life and Death of Michael Servetus 1511-1553*. Boston: Beacon Press, 1953.

Baker, J. Wayne. *Heinrich Bullinger and the Covenant: The Other Reformed Tradition*. Athens, Ohio: Ohio University Press, 1980.

— "Heinrich Bullinger, the Covenant, and the Reformed Tradition in Retrospect." *Sixteenth Century Journal* 29/2 (1998): 359-376.

Balke, Willem. *Calvin and the Anabaptist Radicals*. Trans. William Heynen. Grand Rapids: Eerdmans, 1981.

Balserak, Jon. "'The Accommodating Act Par Excellence?': An Inquiry into the Incarnation and Calvin's Understanding of Accommodation." *Scottish Theological Journal* 55/4 (2002): 408-423.

Bandstra, Andrew J. "Law and Gospel in Calvin and in Paul." In *Exploring the Heritage of John Calvin*. Ed. David E. Holwerda. Grand Rapids: Baker, 1976: 11-39.

Banks, Robert. *Jesus and the Law in the Synoptic Tradition*. Cambridge: Cambridge University Press, 1975.

Baron, Salo W. "John Calvin and the Jews." In *Ancient and Medieval Jewish History: Essays by Salo Wittmayer Baron*. New Brunswick, N.J.: Rutgers University Press, 1972: 338-352, 548-554.

— *Inquisition, Renaissance, and Reformation. A Social and Religious History of the Jews. Late Middle Ages and Era of European Expansion*, vol. 13. New York: Columbia University Press, 1969.

Barth, Karl. *Church Dogmatics*, vol. 2. *The Doctrine of God* 2. Trans. G. W. Bromiley, et al. Edinburgh: T. & T. Clark, 1957.

— "Gospel and Law." In *Community, State and Church: Three essays*. With an Introduction by Will Herberg. Garden City, N.Y.: Doubleday, 1960: 71-100.

— *The Theology of John Calvin*. Trans. Geoffrey W. Bromiley. Grand Rapids: Eerdmans, 1995.

Battles, Ford Lewis. "God Was Accommodating Himself to Human Capacity." *Interpretation* 31/1 (1977): 19-38.

— *Interpreting John Calvin*. Ed. Robert Benedetto. Grand Rapids: Baker, 1996.

Baumgartner, J. *Calvin Hébraïsant et Interprète de l'Ancien Testament*. Paris: Librairie Fischbacher, 1889.
Beardslee, John W. III. Ed. and trans. *Reformed Dogmatics*. New York: Oxford University Press, 1965.
Beintker, Michael. "Calvins Denken in Relationen." *Zeitschrift für Theologie und Kirche* 99 (2002): 109-129.
Benin, Stephen D. *The Footprints of God: Divine Accommodation in Jewish and Christian Thought*. Albany: State University of New York Press, 1993.
Benoît, Jean-Daniel. "The History and Development of the *Institutio*: How Calvin Worked." Trans. the editor. In *John Calvin*. Ed. G. E. Duffield. Courtenay Studies in Reformation Theology, vol. 1. Grand Rapids: Eerdmans, 1966: 102-117.
Bentley, Jerry H. "Biblical Philology and Christian Humanism: Lorenzo Valla and Erasmus as Scholars of the Gospels." *Sixteenth Century Journal* 8, Supplement (1977): 9-28.
Bierma, Lyle D. "Federal Theology in the Sixteenth Century: Two Traditions?" *Westminster Theological Journal* 45 (1983): 304-21.
— *German Calvinism in the Confessional Age: The Covenant Theology of Caspar Olevianus*. Grand Rapids: Baker, 1996.
Blaser, Klauspeter. *Calvins Lehre von den drei Ämtern Christi*. Theologische Studien 105. Zürich: EVZ Verlag, 1970.
Bohatec, Josef. *Budé und Calvin: Studien zur Gedankenwelt des französischen Frühhumanismus*. Graz: Verlag Hemann Bohlaus, 1950.
— "Calvin et le code civil à Genève." *Revue historique du droit français et étranger* 4/17 (1938): 229-303.
— *Calvin und das Recht*. Feudigen in Westphalen: H. Boehlaus, 1934.
— "Calvins Vorsehungslehre." In *Calvinstudien: Festschrift zum 400. Geburtstag Johann Calvins*. Ed. Reformierten Gemeinde Elberfeld. Leipzig: Verlag von Rudolf Haupt, 1909: 339-441.
Boisset, Jean. *Sagesse et Sainteté dans la pensée de Jean Calvin*. Paris: Presses universitaires de France, 1959.
Bolt, John. "Christ and the Law in the Ethics of Herman Bavinck." *Calvin Theological Journal* 28 (1993): 45-73.
Bonfil, Robert. "Aliens Within: the Jews and Antijudaism." In *Handbook of European History, 1400-1600: Late Middle Ages, Renaissance, and Reformation*, vol. 1. *Structures and Assertions*. Ed. Thomas A. Brady, Jr., Heiko A. Oberman, and James D. Tracy. Grand Rapids: Eerdmans, 1994: 263-302.
Bosco, David. "Conscience as Court and Worm: Calvin and the Three Elements of Conscience." *Journal of Religious Ethics* 14/2 (1986): 333-355.
Bouman, Walter R. "The Concept of the 'Law' in the Lutheran Tradition." *Word & World* 3/4 (1983): 413-422.
Bouwsma, William J. *John Calvin: A Sixteenth Century Portrait*. New York and Oxford: Oxford University Press, 1988.
— "The Two Faces of Humanism: Stoicism and Augustinianism in Renaissance Thought." In *Itinerarium Italicum: The Profile of the Italian Renaissance in the*

Mirror of its European Transformations. Dedicated to Paul Oskar Kristeller on the occasion of his 70th birthday. Leiden: E. J. Brill, 1975: 3-60.

Breen, Quirinus. *Christianity and Humanism: Studies in the History of Ideas*. Ed. Nelson Peter Ross. Grand Rapids: Eerdmans, 1968.

— *John Calvin: A Study in French Humanism*. Grand Rapids: Eerdmans, 1931.

Brundage, James A. *Medieval Canon Law*. London: Longman, 1995.

Burnett, Amy Nelson. "Church Discipline and Moral Reformation in the Thought of Martin Bucer." *Sixteenth Century Journal* (1991): 439-456.

Burnett, S. G. "Calvin's Jewish Interlocutor: Christian Hebraism and Anti-Jewish Polemics During the Reformation." *Bibliothèque d'Humanisme et Renaissance* 55/1 (1993): 113-123.

Butin, Philip Walker. *Revelation, Redemption, and Response: Calvin's Trinitarian Understanding of the Divine-Human Relationship*. New York: Oxford University Press, 1995.

Brümmer, Vincent. "Calvin, Bernard and the Freedom of the Will." *Religious Studies* 30 (1994): 437-455.

Brunner, Emil and Barth, Karl. *Natural Theology* ("Nature and Grace" by Brunner and the Reply "No!" by Barth). Trans. Peter Fraenkel. London: The Century Press, 1946.

Büsser, Fritz. "Bullinger as Calvin's Model in Biblical Exposition: An Examination of Calvin's Preface to the Epistle to the Romans." Trans. Christoph Weichert. In *In Honor of John Calvin, 1509-64*. Papers from the 1986 International Calvin Symposium. Ed. E. J. Furcha. Montreal: McGill University Press, 1987: 64-95.

— "The Zurich Theology in Calvin's *Institutes*." In *John Calvin's Institutes: His Opus Magnum*. Proceedings of the Second South African Congress for Calvin Research 1984. Potchefstroom: Potchefstroom Universtiy for Christian Higher Education, 1986: 133-147.

Carbonnier, Jean. "Droit et Théologie chez Calvin." In *Johannes Calvin: Akademische Feier der Universität Bern zu seinem 400. Todestag*. Ed. Hans Merz, Otto Erich Strasser, Jean Carbonnier. Bern: Verlag Paul Haupt, 1965: 18-31.

Carbonnier, Marianne. "Le droit de punir et le sens de la peine chez Calvin." *Revue d'histoire et de philosophie religieuses* 54/2 (1974):187-201.

Cadier, Jean. "Calvin and the Union of the Churches." Trans. P. Rix. In *John Calvin*. Ed. G. E. Duffield. *Courtenay Studies in Reformation Theology*, vol. 1. Grand Rapids: Eerdmans, 1966: 118-130.

— "Calvin et saint Augustin." In *Augustinus Magister*, vol. 2. *Communications*. Congrès International Augustinien (1954). Paris: Études Augustiniennes, 1954: 1039-1056.

Casteel, Theodore W. "Calvin and Trent: Calvin's Reaction to the Council of Trent in the Context of His Conciliar Thought." *Harvard Theological Review* 63 (1970): 91-117.

Choisy, Eugène. *La Théocratie à Genève au temps de Calvin*. Genève: Ch. Eggimann & Cie, 1897.

Cochrane, Arthur C. "Natural Law in Calvin." In *Church-State Relations in Ecumenical Perspective*. Ed. Elwyn A. Smith. Louvain: Duquesne University Press, 1966: 176-217.

Colish, Marcia L. *The Stoic Tradition from Antiquity to the Early Middle Ages: I.*

Stoicism in Classical Latin Literature. Leiden: E. J. Brill, 1985.
— *The Stoic Tradition From Antiquity to the Early Middle Ages: II. Stoicism in Christian Latin Thought through the Sixth Century.* Leiden: E. J. Brill, 1985.
Cottret, Bernard. *Calvin: A Biography.* Trans. M. Wallace McDonald. Edinburgh: T & T Clark, 2000.
Courtenay, William J. "Covenant and Causality in Pierre d'Ailly." *Spectrum* 46 (1971). 97-102.
— "The Dialectic of Divine Omnipotence." In *Covenant and Causality in Medieval Thought: Studies in Philosophy, Theology, and Economic Practice.* London: Variorum Reprints, 1984: 1-37.
Courvoisier, Jacques. "Calvin et les Juifs." *Judaica* 2 (1946): 203-208.
— Une traduction francaise du commentaire de Bucer sur l'évangile selon Saint Matthieu. Paris: Librairie Félix Alcan, 1933.
Cushman, Robert E. "Faith and Reason." In *A Companion to the Study of St. Augustine.* Ed. Roy W. Battenhouse. New York: Oxford University Press, 1956: 287-314.
D'Assonville, V. E. "Observations on Calvin's Responsio to Cardinal Sadoletus's Letter to the Genevans." In *Calvinus Servus Christi.* Ed. Wilhelm H. Neuser. Budapest: Presseabteilung des Ráday-Kollegiums, 1988: 151-164.
De Greef, W. *The Writings of John Calvin: An Introductory Guide.* Trans. Lyle D. Bierma. Grand Rapids: Baker, 1989.
De Jonge, Henk Jan. "Sixteenth-century Gospel Harmonies: Chemnitz and Mercator." In *Théorie et pratique de l'exégèse.* Ed. Irena Backus et Francis Higman. Genève: Droz, 1990: 155-166.
De Kroon, Marijn. *Bucer en Calvijn.* Zoetemeer: Meinema, 1991.
— "Freedom and Bondage." In *Calvin's Books: Festschrift for Peter de Klerk.* Ed. Wilhelm H. Neuser, Herman J. Selderhuis, and Willem van't Spijker. Heerenveen: Groen, 1997: 271-282.
De La Garanderie, Marie-Madeleine. "Guillaume Budé, A Philosopher of Culture." *Sixteenth Century Journal* 19/3 (1988): 378-387.
Demura, Akira. "Two Commentaries on the Epistle to the Romans: Calvin and Oecolampadius." In *Calvinus Sincerioris Religionis Vindex: Calvin as Protector of the Purer Religion.* Ed. Wilhelm H. Neuser and Brian G. Armstrong. Kirkville, Mo.: Sixteenth Century Journal Publishers, 1997: 165-188.
De Savignac, Jean. "Une Réédition du '*De Clementia*' de Jean Calvin." *La Revue Réformée* 21/84 (1970): 39-46.
Detmers, Achim. "Zu den Fragen und Einwürfen irgendeines Juden." In *Calvin-Studienausgabe*, vol. 4. *Reformatorische Klärungen.* Neukirchen: Neukirchener Verlag, 2002: 357-405 (text and translation, 365-405).
DeVries, Dawn. *Jesus Christ in the Preaching of Calvin and Schleiermacher.* Louisville: Westminster/John Knox, 1996.
Diehl, Wilhelm. "Calvins Auslegung des Dekalogs in der ersten Ausgabe seiner *Institutio* und Luthers Katechismen." *Theologische Studien und Kritiken* (1898): 141-162.
Dominicé, Max. *L'humanité de Jésus d'après Calvin.* Paris: Éditions "Je Sers," 1933.

Douglass, Jane Dempsey. "The Image of God in Humanity: A Comparison of Calvin's Teaching in 1536 and 1559." In *In Honor of John Calvin, 1509-64*. Papers from the 1986 International Calvin Symposium. Ed. E. J. Furcha. Montreal: McGill University Press, 1987: 175-203.

Doumergue, Emil. Le *caractère de Calvin: l'homme. le systeme. l'église. l'état*. Neuilly: La Cause, 1931.

— *Jean Calvin: Les hommes et les choses de son temps*. 7 vols. Lausanne: G Bridel, 1899-1927.

Dowey, Edward, Jr. *The Knowledge of God in Calvin's Theology*. Grand Rapids: Eerdmans, 1993.

— "Law in Luther and Calvin." *Theology Today* 41/2 (1984): 146-153.

— "The Third Use of the Law in Calvin's Theology." *Social Progress* 49/3 (1958): 20-27.

Doyle, Robert C. "The Preaching of Repentance in John Calvin: Repentance and Union with Christ." In *God Who is Rich in Mercy: Essays Presented to Dr. D. B. Knox*. Sydney: Moore Theological College, 1986: 287-321.

Droz, Eugénie. *Chemins de l'hérésie: Textes et documents*, vol. 1. Geneva: Slatkine, 1970.

Ebeling, Gerhard. "On the Doctrine of the *Triplex Usus Legis* in the Theology of the Reformation." In *Word and Faith*. Trans. James W. Leitch. London: SCM Press, 1963: 62-78.

Edwards, John. *The Jews in Christian Europe 1400-1700*. London: Routledge, 1988.

Eire, Carlos M. N. *War Against Idols: The Reformation of Worship from Erasmus to Calvin*. Cambridge: Cambridge University Press, 1986.

Elert, Werner. *Law and Gospel*. Philadelphia: Fortress, 1967.

Engammare, Max. "Joannes Calvinus Trium Linguarum Peritus? La Question de l'Hébreu." *Bibliothèque d'Humanisme et Renaissance* 58/1 (1996): 35-60.

Engelsma, David J. "Calvin's Doctrine of the Trinity." *Protestant Reformed Theological Journal* 23 (1989): 19-37.

Engel, Mary Potter. "Calvin and the Jews: A Textual Puzzle." *Princeton Seminary Bulletin*. Supplement 1 (1990): 106-123.

— *John Calvin's Perspectival Anthropology*. Atlanta: Scholars Press, 1988.

— [Potter, Mary Lane]. "The 'Whole Office of the Law' in the Theology of John Calvin." *Journal of Law and Religion* 3/1 (1985): 117-139.

Esser, Hans Helmut. "Zur Anthtopologie Calvins Menschenwürde—Imago dei Zwischen Humanistischem und Theologischem Ansatz." *Hervormde Theologiese Studies* 35/1-2 (1979): 22-40.

Faber, J. *Essays in Reformed Doctrine*. Alberta, Canada: Inheritance Publications, 1990.

Feld, Helmut. "Um die reinere Lehre des Evangeliums: Calvins Kontroverse mit Sadoleto 1539." *Catholica* 36 (1982): 150-180.

Fischer, Danielle. "L'Élément historique dans la prédication de Calvin: Un aspect original de l'homilétique du Réformateur." *Revue d'histoire et de philosophie religieuses* 64/4 (1984): 365-386.

— "Ministères et instruments d'unité de l'Eglise dans la pensée de Luther et de Calvin."

Istina 30 (1985): 8-46.

— "Nouvelles réflexions sur la conversion de Calvin." *Etudes théologiques et religieuses* 58 (1983): 203-220.

Foxgrover, David L. "John Calvin's Understanding of Conscience." PhD dissertation. Claremont Graduate School, 1978.

Fraenkel, P. "Trois passages de l'*Institution* de 1543 et leurs rapports avec les colloques interconfessionnels de 1540-41." In *Calvinus Ecclesiae Genevensis Custos*. Ed. Wilhelm H. Neuser. Frankfurt a. M.: Peter Lang, 1984: 149-157.

Frend, W. H. C. *The Rise of Christianity*. Philadelphia: Fortress Press, 1984.

Friedman, Jerome. *Michael Servetus: A Case Study in Total Heresy*. Genève: Droz, 1978.

— "Michael Servetus: the Case for a Jewish Christianity." *Sixteenth Century Journal* 4/1 (1973): 87-110.

— *The Most Ancient Testimony: Sixteenth-Century Christian-Hebraica in the Age of Renaissance Nostalgia*. Athens, Ohio: Ohio University Press, 1983.

— "Protestants, Jews, and Jewish Sources." In *Piety, Politics, and Ethics: Reformation Studies in Honor of George Wolfgang Forell*. Ed. Carter Lindberg. Kirksville, Mo.: Sixteenth Century Journal Publishers, 1984: 139-156.

— "Sebastian Münster, the Jewish Mission, and Protestant Antisemitism." *Archiv für Reformationsgeschichte* 70 (1979): 238-259.

— "Servetus and the Psalms: The Exegesis of Heresy." In *Histoire de l'exégèse au XVIe siècle: texts du colloque international tenu à Genève en 1976*. Ed. Olivier Fatio and Pierre Fraenkel. Genèva: Droz, 1978: 164-178.

Froehlich, Karlfried. "Johannes Trithemius on the Fourfold Sense of Scripture: The Tractatus de Inuestigatione Sacrae Scripturae (1486)." In *Biblical Interpretation in the Era of the Reformation: Essays Presented to David Steinmetz in Honor of His Sixtieth Birthday*. Ed. Richard A. Muller and John L. Thompson. Grand Rapids: Eerdmans, 1996: 23-60.

Frost, Ronald N. "Aristotle's Ethics: The Real Reason for Luther's Reformation?" *Trinity Journal* 18 (1997): 223-241.

— "'Scholasticism, Reformation, Orthodoxy, and the Persistence of Christian Aristotelianism': A Brief Rejoinder." *Trinity Journal* 19 (1998): 97-101.

Gaffin, Richard B., Jr. "Calvin and the Sabbath." ThM thesis, Westminster Theological Seminary, 1962.

Gamble, Richard C. "Calvin and Sixteenth-Century Spirituality: Comparison with the Anabaptists." In *Calvin Studies Society Papers, 1995, 1997: Calvin and Spirituality, Calvin and His Contemporaries*. Ed. David Foxgrover. Grand Rapids: CRC Product Services, 1998: 31-51.

— "Calvin as Theologian and Exegete: Is There Anything New?" *Calvin Theological Journal* 23 (1998): 178-194.

Ganoczy, Alexandre. *Ecclesia Ministrans: dienende Kirche und kirchlicher Dienst bei Calvin*. Freiburg: Herder, 1968.

— *The Young Calvin*. Trans. David Foxgrover and Wade Provo. Philadelphia: Westminster Press, 1987.

Ganoczy, Alexandre and Scheld, Stefan. *Die Hermeneutik Calvins: geistesgeschichtliche Voraussetzungen und Grundzüge*. Wiesbaden: Franz Steiner Verlag, 1983.

— *Herrschaft – Tugend – Vorsehung: hermeneutische Deutung und Veröffentlichung handschriftlicher Annotationen Calvins zu sieben Senecatragödien und der Pharsalia Lucans*. Wiesbaden: Franz Steiner Verlag, 1982.

George, Timothy. "Calvin's Psychopannychia: Another Look." In *In Honor of John Calvin, 1509-64*. Papers from the 1986 International Calvin Symposium. Ed. E. J. Furcha. Montreal: McGill University Press, 1987: 297-329.

Gerrish, Brian A. *Grace and Reason. A Study of the Theology of Luther*. Oxford: Clarendon Press, 1962.

Gessert, Robert A. "The Integrity of Faith: An Inquiry into the Meaning of the Law in the Thought of John Calvin." *Scottish Journal of Theology* 13/3(1960): 247-261.

Gilby, Thomas. Trans. and notes. *Saint Thomas Aquinas: Philosophical Texts*. Oxford: Oxford University Press, 1967.

Gilmont, Jean-François and Peter, Rodolphe. *Bibliotheca Calviniana: Les œuvres de Jean Calvin publiées au XVIe siècle*. 3 vols. Gèneve: Droz, 1991-2000.

Gilmore, Myron P. *Humanists and Jurists: Six Studies in Renaissance*. Cambridge, Mass.: Harvard University Press, 1963.

Girardin, Benoît. *Rhétorique et Théologique: Calvin, Le Commentaire de l'Épître aux Romains*. Paris: Beauchesne, 1979.

Gloede, Günter. *Theologia Naturalis bei Calvin*. Stuttgart: Verlag von W. Kohlhammer, 1935.

Graafland, Cornelis. "Alter und neuer Bund: Calvins Auslegung von Jeremia 31, 31-34 und Hebräer 8, 8-13." In *Reformiertes Erbe: Festschrift für Gottfried W. Locher zu seinem 80. Geburtstag*, vol. 2. Zürich: Theologischer Verlag, 1993: 127-145.

— "Hat Calvin einen Ordo salutis gelehrt?" In *Calvinus Ecclesiae Genevensis Custos*. Ed. Wilhelm H. Neuser. Frankfurt a. M.: Peter Lang, 1984: 221-244.

Grin, Edmond. "L'unité des deux Testaments selon Calvin." *Theologische Zeitschrift* 17 (1961): 175-186.

Grislis, Egil. "Calvin's Use of Cicero in the *Institutes* I:1-5: A Case Study in Theological Method." *Archiv für Reformationsgeschichte* 62/1 (1971): 5-37.

— "Seneca and Cicero as Possible Sources of John Calvin's View of Double Predestination: An Inquiry in the History of Ideas." In *In Honor of John Calvin, 1509-64*. Papers from the 1986 International Calvin Symposium. Ed. E. J. Furcha. Montreal: McGill University Press, 1987: 28-63.

Hall, Basil. "Calvin and Biblical Humanism," *Huguenot Society Proceedings* 20 (1959-64): 195-209.

— *Humanists and Protestants 1500-1900*. Edinburgh: T & T Clark, 1990

— "John Calvin, the Jurisconsults and the *Ius Civile*." In *Studies in Church History*, vol. 3. Ed. G. J. Cuming. Leiden: E. J. Brill, 1966: 202-216.

Harnack, Adolph. *History of Dogma*, vol. 4. New York: Dover Publications, 1961.

Harrington, Joel F. *Reordering Marriage and Society in Reformation Germany*. Cambridge: Cambridge University Press, 1995.

Hart, Trevor. "Humankind in Christ and Christ in Humankind: Salvation as Participation in Our Substitute in the Theology of John Calvin." *Scottish Journal of Theology* 42 (1989): 67-84.

Haas, Guenther H. *The Concept of Equity in Calvin's Ethics*. Canada: Wilfred Laurier University Press, 1977.

Hausammann, Susi. *Römerbriefauslegung zwischen Humanismus und Reformation: Eine Studie zu Heinrich Bullingers Römerbriefauslegung von 1525*. Zürich: Zwingli Verlag, 1970.

Helm, Paul. "Calvin and Bernard on Freedom and Necessity: A Reply to Brümmer." *Religious Studies* 30 (1994): 457-465.

— "Calvin and Natural Law." *Scottish Bulletin of Evangelical Theology* 2 (1984): 5-22.

— *Calvin and the Calvinists*. Edinburgh: Banner of Truth, 1982.

Heppe, Heinrich. *Reformed Dogmatics: Set Out and Illustrated from the Sources*. Ed. Ernst Bizer. Trans. G. T. Thomson. London: George Allen & Unwin, 1950.

— *Schriften für reformirten Theologie*, vol. 2. *Die Dogmatik der evangelisch-reformirten Kirche*. Elberfeld: Verlag von R. L. Friderichs, 1861.

Hesselink, I. John. *Calvin's Concept of the Law*. Allison Park, Pa.: Pickwick Publications, 1992.

— *Calvin's First Catechism, A Commentary: Featuring Ford Lewis Battles' translation of the 1538 Catechism*. Westminster/John Knox: Louisville, 1997.

— "Calvin, Theologian of Sweetness." *Calvin Theological Journal* 37 (2002): 318-332.

— "Calvin's Understanding of the Relation of the Church and Israel Based Largely on His Interpretation of Romans 9-11." *Ex Auditu* 4 (1988): 59-69.

— "Christ, the Law, and the Christian: An Unexplored Aspect of the Third Use of the Law in Calvin's Theology." In *Reformatio Perennis. Essays on Calvin and the Reformation in Honor of Ford Lewis Battles*. Ed. B. A. Gerrish. Pittsburgh: Pickwick Press, 1981: 11-26.

— "Law and Gospel or Gospel and Law? Calvin's Understanding of the Relationship." In *Calviniana: Ideas and Influence of Jean Calvin*. Ed. Robert V. Schnucker. Kirksville, Mo.: Sixteenth Century Essays & Studies, 1988: 13-32.

— "Luther and Calvin on Law and Gospel in Their Galatians Commentaries." *Reformed Review* 37/2: 69-82.

Higman, Francis M. "Farel, Calvin et Olivétan, sources de spiritualité gallicans." In *Actes du Colloque Guillaume Farel*, vol. 1. *Communications*. Ed. Pierre Barthel, Remy Scheurer, Richard Stauffer. Geneve: Revue de théologie et de philosophie, 1983: 45-61.

Hillerbrand, Hans J. "Martin Luther and the Jews." In *Jews and Christians: Exploring the Past, Present, and Future*. Ed. James H. Charlesworth. New York: Crossroad, 1990: 127-150.

Hobbs, R. Gerald. "*Hebraica Veritas* and *Traditio Apostolica*: Saint Paul and the Interpretation of the Psalms in the Sixteenth Century." In *The Bible in the Sixteenth Century*. Ed. David C. Steinmetz. Durham, N.C.: Duke University Press, 1990: 83-99.

— "Martin Bucer on Psalm 22: A Study in the Application of Rabbinic Exegesis by a Christian Hebraist." In *Histoire de l'exégèse au XVIe siècle: Textes du Colloque*

International Tenu à Genève en 1976. Ed. Olivier Fatio and Pierre Fraenkel. Genève: Droz, 1978: 144-163.

Hoekema, Anthony A. "The Covenant of Grace in Calvin's Teaching." *Calvin Theological Journal* 2/2 (1967): 133-161.

Hoitenga, Dewey J., Jr. *John Calvin and the Will: A Critique and Corrective.* Grand Rapids: Baker, 1997.

Holler, Z. N. "Calvin's Exegesis of the Sermon on the Mount." In *Calvin Studies III.* Ed. John H. Leith. Richmond: Union Theological Seminary, 1986: 5-20.

Hughes, Philip E. "Jacques Lefévre d'Etaples (c. 1455-1536). Calvin's Forerunner in France." In *Calvinus Reformator.* Potchefstroom: Potchefstroom University for Christian Higher Education, 1982: 93-108.

— *Lefèvre: Pioneer of Ecclesiastical Renewal in France.* Grand Rapids: Eerdmans, 1984.

— "Some Observations on the History of the Interpretation of Holy Scripture." In *Church, Word, and Spirit: Historical and Theological Essays in Honor of Geoffrey W. Bromiley.* Ed. James E. Bradley and Richard A. Muller. Grand Rapids: Eerdmans, 1987: 93-106.

— Ed. and trans. *The Register of the Company of Pastors of Geneva in the Time of Calvin.* Grand Rapids: Eerdmans, 1966.

Hyma, Albert. *The Christian Renaissance: A History of the "Devotio Moderna."* 2nd ed. Hamden, Conn.: Archon Books, 1965.

Imbart de la Tour, Pierre. *Les Origines de la Réforme*, vol. 4. *Calvin et l'Institution Chrétienne.* Paris: Firmin-Didot, 1935.

Jansen, J. F. *Calvin's Doctrine of the Work of Christ.* London: James Clarke, 1956.

Jedin, Hubert. *A History of the Council of Trent.* 2 vols. London: Thomas Nelson, 1957-1958.

Joest, Wilfried. *Gesetz und Freiheit: Das Problems des tertius usus legis bei Luther und die Neutestementiliche Parainess.* 2nd ed. Göttingen: Vandenhoeck & Ruprecht, 1956.

Johnson, Merwyn S. "Calvin's Ethical Legacy," In *The Legacy of John Calvin: Papers Presented at the 12th Colloquium of the Calvin Studies Society (1999).* Ed. David Foxgrover. Grand Rapids: CRC Product Services, 2002: 63-83.

— "Calvin's Handling of the Third Use of the Law and Its Problems." In *Calviniana: Ideas and Influence of Jean Calvin.* Ed. Robert V. Schnucker. Kirksville, Mo.: Sixteenth Century Essays & Studies, 1988: 33-50.

Jones, Serene. *Calvin and the Rhetoric Piety.* Louisville: Westminster/John Knox, 1995.

Kelly, Donald R. *Foundations of Modern Historical Scholarship: Language, Law, and History in the French Renaissance.* New York: Columbia University Press, 1970.

Kendall, R. T. *Calvin and English Calvinism to 1649.* New York: HarperSanFrancisco, 1978.

Kerridge, Eric. *Usury, Interest and the Reformation.* Aldershot: Ashgate, 2002.

Kevan, Ernest F. *The Grace of Law: A Study in Puritan Theology.* London: Carey Kingsgate Press, 1964.

Kingdon, Robert M. *Adultery and Divorce in Calvin's Geneva.* London: Harvard University Press, 1995.

—"Calvin and Constitutionalism: His Work on the Laws of Geneva." *Pacific Theological Review* 19/1 (1985): 40-53.

—"Calvin and the Establishment of Consistory Discipline in Geneva: The Institution and the Men Who Directed it." *Nederlands Archief voor Kerkgeschiedenis* 70 (1990): 158-172.

—"*Calvinus Legislator*: The 1543 'Constitution' of the City-State of Geneva." In *Calvinus Servus Christi*. Ed. Wilhelm H. Neuser. Budapest: Presseabteilung des Ráday-Kollegiums, 1988: 225-232.

Kingdon, Robert M, General Editor. Lambert, Thomas A. and McDonald, M. Wallace, Editors. *Registers of the Consistory of Geneva in the Time of Calvin*, vol. 1. *1542-1544*. Grand Rapids: Eerdmans, 2000.

Klempa, William. "Calvin and Natural Law." In *Calvin Studies IV*. Ed. John H. Leith and W. Stacey Johnson. Davidson, N.C.: Davidson College Presbyterian Church, 1988: 72-95.

Kraus, Hans-Joachim. "Calvin's Exegetical Principles." *Interpretation* 31/1 (1977): 8-18.

—"Israel in the Theology of Calvin—Towards a New Approach to the Old Testament and Judaism." *Christian Jewish Relations* 22 (1989): 75-86.

Krodel, Gottfried G. "Law, Order, and the Almighty Taler: The Empire in Action at the 1530 Diet of Augsburg." *Sixteenth Century Journal* 12/2 (1982): 75-106.

Krusche, Werner. *Das Wirken des Heiligen Geistes nach Calvin*. Göttingen: Vandenhoeck & Ruprecht, 1957.

Lane, Anthony N. S. "Calvin and Article 5 of the Regensburg Colloquy." Unpub. Presented at International Calvin Congress (Princeton, 2002). Forthcoming in *Calvinus Praeceptor Ecclesiae*. Ed. Herman Selderhuis (Genève: Droz, 2004): 231-261.

—*Calvin and Bernard of Clairvaux*. Studies in Reformed Theology and History New Series, no. 1. Princeton: Princeton Theological Seminary, 1996.

—"Did Calvin Believe in Free Will?" *Vox Evangelica* 12 (1981): 72-90.

—*John Calvin Student of the Church Fathers*. Grand Rapids: Baker, 1999.

—*Justification by Faith in Catholic-Protestant Dialogue: An Evangelical Assessment*. Edinburgh: T & T Clark, 2002.

Lang, A. "Die Bekehrung Johannes Calvins." *Studien zur Geschichte der Theologie und der Kirche* 2 (1897): 1-56.

—*Der Evangelienkommentar Martin Butzers und die Grundzüge seiner Theologie. Studien zur Geschichte der Theologie und der Kirche, 2/2*. Leipzig: 1900; repr. Aalen: Scientia, 1972.

—"The Reformation and Natural law." In *Calvin and the Reformation*. Ed. William P. Armstrong, repr. Grand Rapids: Baker, 1980: 56-98.

—"The Sources of Calvin's *Institutes* of 1536." *Evangelical Quarterly* 8 (1936): 130-141.

Laver, Mary Sweetland. "Calvin, Jews, and Intra-Christian Polemics." PhD dissertation. Temple University, 1988.

Lazareth, William H. "Love and Law in Christian Life." In *Piety, Politics, and Ethics:*

Reformation Studies in Honor of George Wolfgang Forell. Ed. Carter Lindberg. Kirksville, Mo.: Sixteenth Century Journal Publishers, 1984: 103-117.

Lecoultre, H. "La Conversion de Calvin," *Revue de théologie et de philosophie* (1890): 5-30.

Le Gal, Patrick. *Le droit canonique dans la pensée dialectique de Jean Calvin*. Fribourg: Editions Universitaires, 1984.

Leith, John H. "Creation and Redemption: Law and Gospel in the Theology of John Calvin." In *Marburg Revisited: A Re-examination of Lutheran and Reformed Traditions*. Ed. Paul C. Empie and James I. McCord. Minneapolis: Augsburg Pub., 1966: 141-152.

—*John Calvin's Doctrine of the Christian Life*. Louisville: Westminster/John Knox, 1989.

Leithart, Peter J. "Stoic Elements in Calvin's Doctrine of the Christian Life: Part II. Mortification." *Westminster Theological Journal* 55 (1993): 191-208.

—"That Eminent Pagan: Calvin's Use of Cicero in *Institutes* 1.1-5." *Westminster Theological Journal* 52 (1990): 1-12.

Letham, Robert. "Faith and Assurance in Early Calvinism: A Model of Continuity and Diversity." In *Later Calvinism: International Perspectives*. Ed. W. Fred Graham. Kirksville, Mo.: Sixteenth Century Essays & Studies: 355-384.

Lillback, Peter A. *The Binding of God: Calvin's Role in the Development of Covenant Theology*. Grand Rapids: Baker, 2001.

Little, David. "Calvin and Prospects for a Christian Theory of Natural Law." In *Norm and Context in Christian Ethics*. Ed. Gene H. Outka and Paul Ramsey. New York: Charles Scribner's Sons, 1968: 175-197.

—"Natural Law Revisited: James Luther Adams and Beyond." *Union Seminary Quarterly Review* 37/3 (1982): 217-228.

Lobstein, P. *Die Ethik Calvins in ihren Grundzügen entworfen: Ein Beitrag zur Geschichte der Christlichen Ethik*. Strasbourg: C. F. Schmidt, 1877.

Locher, Gottfried W. "Calvin Spricht zu den Juden." *Theologische Zeitschrift* 23 (1967): 180-196.

—"The Shape of Zwingli's Theology: A Comparison with Luther and Calvin." *Pittsburgh Perspective* 8 (1967): 5-26.

—"Zwingli between Luther and Calvin: Reformation of Faith, Community, and Church." In *Huldrych Zwingli, 1484-1531: A Legacy of Radical Reform*. Papers from the 1984 International Zwingli Symposium. Ed. E. J. Furcha. Montreal: McGill University, 1985: 13-33.

Macleod, Donald. "Living the Christian Life: Luther and Calvin on the Place of the Law." In *Living the Christian Life*. Papers read at Westminster Conference. Huntingdon, U. K., 1974: 5-13.

Manschreck, Clyde L. "The Role of Melanchthon in the Adiaphora Controversy." *Archiv für Reformationsgeschichte* 48/1 (1957): 165-182.

Marie, C. P. "Calvin's God and Humanism." In *Our Reformation Tradition: A Rich Heritage and Lasting Vocation*. Potchefstroom: Potchefstroom University for Christian High Education, 1984: 353-365.

Matter, E. Ann. "The Church Fathers and the *Glossa Ordinaria*." In *The Reception of the Church Fathers in the West: From the Carolingians to the Maurists*. 2 vols. Ed. Irena Backus. Leiden: E. J. Brill, 1997: 83-111.

McCoy, Charles S. and Baker, J. Wayne. *Fountainhead of Federalism: Heinrich Bullinger and the Covenant Tradition with a Translation of De testamento seu foedere Dei unico et aeterno (1534) by Heinrich Bullinger*. Louisville: Westminster/John Knox Press.

McDonough, Thomas. *The Law and Gospel in Luther*. London: Oxford University Press, 1963.

McGiffert, Michael. "From Moses to Adam: The Making of the Covenant of Works." *Sixteenth Century Journal* 19/2 (1988): 129-155.

— "Grace and Works: The Rise and Division of Covenant Divinity in Elizabethan Puritanism." *Harvard Theological Review* 75 (1982): 463-502.

McGrath, Alister E. "Homo Assumptus? A Study in the Christology of the *Via Moderna*, with Particular Reference to William of Ockham." *Ephemerides Theologicae Lovanienses* 60 (1984): 283-297.

— "Humanist Elements in the Early Reformed Doctrine of Justification." *Archiv für Reformationsgeschichte* 73 (1982): 4-20.

— *The Intellectual Origins of the European Reformation*. Grand Rapids: Baker, 1987.

— *Iustitia Dei: A History of the Christian Doctrine of Justification*. 2nd ed. Cambridge: Cambridge University Press, 1998.

— *A Life of John Calvin: A Study in the Shaping of Western Culture*. Oxford: Blackwell Publishers, 1990.

— *Luther's Theology of the Cross: Martin Luther's Theological Breakthrough*. Oxford: Basil Blackwell, 1985.

— *Reformation Thought: An Introduction*. 2nd ed. Grand Rapids: Baker, 1993.

McKane, W. "Calvin as an Old Testament Commentator." *Nederduitse Gereformierde Teologiese Tydskrif* 25 (1984): 205-50.

McKee, Elsie. "Calvin's 1536 *Institutes*: The Church's Book." In *Calvin Studies III*. Ed. John H. Leith. Richmond: Union Theological Seminary, 1986: 33-38.

McNeil, David O. *Guillaume Budé and Humanism in the Reign of Francis I*. Genève: Droz, 1975.

McNeill, John T. "The Democratic Elements in Calvin's Thought." *Church History* 18/3 (1949): 153-171.

— *The History and Character of Calvinism*. New York: Oxford University Press, 1954.

— "Natural Law in the Teaching of the Reformers." *Journal of Religion* 26 (1946): 168-182.

Meylan, Edward A. "The Stoic Doctrine of Indifferent Things and the Conception of Christian Liberty in Calvin's *Institutio Religionis Christianae*." *Romanic Review* 28 (1937): 135-145.

Millet, Olivier. *Calvin et la dynamique de la Parole: Etude de rhétorique réformée*. Genève: Editions Slatkine, 1992.

— "Le premier 'Catéchisme' de Genève (1537/1538) et sa place dans l'oeuvre de Calvin." In *Catéchismes et Confessions de foi*. Ed. Jean Boisset. Montpellier:

Université de Montpellier, 1995: 209-229.
— "Rendre raison de la foi: Le Catéchisme de Calvin (1542)." In *Aux origins du catéchisme en France*. Ed. Pierre Colin. Paris: Desclée, 1989: 188-203.
— "Le thème de la conscience libre chez Calvin." In *La liberté de conscience (XVIe - XVIIe siècles)*. Ed. Hans R. Guggisberg, Frank Lestringant, and Jean-Claude Margolin. Genève: Droz, 1991: 21-37.
Monheit, Michael L. "Guillaume Budé, Andrea Alciato, Pierre de l'Estoile: Renaissance Interpreters of Roman Law." *Journal of the History of Ideas* 58/1 (1997): 21-40.
— "Passion and Order in the Formation of Calvin's Sense of Religious Authority." PhD dissertation. Princeton Seminary, 1988.
— "Young Calvin, Textual Interpretation and Roman Law." *Bibliothèque d'Humanisme et Renaissance* 59/2(1997): 263-282.
Monter, E. William. *Calvin's Geneva*. New York: John Wiley & Sons, 1967.
Moreau, Pierre-François. "Le Stoicisme aux XVII et XVIII siècles: Calvin et le Stoicisme." In *Cahiers de Philosophie et Juridique*. Caen: Publications de l'Université de Caen, 1994: 11-23.
Muller, Richard A. "Biblical Interpretation in the Era of the Reformation." In *Biblical Interpretation in the Era of the Reformation: Essays Presented to David Steinmetz in Honor of His Sixtieth Birthday*. Ed. Richard A. Muller and John L. Thompson. Grand Rapids: Eerdmans, 1996: 3-22.
— *Christ and the Decree: Christology and Predestination in Reformed Theology from Calvin to Perkins*. Grand Rapids: Baker, 1988.
— "The Covenant of Works and the Stability of Divine Law in Seventeenth-Century Reformed Orthodoxy: A Study in the Theology of Herman Witsius and Wilhelmus à Brakel." *Calvin Theological Journal* 29 (1994): 75-100.
— "*Fides* and *Cognitio* in Relation to the Problem of Intellect and Will in the Theology of John Calvin." *Calvin Theological Journal* 25/2 (1990): 207-224.
— "The Hermeneutic of Promise and Fulfillment in Calvin's Exegesis of the Old Testament Prophecies of the Kingdom." In *The Bible in the Sixteenth Century*. Ed. David C. Steinmetz. Durham, N.C.: Duke University Press, 1990: 68-82.
— *Post-Reformation Reformed Dogmatics, vol. 2. Holy Scripture: The Cognitive Foundation of Theology*. Grand Rapids: Baker, 1993.
— "Scholasticism, Reformation, Orthodoxy, and the Persistence of Christian Aristotelianism." *Trinity Journal* 19/1 (1998): 81-96.
— *The Unaccommodated Calvin*. Oxford: Oxford University Press, 2000.
Müller, Denis. *Puissance de la Loi et limite du Pouvoir*. Paris: Èditions Michalon, 2001.
Müller, K. "Calvins Bekehrung." Nachrichten von der (Königlichen) Gesellschaft der Wissenschaft zu Göttingen (1905): 188-255.
Müller, Richard. *Adventisten – Sabbat – Reformation: Geht das Ruhetagsverständnis der Adventisten bis auf die Zeit der Reformation Zurück? Eine Theologiegeschichtliche Untersuchung*. Malmö, Sweden: GWK, 1979.
Naphy, William G. *Calvin and the Consolidation of the Genevan Reformation*. Manchester: Manchester University Press, 1994.
Neuser, Wilhelm H. "Calvin's Conversion to Teachableness." In *Calvin and Christian*

Ethics. Ed. Peter de Klerk. Grand Rapids: Calvin Studies Society, 1987: 57-77.
— "Calvins Urteil über den Rechtfertigungsartikel des Regensburger Buches." In *Reformation und Humanismus.* Ed. M. Greschat and J. F. G. Goeters. Witten: Luther-Verlag, 1969: 176-194.
— "The Development of the *Institutes* 1536 to 1559." In *John Calvin's Institutes: His Opus Magnum.* Ed. Bahrend Johannes van der Walt et al. Potchefstroom: Institute for Reformational Studies, 1986: 33-54.
Newman, Louis I. *Jewish Influence on Christian Reform Movements.* New York, Columbia University Pressw, 1925.
Niesel, Wilhelm. "Calvin wider Osianders Rechtfertigungslehre." *Zeitschrift für Kirchengeschichte* 46 (1927), 410-430.
— "Descriptio et historia editionum Institutionis latinarum et gallicarum Calvino vivo emissarum." In *Johannis Calvini Opera Selecta* 3: vi-l.
— *Die Theologie Calvins.* 2nd ed. München: Chr. Kaiser Verlag, 1957.
— *The Theology of Calvin.* Trans. Harold Knight. Philadelphia: Westminster Press, 1956.
Nijenhuis, W. *Ecclesia Reformata: Studies on the Reformation.* Leiden: E. J. Brill, 1972.
Oakely, Francis. "The Absolute and Ordained Power of God in Sixteenth-and Seventeenth-Century Theology." *Journal of the History of Ideas* 59/3 (1988): 437-461.
Obendiek, Harmannus. "Die Institutio Calvins als 'Confessio' und 'Apologie'." In *Theologische Aufsätze: Karl Barth zum 50. Geburstag.* München: Chr. Kaiser Verlag, 1936: 417-431.
Oberman, Heiko A. *The Dawn of the Reformation: Essays in Late Medieval and Early Reformation Thought.* Grand Rapids: Eerdmans, 1992.
— "*Facientibus Quod in se est Deus non Denegat Gratiam*: Robert Holcot O. P. and the Beginnings of Luther's Theology." *Harvard Theological Review* 55 (1962): 317-342.
— *The Harvest of Medieval Theology: Gabriel Biel and Later Medieval Nominalism.* Repr. Durham, N.C.: Labyrinth Press, 1983.
— *The Impact of the Reformation.* Grand Rapids: Eerdmans, 1994.
— "*Initia Calvini*: The Matrix of Calvin's Reformation." In *Calvinus Sacrae Scripturae Professor: Calvin as Confessor of Holy Scripture.* Ed. Wilhelm H. Neuser. Grand Rapids: Eerdmans, 1994: 113-154.
— *The Reformation: Roots and Ramifications.* Trans. Andrew Colin Gow. Grand Rapids: Eerdmans, 1994.
— *The Roots of Anti-Semitism in the Age of Renaissance and Reformation.* Trans. James I. Porter. Philadelphia: Fortress Press, 1984.
— "*Subita Conversio*: The Conversion of John Calvin." In *Reformiertes Erbe: Festschrift für Gottfried W. Locher zu Seinem 80. Geburtstag,* vol. 2. Zwingliana, 19/1-2. Ed. Heiko A. Oberman, Ernst Saxer, Alfred Schindler, and Heinzpeter Stucki. Zürich: Theologischer Verlag, 1992-1993, 2:279-295.
Olson, Jeannine E. "The Friends of John Calvin: the Budé Family." In *Calvin Studies Society Papers, 1995, 1997: Calvin and Spirituality, Calvin and His Contemporaries.* Ed. David Foxgrover. Grand Rapids: CRC Product Services, 1998: 159-168.

Opitz, Peter. *Calvins Theologische Hermeneutik*. Neukirchen: Neukirchener Verlag, 1994.
Ozment, Steve. *The Age of Reform 1250-1550: An Intellectual and Religious History of Late Medieval and Reformation Europe*. New Haven: Yale University Press, 1980.
Pancaro, Severino. *The Law in the Fourth Gospel: The Torah and the Gospel, Moses and Jesus, Judaism and Christianity according to John*. Leiden: E. J. Brill, 1975.
Pannier, Jacques. *Recherches sur la formation intellectuelle de Calvin*. Paris: Librairie Alcan, 1931.
Parker, T. H. L. *Calvin: An Introduction to His Thought*. Louisville: Westminster/John Knox, 1995.
— *Calvin's New Testament Commentaries*. Louisville: Westminster/John Knox, 1993.
— *Calvin's Old Testament Commentaries*. 2nd ed. Louisville: Westminster/John Knox, 1993.
— *Commentaries on Romans 1532-1542*. Edinburgh: T & T Clark, 1986.
— *The Doctrine of the Knowledge of God*. Rev. ed. Grand Rapids: Eerdmans, 1959.
— *John Calvin: A Biography*. Philadelphia: Westminster Press, 1975.
Partee, Charles B. *Calvin and Classical Philosophy*. Leiden: E. J. Brill, 1977.
— "Calvin and Determinism." *Christian Scholar's Review* 5/2 (1975): 123-128.
— "Calvin's Central Dogma Again." In *Calvin Studies III*. Ed. John H. Leith. Richmond: Union Theological Seminary, 1986: 39-46.
— "Farel's Influence on Calvin: A Prolusion." In *Actes du Colloque Guillaume Farel*, vol. 1. *Communications*. Ed. Pierre Barthel, Remy Scheurer, Richard Stauffer. Geneve: Revue de théologie et de philosophie, 1983: 173-185.
Pater, Calvin Augustine. "Calvin, the Jews and the Judaic Legacy." In *In Honor of John Calvin, 1509-64*. Papers from the 1986 International Calvin Symposium. Ed. E. J. Furcha. Montreal: McGill University Press, 1987: 256-295.
Pauck, Wilhelm. "Calvin and Butzer." *Journal of Religion* 9/2 (1929): 237-256.
Payton, James R. "Calvin and the Legitimation of Icons: His Treatment of the Seventh Ecumenical Council." *Archiv für Reformationsgeschichte* 84 (1993): 222-241.
Pelikan, Jaroslav. *The Christian Tradtion: A History of the Development of Doctrine*, vol. 4. *Reformation of Church and Dogma (1300-1700)*. Chicago: University of Chicago Press, 1984.
Pelkonen, J. Peter. "The Teaching of John Calvin on the Nature and Function of the Conscience." *Lutheran Quarterly* 21/1 (1969): 74-88.
Peterson, Robert A. *Calvin's Doctrine of the Atonement*. Phillipsburg, N.J.: Presbyterian and Reformed Publishing, 1983.
Pfisterer, Ernst. *Calvins Wirken in Genf*. Neukirchen: Neukirchener Verlag, 1957: 29-63.
Phillips, Darryl. "An Inquiry into the Extent of the Abilities of John Calvin as a Hebraist." D. Phil. dissertation. Oxford University, 1998.
Primus, John H. "Sunday: The Lord's Day as a Sabbath—Protestant Perspectives on the Sabbath." In *The Sabbath in Jewish and Christian Traditions*. Ed. Tamara C. Eskenazi. New York: Crossroad, 1991: 98-121.
Puckett, David L. *John Calvin's Exegesis of the Old Testament*. Louisville: Westminster/John Knox, 1995.

Quack, Jürgen. "Calvins Bibelvorreden (1535-1546)." In *Evangelische Bibelvorreden von der Reformation bis zur Aufklärung*. Gütersloh: Gütersloher, 1975: 89-116.

Quistorp, Heinrich. *Calvin's Doctrine of the Last Things*. Trans. Harold Knight. Richmond: John Knox Press, 1955.

Raitt, J. "Calvin's Use of Persona." In *Calvinus Ecclesiae Genevensis Custos*. Ed. Wilhelm H. Neuser. Frankfurt a. M.: Peter Lang, 1984: 273-287.

— "The Person of the Mediator: Calvin's Christology and Beza's Fidelity." *Occasional Papers of the Society for Reformation Research*, vol. 1 (1977): 53-80.

Reid, W. Stanford. "John Calvin, Lawyer and Legal Reformer." In *Through Christ's Work: A Festschrift for Dr. Philip E. Hughes*. Ed. W. Robert Godfrey and Jesse L. Boyd III. Phillipsburg, N.J.: Presbyterian and Reformed Publishing, 1985: 149-164.

Reulos, Michel. "Les Juristes: En Contact avec Calvin." In *Calvin et ses contemporains*. Ed. Olivier Millet. Genève: Droz, 1998: 213-218.

Reuss, E. "Fragments littéraires relatifs à l'histoire de la Bible française." *Revue de théologie* 3 (1865): 217-252, and 4 (1866): 1-48, 281-322.

Reuter, Karl. *Grundverständnis der Theologie Calvins: Unter Einbeziehung ihrer geschichtlichen Abhängigkeiten*. Neukirchen: Neukirchener Verlag, 1963.

Richard, Lucien Joseph. *The Spirituality of John Calvin*. Atlanta: John Knox Press, 1974.

Rilliet, Albert. "Notice Historique." In *Le Catéchisme Français de Calvin publié en 1537, réimprimé pour la première fois d'après un exemplaire nouvellement retrouvé, et suivi de la plus ancienne Confession de foi de l'église de Genève, avec deux notices*. Ed. Albert Rilliet and Théophile Dufour. Genève, 1878: 5-98.

Ritschl, Dietrich. "Some Comments on the Background and Influence of Augustine's Lex Aeterna Doctrine." In *Creation Christ and Culture: Studies in Honour of T. F. Torrance*. Ed. Richard W. A. McKinney. Edinburgh: T & T Clark, 1976: 63-81.

Robinson, Jack Hughs. *John Calvin and the Jews*. American University Studies, series 7. Theology and Religion, vol. 123. New York: Peter Lang, 1992.

Rogers, Jack B. & McKim, Donald K. *The Authority and Interpretation of the Bible*. New York: Harper & Row, 1979.

Rohls, Jan. *Reformed Confessions: Theology from Zurich to Barmen*. Trans. John Hoffmeyer. Louisville: Westminster/John Knox, 2000.

Röthlisberger, Hugo. *Kirche am Sinai. Die Zehn Gebote in der Christlichen Unterweisung*. Zürich: Zwingli Verlag, 1965.

Rott, Jean. "Documents strasbourgeois concernant Calvin." *Revue d'histoire et de philosophie religieuses* 44 (1964): 290-311 (including text, "Un Manuscrit autographe: La Harangue du recteur Nicolas Cop," 305-311).

Roussel, Bernard. "Francois Lambert, Pierre Caroli, Guillaume Farel ... Et Jean Calvin (1530-1536)." In *Calvinus servus Christi*. Congrès International des Recherches Calviniennes (1986). Ed. Wilhelm H. Neuser. Budapest: Presseabteilung Des Ráday-Kollegiums, 1988: 35-52.

Russell, S. H. "Calvin and the Messianic Interpretation of the Psalms." *Scottish Journal of Theology* 21 (1968): 37-47.

Salley, Louise L. "A French Humanist's Chef-d'Oeuvre: The Commentaries on Seneca's

'*De Clementia*' by John Calvin." *Renaissance Papers* (1968): 41-53.
Santmire, H. Paul. "Justification in Calvin's 1540 Romans Commentary." *Church History* 33 (1964): 294-313.
Saxer, Ernst. "Calvins Vorrede zur Olivetanbibel (1535)." In *Calvin-Studienausgabe*, vol. 1/1. *Reformatorische Anfänge (1533-1541)*. Neukirchen: Neukirchener Verlag, 1994: 27-57 (text and translation, 34-57).
Scheld, Stefan. *Media Salutis: Zur Heilsvermittlung bei Calvin*. Stuttgart: Franz Steiner Verlag, 1989.
Schellong, Dieter. *Calvins Auslegung der synoptischen Evangelien*. München: Chr. Kaiser Verlag, 1968.
— *Das evangelische Gesetz in der Auslegung Calvins*. München: Chr. Kaiser Verlag, 1948.
Schlingenseipen, Hermann. *Die Auslegung der Bergpredigt bei Calvin*. Berlin: Emil Ebering, 1928.
Scholl, Hans. "Nicolaus Cop—Pariser Rektoratsrede vom. 1. November 1533." In *Calvin-Studienausgabe*, vol. 1/1. *Reformatorische Anfänge (1533-1541)*. Neukirchen: Neukirchener Verlag, 1994: 1-25 (text and translation, 10-25).
Schreiner, Susan. "Calvin's Use of Natural Law." In *A Preserving Grace: Protestants, Catholics, and Natural Law*. Ed. Michael Cromartie. Grand Rapids: Eerdmans, 1997: 51-76.
— "Exegesis and Double Justice in Calvin's Sermons on Job." *Church History* 58/3 (1989): 322-338.
— *The Theater of His Glory: Nature and the Natural Order in the Thought of John Calvin*. Studies in Historical Theology 3. Durham, N.C.: Labyrinth Press, 1991.
Schümmer, Léopold. "Le Mystère d'Israël et de l'Église, postérité d'Abraham." *Irénikon* 1988/2: 207-242.
— "Le Sabbat, le Dimanche: Un jour pour Dieu, un jour pour l'homme." *Revue Réformée* 45/181 (1994): 39-51.
Schurb, Ken. "Sixteenth-Century Lutheran–Calvinist Conflict on the Protevangelium." *Concordia Theological Quarterly* 54/1 (1990): 25-47.
Schwendemann, Wilhelm. *Leib und Seele bei Calvin: Die erkenntnistheoretische und anthropologische Funktion des platonischen Leib-Seele-Dualismus in Calvins Theologie*. Stuttgart: Calwer Verlag, 1996.
Seebaβ, Gottfried. "Osiander, Andreas." In *The Oxford Encyclopedia of the Reformation*, vol. 3. Ed. Hans J. Hillerbrand. Oxford: Oxford University Press, 1996: 183b-185a.
Seeberg, Reinhold. *Textbook of the History of Doctrines*, 2 vols. Grand Rapids: Baker, 1952.
Selderhuis, Herman J. "Calvin as an Asylum Seeker." In *Calvin's Books: Festschrift for Peter de Klerk*. Ed. Wilhelm H. Neuser, Herman J. Selderhuis, and Willem van't Spijker. Heerenveen: Groen, 1997: 283-300.
— "Church on Stage: Calvin's Dynamic Ecclesiology." In *Calvin and the Church*. Ed. David Foxgrover. Grand Rapids: CRC Production Services, 2002: 46-64.
— *Marriage and Divorce in the Thought of Martin Bucer*. Trans. John Vriend and Lyle

D. Bierma. Kirksville, Mo.: Thomas Jefferson University Press, 1999.
Sharp, Larry D. "The Doctrines of Grace in Calvin and Augustine." *Evangelical Quarterly* 52/2 (1980): 84-96.
Sigal, Phillip. *The Emergence of Contemporary Judaism*, vol. 3. Allison Park, Pa.: Pickwick Publications, 1986.
Spencer, Stephen R. "Francis Turretin's Concept of the Covenant of Nature." In *Later Calvinism: International Perspectives*. Ed. W. Fred Graham. Kirksville, Mo.: Sixteenth Century Essays & Studies, 1994: 71-91.
Sprenger, P. *Das Rätsel um die Bekhrung Calvins*. Beitrage zur Geschichte und Lehre der Reformierten Kirche 11. Neukirken: Neukirchener Verlag, 1960.
Stadtland-Neumann, Hiltrud. *Evangelische Radikalismen in der Sicht Calvins: Sein Verständnis der Bergpredigt und der Aussendungsrede (Matth. 10)*. Neukirchen: Neukirchener Verlag, 1966.
Stauffer, Richard. *The Humanness of John Calvin*. Tr. George Shriver. New York: Abingdon Press, 1971.
— *Interprètes de la Bible: Études sur les Réformateurs du XVIe*. Paris: Éditions Beauchesne: 1980.
— "Quelques aspects insolites de la théologie du premier article dans la prédication de Calvin." In *Calvinus Ecclesiae Doctor*. Ed. Wilhelm H. Neuser. Kampen: Kok, 1978: 47-68.
Stephens, W. P. *The Holy Spirit in the Theology of Martin Bucer*. Cambridge: Cambridge University Press, 1970.
— *The Theology of Huldrych Zwingli*. Oxford: Clarendon Press, 1986.
— *Zwingli: An Introduction to His Thought*. Oxford: Clarendon Press, 1992.
Steinmetz, David C. *Calvin in Context*. Oxford: Oxford University Press, 1995.
— "The Judaizing Calvin." In *Die Patristik in der Bibelexegese des 16. Jahrhunderts*. Wolfenbütteler Forschungen, vol. 85. Ed. David C. Steinmetz. Wiesbaden: Harrassowitz Verlag, 1999: 135-45.
— "The Reformation and the Ten Commandments." *Interpretation* 43/3 (1989): 256-266.
— *Reformers in the Wings: From Geiler von Kaysersberg to Theodore Beza*. 2nd ed. Oxford: Oxford University Press, 2001.
— "The Superiority of Pre-Critical Exegesis." *Theology Today* 37 (1980-1981): 27-38.
— "Theology and Exegesis: Ten Theses," In *Histoire de l'exégèse au XVIe siècle: Textes du Colloque International Tenu à Genève en 1976*. Ed. Olivier Fatio and Pierre Fraenkel. Genève: Droz, 1978: 382.
Street, Thomas W. "John Calvin on Adiaphora: an Exposition and Appraisal of his Theory and Practice." PhD dissertation. Union Theological Seminary, 1955.
Strehle, Stephen. "Calvinism, Augustinianism, and the Will of God." *Theologische Zeitschrift* 48/2 (1992), 221-237.
Strohm, Christoph. Ed., *Martin Bucer und das Recht*. Genève: Droz, 2002.
Sundquist, Ralph R., Jr. "The Third Use of the Law in the Thought of John Calvin." PhD dissertation. Columbia University, 1970.
Tamburello, Dennis E. *Union with Christ: John Calvin and the Mysticism of St. Bernard*.

Louisville: Westminster/John Knox, 1994.

Tappert, Theodore G. Trans. and ed. *The Book of Concord*. Philadelphia: Fortress, 1959.

Tavard, George H. *The Starting Point of Calvin's Theology*. Grand Rapids: Eerdmans, 2000.

Taylor, Hannis. *Cicero: A Sketch of His Life and Works, A Commentary on the Roman Constitution and Roman Public Life, Supplemented by the Sayings of Cicero Arranged for the First Time as an Anthology*. 2nd ed. Chicago: A. C. McClurg, 1918.

Tedeschi, John A. Ed. *Italian Reformation Studies in Honor of Laelius Socinus*. Firenze: F. Le Monnier, 1965.

Torrance, James B. "The Concept of Federal Theology—Was Calvin a Federal Theologian?" In *Calvinus Sacrae Scripturae Professor: Calvin as Confessor of Holy Scripture*. Ed. Wilhelm H. Neuser. Grand Rapids: Eedrmans, 1994: 15-40.

Torrance, Thomas F. *Calvin's Doctrine of Man*. London: Lutterworth Press, 1952.

— *The Hermeneutics of John Calvin*. Edinburgh: Scottish Academic Press, 1988.

Troeltsch, Ernst. *The Social Teachings of the Christian Churches*, 2 vols. Trans. Olive Wyon. New York: Macmillan, 1949.

Tylenda, Joseph N. "Calvin's First Reformed Sermon? Nicholas Cop's Discourse—1 November 1533." *Westminster Theological Journal* 38 (1975-76): 300-318.

— "Calvin's Understanding of the Communication of Properties." *Westminster Theological Journal* 38/1 (1975): 54-65.

— "Christ the Mediator: Calvin versus Stancaro." *Calvin Theological Journal* 8/1 (1973): 5-16.

— "The Controversy on Christ the Mediator: Calvin's Second Reply to Stancaro." *Calvin Theological Journal* 8/2 (1973): 131-57.

— "The Warning that Went Unheeded: John Calvin on Giorgio Biandrata." *Calvin Theological Journal* 12/1 (1977): 24-62.

Van Buren, Paul. *Christ in Our Place: The Subsitutionary Character of Calvin's Doctrine of Reconciliation*. Edinburgh: Oliver and Boyd, 1957.

Van Engen, John. Trans. *Devotio Moderna: Basic Writings*. New York: Paulist Press, 1988.

Van Oort, Johannes. "John Calvin and the Church Fathers." In *The Reception of the Church Fathers in the West: From the Carolingians to the Maurists*. 2 vols. Ed. Irena Backus. Leiden: E. J. Brill, 1997: 661-700.

Van Ravenswaay, J. Marius J. Lange. "Calvin und die Juden- Eine Offene Frage?" In *Reformiertes Erbe: Festschrift für Gottfried W. Locher zu Seinem 80. Geburtstag*. Ed. Heiko A. Oberman, Ernst Saxer, Alfred Schindler, and Heinzpeter Stucki. Zwingliana, 19/1-2, Zürich: Theologischer Verlag, 1992-1993, 2: 183-194.

Van't Spijker, Willem. "Bucer's influence on Calvin: church and community." In *Martin Bucer: Reforming church and community*. Ed. David F. Wright. Cambridge: Cambridge University Press, 1994: 32-44.

— "Calvin's Friendship with Martin Bucer: Did It Make Calvin a Calvinist?" In *Calvin Studies Society Papers, 1995, 1997: Calvin and Spirituality, Calvin and His Contemporaries*. Ed. David Foxgrover. Grand Rapids: CRC Product Services, 1998: 169-186.

— *The Ecclesiastical Offices in the Thought of Martin Bucer.* Trans. John Vriend and Lyle D. Bierma. Leiden: E. J. Brill, 1996.
— "The Influence of Bucer on Calvin as Becomes Evident from the *Institutes.*" In *John Calvin's Institutes His Opus Magnum.* Ed. Bahrend Johannes van der Walt et al. Potchefstroom: Institute for Reformational Studies, 1986: 106-132.
— "The Influence of Luther on Calvin according to the *Institutes.*" In *John Calvin's Institutes His Opus Magnum.* Ed. Bahrend Johannes van der Walt et al. Potchefstroom: Institute for Reformational Studies, 1986: 83-105.
— "The Kingdom of Christ According to Bucer and Calvin." In *Calvin and the State.* Ed. Peter de Klerk. Grand Rapids: Calvin Studies Society, 1993: 109-132.
Viard, Paul Émile. *André Alciat 1492-1550.* Paris: Société Anonyme du Recueil Sirey, 1926.
Vischer, Wilhelm. "Calvin, exegete de l'Ancien Testament." *Revue Réformée* 18/69 (1967): 1-20.
Vos, Arvin. "Calvin: The Theology of a Christian Humanist." In *Christianity and the Classics: The Acceptance of a Heritage.* Ed. Wendy E. Helleman. Landham: University Press of America, 1990: 109-118.
Walker, Williston. *John Calvin: The Organizer of Reformed Protestantism 1509-1564.* 3rd ed. New York: Schocken Books, 1969.
Wallace, Ronald S. *Calvin's Doctrine of The Christian Life.* Edinburgh: Oliver and Boyd, 1959.
— *Calvin's Doctrine of the Word and Sacrament.* Edinburgh: Oliver and Boyd, 1953.
Warfield, Benjamin B. *Calvin and Augustine.* Philadelphia: Presbyterian and Reformed Publishing Company, 1956.
— "On the Literary History of Calvin's *Institutes.*" In John Calvin, *Institutes of the Christian Religion.* Trans. John Allen. 7th ed. Philadelphia: Presbyterian Board of Christian Education, 1936: v-lvi.
Watanabe, Nobuo. "Calvin's Second Catechism: Its Predecessors and Its Environment." In *Calvinus Sacrae Scripturae Professor: Calvin as Confessor of Holy Scripture.* Ed. Wilhelm H. Neuser. Grand Rapids: Eedrmans, 1994: 224-232.
Watt, Jeffrey R. "The Control of Marriage in Reformed Switzerland, 1550-1800," In *Later Calvinism: International Perspectives.* Ed. W. Fred Graham. Kirksville, Mo.: Sixteenth Century Essays & Studies, 1994: 29-53.
Wawrykow, Joseph. "John Calvin and Condign Merit." *Archiv für Reformationsgeschichte* 83 (1992): 73-90.
Weir, David A. *The Origins of the Federal Theology in Sixteenth-Century Reformation Thought.* Oxford: Clarendon Press, 1990.
Weis, James. "Calvin versus Osiander on Justification." *Springfielder* 30/3 (1965): 31-47.
Wendel, François. *Calvin: The Origins and Development of His Religious Thought.* Trans. Philip Mairet. New York: Harper and Row, 1973.
— "Justification and Predestination in Calvin." In *Readings in Calvin's Theology.* Ed. Donald K. McKim. Grand Rapids: Baker, 1984: 153-178.
Wengert, Timothy J. *Law and Gospel: Philip Melanchthon's Debate with John Agricola*

of Eisleben over Poenitentia. Grand Rapids: Baker, 1997.

— "'We Will Feast Together in Heaven Forever': The Epistolary Friendship of John Calvin and Philip Melanchthon." In *Melanchthon in Europe*. Ed. Karin Maag. Grand Rapids: Baker, 1999: 19-44.

Werchkmeister, Jean. "The Reception of the Church Fathers in Canon Law." In *The Reception of the Church Fathers in the West: From the Carolingians to the Maurists*. 2 vols. Ed. Irena Backus. Leiden: E. J. Brill, 1997: 51-81.

Wernle, Paul. *Der evangelische Glaube nach den Hauptschriften der Reformatoren*, vol. 3. *Calvin*. Tübingen: J. C. B. Mohr, 1919.

Whale, J. S. *The Protestant Tradition*. Cambridge: Cambridge University Press, 1955.

Williams, George Huntston. *The Radical Reformation*. 3rd ed. Sixteenth Century Essays & Studies, vol. 15. Ann Arbor, Mic.: Edwards Brothers, 1992.

Willis, David E. *Calvin's Catholic Christology: The Function of the So-Called Extra Calvinisticum in Calvin's Theology*. Leiden: E. J. Brill, 1966.

— "Calvin's Use of *Substantia*." In *Calvinus Ecclesiae Genevensis Custos*. Ed. Wilhelm H. Neuser. Frankfurt a. M.: Peter Lang, 1984: 289-301.

— "The Influence of Laelius Socinus on Calvin's Doctrines of the Merits of Christ and the Assurance of Faith." In *Italian Reformation Studies in Honor of Laelius Socinus*. Ed. John A. Tedeschi. Firenze: F. Le Monnier, 1965: 231-241.

— "Persuasion in Calvin's Theology: Implications for his Ethics." In *Calvin and Christian Ethics*. Ed. Peter de Klerk. Grand Rapids: Calvin Studies Society, 1987: 83-94.

— "Rhetoric and Responsibility in Calvin's Theology." In *The Context of Contemporary Theology*. Ed. Alexander J. Mckelway and E. David Willis. Atlanta: John Knox Press, 1974: 43-63.

Willis. R. *Servetus and Calvin: A Study of an Important Epoch in the Early History of the Reformation*. London: Henry S. King, 1877.

White, Robert. "An Early Reformed Document on the Mission to the Jews." *Westminster Theological Journal* 53 (1991) 93-108.

Witte, Johannes L. "Die Christologie Calvins." In *Das Konzil von Chalkedon: Geschichte und Gegenwart*. Ed. Aloys Grillmeier and Heinrich Bacht. Würzburg: Echter-Verlag, 1954: 487-529.

Witte, John, Jr., "Between Sacrament and Contract: Marriage as Covenant in John Calvin's Geneva." *Calvin Theological Journal* 33 (1998): 9-75.

— *Law and Protestantism: The Legal Teachings of the Lutheran Reformation*. Cambridge: Cambridge University Press, 2002.

Wolf, Ernst. "Deus Omniformis: Bemerkungen zur Christologie des Michael Servet." In *Theologische Aufsätze: Karl Barth zum 50. Geburtstag*. München: Chr. Kaiser Verlag, 1936: 443-466.

Wolf, H. H. *Einheit des Bundes. Das verhältnis von Alten und Neuen Testament bei Calvin*. Neukirchen Kr. Moers: Buchhandlung des Erziehungsvereins, 1958.

Wright, David F. "Accommodation and Barbarity in John Calvin's Old Testament Commentaries." In *Understanding Poets and Prophets: Essays in Honour of George Wishart Anderson*. Ed. A. Graeme Auld. Sheffield: Sheffield Academic Series, 1993:

413-427.

— "Calvin's Accommodating God." In *Calvinus Sincerioris Religionis Vindex: Calvin as Protector of the Purer Religion*. Ed. Wilhelm H. Neuser and Brian G. Armstong. Kirksville, Mo.: Sixteenth Century Essays & Studies, 1997: 3-19.

— "Calvin's 'Accommodation' Revisited." In *Calvin as Exegete*. Ed. Peter De Klerk. Grand Rapids: Calvin Studies Society, 1995: 171-190.

— "Calvin's Pentateuchal Criticism: Equity, Hardness of Heart, and Divine Accommodation in the Mosaic Harmony Commentary." *Calvin Theological Journal* 21/1 (1986): 33-50.

— "The Ethical Use of the Old Testament in Luther and Calvin: A Comparison." *Scottish Journal of Theology* 36/4 (1983): 463-485.

— "*Non posse peccare* in this life? St. Augustine, *De correptione et gratia* 12:33." In *St Augustine and his Opponents, Other Latin Writers*. Studia Patristica, vol. 38. Leuven: Peeters, 2001: 348-353

— "Robert Estienne's *Nova Glossa Ordinaria*: A Protestant Quest for a Standard Bible Commentary." In *Calvin: Erbe und Auftrag. Festschrift für Wilhelm H. Neuser zum 65. Geburtstag*. Ed. Willem van't Spijker. Kampen: Kok, 1991: 40-51.

Wright, Richard. *An Apology for Dr. Michael Servetus: Including an Account of His Life, Persecution, Writings and Opinions*. Wisbech: Printed by F. B. Wright, 1806.

Wyatt, Peter. *Jesus Christ and Creation in the Theology of John Calvin*. Allison Park, Pa.: Pickwick Publications, 1996.

Wyneken, Karl H. "Calvin and Anabaptism." *Concordia Theological Monthly* 36/1 (1965): 18-29.

Zachman, Randall C. *The Assurance of Faith: Conscience in the Theology of Martin Luther and John Calvin*. Minneapolis: Fortress, 1993.

— "Jesus Christ as the Image of God in Calvin's Theology," *Calvin Theological Journal* 15/1 (1990): 45-62.

Zur Mühlen, Karl-Heinz. "Law." In *The Oxford Encyclopedia of the Reformation*, vol. 2. Ed. Hans J. Hillerbrand. Oxford: Oxford University Press, 1996: 404b-407b.

Index of Scripture References

Genesis
1:1	141
1:26	153
2:2	195
2:16	214, 215
3:8	215
3:15	142, 172
4:5	88
4:7	100
8:20	87, 100
12:3	87
14:18	254
14:19	255
15:4-5	253
15:6	19, 233, 236, 250, 256
16:10	87, 155
17:13	89, 156
18:2	87, 155
18:13	104, 110, 147
19:1	55
19:24	141
20:7	87
22:2	87
28:12	87, 102, 103, 110, 140, 142, 148, 149, 155
29:29	186
35:7	142
48:16	154

Exodus
1:1-7	127
3:2	87, 90, 104, 110, 151, 152
3:15	156
12:5-11	158
12:21-22	102
12:46	101
13:1-2	158
13:21-22	149
14:19	88
14:19-20	152, 156
19:1-2	19, 97, 214, 215, 216, 249
20:3	158
20:4-6	100
20:8	101, 160
20:12	162
20:13	100, 162
20:13 et al.	161
20:14	162
20:15 et al.	161, 162
20:17	100
21:7-11	116
21:12	120
21:14	162
21:15-17	162
21:18	120
21:18-19	116
21:1 et al.	117
22:1-4	116, 162
22:7-8	162
22:19 et al.	162
22:25	161, 162
22:25 et al.	162
22:28	160
23:20	87, 89, 110, 156
23:34	117
25:8-15	100, 116, 160
25:17	100
25:31-39	100
26:1-37	101
26:31-37	100
27:1-8	101
27:20-21	101

28:1-43	102	19:35-36	162
28:42	124	20:11-12	162
28:4-8	104, 160	20:18	162
28:42	88	20:25-26	160
28:42-43	101	21:1-2	101
29:38-41	101	21:17-21	102
29:38-46	88, 100	22:17-21	101
30:1-9	101	23:34-35	101
30:11-16	158	26:3-8	160
30:17	100		
30:23	87	**Numbers**	
30:23-24	102	17:8	90
30:25-33	101	18:20-24	160
31:13-17	101	35:1-3	104
		35:16-18	162
Leviticus		35:19-27	116
1:1-4	149, 157, 158		
1:1-17	100, 101	**Deuteronomy**	
2:1-10	101	4:12-18	100
3:16-17	158	5:1-3	233
4:22-24	149	5:4	111
6:1-7	101	5:4-7	115
10:9-11	104	5:8-10	115
11:2	116	5:11	115
14:17-21	162	5:16	115, 162
16:3	87	5:17	103, 115, 162
16:3-6	102	5:18	162
16:7-11	101	5:19	162
16:16	101	5:22	19, 115
17:1	88, 100	5:23-27	115
17:10-14	101, 116, 161	5:28-33	114, 115
18:1-18	162	6:20-25	19
18:5	97	7:21	256
18:6-17	162	9:17	255
18:18	117, 118	9:25-29	87
18:26-30	116	10:17-19	100, 160
19:14	162	11:26-32	102
19:27-28	118	13:5	100
19:32	162	15:1-2	162
19:33	160	17:8-11	104

Index of Scripture References

19:14	162	23:1-7	216, 251
20:12-14	116	27:1-4	251
21:18-20	162		
22:22	162	**Psalms**	
22:23-27	116	45:6-7	88, 153, 154
23:21-23	118	45:8-11	169
23:24-25	162	48:9-15	254
24:1-4	116, 162, 185, 186	50:14-15	112
24:6	162	89:30	156
24:14-15	100, 161, 162	89:31-39	252, 253
24:16	100, 119, 162	119:12	245
25:1-3	162	119:18	244, 245
25:5-10	115	119:26	245
26:1-11	158	119:27	245
26:17-19	100	119:33	245
26:25	217	119:34	245
27:2-6	254	119:64	245
27:11-15	217	119:108	88, 100
27:24-26	217	119:125	245
28:1	216	132:10	153
28:1-2	217	147:18-20	253
29:22-28	100		
29:29	113, 114	**Isaiah**	
30:11-14	113, 114	6:1	103
30:14	114	19:20	104, 110, 148
32:11-15	90	29:11-12	88
33:9-11	88	32:6	215
		53:7-8	23
Joshua		53:12	88, 102
5:13-14	87, 89, 110, 152, 156	63:17	90, 105, 148
20:1-6	16	64:6	227
II Samuel		**Jeremiah**	
8:15	255	11:13	87, 155
		31 f.	138
Job		31:33	204
10:16-17	216, 217, 251		
11:1-6	251	**Ezekiel**	
13:16-22	251	1:25-26	146, 148, 152, 154
15:11-16	94, 251	16:61	88

Daniel
2:11	87, 155
2:44-45	126
7:13	110
7:27	87, 156
8:15	110, 150
9:18	88
9:23	102

Hosea
8:4	102
12:3-5	146, 152, 154

Micah
3:11-4:9	254
4:2	256
4:9	254
5:2	143, 143
5:4	144

Habakkuk
2:5	88

Zechariah
1:8-21	155, 159
3:3-4	88, 153
12:8	87, 155

Malachi
2:14	186
3:1	88

Matthew
1:21	205
1:22	255
1:23	100, 105, 148, 206, 256
3:13	207
4:1-2	207
5:1	179
5:1-12	207
5:11-12	208
5:17	101
5:17-19	199, 201, 204
5:17-48	117, 205
5:18	204
5:19	204
5:20	117, 178, 217
5:21	178, 182, 193, 211, 214
5:22	178, 182
5:23-24	182
5:25	163
5:27-30	189
5:31-32	186, 187, 216
5:38-41	193
5:39	191
5:43	163, 192
5:44	163, 192, 193
5:45	192
5:46	163
5:48	163, 192
6:9	102
6:9-12	207
7:12	162
8:1-4	194, 207
12:3-4	196
12:5-6	196, 197
12:7	196
12:8	195, 197
12:9	197, 198
14:23	108
15:1	194
15:2	194
17:5	207
19:1 f.	184
19:3-4	185, 186
19:6	186
19:7-8	185
19:9	185, 186, 192
19:10-12	185, 188
24:20	195

Index of Scripture References

24:36	108	14:1-6	197
25:51-66	208	14:3-4	194
26:36	169	19:41	108, 169
26:36-39	105, 208	24:47	218
26:36-42	168		
26:40-50	208	**John**	
26:67-27:10	105, 208	1:1	86, 133, 205, 206
27:45-54	208	1:1-5	206
27:51	208	1:4	206
27:55-60	208	1:5	91
27:51	108	1:17	206, 240, 248
28:1-10	209	1:18	103
28:18	110	3:13	104
		5:1	195
Mark		5:17	195, 197
2:24	196	5:29	102
2:27	195, 197	5:46	105, 150, 198
2:28	195	6:45	102
		6:56	110
Luke		7:21-24	198
1:26	205	8:17	112
1:31	205	8:17-18	195
1:31-35	253	10:7	102
1:32	205	10:15	102
1:32-33	205, 253	10:17	169
1:35	205	14:10	86, 103
1:68	206	14:16	108, 209
1:75	215	14:20	209
1:78	206	15:9	210
2:21	207	16:23-24	105
2:22-24	207	16:26	105
2:46	207	17:1	169
2:49	207	17:3	102
4:16-22	207	17:8	102
5:12-14	194	17:12	108
6:1 f.	179	17:21	156
6:5	195	19:30	208
6:22-26	218		
6:35	191	**Acts**	
11:31-41	194	1:1-4	211

1:5	209	7:11	214
1:9-11	209	7:12	236
2:1-4	209	7:13	234
2:13-17	209	7:21	238
2:17-21	209	7:21-23	238
2:33	108	8:2	240
5:13-16	256	8:3	111, 251
5:20	256	8:4	251
7:30	249	8:10	240
7:35-37	19	8:13	244
7:36	253	9:1 f.	154
7:38	255	10:4-5	217, 245
7:42-44	254	13:1	54
7:44	256		
17:18	105	**I Corinthians**	
		1:6-11	79
Romans		1:30	259
1:4	108	10:4	152
1:17	228, 239, 251	10:9	87
1:20	92	11:1	68
2:14-15	92	15:12-13	246
2:15	91	15:39	246
3:20	229		
3:21	229, 239, 250	**II Corinthians**	
3:22	216, 239, 244, 250, 251	3:1 f.	242
3:27-28	250	3:6	108, 234
3:31	248	3:7 f.	234, 240
4:15	223	3:16	242
5:17	239	3:17	ix, 242
5:18	237	4:4	103
5:19	239		
6:1	239	**Galatians**	
6:3	239	1:6-8	89
6:4	160	1:22	254
6:7	239	2:4	254
6:10	239	2:17-18	257
6:22-23	239	2:19	251
7:2-3	235	3:10-14	250
7:4	234, 235	3:13-14	105, 150
7:9-12	234, 251	3:15-18	105, 253

3:19	19, 98, 202, 219	**II Timothy**	
3:19-20	19, 89, 99	1:5	90, 111, 150
3:20	219		
3:24	75, 223, 226	**Hebrews**	
4:1-2	156	1:5	87, 103, 120
4:3	219, 220, 236	2:16	154
4:9-10	254	5:6	255
5:1-3	257	7:12	249
5:6	259	8:5	111, 150
6:2	260	8:6	111, 150
		9:6-12	101
Ephesians		9:11	108
1:1	255		
1:15	215	**I Peter**	
1:17-18	253	1:20	112
1:21-23	253	3:18	168, 169
2:10	256		
2:14-15	256	**I John**	
3:9	254	1:7-8	235
3:14-19	255	4:10	100
3:16	253		
4:10	255		
4:15-16	109, 253		
4:24	256		
5:8-9	254		
5:30	253		

Philippians
2:10   209

Colossians
1:15   103, 143
2:3   245
2:17   101, 206
2:18   87

I Timothy
1:5   256, 233
1:7   215
1:8   227, 233

General Index

Accommodation, God's, 9; 10; 54-55; 59; 79 n.64; 89; 102; 105; 111-118; 120-121; 151; 159; 172; 182; 216; 217-218; 249; 260
Ad fontes, 26; 30 n.28; 32; 37; 47; 50; 57
Ad quaestiones et obiecta Iudaei cuiusdam responsio, 163-170
Adiaphora, 4; 13; 14; 91; 117-118; 190; 194; 258; 260
Agricola, John, 18; 73; 213; 220-221
Alciati, Andrea, 31; 33-35; 37; 56
Althaus, Paul, 7 n.28
Ames, William, 1 n.1; 3
Anabaptists, 74; 80; 81; 125-126; 129; 131; 172; 190 n.111; 191; 193 n.132; 204
Anselm, 15 n.69
Anti-Semitism, 127-129
Apostles' Creed, 71; 77
Aquinas, Thomas, 41 n.86; 42; 43 n.96; 50; 74 n.45; 82; 121 n.142
Aristotle, 36; 50; 51; 53 n.143; 83; 95 n.53
Atonement, 2; 84-86; 101; 108
Augustine of Hippo, 40; 47; 48 n.122; 51; 58; 69; 75; 96; 102 n.80; 106; 107; 113; 121 n.142; 127 n.15; 155 n.156; 179; 184; 185 n.79; 224 n.64; 228; 229; 246 n.2; 250

Backus, Irena, 144 n.104; 247 n.8
Bainton, Roland H., 134 n.51, 53
Baker, J. Wayne, 2 n.3
Balke, Willem, 74 n.46
Balserak, Jon, 111 n.119; 114 n.127
Bandstra, Andrew J. 84 n.2
Banks, Robert, 195 n.144
Baron, Salo W., 126 n.8; 171 n.231
Barth, Karl, 5-6

Battles, Ford Lewis, 29; 36; 47 n.117; 50 n.131; 52 n.139; 53 n.143; 69; 131-132
Baumgartner, J., 147
Beintker, Michael, 78 n.61
Benin, Stephan D., 151 n.138
Benoît, Jean-Daniel, 65
Bentley, Jerry H., 37 n.66
Bernard of Clairvaux, 41 n.84; 93; 227 n.80
Biandrata, Giorgio, 87; 102 n.77; 121; 129
Biel, Gabriel, 39; 40 n.77; 43; 121 n.142
Bierma, Lyle D., 3 n.3; 4; 42 n.89
Blaser, Klauspeter, 98 n.62; 99 n.66
Bohatec, Josef, 5; 37; 174; 186 n.84
Boisset, Jean, 47 n.117; 48 n.124
Bolt, John, 9 n.40
Bonfil, Robert, 126 n.9; 128 n.18
Bosco, David, 51 n.133
Bouman, Walter R., 234
Bourges, college of, 33
Bouwsma, William J., 25; 47 n.120; 51 n.134; 55 n.147
Breen, Quirinus, 24 n.4; 26 n.14; 30 n.27-29; 33 n.40, 37
Brevitas, 37; 180
Brümmer, Vincent, 93 n.46
Brundage, James A., 83 n.74
Brunner, Emil, 5-6
Bucer, Martin, 14 n.65; 44; 64 n.21; 66; 69; 70; 72; 80; 128; 129; 165; 171 n.231; 173; 180-181; 183-184; 186-188; 190-191; 193-194; 198-199; 201-204; 210-211; 228-231; 238; 240-242; 257-258
Budé, Guillaume, 34; 35-38; 50; 56; 57; 247
Bullinger, Heinrich, 2-3; 62 n.7; 173; 179; 187 n.88; 211 n.247; 224-

General Index

228; 258
Burnett, Amy Nelson, 181 n.42
Burnett, S. G., 165 n.204
Büsser, Fritz, 179 n.33
Butin, Philip Walker, 86 n.10; 176 n.18

Cadier, Jean, 69 n.35; 75 n.49
Calvin: a man of law, 26-27; *Iudaizans*, 15; 131; 139-144; 171-172; three images, 27-28
Canon law, 26; 30; 32; 33 n.40; 57 n.152; 83 n.74; 186 n.79
Capito, Wolfgang, 126; 127; 164 n.201
Carbonnier, Jean, 27 n.16
Carbonnier, Marianne, 58 n.155
Caroli, Pierre, 85 n.8; 129; 151 n.139
Casteel, Theodore W., 14 n.66
Castellio, Sebastian, 15 n.70; 134 n.51
Catechisms: the First, 13; 62-64; 216; 233; the Second, 62; 64; 98; 233
Catholic formalism, 123-125
Central dogma, 18-19
Choisy, Eugène, 27 n.17
Christ: Adonai, 88; Communicatio with the righteousness of (*communicatio cum iustitia Christi*), 210; 213; 217; 222; 239; 244; 251; 256; 260; Communion with (*communio cum Christo*); 209; 230; 238; 239; 241; 251; 253; 254; 260; Elohim, 88; 133; 140-141; 151-153; 154; 169; end of the law, 11; 81; 88; 208; 256; example and type of the law, 9; 17; 18; 19; 46; 84; express and living image of God, 103; 158; 215; 243 n.166; fulfilment of the law, 7; 10; 11; 16; 44; 61; 81-82; 83; 97; 120; 138; 159; 160; 170-171; 172; 199-212; 226; 243; 247; 250; 252; 257; 258; 260; head of the covenant, 150; head of the church and angels, 89; 108-109; 142-145; 153; 154-157; 213; 243; 252; 253; 255; 257; *hypostasis* of; 85; 103; 107; 120; 130; 133; 135; 138; 149; 151; 153; 205; 206; 246; Immanuel, 100; 148; 206; 256; interpreter of the law, 9; 35; 57; 68; 104; 163; 174; 177-199; 212; Jehovah, 71; 88; 144; 151-153; 154; 155; Leader of the Israelites, 88; 151; 154; 156; 167; merit of (*meritum Christi*), 38-43; 56; 72; 82; 99; 102; 216; 229; 240; 242; 247; 252; 253; office of Christ, threefold (*munus triplex Christi*), 98-99; *persona* of, 39-40; 85-86; 103; 107-108; 113; 120-123; 131; 133-139; 142; 144; 145-147; 148-151; 152-154; 156; 157; 167-172; 205; 209-211; 255; presence of (*praesentia* Christi), 106-107; 148-154; 156; 157; 167; 172; 208; 209; 211; 213; 243; 250; 255; 256; 258; *proprietas* (*proprium, qualitas*)of, 136; 145; 153; representation of (*repraesentaio Christi*), 160; 133; 213; rightousness of (*iustitia Christi*), 19; 63; 64; 68; 97; 108; 148; 197; 198; 200; 208; 211; 213; 218; 226; 236; 237; 238; 240; 241; 244; 251; 253; 254; 255; 256; 257; 260; soul of the law, 19; 88; 198; 246 n.2; 248; 255; Spirit of (*Spiritus Christi*), 19; 64; 68; 71; 97; 105; 108-109; 138; 139; 167; 176; 177; 183; 184; 190; 191; 193; 196; 197; 201-204; 205; 208; 209-210; 217; 221; 225-227; 230-231; 239; 240; 241-243; 251; 253; 255-256; 257; spirit of the law, 34; 203; 227; 242; substance of the law

(*substantia legis*), 10; 11; 12; 16; 17; 61; 68; 74; 81; 82; 83; 88; 101; 120; 150; 157; 158; 159; 160; 166; 171-172; 173; 174; 177; 203; 205; 206; 211; 215; 228; 230; 237; 248; 250; 253; 254; 255; 256; 257; 258; 260; the Angel, 87; 104; 110; 146; 151-152; 154; 156; 167; truth of the law; 10; 11; 16; 19; 39; 68; 81; 83; 88; 123; 124; 158; 159; 163; 203; 204; 206; 215; 237; 250; 253; 257; 260; union with (*mystica unio cum Christo*), 19; 66; 70; 91 n.43; 129; 131; 149; 217; 244; 248; 252; 256; 259 n.43; *unitas in unio*, 107-110; 131; 135; 136; 170; 171

Christian life, doctrine of, 17; 37-38; 42-43; 46-47; 64; 68; 75; 78; 80; 84; 183; 199; 201; 213; 215; 220; 235; 243; 252; 259; 260

Christus mediator legis, 20; 71; 77-82; 84, n.1; 86-89; 98-104; 104-105; 114; 121; 157; 171; 243; 246-247; 257; 260; *mediator reconciliationis*, 19; 98; 99-100; *mediator patrocinii*, 19; 98; 101-102; *mediator doctrinae* 19; 98; 102-104

Church; *ecclesiola in ecclesia*, 154; discipline, 12; 14; 53; 181; 193; as *domesticus (familia Dei)*, 156; *pueritia ecclesiae*, 116; unity and continuity of, 99; 112; 125-126; 142; 154; 156; 157; 253-255; visible and invisible, 75-77

Cicero, 12; 31; 49; 52; 53; 54

Civil law (positive law), 26; 32; 48; 58; 83; 186; 187; 252

Cocceius, Johannes, 1 n.1; 2 n.2

Cochrane, Arthur C., 161 n.188

Colish, Marcia L., 48 n.120, 122; 52 n.138

Commentary on Seneca's *De Clementia*, 47-55; judicial proceedings, 50; prince as a vicar of God, 54-55; three uses of punishment, 52-54; pessimistic view of humanity, 50-51

Communicatio idiomatum, 85; 105; 107; 121; 167; 168; 171; 176; 177; 211

Confession de la foy, 62

Conscience, 54; 76-77; 90-92; 123; 220; 222-223

Consensus Tigurinus, 106

Consistory of Geneva, 12; 27; 35; 184

Cop, Nicolas, 12; 60-61

Cordier, Mathurin, 31; 46

Cottret, Bernard, 15 n.68; 46 n.112; 173 n.1

Counsels (*consilia*), 175; 192-194

Courtenay, William J., 42 n.89, 90; 186 n.86

Courvoisier, Jacques, 64 n.21; 165 n.207; 180 n.39

Covenant theology, 1-3; 20: on the two Reformed traditions, 2

Covenant: conditionality of, 20; 215; 216; 249; 260; mutuality of, 20; 216; 260; new covenant, 138; 211; 230; of grace, 16; 43; 214; 217; 226; 234; of works, 9; unity of 125; 159

Cushman, Robert E., 102 n.80

D'Assonville, V. E., 259 n.88

De Greef, W., 60 n.1; 164 n.201; 173 n.2

De Jonge, Henk Jan, 179 n.29

De Kroon, Marijn, 199 n.168; 201 n.184

De La Garanderie, Marie-Madeleine, 36 n.59

De Savignac, Jean, 52 n.138

Decree, God's, 2; 4; 9; 166 n.212; 200; 225; 249

Demura, Akira, 231 n.109; 250 n.21

Detmers, Achim, 164 n.200
Devotio moderna, 45-47; 57; 247
DeVries, Dawn, 252 n.38
Diehl, Wilhelm, 13 n.62; 65 n.23
Docet (edocet) lex, 67; 160; 97 n.56
Dominicé, Max, 207 n.224
Douglass, Jane Dempsey, 79 n.62
Doumergue, Emil, 8; 23 n.2; 34; 48 n.124; 55; 56; 60 n.1; 164 n.201; 173 n.2; 235 n.129; 244 n.167
Dowey, Edward, Jr., 9-10; 18 n.74; 44 n.97; 65 n.23; 91 n.33; 161 n.188; 234 n. 121; 235 n.129
Doyle, Robert C., 69 n.33
Droz, Eugénie, 164 n.201
Ducemin, Nicolas, 34

Ebeling, Gerhard, 4 n.9; 219; 236 n.132
Edwards, John, 128 n.17
Eire, Carlos M. N., 117 n.133
Elert, Werner, 7; 214; 219 n.31
Engammare, Max, 127 n.13; 16
Engel, Mary Potter, 94 n.50; 154 n.151; 233 n.117
Engelsma, David J., 86 n.10
Epicureans (*deus etiosus*), 38; 48
Equity, 14; 26; 28; 36; 49; 56; 76; 83; 119; 120; 161 n.188; 162 n.194; 163; 247
Erasmus, Desiderius, 27; 28; 35; 36; 37; 79 n.63; 179 n.28; 181 n.45
Esser, Hans Helmut, 103 n.81
Estoile, Pierre de L', 30 n.29; 31; 32-33; 34; 56-57; 247
Extra legem, 21; 106; 120-121

Faber, J., 103 n.81, 83
Facientibus quod in se est, 40; 247
Facilitas, 180
Faith: 3-4; 16; 19; 56; 60; 63; 68; 75; 78; 79; 80; 81; 105; 109; 112; 118; 138; 150; 158; 160; 183; 188; 198; 209; 215; 216; 217; 218; 220; 221; 223; 229; 235; 240; 244; 248; 250; 257; *fides efficax caritate*, 259; *fides mutila*, 244; *fides nuda*, 250; *fides viva*, 68; 138; 220; 221; 250; 258; 259; *persuasio*, 68; 92; 259;
Farel, Guillaume, 62; 67 n.28; 134
Feld, Helmut, 239 n.150
Fischer, Danielle, 24 n.3; 59 n.156; 156 n.161
Foxgrover, David L., 50 n.132
Fraenkel, P., 75 n.49
Francis I, 66
Free will, 71; 73; 92-98; 113; 215
Freedom from necessity, 93-95; 96-97
Frend, W. H. C., 125 n.4
Friedman, Jerome, 128 n.19, 20, 21; 132; 138 n.73; 145 n.107, 108, 110, 111
Froehlich, Karlfried, 29 n.23
Frost, Ronald N., 95 n.53

Gaffin, Richard B., Jr., 195 n.146
Gamble, Richard C., 38 n.71; 55 n.146; 71 n.40
Ganoczy, Alexandre, 24; 25 n.11; 45; 46 n.111; 47; 58 n.155; 152 n.141; 177 n.19; 250 n.25
George, Timothy, 46 n.110
Gerrish, Brian A., 220 n.39
Gessert, Robert A., 236 n.134
Gilby, Thomas, 82 n.73
Gilmont, Jean-François, 173 n.2
Gilmore, Myron P., 28 n.21
Girardin, Benoît, 71 n.40; 218 n.24; 221 n.47; 251 n.33
Gloede, Günter, 161 n.188
God: Lawgiver, 34; 35; 56; 74; 100; 119; 161; 216; 249; *paterna indulgentia*, 114; righteousness of (*iustitia Dei*): 15; 21; 66; 67; 69; 72; 77; 80; 96; 114; 121; 173; 178; 182; 213; 221; 226; 228; 229; 230; 231; 233; 235; 239; 240; 244; 249;

251; 256
Good works [of the law], 2; 28; 43; 68; 69; 72; 82; 96-98; 216; 217; 223; 234; 241; 250; merit of, 164 n.202; 234; 250; righteousness of, 28; 222; 234; 236; 241
Graafland, Cornelis, 78 n.61; 211 n.247
Gratia infusa, 15 n.69
Grin, Edmond, 84 n.2
Grislis, Egil, 52 n.130; 52 n.138; 95 n.52

Haas, Guenther H., 33 n.40; 36 n.58; 47 n.117; 49 n.127
Hall, Basil, 13 n.63; 24 n.4; 34 n.47
Harmonia of the last four books of Moses, 17 n.73
Harnack, Adolph, 39 n.74
Harrington, Joel F., 184 n.70; 185 n.79
Hart, Trevor, 15 n.69
Hausammann, Susi, 227 n.78
Helm, Paul, 3; 93 n.46; 161 n.180
Heppe, Heinrich, 1 n.1; 2 n.2; 44 n.97
Heshusius, Tilemann, 106
Hesselink, I. John, 4 n.11; 8-9; 17 n.74; 52 n. 139; 63 n.11; 67; 84 n.2; 154 n.151; 234 n.121; 243; 244 n.167; 245 n.171
Higman, Francis M., 67 n.29
Hillerbrand, Hans J., 128 n.20
Hobbs, R. Gerald, 127 n.15; 129 n.22
Hoekema, Anthony A., 2 n.2
Hoitenga, Dewey J., Jr., 97 n.59
Holler, Z. N., 179 n.28
Holy Spirit, 17; 19; 32; 38; 60; 64; 66; 68; 69; 70; 71; 75; 76; 77; 79; 92; 97; 108; 131; 135-136; 141; 160; 168; 175; 176; 181; 189; 192; 197; 200; 208; 220; 229; 237; 238; 240; 243; 253; *hypostasis* of, 135-136
Hughes, Philip E., 29 n.23; 46 n.111; 131 n.30; 133 n.42
Human soul, 50; 51; 90-95; 215; 246
Hunnius, Aegidius, 139-144; 148; 157; 172
Hyma, Albert, 46; 47 n.113

Image of God, 2 n.2; 79 n.62; 103; 158; 215
Imbart de la Tour, Pierre, 67 n.28; 70 n. 39; 82 n.72
Imputatio duplex, 14 n.67; 19; 40; 69; 78; 97; 103 n.83; 114; 121; 238; 239 n.150; 248; 249; 251, 255; 256; 257
Institutes of Christian Religion, 13; 14; 16-17; 65-82; 1536 edition, 13; 17; 58; 62; 65-70; 125; 193; 216; 252; 1539 edition, 13; 64; 70-74; 98; 125; 232; 252; 1543-1550 edition, 13; 14; 73; 74-77; 80; 155; 238-239; 252; 1559 edition, 16-17; 39; 58; 70; 77-82; 98-99; 106; 125-126; 131-132; 233; 252
Irenaeus, 133
Iustificatio duplex, 66; 68; 97
Iustitia duplex, 14 n.67; 18 n.76
Iustitia substantialis, 90

Jansen, J. F., 85 n.5
Jedin, Hubert, 13 n.63
Jewish monotheism, 145
Joest, Wilfried, 4 n.9
Johnson, Merwyn S., 13 n.63; 17 n.74; 84 n.2; 91 n.33; 235 n. 129; 242 n.163
Jones, Serene, 50 n.130
Josel of Rosheim, 128, 165
Justification, 13; 15; 16; 17-18; 26-27; 40; 42-43; 66; 69; 70; 71; 73; 78; 89; 200; 217; 218; 220; 226; 227; 229-230; 235; 238-239; 244; 248; 249; 251-252

Kelly, Donald R., 33 n.43; 34 n.44, 48
Kendall, R. T., 1 n.1; 3
Kerridge, Eric, 194 n.138
Kevan, Ernest F., 1 n.1; 8 n.33
Kingdon, Robert M., 12 n.59; 27 n.17; 184 n.68
Klempa, William, 91 n.33; 161 n.188
Kraus, Hans-Joachim, 127 n.11; 157 n.164
Krodel, Gottfried G., 5 n.12
Krusche, Werner, 176 n.16

Lane, Anthony N. S., 13 n.63; 18 n.76; 44 n.101; 93 n.44, 46; 94 n.48; 95 n.53; 241 n.156; 250 n.23; 259 n.88
Lang, A., 24 n.3; 65 n.23
Latria and *dulia*, 74; 123
Laver, Mary Sweetland, 163 n.200; 166 n.209
Law and gospel, 7; 9; 18; 74; 81; 82; 84; 159; 165; 219
Law in Calvin's theology: accusing office of the law (*lex accusans*), 7; 20; 81; 214; 216; 218; 224; 229; 231; 232; 233; 234; 249; 257; 258; 260; Christolgical formation and development, 60-83, deployed by theologians, 1-12; *lex nuda*, 97 n.58; 235 n.128; *lex tota*, 97 n.58; 235; *non quid possint homines sed quid debeant*, 96; 186; 193; 204; 216; 249; [original] normative nature, 8; 12; 15; 16; 19 n.79; 20; 42; 63; 73; 81; 82; 83; 100; 111; 121; 163; 173; 178; 213; 214-218; 225; 232 n.112; 234; 235; 236; 237; 243; 244; 247; 248; 252; 256; 257; 259; 260; of grace (*lex gratiae*), 68; 69; 193; of the gospel (*lex evangelicae*), 68; 73; 74; revelation of God's will, 9; 11; 66; 67; 93; 100; 216; 227; 249; 256; of covenant, 6; 9; 17; 79; original righteousness of (*iustitia originalis legis*), 163; 174; 183; 189; 192; 224; 228; 234; 257; precept of (*praeceptum legis*), 113; 183; 187; 193; 200; 202; 216; promise of (*primissio legis*), 16; 113; 216-218; 224; 234; 249; 250; righteousness of (*iustitia legis*), 16; 18; 73; 163; 174; 178; 183; 184; 188; 196; 198; 199; 201; 211; 221; 217; 218; 221; 224; 225; 226; 227; 229; 234; 240; 248; 251; 252; rule of life and living(*lex vivendi*), 7; 10; 62; 67; 71; 82; 96; 98; 163; 215; 216; 217; 231-235; 242; 244; 256; rule of life-giving(*lex vivificandi*), 82; 98; 214 n.3; 231-235; 242; 247; 255; rule of righteousness (*regula iustitiae*), 63; 64; 67; 72; 94; 95; 173; 238; significance, 9 n.32; sweetness of, 245; three classes of, 71; 232
Law, double office of (*duplex officium legis*), 81; 229; 232-235; 252-253
Law, triple use of (*triplex usus legis*) in Calvin: first use, 73; 75; 223; 226; 235-237; 242; 256; second use, 53; 73; 75-77; 223; 235; 237; 256; third use, 53; 63-64; 69; 72-73; 75; 201; 222-224; 227; 235; 237-245; 256; exhortative use: 69; 71; 73; 92; 97; 222; 227; 238; 240-243; 244; 257; 260
Lazareth, William H., 242 n.162
Le Gal, Patrick, 30 n.26; 44
Lecoultre, H., 24 n.3
Lefèvre d'Etaples, Jacques, 29; 38; 46
Leith, John H., 19 n.77; 51 n.135; 84 n.2
Leithart, Peter J., 50 n.130
Letham, Robert, 59 n.157
Lillback, Peter A., 2 n.2
Little, David, 161 n.188

Lobstein, P., 5
Locher, Gottfried W., 66 n.28; 85 n.7; 126 n.8; 163 n.200
Logos, 44 n.97; 48; 49; 51; 86; 104; 107 n.102; 133
Lombard, Peter, 39; 41 n.84; 106; 107 n.101; 121 n.142; 185 n.79
Loyola, Ignatius, 46; 80
Luther, Martin, 4; 8; 24; 28; 41 n.84; 65; 66; 82; 91 n.38; 95 n.53; 107; 117; 128 n.21; 172; 174; 179; 182; 193; 199; 204; 210; 214; 218-224; 226; 227; 233; 234; 236; 244 n.167; 258; 259
Lutheran controversies over law and gospel, 4; 13; 73; 213

Macleod, Donald, 237 n.138
Major, John (Reuter's thesis), 44-45
Manschreck, Clyde L., 260 n.89
Marcion, 125, 129
Marie, C. P., 49 n.124
Marot, Clément, 14 n.68
Matter, E. Ann, 48 n.121
McDonough, Thomas, 4 n.10
McGiffert, Michael, 1 n.1
McGrath, Alister E., 26 n.11; 38 n.72; 39; 42 n.89; 45; 241 n.157; 240; 247 n.10
McKane, W., 156 n.161
McKee, Elsie, 65 n.23
McNeil, David O., 36 n.58; 52 n.138
McNeill, John T., 26 n.15; 65 n.23; 161 n.188; 182 n.56
Medieval Pelagianism, 41 n.84
Melanchthon, Philip, 12; 18; 21; 54 n.125; 66; 69; 70; 72; 74 n.45; 80; 95 n.52; 117; 173; 180; 181 n.45; 182-183; 186 n.84; 189; 191; 193; 198; 199-201; 210; 211; 213; 220-224; 226; 227; 228 n.86; 232; 236; 257; 258; 260 n.89
Meritum de condigno, 41-42
Meritum de congruo, 40-41
Meylan, Edward A., 117 n.132

Millet, Olivier, 25; 37 n.61; 62 n.8; 64 n.16, 21; 247 n.8
Monheit, Michael L., 30 n.26; 32 n.39; 34 n.48; 37 n.65
Monter, E. William, 27 n.17
Moreau, Pierre-François, 48 n.124; 59 n.157
Mos novus, 28-38; 247
Müller, Denis, 237 n.137
Müller, K., 24 n.3
Muller, Richard A., 1 n.1; 3 n.5; 4 n.7; 9 n.38; 28; 29 n.23; 65 n.24; 70 n.37; 77 n.56; 90 n.31; 93 n.43; 95 n.53
Müller, Richard, 195 n.146

Naphy, William G., 15 n.68
Natural law debate between Barth and Brunner, 4-7
Natural law, 10; 14; 36; 48-50; 52; 54 n.145; 58; 70; 82; 83; 90; 92; 119; 138; 160-163; 223; 234; 247; 252; 258; order of nature, 86 n.10; 161 n.188; 185; 192.
Necessitas, 48-49; 93-97
Neo-Platonism, 136; 146; 172
Neuser, Wilhelm H., 13 n.62; 18 n.76; 24 n.3; 65 n.23; 81 n.70
Newman, Louis I., 130 n.25; 132 n.34, 36
Nicholas of Lyra, 28-29
Niesel, Wilhelm, 7; 15 n.69; 71 n.41; 84 n.4; 161 n.188
Nijenhuis, W., 128 n.21
Non posse peccare, 96, 97

Oakely, Francis, 42 n.89; 45 n.106
Obendiek, Harmannus, 66 n.25
Oberman, Heiko A., 4 n.8; 26 n.11; 39 n.75; 40 n.77, 78, 81, 82; 41 n.83, 84; 42 n.91; 43 n.96; 82 n.73; 106 n.92,93; 127 n.13
Ockham, William, 39; 41 n.84; 96
Olivétan, Pierre Robert (Olivetanus),

General Index

12; 62 n.7; 163; 164 n.201, 202
Olson, Jeannine E., 36 n.60
Opitz, Peter, 112 n.122
Ordo docendi, 16-17; 70; 232; 252
Ordo Salutis, 78; 232; 241 n.157; 244
Orléans, college of, 32-33
Osiander, Andreas, 14 n.65, 67; 15; 90; 103; 179; 239 n.146
Ozment, Steve, 42 n.89

Pancaro, Severino, 195 n.145
Pannier, Jacques, 31 n.30; 62 n.7
Pareus, David, 140; 142 n.94; 144
Parker, T. H. L., 17 n.73; 33; 35 n.52; 49 n.124; 60 n.1; 71 n.40; 148; 157 n.166; 159; 173 n.3; 179; 224 n.64; 231 n.109
Partee, Charles B., 19 n.77; 24 n.4; 48 n.122; 59 n.157; 67 n.28
Pater, Calvin Augustine, 166 n.213
Pauck, Wilhelm, 181
Payton, James R., 117 n.133
Pelikan, Jaroslav, 41 n.86; 47 n.113; 57 n.151
Pelkonen, J. Peter, 91 n.33
Peter, Rodolphe, 62 n.8
Peterson, Robert A., 85 n.5, 6
Pfisterer, Ernst, 27 n.17
Phillips, Darryl, 127 n.11, 14
Philosophia christiana, 60
Pietas, 66; 183; 196; 201; 233
Pighius, Albertus, 96 n.54
Plato, 50; 51; 52; 53; 87; 155; 157; 183; 246 n.2
Potentia Dei ordinata, 8 n.34; 40; 42; 45; 94
Primus, John H., 195 n.146
Promissio-perfectio analogia, 29 n.23; 173; 250;
Providence, 48; 49 n.125; 54; 58 n.155; 59; 94-95; 100; 120; 170; 217; 251
Puckett, David L., 55 n.146; 140

n.86; 148; 158

Quack, Jürgen, 62 n.7
Quistorp, Heinrich, 246 n.2

Raitt, J., 144 n.105; 145 n.108; 91 n.33
Regensburg Colloquy, 14 n.65; 18; 75 n.49; 259 n.88
Reid, W. Stanford, 24 n.4
Repentance, 21; 40; 69; 70; 75; 78; 80-81; 201; 213; 218; 220-224; 229; 230-231; 244; 248
Reuchlin, Johannes, 127-128
Reulos, Michel, 57 n.152
Reuss, E., 164 n.201
Reuter, Karl, 44-45; 46 n.113
Richard, Lucien Joseph, 46 n.108
Rilliet, Albert, 62 n.8, 9, 10; 64 n.24
Ritschl, Dietrich, 48 n.122
Robinson, Jack Hughs, 148 n.122
Rohls, Jan, 85 n.6
Roman law (common law, *Corpus Iuris Cilivis*), 12; 29-30; 32; 33; 35; 37; 49; 162; 247
Röthlisberger, Hugo, 7 n.25; 243
Rott, Jean, 60 n.1
Roussel, Bernard, 164 n.201
Russell, S. H., 156 n.163

Sabbath, 194-199
Sadolet, Jacopo, 13; 239 n.150; 259 n.88
Salley, Louise L., 26 n.12
Sanctification, 17; 18; 21; 27; 42; 78; 89; 108; 160; 175; 203; 213; 217; 223; 228; 232; 235; 238; 239; 241; 244; 248; 251
Santmire, H. Paul., 251 n.29, 30
Saxer, Ernst, 61 n.6
Scandalum, 117; 194 n.143
Scheld, Stefan, 46 n.111; 58 n.155; 85 n.6; 250 n.25
Scheld, Stefan, 46 n.111; 85 n.6

Schellong, Dieter, 174-175; 211
Schlingenseipen, Hermann, 181 n.45
Schola Augustiniana moderna, 45
Scholl, Hans, 60 n.1
Schreiner, Susan, 14 n.67; 49 n.126; 94 n.49; 161 n.188
Schümmer, Léopold, 197 n.152
Schurb, Ken, 140 n.85; 142 n.94
Schwendemann, Wilhelm, 246 n.2
Scotus, Duns, 39 n.73; 41 n.86; 82 n.73
Seebaß, Gottfried, 15 n.69
Seeberg, Reinhold, 7
Selderhuis, Herman J., 76 n.52; 186 n.87; 253 n.48
Semen iustitiae, 91
Semen religionis, 91
Sermo, 10; 79; 86; 206
Servetus, Michael, 15; 21; 74; 90 n.30; 123; 125; 129; 130-139; 144-147; 148; 149; 154; 157; 171-172; 253 n.43
Sharp, Larry D., 69 n.35
Sigal, Phillip, 126 n.8
So-called *extra Calvinisticum*, 21; 40 n.77; 43; 84-85; 86; 102-103; 105-111; 126; 148-149; 167; 168; 171; 176; 177 n.19; 212; 252; 254; 255
Socinus, Laelius, 38-39
Sola fide, 13; 14 n.67; 41; 68; 78; 213; 229; 238; 260
Sola gratia, 2; 4; 5; 6; 9; 40; 41; 83; 260
Spencer, Stephen R., 1 n.1
Spiritual insight, three kinds of, 90
Spirituality, 38; 46; 57; 248
Sprenger, P., 24 n.3
Stadtland-Neumann, Hiltrud, 175 n.11
Stancaro, Francesco, 87; 88; 99 n.63; 121, 129
Stauffer, Richard, 23 n.2; 94 n.49; 141 n.88
Steinmetz, David C., 45 n.107; 54 n.145; 93 n.47; 140 n.85; 157; 224 n.66; 258 n.86
Stephens, W. P., 3 n.7; 181 n.42
Stoics (*fatum*), 38; 48; 49; 51; 54; 57; 59; 83; 120
Street, Thomas W., 117 n.132
Strehle, Stephen, 42 n.89
Strohm, Christoph, 128 n.21
Subita conversio, 23-26
Substantial unity between the Old and New Testaments, 3; 14; 16; 32; 70; 74; 78-79; 84; 89; 125; 142; 151; 159; 202; 224; 225; 228; 249; 255
Sundquist, Ralph R., Jr., 242 n.161
Sursum corda, 101-102; 108-109
Symbolum nudum, 101
Synecdoche, 36; 161; 166; 182; 196

Tamburello, Dennis E., 92 n.43
Tavard, George H., 46 n.110; 47 n.113
Taylor, Hannis, 51 n.136
Tedeschi, John A., 38 n.72
Ten Commandments, 10; 63; 64; 115 n.128; 157; 214; First Table, 56; 157-160; 162 n.194; 182 n.56; 215; 247; Second Table, 56; 90; 160-163; 181; 182 n.56; 196; 215
Tertullian, 133
Thomas à Kempis, 46-47
Timor Dei, 69; 80; 224; 232; 255
Torrance, James B., 2 n.2
Torrance, Thomas F., 31 n.31, 33; 44; 161 n.188
Total depravity, 51; 53; 82; 83; 90; 192
Totus ubique, sed non totum, 105-109; 121; 167; 243
Trent, Council of, 14, 18 n.76
Troeltsch, Ernst, 5
Troeltsch, Ernst, 5
Two-kingdom theory, 4, 76
Tylenda, Joseph N., 60 n.1; 85 n.7; 87 n.17; 88 n.18; 108 n.87

General Index

Umbra-substantia analogia, 101 n.73; 159; 166; 173; 199; 200; 210; 250

Valla, Lorenzo, 30-31; 37
Van Buren, Paul, 85 n.5
Van Engen, John, 45 n.108
Van Oort, Johannes, 69 n.34; 75 n.50
Van Ravenswaay, J. Marius J. Lange, 154 n.151
Van't Spijker, Willem. 66 n.28; 129 n.23; 181 n.41, 42, 44; 202 n.191; 210 n.245
Verbum, 71; 86; 133
Veritas Hebraica, 126-129
Via moderna, 38-45; 247; 250
Viard, Paul Émile, 35
Viator, 25; 42; 122
Vischer, Wilhelm, 127 n.13
Voluntas Dei, 8; 34; 38; 41 n.87; 56; 82 n.73; 93; 94; 95; 119; 121; 206; 237; unity and continuity, 18; 119
Vos, Arvin, 24 n.4

Walker, Williston, 24 n.3; 26 n.11
Wallace, Ronald S., 84 n.3; 257
Warfield, Benjamin B., 66 n.25; 258 n.85
Watanabe, Nobuo, 64 n.20
Watt, Jeffrey R., 185 n.75
Wawrykow, Joseph, 41 n.86, 87
Weir, David A., 1 n.1
Weis, James, 15 n.69
Wendel, François, 11; 24 n.3; 32 n.37; 48 n.124; 60 n.1; 65 n.23; 77 n.56; 186 n.85; 241 n.157
Wengert, Timothy J., 4 n.9; 18 n.75; 220 n.41; 221 n.44; 260 n.89
Wernle, Paul, 66 n.27, 28; 68 n.30; 70 n.36; 243
Westphal, Joachim, 107 n.99; 109 n.106; 173 n.2
Whale, J. S., 27 n.20
White, Robert, 164 n.201

Williams, George Huntston, 129 n.24
Willis, David E.,
Willis. R., 38 n.72; 39 n.73; 47 n.118; 85 n.6, 7; 86 n.10; 92 n.40; 99 n.64; 102 n. 80; 107 n.101; 105-106; 109 n.109; 110 n.113; 145 n.106; 176-177
Witte, Johannes L., 175-176; 187 n.88; 211
Witte, John, Jr., 5 n.12; 184 n.68; 186 n.84
Wolf, Ernst, 136 n.64
Wolf, H. H., 7; 154 n.151
Wright, David F., 17 n.73; 55 n.146; 59 n.156; 96 n.55; 111 n.118; 114 n.125, 127; 115 n.129; 133 n.41; 139 n.82; 174 n.3; 186 n.86; 228 n.82; 229 n.88
Wright, Richard, 131 n.32; 132 n.37; 134 n.52
Wyatt, Peter, 104 n.83
Wyneken, Karl H., 74 n.46

Zachman, Randall C., 91 n.38; 103 n.81; 117 n.132, 133; 260 n.89
Zasius, Ulrich, 32; 57
Zur Mühlen, Karl-Heinz, 220 n.39
Zwingli, Ulrich, 3; 8 n.34; 13 n.62; 66; 81; 85 n.7; 179 n.33; 181 n.45

Studies in Christian History and Thought

(All titles uniform with this volume)
Dates in bold are of projected publication

David Bebbington
Holiness in Nineteenth-Century England
David Bebbington stresses the relationship of movements of spirituality to changes in their cultural setting, especially the legacies of the Enlightenment and Romanticism. He shows that these broad shifts in ideological mood had a profound effect on the ways in which piety was conceptualized and practised. Holiness was intimately bound up with the spirit of the age.
2000 / 0-85364-981-2 / viii + 98pp

J. William Black
Reformation Pastors
Richard Baxter and the Ideal of the Reformed Pastor
This work examines Richard Baxter's *Gildas Salvianus, The Reformed Pastor* (1656) and explores each aspect of his pastoral strategy in light of his own concern for 'reformation' and in the broader context of Edwardian, Elizabethan and early Stuart pastoral ideals and practice.
2003 / 1-84227-190-3 / xxii + 308pp

James Bruce
Prophecy, Miracles, Angels, *and* Heavenly Light?
The Eschatology, Pneumatology and Missiology of Adomnán's Life of Columba
This book surveys approaches to the marvellous in hagiography, providing the first critique of Plummer's hypothesis of Irish saga origin. It then analyses the uniquely systematized phenomena in the *Life of Columba* from Adomnán's seventh-century theological perspective, identifying the coming of the eschatological Kingdom as the key to understanding.
2004 / 1-84227-227-6 / xviii + 286pp

Colin J. Bulley
The Priesthood of Some Believers
Developments from the General to the Special Priesthood in the Christian Literature of the First Three Centuries
The first in-depth treatment of early Christian texts on the priesthood of all believers shows that the developing priesthood of the ordained related closely to the division between laity and clergy and had deleterious effects on the practice of the general priesthood.
2000 / 1-84227-034-6 / xii + 336pp

Anthony R. Cross (ed.)
Ecumenism and History
Studies in Honour of John H.Y. Briggs

This collection of essays examines the inter-relationships between the two fields in which Professor Briggs has contributed so much: history—particularly Baptist and Nonconformist—and the ecumenical movement. With contributions from colleagues and former research students from Britain, Europe and North America, *Ecumenism and History* provides wide-ranging studies in important aspects of Christian history, theology and ecumenical studies.

2002 / 1-84227-135-0 / xx + 362pp

Maggi Dawn
Confessions of an Inquiring Spirit
Form as Constitutive of Meaning in S.T. Coleridge's Theological Writing

This study of Coleridge's *Confessions* focuses on its confessional, epistolary and fragmentary form, suggesting that attention to these features significantly affects its interpretation. Bringing a close study of these three literary forms, the author suggests ways in which they nuance the text with particular understandings of the Trinity, and of a kenotic christology. Some parallels are drawn between Romantic and postmodern dilemmas concerning the authority of the biblical text.

2006 / 1-84227-255-1 / approx. 224 pp

Ruth Gouldbourne
The Flesh and the Feminine
Gender and Theology in the Writings of Caspar Schwenckfeld

Caspar Schwenckfeld and his movement exemplify one of the radical communities of the sixteenth century. Challenging theological and liturgical norms, they also found themselves challenging social and particularly gender assumptions. In this book, the issues of the relationship between radical theology and the understanding of gender are considered.

2005 / 1-84227-048-6 / approx. 304pp

Crawford Gribben
Puritan Millennialism
Literature and Theology, 1550–1682

Puritan Millennialism surveys the growth, impact and eventual decline of puritan millennialism throughout England, Scotland and Ireland, arguing that it was much more diverse than has frequently been suggested. This Paternoster edition is revised and extended from the original 2000 text.

2007 / 1-84227-372-8 / approx. 320pp

Galen K. Johnson
Prisoner of Conscience
John Bunyan on Self, Community and Christian Faith
This is an interdisciplinary study of John Bunyan's understanding of conscience across his autobiographical, theological and fictional writings, investigating whether conscience always deserves fidelity, and how Bunyan's view of conscience affects his relationship both to modern Western individualism and historic Christianity.
2003 / 1-84227-223-3 / xvi + 236pp

R.T. Kendall
Calvin and English Calvinism to 1649
The author's thesis is that those who formed the Westminster Confession of Faith, which is regarded as Calvinism, in fact departed from John Calvin on two points: (1) the extent of the atonement and (2) the ground of assurance of salvation.
1997 / 0-85364-827-1 / xii + 264pp

Timothy Larsen
Friends of Religious Equality
Nonconformist Politics in Mid-Victorian England
During the middle decades of the nineteenth century the English Nonconformist community developed a coherent political philosophy of its own, of which a central tenet was the principle of religious equality (in contrast to the stereotype of Evangelical Dissenters). The Dissenting community fought for the civil rights of Roman Catholics, non-Christians and even atheists on an issue of principle which had its flowering in the enthusiastic and undivided support which Nonconformity gave to the campaign for Jewish emancipation. This reissued study examines the political efforts and ideas of English Nonconformists during the period, covering the whole range of national issues raised, from state education to the Crimean War. It offers a case study of a theologically conservative group defending religious pluralism in the civic sphere, showing that the concept of religious equality was a grand vision at the centre of the political philosophy of the Dissenters.
2007 / 1-84227-402-3 / x + 300pp

Byung-Ho Moon
Christ the Mediator of the Law
Calvin's Christological Understanding of the Law as the Rule of Living and Life-Giving

This book explores the coherence between Christology and soteriology in Calvin's theology of the law, examining its intellectual origins and his position on the concept and extent of Christ's mediation of the law. A comparative study between Calvin and contemporary Reformers—Luther, Bucer, Melancthon and Bullinger—and his opponent Michael Servetus is made for the purpose of pointing out the unique feature of Calvin's Christological understanding of the law.

2005 / 1-84227-318-3 / approx. 370pp

John Eifion Morgan-Wynne
Holy Spirit and Religious Experience in Christian Writings, c.AD 90–200

This study examines how far Christians in the third to fifth generations (c.AD 90–200) attributed their sense of encounter with the divine presence, their sense of illumination in the truth or guidance in decision-making, and their sense of ethical empowerment to the activity of the Holy Spirit in their lives.

2005 / 1-84227-319-1 / approx. 350pp

James I. Packer
The Redemption and Restoration of Man in the Thought of Richard Baxter

James I. Packer provides a full and sympathetic exposition of Richard Baxter's doctrine of humanity, created and fallen; its redemption by Christ Jesus; and its restoration in the image of God through the obedience of faith by the power of the Holy Spirit.

2002 / 1-84227-147-4 / 432pp

Andrew Partington,
Church and State
The Contribution of the Church of England Bishops to the House of Lords during the Thatcher Years

In *Church and State*, Andrew Partington argues that the contribution of the Church of England bishops to the House of Lords during the Thatcher years was overwhelmingly critical of the government; failed to have a significant influence in the public realm; was inefficient, being undertaken by a minority of those eligible to sit on the Bench of Bishops; and was insufficiently moral and spiritual in its content to be distinctive. On the basis of this, and the likely reduction of the number of places available for Church of England bishops in a fully reformed Second Chamber, the author argues for an evolution in the Church of England's approach to the service of its bishops in the House of Lords. He proposes the Church of England works to overcome the genuine obstacles which hinder busy diocesan bishops from contributing to the debates of the House of Lords and to its life more informally.

2005 / 1-84227-334-5 / approx. 324pp

Michael Pasquarello III
God's Ploughman
Hugh Latimer: A 'Preaching Life' (1490–1555)

This construction of a 'preaching life' situates Hugh Latimer within the larger religious, political and intellectual world of late medieval England. Neither biography, intellectual history, nor analysis of discrete sermon texts, this book is a work of homiletic history which draws from the details of Latimer's milieu to construct an interpretive framework for the preaching performances that formed the core of his identity as a religious reformer. Its goal is to illumine the practical wisdom embodied in the content, form and style of Latimer's preaching, and to recapture a sense of its overarching purpose, movement, and transforming force during the reform of sixteenth-century England.

2006 / 1-84227-336-1 / approx. 250pp

Alan P.F. Sell
Enlightenment, Ecumenism, Evangel
Theological Themes and Thinkers 1550–2000

This book consists of papers in which such interlocking topics as the Enlightenment, the problem of authority, the development of doctrine, spirituality, ecumenism, theological method and the heart of the gospel are discussed. Issues of significance to the church at large are explored with special reference to writers from the Reformed and Dissenting traditions.

2005 / 1-84227-330-2 / xviii + 422pp

Alan P.F. Sell
Hinterland Theology
Some Reformed and Dissenting Adjustments

Many books have been written on theology's 'giants' and significant trends, but what of those lesser-known writers who adjusted to them? In this book some hinterland theologians of the British Reformed and Dissenting traditions, who followed in the wake of toleration, the Evangelical Revival, the rise of modern biblical criticism and Karl Barth, are allowed to have their say. They include Thomas Ridgley, Ralph Wardlaw, T.V. Tymms and N.H.G. Robinson.

2006 / 1-84227-331-0 / approx. 350pp

Alan P.F. Sell and Anthony R. Cross (eds)
Protestant Nonconformity in the Twentieth Century

In this collection of essays scholars representative of a number of Nonconformist traditions reflect thematically on Nonconformists' life and witness during the twentieth century. Among the subjects reviewed are biblical studies, theology, worship, evangelism and spirituality, and ecumenism. Over and above its immediate interest, this collection provides a marker to future scholars and others wishing to know how some of their forebears assessed Nonconformity's contribution to a variety of fields during the century leading up to Christianity's third millennium.

2003 / 1-84227-221-7 / x + 398pp

Mark Smith
Religion in Industrial Society
Oldham and Saddleworth 1740–1865

This book analyses the way British churches sought to meet the challenge of industrialization and urbanization during the period 1740–1865. Working from a case-study of Oldham and Saddleworth, Mark Smith challenges the received view that the Anglican Church in the eighteenth century was characterized by complacency and inertia, and reveals Anglicanism's vigorous and creative response to the new conditions. He reassesses the significance of the centrally directed church reforms of the mid-nineteenth century, and emphasizes the importance of local energy and enthusiasm. Charting the growth of denominational pluralism in Oldham and Saddleworth, Dr Smith compares the strengths and weaknesses of the various Anglican and Nonconformist approaches to promoting church growth. He also demonstrates the extent to which all the churches participated in a common culture shaped by the influence of evangelicalism, and shows that active co-operation between the churches rather than denominational conflict dominated. This revised and updated edition of Dr Smith's challenging and original study makes an important contribution both to the social history of religion and to urban studies.

2006 / 1-84227-335-3 / approx. 300pp

Martin Sutherland
Peace, Toleration and Decay
The Ecclesiology of Later Stuart Dissent
This fresh analysis brings to light the complexity and fragility of the later Stuart Nonconformist consensus. Recent findings on wider seventeenth-century thought are incorporated into a new picture of the dynamics of Dissent and the roots of evangelicalism.
2003 / 1-84227-152-0 / xxii + 216pp

G. Michael Thomas
The Extent of the Atonement
A Dilemma for Reformed Theology from Calvin to the Consensus
A study of the way Reformed theology addressed the question, 'Did Christ die for all, or for the elect only?', commencing with John Calvin, and including debates with Lutheranism, the Synod of Dort and the teaching of Moïse Amyraut.
1997 / 0-85364-828-X / x + 278pp

David M. Thompson
Baptism, Church and Society in Britain from the Evangelical Revival to
Baptism, Eucharist and Ministry
The theology and practice of baptism have not received the attention they deserve. How important is faith? What does baptismal regeneration mean? Is baptism a bond of unity between Christians? This book discusses the theology of baptism and popular belief and practice in England and Wales from the Evangelical Revival to the publication of the World Council of Churches' consensus statement on *Baptism, Eucharist and Ministry* (1982).
2005 / 1-84227-393-0 / approx. 224pp

Mark D. Thompson
A Sure Ground on Which to Stand
The Relation of Authority and Interpretive Method of Luther's Approach to Scripture
The best interpreter of Luther is Luther himself. Unfortunately many modern studies have superimposed contemporary agendas upon this sixteenth-century Reformer's writings. This fresh study examines Luther's own words to find an explanation for his robust confidence in the Scriptures, a confidence that generated the famous 'stand' at Worms in 1521.
2004 / 1-84227-145-8 / xvi + 322pp

Carl R. Trueman and R.S. Clark (eds)
Protestant Scholasticism
Essays in Reassessment

Traditionally Protestant theology, between Luther's early reforming career and the dawn of the Enlightenment, has been seen in terms of decline and fall into the wastelands of rationalism and scholastic speculation. In this volume a number of scholars question such an interpretation. The editors argue that the development of post-Reformation Protestantism can only be understood when a proper historical model of doctrinal change is adopted. This historical concern underlies the subsequent studies of theologians such as Calvin, Beza, Olevian, Baxter, and the two Turrentini. The result is a significantly different reading of the development of Protestant Orthodoxy, one which both challenges the older scholarly interpretations and clichés about the relationship of Protestantism to, among other things, scholasticism and rationalism, and which demonstrates the fruitfulness of the new, historical approach.

1999 / 0-85364-853-0 / xx + 344pp

Shawn D. Wright
Our Sovereign Refuge
The Pastoral Theology of Theodore Beza

Our Sovereign Refuge is a study of the pastoral theology of the Protestant reformer who inherited the mantle of leadership in the Reformed church from John Calvin. Countering a common view of Beza as supremely a 'scholastic' theologian who deviated from Calvin's biblical focus, Wright uncovers a new portrait. He was not a cold and rigid academic theologian obsessed with probing the eternal decrees of God. Rather, by placing him in his pastoral context and by noting his concerns in his pastoral and biblical treatises, Wright shows that Beza was fundamentally a committed Christian who was troubled by the vicissitudes of life in the second half of the sixteenth century. He believed that the biblical truth of the supreme sovereignty of God alone could support Christians on their earthly pilgrimage to heaven. This pastoral and personal portrait forms the heart of Wright's argument.

2004 / 1-84227-252-7 / xviii + 308pp

Paternoster
9 Holdom Avenue,
Bletchley,
Milton Keynes MK1 1QR,
United Kingdom
Web: www.authenticmedia.co.uk/paternoster

www.ingramcontent.com/pod-product-compliance
Lightning Source LLC
Chambersburg PA
CBHW071230230426
43668CB00011B/1369